Y0-DVQ-514

CITY LIGHTS

CITY LIGHTS
An Introduction to Urban Studies

E. BARBARA PHILLIPS
San Francisco State University

RICHARD T. LeGATES
San Francisco State University

New York Oxford
OXFORD UNIVERSITY PRESS
1981

Library of Congress Cataloging in Publication Data

Phillips, E Barbara.
City lights.

Bibliography: p.
Includes index.
1. Sociology, Urban. 2. Urban economics.
I. LeGates, Richard T., joint author. II. Title.
HT151.P513 307.7'6 80-16234
ISBN 0-19-502797-3
Printing (last digit): 9

Printed in the United States of America

Page 8 From Saul Bellow, *The Adventures of Augie March*. Copyright © 1949, 1951, 1952, 1953 by Saul Bellow. Reprinted by permission of The Viking Penguin, Inc.

Page 10 From "Chicago" in *Chicago Poems* by Carl Sandburg. Copyright 1916 by Holt, Rinehart and Winston, Inc.; copyright 1946 by Carl Sandburg. Reprinted by permission of Harcourt Brace Jovanovich, Inc.

Page 17 From *Dissertations by Mr. Dooley* by Finley Peter Dunne. Copyright 1906 by Harper and Row, Publishers, Inc.

Page 20 "Elephants are Different to Different People" in *Complete Poems* by Carl Sandburg. Copyright 1950 by Carl Sandburg. Reprinted by permission of Harcourt Brace Jovanovich. Inc.

Page 26 From *The Little Prince* by Antoine de Saint-Exupéry. Copyright 1943, 1971 by Harcourt Brace Jovanovich, Inc. Reprinted by permission.

Page 44 From *Hard Times* by Charles Dickens. Reprinted by permission of E.P. Dutton and Everyman's Library.

Page 173 "Prelude" from *Western Star* by Stephen Vincent Benet. Copyright © 1943 by Stephen Vincent Benet. Copyright renewed © 1971 by Thomas C. Benet, Stephanie B. Mahen, and Rachel Benet Lewis. Reprinted by permission of Brandt & Brandt Literary Agents, Inc.

Page 178 From *How the Other Half Lives* by Jacob Riis. Copyright © New York, Dover [1901] 1970, p. 41. Reprinted by permission of Dover Publications, Inc.

Page 178 "Haiku" by Sankuro Nagano in *Nisei: The Quiet Americans* by Bill Hosokawa. Copyright © 1969 by William Hosokawa. By permission of William Morrow and Co.

Page 178 From *The Autobiography of Malcolm X* by Malcolm X, with the assistance of Alex Haley. Copyright © 1964 by Alex Haley and Malcolm X; copyright © 1965 by Alex Haley and Betty Shabazz. Reprinted by permission of Random House, Inc.

Page 179 From *La Raza: The Mexican Americans* by Stan Steiner. Copyright © 1969, 1970 by Stan Steiner. Reprinted by permission of Harper and Row Publishers, Inc.

Page 432 From *Even Cowgirls Get the Blues* by Tom Robbins. Copyright © 1976 by Thomas Robbins. Reprinted by permission of Bantam Books, Inc. All rights reserved.

To
my Father and the memory of my Mother, wonderful parents, who encouraged me to explore the urban world

e.b.p.

and
my daughter, Becky, who is just discovering what this book is about

r.t.l.

Preface

Historian Arthur Schlesinger once remarked that there are only two kinds of historians: "Those who admit their bias and those who shoot from ambush." This applies to urbanists too, so we begin by stepping out from behind the bushes. Here are our biases and assumptions revelant to writing—and reading—this book about urban life.

WHAT YOU SEE DEPENDS ON HOW YOU LOOK AT IT

We start with a very basic assumption: nobody has cornered the market on knowledge. No one ideology, intellectual discipline, perspective, or guru has a monopoly on truth. Hence, we stress the relativity of views on city life. Instead of saying, "This is the way it is," we show *how* and *why* observers of the urban scene so often disagree on important issues: *what* they see, the *meaning* of what they see, and *what to do* about what they see.

Take the case of urban poverty. Scholars and citizens don't agree on its causes, nature, or cure. The U.S. President and Chicago's Mayor, the urban planner and sociologist, the banker and autoworker, the socialist and conservative all bring different perspectives to the issue of poverty. And they don't agree on how to fight it. If, for example, Mayors see their cities' problem as lack of money, they may lobby for more federal and state funds. They may try to attract new tax-paying industry into their boundaries. But if they define poverty as a problem rooted in the unequal distribution of existing resources, the Mayors will pursue different policies, ones aimed at changing institutional structures and redistributing existing resources. In other words, how they define the problem determines how they try to solve it.

This approach means that we recognize controversy and don't try to sweep it under a rug. Accordingly, we see our task as laying out appropriate ways of thinking about an issue, not as peddling a particular point of view.

But we don't think all perspectives on the urban world are equally valid. For instance, we reject the idea that poor people are poor because they're lazy. Yet, the general tone of this book is tentative. As poet William Blake wrote, "What is now true was once only imagined." He might have added that what now seems self-evident truth may be considered mere nonsense in the future.

Given our commitment to the relativity of perspectives, we don't often provide definitive answers to anything you may have wanted to know about cities. But we do help readers to choose more intelligently for themselves among competing claims and truths about how cities work. Alas, there are no easy routes. We spend our entire lives sifting sense from nonsense, trying to decide which is which. Here we present (1) information—ammunition for asking better questions about city life and (2) concepts, visions, and frameworks to better understand information about cities.

THE PLACE OF URBAN "PROBLEMS"

Are there really any urban problems? A strange question? Perhaps, but nobody talked about them until this century. People did talk about disagreeable urban conditions and conflicts, but the idea of clearly definable urban problems is recent. It came into style in the early 1900s as social scientists, eager to play the role of social doctors, began to apply medical language to the city. A city was compared to a human body. Just as people had diseases complete with symptoms and (under a doctor's care) cures, cities had problems that could be cured. Today, it is common to hear a city diagnosed as sick. More optimistically, an urban area might be described as healthy or showing good vital signs.

We avoid this terminology because talk of sick, problem-ridden cities masks an important idea: There is no general agreement on what constitutes an urban problem. What is recognized as an urban problem depends basically on two factors: Who's doing the talking and the intellectual-political fashion of the times. Drug use, for one example, has been a feature of American city life for decades. When did it become a problem? Just about the time that drugs spread from lower-class, ethnic neighborhoods to affluent metropolitan homes.

A number of urban conditions and issues are discussed here, but we do not organize our discussion around drug use, housing, energy shortages, or other so-called problems. To do so would only perpetuate the wrongheaded idea that people agree on what the problems are. Also, the urban problems approach places undue emphasis on the seamy side of city life, ignoring the richness of the urban experience.

THINGS URBAN ARE BEST UNDERSTOOD IN A BROADER CONTEXT FROM AN INTERDISCIPLINARY PERSPECTIVE

Today there is no substantial consensus and no simple analytic framework that unite urban researchers. What we have are fragments of knowledge, bits and pieces of understanding about cities that come from a number of intellectual professional and artistic fields.

How can we deal with the lack of coherence and consensus that we find in urban studies? Here we cope with incoherence and dissensus in the following ways. First, as mentioned earlier, we lay out competing frameworks through which to think about how cities work. Of course, detailing the bases of disagreements among urban observers doesn't result in a new synthesis, but it does reduce the tension level by clarifying the nature of dissensus.

Second, we approach urban phenomena by placing them in broader contexts. Sometimes this means putting an "urban" issue into a national and/or international framework. Sometimes this means putting an issue into the framework of general theory before examining its urban applications. For instance, to contrast boomtown Houston and bust-town Detroit, we link their economic fates to national and worldwide trends; these include shifts in population and power from Frostbelt to Sunbelt and changes from an industrial to a postindustrial economy. To understand why a larger percentage of people in Detroit than Houston live below the poverty line requires some knowledge of the broader context in which these two cities find themselves. So we pay a great deal of attention to these broader contexts, much more so than most urban texts.

Finally, we try to bring together a wide variety of perspectives on urban phenomena and to suggest some connections between perspectives. In an age of information explosion and specialization, this is not easy for any of us. Here our aim is to expand the vision of things urban. An interdisciplinary approach is essential to this goal. When discussing the economy of cities, to take one example, we blend insights from sociology, geography, literature, political science, and other relevant disciplines with economic theory and data. Why? Because economic concepts alone don't tell the whole story. Certainly they add nothing to our understanding of human reactions to economic change. That's why we also examine value systems, community power structures, federal policies, and other factors related to a city's economy.

SOCIAL ACTION CANNOT BE SEPARATED FROM SOCIAL THEORY

We try to provide a solid theoretical base for action-oriented people. Throughout this book, we emphasize theory and practice because there is no good social action without good social theory; the two are inextricably linked.

Using case studies, we highlight individuals and groups who have acted upon their urban world. And we link their practice to theories about urban life. For instance, we examine how New York City's masterbuilder Robert Moses and Chicago's Mayor Richard Daley exercised enormous influence and power. We also follow the progress of Bananas, a group of California women who set out to perform a community service: Providing harried parents with information about kids' activities—to save them from "going bananas." Bananas learned how the political system works and, with much hard work and persistence, got something done.

Both of us bring practical experience to these issues. Collectively, we have worked for government and citizens' groups on such concerns as urban renewal, low-income housing, land use policies, antipoverty campaigns, public access to the mass media, energy policy, legal assistance for the poor, international understanding via cultural exchange, and community development. Among other lessons, we learned that fighting a war against poverty armed only with false hopes is a losing battle. We hope that this book will lay the groundwork for better understanding of how cities work and, hence, more effective social action.

REVELATIONS IN ORDINARY PLACES

Taking a closer look at ordinary people doing ordinary things—like riding a city bus—can reveal a great deal about urban life. For instance, when riding a crowded bus, we expect to be left alone. If, perchance, a seatmate strikes up a conversation, we note how unusual this is. The next time we may bury our heads in a newspaper or stare out the window to avoid conversation. Now, nobody taught us how to stave off urban strangers. Or that rules—not talking to strangers, for example—govern bus behavior. Yet most of the time, most of us follow these implicit rules.

By observing routine activities, we can begin to understand what rules govern urban social behavior and what purposes these rules serve. And so we devote a chapter to such ordinary behavior as walking down a busy street, riding a subway, and going to a bar.

ANYTHING ELSE?

Other assumptions and biases can be read between the lines of the following 17 chapters. Choices (what issues to include? how to present them? which theorists to exclude?) are inevitable. No doubt some choices were barely conscious, stemming from our own backgrounds, life experiences, professional training, and personal reactions to the currents of our times. Surely this book was influenced by our academic training: Dick is a lawyer and city planner; Barbara holds advanced degrees in international relations, public administration, and interdisciplinary social science. This book would have been different if each of us, at different times, had not studied in Europe, worked in the Third World, and fought the War against Poverty in the United States. Certainly, it would have been different, and poorer, had we not spent years teaching Introduction to Urban Studies, Urban Sociology, Urban Housing, and other urban-oriented courses at a large urban university with diverse and exciting students. In large measure, our students' interests and suggestions shaped this book.

At least two important biases pervade this book, and for them we are unrepentant. One is toward a comparative approach. Although this book centers on urban life in the United States, we draw on personal experience and research, whenever applicable, to compare and contrast varieties of urban lifestyles. The other is an unabashed pro-urban bias. We like cities, especially big ones. Neither of us yearns to get away from it all, joining the exodus to rural America. We don't hide our preference for city living. To the contrary, we hope our enthusiasm for cities will be apparent. Even rub off a little.

Lastly, studying urban life can be overwhelming because cities are such complex entities. We attempt to give readers as much help along the way as possible: key terms in bold print; biographical sketches of theorists and practitioners; case studies of real people setting urban policy or trying to change the way things are done in cities; excerpts from the work of folksingers, novelists, poets, and New Journalists; graphs, cartoons, and photographic essays; and boxed selections from classic essays relating to urban life. Most especially, you are invited to participate directly in studying and discovering the city. We hope that carrying out the projects in each chapter will bring the city alive and encourage serious discussion, even theory building. We would like to know what you find when doing the projects. Write us! About them or anything else related to this book.

So, that is where this book is "coming from," to use the vernacular. From us, two individuals shaped by personal experiences, places we've been, and the urban world we live in. Of course, how we interpret that world depends on all that we have met. That's why we've tried to reveal some of those influences instead of shooting from ambush.

Berkeley E.B.P.
December 1980 R.T.L.

Acknowledgments

This book was very much a joint enterprise. Without our students, colleagues, friends, families, inspirers, and editors at Oxford University Press, it would not have been started or finished.

Our students at San Francisco State encouraged us, and through their comments on draft chapters used in our courses, shaped the book's contents. Students at Stanford helped to refine the projects at the end of each chapter. Former students Mary Garrett and Mary Bankston assisted with data collection and a keen eye.

San Francisco State colleagues made suggestions on draft chapters: Roger Crawford, Rich DeLeon, Marsh Feldman, Lenny Goldberg, Bill Issel, Debbie LeVeen, Lynn McAllister, Norm Schneider, Jules Tygiel, David Wilmoth, and Jean Vance of the interdisciplinary Urban Studies Program, and Rick Boussaka, Rufus Browning, John Gemello, Rachel Kahn-Hut, John Huttman, Terry McDonald, Ray Miller, Pete Phillips, Elizabeth Rooney, Ruth Shen, and Dan Vencill of various social science departments. Special thanks go to the entire sociology department; members reasoned together on approaches to synthesizing ideas about urban life.

Bay Area colleagues shared their time, insights, and comments: Donald Appleyard, George Break, Galen Cranz, Mary Lou FitzGerald, Claude Fischer, Kathy Gerson, Ira Lapidus, Bonnie Loyd, Dale Marshall, John Mollenkopf, Roger Montgomery, Anne Steuve, Fred Stout, and Dick Walker. Chester Hartman read every word of the manuscript, very carefully. Not only did we benefit from his remarks, we take heart from his commitment to improving the quality of urban life through social action. Colleague and friend Margaret Fay, who died in 1979, contributed her passion for ideas, social activism, and blithe spirit.

Colleagues elsewhere read draft chapters and advised: Brack Brown, Peter Knauss, Allen Schick, Manfred Stanley, Larry Susskind, and Bill Tabb.

Practitioners pointed out many gaps between urban theory and practice: Bill Barnes, Harvey Bragdon, Barbara Cohen, Arlyce Currie, Lew Feldstein, John Field, Sonia Hammam, Tom Hargadon, Anya Miller, and Bob Snyder. A. M. Babu, former Minister of Economic Planning in Tanzania, reminded us of some connections between urban, national, and international policies.

Photographers and artists helped with ideas for this book's visual presentation: Andrée Abecassis, Ben Achtenberg, Richard Hedman, Alan Jacobs, Bill Owens, John Pearson, and Mary Swisher.

Reference librarians at Berkeley were invaluable resources, finding obscure bits of information.

Lorraine Whitmore of San Francisco State's manuscript service caught stylistic inconsistencies. Helen Greenberg gave encouraging words while copyediting the manuscript. Joyce Berry and Patricia Loewe of Oxford University Press helped to secure copyright permissions and assemble the art work. Linda Coleman, Aspasia Gard, and Meredith Hoffman typed the bulk of the manuscript.

Jim Anderson and Spencer Carr, our editors at Oxford University Press, believed in this project and treated us very well. They chose anonymous reviewers who added helpful suggestions.

And our deep appreciation to dear friends who provided support services, a sounding board, and an understanding ear.

Contents

List of Boxes

PART ONE
An Invitation to the City

Brack Brown

Oscar Graubner

CHAPTER 1 The Knowing Eye and Ear

Welcome to the city . . . to the City of Angels, the Windy City, the Big Apple, the Big D, and the Twin Cities . . . to Liberty, Defiance, Friendly, and Eden . . . to Gary, Indiana, the town that steel built . . . and to supercity Houston and tiny Placerville, California, constructed on black and yellow gold.

Enter Oak Park, Illinois, the world's largest village, and Castroville, California, the artichoke capital of the world. . . . Visit Little Switzerland, Germantown, Cherokee, San Juan, and Havre de Grace. Look at the plans for Soul City, North Carolina.

Welcome to Cottondale, Mechanicsville, Mineralville, and Thermopolis . . . and all the Georgetowns, Charlestons, and Yorktowns. Welcome to the marvelous variety of cities and towns that Americans from Africa, China, Europe, Great Britain, and all over the world have built and rebuilt—and are still building.

Walk down Main Street. Walk through Chinatown. Sit down to an espresso at the café. Trace your roots at the Newberry Library. Pack a picnic and hear Shakespeare in the park. See a play on the Great White Way.

Stand up and fly a kite on the Boston Common. Go to a game in the Astrodome.

Browse the boutiques at Lorimer Square. Listen—to the sounds of the city: foghorns, squeaky brakes, ambulance sirens, jazz, and salsa . . . and the lilt of the languages spoken on the city streets. Hear the messages that buildings subtly send.

Look at the art on subway walls and sidewalks. See gargoyles peering from towering buildings and portraits of all the people passing by. Read all about it—in the World's Greatest Newspaper in Chicago and the Whitesburg *Eagle* of Kentucky. See what's doing in town from bulletin boards, telephone poles, and kiosks.

Smell the aroma of Mongolian hot pot, hash browns, Indian curries, and enchiladas cooking on the restaurant stoves. Touch the baby elephant in the children's zoo and the sculpture in the museum garden. Feel the smooth bank marble and the rough pavement.

And the people. Living in tenements and tracts, glass houses, red-brick Georgians, forty-story apartment houses, ticky-tacky boxes, geodesic domes, penthouses, mobile homes, shacks by the railroad tracks. Going by foot, ferryboat, car, bus, subway, bicycle, and train to work in offices, factories, shopping malls, TV studios, and schools. Selling shoes, waiting tables, unloading the supermarket trucks, reporting the daily news, repairing potholes, and keeping the cities moving.

And troubles? Yes, those too. Breathe exhaust fumes and watch belching smokestacks pollute the air. Look at the dilapidated apartments and hear cries of loneliness in the night. See litter and rats. Gaze into the eyes of the poor. Feel what it means to be going nowhere in a hurry.

Experience the city. Use all your senses to feel its promise, its troubles. And reflect: What's going on here? Must it be this way? What can people do, working together, to make the city more livable, more humane?

a

b

Toshiko Akiyoshi/
Lew Tabackin Big Band
Joachim Kuhn
Turk Murphy
Harry "Sweets" Edison &
Eddie "Lockjaw" Davis
CRIME
FRIDAY & SATURDAY
SEPTEMBER 8 AND 9
MUTANTS
THE BLANK
THE BRANCH
KEYSTONE
ROCKY SULLIVAN
JOHN CIPOLLINA
JOE COVINGTON SISCO
MARIO CIPOLLINA
JOHNNY FONTAYN
NICKY HOPKINS
MISTRESS
TOMMY TUTONE
SAT. SEPT. 16
BERKELEY
Mario Murillo
Night of Miracles
7:pmSat.Sept.16
Oakland Aud.Theater
843-5724
Women in Music
Festival
THE NATIVES
DEBATE ON
BUILDING THE NEW
COMMUNIST PARTY
MOE ARMSTRONG
KEYSTONE
SEPT. 2 & 3
c

d

e

f

Fig. 1-1 CITY LIFE. Where else can you hug a bear, hear a musical saw over lunch, read all about it, see or join the passing parade, play with a dolphin, or sit down for an espresso break? (*a,c,e,f,* Brack Brown; *b,d* Michael Schwartz)

TWO PATHS TO UNDERSTANDING THE CITY

"Acquaintance with" and "Knowledge about" Urban Life

Personal experience and systematic reflection offer two different ways of understanding city life. Each provides a special kind of knowledge. They work in dissimilar ways, and sometimes they can be incompatible.

Firsthand, concrete experience gives an **"acquaintance with"** the city: direct, personal knowledge. This mode of understanding is intuitive, nonlinear, and holistic. Psychologists associate it with right-brain thinking.

By contrast, **"knowledge about"** the city comes from abstract, logical thought. It is analytical, linear, and rational. This sequential, rational mode orders information by breaking it down into component parts. Psychologists associate it with left-brain thinking.

Word pictures and photographic images often transmit acquaintance with an urban scene: a sense of being there, an immediate emotional reaction. For instance, Jacob Riis's photo in Fig. 1-2 allows us to witness the life of poverty in New York City around 1900. It touches our feelings as well as our intellect, and that was social reformer Riis's intent—to touch people's hearts, to make them understand emotionally *How the Other Half Lives* ([1901] 1971).

On the other hand, Table 1-1 provides information about poverty to be rationally and systematically analyzed. From this information, we might logically ask, "Why is there a wide disparity between cities and 'outside central cities' (suburbs and all places in the metropolitan area minus the core or 'central city') in terms of poverty rates?" To figure out why, we would construct systematic, formal statements, leading to knowledge about poverty.

Often poets, music makers, and other artists touch our emotions in ways that statistical tables and abstract theory cannot. Such is the case with Riis's photos. Here is another: Nobel Prize winner Saul Bellow's ironic assessment of social mobility in the modern industrial city, excerpted from *The Adventures of Augie March* (1949). It is the obituary of a real estate broker in Chicago, written by the broker's son. The son writes that his father

> found Chicago a swamp and left it a great city. He came after the Great Fire [in 1871] said to be caused by Mrs. O'Leary's cow, in flight from the conscription of the Hapsburg tyrant, and in his life as a builder proved that great places do not have to be founded on the bones of slaves, like the pyramids of Pharaohs. . . . The lesson of an American life like my father's . . . is that achievements are compatible with decency. (Bellow, [1949] 1964:104)

Literary artists like Bellow give readers a sense of the richness of life, particularly through the use of detail. Readers feel as if they are personally acquainted with the characters and their settings.

Of course, great artists do more than that. They go beyond portraying particular people in specific settings. They represent typical characters in typical situations, that is, general types. As one literary critic notes, "The goal for all great art is to provide a picture of reality in which the contradiction between appearance and reality, the particular and the general, the immediate and the conceptual, etc., is so resolved that the two converge . . . and provide a sense of an inseparable integrity" (Lukács, 1971:34). Art, then, or "great art," offers both personal acquaintance with and knowledge about a subject.

Note that literary critics, philosophers, and scientists don't agree on the functions or procedures of art—or science. Some think that the very distinction between acquaintance with and knowledge about something is false. It is argued, for instance, that there is no such thing as objectivity, for every individual personally participates in all acts of understanding; all knowledge, therefore, is personal knowledge (e.g., Polanyi, 1958). Members of the so-called New Physics claim that observers can't eliminate themselves from the picture. Thus, people can't observe reality without changing it. And people can't study the world *except* from a point of view that affects what they see (see Zukav, 1979). If correct, this means that facts cannot be separated from values.

The debate over how we know what we know has engaged thinkers for at least 2,500 years. And like most questions worth asking, it will undoubtedly continue to be debated long past our lifetimes. Meanwhile, for **heuristic** purposes, we will draw the distinction between subjective personal acquaintance with and objective knowledge about the world around us.

In light of this heuristic distinction, let us examine a poem: Carl Sandburg's "Chicago." It may be folk art, not great art—that is a question for literary critics. But we can read it

Fig. 1-2 TWO PATHS TO KNOWLEDGE. A coal-heaver's home on West 28th Street. Social reformer Jacob Riis's photos of poverty at the turn of the twentieth century give a firsthand "acquaintance with" New York City's tenement life. Data from the U.S. census in Table 1-1 gives facts upon which more abstract "knowledge about" poverty can be founded. (Library of Congress)

Table 1-1 Twenty Largest Standard Metropolitan Statistical Areas—Persons and Families by Poverty Status in 1977 and Central City Residence (numbers in thousands)

	Persons						*Families*					
	Total		*Below poverty level*		*Poverty rate*		*Total*		*Below poverty level*		*Poverty rate*	
Standard metropolitan statistical areas	*Number*	*Standard error*	*Number*	*Standard error*	*Percent*	*Standard error*	*Number*	*Standard error*	*Number*	*Standard error*	*Percent*	*Standard error*
New York, N.Y.	10,996	211	1,490	95	13.6	0.8	2,889	63	322	18	11.1	0.6
New York	7,087	171	1,312	89	18.5	1.1	1,868	51	288	17	15.4	0.9
Outside central city	3,909	128	178	28	4.6	0.7	1,021	38	34	7	3.3	0.7
Los Angeles–Long Beach, Calif.	7,224	172	769	69	10.6	0.9	1,839	50	175	14	9.5	0.7
Los Angeles–Long Beach	3,173	115	380	48	12.0	1.4	770	33	78	9	10.1	1.1
Outside central cities	4,051	130	389	41	9.6	1.0	1,069	38	97	12	9.1	1.0
Chicago, Ill.	6,987	170	785	69	11.2	0.9	1,812	50	162	13	8.9	0.7
Chicago	2.942	111	669	64	22.7	1.9	711	31	135	12	19.0	1.5
Outside central city	4,045	130	116	22	2.9	0.5	1,101	39	27	6	2.5	0.6
Philadelphia, Pa.	4,532	137	504	56	11.1	1.2	1,182	40	108	11	9.2	0.9
Philadelphia	1,671	84	327	45	19.6	2.4	427	24	71	9	16.6	1.9
Outside central city	2,859	110	177	27	6.2	0.9	755	32	37	7	4.9	0.9
Detroit, Mich.	4,058	130	316	44	7.8	1.0	1,066	38	65	8	6.1	0.8
Detroit	1,186	71	174	33	14.7	2.5	287	20	34	6	11.8	2.0
Outside central city	2,872	110	142	25	4.9	0.8	779	33	31	7	4.0	0.8
San Francisco–Oakland, Calif.	3,093	114	213	36	6.9	1.1	826	34	45	7	5.5	0.8
Washington, D.C.–Md.–Va.	3,175	115	222	37	7.0	1.1	814	34	41	7	5.0	0.8
Boston, Mass.	2,394	100	278	41	11.6	1.6	634	30	66	8	10.4	1.3
Pittsburgh, Pa.	2,306	98	146	30	6.3	1.3	611	29	26	5	4.3	0.8
St. Louis, Mo. –Ill.	2,233	97	295	43	13.2	1.8	583	28	64	8	11.0	1.3
Baltimore, Md.	2,137	95	243	39	11.4	1.7	556	28	47	7	8.5	1.2
Cleveland, Ohio	2,001	92	178	33	8.9	1.6	516	27	40	7	7.8	1.2
Houston, Tex.	2,407	101	253	39	10.5	1.5	618	29	57	8	9.2	1.2
Newark, N.J.	1,672	84	208	36	12.4	2.0	417	24	42	7	10.2	1.5
Minneapolis–St. Paul, Minn.	1,840	88	98	25	5.3	1.3	472	26	15	4	3.3	0.8
Dallas, Tex.	1,852	88	219	37	11.8	1.9	506	26	50	7	10.0	1.4
Seattle–Everett, Wash.	1,447	78	113	26	7.8	1.7	366	23	23	5	6.2	1.3
Anaheim–Santa Ana–Garden Grove, Calif.	1,820	88	56	19	3.1	1.0	496	26	10	3	2.0	0.6
Milwaukee, Wis.	1,485	79	94	24	6.3	1.6	383	23	21	5	5.6	1.2
Atlanta, Ga.	1,472	79	191	34	12.9	2.2	392	23	43	7	10.9	1.6

NOTE: Persons and families as of March 1978.

SOURCE: U.S. Bureau of the Census, *Current Population Reports* Series p-60, No. 119, "Characteristics of the Population Below the Poverty Level: 1977" (Washington, D.C.: U.S. Government Printing Office, 1979), Table 46, p. 197.

to see what and how it communicates to readers. Here is an excerpt from Sandburg's 1914 word picture of his adopted city.

Chicago

HOG Butcher for the World,
Tool Maker, Stacker of Wheat,
Player with Railroads and the Nation's
  Freight Handler;
Stormy, husky, brawling,
City of the Big Shoulders:
They tell me you are wicked and I believe
  them, for I have seen your painted
  women under the gas lamps luring the
  farm boys.
And they tell me you are crooked and I
  answer: Yes, it is true I have seen the
  gunman kill and go free to kill again.
And they tell me you are brutal and my
  reply is: On the faces of women and
  children I have seen the marks of wan-
  ton hunger.
And having answered so I turn once more
  to those who sneer at this my city, and I
  give them back the sneer and say to
  them:
Come and show me another city with
  lifted head singing so proud to be alive
  and coarse and strong and cunning.
Flinging magnetic curses amid the toil of
  piling job on job, here is a tall bold slug-
  ger set vivid against the little soft
  cities. . . . (in Williams, 1952:579)

Sandburg's strong images paint a two-sided face of Chicago: vitality and brutality. A proud, strong, cunning and crooked, hungry, wicked city.

a

b

Fig. 1-3 SANDBURG'S CHICAGO. (*a*) The intense energy that characterized Chicago in 1905 is reflected in the street life. This photo was taken at State and Madison Streets, said to be the busiest streetcorner in the world at the time. Note Louis Sullivan's skyscraper (later the Carson Pirie & Scott Company) at the right; Sullivan's Art Nouveau decoration frames the store's display windows. It has been called one of the great works of modern commercial architecture. (*b*) Chicago's five-term mayor, Carter H. Harrison II (whose father also served five terms as mayor), was considered incorruptible, despite the widespread city corruption of his day by financiers such as Charles T. Yerkes (immortalized as *The Financier* and *The Titan* in Dreiser's novels). About himself, Mayor Harrison said, "Chicago is fortunate in having a mayor who keeps his hands in his own pockets." (*c*) George A. Regan's tavern on South Halsted Street, which could have served as Finley Peter Dunne's model when he created "Mr. Dooley," one of America's foremost social critics. (*a,b,c* Chicago Historical Society)

c

Aside from communicating the feel of an industrial city on the move, Sandburg's poem offers insight into the services that Chicago performs: "HOG Butcher for the World," "Tool Maker, Stacker of Wheat," and "Player with Railroads and the Nation's Freight Handler." Compare that listing with a more systematic classification of city functions by Harris and Ullman (1945). According to these geographers, there are three different kinds of cities, although one city may perform all three functions: (1) *central place cities*—performing central services, such as retail trade, for their surrounding area; (2) *transport cities*—including railroad centers and ports; and (3) *specialized function cities*—performing one particular service, such as mining or meat packing. From the first three lines of Sandburg's poem, we know that Chicago is a city that performs all three functions: (1) central place—"Tool Maker, Stacker of Wheat"; (2) transport—"the Nation's Freight Handler"; and (3) specialized function—"HOG Butcher for the World." Thus, the kind of city Chicago is can be derived from Sandburg's poem as well as from the Harris and Ullman classification scheme.

Writers, artists, and social scientists often communicate similar messages but use different methods and styles. The awareness of industrial city life is more intimate and direct in Sandburg's poetic vision than in the geographers' scheme. As a Chicagoan of Sandburg's era, sociologist Robert E. Park, said in his classic essay on the city in 1916 (1974:3), "We are mainly indebted to writers of fiction for our more intimate knowledge of contemporary urban life." Park continued, however, that urban life "demands a more searching and disinterested study"—a marriage of personal acquaintance with and knowledge about the city. And that is what Park and the distinguished urban-oriented scholars at the University of Chicago proposed to do in 1916.

UNDERSTANDING CHICAGO IN ITS HEYDAY, 1900–1920

Using Social Science and Literature as Paths to Knowledge

To novelist Nelson Algren, Chicago is the

> Most native of American cities, where the chrome-colored convertible cuts through the traffic ahead of the Polish peddler's pushcart. And the long, low-lighted parlor-cars stroke past in a single, even yellow flow. . . . Big-shot town, small-shot town, jet-propelled old-fashioned town, by old-world hands with new-world tools built into a place whose heartbeat carries farther than its shout. . . . (Algren, [1952] 1961:59–60)

Around the time that Park and his University of Chicago colleagues were scientifically studying the city—using Chicago as their sociological laboratory—a world literature was being produced in the Windy City. From the beginning of this century until roughly 1920, Chicago produced writers in the same way that it created the nation's first skyscrapers in the 1880s. Writers became so numerous in Chicago in the period 1900–1920 that literary critic H. L. Mencken observed that it had nearly taken over the entire field of American letters.

Why was Chicago like a magnet, attracting writers speaking with a new American voice? Why was Chicago also an architect's dream town, with Louis Sullivan's skyscrapers and Frank Lloyd Wright's prairie houses? And why was Chicago a social scientist's town, a lab for urban research? Why? For many of the same reasons.

Novelist Nelson Algren suggests that Chicago's great literary scene did not happen accidentally:

Chicago is the . . . city in which a literature bred by hard times . . . once became a world literature. . . . For it was here that those arrangements more convenient to owners of property than to the propertyless were most persistently contested by the American conscience. ([1952] 1961:12–13)

"Those arrangements more convenient to owners of property" had been contested even before the turn of the century. Indeed, Chicago was a center of industry and industrial conflict by the 1870s.

Labor Radicalism, Industrial Progress, and Social Reform

Several events before 1900 give a feeling for the conflicting currents in Chicago. First, there was the railroad strike in 1877, which prepared fertile ground for socialist and anarchist organizers among the workers. Second, there was the Haymarket Square affair in 1886. This was a labor meeting in Haymarket Square, called to protest police violence against locked-out employees at the Cyrus McCormick Harvester Works. It ended when an unknown person or persons threw a bomb into the crowd. (Later, four labor organizers, thought to be anarchists, were found guilty of bomb throwing and hanged.) The Haymarket Square affair, according to one urban historian, "symbolized an era in American history; it dramatized the determination of the business interests to maintain the status quo" (Spear, 1967:3).

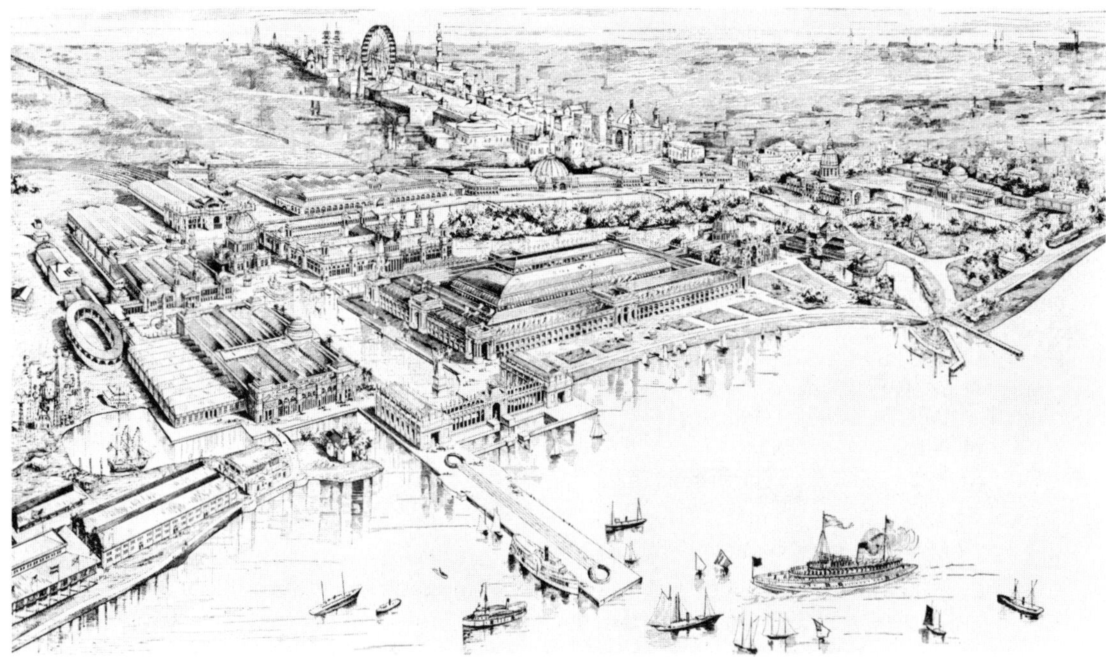

Fig. 1-4 BIRD'S-EYE VIEW OF THE CHICAGO WORLD'S FAIR, 1893. The monumental neoclassical architecture of the Columbian Exposition was an inspiration for the City Beautiful movement throughout America. (Hubert Howe Bancroft, *The Book of the Fair*, Chicago, 1893, p. 71)

Box 1-1

CHICAGO'S "OFFICIAL" HISTORY

What Schoolchildren Learned about Their City

What an elementary school textbook writer chooses to include—and exclude—gives clues to the "official" version of history at a particular time. Thus, examining the content of a grammar school history book can be most instructive.

One widely used elementary text in the 1910s and 1920s was Jennie Hall's *The Story of Chicago*, published in 1911 and revised in 1929. Interestingly, this text, distributed to schools by the Chicago Board of Education, contains no mentions of certain facets of the city's history: political corruption, labor history, industrial conflict, or ethnic prejudice and discrimination. One does find Haymarket Square, complete with a line drawing of its hustle-bustle, but the incident that immortalized it—the Haymarket Square affair in 1886—goes unmentioned. Here is is what Chicago schoolchildren learned about its function: "There is another place in Chicago besides the market on 14th Street where vegetables are sold. It is Haymarket Square on the west side. . . . Haymarket tells you a story of the many truck gardens near this great city" (p. 250). Yes, but Haymarket, of course, symbolizes quite another story.

Somewhat ironically, Hall (a teacher at one of Chicago's elite private schools) hoped that her book would be "a finger pointing to real material for study" (p. 303). What is "real material," however, is usually a matter of some controversy.

In the following excerpt from *The Story of Chicago*, note particularly how the text handles the problems of the city and the proposed solutions. Compare Hall's "official" textbook version of history to the IWW's "unofficial" competing vision contained in Chaplin's songs. Clearly, their views of reality do not coincide.

> Why did Chicago, built in a swampy wilderness, become a great city? Where will a large city grow up? There must be people living about with things to sell. Good land roads or water roads must lead to her. . . . [In Chicago] land travel met lake travel. That is why we are a railroad center. That is why cattle are brought here. . . . That is why grain comes here. . . . All these industries bring workers. These people need stores, theatres, churches, schools. . . . So the city keeps adding to itself. Soon it comes to need officers to take care of it and its people—mayor, policemen, firemen, board of health, street commissioners. Then it gets into trouble because it is so big. In some places its houses are so close together that people get no sunshine and children no place to play. Some of its tenements are too crowded. The air is smoky from factories. Many of the people are poor. The city need try no more to be large and rich. But it must try to be clean and comfortable and happy. That is the great problem now, and there is much work to be done in solving it.
>
> There are many fine public schools in Chicago. . . . Americanization schools help the foreigner to become a good citizen. . . . But there is still much to be done in making the schools as useful to all as they can be. People must be taught to make even better use of . . . the public libraries and the Art Institute. . . . (Hall, [1911]1929:261–264; 287–288)

Third, there was the Chicago World's Fair—the Columbian Exposition in 1893. Led by the famous architect and planner Daniel Burnham (remembered by his quip, "Make no little plans"), a group of architects, promoters, and planners constructed a White City, part of the City Beautiful, on Chicago's South Side. It was a monument to industrial progress, showing off the technology that was making the United States a world economic power. Visitors came from all over the world to see the exposition's midway, the world's first Ferris wheel, and the Woman's Building (designed by a woman and featuring art and exhibits by women exclusively).

Fourth, there was the Pullman railroad

Box 1-1 (*continued*)

CHICAGO'S UNOFFICIAL HISTORY

What Some People Were Singing About

The Industrial Workers of the World (IWW), nicknamed the "Wobblies," were organized in Chicago in 1905. Their goal was to organize unskilled workers in the factories and fields throughout the nation. They focused their efforts on groups considered to be dispossessed and downtrodden, including textile mill workers in the Northeast, coal and iron miners in West Virginia and Minnesota, migrant workers, and Northwest lumberjacks.

"Sing and fight" was a Wobblie slogan. Many organizers shaped their protests into songs as tools for agitation. About 1909, the first edition of their "Little Red Song Book" appeared, with its cover announcing: "IWW Songs—to Fan the Flames of Discontent."

The most popular union song in the United States, "Solidarity Forever," was written by Wobblie organizer Ralph Chaplin after his return from a coal miners' strike near Charleston, West Virginia, in 1915. Sung to the tune of "John Brown's Body," the song is full of revolutionary fervor. One stanza reveals the Wobblie view of the new industrial order—class struggle—in which people are divided into two camps: THEM (owners of mines and factories, the capitalists) and US (the exploited workers):

> They have taken untold millions that they never toiled to earn,
> But without our brain and muscle not a single wheel could turn.
> We can break their haughty power, gain our freedom when we learn
> That the union makes us strong.

Wobblie organizer Joe Hill was one of the IWW's best songwriters, as well as a leading agitator. In 1914, Hill was arrested in Salt Lake City on a murder charge and executed there. The day before his execution in 1915, he sent IWW head Big Bill Haywood a wire in Chicago: "Don't waste time mourning. Organize." Joe Hill's body was brought to Chicago, where a great funeral procession was held. One of the songs sung by the approximately 30,000 sympathizers was Ralph Chaplin's "The Commonwealth of Toil" (in Fowke and Glazer, 1961:14–16):

> In the gloom of mighty cities,
> Midst the roar of whirling wheels,
> We are toiling on like chattel slaves of old,
> And our masters hope to keep us
> Ever thus beneath their heels,
> And to coin our very life blood into gold.
>
> CHORUS
> But we have a glowing dream
> Of how fair the world will seem
> When each man can live his life secure and free;
> When the earth is owned by labor
> And there's joy and peace for all
> In the Commonwealth of Toil that is to be.
>
> They would keep us cowed and beaten,
> Cringing meekly at their feet.
> They would stand between each worker and his bread.
> Shall we yield our lives up to them
> For the bitter crust we eat?
> Shall we only hope for heaven when we're dead?
>
> They have laid our lives out for us
> To the utter end of time.
> Shall we stagger on beneath their heavy load?
> Shall we let them live forever
> In their gilded halls of crime,
> With our children doomed to toil beneath their goad?

strike in 1894. The strike shut down the nation's railroads and brought federal troops to the city. Railroad magnate George Pullman had constructed a model industrial town for his workers just south of Chicago; the privately owned company town was a totally planned community, with decent housing for the workers, attractive shopping arcades, a library, and a hotel. But no matter how lovely the parklike setting and the amenities for workers in Pullman's town, it was still Pullman's town. His ownership and control bore the seeds of industrial conflict, not peace.

And finally, there was a variety of efforts aimed at social reform. These ranged from Jane Addams's work at Hull House on the West Side to attempts to reform City Hall and improve sanitary conditions in the slums led by local merchants and their wives.

All this—industrial conflict, attempts at reform, monuments to "progress" and technology—was taking place in the world's fastest-growing metropolis of the era: Chicago. And all this so shortly after Mrs. O'Leary's cow had allegedly started the 1871 fire that ravaged one-third of the city.

In its heyday, Chicago was many things to many people. It had the reputation of being the most politically radical of all American cities. Among others, it was the town of socialist Eugene V. Debs and Big Bill Haywood, leader of the Industrial Workers of the World. (See Box 1-1.)

Urban Researchers and Writers: Convergent Goals

The "City of the Big Shoulders" was also the cradle of urban research in the United States. Why? For many of the same reasons that made Chicago the most stimulating literary scene of its day. As writer Algren put it, it was in Chicago that challenges were made to the existing economic and social arrangements by "a conscience in touch with humanity." Social scientists at the University of Chicago who pioneered urban research were an important part of that conscience.

As two University of Chicago sociologists later recalled about this period:

> By the time our studies began, the various ethnic neighborhoods were well established. . . . By this time, too, public sentiment had crystallized into rather firm prejudice and discrimination against the new arrivals from Eastern Europe and Southern Europe. . . . Landlords were taking advantage of the crowded housing situation. . . . The city administration was commonly regarded as corrupt. . . . Many families were desperately poor. (Burgess and Bogue, 1964:5)

Sociologists tried to understand and interpret social and economic forces at work in the slums and their effect on slum dwellers. Their objective was scientific analysis. But their hope was a moral one, and it was policy-oriented: "To dispel prejudice and injustice" and to help change the plight of the slum dwellers.

The numerous poets and novelists inspired or formed by the Chicago scene didn't aim for scientific analysis. Yet, they shared the social scientists' goal: to dispel prejudice and injustice.

Here are a few injustices exposed by Chicago's literary figures. There was the injustice of grain speculators in Chicago's wheat market, exposed by Frank Norris. Norris's *The Pit* ([1903] 1970:41) paints Chicago's Board of Trade building, the global center of the wheat trade, in dark colors: "black, monolithic, crouching on its foundations like a monstrous sphinx with blind eyes, silent, grave."

There was political corruption, exposed by novelist Theodore Dreiser. The story of financier Charles T. Yerkes's buying and selling of Chicago—by corrupting city officials—is told in Dreiser's *The Financier* (1912) and *The Titan* (1914).

There were the savage practices at the Union Stockyards, the place that made Chicago "HOG butcher for the World." Socialist Upton Sinclair exposed the unsanitary conditions and adulteration of food at the nation's stockyards in the greatest muckraking novel of all, *The Jungle* (1905). This exposé had public policy impact, too, influencing the passage of the Pure Food and Drug Act by Congress.

Chicago's urban literature ranged in tone from reformist muckraking to socialist outrage. Some described what they saw as "capitalist decay" and the oppression of the many by the few. Like West Coast writer Jack London, Upton Sinclair saw the evils of capitalism in the new industrial order, represented by Chicago. Sinclair measured *what was* against *what could be* in his ideal society under socialism. By contrast, Theodore Dreiser accepted the new industrial order and its corruption as the American destiny, as "natural."

There was also a bit of nostalgia for less complex times. Some novelists idealized the Jeffersonian ideal of the small town. Big-city

Box 1-2

POLITICS AND THE NOVEL

The Impact of Upton Sinclair's The Jungle

In *The Jungle* (1905), novelist Sinclair tells the tragic story of Jurgis Rudkus, a Lithuanian immigrant, and his relatives and friends who work at the Union Stockyards and live nearby, in the "back of the yards" neighborhood. There, in what Sinclair called Packingtown, immigrants were victimized by those who had control or influence over them: landlords, real estate brokers, meatpacking bosses, first-line supervisors, and political bosses. Sinclair paints a dreary picture of crushed lives and wretchedness under these conditions. In the end, Rudkus turns to socialism as the only hope for a decent life.

Ironically, very few pages of Sinclair's novel are devoted to the brutality, filth, and smell of the stockyards. But that is what caught the public eye—and stomach. Sinclair's purpose was much broader: to expose what he considered the evils of capitalism, especially "wage slavery," and to make an appeal for socialism. But, as he said of his own work, "I aimed at the public's heart and by accident I hit it in the stomach."

The Jungle had immediate political impact, if not the kind Sinclair had hoped for. President Theodore Roosevelt, who had seen an advance copy of the book, wired Sinclair to visit him in Washington, D.C., to talk about stockyard conditions. Six months later, over violent opposition by the meatpacking industry, a Pure Food and Drug Act and a Beef Inspection Act were passed by Congress.

One of the leading social critics of the day, Chicago journalist Finley Peter Dunne's fictional Irish bartender, "Mr. Dooley," had this to say about Roosevelt's reaction:

> Tiddy was toying with a light breakfast an' idly turnin' over th' pages iv th' new book with both hands. Suddenly he rose fr'm th' table, an' crin': "I'm pizened," begun throwin' sausages out iv th' window. Th' ninth won sthruck Sinitor Biv'ridge on th' head an' made him a blond. It bounced off, exploded, an' blew a leg off a secret-service agent, an' th' scatthred fragmints desthroyed a handsome row iv' ol' oak-trees. Sinitor Biv'ridge rushed in, thinin' that th' Presidint was bein' assassynated be his devoted followers in th' Sinit, an' discovered Tiddy engaged in a hand-to-hand conflict with a potted ham. Th' Sinitor fr'om Injyanny, with a few well-directed wurruds, put out th' fuse an' rendered th' missile harmless. Since thin th' Prisidint, like th' rest iv us, has become a viggytaryan. . . . (Dunne, 1906:247–54)

life was sometimes viewed as destructive of human and humane values.

In general, then, writers reacted in two different ways to Chicago and the new republic for which it stood. Some looked backward and others looked forward. Novelists of the Progressive Era (1904–1917)

> based their values either on the traditional individualism and amenity of an agricultural and small owner's way of life (which was the ideal of the Progressive movement), or on . . . Socialism . . . (Kazin, [1942] 1956: 64–5)

Urban research started by the Chicago sociologists, beginning in the Progressive Era, arose from the same mix of responses to the new industrial order. Robert Park, for instance, had some nostalgia for the small town in Minnesota where he grew up. At the same time, Park was deeply ambivalent about the limitations of small-town life and the sense of community it supposedly offered. Before teaching at the University of Chicago, he had been a reformist-minded news reporter in the Midwest and publicity person for Booker T. Washington's Tuskegee Institute. Park's colleague, Ernest W. Burgess (who constructed a classic model of urban space and growth, detailed in Chapter 13), was concerned with the fragmentation of community and what he assumed to be a result of urban-industrial life: social disorganization, indicated by crime, delinquency, family breakdown, and so forth.

The City Beautiful

Urban research . . . social reform . . . big novels. All responses to Chicago, "the capital of the frontier world of acquisitive energy" (Kazin, [1942] 1956: 94) and the pulse-beat of the heartland. But what about other professionals and interested parties—how did they react to the expanding industrial city?

Chicago's business executives focused their energy on promoting the city's industrial development and facilitating suburbanization. City planners concentrated their efforts on making the city more beautiful.

It was in the Plan of Chicago that the expertise and ideas of planner extraordinaire Daniel Burnham came together with the interests of Chicago's business leaders. Labeling his idea the **"City Beautiful,"** Burnham persuaded the influential Chicago Commercial Club to back the Chicago Plan of 1909: a giant, even superhuman-scale, city plan. Burnham's idea was to create romantic parks and lovely waterfront landscapes by Lake Michigan with huge plazas and broad thoroughfares. This was to serve as a contrast to city life. According to Burnham,

> Natural scenery furnishes the contrasting element to the artificiality of the city. *All of us should often run away . . . into the wilds, where mind and body are restored to a normal condition,* and we are enabled to take up the burden of life in our crowded streets and endless stretches of buildings with renewed vigor and hopefulness. . . . (Burnham and Bennett in Glaab and Brown, 1976:241; italics ours)

Clearly, Burnham thought the city was a place to escape from.

Interestingly, the Chicago Plan hardly mentioned the "burden of life" on those shoulders which carried more than their measure: the urban poor. As the University of Chicago researchers and the novelists had well noted, by 1909 parts of Chicago were one immense slum, housing new immigrants from Eastern and Southern Europe in crowded, overpriced, deteriorated tenements. But only two short paragraphs of Burnham's Chicago Plan are devoted to the problems of the widespread slums. And what were the suggested solutions? The plan, in familiar-sounding language, suggested two ways of dealing with what it termed "the unwholesome district": (1) cutting broad boulevards through it and (2) enforcing sanitation and cleanliness codes.

So, Chicago became a proving ground for Burnham's City Beautiful concept: that cities could be improved physically without any restructuring of economic, social, or political institutions. Most of the improvements that Burnham counseled, aside from the glorious parks for people wishing to flee the city, were meant to spur commerce and industry. For instance, Michigan Avenue and other streets were to be widened to facilitate downtown traffic. "No wonder," writes one of Chicago's biographers, "the cry went up that the Chicago Plan was in reality a scheme to tax the poor for improvements desired by the rich" (Lowe, 1978:173–74).

The Chicago Plan emphasized civic beauty, for Burnham was convinced that human nature craved beauty so much that "people will travel far to find and enjoy it." This vision of human nature and what people need to lead healthy, fulfilling urban lives was distinctly different from what Chicago's novelists and urban researchers believed.

The City Beautiful. The squalor of the slums. Industrial progress and poverty. Chicago was all of these. And it was a poet—Carl Sandburg—who perhaps best captured the promise and the problems of the city. In "Chicago" and other poems, Sandburg draws an image of the Windy City as a wondrous thing, a bold human enterprise. Yet Chicago, this new city, this representative of the new industrial order, corrupts what he considered human emotions. That is, in the shuffle for the almighty dollar and industrial development, Sandburg feared that friendship, mutual caring, and human dignity were lost amid the skyscrapers and the steel.

Sandburg's view of Chicago—and more broadly, urban industrial capitalist society—echoes the theories put forward by many nineteenth-century social theorists about urban life. And his views resound in the work of the Chicago school of sociology. As we discuss in Chapter 5, University of Chicago urban theorist Louis Wirth viewed "Urbanism as a Way of Life"; several of Wirth's key ideas parallel the images drawn by Sandburg.

Alienation. Rootlessness. Superficial relationships. The loss of human connections. Money instead of personal relations as the bond of association among people. These were what poet Sandburg and theorist Wirth saw as the price to be paid for living in the modern industrial American city. At the same time, both of them noted the energy, the greater mobility, and the increased individual freedom which the new industrial city promised. Such were the contradictions in Chicago, and in the new American industrial order which Chicago symbolized. Using ideas or images, Chicago's urbanists, poets, political organizers, and novelists alerted their different audiences to the promise and conditions of urban life.

To summarize: Both Chicago writers and urbanists responded to the new industrial order that Chicago represented. Both described and labeled new phenomena, whether in the form of personal images which communicated a subjective acquaintance with the city or in the form of abstract, objective maps and models which provided knowledge about urban life. Rooted in the same historical climate, their insights often ran parallel. Some theorists, like Park, had a nostalgic affection for small-town, agricultural communities; they worried about the loss of the sense of community in a big industrial city. Others, like Upton Sinclair, described similar urban conditions but saw the causes of urban problems as part of the economic and social arrangements under capitalism.

Fig. 1-5 SIN CITY. Painter Thomas Hart Benton portrayed his view of urban life in *City Activities with Subway* (1930), a mural painted on the walls of the New School for Social Research in New York City. To Benton, raised in a small town in the Midwest, large cities seemed fragmented and frantic. Worse yet, in his view, great cities were run by gay aesthetes and Marxists, and thus were "dead." The subjects he chose and his style reflect his anticity bias: a burlesque show, boxing match, Salvation Army band, tabloid newspaper, and subway. (© New School for Social Research, New York)

These differences in vision remain to this day. So do controversies about civic beauty and what urbanites need to thrive. Which brings us to another poem by Carl Sandburg (1970:628–29):

Elephants are Different to Different People

Wilson and Pilcer and Snack stood before the zoo elephant.
Wilson said, "What is its name? Is it from Asia or
Africa? Who feeds it? Is it a he or a she? How
old is it? Do they have twins? How much does it cost
to feed? How much does it weigh? If it dies how much
will another one cost? If it dies what will they use
the bones, the fat, and the hide for? What use is it
besides to look at?"

Pilcer didn't have any questions; he was murmuring
to himself, "It's a house by itself, walls and windows,
the ears came from tall cornfields, by God; the
architect of those legs was a workman, by God; he stands like a bridge out across deep water; the face
is sad and the eyes are kind; I know elephants are
good to babies."
Snack looked up and down and at last said to
himself, "He's a tough son-of-a-gun outside and
I'll bet he's got a strong heart, I'll bet he's
strong as a copper-riveted boiler inside."
They didn't put up any arguments.
They didn't throw anything in each other's faces.
Three men saw the elephant three ways
And let it go at that.
They didn't spoil a sunny Sunday afternoon.
"Sunday comes only once a week," they told each other.

Our aim is to see the elephant (in this case, the city) in more than three ways—and *not* let it go at that. Why? Are we just spoilers? No. We think that working through the grounds of controversy, not sweeping them under the rug for the sake of a sunny Sunday afternoon, is essential to understanding. We think that wide-angle vision and spirited debate are needed to reclaim the promise of the city and to deal effectively with urban conditions. We respect and honor both the famous and the unknown who have spent their lives, even given their lives, fighting for different visions of what *could* be and what *should* be in the city good, true, and beautiful.

Thus, this book is not full of definitive answers or solutions to long-standing urban conditions. Nor is it a tract for a particular point of view. Rather, it is an invitation to learn about urban life, a request to open your eyes, ears, heart, and mind to experiencing and reflecting upon the city. We hope to provide tools, information, and perspectives that will assist in deciding whether Wilson, Pilcer, or Snack sees the beast most clearly—or whether they all suffer from tunnel vision.

PROJECTS

1. **Understanding the city through social science and art**. Compare the treatment of one U.S. city by artists and social scientists. Taking Los Angeles, for example, what impressions does one get from the film *Welcome to L.A.* (1976) and the movie version of Nathanael West's novel *The Day of the Locust* (1975)? What impressions does one get from looking at statistical data on Los Angeles (and Hollywood) that relate to subjects treated in the artistic works?

2. **An eye-ear tour of one city**. Walk around a city with a notebook or camera and tape recorder, recording the following: the *soundscape* of the city (are some areas more noisy than others? what different sounds typify different neighborhoods—e.g., are there chidren's voices everywhere? are there any street sellers or knife sharpeners calling out their services in any areas?) and the *landscape* (what are the city's most imposing buildings and what functions are performed in them? are church spires, factory smokestacks, or office buildings the tallest structures? what do the bulletin boards and signs advertise? if street murals exist, what do they portray?how many different forms of art can you find in the city?).

SUGGESTIONS FOR FURTHER LEARNING

The tendency in American thought and literature to romanticize rural and small-town life and denigrate urban life is detailed in Morton and Lucia White's *The Intellectual versus the City: From Thomas Jefferson to Frank Lloyd Wright* (New York: Mentor, 1964). For an opposite view—that "civilization in the United States survives only in the big cities"—see H. L. Mencken, *The Vintage Mencken*, edited by Alistair Cooke (New York: Vintage, 1956).

Works of art, literature, and films that take cities as their settings or subjects are too numerous to mention. Examples which show the range of popular films include Willard Van Dyke's early documentary film *The City* (1939), with narration by Lewis Mumford; it romanticizes the New England small town, focuses on the lack of humanity in big industrial cities, and calls for new greenbelt communities; Fritz Lang's classic feature film *Metropolis* (1927), whose setting is a robotlike underground city composed of workers and an affluent overground city of their bosses; and Charlie Chaplin's *City Lights* (1931), a tale of any city (the plot turns on a meeting between the Little Tramp and a millionaire). The novels of small-town America include Sinclair Lewis's *Main Street* (New York: Harcourt Brace, 1920), set in Sauk Centre, Minnesota, and Sherwood Anderson's *Winesburg, Ohio* (New York: Modern Library, 1947) (in actuality his hometown of Clyde, Ohio, near Toledo). Both Lewis and Anderson deromanticized small-town life.

Saul Bellow's *The Adventures of Augie March* (New York: Viking, [1949] 1964) and James Farrell's *Studs Lonigan* (New York: Modern Library, 1938) trilogy give different views of Chicago life in the post-World War I era. In *The Moviegoer* (New York: Popular Library, 1962), Walker Percy captures what he calls "the genie-soul" of the city: "here is Chicago . . . the buildings are heavy and squarish and set down far apart and at random like monuments on a great windy plain. And the Lake . . . Here the Lake is the North itself: a perilous place from which the spirit winds come pouring forth all roused up and crying out alarm. . . . This is a city where no one dares dispute the claim of the wind and the skyey space to the out-of-doors. This Midwestern sky is the nakedest, loneliest sky in America. To escape it, people live inside and underground." Novelist James Baldwin gives another view of the city—the black ghetto of New York's Harlem in *Go Tell It on the Mountain* (New York: Dell, 1952).

Alienation and dehumanization in the modern city is a continuing theme in the drawings of *Saul Steinberg* (by Harold Rosenberg, New York: Knopf, 1978). But in the paintings of Ralph Fasanella, the city is depicted as a joyous place, with stickball games, as well as a place of aloneness. See Patrick Watson's *Fasanella's City* (New York: Ballantine, 1973).

An excellent study of a city's architecture and its relationship to the social context is David Lowe's *Lost Chicago* (Boston: Houghton Mifflin, 1978); it proceeds from the comment by the architect of the American skyscraper and inventor of Art Nouveau in the United States, Louis Sullivan: "Our architecture reflects us, as truly as a mirror. . . . "

Books by visual anthropologist-photographer Bill Owens give an intimate view of *Suburbia* (San Francisco: Straight Arrow Press, 1973); *Our Kind of People* (San Francisco: Straight Arrow Press, 1975); and *Working* (New York: Simon & Schuster, 1977).

Of special interest are two documentaries which provide the opportunity to link personal acquaintance with knowledge about city life. In *The Writer and the City* (1970) Alfred Kazin narrates, reading the words of writers about Chicago and New York City, while powerful visual images invade the screen. In "Calcutta" (1968), a section of Louis Malle's prize-winning *Phantom India*, intellect and emotions are both stretched.

KEY TERMS

Acquaintance with Personal, direct, intuitive, holistic, nonlinear, concrete, subjective knowledge.

City Beautiful A movement inspired by architect-city planner Daniel Burnham around the turn of the twentieth century. City Beautiful planners believed that people needed to escape from the burden of city life to natural surroundings, such as large parks, and that cities could be improved physically without restructuring basic institutions.

Heuristic A model, assumption, or device that is not necessarily scientifically true but is a useful tool to aid in the discovery of new relationships. For example, classifying people as urbanites or rural dwellers is a heuristic device that assumes urbanites share common traits in contrast to rural people.

Knowledge about Systematic, abstract, linear, theoretical, objective knowledge.

REFERENCES

Algren, Nelson
[1952]
1961 Chicago: City on the Make. Sausalito, Calif.: Contact Editions.

Bellow, Saul
[1949]
1964 The Adventures of Augie March. New York: Viking.

Burgess, Ernest W. and Donald J. Bogue (eds.)
1964 Contributions to Urban Sociology. Chicago: University of Chicago Press.

Dreiser, Theodore
1912 The Financier. New York: Burt.
1914 The Titan. New York: Boni & Liveright.

Dunne, Finley Peter
1906 "The food we eat". Pp. 247–54 in Finley Peter Dunne, Dissertations by Mr. Dooley. New York: Harper and Brothers.

Fowke, Edith and Joe Glazer (eds.)
1961 Songs of Work and Freedom. Garden City, N.Y.: Dolphin Doubleday.

Glaab, Charles N. and A. Theodore Brown
1976 A History of Urban America. New York: Macmillan.

Hall, Jennie
[1911]
1929 The Story of Chicago. Chicago: Rand McNally.

Harris, Chauncy D. and Edward L. Ullman
1945 "The nature of cities." Annals of the American Academy of Political and Social Science 242:7–17.

Kazin, Alfred
[1942]
1956 On Native Grounds: A Study of American Prose Literature from 1890 to the Present. Garden City, N.Y.: Doubleday Anchor.

Lomax, Alan
1960 The Folk Songs of North America in the English Language. Garden City, N.Y.: Doubleday.

Lowe, David
1978 Lost Chicago. Boston: Houghton Mifflin.

Lukács, Georg
1971 Writer & Critic and Other Essays. New York: Grosset & Dunlap.

Norris, Frank
[1903]
1970 The Pit. Columbus, Ohio: Charles E. Merrill.

Park, Robert Ezra
[1916]
1974 "The city: suggestions for the investigation of human behavior in the urban environment." Pp. 1–46 in Robert E. Park, Ernest W. Burgess, and Roderick D. McKenzie, The City. Chicago: University of Chicago Press.

Polanyi, Michael
1958 Personal Knowledge. Chicago: University of Chicago Press.

Riis, Jacob A.
[1901]
1971 How the Other Half Lives: Studies among the Tenements of New York. New York: Dover.

Sandburg, Carl
1970 The Complete Poems of Carl Sandburg. New York: Harcourt Brace Jovanovich.

Sinclair, Upton
1905 The Jungle. New York: Vanguard.

Spear, Allan H.
1967 Black Chicago: The Making of a Negro Ghetto, 1890–1920. Chicago: University of Chicago Press.

Williams, Oscar (ed.)
1952 A Little Treasury of Modern Poetry. New York: Scribner's.

Wirth, Louis
1938 "Urbanism as a way of life." American Journal of Sociology 44: 1–24.

Zukav, Gary
1979 The Dancing Wu Li Masters: An Overview of the New Physics. New York: Morrow.

Richard Hedman

urbanists see different aspects of city life, depending on what parts they explore

CHAPTER 2 Thinking about Cities

WHAT YOU SEE DEPENDS ON HOW YOU LOOK AT IT

Reality is in the eye of the beholder. This truism is whimsically illustrated in Antoine de Saint-Exupéry's tale, *The Little Prince:*

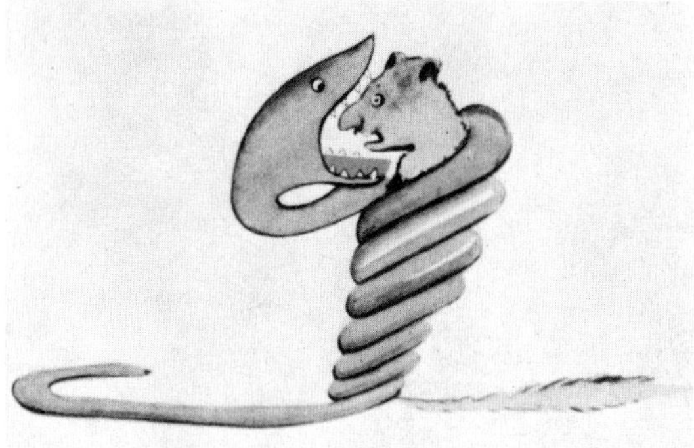

Once when I was six years old I saw a magnificent picture in a book, called *True Stories from Nature*, about the primeval forest. It was a picture of a boa constrictor in the act of swallowing an animal. Here is a copy of the drawing.

In the book it said: "Boa constrictors swallow their prey whole, without chewing it. After that they are not able to move, and they sleep through the six months that they need for digestion."

I pondered deeply, then, over the adventures of the jungle. And after some work with a colored pencil I succeeded in making my first drawing. My Drawing Number One. It looked like this:

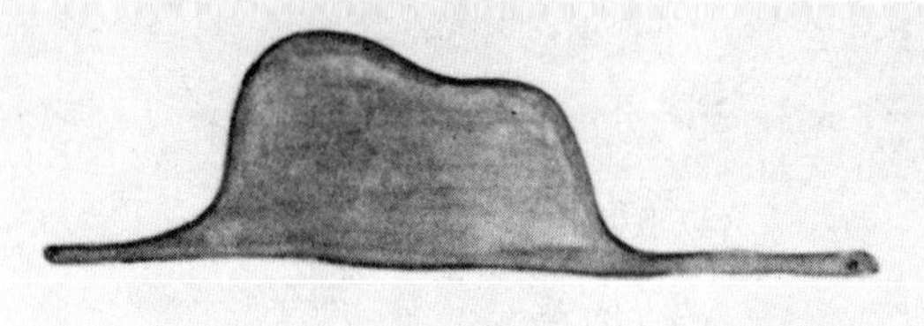

I showed my masterpiece to the grown-ups, and asked them whether the drawing frightened them.

But they answered: "Frighten? Why should anyone be frightened by a hat?"

My drawing was not a picture of a hat. It was a picture of a boa constrictor digesting an elephant. But since the grown-ups were not able to understand it, I made another drawing: I drew the inside of the boa constrictor, so that the grown-ups could see it clearly. They always need to have things explained. My Drawing Number Two looked like this:

The grown-ups' response, this time, was to advise me to lay aside my drawings of boa constrictors, whether from the inside or the outside, and devote myself instead to geography, history, arithmetic and grammar. . . . Grown-ups never understand anything by themselves, and it is tiresome for children to be always and forever explaining things to them.

So then I chose another profession, and learned to pilot airplanes. I have flown a little over all parts of the world; and it is true that geography has been very useful to me. At a glance I can distinguish China from Arizona. If one gets lost in the night, such knowledge is valuable.

In the course of this life . . . [whenever I met a grown-up]who seemed to me at all clear-sighted, I tried the experiment of showing him my Drawing Number One. . . . I would try to find out, so, if this was a person of true understanding. But, whoever it was, he, or she, would always say: "That is a hat."

Then I would never talk to that person about boa constrictors, or primeval forests, or stars. I would bring myself down to his level. I would talk to him about bridge, and golf, and politics, and neckties. And the grown-up would be greatly pleased to have met such a sensible man. (Saint-Exupéry, [1943] 1970:3–5)

Whether we identify with the imaginative pilot or the sensible grown-ups in Antoine de Saint-Exupéry's modern fable, the point is clear: What you see depends on how you look at it. People can look at the same thing and see it through different lenses. Urbanists are no exception. Like all other human beings, urbanists filter what they see through lenses. Whatever lens we use, our vision is necessarily limited, for some things are not focused on (like the inside of the boa constrictor) or are seen only partially or with distortion.

Here's a more concrete example: an urban street scene. Walking down a familiar street every day, you may not see birds overhead or hear teenagers singing. You may filter out information that seems extraneous, missing the less visible and missing the overall picture.

How people see and make sense out of their world depends on many factors, including their age, sex, social background, past experience, present purposes, and so on. For a moment, we want to concentrate on ways of seeing based on different (1) modes of understanding and (2) academic and occupational perspectives.

Different Modes of Understanding

Chapter 1 suggested that acquaintance with and knowledge about urban life are two different paths to understanding. Most of us are routinely trained to use what Saint-Exupéry calls the grown-ups' path: knowledge about. Schools stress reason and logic, not emotion or holistic thought. We aren't taught to see "boa constrictors, or primeval forests, or stars." We are taught to break down wholes into their component parts, to logically dissect complex phenomena. Of course, the sequential, analytic-rational mode is very useful, even essential, to science. After all, as Saint-Exupéry said (tongue-in-cheek), reason helped him to know whether he was flying over China or Arizona.

However, the analytic-rational mode (knowledge about) leads to a particular distortion of reality. Another elephant story will illustrate the point. According to an ancient Indian folktale, six blind men set out to investigate an elephant. After each man touches some part of the beast, they quarrel about what exactly they saw. "It is rough and scaly," says the man who touched the skin. "Not at all," says the one who held the trunk, "it is narrow and soft." Others say the elephant is big, small, round, and hard. None understands the nature of an elephant, for each lacks an overall perspective. Each observation is partially correct. But the whole is more than the sum of its parts, and in this case, the observations don't add up to a whole elephant.

Seeing only part of the beast, whether an elephant or a city, leads to distorted vision. It doesn't result in seeing the big picture.

In his fable, Saint-Exupéry isn't advising that intuition and acquaintance with something should replace reason and systematic thought. Rather, he seems to say: Isn't it a shame that sensible grown-ups have lost the childlike quality of imagining, of seeing beyond the information given. Grown-ups who don't use holistic thought and flashes of intuitive insight are robbed of an entire dimension of understanding.

This brings us to another way of ordering information that floods our senses: academic and occupational perspectives. While useful, they too can lead to partial or distorted vision.

Academic and Occupational Perspectives

People's perception of the world around them is influenced by their academic training and occupation. An exercise developed by Prof. Larry Susskind of the Department of Urban Studies and Planning at the Massachusetts Institute of Technology illustrates these perceptual differences.

Susskind begins by drawing a series of maps on the blackboard. Each one represents a different way of seeing a city. Taking San Francisco as our example here, Fig. 2-1 presents several subjective maps of the city, that is, **cognitive maps**. The bare outline of San Francisco (2-1*a*) is shared by all; the other

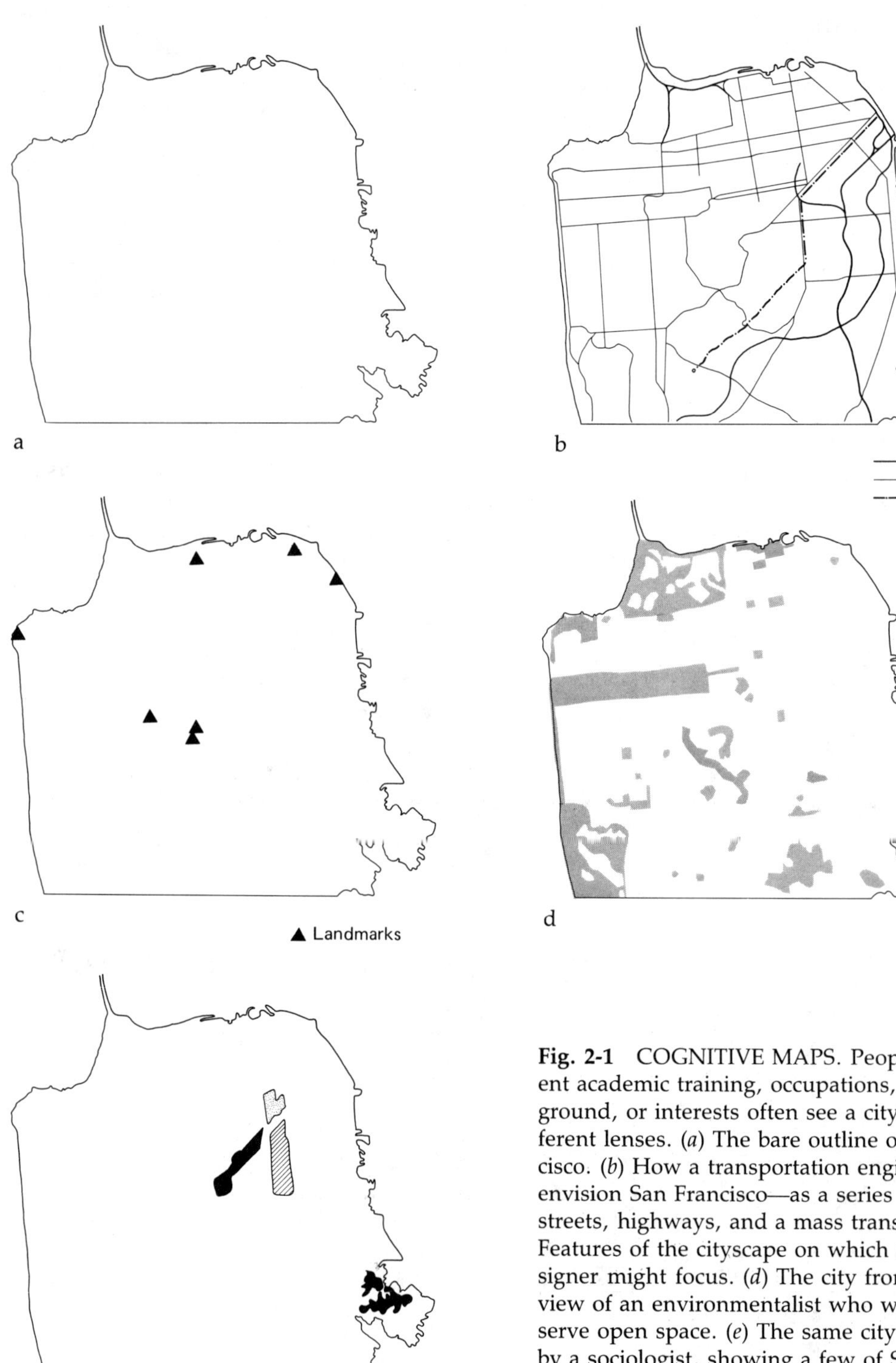

Fig. 2-1 COGNITIVE MAPS. People with different academic training, occupations, social background, or interests often see a city through different lenses. (*a*) The bare outline of San Francisco. (*b*) How a transportation engineer might envision San Francisco—as a series of major streets, highways, and a mass transit line. (*c*) Features of the cityscape on which an urban designer might focus. (*d*) The city from the point of view of an environmentalist who wants to preserve open space. (*e*) The same city as perceived by a sociologist, showing a few of San Francisco's many ethnic communities.

maps are not. Fig. 2-1*b* shows how transportation engineers might see the city. From this perspective, San Francisco is a vast array of transport networks: a ferry terminal, bus lines, cable car tracks, an underground rapid transit system, major arteries, and a street grid. Blank spots on this map (Golden Gate Park, for instance, located in the upper left quadrant) would be of little interest. Transportation engineers might see the city in ways common to the profession, focusing on traffic flows, cost/distance ratios, and the like. Clearly, if this were the major way of seeing San Francisco, a transportation engineer would suffer from tunnel vision.

The environmentalist might see an entirely different city (Fig. 2-1*d*). From this perspective, hilltops, vacant lots, and parks—places omitted from the transportation engineer's map—would be of great interest.

Others would see still another city. The urban designer (Fig. 2-1*c*) may pick out the Transamerica "Pyramid," the city's most visually dominant structure, and visual corridors that offer Bay views. A sociologist (Fig. 2-1*e*) concerned with issues of class and race might focus on neighborhoods of extreme contrast, such as white, affluent Pacific Heights and Chinatown, one of the most densely settled areas in the world. Other parts of the city might be blurry or fade out altogether.

Is it possible that people just don't see parts of the city? Doesn't this exercise using cognitive maps grossly overstate the case? Empirical evidence suggests not. When Kevin Lynch ([1960] 1974) asked Bostonians to draw maps of their city, he found that interviewees consistently left out whole areas.

What this implies is that all of us have blind spots. The question is how to reduce them and expand our vision.

Box 2-1

A NOVELIST'S VIEW OF MAPS

"Only the Dead Know Brooklyn"

"How'd yuh know deh was such a place," I says, "if you neveh been deh befoeh?"

"Oh," he says, "I got a map."

"A map?" I says.

"Sure," he says, "I got a map dat tells me about all dese places. I take it wit me every time I come out heah," he says.

And Jesus! Wit dat, he pulls it out of his pocket, an' so help me, but he's got it—he's tellin' duh troot—a big map of duh whole f——— place with all duh different pahts mahked out. You know—Canarsie an' East Noo Yawk an' Flatbush, Bensonhoist, South' Brooklyn, suh Heights, Bay Ridge, Greenpernt—duh whole goddam layout, he's got it right deh on duh map.

So den duh guy begins to ast me all kinds of nutty questions: how big was Brooklyn an' could I find my way aroun' in it, an' how long would it take a guy to know duh place.

"Listen!" I says, "You get dat idea outa yoeh head right now," I says. "You ain't neveh gonna get to know Brooklyn," I says, "an I don't even know all deh is to know about it, so how do you expect to know duh town," I says, "when you don't even live heah?"

"Yes," he says, "but I got a map to help me find my way about."

"Map or no map," I says, "yuh ain't gonna get to know Brooklyn wit no map," I says. (Wolfe, [1932] 1963:93, 95. Used by permission of Charles Scribner's Sons from *From Death to Morning* by Thomas Wolfe. Copyright 1935 by Charles Scribner's Sons; renewal copyright © 1963 by Paul Gitlin.)

EXPANDING OUR VISION OF THE CITY

One way to reduce the blind spots is to look at urban life from many perspectives and then to combine our insights. Alas, this is easier said than done. For one thing, hardly anyone today is a Renaissance person who, like Leonardo da Vinci, is a serious student of the social and physical sciences as well as a creative artist.

Fragmentation of the Social Sciences

The expansion and specialization of knowledge in today's technological society make it difficult for anyone to systematically study the many facets of any complex phenomenon, including the city. Academically speaking, this proliferation of knowledge has led to a splitting up of the world into specialist disciplines and professional territories: sociology, history, economics, policy analysis, geography, and so forth. Subdisciplines (e.g., urban sociology) and hybrids have also developed as further responses to the knowledge explosion and to real-world concerns. Today academics may see themselves as urban economists, gerontologists, and so forth.

This was not always the case. In the nineteenth century (before the knowledge explosion and computerized data banks), influential social thinkers argued vigorously against carving up the world into narrow, specialized disciplines. Essentially, thinkers like sociology's founder Auguste Comte, Karl Marx, and John Henry Cardinal Newman believed that social phenomena are so inextricably linked that studying one small category of the social world was fruitless. Cardinal Newman summed up this point of view in 1852. He wrote ([1852] 1919:137) that a true university education should provide the power of viewing many things at once as "one whole, and referring them severally to their true places in the universal system, and understanding their respective values, and determining their mutual dependence."

Despite Cardinal Newman's lofty vision—encouraging us to seek a comprehensive, holistic view of things—specialist disciplines have continued to multiply. Instead of a unified social science, a number of social sciences came into existence for many reasons, including the growing complexity of the social world itself and the variety of research tools used to observe it. On one hand, this fragmentation can lead to expertise in a specialized area, say, ethnic voting behavior. But, on the other hand, it can result in narrow vision: scholars may know more and more about less and less.

Some theorists (e.g., Duverger, 1964) say that there is no rational way to classify the social sciences, for distinctions among them are artificial. Nonetheless, higher education is organized that way—along disciplinary lines. Thus, there are departments of sociology, history, geography, and so forth. And each discipline has developed particular perspectives on the world it tries to better understand.

What constitutes a discipline's perspective on the world? Its substantive content, **paradigms** for doing research, and research methods used to investigate its subject matter combine to produce a unique disciplinary outlook. Thus, an economist looks at the world through particular lenses. So do sociologists, geographers, political scientists, and other social scientists.

Ways of Expanding our Vision

This book will attempt to expand our vision of things urban in several different ways: (1) by drawing on the insights of different disciplines and professional fields as well as the literary and visual arts; (2) by trying to draw together and make connections between insights from various disciplines and fields of study; (3) by presenting a range of ideological perspectives on urban conditions and policies; (4) by examining the bases of disagreements among students of urban life and then trying to see patterns of difference; (5) by reexamining what seems so obvious, such as the way people walk down busy city streets or behave on subways; and (6) by encouraging the development of both modes of seeing urban life—intuition and acquaintance with the urban world as well as analytic knowledge about it. In these ways, we hope to increase our understanding of things urban.

Our approach will be from the point of view of urban studies. A word about this subject area is appropriate here.

Urban Studies

Urban studies is a new addition to academia. It developed in recent decades as a response to the needs of social scientists, city planners, and others who desired a broader approach to urban phenomena that they had been studying piecemeal.

At present, academics don't agree on what to call it or where to put it. It is variously called "urban studies," "urban affairs," "metropolitan studies," "urban life," and "urban and metropolitan studies." It is sometimes a department, a program, or an entire school. No one label identifies its theorists and researchers. Some call themselves urbanists or urbanologists; others shrink from such labels.

Whatever it's called and wherever it's housed within colleges and universities, urban studies is a *field of study*, not a discipline. It is often viewed as either a **multidisciplinary** or **interdisciplinary** field focusing on urban-related theory, issues, and policies. Popularly, it is often associated with the attempt to solve urban problems.

As a field of study, urban studies has rather ill-defined boundaries. Does it include life beyond the city limits? Beyond the suburbs? Does it include the study of solid waste disposal (garbage, to the uninitiated)? Neither the physical nor the intellectual boundaries are well delineated.

Indeed, some scholars maintain that it is no longer possible to make meaningful distinctions between things urban and nonurban in complex societies like the United States. In addition, they argue, and we agree, that in an interdependent world, urban life cannot be divorced from national (and often international) life. We call this the "urban-schmurban" stance. It was tartly summarized by the late sociologist Talcott Parsons when he commented, "Putting the word 'urban' before sociology [or political science, economics, etc.] is like putting the word 'horse' before doctor."

Despite its ill-defined boundaries and scope, urban studies does have a special focus: the city and its surrounding area. Students are encouraged to use the theoretical perspectives and methods of various intellectual disciplines in order to better understand metropolitan phenomena.

Ideally, students of the city are also encouraged to achieve interdisciplinarity. But coordinating, synthesizing, and blending information and insights *among* disciplines is difficult at best and sometimes impossible. One urbanist describes the recipe for many so-called interdisciplinary studies like this: "Take a physical planner, a sociologist, an economist; beat the mixture until it blends; pour and spread" (Alonso, 1971:169). In other words, synthesizing unlike insights or data sets is like blending oil and water; it won't work. Without basic agreement on conceptual frameworks and meaningful consensus among urbanists—neither of which presently exists—interdisciplinarity remains an ideal. Meanwhile, scholars often achieve some minor degree of integration when they work together in an interdisciplinary team.

Most commonly, scholars working on a team study of some urban condition each approach the city from the perspective of their particular discipline. An example will help to clarify the various disciplinary approaches to the same phenomenon: slums.

DISCIPLINARY PERSPECTIVES: THE EXAMPLE OF SLUMS

According to the *Oxford English Dictionary* (1971:2874), a slum is

> A street, alley, court, etc., situated in a crowded district of a town or city and inhabited by people of a low class or by the very poor; a number of these streets or courts forming a thickly populated neighbourhood or district where the houses and the conditions of life are of a squalid and wretched character.

People concerned with the history and use of language would be interested in the derivation of the word "slum" (British provincial

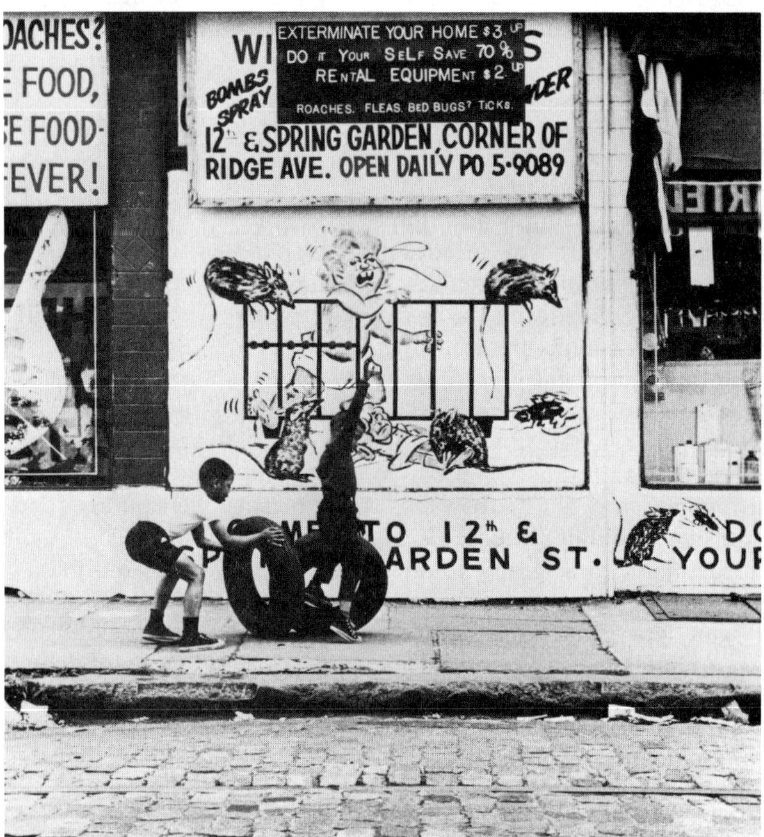

Fig. 2-2 SLUM. According to the *Oxford English Dictionary*, a slum may be defined as "a thickly populated neighbourhood or district where the houses and the conditions of life are of a squalid and wretched character." People living in areas called slums may not see it that way. (Ben Achtenberg)

slang); its first recorded usage (1825, in England), and its changing meanings over time (by the 1890s it connoted crime, viciousness, and debauchery, in other words, bad people as well as bad physical conditions). People living in areas called slums (by people who don't live there) would undoubtedly have more pressing concerns than understanding where the word "slum" came from. In other words, what is of utmost importance to one group of people may be of much less concern to another.

This observation also holds true for urbanists: What is of primary importance to people trained in one discipline or field may be peripheral, even neglected, by those trained in another. To illustrate, we'll look at various disciplinary approaches to slums.

Economics

Economics, once called the "dismal science," is primarily concerned with choice: how individuals or whole societies choose to use their scarce productive resources (land, labor, capital, know-how) to produce and distribute goods and services. Whether economists study a complex economic system, such as that of the United States, or the economic organization of a single urban commune, they ask three basic and interrelated questions:

1. *What* goods and services are produced, and *how much* of alternative commodities is produced? For example, does the U.S. economy produce many weapons for national defense and few housing units? A mix of both? Or many housing units and few weapons?
2. *How* are goods produced? For instance, is high technology used? What resources are used?
3. *For whom* are the goods produced? For example, how are certain kinds of housing distributed among the affluent and the poor, whites and nonwhites?

These questions—*what, how,* and *for whom*—inform an economist's perspective on the issue being investigated. To answer these questions, economists use a variety of tools, mainly quantitative in nature. In an economics text, for instance, we would expect to find numbers, statistics, mathematical equations, graphs of relationships between factors involved, and econometric projections. It is the rare economist who is trained in or uses qualitative research methods common to anthropology and sociology, such as in-depth interviewing and participant-observation.

Looking at urban housing, one does not have to be a computer-competent, sophisticated economist to understand *what* poor people get: high-density, physically deteriorating slums. Indeed, it has been said that if all of New York City were as densely populated as parts of Harlem, the entire population of the United States would fit into three of New York City's boroughs (Harrington in Hunter, 1964:37).

Why do the poor live in densely populated dwellings, usually near the center of the city, rather than on the city's fringes? The answer is not so obvious. Here, economists' logic and models can help to explain. The key to their explanation is a heuristic device showing the way urban land prices vary in a market-based economy: the **bid rent curve**. Fig. 2-3 is a residential bid rent curve. It depicts the relationship between two factors that economic analysts consider essential to explain urban land use: (1) the price of land per square foot and (2) the distance of the land from the Central Business District (CBD).

Near the center of the city, land is expensive—the most expensive in the city. In our example, it is $240 per square foot. Land is expensive near the center because centrally located land is prime land, close to the nerve center of the city with its corporate headquarters, large department stores, banks, and so forth. At the city's edges, land is cheaper because it is not as convenient to jobs or amenities.

Why urban slums are found near the center of cities rather than on the periphery, where land is cheaper, is a seeming paradox. Studying this phenomenon, regional planner William Alonso (1973:54) concludes that the reasons are connected to the amount of land affordable by rich and poor. "At any given location," Alonso says, "the poor can buy less land than the rich, and since only a small quantity of land is involved [for living space], changes in its price are not as important for the poor as the costs and inconvenience of commuting." What Alonso claims, then, is that the rich make a trade-off. They are willing to take more trouble and time commuting to work in exchange for living farther away from the city center (where, presumably, it is more comfortable and pleasant).

In Alonso's simple model shown in Fig. 2-3, the value of land declines from $240 per square foot at the city center to $20 per square foot at the city's edge. How does this relationship between the price of land and its location help us understand why the poor live in crowded settlements called slums? The economic analyst would point out that since centrally located land is expensive, any housing built there must try to minimize land costs: by building up or by packing people in. In the case of poor people with little money, both situations occur, resulting in slums.

To answer the *what* question, economists frequently employ the concepts of supply

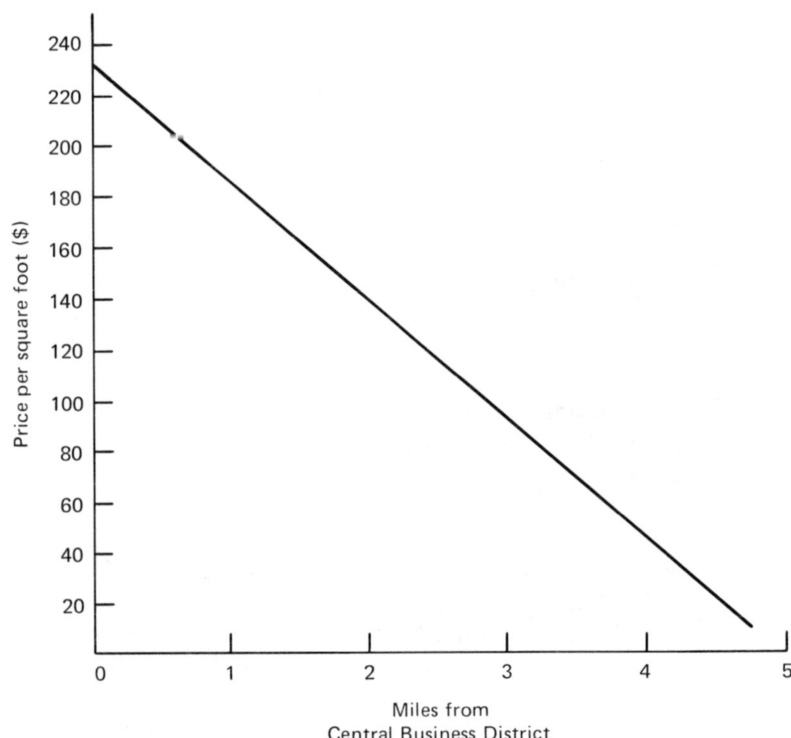

Fig. 2-3 ECONOMIC MODEL. This residential bid rent curve shows that the price of land per square foot decreases as the distance from the CBD increases.

and demand. In a market economy (also called "free enterprise" or "competitive" economy), classical or market theory holds that goods will be supplied in the marketplace according to people's ability to pay for them. However, in the case of housing, some economists say that there is a large "noneffective" demand—that is, a group of people who want decent housing but can't afford to pay for it. The logic is this: The laws of the market work to give them only what they can pay for—physically deteriorating housing.

How is slum housing provided? With the exception of a small amount of publicly assisted housing, no new housing is produced by the market for poor people. Instead, older housing units are occupied by successively lower-income groups, and this housing eventually "trickles down" to the poor slum dweller. Urban economists call this the **filtering** process. Some economists argue in favor of public policies to provide more housing to upper- and middle-income people on the assumption that more and better housing will then filter down to the poor more rapidly.

To summarize: Economists tend to see the provision of slum housing in a market economy as an outcome of the workings of the laws of supply and demand. Such factors as land costs and the journey-to-work determine the behavior of urbanites, whether as buyers or renters of urban land, owners of slum property, or slum dwellers. Crowded, physically deteriorated slum housing, in this way of thinking, tends to trickle down to poor people because of underlying market forces.

Geography

While economists ask what, how, and for whom, geographers focus on *where* people or activities cluster. Concern for the management of space gives geographers a particular disciplinary perspective. Mapping is a key tool, but geographers also use mathematical and computer-assisted models, field observation, and other social science methods. Investigating slums, a geographer might map out where they are located in city space or construct a model to predict where they will be located fifty years later.

A starting point for the description of residential spatial patterns, including the location of slums, is sociologist Ernest W. Burgess's model of urban space: the **Burgess hypothesis**. This hypothesis, developed by Burgess at the University of Chicago in the 1920s, has since become central to urban geography, showing the interdisciplinary roots of much urban theory.

Fig. 2-4 depicts the Burgess model of urban space. It suggests that cities expand outward from the CBD in a nonrandom way—through a series of zones or rings. One implication of this model (discussed in more detail in Chapter 13) is that poor people live in slums because changes in the city's land use patterns push them there. Briefly, the logic is this: The city's changing environment leads to the sorting and sifting process which segregates individuals by social class, ethnic background and race, and family composition. As a city's population grows, demand for land in the CBD (the city's core) can be satisfied only by expanding outward. Property owners in and around the CBD will let their housing units deteriorate, for they can profit by selling their land to businesses expanding there. The result of this growth process, the Burgess model predicts, is that the poor living in slums near the CBD will be pushed out into new slums a bit farther out from the CBD.

Burgess's model is of special interest here because it is essentially interdisciplinary in nature; it combines economic assumptions about the way the world works (economic competition for urban space) with patterns of

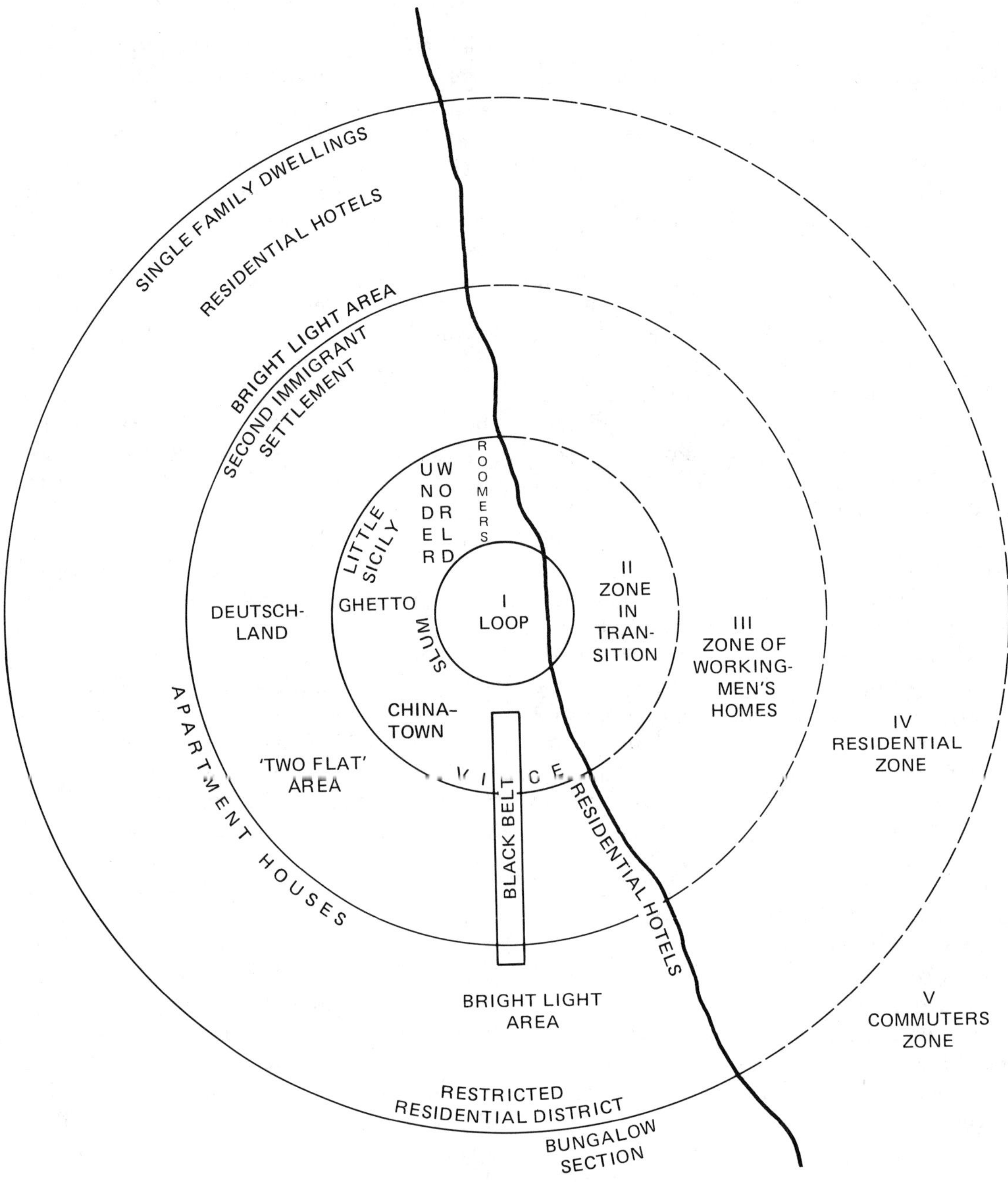

Fig. 2-4 BURGESS'S CONCENTRIC ZONE MODEL. Applied to Chicago, the zonal model shows that the Loop (Chicago's CBD) is surrounded by low-income neighborhoods in Zone II. (Robert E. Park, Ernest W. Burgess, and Roderick D. McKenzie, *The City*, Chicago: University of Chicago Press [1925] 1974, p. 55. Copyright © 1967 by the University of Chicago. Reproduced by permission of the University of Chicago Press. All rights reserved.)

spatial and social order. For instance, it predicts that the higher people move up the socioeconomic ladder, the farther away they will live from the CBD, Zone I.

Sociology

Sociologists study people: how they act, think, produce things and ideas, and live. They may study social interaction between as few as two individuals or as many as the entire world population. Their major interest lies in better understanding human action. Normally, sociologists are not concerned with one person's action.

Sociologists start with the assumption that things are not always the way they seem. For instance, universities exist, according to their high-principled mottos and public relations brochures, to expand the frontiers of knowledge and (more recently) to provide career training. Those are their official reasons for existence, their **manifest functions**. Looking below the surface, however, sociologists may uncover some hidden or unintended purposes of universities, their **latent functions**. These include lowering the unemployment rolls by keeping people off the streets and instilling habits useful in the labor market, such as following orders from authority figures. These latent functions can't be seen with the naked eye or discovered by common sense; they emerge as one explores the interconnections between people, institutions, and ideas.

The sociological perspective attempts to better describe and understand the social forces that mold the lives of individuals, perhaps without their own realization. It can be applied to many events that, on the surface, seem to be purely personal experiences.

A sociologist investigating any topic, including slums, might ask the following kinds of questions:

1. *What* are people doing and thinking here? For instance, do slum dwellers vote, join church groups, feel satisfied with their lives?
2. *What kinds* of people are here—what are their social characteristics?
3. *What rules* govern behavior here? In the case of slum dwellers, are they expected to passively accept their substandard housing?
4. *Who says so?* For example, in slum buildings, who or what groups have the power to make rules and enforce them?
5. *Whose interests* do these social arrangements serve? For example, what social functions do slums serve? Do some groups in society benefit more than others from their existence?

The work of John R. Seeley represents one approach to the study of slums. Seeley (1970) argues that slums will not—cannot ever—be eradicated because the definition of the word "slum" is relative to how other people live. He reasons that people at the bottom of the social ladder will still be perceived by those higher up as living in slums even if living conditions are improved. Further, Seeley maintains that in a society where economic and social inequality exist, as in the United States, there are bound to be those who will be labeled "slum dwellers."

In his analysis of slums, Seeley employs a device common to many scientific disciplines: a **typology** or classification scheme. His typology differentiates slum dwellers on the basis of length of residence and reasons for residing in the slums. He distinguishes between four major types or classes of people who live in slums: (1) the "permanent necessitarians" (who live there permanently and by necessity); (2) the "temporary necessitarians" (who aspire to leave the slums but live there out of necessity); (3) the "permanent opportunists" (who stay in the slums primarily because it affords them opportunities to escape the law or live the high life); and (4) the "temporary opportunists" (who want to pursue dominant cultural values, like success; these include recent arrivals to the city).

Other sociologists may explore face-to-face encounters among slum dwellers, paying special attention to how people interpret each other's actions and bring meaning to their interaction; this approach typifies the symbolic interaction school of sociology. But whatever approach or method is used (ranging from mathematical models to firsthand participation and observation), sociologists focus on the social forces that shape individual lives. They look for traits that cannot be explained simply by referring to individual psychological states.

Political Science

Traditionally, political scientists have been concerned with questions of power and governance: Who governs? How do they govern? To what end? Or, as one political scientist so neatly put it, "*Who gets what, how,* and *why*?"

As in other disciplines, the range of topics within political science is broad. But the nature of political processes and political outcomes are central to the discipline. The research tools of political science include mathematical models, content analysis, attitude surveys, and firsthand observation of events.

In the case of slums, political scientists investigate a number of issues. Some study citizens' attitudes toward government housing policy; others explore the relations between different levels of government (federal, state, local) in establishing housing policy. Still others look at comparative political systems, exploring how different countries handle housing problems. A political scientist exploring local power relationships might be drawn into studying conflicts of interest in which decisionmakers stand to gain personally from land deals to raze slums. And a political philosopher might question the nature of a political system that either allows or perpetuates slums.

One of the many studies of slums from the perspective of political science is *Politics, Planning, and the Public Interest* (1955) by Edward Banfield and Martin Meyerson. This study centers on the decision-making process that led to the construction of low-income public housing projects in Chicago. (These housing units, meant—at least by government definition—to provide standard housing for the poor, came to be known as slums.)

Banfield and Meyerson found that Chicago's aldermen (city councillors) had effective veto power over public housing construction in their wards. The proposed housing projects were going to house poor people, the majority of whom were black. Middle- and upper-class residents of predominantly white neighborhoods vigorously opposed the suggestion that such public housing projects should be located in their neighborhoods. These affluent whites believed that if the projects came in, crime would increase, property values would decrease, and the aesthetic character of their areas would change. Their opposition to public housing was sufficient to block the original proposal: that public housing projects be scattered throughout the city. Eventually, much less public housing than originally contemplated was built, and virtually all units were placed in a very few wards that were already nearly all black.

Banfield and Meyerson would not dispute the importance of economic and social processes in determining the distribution of different kinds of housing within a city. What they stress, however, are political factors. They focus on the politics of class and race as well as on what Chicagoans call "clout" (influence and power), rather than on concepts central to other disciplines, such as urban growth over space.

Anthropology

Starting in the nineteenth century, anthropologists have made significant contributions to the study of urbanization and cultural change from a cross-cultural point of view. In recent years, they have been turning their attention away from "folk" or "primitive" cultures, such as that of the Trobriand Islands, and have focused on urbanizing and urban cultures. Wherever anthropologists work, their primary method of investigation remains fieldwork.

The late American anthropologist Oscar Lewis used fieldwork methods to get an insider's view of family life in Mexico City. He wanted to find out what it meant to grow up in a slum tenement within a city undergoing rapid social and economic change, such as Mexico City. Using a tape recorder to take down the life histories of one Mexican family, *The Children of Sanchez* (1961), Lewis recorded their personal statements and feelings about a wide range of issues, including religion, kinship patterns, interpersonal relations, and social mobility. But he was interested in much broader issues: the effects of industrialization and urbanization on the peasant and urban masses. He sought to develop a conceptual model of what he called the "culture of poverty," that is, "a design for living which is passed down from generation to generation" among "those people who are at the very bottom of the socio-economic scale" (1961:xxiv–xxv).

In recent years, a subdiscipline of urban anthropology, urban archeology, has been tapping a rather ingenious source of information: garbage. As the head of a "dig" in Atlanta, Georgia, put it, "People's garbage never lies. It tells the truth if you know how to read it" (in Weathers et al., 1979:81). From a Newburyport, Massachusetts, garbage dig, urban archeologists discovered evidence that nineteenth-century Irish and Canadian immigrants, long presumed illiterate, could read and write.

Wherever they go to study people—the towns of Massachusetts; the garbage dumps of Atlanta; native American reservations and city dwellings; or remote areas of the Philippines (where the Tasaday, a small Stone Age tribe, was discovered in the 1970s)—anthropologists seek "to provide convincing accounts of what is happening to people in varied real life situations and to set these in a broader framework of time and space" (Southall, 1973:4). Their emphasis on the diversity of human experience as well as the search for common or universal themes gives anthropologists a particular perspective on the social and material world.

History

His-story and her-story—the range of humankind's experience over time—is the subject matter of historians. Some focus on a small piece or area of the whole, while other grand (some say grandiose) thinkers try to see patterns throughout the whole human experience.

Historians have contributed a variety of studies about urban life and culture, starting with the earliest known settlements in the Middle East. To investigate various aspects of urban life, historians use a range of tools, including the analysis of written records, oral histories, and, more recently, quantitative techniques such as computer-aided statistical analysis.

One of the most influential historians of urban culture is Lewis Mumford. In *The City in History: Its Origins, Its Transformations, and Its Prospects* (1961), Mumford paints a picture of the forms and functions of the city throughout the ages. He also pleads for a "new urban order" which emphasizes "local control over local needs". In his historical tour from the early origins of the city to the contemporary megalopolis, Mumford stops to comment on the development of European industrial cities between 1830 and 1910. First, he quotes his mentor, the Scots planner Patrick Geddes, who influenced a generation of U.S. city planners, and then he offers his own comments on slums:

> "Slum, semi-slum, and super-slum—to this has come the evolution of cities." Yes: these mordant words of Patrick Geddes apply inexorably to the new environment. Even the most revolutionary of contemporary critics [like Friedrich Engels] lacked genuine standards of building and living: they had no notion how far the environment of the upper classes themselves had become impoverished. . . . [Even Engels, the revolutionary critic] was apparently unaware of the fact that the upper-class quarters were, more often than not, intolerable super-slums. (Mumford, 1961:464–65)

Thus, according to Mumford, the new industrial cities were not only bleak environments for the poor; they were just as intolerably overcrowded, ugly, and unhygienic for the nonpoor.

A pioneering work in U.S. urban history, Arthur M. Schlesinger's *The Rise of the American City, 1878–1898* (1933), makes the claim that innovation and social change are uniquely associated with city life. Schlesinger maintains that overcrowding in slums, intense economic and social interactions in the CBD, and other aspects of urban life lead city dwellers to adopt new lifestyles in order to survive. This theme echoes the findings of theorists from other disciplines, including the Chicago school of sociology.

Other historians trace changes within one city, often using the case study approach to illuminate issues common to other cities or to generate broader theory. Sam Bass Warner, Jr.'s, "If All the World Were Philadelphia: A Scaffolding for Urban History, 1774–1930" (1968), is a case in point. In this article, Warner looks at housing patterns in Philadelphia at three points in time: 1774, 1860, and 1930. Using historical data, Warner argues that at the time of the American Revolution, poor people in Philadelphia lived around the fringes of the city, not near the city's core. He maintains that both racial segregation and the relocation of slums near the CBD in Philadelphia were nineteenth century phenomena. What caused these changes in settlement patterns? Warner says that improvements in transportation within the city and the creation of large business organizations led to the changing residential patterns. In conclusion, Warner (1968:35) states that the organizing principle of the big city in the nineteenth century became "intense segregation based on income, race, foreign birth, and class."

Psychology, Social Psychology, and Social Psychiatry

Is there an "urban personality" or an "urban way of life"? Do city folk suffer more mental illness than rural people? What effects does growing up poor, or rich, have on urbanites' beliefs about themselves and others? These are some questions explored by psychologists, social psychologists, and social psychiatrists.

A classic study in social psychology is Louis Wirth's "Urbanism as a Way of Life" (1938). This still controversial essay, excerpted in Chapter 5, contends that city dwellers—whether slum residents or super-rich—share certain characteristics, including indifference to others, sophistication, rationality, and calculating behavior. Presumably, urbanites develop these personality traits in order to defend themselves and preserve their sanity amid the intensity and stimulation of city life.

More recently, Robert Coles has explored

the psyches of rich and poor children in both urban and rural America. In so doing, he has created a new subdiscipline: social psychiatry. In his five-volume series, *Children of Crisis*, Coles uses a mixture of clinical observation, oral history, narrative description, psychiatric approaches, and social comment to look at how wealth, power, cultural background, and historical influences mold the character of children and their expectations of what life can offer them. In the latter two volumes of his study, *Eskimos, Chicanos, Indians* (1977a) and *Privileged Ones: The Well-Off and the Rich in America* (1977b), Coles paints a portrait of growing up poor, outside the mainstream of American culture, versus growing up wealthy. He notes striking differences. Rich children, for instance, are routinely trained to believe that their way of life is worthwhile; they grow up believing they're special. In Coles's words (1977b:380), the children of the wealthy have a "continuous and strong emphasis . . . on the 'self.' " In contrast, poor children, some trapped in the slums, are discouraged from being independent and assertive. They are routinely trained by parents and their environment to keep their thoughts to themselves and not to cultivate a sense of being special persons.

Public Administration

Historically, the professional field of public administration emerged from the discipline of political science in the United States. The field is intimately connected with the efforts to reform the U.S. city. As Dwight Waldo states in his influential study of *The Administrative State* (1948:73), "Much of the impetus to public administration came from the municipal reformers [of the early 1900s], who were genuinely inspired by a City of the Future." Interestingly, in contrast to the intellectual bias against the city held by many social scientists in the first quarter of this century, public administration writers thought that "The Good Life is an urban life . . . . [They] rejected the Jeffersonian idea that cities are sores on the body politic and menaces to democracy."

It is tempting to say that what public administrators do is to manage the public business, carrying out decisions made by political leaders. But this creates a false distinction between administrators and politicians. Early theorists of public administration attempted to distinguish between administration and politics, but current thinkers reject the distinction, demonstrating that administration *is* politics. In other words, the administration of public programs, such as the War on Poverty or school busing, is a highly political process. Indeed, bureaucratic politics (e.g., the politics of constructing a city or national budget, discussed in Chapter 17) has increasingly captured the imagination of public administration scholars.

In the case of slums, theorists and practitioners in the field have written about a number of issues, ranging from the interface between professionals and their welfare clients to evaluations of government programs designed, in theory at least, to alleviate poverty and slum conditions. One study by a city councillor in California concludes that the effect of government-sponsored urban renewal programs has not been the scattering of minorities throughout cities but rather the further concentration of "minorities into more densely packed ghetto areas" (Denton, 1971:183).

City Planning and Urban Design

Like public administration in the United States, city planning and urban design are relatively young professional fields. Initially, they were heavily influenced by the ideas and methods of architecture, engineering, and landscape architecture. Today, graduate

Fig. 2-5 ONCE IT LEAVES THE DRAWING BOARD . . . What pleases the planners and urban designers may not suit various interest groups, both public and private. Drawing a plan is only the first step in the long, highly political process of getting it implemented. These drawings, from the *San Francisco Urban Design Plan* (1971), reveal the planners' preference for long vistas of the Bay, unobstructed by tall buildings. (Reprinted by permission of the San Francisco City Planning Department.)

programs in city planning usually offer training in economics, information science, and policy analysis in their curriculum as well as the more traditional fare.

Planning—whether for city growth, economic development, or social purposes—has not had the acceptance in the United States that it enjoys in many other nations, including England, France, and the socialist countries. In large part this reflects American individualism and nonconformity dating from frontier days, captured in these lines from an old backwoods lyric:

> I'll buy my own whiskey, I'll drink my own dram,
> And for them that don't like me, I don't give a damn!

It also reflects many Americans' long-standing preference for private enterprise and the market of supply and demand (rather than government) to regulate economic matters, including what gets built where. However, with the enlarged scope and reach of corporate business and the expansion of federal, state, and local government since World War II, increased numbers of economic and physical (but relatively few social) planners have been added to private and public payrolls.

Wherever they work, city planners and urban designers are, of necessity, political animals. More than most urban professionals, they find themselves at the center of perpetual controversy. They can hardly ignore the clout of private developers; citizens' preferences either for preserving the character of the community or attracting new people, business, and money; federal regulation of local programs; the political environment in which they work; and differences in aesthetics and perceived needs among local groups. Even the most functional and aesthetically pleasing (in the planners' minds, at least) design plan remains a plan until both private and public interests decide to fund it and back it.

Mass Communications

"*Who* says *what* in *which channel* to *whom* with *what effect?*" That was the question a pioneer in the interdisciplinary field of mass communications, political scientist Harold Lasswell (1943), asked years ago that summarizes the field's concerns. Usually, researchers focus on one of the five Ws: who (communicators), what (message content), which channel (medium of communication), to whom (audience analysis), or what effect (impact).

Since World War II, mass communications research has expanded along with the means of mass communication. Such innovations as microcomputerization; broadcast satellites; computer-allied TV that promises home video information centers; and fiber optics have revolutionized the way people and organizations receive and send information.

These new computer and communications technologies, collectively dubbed "compunications," may be just the beginning. Some futurists talk about the ways social, political, and economic life will change dramatically in the near future as a result of even more technological innovations. Moviemaker Francis Ford Coppola expressed this view when speaking at the 1979 Oscar awards. He said that the oncoming communications revolution will make the Industrial Revolution look like a "small-time tryout out of town."

As the United States enters the stage of **post-industrialism**—where more people manage things, serve things, think about things, and communicate about things than produce things—these new information technologies will undoubtedly increase in both economic and sociopolitical importance.

Particularly relevant to our example of slums are several studies dealing with information and access to information in mass society. In *The Politics of Communication* (1973), political sociologist Claus Mueller contends that lower-class people in advanced technological societies like the United States lack both the linguistic ability and the conceptual frameworks which would allow them to gain access to necessary information to effectively participate in politics. He argues that the mass media reinforce consumerism and leisure, thus integrating the poor into the political system. Others (e.g., Novak, 1971; Phillips, 1975) maintain that news reportage routinely ignores issues which concern the city's poor and ethnic groups; such issues become defined as nonnews and don't even reach the arena of public debate. This suggests that even so-called objective news reports are biased, not in the way that Spiro

Agnew once charged (calling reporters "nattering nabobs" and purveyors of "ideological plugola") but in a more subtle way: toward a particular view of the social world—a cosmopolitan, middle- and upper-class, educated viewpoint that reflects the news reporters' own outlook on reality.

Literature and the Arts

How often poets, writers, songwriters, and artists speak to the soul, clarifying the human condition in ways that statistics or theoretical models cannot! Those familiar with the poor Southern sharecroppers in Walker Evans's photos in Agee's *Let Us Now Praise Famous Men* ([1939] 1960) or the Kinte clan in Alex Haley's *Roots* (1976) get a sense of personal acquaintance with these people and their lives, an acquaintance that touches the emotions as well as the intellect.

Poverty and slum conditions have been a continuing theme in the arts since the Industrial Revolution, which gave us both the word "slum" and the condition called slums. To take but one example, here novelist Charles Dickens ([1854] 1967:17) draws a portrait of "Coketown," a new industrial town that could be one of many English cities in the mid-nineteenth century:

> It was a town of red brick or of brick that would have been red if the smoke and ashes had allowed it; but as matters stood it was a town of unnatural red and black like the painted face of a savage. It was a town of machinery and tall chimneys, out of which interminable serpents of smoke trailed themselves. . . . It had a black canal in it, and a river that ran purple with ill-smelling dye, and vast piles of buildings full of windows where there was a rattling and a trembling all day long. . . . It contained several large streets . . . inhabited by people equally like each other, who all went in and out at the same hours, with the same sound upon the same pavements, to do the same work, and to whom every day was the same as yesterday and tomorrow, and every year the counterpart of the last and the next.

No statistical table can capture the monotonous rhythm of life, the squalor and dirt, and the pervasive gloom of working conditions in nineteenth-century England as well as Dickens's word portrait.

Likewise, the photographs of reformer Jacob Riis ([1901] 1971) and Bill Owens (1977) freeze a way of life, a moment of time. A keen observer trained in visual anthropology, Owens lets people speak for themselves. By recording his subjects' statements as well as providing his own observations, he offers two perspectives on people's lives and work. Owens and others like him portray the texture of urban life in rich detail. Often a viewer can feel what vacant hopes lie beyond the vacant eyes, as in the case of a woman packing cauliflower (see Fig. 2-6).

The image of poverty and slums has also been poignantly captured by the motion picture camera. Most often, Hollywood movies focus on the social disorder presumed to accompany slum life. *West Side Story* (1961) is a case in point. Yet, on close inspection, the film also shows what sociologist Gerald D. Suttles calls *The Social Order of the Slum* (1968): a well-defined moral order rooted in personalistic relations and provincialism. To be sure, the rules of the gangs (the Jets and Sharks) are not exactly those of middle-class block groups, but they are widely understood by people in the neighborhood, and they serve to regulate daily life. By contrast, Willard Van Dyke's classic documentary *The City* (1939) portrays the slum only as a bastion of social disorganization. Juxtaposing images of lovely old New England small towns with blighted buildings, the film makes its point in unsubtle terms: Americans cannot afford *not* to build new, open garden cities. The film's narrative (written by Lewis Mumford) tells viewers that the United States has a choice: "Shall we build and re-build our cities, clean again: close to the earth—open to the sky?" The narrator asks, "Maybe the question is can we afford all this disorder, the hospitals, the jails, reformatories, the wasted years of childhood? . . . Chaos—or order? . . . Which shall prevail?"

Other forms of popular culture and folk culture—from graffiti and street murals to best-sellers—are important sources of information for understanding people's responses to poverty and slum life. Consider, for instance, one American musical tradition: the blues. The blues speak of melancholy, what early American settlers from England called the "blue devils." Immigrants coming from the villages and small towns of the British Isles to the hills and hollows of the American

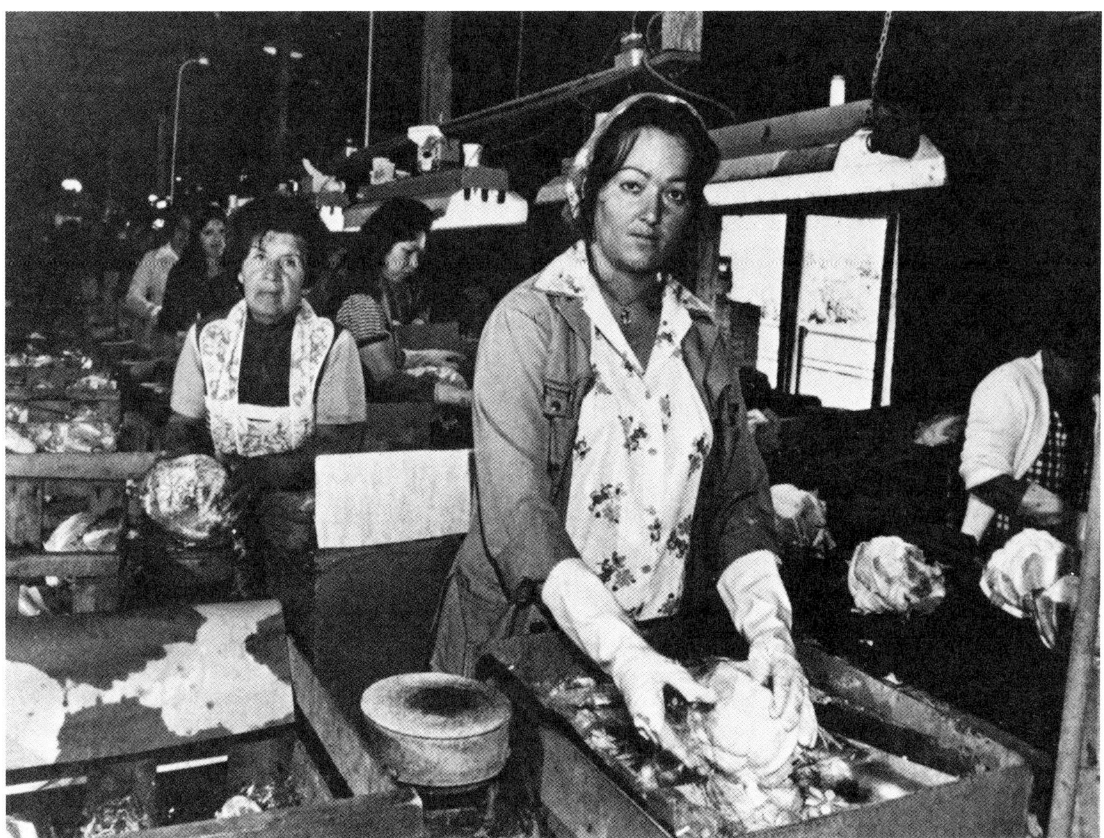

"As long as I can work here, I will. It's better than housework. Cauliflower packing is hard work but I don't even think about it. My hands go through the motions, my mind's somewhere else. The season lasts six months, then I pack tomatoes and collect unemployment for the rest of the year."

Fig. 2-6 CAULIFLOWER PACKERS. (Bill Owens)

wilderness apparently suffered from the blue devils of homesickness, and they sang about it. In the words of novelist Thomas Wolfe, the pioneers were "lost and wind-grieved" in the vast, raw spaces of the New World. Later, in the nineteenth century, white and black migrants from the rural countryside to the city started singing the blues. Some sang "The House of the Rising Sun Blues," the story of the poverty which forced poor country girls, perhaps as early as the 1840s, into a life of prostitution in New Orleans. Freed slaves during the Reconstruction era sang of their kinship with the boll weevil, who "was lookin' for a home, just a'lookin' for a home." And around 1900, when some blacks left Southern sharecropping and headed north, they "found the blues waiting . . . at every station down the line. [They had] the *Alabama Blues, The Atlanta Blues, The New Orleans Hop Scop Blues, The Fort Worth Blues and the Dallas Heart Disease, The St. Louis Blues* (like a rock cast in the sea), *The Michigan Water Blues, The Wabash Blues, The State Street Blues* (in Chicago), *The Harlem Blues* " (Lomax, 1960:576). And in the textile mill towns, people sang "The Winnsboro Cotton Mill Blues" and the "Cotton Mill Colic":

When you go to work, you work like the Devil,
At the end of the week you're not on the level.
Pay day comes, you pay your rent,
When you get through, you've not got a cent
To buy fat-back meat, pinto beans;
Now and then you get a turnip green.
No use to colic, they're all that way,
You can't get the money to move away.

Chorus:
I'm a-gonna starve, ev'rybody will,
You can't make a livin' at a cotton mill. (in Lomax, 1960:287)

By the 1920s, blues singers like Big Bill Broonzy began recording their songs for the whole world to hear. As folk song historian Alan Lomax (1960:576) comments, "If all the verses of the recorded blues were laid end to end, it would make a lonesome moan that could be heard on the moon. These songs speak plainly, pithily, and powerfully about the emotional disturbances of urban society in the west. The jobless, dispossessed, unwanted predatory Negro male was the first character in our civilization to experience and express these feelings. Now we are all aware of them, and the big sad wind of the blues sings through the heart-strings from Memphis to Moscow."

To summarize: Each intellectual discipline has its own angle of vision on the world it studies. For instance, in investigating slums and poverty, an economist would concentrate on such issues as the price of land and the profitability of different land uses. A mass communications researcher would focus on a different set of issues: where slum dwellers get their information about the world (radio? TV? newspapers?), how they process information and so forth. Geographers, political scientists, and others approach the topic with concepts central to their discipline.

MAKING SOME CONNECTIONS

After this brief look at how various disciplines and fields of knowledge might view one urban condition through their own special lenses (and blinders), we might ask whether any common foci appear. And you might wonder, quite sensibly, whether any connections, however desirable, can be made.

We think that some common themes and factors do emerge from this potpourri of information about slums. For one thing, the impact of economic forces in shaping and molding people's lives is a theme that cuts across many disciplines and fields. Economic logic underpins Burgess's model of urban growth and Alonso's model of residential bid rent. Economic forces are also emphasized in Lewis's anthropological studies of the culture of poverty, Warner's historical look at Philadelphia, Coles's social psychiatric research on children, and Mueller's analysis of communication in mass society. Other factors important to urban life that cross-cut disciplines and fields include the importance of power relations, social organization, environment, and technology in influencing individual lives.

For another thing, this brief look at varying perspectives on slums shows that while intellectual disciplines may have unique outlooks, scholars don't stop at disciplinary boundaries. Lewis Mumford, for instance, writes urban history with special emphasis on city planning. However, the scope of his research and learning ranges from religion in ancient Babylonian cities to interior decoration of working-class houses in nineteenth-century England. Similarly, sociologist Burgess constructed a model of urban spatial growth that has guided generations of geographers. Lewis's culture of poverty thesis is debated by political scientists, sociologists, and policymakers, as well as by his anthropology colleagues. And so it goes.

Another theme emerges: People living in a certain situation, say, in Appalachian poverty, may understand their subjective experience differently than "objective" social scientists do. As we've already implied by starting this book with a list of our own biases, the notion of an objective, value-free social science is a mythic ideal, not a practical possibility. Worse, it often serves as a cover, turning a professional, upper-middle-class view of what's real into the official definition of reality. This can be especially dangerous when urbanists advise policymakers. Projecting what they think is objectively good for other people (especially people who don't share the same dreams, material possessions, or values), urbanists have often imposed their values on others in the name of objectivity.

Throughout this book, we try to make some connections between insights and to draw on various modes of knowing in order to expand our urban vision. Unfortunately, no synthesis of views or information is on the horizon; the current lack of a single, agreed-upon conceptual framework and the absence of meaningful consensus among urbanists prevent it. Still, we can begin the project of weaving some threads together to better understand the urban world.

As we begin that difficult long-term project, let us recall Gertrude Stein. Her life as a writer exemplifies the quest to see beyond a mere litany of facts. On her deathbed, Stein turned to her assembled friends and asked, "What is the answer?" After a moment of stunned silence, she asked, "What, then, is the question?" Then she died.

The next chapter suggests some worthwhile questions to ask. It also looks at even more reasons why urban observers disagree on answers.

PROJECTS

1. **What you see depends on how you look at it**. Select four individuals of differing occupations and professions (for instance, an architect, environmentalist, downtown business executive, suburban housewife, bus driver, athletic coach) and ask each one to draw a simple sketch of the city you're in (or near), noting its most important places and outstanding features. Do these cognitive maps differ? If so, how?

2. **Disciplinary perspectives**. Select one urban issue—for instance, transportation, crime, violence, or unemployment—and examine how basic

texts in at least three different disciplines or fields approach it, noting what factors they stress in their analysis. Do themes emerge?

3. **The people speak and sing**. Using the same issue selected for Project 2, investigate what novelists, folk singers, and cartoonists have written, sung, or drawn about it. In what ways, if any, do these approaches vary from those of the three intellectual disciplines and/or professional fields?

SUGGESTIONS FOR FURTHER LEARNING

Of the many urban readers available, Eliot Hurst's *I Came to the City* (Boston: Houghton Mifflin, 1975) offers a range of exciting selections, both intellectual and emotional, for the beginning student. A geographer by training, Hurst pays attention to interdisciplinary analysis, aesthetics, and radical theory.

One effort to explain the meaning(s) of urban studies is David Popenoe's "On the Meaning of 'Urban' in Urban Studies"in Paul Meadows and Ephraim Mizruchi (eds.), *Urbanism, Urbanization, and Change: Comparative Perspectives* (Reading, Mass.: Addison-Wesley, [1963] 1967).

For scholarly overviews of urban research, see Philip M. Hauser and Leo F. Schnore, *The Study of Urbanization* (New York: Wiley, 1967); it contains state-of-the-art essays by noted urbanists, including Oscar Lewis and Eric Lampard. Charles Tilly's edited anthology *An Urban World* (Boston: Little, Brown, 1974) attempts to identify some new ideas in the field, and Leo F. Schnore's edited anthology *Social Science and the City* (New York: Praeger, 1968) presents research priorities in a discipline-by-discipline manner.

For a closer look at disciplinary perspectives on the world, the best bet is introductory texts in each field, with key concepts and treatment of urban-related topics. For sociology, as one example, see the best-selling text by Donald Light, Jr., and Suzanne Keller, *Sociology* (New York: Knopf, 1978); they present the sociological perspective in Chapters 1 to 3 and discuss urban life and technology in Chapter 18. The best-selling text in economics remains Paul Samuelson's *Economics* (New York: McGraw-Hill).

Too numerous to mention, of course, are the works of literary and visual art that expand our vision of the urban world. For poetic commentaries on folk music, see Alan Lomax, *The Folk Songs of North America in the English Language* (Garden City, N.Y.: Doubleday, 1960). Lomax himself collected many of these songs as he traveled throughout the United States. Hear Bob Marley's reggae music for the sound of "sufferation and iration" in the Jamaican ghetto.

For a flight into fantasy, we recommend Saint-Exupéry's *The Little Prince*, available both in French and English (in English paperback, New York: Harbrace, 1970). The feature film made of this fable gets high marks from some children, but for us, it fails to capture that poetic, even mystical, sense of Saint-Exupéry's own words and drawings on the printed page.

KEY TERMS

Bid rent curve Economist's description of how much a residential buyer will "bid" (pay) for land or rent at varying locations from the CBD of a city.

Burgess hypothesis Hypothesis constructed by sociologist Ernest W. Burgess concerning the spatial and social structure of the U.S. industrial city and its expansion over time. The hypothesis explains that a city's population is organized in a series of five concentric rings or zones, starting from the CBD.

Cognitive maps Subjective, personal, internal maps which usually bear little resemblance to official tourist maps of a city or neighborhood. Images of a city—outstanding features, landmarks, important places, etc.—differ among individuals and social groups.

Discipline A division of intellectual labor associated with higher education. As specialization increased and knowledge about the physical and social world expanded in the nineteenth century, social science split up into disciplines: economics, political science, sociology, and so forth.

Filtering The process by which housing passes downward from higher-income to lower-income residents as it ages and becomes less desirable. Thus, a mansion built in 1860 for a very rich family may have filtered down to house a moderate-income family by 1920. By 1980 the same house might have filtered down still further to house four very low-income families. If there is a housing shortage, old housing may filter up; this process is called "gentrification."

Interdisciplinary Having a degree of integration among several disciplines. The concepts, methodology, procedures, terminology, or data may be more or less connected among two or more disciplines in an interdisciplinary study. To some, "interdisciplinary" connotes the attempt to bridge disciplines and apply research tools and/or perspectives from more than one discipline; to others, it is synonymous with multidisciplinary studies.

Latent function A function or purpose hidden from view and often unintended. For example, a city public works department exists officially to build roads. Its latent function may be to provide patronage opportunities, such as jobs for political supporters and ethnic voting groups.

Manifest function The officially stated, visible reason for existence. For example, building roads is the manifest function of a city's public works department.

Multidisciplinary Involving more than one academic discipline. In practice, multidisciplinary and interdisciplinary efforts are not always distinguishable.

Paradigm A model or patterned way of seeing the world. In the scientific disciplines, the dominant paradigm defines the problems and methods of a research field; it makes legitimate what counts as facts, what assumptions are valid, and what procedures are deemed scientific. Today, there are competing paradigms in the social science disciplines.

Post-industrialism As distinguished from preindustrialism and industrialism, a society and economy characterized by high technology which permits most people to work at jobs in the information and service sectors rather than the agricultural and manufacturing sectors.

Typology A classification scheme composed of two or more ideal types, used to organize data and guide research—for example, four types of slum dwellers, distinguished by length of residence and reasons for being there.

Urban studies A multidisciplinary or interdisciplinary field of study whose central focus is the city and its surrounding area. Its intellectual boundaries are not well defined, and programs of urban studies vary in content from one academic institution to another.

REFERENCES

Agee, James and Walker Evans
[1939]
1960 Let Us Now Praise Famous Men. Boston: Houghton Mifflin.

Alonso, William
1971 "Beyond the inter-disciplinary approach to planning." American Institute of Planners Journal 37:169–73.
1973 "A theory of the urban land market." Pp. 45–55 in Ronald E. Grieson (ed.), Urban Economics. Boston: Little, Brown.

Banfield, Edward and Martin Meyerson
1955 Politics, Planning, and the Public Interest. Glencoe, Ill.: Free Press.

Coles, Robert
1977a Eskimos, Chicanos, Indians. Boston: Little, Brown.
1977b Privileged Ones: The Well-Off and the Rich in America. Boston: Little, Brown.

Denton, John
1971 "The National Association of Real Estate Boards and the ghetto system." Pp. 161–90 in Robert S. Ross (ed.), Public Choice and Public Policy. Chicago: Markham.

Dickens, Charles
[1854]
1967 Hard Times. New York: Dutton.

Duverger, Maurice
1964 An Introduction to the Social Sciences. New York: Praeger.

Haley, Alex
1976 Roots. Garden City, N.Y.: Doubleday.

Hunter, David R.
1964 The Slums. New York: Free Press.

Lasswell, Harold
1943 "The structure and function of communications in society." Pp. 37–51 in Lyman Bryson (ed.), The Communication of Ideas. New York: Institute for Religious and Social Studies.

Lewis, Oscar
1961 The Children of Sanchez. New York: Random House.

Lomax, Alan
1960 The Folk Songs of North America in the English Language. Garden City, N.Y.: Doubleday.

Lynch, Kevin
[1960]
1974 The Image of the City. Cambridge, Mass.: MIT Press.

Mueller, Claus
1973 The Politics of Communication: A Study in the Political Sociology of Language, Socialization, and Legitimation. New York: Oxford University Press.

Mumford, Lewis
1961 The City in History: Its Origins, Its Transformations, and Its Prospects. New York: Harcourt Brace & World.

Newman, John Henry Cardinal
[1852]
1919 The Idea of a University. London: Longmans, Green.

Novak, Michael
1971 The Rise of the Unmeltable Ethnics. New York: Macmillan.

Owens, Bill
1977 Working [I Do It For the Money]. New York: Simon & Schuster.

Oxford University Press
1971 The Compact Edition of the Oxford English Dictionary. New York: Oxford University Press.

Phillips, E. Barbara
1975 The Artists of Everyday Life: Journalists, Their Craft, and Their Consciousness. Unpublished Ph.D. dissertation, Syracuse University.

Riis, Jacob A.
[1901]
1971 How the Other Half Lives: Studies among the Tenements of New York. New York: Dover.

Saint-Exupéry, Antoine de
[1943]
1970 The Little Prince. Tr. from the French by Katherine Woods. New York: Harbrace.

Schlesinger, Arthur M.
1933 The Rise of the American City: 1878–1898. New York: Macmillan.

Seeley, John R.
[1959]
1970 "The slum: its nature, use and users." Pp. 285–96 in Robert Gutman and David Popenoe (eds.), Neighborhood, City, and Metropolis. New York: Random House.

Southall, Aidan (ed.)
1973 Urban Anthropology: Cross-Cultural Studies of Urbanization. New York: Oxford University Press.

Susskind, Lawrence
1978 Personal conversation. Berkeley, Calif.

Suttles, Gerald D.
1968 The Social Order of the Slum: Ethnicity and Territory in the Inner City. Chicago: University of Chicago Press.

Waldo, Dwight
1948 The Administrative State. New York: Ronald Press.

Warner, Sam Bass, Jr.
1968 "If all the world were Philadelphia: a scaffolding for urban history, 1774–1930." American Historical Review 74:182–95.

Weathers, Diane et al.
1979 "Urban archeology." Newsweek 83 (Apr. 16):81–82.

Wirth, Louis
1938 "Urbanism as a way of life." American Journal of Sociology 44:1–24.

Wolfe, Thomas
[1932]
1963 Death to Morning. New York: Scribner's.

Mary Swisher

CHAPTER 3
Posing the Questions

DOING SCIENCE

At their best, urbanists make the world more understandable. In their struggle to reach this goal, they think in ways common to all intellectual disciplines. To begin with, they are skeptical. As astronomer Carl Sagan (1978:xiv) puts it, "skeptical scrutiny is the means, in . . . science . . . by which deep insights can be winnowed from deep nonsense."

Also, more often than might be suspected, urbanists bring eagerness and passion to their work. When this happens, it results in what Sagan calls "the romance of science." An ecstatic sense of discovery, of following up on hunches, and of creatively searching for meaning—these are at the heart of doing science too.

Qualities like ecstasy are best experienced firsthand or vicariously through the words and images of inspired communicators, including Sagan. Instead of dwelling on these qualities here, we'll focus on common elements of doing science that can be transmitted from generation to generation: reasoning processes, systematic analysis, and hypothesis construction.

Reasoning, Deductive and Inductive

Deductive and inductive reasoning processes represent two ways of gaining knowledge about a subject. **Deductive reasoning** proceeds from general principles to particular examples. A **model** of how something works is speculatively constructed in the theorist's mind, then tested by gathering data. **Inductive reasoning** proceeds from particular instances to the general. A researcher first collects and sifts through pieces of **empirical evidence** and then derives **hypotheses** and generates **theories** about how something works.

In practice, however, the two kinds of reasoning processes are not clearly separate. None of us starts with a blank mind. We have some preconceived notions about how something might work or couldn't work; these models influence how we interpret new information. Without some assumptions or working models, we wouldn't even know what data to start gathering. So, most social science thinking develops as a result of both inductive and deductive reasoning.

This was the case for Ernest W. Burgess. This University of Chicago sociologist started with a hunch: that human communities are organized in ways similar to plant communities along Chicago's lakefront. Then he sent his students out to collect any data they could find—where pool hall hustlers gathered, where the rich and poor lived, what crimes were committed in which neighborhoods, and so forth. On the basis of this empirical evidence, he derived his refined concentric zone hypothesis of urban space.

To summarize: Most researchers start with a model, or at least a hunch, and proceed from there—observing real-world phenomena, formulating hypotheses, testing them, and reformulating hypotheses.

Systematic Analysis

Whatever their disciplinary background, scholars are routinely taught how to use the scientific method. This name—the **scientific method**—makes doing science sound much more methodical than is usually the case. It also masks the guesswork and creativity involved. Nonetheless, it is the model for doing science in the West, setting the step-by-step procedures for collecting, checking, classifying, and analyzing data. In theory, the scientific method proceeds as follows:

Step 1 Defining the problem and stating it in terms of existing research.

Step 2 Classifying or categorizing facts, often by constructing categories or typologies (e.g., types of slum dwellers by reasons for residence).

Step 3 Constructing hypotheses related to the problem—that is, looking for possible relationships between phenomena or factors. (For instance, in the Burgess model, it is hypothesized that an individual's social status is linked to his or her place of residence in the city; the higher the status, the farther out from the CBD the person lives.)

Step 4 Determining what methods to use for data gathering and then gathering the data.

Step 5 Analyzing the data gathered to see if hypotheses are confirmed or disconfirmed; relating findings to the existing body of theory.

Step 6 Predicting facts on the basis of findings.

In practice, scientific research doesn't usually proceed in such well-ordered, successive steps. First, the steps are often interwoven. For instance, constructing categories entails some prior observation. Second, the scientific method has no provision for intuitive flashes or acquaintance with something. It is a **positivistic** model which assumes that anything worth knowing can be known through sensory experience and verified by procedures outlined in the six steps above. But we know, by Einstein's own declaration, that intuitive insight inspired his theory of relativity, a theory which forever changed our way of seeing the universe. Indeed, scientific breakthroughs often result from minds not hemmed in by the reigning paradigms of doing science (see Kuhn, [1962] 1970).

The scientific method is now questioned by a host of scholars—philosophers of science, the New Physicists, phenomenological philosophers, and social scientists (see Bernstein, 1978; Zukav, 1979). Under attack are the scientific method's assumptions that there are causes and effects that can be tested; that objectivity can be achieved; and that subjective insight plays no role in actual scientific endeavors.

To conclude: The validity of so-called objective science is currently under heavy attack. The very notion of objectivity is now suspect. So is the positivists' clear distinction between facts and values. Today, neither physical nor social scientists agree on what doing science really means.

Facts, Hypotheses, and Value Judgments

For a moment, let's play the "as if" game, returning to the scientific method *as if* facts can be separated from values, *as if* there are causes and effects that can be tested.

Like other scholars, urbanists are trained to use the scientific method. This method makes clear distinctions among statements of fact, statements of suggested relationships among facts, and value judgments about facts. Respectively, these are called *empirical statements, hypotheses,* and *normative statements.* The ability to differentiate among these three types of statements is a prerequisite to critical analysis.

Consider the following sentences that could appear in a report about government-subsidized housing:

1. In Our Town, 5,000 black families live in low-income public housing; 80 percent of these families live in a single neighborhood which is virtually all black.
2. Our Town's City Council decides on public housing sites. It has probably vetoed the construction of public housing in upper-income white neighborhoods since 80 percent of black families living in public housing are located in a virtually all-black neighborhood.
3. This situation of racially segregated, clustered housing should be changed so that low-income housing is scattered throughout Our Town.

Statement 1 is presented as an empirical or factual statement. It appears to be based on scientifically gathered and accurately reported data. These facts can be checked and verified by independent researchers.

Statement 2 is a hypothesis—that is, a statement of relationship between two or more **variables** (factors subject to change). In this case, there are two variables: (a) clustered public housing and (b) the City Council's veto power. Statement 2 can be restated in the form of a hypothesis using these two variables: Our Town's clustered pattern of public housing is a result of the City Council's veto power, preventing the scattering of public housing throughout the city.

The independent variable (the factor that

Box 3-1

RATIONAL ANALYSIS

Hypotheses

Distinguishing between mere assertion and hypotheses is a critical step in rational analysis. For example, the statement that "People are basically evil" (or "good") is a mere assertion. It fails to meet the basic requirements of a hypothesis on two grounds: (1) it is not testable by scientific methods and (2) it does not contain a statement of suggested relationship. By contrast, the following is a hypothesis containing an independent and a dependent variable:

The suicide rate among Protestants is higher than the suicide rate among Catholics and Jews.

This hypothesis suggests a relationship between *religion* and *suicide rate*. The independent variable is religion; the dependent variable is suicide rate. It suggests that a group's religious background affects its propensity to commit suicide.

The graphic model below contains an implied hypothesis: a statement of relationship between two variables, cost of land and distance of land from the city center. In this model, distance determines land cost or rent: As distance from the city center increases, land cost decreases. Thus, distance is the independent variable and cost is the dependent variable.

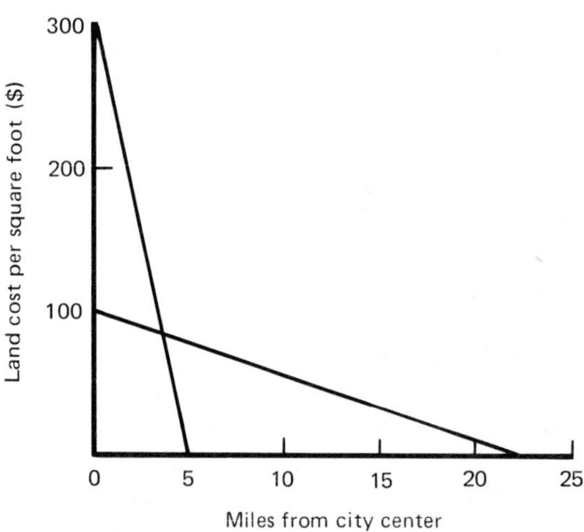

The following statement is a hypothesis containing several variables:

Teenage urban males who are unemployed are more alienated from the political system than unemployed teenage females or unemployed rural teenagers.

This hypothesis suggests a relationship between place of residence (urban or rural) and sex (male or female) and attitudes toward government. Age is a *constant*—not a variable—here, for all involved are teenagers. The dependent variable is attitude toward the political system; the hypothesis suggests that attitude toward the political system depends on both sex and place of residence.

The following paragraph contains an implied hypothesis, empirical statements, and a normative statement:

In 1966 there were 900,000 large families (five or more children) in the United States living below the poverty line. A child born into a large family was 3.5 times as likely to be poor as a child born into a small family (less than three children). To decrease the number of people below the poverty line, governmental programs should encourage the use of contraceptives among persons who already have two children.

The implied hypothesis here is that family size is related to income level. Family size is the independent variable and poverty status is the dependent variable. The first sentence of the paragraph is an empirical statement. The last sentence is a normative statement. An alternative normative statement, derived from the same empirical information, is this: To decrease the number of people below the poverty line, government should guarantee large families an annual income.

causes or influences something; in this case, the resulting clustered housing) is the City Council's veto power. The dependent variable (the factor determined or influenced by the independent variable) is the clustered housing pattern.

Hypotheses must satisfy two requirements. First, they must be testable; second, they must contain a statement of relationship. The statement that "the Devil controls the world" satisfies neither requirement. It is not testable by empirical scientific methods. Nor is it a statement of relationship; it is merely an assertion. By contrast, the suggested relationship between clustered housing patterns and the veto power of elected officials satisfies both requirements, for it can be tested by the scientific method and it contains a statement of relationship between two variables.

Statement 3 is neither a statement of fact nor a hypothesis. It is a normative statement, a value judgment about what should be. It is based on the researcher's own values of what is good and right. One can agree or disagree with a normative statement, depending on one's values.

Often it is hard to separate empirical statements, hypotheses, and normative statements. For instance, the statement that "people on welfare don't want to work" is actually a hypothesis in disguise. (It states a relationship between being poor and being lazy.) In this case, the thrust of social science research (e.g., Goodwin, 1972) shows that welfare recipients prefer working to receiving government assistance. Thus, the hypothesis is generally invalid or nul.

WHY SOCIAL SCIENTISTS DISAGREE

Ideally, social scientists are supposed to seek the truth at all times and apply scientific methods to their research. Why, then, can they look at the very same phenomenon, say, poverty and slums, and disagree on what they see and what should be done about it?

To explore this knotty question, let us take the example of poverty in urban America. Suppose that the President of the United States declares a war against poverty. Before deciding how best to fight the war, the President appoints a task force of highly respected social scientists. Their mission: to produce a joint report on the causes, nature, and extent of poverty in the nation's cities. Eighteen months and $1.5 million later, the report is submitted for policy action. It contains a majority opinion and three separate minority reports. It is clear that the researchers disagree among themselves on basic issues. To begin with, they disagree on whether or not poverty even constitutes a problem. In addition, those who think it is a problem don't agree on whether or not it can be solved or the means to solve it.

Disagreements among task force members might be based on the following kinds of differences: (1) theoretical orientations; (2) disciplinary perspectives; (3) research methods; (4) levels of analysis; (5) ideological assumptions and values; (6) subtle influences, such as the funding source; and (7) attitudes toward social problem solving. These differences can affect what questions a researcher asks, what a researcher finds, how a researcher defines the problem and thus the solution, and/or what the researcher advises doing about it.

Theoretical Orientations

First, social scientists do not share a common theoretical orientation. Within any one discipline, there may be competing models or paradigms of how the world works.

Taking sociology as an example, let's exam-

Fig. 3-1 FACTS DON'T SPEAK FOR THEMSELVES. (© 1976 Richard Hedman)

ine how two major theoretical orientations filter the social world through different lenses: structural-functionalism and symbolic interaction. Very briefly, structural-functionalists are concerned with the structures of society and their functions (purposes). They look for the interconnections between different parts of a social system, assuming that society, like the human body, is organized in systems and subsystems. Just as each system of the body (circulation, defense against disease, etc.) serves different functions and contributes to the whole organism's welfare, so do different institutional structures in society. In this view, systems (both the human organism and the social system) seek equilibrium, balance, stability, and order. Structural-functionalists think that whatever exists—poverty, for instance—serves a social function or it would cease to exist. Critics of structural-functionalism hold that this theoretical perspective is inherently conservative because it focuses on social order (rather than social change) and things as they are (rather than things as they might be).

Symbolic interactionists have a very different focus. Instead of social systems or institutional structures, symbolic interactionists focus on *meaning*—how people construct meanings, how they define social reality in different ways. They deal with small, microworlds of social behavior, such as face-to-face encounters and small group behavior. The language people use to express themselves (both in words and gestures) and the way these words and gestures are understood by others are especially interesting to symbolic interactionists. They may explore the subtle ways in which meaning is transmitted between parents and children in the slums or the interpretation of action from the actor's point of view. Researchers in this tradition are routinely trained in qualitative techniques such as participant-observation and in-depth interviewing. Herbert Gans's study of a Boston slum, *The Urban Villagers* (1962), examines group life of Italian-Americans using participant-observation as a research method.

Each theoretical orientation looks at poverty (as a research problem) in a particular way. And in large measure, each approach determines what questions will be asked. In turn, what questions are asked influences one's findings about the nature and causes of poverty.

Disciplinary Perspectives

As with background pictures or cognitive maps, urbanists bring their disciplinary perspectives with them when they investigate an issue. The example of slums in Chapter 2 illustrated how various social science disciplines, professional fields, and the humanities might see slums and poverty. Recall that some concepts and research tools cross disciplines, but each one retains its central focus. This means that scholars in the same discipline may differ in their theoretical orientations, even their ideologies and methods, but still share a disciplinary perspective that sets them apart from other social scientists. This was pointed out by two economists who are poles apart, free market theorist Milton Friedman and liberal economist Walter Heller. Discussing what economists do and why they disagree, Friedman and Heller both said on a public television show in 1979 that when economists of varying ideologies discuss issues with colleagues from political science and other social science disciplines, the economists as a group find themselves agreeing with one another.

Research Methods

Urbanists use different strategies for observing and analyzing facts. Research methods may vary from discipline to discipline, from subdiscipline to subdiscipline, and from one theoretical orientation to another. Most economists today, for instance, use quantitative techniques (econometrics, mathematical equations and models, statistical analysis). Anthropologists, on the other hand, depend primarily on qualitative techniques—direct, intensive observation of social life through fieldwork, or what sociologists call **participant-observation.** This means observing people firsthand to get an intimate, personal acquaintance with their situation or way of life.

Within a single discipline techniques vary, so much so that researchers often find it difficult to communicate or understand each other—although both call themselves by the same disciplinary name, such as political scientist or sociologist. This situation is reflected in the learned journals within a discipline; usually, journals will contain a few articles that appeal to a broad audience within the discipline and more specialized articles that only a portion of the audience will—perhaps can—read. In history, for example, those trained before the 1970s often find it hard to read recent research that is based on quantitative techniques, including sophisticated computer-based statistical analyses.

Members of one "school" or theoretical orientation are routinely trained in particular methods. In sociology, symbolic interactionists are trained in methods of participant-observation. This method encourages inductive reasoning. Theory is grounded in and generated from direct observation. In contrast, structural-functionalists (and Marxist-oriented sociologists) are more commonly trained in quantitative research methods and tend to begin with more complete models of how things work, thus applying deductive reasoning to the facts they find.

Comparison—the analysis of similarities or differences among phenomena—is considered by many theorists to be the basic method of the social sciences. But researchers use varying techniques to gather and analyze comparative data. Some study written and other social documents: official statistics, diaries, graffitti, paintings, tombstones, organizational records, census data, and so on. Others gather information by conducting polls and interviewing random samples of the population (survey research) or setting up controlled experiments. To express the results of these various data-gathering techniques, urbanists use a number of aids: graphs, organization charts, diagrams, flow charts, statistical tables, verbatim conversational reports, narrative description, and abstract models.

Why do the techniques used to investigate and analyze a research problem like poverty make a difference? As philosophers of science point out, the techniques used to investigate a research topic help to determine what the findings will be. Here is one example, discussed in Chapter 12 in greater detail. Two social scientists, political scientist Robert Dahl and sociologist Floyd Hunter, set out to study the same questions: Who runs this

Fig. 3-2 DOING SOCIAL SCIENCE. (Richard Hedman)

town? How are political decisions made at the city level? Hunter ([1953] 1963) used a technique called the "reputational method" to explore the question, asking influential people in Atlanta, Georgia, to assess the relative power of reputed leaders in local decision making. Dahl (1961), investigating who runs New Haven, Connecticut, used "decision analysis," examining local decisions (e.g., urban renewal) to see who participated in making them. The two researchers found different patterns of influence and power. Hunter found a power structure that was highly centralized and monolithic. Dahl found a pluralistic structure in which various elites shared power. To a significant degree, the research methods that Dahl and Hunter used helped to determine what kind of power structure each found.

Each method of investigation has its own strengths and weaknesses. Participant-observation can provide direct acquaintance with poverty; no questionnaire survey can do that. But on the other hand, no direct observation of a few people living in poverty can yield general statements about all people living in poverty; the group under study may be atypical. Then again, a person constructing a questionnaire may miss salient questions without firsthand acquaintance with poverty situations. Similarly, those who depend on official statistics can be misled, even if the statistics represent the best available data. Suicide rates are illustrative. Whether a death is reported as natural or suicide is often problematic; high-status individuals may not be listed as suicides as often as low-status, low-income individuals, for family doctors can list deaths as natural to protect the high-status family from embarrassment, while the poor have fewer means to protect themselves. For these kinds of reasons, methodologists counsel social science researchers to use a variety of techniques in their work—for example, to combine fieldwork (participant-observation and interviewing) with survey research and **unobtrusive measures** (i.e., methods that don't influence the research subjects or have reactive effects, such as analyzing the content of documents or TV shows).

Levels of Analysis

"Science," says astronomer Carl Sagan (1978:13), "is a way of thinking much more than it is a body of knowledge." For some, doing science means reflecting on a grain of salt; for others, it means trying to understand the entire universe. And for others, it means trying to make the connections between the grain of salt and the entire universe.

Those who study grains of salt use the micro-level approach, focusing on small-scale phenomena. Micro-sociology is the study of small groups. Micro-economics is the study of economic behavior of individuals, households, and business firms.

Those who study the universe, so to speak, use the macro-level approach. Macro-sociology is thus the study of large-scale social systems, and macro-economics investigates how fiscal and monetary policy and other large-scale factors keep an economic system working.

Used in combination, the micro and macro approaches can give a very different view of a phenomenon, such as poverty, than either could do alone. Elliot Liebow's study of black streetcorner men in Washington, D.C., *Tally's Corner* (1967), demonstrates the wisdom of using both levels of analysis to explore the same issue. In *Tally's Corner*, Liebow gives an account, based on his participant-observation, of how this group of men spend much of their daily life hanging out on streetcorners in the nation's capital. But he doesn't stop there. He goes on to relate their everyday activities to larger social forces—racial discrimination, structures of economic opportunity, and other factors which shape their everyday lives. Had he looked only at the macrolevel (the larger social forces which influenced the men's self-perceptions and lifestyles) or only at the microsocial structure (the streetcorner), he could not have traced the interrelationships between individual behavior and structural opportunities. Connecting micro and macro levels of analysis, Liebow finds that the behavior of Tally and his buddies is a response to their failure to reach the goals of the dominant culture—goals that the men share. Liebow concludes that it is a lack of economic opportunity and lack of skills—not distinctive cultural traits (as Oscar Lewis's "culture of poverty" thesis would have it)—or laziness that mold the lives of the twenty-four men who stand around the New Deal Carry-out shop at Tally's corner.

Ideologies and Values

In 1960 Harvard sociologist Daniel Bell proclaimed *The End of Ideology*. Bell reasoned that in the postindustrial society, intellectuals (including urbanists) would not have deep-seated ideological differences. Believing that political ideas had been exhausted in the 1950s, Bell said that American intellectuals basically agreed on the *ends* of public policy. Public debate, therefore, would center on the *means* of implementing public policy, not on the ends themselves. In his view, public choices in the postindustrial society would be technical, not political, in character.

Bell's obituary for ideology has since proved premature. Scholars, policymakers, and citizens alike fail to agree on basic ideological issues, including government's proper role in American life. Urbanists themselves reflect the range of ideological positions current in the United States today: conservative and neo-conservative (Bell is now dubbed a "neo-conservative"), liberal, and radical. And some cross-cut these ideological positions with another dimension, centralism or decentralism.

The labels "conservative," "liberal," and "radical" are now used fairly loosely. For instance, a TV newscaster in Syracuse, New York, once described his town as "conservative." Pressed to specify what he meant by this label, he answered, "You know, Syracusans don't get married in drive-in churches or buy everything on credit." What he apparently meant was that conservatism refers to traditional values. To some, a "liberal" is one who is "open-minded" or in favor of school busing to integrate schools. And "radical" may conjure up the image of a wild-eyed, bearded bomb thrower.

However, these loosely applied labels do have more precise meanings. Conservative social thinkers have had a consistent view of human nature for hundreds of years, and a rather pessimistic one at that. Radicals, on the contrary, have maintained a much rosier picture of human motivation, tending to see bad social systems, not inherently bad people. This is a more optimistic view of social change, for it follows that if a social system is altered, the personalities of the people who live under it will also change.

The liberal label once had a very precise denotation. To be a liberal in the nineteenth century meant holding certain ideas about how the social and economic order did and should work. "Classical liberalism" (also called "laissez-faire economics") provides the basis for what is today called "economic conservatism." In other words, a nineteenth-century classical liberal would be called an economic conservative today.

The Liberal Perspective: All **ideologies** pivot on a view of human nature, a view which can neither be defended nor refuted on strictly empirical grounds. Originally, the liberal perspective saw humankind through the eyes of English philosopher Thomas Hobbes (1599–1679). According to Hobbes, the human condition is one of "the war of all against all." People are driven by personal gain, glory, and selfishness. Their lives are "solitary . . . nasty, brutish, and short." In order to bypass people's assumed selfishness and greed, liberal philosophers assigned all social and political decision making to a mechanism they believed neutral and self-regulating: the market of supply and demand.

Over the centuries, liberalism changed significantly. Liberals today tend to be more optimistic about the slow but sure progress of individuals and society. They also think that the market mechanism doesn't always work to prevent major social and economic trauma, such as worldwide economic depression. Yet, through all these changes, Hobbes's materialist conception of human nature and his atomistic individualism remain at the heart of the liberal perspective.

Before detailing the points of difference between liberals and conservatives today, let's examine their shared assumptions. These assumptions are rooted in the political economy of Adam Smith (1776), and they can be found today between the lines of one of liberalism's most well-read works: Paul Samuelson's best-selling introductory text, *Economics*. Liberals, both classical and modern, make the following assumptions:

1. *People act in their own rational self-interest.* Individuals and decision-making units (such as business firms) act in a rational way to maximize their own welfare.
2. *Consumers are sovereign in the marketplace.* Given simple constraints, individuals are free to determine how to use their scarce resources, choosing goods and services from a wide range of alternatives in the marketplace.
3. *The market is self-regulating.* The market mechanism of supply and demand "still works to solve the WHAT, HOW and FOR WHOM questions" (Samuelson, 1964:53).
4. *The "invisible hand" works to serve the public interest and bring about social equilibrium.* Adam Smith theorized in 1776 that each individual would act in the general interest "as if guided by an invisible hand." In other words, individual and social interests automatically harmonize; if you do well for yourself, you also benefit the entire community.
5. *A rising tide lifts all boats.* National growth and prosperity benefit all citizens. Also, wealth trickles down from top to bottom so that money spent at the top eventually filters down to those at the bottom of the social ladder, thereby benefiting everyone. Or as a president of General Motors put it in the 1950s: "What's good for GM is good for the country."

These key assumptions underlie classical liberalism. Generally speaking, they are shared by liberals and conservatives today. It is evident that the role of the free market is central to their analysis.

The major area of disagreement between liberals and conservatives today is the role of government in modern American life. Liberals tend to believe that the market does not always work to provide opportunities for those at the lower end of the social ladder. Thus, liberals hold, government should intervene in the competitive market to affect public welfare and help individuals do better for themselves (thus benefiting the entire community). In practice, this means that liberals support the expansion of opportunities for all (through job training, education, etc.) and income redistribution (through tax policy, resource allocation policies, etc.).

Liberals today also support government intervention to promote economic stability.

Fig. 3-3 GET THE LIFE JACKETS! Liberals favor government intervention to address some failures of the free market system. (© 1976 Richard Hedman)

They want to avoid the unemployment and instability that accompanied the Great Depression of the 1930s. To prevent another ruinous depression and lessen the effects of massive unrest in the 1930s, Lord John Maynard Keynes advocated vast government spending to create jobs for countless millions out of work and to intervene in the private market. Since the 1930s, Keynesian prescriptions and economic analysis have dominated liberal economic thought.

Traditionally, liberals have favored government intervention at the federal level, viewing state and local governments as either incompetent, corrupt, and/or agents of the status quo. In recent years, however, some liberals have changed their tune, stressing grass roots efforts for social change. Liberals were at the forefront of programs during the 1960s aimed at increasing citizen participation in local decision making.

Generally speaking, liberals view urban problems (such as poverty) as capable of solution, or at least amelioration. Their method for solving problems is to make incremental and marginal changes around the edges of social and economic institutions, not to restructure basic institutions. A major tool of liberal social policy is the federal income tax. Liberals view the federal income tax as a key instrument in redistributing goods and services that the market fails to provide for citizens at the bottom (and sometimes middle) of the economic ladder.

Another liberal solution to urban problems is pouring in money to create conditions of supposedly equal opportunity for citizens deemed disadvantaged. The federally sponsored Office of Economic Opportunity (the War on Poverty) was based on the liberal tenet of providing equal opportunity for all.

Another key liberal assumption bears special notice. An extension of classical liberal thought, it joins liberal politics to liberal economics: pluralist democracy. Liberals assume that power is fairly widely dispersed among a multiplicity of interest groups, each representing its members' self-interest.

The liberals' notion of pluralist democracy in America—where diverse interest groups bargain and negotiate in the political arena to protect their rational self-interest—helps account for their almost total inattention or dismissal of the issue of social class. Both conservatives and radicals use the concept of social class in their analysis of society and social problems (albeit in very different ways), but liberals tend to act "as if the subject did not exist" (Hacker, 1973:65).

In brief, then, liberals today tend to sponsor social change within prescribed limits: social change that can be managed and directed by government action, that is incremental in nature, and that does not alter basic economic and social institutions. Government is viewed as the proper agent of managed social change.

Liberal spokespersons today include economists John Kenneth Galbraith and Paul Samuelson; Brookings Institution analysts in Washington, D.C.; and Edward Kennedy. Their policy proposals—more funds to cities, more social programs, fewer tax loopholes, government-sponsored health programs, etc.—reveal their belief that government action can lessen, if not remedy, social injustice, poverty, and other conditions deemed urban problems.

The Conservative and Neo-conservative Perspective: As outlined above, conservatives today remain classical liberals in their economic doctrine. They tend to see big government as the enemy, a threat to individual freedom and prosperity. In their view, business interests—if left alone and unhampered by government interference or regulations—would do a better job than government of managing the economy. This preference for the free market to determine social and political outcomes means that conservatives tend to fear big government more than big business. In contrast, contemporary liberals tend to fear big business more.

Again in contrast to liberals, most conservatives today do not favor social reforms. To understand why, we must look at the conservatives' assumptions about human nature and the social order. Basically, conservatives are pessimistic about the human condition. In the words of a classic conservative thinker, Edmund Burke (1729–1797), people have "disorderly appetites" such as pride, avarice, lust, and ambition. Or, in the words of contemporary conservative James Burnham: "man is partly corrupt as well as limited in his potential" (in Hacker, 1973:13). In other words, individuals are marked with what Christian theologians call "original sin." It follows that people are not essentially good and that even the best-intentioned social reforms are self-defeating because people are prone to perversity. Given this view of human nature, it also follows that conservatives prize social stability, social order, and authority above all else.

So-called neo-conservatives share the basic assumptions of laissez-faire economic doctrine and conservative social thought. This group emerged in the late 1960s in the wake of what they considered to be the excesses of liberalism: the Great Society programs of President Lyndon B. Johnson (including the War on Poverty), New Left politics, and countercultural lifestyles. What makes them "neo" or new conservatives is not their pessimism about human nature or their distrust of the masses, for these are traditional conservative ideas. Rather, it is their perception of the current American situation. They fear a crisis of authority, a breakdown in morality, and government's inability to govern. The neo-conservatives fear liberal and radical proposed solutions to poverty and social injustice more than they fear the injustices themselves (see Steinfels, 1979).

Senator Daniel Patrick Moynihan (Democrat-New York) is the neo-conservatives' leading spokesperson today. Formerly a university professor and urbanist (among other roles), Moynihan is joined by other urbanists at the core of this school of thought, particularly Edward Banfield and Nathan Glazer; their doctrines can be found in the pages of their journals, *The Public Interest* and *Commentary*.

Edward Banfield sums up the neo-conservative stance in his widely read, controversial book *The Unheavenly City* ([1968] 1970). Banfield argues that "social problems will sometimes disappear in the normal course of events" and "government cannot solve the problems of the cities and is likely to make them worse by trying" (257). Further, Banfield discusses class characteristics openly, claiming that "So long as the city contains a sizable lower class nothing basic can be done about its most serious problems" (210).

Moynihan states his position much more succinctly, in a single-word title: *Coping* (1973). He does not hold out a vision of a better world to come through reform (as the liberals do) or eventual revolution (as the radicals propose). Instead, he advises "benign neglect" of problems and muddling through.

The Radical Perspective: *The* radical perspective is a misnomer. So many branches of radical thought exist today that it is impossible to single out a particular stance as the radical position. Here we focus on one aspect of radical thought rooted in the theories of Karl Marx. As we discuss in more detail later, Marx's analysis of political economy—whether one agrees or dissents—has been so influential that it cannot be overlooked. No matter how one judges Marx's notions of the nature of the social system and the human condition, his ideas are inescapable.

Marxists think that most social problems can be solved—but not within the context of the present institutional structure. This is in contrast to (1) conservatives and neo-conservatives, who think that few social problems can be solved (especially by government programs), and (2) liberals, who think that government action can improve social life. Marxists reject the liberal problem-solving approach of incremental change at the edges of basic social and economic institutions. They say that only by going to the roots ("radical" means root) of economic instability and social injustice can problems be solved. Fiddling around with marginal changes, radicals claim, is like applying Bandaids to social cancers; superficial responses won't cure the root problem. For Marxists, it is not possible to abolish poverty and leave the present economic system intact. In their view, the present economic system and authority structures that grow out of that system are the roots of the problem.

Urban geographer David Harvey (1973) is one spokesperson for the Marxist perspective today. Harvey starts with this assumption: Poverty is a manifestation of social structural problems in the national and international socioeconomic system. These problems can be only solved by a radical restructuring of this system of monopoly capitalism. In this view, what is needed is not liberal reform or conservative benign neglect of social problems. What is needed is socialist revolution.

Marxists point to such conditions as the unequal distribution of wealth and income among social classes and the capitalist state's alliance with business interests and elite groups as forces that perpetuate poverty. Since Marxists think that government is part of the problem, they don't look to government for the solution.

The Marxist analysis of society proceeds from the following assumptions:

1. *The productive forces in society determine its essential character.* The prevailing beliefs, legal system, politics, and social relationships in a society are determined by that society's mode of production (e.g., the state of technology, the ownership and management of scarce resources, and the authority relations that result from a particular productive mode, such as feudalism or capitalism).

2. *There is no such thing as "human nature."* This follows from the first assumption that the ways people think, relate to other people and their work, even feel, are linked to the prevailing mode of production. For instance, people tilling the soil in preindustrial rural societies, fashioning handicrafts in medieval towns, or attaching left-rear bumpers on an assembly line in capitalist urban-industrial societies will necessarily interpret their worlds in very different ways. People are formed by the productive activities in society. They are not basically "economic animals," as the liberal perspective maintains; rather, they are active agents who transform the material world and master nature. Marx used the term *homo faber* (man the maker or producer) to express this notion.

3. *Social conflict between classes dominates capitalist societies.* Under the capitalist mode of production, social harmony does not exist (as liberals maintain). Rather, economic and political life is primarily determined by the conflict between two great social classes: those who own and control the factories and other productive forces in society (the bourgeoisie) and those who neither own nor control the society's productive forces (the have-nots, or the proletariat). Under capitalism, a few "continue to obtain enormous shares of wealth and leisure, while others continue to support themselves and others with their labor" (Gordon, 1977:7). In other words, Marxists see a necessary connection between poverty and wealth under capitalism: Some are poor because others are rich.

4. *Government (the state) under capitalism is not neutral.* Whereas liberals see diverse interest groups bargaining and negotiating for scarce resources in the political arena in the context of a neutral government, Marxists see the state as a tool of the bourgeoisie. Decision making is dominated by those who own and control society's productive forces or civil servants who act to protect their interests. In short, public policy under capitalism is dominated by urban business and creditor classes.

5. *Under capitalism today, the self-regulating market mechanism doesn't work.* The theory of the free market as self-regulating neglects the facts of monopoly price-fixing, the creation of needs by advertising, the corporate political economy which tries to avoid competition in its own interest, and government intervention on behalf of private enterprise.

6. *The sum of the private interests does not equal the public interest.* Believing, as classical liberals do, that the "invisible hand" works to assure social harmony and individual well-being is illogical. It assumes that "the lead of private greed [can be transmuted] into the gold of public welfare" (Wolfson and Stanley, 1969:1).

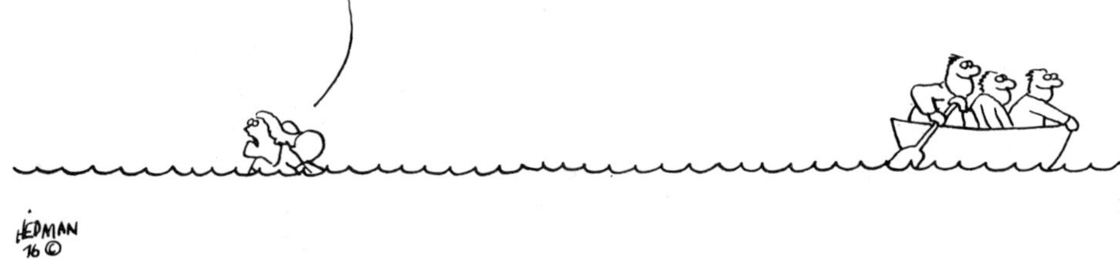

Fig. 3-4 GET SOME NEW BOATS! Radicals call for basic changes in the relationships between social classes in order to meet the problems of people and cities in distress. (© 1976 Richard Hedman)

In sum, Marxists don't expect the capitalist state to change its basic institutional structure. On the contrary, they see government policies and programs—poverty programs, for example—as means of upholding the status quo by diverting attention away from structural problems inherent under capitalism. Thus, according to sociologist Irving Louis Horowitz (1966:104), the War on Poverty may have been an effort to "stave off economic class struggle" by substituting tension release, symbolic reassurance of permanent change, and racial conflict for problems of income inequality.

Centralists and Decentralists: By tradition, Marxists and other radicals are considered to fall on the left of the political spectrum, while liberals occupy the center and conservatives the right. Most probably, this left-center-right distinction originated in the seating arrangements of the eighteenth-century French national assembly; socialists and other radicals took the chamber's left wing, moderates were seated in the middle, and social conservatives of the day took the right wing.

People still identify political ideologies as left-wing, right-wing, and middle-of-the-road. Yet, this one-dimensional distinction obscures issues that cross-cut traditional politics. In particular, it obscures the big-small or centralist-decentralist dimension.

Slogan makers might express the big-small difference as follows: "small is beautiful" versus "big is better." Decentralists, proclaiming "small is beautiful," tend to be anti-bigness, whether big government, big business, or big technology. Their ideals center on self-sufficiency and small community. Decentralists of the left and right come together on such concerns as ecological consciousness; the need to find alternative energy sources and reduce total energy consumption; the desire for human-scale institutions and appropriate technology; and the need to meet human needs rather than to encourage economic growth.

By contrast, centralists tend to be pro-bigness: either big government or big business plus big technology. Centralists of the left and right come together on such issues as the preference for large-scale organizations (assumed to be efficient and economic) as providers of goods and services; economic growth as a necessary condition of human welfare; and functional interdependence among regions of a country and among the family of nations.

As Fig. 3-5 illustrates, the two-axis political world does make for some new seating arrangements. Decentralists may be libertarians, populists, anarchists, or utopian communalists; centralists may be liberals, Marxists, conservatives, or neo-conservatives.

The "small is beautiful" versus "big is better" distinction runs deep in social

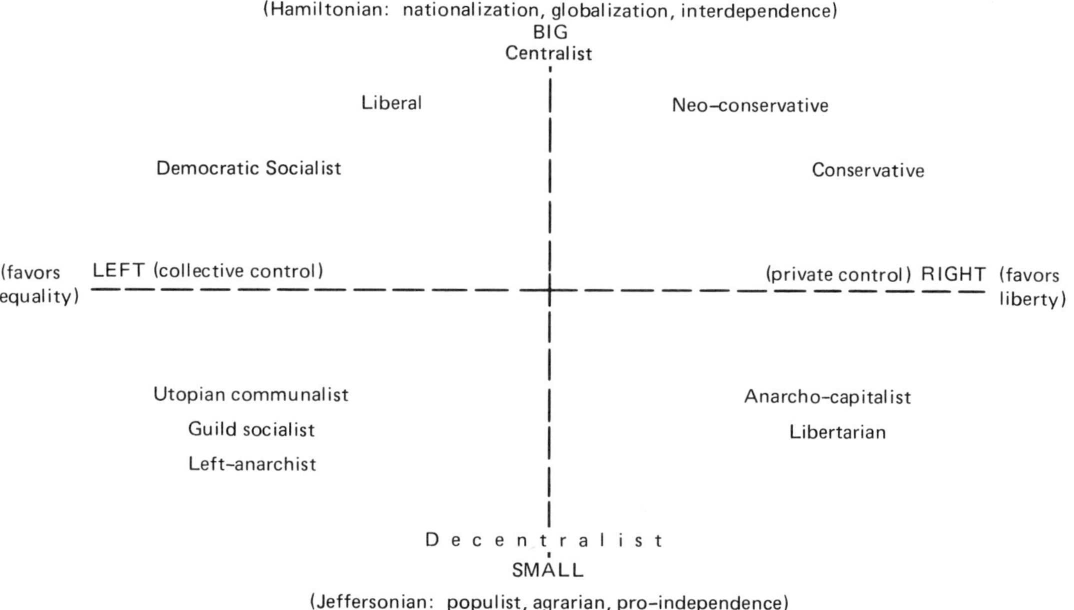

Fig. 3-5 THE TWO-AXIS POLITICAL WORLD. Combining the left-right political spectrum with the big-small dimension provides clues to possible political coalitions in the postindustrial society. (Michael Marien, "The New Path of Progress and the Devolution of Services: Viewing the Present and Future without Industrial Era Bias," paper presented at the conference on the Service Sector of the Economy, San Juan, Puerto Rico, 1978)

thought. These countervisions of the good society lie at the base of historical debates over the nature (and wisdom) of urban-industrial society, as we shall see in Chapter 5. These opposing visions are involved in the controversy over the causes and cures of alienation in urban society, as we note in Chapter 16. And they form the basis of hope—and despair—in visions of the coming postindustrial society, as we note throughout this book.

Centralists and decentralists have little respect for each other's position. Centralists, advocating a consumer-service society built on bigness, tend to treat decentralists as romantic, anti-progress, and anti-science moralists—in a word, as naive primitives. Decentralists tend to paint their opponents as elitist technocrats, as materialistic and amoral tools of big government and/or big business who suffer from nonexpanded consciousness. While centralists put forth their views as objective scientific forecasts, decentralists tend to express their values explicitly, emphasizing alternative futures. Each side discounts the other's methods and visions. E. F. Schumacher (1973:146), a prophet of the decentralists, described the *Small Is Beautiful* people as "the homecomers" who want to "return to certain basic truths about man and his world." Speaking for the other side, futurist Alvin Toffler (1970) described decentralists as "people of the present" and "people of the past," while centralists are "people of the future."

To conclude: Urbanists disagree on fundamental issues of political ideology. Personal preferences—for left- or right-wing politics, for big or small community—influence how they see the world. These ideological preferences also influence how they advise policymakers to cope with the world or try to change it.

Subtle Influences on Researchers

Disagreements among urbanists can also stem from another factor: dependence on funding sources. In an era of government- and corporate-sponsored research, it is almost impossible for researchers to be independent intellectuals, answerable to nothing but their own conscience and the long search for knowledge.

Often researchers are channeled into investigating certain topics, including poverty, because research money is available. "Going where the money is"—allowing private and public funding sources to set the research priorities—often robs scholars of their initiative to explore the issues they consider important. In addition, fear that the pipeline to future research grants can be cut if "controversial" results are submitted to funding agencies may have a chilling effect on researchers.

Scholars of various ideologies decry the ever-increasing dependence on corporate and government funding sources. Conservatives and radicals alike often see the "grants economy" as an intrusion on scholarly freedom of thought. In particular, academic links with various covert projects funded by the Central Intelligence Agency have been severely criticized.

One major objection to the grants economy is that "he who pays the piper calls the tune." A related objection is raised by radicals. They argue that the poor and powerless, often the subjects (or objects) of social research, can't hire academic consultants and consequently have little input into proposed policies that may affect their lives.

Attitudes toward Solving Social Problems

Can social science solve social problems? Should social scientists play key roles in

Box 3-2

WHERE YOU STAND DEPENDS ON WHERE YOU SIT

Handy Guide to Public Policy Proposers and Their Proposals

IDEOLOGICAL POSITION	VIEW OF PRESENT AND FUTURE	PROPOSALS FOR FUTURE
Languishing Liberal	Troubled times	More money and programs, racial integration
Counteracting Conservative	Crime, centralization, and crumbling civilization	Law, order, soap, haircuts, truth and morality
Rabid Rightist	It's getting REDder all the time	Wave flags and stockpile arms (public and private)
Primitive Populist	Domination by pointy-headed pseudo-intellectuals	Throw briefcase in Potomac; restore common sense
Passionate Pacifist	A garrison state	A peaceable kingdom
Rumbling Revolutionary	A repressive, racist, imperialist, capitalist establishment	Confront and destroy The System (other details to be worked out later)
ROLE–RELATED POSITIONS		
Urgent Urbanist	Decline and fall of cities	More funds and programs, side-stepping states
Emphatic Ecologist	Decline and fall of everything else	Control contaminators and restore nature
Stultified Student	Entrapment in *their* world	Inner and interpersonal exploration and other relevant learning
Tortured Taxpayer	Growing gaps between income, aspirations, and expenditures	Cut, cut, cut, cut
Contracting Conglomerator	Cybernation, diversification, and internationalization	Withering of the state

SOURCE: Michael Marien, *Public Administration Review* 30, 2:154.

formulating social policy? Among themselves, social scientists don't agree, and their opinions often are linked to their ideologies.

First, a note on the term "social problem." One hundred years ago, there were disagreeable social conditions, issues, and conflicts—but no social problems or social ills. The idea that society can be "sick" and need "treatment" for "chronic disease" is relatively recent, probably dating from the early twentieth century. The Chicago school of sociology (Park, Burgess, etc.) was partially responsible for this linguistic change that altered people's way of seeing the world, for they were convinced that urban industrial life led to "social disorganization" and "social pathology". Thus, as they studied crime, deviance, juvenile delinquency, and other "pathologies," they helped to transfer medical and clinical language to the realm of urban life (Rule, 1978:16). At about the same time, the new field of psychoanalysis, in an attempt to legitimate the fledgling field, began to apply the medical model to individual behavior. Where people were formerly labeled "sinful," "strange," or "eccentric," they now became mentally "ill."

Today we routinely use medical language to describe people and societies. What we often forget is that the medical model of illness and problems is a mere metaphor, a rhetorical device, that masks other ways of seeing and understanding. In particular, seeing disagreeable social conditions as problems conceals the political conflicts of interests that belie social problems: "A conflict, after all, inescapably requires one to take a stand. A 'problem,' on the other hand, is something everyone can safely oppose. . . . Social problem solving . . . is a profoundly *political* enterprise from beginning to end" (Rule, 1978: 18–19, 23).

When problems were merely disagreeable social conditions, they were thought to be approachable through either the market mechanism or the political process. But once something is defined as a social *problem*, it logically calls for a *technical* solution. Here is the logic: Just as medical experts are needed to cure physical illness, social experts (social scientists) are needed to cure society's chronic ailments. Using technical experts—urbanists, for example—to solve social problems means transferring issues out of the political arena. This sidesteps public debate. It also turns social scientists into technocrats—as if they were value-free and objective, with no ideological axes to grind or visions to promote. We have already seen how faulty that assumption is.

A case study by sociologist Scott Greer (1961) illustrates the problematic nature of problem solving. Looking at urban traffic and transportation, Greer asks: Whose problem is it? What kind of people, playing what social roles, define the nature of the metropolitan transportation problem? Who is concerned about it? After all, Greer says, traffic may not be a problem to drivers sitting and listening to car radios. Nor is traffic a major concern to suburbanites, who may pay the price of driving slowly through fumes rather than paying for anti-pollutants. But congestion may indeed be a major concern for downtown business merchants or suburban shopping mall developers. In other words, it is wrong to assume that a social problem is everyone's problem. Greer advises the use of extreme skepticism when analyzing the slogans of public discourse, such as "problems." And he counsels researchers to analyze what groups in society have power to define a problem as well as what interest groups benefit most from its solution.

Having looked at the transformation of social conflicts and conditions into more neutral social problems, let us touch briefly on a related matter: the proper role of social scientists in solving problems. This issue is rooted in much larger questions: Who should govern? Will government by experts turn out to be government in the interest of experts?

Since World War II, social scientists have become part of a giant knowledge industry. Armed with sophisticated research tools and computers, many social researchers think they can—and should—use their knowledge to build better cities. Even a better world. Indeed, some see themselves as a priestly caste, possessing reason and analytical skills that can lead people into the good society (e.g., Hoult, 1968). Others (e.g., Lindblom and Cohen, 1979) aren't so sure that social scientists should play the role of physician or social engineer. This view is epitomized by neo-conservative urbanist Daniel Patrick Moynihan in his book *Maximum Feasible Misunderstanding* (1969), a stinging appraisal of social scientists as problem solvers in the War on Poverty. Moynihan concludes that social scientists should measure and evaluate the outcomes of public policy, not formulate or implement it. Still others argue that the debate over the proper role of the scientific expert is academic, for professionals, afraid to risk the loss of community standing, are inherently conservative and thus end up serving the ends of those in political power.

How social scientists view their proper role in defining and solving problems is significant because it influences their research. Indeed, urbanist Nathan Glazer (in Scully, 1978:7) claims that problem solving has already supplanted theoretical concerns as the mission of the social sciences. Since the 1960s, he says, there has been a striking shift: away from pure theory toward policy studies aimed at making social institutions more effective.

What is the wider impact of this shift? One implication is that social scientists are now taking the place of novelists, poets, and artists (cf. Chapter 1) as observers and critics of good and evil in social life. In other words, social scientists have become the moralists of our time. This, of course, represents a significant departure from what doing science once meant. For it completely blurs the distinction between facts and values.

WHAT QUESTIONS TO ASK

Understanding the bases of disagreements among urban observers permits us to be more critical and self-aware, both as consumers and as producers of research. And by understanding the underlying vision and assumptions of a researcher or artist, we can better assess the messages they communicate and the evidence they present.

Here are some worthwhile questions to ask of any urban study in order to more critically assess it and the policy recommendations that may flow from it:

1. *Who says so?* What do we know about the author? Specifically, what is his or her (a) disciplinary background, (b) theoretical orientation, (c) practical experience that may be relevant, (d) assumptions and values, and (e) funding sources?

What is the author's political ideology? Is it explicit, or can you tell by reading between the lines? Is the study sponsored or published by an organization or magazine with a known point of view, such as the American Enterprise Institute (generally labeled conservative), the Brookings Institution (the liberal middle), the Institute for Policy Studies (radical), or the libertarian Cato Institute?

How do your own values and biases affect your evaluation of information? Specifically, do you automatically accept as objective what some sources, such as the *New York Times* or your favorite journal of opinion, report but reject as slanted information (perhaps the same information) appearing in a French or Russian newspaper?

2. *What's been neglected?* Is there evidence which might contradict the basic point of the study? Does the author use micro-level analysis alone when macro-level analysis would have added an important dimension, or vice versa? Could the study have been improved by combining several methods of investigation? What points of view seem to be overlooked? These are important questions because in research, as in life, sins of omission can be as deadly as sins of commission.

3. *So what?* Some urban studies may be sophisticated methodologically. But their findings may be trivial, their conclusions relatively meaningless. Hence the "so what?" question: Does the study enrich our understanding of the topic under investigation?

To conclude: By routinely asking and trying to answer these questions— who says so? what's been overlooked? so what?—we can begin to sort sense from nonsense. And we can strengthen our ability to understand and act upon the urban world in which we live.

PROJECTS

1. **Constructing hypotheses**. Using *poverty status* as the dependent variable, construct three different hypotheses (with different independent variables) to explain why some people are poor. These three hypotheses should reflect the liberal, conservative, and radical points of view.

2. **Reading between the lines**. Examine two works of urban scholarship on the same topic—for instance, slums or urban unemployment. Do the authors agree? If not, why not? Try to analyze their assumptions, research methods, political biases, disciplinary perspectives, and levels of analysis used.

SUGGESTIONS FOR FURTHER LEARNING

For an introduction to social science reasoning, see David and Chava Nachmias, *Research Methods in the Social Sciences* (New York: St. Martin's, 1976). Chapter 2 contains a clear discussion of variables, hypotheses, and concepts. Alice Rivlin, *Systematic Thinking for Social Action* (Washington, D.C.: Brookings Institution, 1971), is a classic work on applied social science reasoning; it deals with questions of hypothesis testing and evaluation.

Two more specialized works contain excellent background chapters relevant to this chapter. Eugene J. Webb et al., *Unobtrusive Measures: Nonreactive Research in the Social Sciences* (Chicago: Rand McNally, 1966), primarily deals with techniques for understanding social phenomena without disturbing or altering them in the process of studying them. Carol Weiss, *Evaluation Research* (Englewood Cliffs, N.J.: Prentice-Hall, 1972), is particularly strong in explaining how to work with imperfect data and what it is like to conduct social science research under various constraints.

David Gordon's edited book of readings, *Problems in Political Economy: An Urban Perspective* (Lexington, Mass.: D.C. Heath, 1977), is organized to describe the role of competing ideologies—radical, liberal, and conservative—in urban analysis. This work discusses issues (employment, race, education, poverty and welfare, crime, etc.) from various ideological standpoints and provides short articles from each perspective. Milton Friedman's public television series "Freedom of Choice" (1980) lets Friedman speak for himself, defending the free market and debating with audience members.

For varying points of view on the role of the functional specialist—the expert—in social problem solving, see Michael Halberstam, "The M.D. Should Not Try to Cure Society" in the *New York Times* magazine (November 9, 1969, pp. 32ff); Thorstein Veblen's defense of a form of technocracy in advanced technological society, *The Engineers and the Price System* (New York: Kelley, [1921] 1965); and Robert Boguslaw's description of *The New Utopians* (Englewood Cliffs, N.J.: Prentice-Hall, 1965). The last title refers to the computer manufacturers, operations researchers, systems engineers, and other technological experts who aspire to transcend present reality.

For differing visions of the nature of human beings and their effect on political ideology, see

Sheldon Wolin, *Politics and Vision* (Boston: Little, Brown, 1960), and C.B. Macpherson, *Political Theory of Possessive Individualism: Hobbes to Locke* (New York: Oxford University Press, 1962).

KEY TERMS

Deductive reasoning The process of reasoning from general principles to particular examples.

Empirical evidence Evidence derived from direct observation and sense experience—not intuitive insight, metaphysical speculation, or pure logic.

Hypothesis A tentative statement suggesting a relationship between two or more variables. A hypothesis is intended to be tested empirically, or at least to be testable.

Ideology A set of beliefs and ideas that justify certain interests. An ideological position reflects and rationalizes particular political, economic, institutional, and/or social interests.

Inductive reasoning The process of reasoning from particular examples to general principles.

Model A tentative and limited tool that represents some aspect of the world in words, mathematical symbols, graphs, or other symbols. Models attempt to duplicate or illustrate by analogy a pattern of relationships found in the empirical world. They are used to guide research and build theory in the sciences.

Participant-observation A research method commonly used by sociologists, anthropologists, and news feature writers. The investigator becomes or poses as a member of a group under study in an attempt to gain an intimate, firsthand acquaintance with the group and understand how group members interpret the world.

Positivistic science or **positivism** The philosophical stance claiming that all true knowledge can be derived from sense experience. It rejects intuitive insight, subjective understanding, and metaphysical speculation as bases of knowledge.

Scientific method A method for doing science based on the assumption that all true knowledge is verifiable using empirical evidence. Well-ordered, successive stages—defining a research problem, constructing hypotheses, data gathering and analysis, and prediction of facts—are outlined.

Theory A comprehensive explanation of something. The function of a social theory is to summarize and order information meaningfully; to permit prediction; and to suggest new lines of scientific inquiry. Theories are composed of a set of interrelated generalizations which form a logical system of explanation. A theory is a generalization that is intermediate in degree of verification between a scientific law and a hypothesis.

Unobtrusive measure A research method which seeks to remove the observer from the event under study and thereby to eliminate possible reactive effects. Examples: content analysis of TV programs; archival research; analysis of data gathered by hidden tape recorders or hidden cameras.

Variable A trait or factor that can vary among a population or from case to case (e.g., sex, size of firm, cost per square foot, social class). A variable that causes another factor to change is the independent variable. A dependent variable is a factor influenced or affected by the independent variable.

REFERENCES

Banfield, Edward
[1968]
1970 The Unheavenly City. Boston: Little, Brown.

Bell, Daniel
1960 The End of Ideology. New York: Free Press.

Bernstein, Richard J.
1978 The Restructuring of Social and Political Theory. New York: Harcourt Brace Jovanovich.

Burgess, Ernest W. and Donald J. Bogue
1964 "Research in urban society: a long view." Pp. 1–14 in Ernest W. Burgess and Donald J. Bogue (eds.), Contributions to Urban Sociology. Chicago: University of Chicago Press.

Burke, Edmund
[1790]
1959 Reflections on the Revolution in France. New York: Holt, Rinehart & Winston.

Dahl, Robert
1961 Who Governs: Democracy and Power in an American City. New Haven: Yale University Press.

Gans, Herbert J.
1962 The Urban Villagers. New York: Free Press.

Goodwin, Leonard
1972 Do the Poor Want to Work? Washington, D.C.: Brookings Institution.

Gordon, David (ed.)
1977 Problems in Political Economy: An Urban Perspective. Lexington, Mass.: D.C. Heath.

Greer, Scott
1961 "Traffic, transportation, and problems of the metropolis." Pp. 605–50 in Robert K. Merton and Robert A. Nisbet (eds.), Contemporary Social Problems. New York: Harcourt Brace & World.

Hacker, Andrew
1973 "On original sin and conservatives." New York Times magazine section (February 25): 13+.

Harvey, David
1973 Social Justice and the City. Baltimore: Johns Hopkins.

Hobbes, Thomas
[1651]
1968 Leviathan: or the Matter, Forme and Power of a Commonwealth Ecclesiasticall and Civil. New York: Collier.

Horowitz, Irving Louis
1966 Three Worlds of Development. New York: Oxford University Press.

Hoult, Thomas F.
1968 " ' . . . Who shall prepare himself to the battle?' " The American Sociologist, 3, 1: 3–7.

Hunter, Floyd
[1953]
1963 Community Power Structure: A Study of Decision Makers. Garden City, N.Y.: Doubleday Anchor.

Kuhn, Thomas S.
[1962]
1970 The Structure of Scientific Revolutions. Chicago: University of Chicago Press.

Liebow, Elliot
1967 Tally's Corner. Boston: Little, Brown.

Lindblom, Charles E. and David K. Cohen
1979 Usable Knowledge: Social Science and Social Problem Solving. New Haven: Yale University Press.

Marien, Michael
1970 "Handy guide to public policy proposers & their proposals." Public Administration Review 30, 2:154.

Moynihan, Daniel Patrick
1969 Maximum Feasible Misunderstanding. New York: Free Press.
1973 Coping: On the Practice of Government. New York: Random House.

Public Broadcasting Service (PBS)
1979 "Economically speaking."

Rule, James B.
1978 Insight and Social Betterment: A Preface to Applied Social Science. New York: Oxford University Press.

Sagan, Carl
1978 Broca's Brain: Reflections on the Romance of Science. New York: Random House.

Samuelson, Paul A.
1964 Economics, 6th ed. New York: McGraw-Hill.

Schumacher, E. F.
1973 Small Is Beautiful: Economics as if People Mattered. New York: Harper & Row.

Scully, Malcolm G.
1978 " 'Striking change' seen reshaping science." The Chronicle of Higher Education 16, 12:7.

Smith, Adam
[1776]
1970 Wealth of Nations. Baltimore: Penguin.

Steinfels, Peter
1979 The Neoconservatives: The Men Who Are Changing America's Politics. New York: Simon & Shuster.

Toffler, Alvin
1970 Future Shock. New York: Random House.

Wolfson, Robert and Manfred Stanley
1969 "Beyond the invisible hand: policy advisors and their clients." Syracuse, N.Y.: Educational Policy Research Center, working draft.

Zukav, Gary
1979 The Dancing Wu Li Masters. New York: Morrow.

PART TWO
Polis, Metropolis, Megalopolis

Bank of California

Mexican National Tourist Office

CHAPTER 4 Small Beginnings

THE FIRST CITIES

Digging into Urban History

Rising like a giant spaceport out of Turkey's Anatolian plain is a fifty-eight-foot mound of earth. Until 1961, it was just a big mound lying in the hot sun. Then, an international team moved in to excavate and analyze this ancient site, named **Catal Hüyük** (pronounced Chatal Hooyook; "mound at the end of the road" in modern Turkish). Under the direction of archeologist James Mellaart, the team dug wide trenches into the urban past. As they cut through the mound, they uncovered a prehistoric community—perhaps a city—constructed about 9500 years ago, or even earlier.

Recent archeological digs such as Catal Hüyük and new scientific techniques for radiocarbon dating of ancient artifacts have been overturning long-held theories about why and where cities first came into existence. New evidence has also called into question the dates for the birth of cities, often referred to as the "dawn of civilization." Until quite recently, it was generally assumed that urban life started in the fertile river valleys of the Near East around 3500 B.C. Newer theories push back the date to 8000 B.C. and suggest that the earliest city dwellers settled in the hills above the valleys or in places far from the great rivers of antiquity.

But these matters are far from settled. The origins of cities remain controversial. And as archeological teams uncover new mounds in their digs, as they probably will in the future, we can expect even more controversy and theorizing about what prerequisites were necessary for the emergence of urban life.

Controversy and tentative knowledge thus typify scholarly discussions of the earliest cities invented by human beings. In fact, controversy and tentative knowledge seem to be our fate in studying many urban phenomena, whether in ancient earth mounds or modern U.S. cities. For some, this may produce anxiety and a desire to enter another field or discipline, perhaps physics with its laws and certainties. Yet, physicists on the cutting edge of research say that they too deal only with tentative knowledge and approximations of truths. Facing the limits on our collective understanding in so many important areas—from the origins of the universe and the birth of cities to the causes and cures for human misery—could throw us into despair. Or it could, and we argue should, encourage us to join the long search for knowledge and meaning by seeking better answers to more informed questions.

In this section, we begin the search by tracing the roots of urban life and culture. Using various analytical techniques discussed in previous chapters, we move through the millennia of city life. En route, we pose questions that have few definitive answers: Why did people form cities? What features do the varied cities invented and sustained by human beings have in common? How do they differ from each other? Why did cities grow and prosper at certain historical periods? What roles do **technology,** social organization, physical environment, and population play in city growth?

What Is a City?

Before attempting to date the origin of cities, we run into a problem of definition: What exactly is a **city?** The ancient Romans made a sharp distinction between the community of people who banded together to form a settlement, which they called *civitas* (from which our word "city" is derived), and the physical place they formed—an *urb* (from which our word "urban" is derived). The earliest Roman cities were created by a solemn religious ceremony—the banding together of a group of people to form a community at a definite site.

Today, "city" has been applied to so many different settlement types that the original Roman use of the word is obsolete. There is no precise definition of the word "city" that social scientists or anyone else agrees upon. That is one reason why it is so difficult to discuss when the first cities were invented or whether some communities are indeed cities.

In most definitions of city, however, there are common elements. Usually these include notions of *permanent residence, large population, high density,* and *heterogeneity*. But how large is large? How densely settled must a community be to be classified as a city rather than a village—200 people per square mile, 400, more? And how differentiated by occupation and kin group must a population be in order to be categorized as heterogeneous? Again, there are no precise criteria.

Another approach is to define a city in terms of its economic character. Using this approach, we can describe a city as a market settlement, a place "where the local inhabitants satisfy an economically substantial part of their daily wants in the local market" (Weber, [1921] 1963:66–67).

Yet another approach states that a city exists only when there are cultural ingredients considered essential to urban life—fine arts, exact sciences, and in particular, writing. In this view, a collection of people—no matter how large—does not form a city unless these characteristics are present.

The First Urban Settlements: An Overview

Using any of the above definitions, should the most ancient sites yet excavated be called cities? It is unclear. Early settlements that might qualify as cities overlap two other settlement forms: agricultural villages and trading posts.

Jarmo, in present-day Iraq, is the most widely studied example of a large neolithic agricultural village. Around 7000–6500 B.C., an estimated 150 people lived there at a low density, about 27 people per square mile. Perhaps it had the stirrings of a barter economy, a simple division of labor, and some cultural life. But it was not a city by anyone's definition.

Ancient **Jericho** is harder to classify. Some archeologists believe that Jericho is indeed the earliest city. Dame Kathleen Kenyon and her team of archeologists started digging up Jericho in the 1950s. They found ruined walls which apparently came tumbling down around 1400 B.C., when Joshua "fit the battle of Jericho" in the biblical story. Beneath these ruined city walls, they kept finding remains of earlier and earlier Jerichos. Finally, some 70 feet down, they unearthed the first Jericho: a neolithic community, inhabited perhaps as early as 10,000 years ago. As Dame Kenyon and her co-workers probed, they were astonished to find that this first Jericho was quite a substantial settlement: a 10-acre site, probably an oasis in mid-desert, covered with well-built rectangular houses made of mud-brick. Dame Kenyon (1957:65) estimates that it contained about 3,000 residents, called the "hog-backed brick people" after the round houses with humps at the top that they built. How the hog-backed brick people did it remains a mystery, but somehow they hauled cut stones for enormous public works, including a 20-foot stone wall and a 27-foot-wide, 9-foot-deep ditch.

Although Dame Kenyon calls ancient Jericho the first "town" (a settlement bigger than a village but smaller than a city), its status remains controversial. To many, it is best thought of as a trading post.

If Jericho's status is disputed and Jarmo is certainly not a city, what is the earliest true city? Was it Catal Hüyük on the Anatolian plain?

Catal Hüyük was probably established shortly after Jericho. Apparently, its population was twice that of Jericho. Residents produced some spectacular art work and engaged in extensive trade. By some people's definitions, it qualifies as one of the earliest cities.

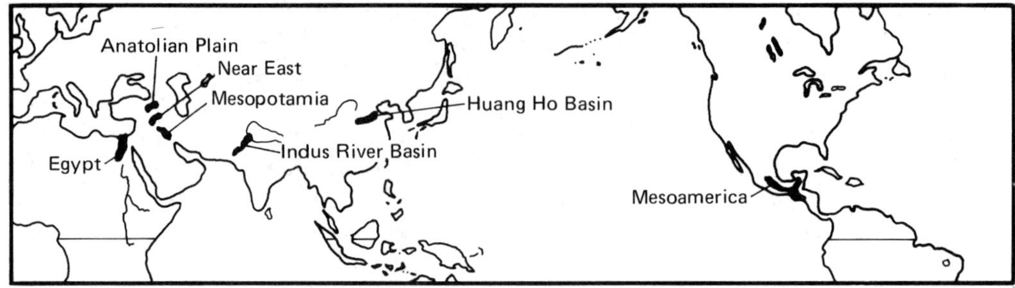

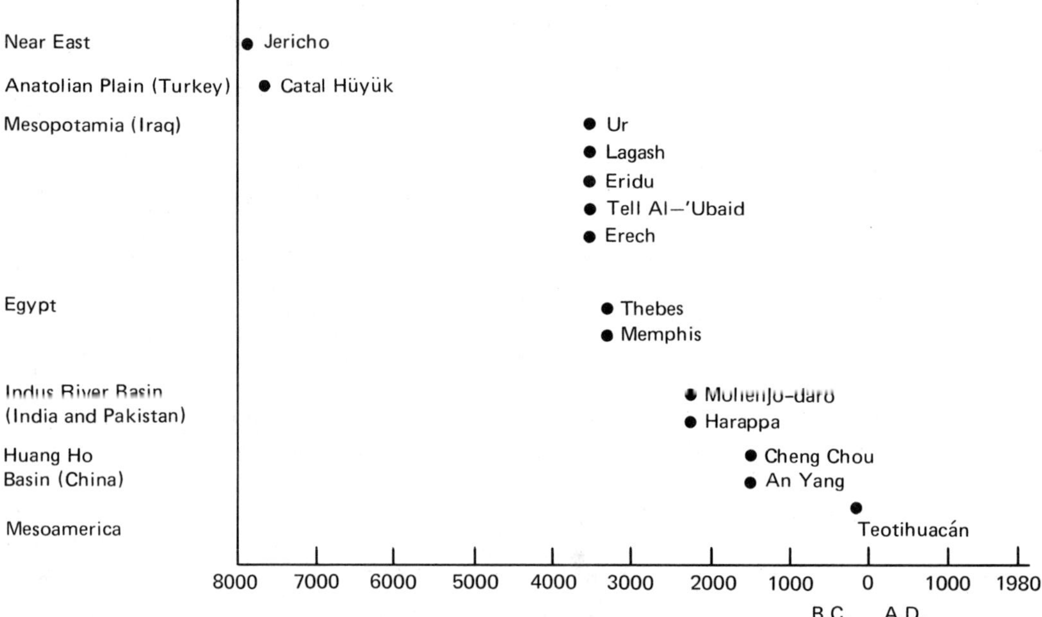

Fig. 4-1 WHERE AND WHEN EARLY CITIES AROSE.

Bigger and much more sophisticated were a number of cities in ancient Mesopotamia which arose about 3500 B.C. Until the discoveries at Jericho and Catal Hüyük, conventional wisdom held that these Mesopotamian cities in the Sumer region were the earliest cities.

Three other centers of early urban civilization have been identified, the first in the Indus Basin in present-day India and Pakistan. Here twin capital cities, Mohenjo-daro and Harappa, flourished around 2300–1750 B.C. Physically, these were large cities, about one square mile in size (Wheeler, 1953; 1966). Carefully built according to identical city plans, they housed perhaps as many as a quarter of a million persons each. And, the archeological record shows, Mohenjo-daro and Harappa were technologically and aesthetically sophisticated centers as well as trade centers. The second early center of urban life was in the valley of the Huang Ho River in China. The first Chinese dynasty, the Shang, built large cities at Cheng Chou and An Yang in approximately 1300–1500 B.C. (Wheatley, 1971). One archeologist estimates that it would take 10,000 workers, working full-time, at least eighteen years to build the massive packed-earth walls which surround An Yang, the largest of the Shang cities. The third urban center was in **Mesoamerica** somewhat later. Various Indian cultures built cities in what are today Mexico, Guatemala, and other parts of Central America. The largest of these early cities, **Teotihuacán,** lies just outside Mexico City. Established about 150 B.C. and flourishing for more than a thousand years, Teotihuacán's ruins today show an impressive city of pyramid-type structures and religious buildings. At its height, the city may have had as many as 200,000 residents.

Teotihuacán poses many questions for scholars. As we will discuss shortly, many historians believe that a fertile environment was a prerequisite for the birth of cities. Yet Teotihuacán emerged on a high arid plain. Furthermore, some view the wheel, plow, writing, and domesticated animals as prerequisites of early urban growth. Yet even at its height, Teotihuacán had none of these inventions. A final puzzle involves cultural diffusion: Could Teotihuacán have borrowed elements from already established urban cultures in Mesopotamia or Egypt? There are striking parallels, including religious pyramids that are similar to Mesopotamian ziggurats. However, few scholars of Mesoamerica believe this diffusion occurred. In one ingenious test of the cultural diffusion thesis, explorer Thor Heyerdahl built a reed boat, the *Ra II,* to demonstrate that Egyptian sailors might have reached Mesoamerica centuries ago. It sank.

Cities in Mesoamerica, Egypt, the Indus Basin, and the Huang Ho river valley were established after those in ancient Sumer. Now our quest to find answers about where and why cities first came into existence brings us back to Mesopotamia.

The Childe Thesis: The Urban Revolution in Mesopotamia

Australian-British archeologist V. Gordon Childe (1892–1957) spent a scholarly lifetime studying the rise of civilization in **Mesopotamia:** the Fertile Crescent located between the Tigris and Euphrates rivers (that flow into the Persian Gulf) in what is now Iraq. In his very readable works *Man Makes Himself* ([1936] 1952) and *What Happened in History* ([1942] 1964), Childe details his thesis about what he considers the evolutionary development and progress of humankind from prehistoric food gatherer to food producer in the neolithic revolution to city builder in the second revolution, the **urban revolution.**

According to the **Childe thesis,** the long march of human development started in the fertile river valleys of the Tigris-Euphrates. At the end of this developmental sequence was the emergence of cities around 3500 B.C.

In brief, Childe's logic is as follows: The transition from hunting and gathering to food cultivation and the domestication of animals—the agricultural revolution—was a necessary precondition for the emergence of village and city life. Agriculture and the production of a food surplus permitted people to stop their nomadic wandering and form settled communities. Agriculture, then, is the key factor in the revolutionary change from nomadic wandering to small-scale agricultural village life.

In a fertile environment such as the Tigris-Euphrates river valley, the Childe thesis continues, farmers could and did produce and store a food surplus. Population in the agricultural villages then increased, for a constant food supply allowed more people to survive. Over the millennia, larger and larger villages developed. In turn, larger villages led to the need for more complex social organization and social control. And to feed the ever-increasing population, intensive agriculture was invented. Eventually, a whole series of technological innovations and political changes followed as a result of larger populations and the need to handle and ensure the food surplus. For instance, the Childe thesis holds that ruling elites or classes developed to oversee the organization of the surplus. These elites invented systems of recording to assure the surplus as well as peace and security. This long historical chain of events set the stage for the emergence of cities in Mesopotamia, the urban revolution.

Childe's thesis assumes that the urban revolution in Mesopotamia is the product of four factors, inextricably linked:

Population—increased numbers encouraged by the agricultural surplus.

Organization—an increasingly complex division of labor, particularly the evolution of ruling religious and secular elites to organize the surplus and a variety of specialists such as craftspeople, metallurgists, and scribes.

Environment—a hospitable physical setting, such as a fertile river valley, capable of producing an agricultural surplus.

Technology—innovations that first brought food cultivation and food surplus and gradually led to such inventions as the wheel and writing.

Thus, according to the Childe thesis, cities resulted from the interaction between these demographic, environmental, social, and technological factors, easily remembered by their acronym, POET.

Childe uses the term "revolution" on purpose, to emphasize a total transformation in a very short period of time. It is as if a chemist slowly added ingredients to a test tube until suddenly the mixture was just right to produce a sudden transformation into a new compound.

What exactly was produced? What were the Mesopotamian cities like? And how well do they fit the several definitions of a city discussed earlier? The case of ancient **Ur,** the largest of the Mesopotamian cities, is instructive.

The population of Ur was large compared with any settlement which had preceded it. At its height, Ur's population may have numbered as many as 34,000 within the walled city itself and perhaps as many as 360,000 people in the "greater Ur" area (Sjoberg, [1960] 1965:36–37). Nonetheless, Ur was small by present-day standards; the walled city was about the size of Texarkana, Arkansas.

Ur was densely settled. The total area within the wall and moat in 3000 B.C. was 220 acres, and the entire population was compressed into this space.

The population of Ur was socially heterogeneous, reflecting a well-developed system of classes and specialization of functions. Wide differences in wealth and power existed between elites and the rest of the population. There were also finely graded occupational divisions, including full-time soldiers, fishermen, herdsmen, craftsmen of different types, musicians, and artisans. Cuneiform clay tablets from Ur record the specialization of labor at the royal palace: gatekeepers, cooks, stewards, servants, messengers, a harem official (hence, a harem), and a royal cupbearer (Adams, 1966:143).

Thus, using conventional criteria, Ur may be defined as a city. It was a relatively large, dense, and heterogeneous community. Ur also qualifies as a city in terms of market functions and urban culture. It served as the marketplace for an extended region. Artifacts unearthed at the site show trade with countries as far away as Egypt, Armenia, and Oman in the Persian Gulf. Culture in Ur also advanced to high levels. The city itself was a handsome, planned area with wide streets and large civic buildings. The dominant architectural feature of Ur and other Mesopotamian cities was a **ziggurat**—a pyramid with stepped sides central to the religious functions of the community. Further, residents developed writing, an accurate solar calendar, musical instruments, and fine art and handicrafts.

Reflecting on how radically different Ur and other cities in the Sumer region were from the scattered and humble farming villages which preceded them, Childe generalized about what distinguishes *any* early city from such villages: 10 criteria, deducible from archeological data. (See Box 4-1.) These criteria remain influential—and controversial.

In other words, Childe set out his own list of prerequisites for urban life. All existed in the Mesopotamian cities by definition, for he deduced them from archeological evidence.

Counter Views on the Origin of Cities: The Role of Trade and Religion

Childe's thesis on the developmental sequence that led to the urban revolution dominated scholarship throughout his lifetime. His views became conventional wisdom. It was generally assumed, for instance, that agriculture was invented as populations started to increase—that is, as a response to social stress, or, alternatively, as a response to shrinking natural resources or environmental pressure. In addition, it was assumed

Box 4-1

CHILDE'S CRITERIA

How to Distinguish an Early City from Other Forms of Human Settlement

1. Larger size and denser population (Ur and other Sumerian cities contained from 7,000 to 20,000 persons by 3000 B.C.).
2. Classes of nonfarming specialists, including craftspersons, merchants, administrators, and priests, all supported by the agricultural surplus.
3. Taxation and capital accumulation (taxes or tithes paid to gods or kings who concentrated the surplus).
4. Monumental public buildings, such as the stately temples of Sumer with their ziggurats.
5. Ruling elites or classes who absorbed, accumulated, and organized the surplus.
6. Exact sciences, needed to predict, measure, and standardize (e.g., arithmetic, geometry, astronomy).
7. The invention of writing or scripts, enabling the "leisured clerks" to elaborate the exact and predictive sciences.
8. Specialists in the arts, supported by the surplus.
9. Long-distance trade in vital materials.
10. Community membership based on residence alone, rather than kinship. (Adapted from Childe, 1950:9–16. Published in Liverpool at the University Press. Reprinted by permission.)

that cities emerged after a long linear sequence: from nomadic wanderings to agricultural villages to cities.

Recent discoveries, however, pose many problems about why agriculture was invented and why cities arose. In 1979, an international team of scientists discovered cultivated barley at a 17,000-year-old Egyptian campsite, putting the origins of agriculture some 10,000 years before previous estimates. According to the discoverers, the finding means that agriculture was not invented as a response to environmental or social stress. The scientists say that they don't know why agriculture started. "Now we have to find a new reason," comments the head of the team (in the Associated Press, 1979:3).

Moreover, shortly after Childe's death, Dame Kenyon's findings at Jericho upset conventional wisdom about the slow progression of agricultural settlements. Later, in 1961, at Catal Hüyük, archeologist James Mellaart dug deep into something Childe said could not exist: a neolithic city.

The settlement lies in south central Turkey about 250 miles from Ankara. It is situated on a high mountain plain, not in a fertile river valley. Environmentally, Catal Hüyük was not particularly favored. In neolithic times a freshwater lake nearby may have made its environment somewhat more fertile, but certainly far less so than the swampland of Mesopotamia.

Catal Hüyük's population was probably 5,000 to 6,000 (Mellaart in Todd, 1976:122). Since the mound from which the settlement is being excavated covers only 32 acres, it was densely settled.

While Catal Hüyük had a somewhat heterogeneous population, there is no evidence of anything like the elaborate class structure of the Mesopotamian cities. Distinct skeletal types unearthed show that at least two different racial groups inhabited the settlement. Religious buildings suggest the existence of a priestly class, and art and trade artifacts suggest some social differentiation and specialization of functions. But this is far removed from the elaborate Mesopotamian social structure with a royal cupbearer.

Does Catal Hüyük qualify as a city in terms of its cultural level? In the judgment of Mellaart (1967:77), it "shines like a supernova among the rather dim galaxy of contemporary peasant cultures." Representational and abstract wall paintings include striking scenes of bulls, people, and cattle, and one macabre room is decorated with vultures and decapitated human beings. Other artifacts reveal rather subtle clay baked seals, woven mats, fine obsidian daggers, and sculpted figurines. But there was no writing. Thus, by Childe's standards—which placed great weight on the invention of writing—Catal Hüyük appears to fall short of city culture. But in Mellaart's view, it was a stellar cultural achievement even when compared with some cultures today.

Catal Hüyük would qualify as a city under Weber's definition, for it was a market center. Catal Hüyük apparently carried on brisk trade with its neighboring region.

In *The Economy of Cities* (1970), urbanist Jane Jacobs describes New Obsidian, the "first city." While it is an imaginary creation, Jacobs draws heavily on the discoveries and theories of Mellaart. In fact, New Obsidian closely parallels Catal Hüyük. Mellaart, the patient archeologist taking years to sort through the dust and rubble, is more cautious about constructing theories than Jacobs. Yet, their ideas on the possible role of trade in Catal Hüyük are similar.

Jacobs's **trade thesis** turns Childe's thesis on its head. In her imaginary scenario, the city becomes the independent variable, ex-

Box 4-2

JANE JACOBS'S THEORY OF CITY ORIGINS

New Obsidian

I am choosing to imagine . . . a city I shall call New Obsidian and I am pretending that it is the center of a large trade in obsidian, the tough, black, natural glass produced by some volcanoes. The city is located on the Anatolian plateau of Turkey. . . .

How Early Trade Worked

In 8,500 B.C., New Obsidian's population numbers about two thousand persons. . . . [T]he buildings are made of timber and adobe; later in the millennium there will also be buildings made of shaped mud bricks. The "center" or barter space of the little city is physically on the edge where the routes join and approach the settlement. . . .

The system of trade that prevails runs this way: The initiative is taken by the people who want to buy something. Traveling salesmen have not yet appeared on the scene; the traders, rather, regard themselves, and are regarded as traveling purchasing agents. Undoubtedly they take trade goods of their own to the place of purchase, but this is used like money to buy whatever it is they came for. Thus, the traders who come to New Obsidian from greater and greater distances come there purposely to get obsidian, not to get rid of something else. For the most part, the barter goods they bring consist of the ordinary produce of their hunting territories. When the New Obsidian people want special treasures like copper, shells or pigments that they themselves do not find in their territory, parties of their own traders go forth to get these things from other settlements. With them they take obsidian, as if it were money. . . .

To understand why New Obsidian has become a trading center of such importance, the goal of people from great distances, it is necessary to understand the enormous value of obsidian to hunters. . . . Obsidian makes the sharpest cutting tools to be had. . . . Obsidian is not steel, but it is the nearest thing to it in the world of New Obsidian.

Why Agriculture Arose in Cities

The food of New Obsidian is derived in two ways. Part of it comes from the old hunting and gathering territory. . . . But a large proportion of the food is imported from foreign hunting territories. This is food that is traded at the barter square for obsidian and for other exports of the city. . . . Wild food of the right kind commands a good exchange. . . . Except in times of great shortage and unusual hunger when anything is welcome, only nonperishable food is accepted. . . . [U]nless the customers are from territories very nearby, nonperishable food stands the trip to the city best. . . . [M]ore important, the people of New Obsidian like to store the food and mete it out rationally rather than gorge upon it and perhaps go hungry later. Thus the imported food consists overwhelmingly of live animals and hard seeds. . . . Nonperishable plant food is easier to handle than animals, and traders carrying it can travel more swiftly. Thus, especially from the greater distances, beans, nuts and edible grass seeds pour into New Obsidian. . . .

When seeds remain after the winter, they are used for wild patch sowing, a practice not productive of much food; it just makes gathering wild seeds more convenient. . . .

Whether spill sown, patch sown, or sown by little predators—rats, mice, and birds—these plants cross in unprecedented combinations. It is no problem to get grain crosses in New Obsidian, or crossed beans and peas either. Quite the contrary; crosses cannot be avoided.

The crosses and hybrids do not go unobserved. They are seen, in fact, by people who are experts at recognizing the varieties and estimating the worth of barter seeds, and who are well aware that some of these city seeds are new. . . .

Some of the households of New Obsidian [select high-potential seeds]. Selection happens because some patches of sown seed yield much more heavily than other patches do. . . .

Box 4-2 (*continued*)

The unprecedented differentials in yields from New Obsidian's best and poorest seed patches lead to an arrangement formerly unheard of: some people *within* the city trade seeds to others. . . .

Owing to this local dealing in seeds from patches that yield most heavily, all the grain grown in New Obsidian eventually yields heavily in comparison with wild grains. . . . And in the second stage of the process, selection becomes more deliberate and conscious. The choices made now are purposeful, and they are made among various strains of already cultivated crosses, and their crosses, mutants, and hybrids.

It takes many generations—not just of wheat and barley but of people—to differentiate the New Obsidian seeds into sophisticated cultivated grains. . . .

The traders of New Obsidian, when they go off on their trips, take along New Obsidian food to sustain themselves. . . . And the traders of other little cities who come to New Obsidian sometimes take back food with them and tell what they have seen in the metropolis. Thus, the first spread of the new grains and animals is from city to city. The rural world is still a world in which wild food and other wild things are hunted and gathered. The cultivation of plants and animals is, as yet, only city work. It is duplicated, as yet, only by other city people, not by hunters of ordinary settlements. (Jacobs, 1970:18–31. Copyright © 1969 by Jane Jacobs. Reprinted by permission of Random House.)

plaining the development of agriculture—not the reverse. Moreover, factors that Childe stressed as vital in setting the stage for the urban revolution (a favorable environment, technology, a large population base, and elaborate social organization) are relatively unimportant in her vision. To Jacobs, the first cities arose because of trade. Location was a key factor; early cities had to be located near the source of prized goods such as salt and obsidian. And they had to be situated along trade routes that bypassed geographical barriers. In Jacobs's scenario, the survival of the first city dwellers, the New Obsidianites, was based on exchanges of vital commodities for food from their trading partners, not on agriculture. Moreover, Jacobs believes that agriculture was invented by ancient city dwellers and diffused by trade (see Box 4-2). In her view, then, intensive farming didn't cause the development of cities. To the contrary, agriculture developed because of cities.

If correct, the trade thesis does overturn Childe's thesis. It implies that agriculture was not an absolute prerequisite for the rise of cities. It also implies that Childe's notion of slow evolutionary development—a Darwinian concept whereby each stage of life represents an advance over the previous stage—is wrong. In other words, some cities could have been established as cities from the start, without a gestation period of several millennia and without the linear progression from nomadic wandering to food production to settled village life to the rise of cities. Finally, the trade thesis calls into question Childe's list of ten criteria as universals.

This debate has no definitive conclusion. Moreover, there is a third competing view of city origins and growth: the religous-symbolic thesis. In this view, both the Childe thesis and the trade thesis are incomplete because they neglect *nonmaterial* factors in city development.

Urbanist Lewis Mumford, representing this third viewpoint, writes that "Early man's respect for the dead, itself an expression of fascination with his powerful images of daylight fantasy and nightly dream, perhaps had an even greater role than more practical needs in causing him to seek a fixed meeting place and eventually a continuous settlement" (1961:6–7). While Mumford states that one must not overlook the practical needs that drew families and tribes together in campsites, sacred things were the central concerns, "the very reason for the city's existence": "The first germ of the city, then, is the ceremonial meeting place" which has " 'spiritual' or supernatural powers" that are endowed with a "cosmic image" (10).

Other scholars in this tradition (e.g., Fustel de Coulanges, [1864] 1955; Adams, 1966) emphasize the idea that a strong ideological core, holding together early urbanites in a sense of community, is a key variable in the origin or growth of cities. In this view, then, what brought people together in settlements had to do with much more than physical survival and economic subsistence. As Mumford (1961:8) puts it, "fixed landmarks and holy meetings places called together, periodically or permanently, those who shared the same magical practices or religous beliefs."

Using the religious-symbolic thesis, it could be argued that Catal Hüyük was a shrine city, attracting the faithful. Its central purpose was to serve as a holy meeting place. If so, many materialist social science theories are called into question, for materialist theories assume that culture (including religion) is a *dependent* variable, reflecting the material base of culture, not an independent variable.

To conclude: When thinking about the origin of cities, it is wise to recall what Childe ([1936] 1952: Preface) himself said: "Almost every statement in prehistory should be qualified by the phrase 'On the evidence available today the balance of probability favors the view that.' " Evidence discovered since Childe's death raises even more questions about the invention of agriculture and the rise of cities.

It is also wise to remember that the debate over the emergence of cities is essentially a debate over definitions of what constitutes a city. On this most essential concept, urban scholars disagree.

TRYING TO CLASSIFY CITIES

The controversy about the emergence of cities is just one of many current debates on the nature of urban life. We now turn to another. This debate focuses not on the desirability but rather the success of attempts to generalize about the nature of cities.

Preindustrial versus Industrial Cities (Sjoberg)

Contemporary sociologist Gideon Sjoberg thinks that cities share certain general features and can be classified accordingly. Sjoberg's central hypothesis is that "in their structure or form, preindustrial cities, whether in medieval Europe, traditional China, India or elsewhere—resemble one another closely and in turn differ markedly from modern industrial-urban centers" ([1960] 1965:4–5). In other words, Sjoberg looks for what he calls "structural universals" that typify preindustrial cities and distinguish them from modern industrial cities.

For our purposes, we'll deal only with the preindustrial city. How does Sjoberg define such a city? According to him, all cities that utilize animate energy sources (human beings and animals) rather than inanimate energy sources (steam, electricity, nuclear fission, etc.) are classified as preindustrial. This means, in Sjoberg's view, that cities as diverse in culture and context as ancient Ur, the lost cities of Africa, Periclean Athens, seventeenth-century London, and modern Kathmandu "share numerous patterns in the realms of ecology, class, and the family, as well as in their economic, political, religious,

a

b

c

d

Fig. 4-2 SJOBERG'S PREINDUSTRIAL CITY. Essaouira, Morocco, displays many characteristics that Gideon Sjoberg associates with the preindustrial city: (*a*) a wall that girdles the city, (*b*) narrow passageways, (*c*) the hiding of female attractiveness, and (*d*) governmental and religious structures that dominate the urban horizon. (© Andrée Abecassis 1980)

and educational structures, arrangements that diverge sharply from their counterparts in mature industrial cities" ([1960] 1965:6).

Sjoberg argues that the demographic and ecological structures of all preindustrial cities are remarkably similar and transcend cultural boundaries. For instance, he notes the common features of *small size* (under 100,000 inhabitants); *cramped conditions* (because transportation and building technology are limited, people live close together in low-rise structures within walking distance of central facilities); *widespread residential segregation by ethnic and occupational groups* (the poorest castes or classes live farthest away from the city center, where the elites are concentrated; special quarters are set aside for particular economic pursuits, such as goldsmithing or pottery making); and *little specialization in land use* (due to the lack of industrial technology, such as rapid transit, which permits high specialization of land use in modern industrial cities).

Similarly, Sjoberg hypothesizes that class and status structures in all preindustrial cities share common features. These include a *small elite,* generally composed of political and religious leaders and sometimes including military leaders, educators, and wealthy merchants; a *large lower-class group* of laborers, artisans, and small merchants; and commonly, an *outcaste group,* such as India's "untouchables" or a slave population. These class and caste barriers were and are nearly impossible to cross, for social position is determined by one's family background rather than one's personal achievements, including education. Thus, according to Sjoberg, there is little mobility within the rigid social structure of preindustrial cities.

In many other areas of life—family, the economy, politics, communication, and the nature of education—Sjoberg notes recurring patterns among preindustrial cities. These range from the "purposive adulteration of goods" (211) and periodic public festivals which provide entertainment and promote social cohesion (though outcaste groups may be excluded) to the treatment of books as sacred and holy.

While neat and tidy, how useful is Sjoberg's way of approaching the nature of preindustrial cities? Here urbanists disagree. A few consider the concept of the preindustrial city a notable contribution to urban studies. The majority, however, attack Sjoberg for bringing more confusion than clarity to the study of preindustrial cities. Critics charge him with imprecision on concrete historical matters; technological determinism; and neglect of the role that culture plays in city form and structure. In addition, urbanists point to a basic fallacy in Sjoberg's approach: He incorrectly treats all cities before the Industrial Revolution as dependent subsystems within larger feudal societies. This is historically wrong, critics hold, pointing to such ancient cities as Athens, Rome, and Constantinople, which did not exist under feudalism, and such medieval cities as Venice, which were autonomous—not dependent subsystems within feudalism—to support their challenge. As one critic puts it, "The preindustrial city type lumps so many disparate societal systems [feudalism, capitalism, etc.] that its value as an operational instrument seems nullified" (Cox, [1964] 1969:26). Or, in more straightforward terms, it is useless.

Critics see Sjoberg's classification and characterization of preindustrial cities as limited, even useless. But that does not mean that urbanists disdain any such attempt. To the contrary, a meaningful classification scheme is important for urban theory. But to date, most urbanists would agree, such a scheme for understanding the commonalities—and differences—between cities as diverse as ancient Ur in the Sumer, Athens and Rome, autonomous medieval cities, and present-day Kathmandu does not exist.

VARIETIES OF WESTERN CITIES: A SAMPLER

Since we agree with Sjoberg's critics that the concept of the preindustrial city is, at best, limited, we will not attempt to follow his classification. Neither will we—or can we, given the limits of space and our own knowledge—give creditable accounts of the variety of cities and urban cultures created over the millennia, as in *Lost Cities of Africa* (Davidson, [1959] 1970) or *Victorian Cities* (Briggs, 1963). Instead, we present a sampler. Designed to highlight only a few urban scenes, this sampler focuses on architecture and town planning in ancient Greek cities; the role of trade in medieval cities; and the

Fig. 4-3 THE PARTHENON IN ATHENS. (Alison Frantz)

impact of the Industrial Revolution on nineteenth-century Manchester, England.

The Glory that was Greece

"Frankly, Scarlett, I don't give a damn" may be the best-remembered exit line of the American cinema. Delivered by Rhett Butler (Clark Gable) in *Gone with the Wind* (1939), it signals more than the hero's rejection of a woman. It brings down the curtain on a way of life embodied by Tara, the stately Southern plantation house built during the Greek Revival period of architecture in the United States (1830–1860). In a nation moving toward industrialization after the Civil War, Rhett Butler turns his back on a way of life: an agrarian way of life symbolized by Tara's perfect proportions and pure form in harmony with its natural setting.

Ironically, Greek templelike plantation homes such as Tara (and county courthouses and other public buildings constructed in the Greek Revival period) may be considered some of the many expressions of antiurban tendencies and thoughts in the United States. "The Greek temple," one architectural historian notes, "does not really want to get along with other buildings in a street, but to stand free outside. . . . As revived, it demonstrates the puristic instinct to the utmost" (Scully, 1969:64–65). What's ironic is that the original ancient Greek temples and public monuments crowned the glory that was Greece—an *urban* glory—and celebrated city life.

In ancient Greece, monumental public

buildings—theatres, stadia, gymnasia, and temples—were erected to enrich the beauty of the city. Consistent with the Greek emphasis on collective civic endeavor (detailed in the next chapter), private houses were small and unpretentious. The Greeks devoted their energy to public institutions such as the agora (literally, "the place where people get together"), which dominated the city center. The everyday life of ordinary Greek citizens focused on the agora: a mixture of markets, courts, temple shrines, and government buildings. Here Greeks of the fifth century B.C. could get fish, discuss their leader Pericles's policies toward Persia, pay tribute to their gods and goddesses, and gossip.

In Greek cities before the fifth century B.C., an **acropolis,** such as Athens's famous Parthenon, dominated the city. Built on hills with commanding views, these acropoleis consisted of a fortified palace, temple, and fort complex. Later, as Greeks evolved democratic institutions, the acropolis declined in importance.

Cities built during the height of Greece's glory—the democratic period, particularly Periclean Athens—were constructed mainly on the principles of one architect-town planner, Hippodamus of Miletus, born in the fifth century B.C. Integrating architectural and planning principles, Hippodamus urged simple, functional, and pure forms blended harmoniously with the natural environment. The outcome was not only a magnificent beauty but, according to Thucydides ([411 B.C.] 1956, Vol. I:19), a sense of overwhelming power. In its own day, then, Athens's mix of commanding acropolis and Hippodamian-inspired buildings was recognized as architecture that magnified the city's strength.

Ancient Greeks viewed their cities' monuments from streets laid out in a grid system. The grid, introduced earlier, was continued by Hippodamus in his city plans. Centuries later, it became the dominant scheme in American cities, appearing as early as 1641 in the plan of New Haven, Connecticut.

Medieval Cities

For complex reasons discussed in the next chapter, the glory that was Greece faded. It was later replaced by the grandeur that was Rome. The vast Roman Empire stretched from the Sahara and the Euphrates to Gaul, creating such grandiose structures as the Roman Forum, the Temple of Bacchus at Baalbek, Lebanon, and the Pont du Gard near Nîmes, France.

What produced and sustained this vast empire and its sparkling cities, particularly its jewel, Rome? According to the eminent Belgian historian Henri Pirenne ([1925] 1956), commerce was the key variable. Roman civilization was built on trade, and the Mediterranean Sea was the crucial element in Rome's maritime empire. Even after the fall of Rome in 476 A.D. to the Goths, Vandals, and other invaders, trade continued on the Mediterranean, and the economy of the Mediterranean commonwealth, created by the Roman Empire, remained unified.

But in the seventh century A.D., this long-lived unity and world order that had survived the fall of Rome collapsed. Islamic expansion changed the face of the world, spreading from the China Sea to the Atlantic Ocean. And in its wake, the Mediterranean Sea, which had for so long united the cultures of East and West Europe, became a barrier between them.

According to Pirenne, the closing off of the Mediterranean by the Islamic invasion led to the stagnation of the old Roman cities. But by the twelfth century, conditions stabilized, and Western Europe was back on the road of economic progress: "the new Europe resembled . . . more the ancient Europe than the

Europe of Carolingian times. . . . She regained that essential characteristic of being a region of cities" ([1925] 1956:73).

Pirenne paints a picture of many medieval towns built around the physical shell of an ancient Roman city. These towns contained an old burg (walled fortress or town) occupied by a Catholic bishop or other religious officials but were surrounded by a new burg, a fortified area for storing goods plus living quarters for traders.

It was in twelfth-century towns operating as autonomous trading centers—Venice and Bruges, for instance—that a new merchant class acted as a catalyst, pushing forward the economy and social change. Unlike the vast feudal masses of Western Europe, people in these autonomous cities were not tied to tradition. The secular commercial towns encouraged innovation and entrepreneurial activity.

Residents of commercial suburbs were referred to as "burghers" or members of the "bourgeoisie" (from the root "burg" or "bourg"). From their origins in the twelfth century as a fledgling merchant class, they came to dominate England and other nations in the throes of the Industrial Revolution in the eighteenth century. By the nineteenth century, the word "bourgeoisie" had turned into a contemptuous epithet, and the overthrow of this class had become an objective of revolutionary intellectuals like Karl Marx and Friedrich Engels.

Manchester, England: Symbol of the New Industrial City

Beginning in the late 1700s, a series of technological changes in textile machinery in England made possible large-scale, mechanized, capital-intensive industry unlike anything the world had previously seen. In two generations, textile workers who labored on hand looms in their cottages were replaced by an urban-industrial proletariat toiling in giant spinning factories. Many other sectors of the British economy also experienced the Industrial Revolution. Water and steam power replaced hand labor, machinery grew in complexity, and the small-scale familial workplace was replaced by massive industrial establishments.

In 1760, Engels ([1845] 1950:15) noted, "England was a country like every other, with small towns, few and simple industries, and a thin but *proportionally* large agricultural population. Today [1844] it is a country like *no* other, with a capital of two and a half million inhabitants; with vast manufacturing cities; with an industry that supplies the world, and produces almost everything by means of the most complex machinery; with an industrious, intelligent, dense population, of which two-thirds are employed in trade and commerce, and composed of classes wholly different. . . ."

"Composed of classes *wholly different.*" In Engels's view, that was the key. The bourgeoisie, or capitalist class, formed a relatively small, privileged group. In contrast, a large, oppressed mass—the industrial proletariat—was developing. "What is to become of these destitute millions," Engels asked, "who consume today what they earned yesterday; who have created the greatness of England by their inventions and their toil; who become with every passing day more conscious of their might and demand with daily increasing urgency their share of the advantages of society?" (17). Engels's prescription: socialist revolution.

Manchester is often taken as the symbol of the new industrial city, and few were neutral about it. Like the Chicago painted by Nelson Algren (see Chapter 1), "Manchester forced to the surface the problems of 'class' and the relations between rich and poor" (Briggs, 1963:93).

Box 4-3

PUTREFACTION AND OPEN PRIVIES

Manchester in the Nineteenth Century

Manchester contains, at its heart, a rather extended commercial district, perhaps half a mile long and about as broad, and consisting almost wholly of offices and warehouses. Nearly the whole district is abandoned by dwellers, and is lonely and deserted at night. . . . This district is cut through by certain main thoroughfares upon which the vast traffic concentrates, and in which the ground level is lined with brilliant shops. . . . With the exception of this commercial district, all Manchester proper [and surrounding cities] are all unmixed working-people's quarters, stretching like a girdle, averaging a mile and a half in breadth, around the commercial district. Outside, beyond this girdle, lives the upper and middle bourgeoisie, the middle bourgeoisie in regularly laid out streets in the vicinity of the working quarters . . . the upper bourgeoisie in remoter villas with gardens . . . in free, wholesome country air, in fine comfortable homes, passed once every half or quarter hour by omnibuses going into the city. And the finest part of this arrangement is this, that the members of this money aristocracy can take the shortest road through the middle of all the labouring districts to their places of business, without ever seeing that they are in the midst of the grimy misery that lurks to the right and the left. For the thoroughfares leading from the Exchange in all directions out of the city are lined, on both sides, with an almost unbroken series of shops, and are so kept in the hands of the middle and lower bourgeoisie, which, out of self-interest, cares for a decent and cleanly external appearance . . . they suffice to conceal from the eyes of the wealthy men and women of strong stomachs and weak nerves the misery and grime which form the complement of their wealth.

In one of these [working-class residential] courts there stands directly at the entrance, at the end of the covered passage, a privy without a door, so dirty that the inhabitants can pass into and out of the court only by passing through foul pools of stagnant urine and excrement. . . . Below it on the river there are several tanneries which fill the whole neighborhood with the stench of animal putrefaction. . . . At the bottom flows, or rather stagnates, the Irk, a narrow, coal-black, foul-smelling stream, full of debris and refuse, which it deposits on the shallower right bank. In dry weather, a long string of the most disgusting, blackish green slime pools are left standing on this bank, from the depths of which bubbles of miasmatic gas constantly arise and give forth a stench unendurable even on the bridge . . . behind [weirs] slime and refuse accumulate and rot in thick masses. Above the bridge are tanneries, bonemills, and gasworks, from which all drains and refuse find their way into the Irk, which receives further the contents of all the neighbouring sewers and privies. . . . Below the bridge . . . each house is packed close behind its neighbour, and a piece of each is visible, all black, smoky, crumbling, ancient, with broken panes and window frames . . . and the Workhouse, the "Poor-law Bastille" of Manchester, . . . looks threateningly down from behind its high walls and parapets on the hilltop, upon the working people's quarter below. (Engels, [1845] 1950:46–47, 49–50. First published in 1892. Reprinted 1920, 1926, 1936, 1943, and 1950. Reprinted by permission of George Allen & Unwin [Publishers] Ltd.)

Like Chicago in the 1890s and 1900s, some saw Manchester as a grand city, a symbol of progress and civilization. Engels did not deny the grandeur of parts of Manchester, but he loathed the brutality of the city toward its working-class residents. And he connected "the marvels of civilization" for the few to the "nameless misery" for the many.

The price paid for progress under capitalism, in Engels's view, was "brutal indifference," "unfeeling isolation," and "reciprocal plundering" (24). The accompanying box gives Engels's report on Manchester's physical condition.

Manchester was not what a city planner would call a "planned" community. But Engels thought that private forces—the workings of the capitalist economic system—had patterned the city and its environs in a certain fashion: to serve the interests of the bourgeoisie. Members of the capitalist class, living in villas and breathing the clean air of the suburbs, could catch a horse-drawn omnibus to work and ride along broad boulevards, walled off from human misery by the shops of the petty bourgeoisie. They did not even see the working-class slums.

In many ways, Engels's writing on Manchester prefigures the work of later urban sociologists, as we shall see in the next chapter. According to Engels, the new urbanites

> crowd by one another as though they had nothing in common. . . . The brutal indifference, the unfeeling isolation of each in his private interest becomes the more repellant and offensive, the more these individuals are crowded together. . . . This isolation of the individual, this narrow self-seeking is the fundamental principle of our society everywhere, [but] it is nowhere so shamelessly barefaced, so self-conscious as just here in the crowding of the great city. The dissolution of mankind into monads, of which each one has a separate principle, the world of atoms, is here carried out to its utmost extreme. (Engels [1845] 1950:24)

Thus, atomism for all, crushing poverty for wage earners, and the marvels of civilization for those who owned and controlled the industry that made Manchester and other English towns great—such was, in Engels's view, the new industrial city in the capitalistic society.

A dissenting view: Recall from Chapter 2 what Lewis Mumford (1961:465) says about "slum, semi-slum, and super-slum" in Manchester. According to Mumford, even Engels didn't realize "the fact that the upper-class quarters were, more often than not, intolerable super-slums." In this view, there were few marvels of civilization for any class to enjoy. The new industrial cities were just as intolerably ugly, overcrowded, and unsanitary for rich as for poor.

AMERICAN URBAN ROOTS

Specks in the Wilderness

America's first European settlers founded tiny, compact colonial cities, "specks in the wilderness" (Bridenbaugh, 1938:467). Between their founding in the seventeenth century and the American Revolution, these first settlements matured into larger cities. Let's look at late-eighteenth-century Philadelphia to get a feeling for the colonial city.

Historian Samuel Bass Warner, Jr. (1968) characterizes Philadelphia on the eve of the Revolution as a "private city." The vast majority of its 23,700 residents were artisans or independent shopkeepers, contracting out on a daily basis. A small merchant elite engaged in production and trade, and a small underclass of indentured servants, slaves, and hired servants toiled at the bottom of the heap. Most Philadelphians, however, were modest, independent businessmen (and their families) with a privatistic ethic.

Colonial Philadelphia, according to Warner, was a town of abundant opportunity. Workers were in great demand. People could find work, save money, and move into most trades, for the guilds had failed in their attempts to restrict access to their crafts.

If there was great social mobility in Phila-

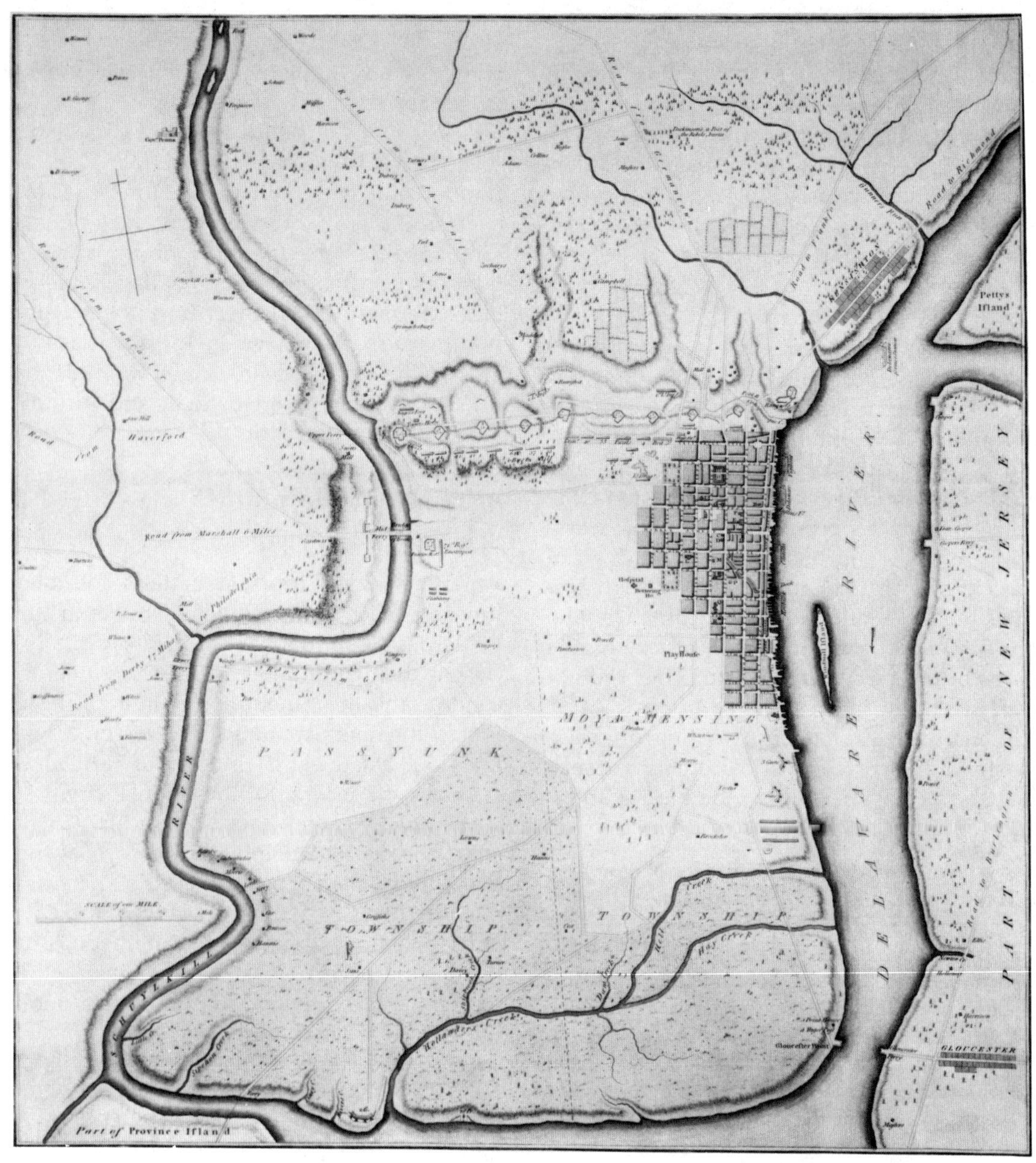

Fig. 4-4 A WALKING CITY—PHILADELPHIA IN 1777. (The New-York Historical Society)

delphia at the time, what was its cause? Property ownership, in Warner's analysis.

The physical form of colonial Philadelphia was consistent with its social structure. The city was compact—a classic **walking city.** All points were easily accessible on foot. Blocks tended to be economically and socially mixed. The clustering effects of ethnic or occupational groups were not consequential.

The political structure also reflected the privatistic ethic. Citizens wanted little government. The formal city government consisted of a "club of wealthy merchants without much purse, power, or popularity" (1968:9). Its only significant functions were to manage the market and run the local records' court; there were no public schools or public water supply; most streets were unpaved. Philadelphia had independent commissions of assessors, street commissioners, city wardens (in charge of the night watch and street lighting), and a board of overseers for the poor. But these groups accomplished little. Warner concludes that things got done in Philadelphia less through formal government structures than through the clubbiness of a small community which functioned by a set of informal rules and power relationships (a common theme in urban government, as we shall see in Chapter 11).

Warner depicts a city of small-scale entrepreneurs, abundant opportunity, and social fluidity, without the geographic segregation which characterized Philadelphia (and other American cities) in later years. But he points out that Philadelphians were not socially or economically equal by any means. Indeed, the tax list for 1774 shows that the upper tenth of the taxpaying households owned 89 percent of the city's taxable property.

The little private city of Philadelphia described by Warner did not have the great extremes of wealth and poverty, the teeming slums, the unhealthy conditions, or the social discord of European industrial cities which emerged shortly thereafter. Nor did it have the urban problems of contemporary Newark, East St. Louis, or Detroit. Nor was much of the American population urban at the time. Indeed, only 5.1 percent of the population was classified as urban by the first U.S. census in 1790. Nonetheless, the predominantly rural intellectuals of the day generally disliked and distrusted the city. As cities grew larger, more heterogeneous, and less tied to rural ways during the nineteenth century, this animosity increased.

Intellectuals Versus the Emerging Nineteenth-century City

"The mobs of great cities," wrote Thomas Jefferson in 1784, "add just so much to the support of pure government, as sores do to the strength of the human body." In this negative judgment, he was in good company—few American intellectuals liked cities. Jefferson's blast at city mobs in 1784 is examined closely by the Whites in *The Intellectual Versus the City* ([1962] 1964). They identify medical, moral, and political reasons for his antiurbanism at that time and trace an evolution in his later thinking.

One reason why the concentration of people in cities in eighteenth-century America was undesirable was purely medical. Periodically, yellow fever ravaged the early colonial cities, and Jefferson based part of his opposition on medical grounds.

But Jefferson's critique went much deeper. In his views on what made for the good life, Jefferson was somewhat torn between the values of the country squire and those of the city gentleman. As a child of the Enlightenment, he enjoyed the good things of civilized urban life: art, literature, witty conversation, painting, science, and other "elegant arts." Yet he more dearly loved the simple pleasures of the country farmer. Further, he feared the effect of cities on the health, virtue, and freedom of the people: "I view great cities as pestilential to the morals, the health and liberties of man. True, they nourish some of the elegant arts, but the useful ones can thrive elsewhere, and less perfection in the others, with more health, virtue, and freedom would be my choice" (in White and White, [1962] 1964:28).

Another basis for his concern was political stability. Jefferson's writings reflect a fear of the political consequences of city mobs. The words of Alexis de Tocqueville, a generation later, echo this fear. De Tocqueville viewed the largest American cities in the 1830s with alarm, even predicting that [the United States and other republics] would "perish from [the unruly, self-interested mobs of cities] unless the government succeeds in creating an armed force which, while it remains under the control of the majority of the nation, will be independent of the town population and able to repress its excesses" (in White and White, [1962] 1964:35). Similarly, Jefferson believed that a dispersed agricultural population, tied to the land and concerned with private property, was most conducive to political stability and personal freedom.

Jefferson's antiurban views survived decades of politics and travel to Paris. But late in life, they changed. During the War of 1812, Britain was able to cut off imports from Europe, and the United States, lacking industries of its own, suffered. Jefferson concluded that the United States must develop its own manufacturing (and by implication, cities) rather than face dependency or want in time of war or national crisis.

During and after Jefferson's time, antiurbanism was a dominant attitude among philosophers, novelists, poets, and social critics. Transcendental poet and essayist Ralph Waldo Emerson reportedly shuddered when approaching New York City (population: 200,000 by the 1830s). He wrote: "That uncorrupted behavior which we admire in animals and young children belongs to the . . . man who lives in the presence of nature. Cities force growth and make men talkative and entertaining, but they make them artificial" (in White and White, [1962] 1964:40). Accordingly, transcendentalists "prefer to ramble in the country and perish of ennui, to the degradation of such charities and such ambition as the city can propose to them." Henry David Thoreau carried the logic of the "cities corrupt—nature restores" philosophy to its logical extreme, repudiating cities, towns, and eventually the society of other human beings. Thus, while Jefferson disliked cities on political grounds, the transcendentalists attacked them on metaphysical grounds.

Meanwhile, major American novelists and poets described the city as a bad dream. Edgar Allen Poe (1886:170) paints a surreal setting in which a nightmarish city, disembodied from space and time, is destroyed:

> And when amid no earthly moans,
> Down, down that town shall settle hence,
> Hell, rising from a thousand thrones,
> Shall do it reverence.

Similarly, Hawthorne, in *The Marble Faun* ([1860] 1950), describes the streets of Rome as "uneasy," "evil," and "stony-hearted" and the city itself as "chilly," "gloomy," "melancholy," "sickly," "dreary," "filthy," and "foul."

American writers, using nightmarish imagery, tended to set their fantasies in Europe, not America. But as America began to experience the first strains of industrialization and urbanization in the 1830s and 1840s, these authors looked with fear at the potential consequences.

How much do the views of novelists and philosophers count? What impact did they have on policymakers and the masses? The

Whites argue that the antiurban bias of American intellectuals and writers helped to shape the values and attitudes of Americans for generations. And, they add, part of the difficulty in focusing public policy on urban problems is rooted in the long tradition of antiurbanism.

From Walking City to Streetcar Suburb

The cities described in nightmarish terms by America's antiurban intellectuals were small and compact by today's standards. Indeed, until the 1850s, even the largest U.S. cities could be crossed on foot in about thirty minutes; hence the name "walking city."

Today, as we think about the potential effects of increased costs and decreased availability of energy on city life, historical studies of the relationship between transport technology and city form take on renewed interest. Speaking in 1895, one observer noted the role of three new technologies: the trolley, bicycle, and telephone. Although their influence on city and country life was "impossible to foresee," the observer said that already they had added five to fifteen miles to the radius of every large town. "It is by such apparently unimportant, trifling, and inconspicuous forces," concluded the observer, "that civilization is swayed and moulded in its evolutions and no man can foresee them or say whither they lead" (F. J. Kingsley in Banfield, 1970:25). In other words, a change in transport or communications technology leads to changes in city structure, and no one can totally predict "whither they will lead."

The demise of the compact walking city can be traced to a series of innovations in transport technology. What trolleys, bicycles, and later, cars did was to expand the limits of the walking city.

The centrifugal forces that ultimately destroyed the walking city were put into motion as early as 1829, when a New York City entrepreneur initiated the first omnibus route in America. A decade later, similar operations had spread to all major U.S. cities. That these omnibuses were far from comfortable or convenient is indicated by a New York City newspaper's comment in 1864: "Modern martyrdom may succinctly be defined as riding in a New York City omnibus" (in Chudacoff, 1975:69). Still, the proliferation of bus companies and the rapid increase in ridership testify to the popular desire for improved transportation. Soon the omnibus was followed by horsedrawn buses on rails and commuter railroads, further accelerating the sprawl of the city.

But it was the invention of the electric trolley in 1886, coupled with the telephone in 1876, that worked a major change in the structure of cities. These two inventions greatly increased people's ability to work in cities and travel to suburban homes, to live on the outskirts of town and communicate to central locations.

In his study of three Boston **streetcar suburbs,** historian Samuel Bass Warner, Jr., notes that the electric trolley pushed Boston's urban fringe out to six miles in the 1880s and 1890s. By 1900, the old walking city had become primarily a region of cheap housing. Warner concludes that early streetcar suburbanization around Boston produced an urban area characterized by housing segregation, both by ethnicity and by class. In addition, the new trolley technology made possible what many builders, large institutions, and upper-class homeowners wanted: the physical separation of work from residence.

To conclude: Despite Jefferson's lament, cities continued to grow apace in nineteenth-century America, changing from colonial walking cities to more sprawling places with suburbs reached by streetcars and trolleys. Such technological innovations in the 1880s influenced the shape of housing patterns as well as other social and political patterns.

URBANIZATION OF THE WORLD'S POPULATION

American cities were growing in population in the nineteenth century, but the majority of people still lived in rural areas. This was true everywhere in the world.

It was not until about the turn of the twentieth century that the first urbanized society came into existence. At that time, Great Britain became the first society in history whose urban population exceeded its rural population. As noted above, at the time of the first U.S. census in 1790, only 5.1 percent of the population lived in cities, and in 1850 no society could be called urbanized. Only in the last eighty years or so has there been a profound change in the number of cities worldwide, their size, and the proportion of the world's population which lives in them. Demographer Kingsley Davis calls this profound change "The Urbanization of the Human Population" (1965).

The Process of Urbanization

Early cities were nothing more than urban specks in a rural world—and small ones at that. Ancient Sumerian cities and Periclean Athens had populations no larger than many contemporary suburbs. Moreover, Ur, ancient Athens, medieval Venice, and all cities before the Industrial Revolution accounted for only a tiny proportion of the population of their societies. In other words, being a city dweller and being urbanized aren't the same thing.

Urbanization refers to population concentration: "the proportion of the total population [in a society or nation] in urban settlements, or else to a rise in this proportion" (Davis, 1965:41). Urbanization may also refer to the process of becoming urban in terms of social, technological, political, and spatial organization.

Urbanization should not be confused with the growth of cities. Since urbanization refers to the proportion of an entire society's or nation's population living in urban places, it is quite possible for cities to expand in population without urbanization taking place. This can occur if the rural population grows as rapidly as, or more rapidly than, the urban population.

Two factors are crucial in the urbanization process: (1) out-migration from rural areas to cities and (2) natural increase (population increase due to an excess of births over deaths). The movement of people from rural land to urban areas can change the total proportion of people living in cities. In the United States, for instance, approximately 700,000 persons each year migrated from farms between 1920 and 1959, contributing significantly to urbanization in the nation. Natural increase can also alter the demographic structure of a society. If birth rates are lower or mortality rates higher in cities than in the countryside, they may retard urbanization. Poor sanitation and health conditions in many eighteenth- and nineteenth century cities led to just such a differential in mortality rates.

Industrialization and Urbanization in the West

Kingsley Davis concludes that between the sixteenth and eighteenth centuries, the average rate of urbanization was barely perceptible—about 6/10 of 1 percent a year for the European cities he examined. Since that time, Western industrialized nations have passed through a recognizable pattern of urbanization: an S-shaped curve, beginning slowly, moving sharply upward, then leveling off. In rural preindustrial societies, urbanization proceeds slowly. Then, if the society experiences an industrial revolution, it shoots up.

At the most advanced stages, it tends to level off.

While Davis offers several explanations for such an S curve, the most important relates to the rural-to-urban shift. In the initial (slowly rising) part of the curve, most people are rural, but there is a small net flow to cities. Then the curve shoots up, usually depleting the pool of rural people. Eventually, the top of the curve is reached and a leveling off begins, in part because the pool of potential migrants has already been largely depleted.

Generally speaking, urbanization accompanied industrialization in England and other Western countries. Thus, when England became the first urban society in human history around 1900, rural migrants to the city were working in the factories and shops of an industrialized nation. But this is not the case in many Third World countries today. There, Davis argues, urbanization results more frequently from a push off the land due to overpopulation, not a pull to the city for work and urban amenities.

Urbanization in the Third World

There is dramatic urban growth in the Third World today. Cities are growing rapidly, more rapidly than in the period of rapid industrialization in the West. National leaders, trying to stem the flow of migrants to the cities of developing countries, are stymied. No policies seem to work. Rural people continue to move to the cities, even without jobs awaiting them.

Davis does not attribute this phenomenal city growth primarily to urbanization. Rather, he suggests, it is happening because the total populations of developing countries are rapidly growing. This population boom, Davis thinks, is the primary cause of urban growth in such countries. Thus, Davis sees high national rates of population growth, not rapid urbanization, as underlying urban problems in the Third World. This population boom is exacerbated by the lack of economic development which accompanied urbanization in the West.

Others are not so sure. Dissenters argue that it is *overconsumption* in the First World (the advanced technological countries, such as the United States)—not overpopulation in the Third World—that underlies urban problems in the less developed countries.

To summarize: In the world's first urban society, Great Britain, industrialization was the key to urbanization. This was also the case in Western Europe and the United States. But the developing countries are becoming urbanized without becoming industrialized. According to Kingsley Davis, the population explosion is responsible for this pattern, a pattern so different from the Euroamerican experience.

In a remarkably short time, then, a world of urban specks was replaced by a predominantly urban world. The evolution may have started at Jericho or Catal Hüyük some 10,000 years ago, or in Mesopotamia around 3500 B.C. Scholars don't agree on when, where, or why the first cities came into existence. But they do agree that, in the West, it was the technology of the Industrial Revolution that spurred urban growth and urbanization.

ANOTHER LOOK

Looking back on this brief tour through several millennia of urban history—from early cities in a rural world to an urban world by the twentieth century—several themes emerge. First, scholars disagree on when, why, and where cities first arose. How these disagreements developed, and what characteristics they may share, have little to do with their disciplinary backgrounds. Clearly, archeologists differ among themselves, as do sociologists and historians. Their dissent turns primarily on the relative weights they assign to various factors associated with the birth and development of cities. Some scholars, notably Childe and Sjoberg, place great emphasis on the role of technology. Others, such as Mumford and Fustel de Coulanges, stress the role of nonmaterial factors such as religion in the development of human institutions. This split—between those who think that ideas and culture can act as independent variables in determining social and political institutions and those who see ideas and culture as dependent upon people's material existence—is deep and irreparable. And it extends to many aspects of urban scholarship.

A second theme concerns conventional wisdom: Today's truth can quickly become tomorrow's folly. New evidence often changes long-accepted explanations of urban-related phenomena. Such is the case with the discovery in 1979 of cultivated barley at an ancient Egyptian campsite. These few grains of barley served to transform scholarly thought about when and why agriculture was invented. Thus, it is wise to consider all urban "truths" as tentative, not self-evident or timeless.

A third theme concerns language and definitions. Often scholars do not share a common definition of a very basic concept, including what is a city. Perhaps the best way to cope is to accept dissensus on basics as a given and then try to understand how a theorist uses a particular concept.

Finally, this chapter points up the difficulty in trying to make sweeping generalizations about all cities or classifying them in some meaningful way. Many scholars feel that the effort to find patterns of similarity or difference, say, between preindustrial and industrial cities, may be worthwhile but thus far unsatisfactory. At least for the present, then, we are left with a sense of the variety of human settlements called cities that people over the millennia have built.

PROJECTS

1. **American urban history.** For the city in which you live (or a nearby one), identify and determine the location of key transportation routes and their history. (For instance, when were major roads, electric trolley lines, railroads, and highways built? What effects on the present form of the city are evident from these early developments?)
2. **American urban history.** Select an old inner-city neighborhood. Conduct a walking tour of the area. Differentiate the architectural styles of the houses; when were they built? for whom? Notice particularly the churches: Do their architectural style and size tell you anything about the ethnic roots of the neighborhood? Do they indicate when various ethnic groups arrived (or were present in large enough numbers with enough wealth) to build a church? Are these churches still used as churches?

SUGGESTIONS FOR FURTHER LEARNING

A readable and nicely illustrated set of readings on the origins of cities is contained in *Scientific American, Cities: Their Origin, Growth and Human Impact* (San Francisco: Freeman, 1974). The selections concern early cities in both the Fertile Crescent and Mesopotamia. Most are case studies by archeologists. Individual case studies are woven together by a general introduction by Kingsley Davis and overview articles by Gideon Sjoberg and Richard S. McNeish.

The urban revolution in Mesopotamia is described in compact and highly readable form in two of V. Gordon Childe's books: *What Happened in History* (New York and Middlesex, England: Penguin [1942] 1950) and *Man Makes Himself* (New York: Mentor [1936] 1952).

Gideon Sjoberg's theories on the nature of the preindustrial city are contained in his book *The*

Preindustrial City (New York: Free Press, 1960). Sjoberg reviews the evidence on the rise of cities in Mesopotamia and Mesoamerica and describes the global spread of urbanization. Most of his book discusses his ideal type, the preindustrial city, in terms of ecology and demography, social class, family and kinship arrangements, and economic, political, and religious structure.

An anthology which draws together a number of seminal articles on the origin of cities and early urbanization is Thelma S. Baker (ed.), *The Urbanization of Man: A Social Science Perspective* (Berkeley, Calif.: McCutchan, 1972). Included are works by V. Gordon Childe, Kingsley Davis, H. D. F. Kitto, and Henri Pirenne.

A series of books on planning and cities published by George Braziller (New York) provide brief, well-illustrated overviews of cities in a variety of cultures and epochs. Relevant to the concerns of this chapter are Paul Lampl, *Cities and Planning in the Ancient Near East* (1968), Jorge Hardoy, *Urban Planning in Pre-Columbian America* (1968), J. Ward-Perkins, *The Cities of Ancient Greece and Italy* (1974), and Howard Sallman, *Medieval Cities* (1968).

For U.S. urban history, see Howard P. Chudacoff, *The Evolution of American Urban Society* (Englewood Cliffs, N.J.: Prentice-Hall, 1975), which is particularly strong on the connection between technological change and the evolution of city form, social and cultural history, and urban politics. Charles A. Glaab and Theodore Brown, *A History of Urban America*, 2d ed. (New York: Macmillan, 1976), attempts to synthesize material on selected themes in American urban history. One chapter on urban technology provides a unique look at the bases of construction techniques (such as the origin of elevators) which made high-density cities possible. Zane Miller, *The Urbanization of Modern America: A Brief History* (New York: Harcourt Brace Jovanovich, 1973) is a lively, eclectic, and interdisciplinary work which examines the historical origins of city form and space, economic bases, social groupings, and political structures. Sylvia Doughty Fries focuses on the antiurban origins of the American city and examines the expectations accompanying the establishment of Boston, New Haven, Philadelphia, Williamsburg, and Savannah in *The Urban Idea in Colonial America* (Philadelphia: Temple University Press, 1977).

Samuel Bass Warner, Jr., *The Urban Wilderness* (New York: Harper & Row, 1972), is a selective and highly interpretive urban history: "a series of present-oriented historical essays which will give the reader a framework for understanding the giant and confusing urban world he must cope with" (4). Warner is concerned with the roots of current urban problems and traces them through case study material to such things as the retention of anachronistic land use law, forms of industrial organization rooted in laissez-faire capitalism, the technological imperatives of railroads, and later the automobile.

Bayard Still, *Urban America: A History With Documents* (Boston: Little, Brown, 1974), is a detailed collection of documents on American urban history with text. The book is divided into a section on early cities, urban growth 1820–1870, urban expansion 1870–1920, and the metropolitan era. Letters, speeches, newspaper accounts, journals, municipal records, and the like are combined to flesh out standard urban history.

Specialized articles on American urban history are collected in various anthologies, including Alexander B. Callow (ed.), *American Urban History* (New York: Oxford University Press, 1973); and Kenneth T. Jackson and Stanley K. Schultz (eds.), *Cities in American History* (New York: Knopf, 1972), which features revisionist interpretations. Allen M. Wakstein (ed.), *The Urbanization of America: An Historical Anthology* (Boston: Houghton Mifflin, 1970), adopts a somewhat different perspective. It is heavy on methodology—how to study urbanization—and it devotes considerable attention to the history of urban services (e.g., police).

Two filmstrips that explore the origin of cities in Mesopotamia are *How Cities Began* (Multimedia Productions, 1974); an accompanying phonodisc traces the development of cities in the Middle East using a variety of maps, models, and artifacts. It explores the agricultural base of the early cities and their intimate connection with religious life and follows the daily life of an early city dweller. Similar is *The Urban Revolution: The First Cities* (The National Film Board of Canada), which shows excavation sites of Mesopotamian cities and includes material on early cities in China. A pair of filmstrips tracing the development of cities from ancient times through the Middle Ages to early colonial U.S. cities and the modern metropolis is *The City in History* (Educational Dimensions Corporation, 1972).

The urbanization of the world population is described in the film strip *The City Explosion: Urban Growth in the Developing Nations* (Visual Education Consultants, 1969). It traces the world population explosion, with particular emphasis on the implications for Third World countries.

Perhaps the most stunning portrayal of ancient cities is D. W. Griffith's remarkable film *Intolerance* (1916). Reviewing the "stupendous spectacle" in 1916, the *New York Times* critic said, "It is the Babylonian portion of the film that will commend it to the public. These pictures of the walls of Babylon, broad enough for chariots to pass at ease, of the great gates thronged with picturesque caravans . . . are indeed masterpieces of the cine."

KEY TERMS

Acropolis In early classical Greek cities, a combined palace-fortress-temple complex built upon a defensible hill within the city.

Catal Hüyük An early (perhaps the earliest) trade city, dating from approximately 9500 years ago. Catal Hüyük was located in high arid land in present-day Turkey. The economy of this prehistoric settlement was apparently based on trade in salt, obsidian, and other goods, not agriculture.

Childe thesis The thesis concerning the origin of cities formulated by V. Gordon Childe. On the basis of Mesopotamian evidence, Childe argued that a fertile environment, increasing population, the growth of social organization, and introduction of technology created an urban revolution.

City What constitutes a city is much debated. Usually, definitions assume a relatively large population, high population density, and heterogeneity. Alternatively, a settlement may be defined as a city only if it performs certain market functions or cultural roles.

Jericho An ancient urban center located in mid-desert, in the Near East. Recent archeological excavations suggest that the "hog-backed brick people" (named after the structures they built) may have formed a trade city of several thousand people by 8000 B.C. or even earlier. The claim that Jericho was the first city remains clouded in empirical and definitional debate.

Mesoamerica The area in which pre-Columbian Indian civilizations flourished, beginning about 150 B.C. It encompasses the southern two-thirds of mainland Mexico, Guatemala, Belize, a western strip of Honduras, El Salvador, the Pacific coast of Nicaragua, and northwestern Costa Rica.

Mesopotamia The Fertile Crescent region (now in Iraq) where some, notably Childe, believe the first true cities arose about 3500 B.C.

Streetcar suburbs The first wave of U.S. suburbs resulting from the improvement in transportation technology during the last quarter of the nineteenth century.

Technology Tools and cultural knowledge used to control the physical environment to achieve practical ends. In Sjoberg's typology, it is the key variable for distinguishing city types.

Teotihuacán The largest of the Mesoamerican cities, located on a high, relatively infertile plain near present-day Mexico City. This Indian city of spectacular pyramids and shrines may have had a population of as many as 200,000.

Trade thesis of the origin of cities. Recent archeological excavations have unearthed settlements which were large, dense, and heterogeneous enough that some characterize them as cities, notably Catal Hüyük. Some theorists claim that unlike the later Mesopotamian cities (which served as distribution points for the agricultural surplus), these early settlements' main economic function was trade. Thus, they argue that trade—not agriculture—was the basis for the emergence of the earliest cities.

Ur The largest of the Mesopotamian cities in the Fertile Crescent. About 3500 B.C., Ur emerged in a fertile, swampy area of Sumer in lower Mesopotamia between the Tigris and Euphrates rivers. It was a well-planned, compact city of perhaps 34,000 persons, serving as a religious and organizational center for a much larger agricultural area.

Urbanization The process by which the *proportion* of the total population in a society living in urban settlements becomes greater, and the proportion living in rural areas decreases. Also, some scholars use the concept to mean the process of becoming urban in terms of social, technological, political, and spatial organization. Urbanization is not to be confused with mere growth of cities.

Urban revolution A term used by archeologist V. Gordon Childe to refer to what he deemed the profound changes in civilization which occurred concurrently with the rise of cities in Mesopotamia.

Walking city An urban historian's term to describe cities prior to the introduction of transportation technologies which expanded their outer limits beyond comfortable walking range. Prior to 1850, all American cities were walking cities: The edge of the urbanized area could be reached in a half-hour walk.

Ziggurat Religious temple in ancient Mesopotamian cities. It was shaped like a pyramid (but had steps rather than smooth sides) with a temple on top.

REFERENCES

Adams, Robert M.
1966 The Evolution of Urban Society: Early Mesopotamia and Prehispanic Mexico. Chicago: Aldine.

Associated Press
1979 "Crop from a farm 17,000 years old." San Francisco Chronicle (Sept. 25):3.

Banfield, Edward
1970 The Unheavenly City Revisited. Boston: Little, Brown.

Bridenbaugh, Carl
1938 Cities in the Wilderness. New York: Knopf.

Briggs, Asa
1963 Victorian Cities. New York: Harper & Row.

Childe, V. Gordon
[1936]
1952 Man Makes Himself. New York: New American Library.
[1942]
1964 What Happened in History? New York and Middlesex, England: Penguin.
1950 "The urban revolution." Town Planning Review 21:3–17.

Chudacoff, Howard P.
1975 The Evolution of American Urban Society. Englewood Cliffs, N.J.: Prentice-Hall.

Cox, Oliver C.
[1964]
1969 "The preindustrial city reconsidered." Pp. 19–29 in Paul Meadows and Ephraim H. Mizruchi (eds.), Urbanism, Urbanization, and Change: Comparative Perspectives. Reading, Mass.: Addison-Wesley.

Davidson, Basil
[1959]
1970 Lost Cities of Africa. Boston: Little, Brown.

Davis, Kingsley
1965 "The urbanization of the human population." Scientific American 213:40–53.

Engels, Friedrich
[1845]
1950 The Condition of the Working Class in England in 1844. London: George Allen and Unwin.

Fustel de Coulanges, Numa Denis
[1864]
1955 The Ancient City. Garden City, N.Y.: Doubleday Anchor.

Hawthorne, Nathaniel
[1860]
1950 The Marble Faun. New York: Arcadia House.

Jacobs, Jane
1970 The Economy of Cities. New York: Vintage.

Kenyon, Kathleen M.
1957 Digging Up Jericho. New York: Praeger.

McKelvey, Blake
1966 The Emergence of Metropolitan America. New Brunswick, N.J.: Rutgers University Press.

Mellaart, James
1967 Catal Hüyük: A Neolithic Town in Anatolia. London: Thames and Hudson.

Mumford, Lewis
1961 The City in History. New York: Harcourt Brace and World.

Pirenne, Henri
[1925]
1956 Medieval Cities. Princeton, N.J.: Princeton University Press.

Poe, Edgar Allan
1886 The Complete Poetical Works of Edgar Allan Poe. Chicago: Belford, Clarke.

Scully, Vincent
1969 American Architecture and Urbanism. New York: Praeger.

Sjoberg, Gideon
[1960]
1965 The Preindustrial City. New York: Free Press.

Thucydides
[411 B.C.]
1956 History of the Peloponnesian War. Books I and II, Vol. I. Tr. by Charles Forster Smith. Cambridge, Mass.: Harvard University Press.

Todd, Ian A.
1976 Catal Hüyük in Perspective. Menlo Park, Calif.: Cummings.

Warner, Samuel Bass, Jr.
1962 Streetcar Suburbs: The Process of Growth in Boston, 1870–1900. Cambridge, Mass.: MIT Press and Harvard University Press.
1968 The Private City: Philadelphia in Three Periods of its Growth. Philadelphia: University of Pennsylvania Press.

Weber, Max
[1921]
1963 The City. Don Martindale and Gertrude Neuwirth (tr., eds.). New York: Free Press.

Wheatley, Paul
1971 The Pivot of the Four Quarters: A Preliminary Enquiry Into the Origins and Character of the Ancient Chinese City. Chicago: Aldine.

Wheeler, Mortimer
1953 The Indus Civilization. Cambridge: Cambridge University Press.
1966 Civilization of the Indus Valley and Beyond. New York: McGraw-Hill.

White, Morton and Lucia White
[1962]
1964 The Intellectual Versus the City. New York: Mentor.

Wide World Photos

CHAPTER 5
The Ties that Bind

Poet John Donne expressed his view of the human condition in a memorable phrase: "No man is an island." If, as Donne implies, people are social animals whose fates are intertwined, then why do so many people feel disconnected and alone in the world? What ties bind people together? How do we prevent insecurity and loneliness? The idea of community is central to such questions of personal security and social connectedness. Although the abstract concept has many meanings, "community" hinges on the notions of togetherness and sharing.

Chapters 5 and 6 focus on the ties that bind people together, both in contemporary metropolitan America and in small-scale rural communities. This chapter begins with a discussion of the concept of community. Then it examines a form of community that Aristotle and many since his time have held up as an ideal: the ancient Greek polis of Athens. Next, the chapter looks at urban theory. Various explanations of the shift from rural to urban life in the West and the effects of this shift on human personality are evaluated in terms of their basic assumptions and contemporary relevance. For example, the rural-to-urban theoretical constructs predict an *inevitable* breakdown in community within urban-industrial society. Is this indeed what has happened?

That leads us back to the issue of metropolitan community today, the major topic of the next chapter. What binds people together in large, sprawling urban-suburban areas? Are suburbs and New Towns new forms of community? Or are they substituting conformity for community? Is the "back to the land" movement essentially a search for lost community? And what about community life in the future—in proposed space age cities beneath the water and above the earth?

These two chapters pose many questions, and not merely abstract ones. What makes us feel like insiders or outsiders in a social group? Why do we tend to trust people like ourselves and mistrust people unlike ourselves? When do we feel cut off and alone, disconnected from the fates of our neighbors? These questions confront us all, often in deeply emotional ways. How beautiful it would be, we may fantasize, to live in peace and harmony like the Tasaday, a small Stone Age tribe living in a Philippine rain forest today. Apparently, the Tasaday live a conflict-free existence. Some observers (e.g., Nance, 1975) portray the Tasaday as living in a garden of Eden. Inspired by visions of such a community built on trust, security, and simple technology, contemporary visionaries have tried to construct isolated, self-sufficient communities in the midst of an advanced technological society. Can they succeed?

So many questions, so few definitive answers. Of course, there are many proposed answers to questions of community. The essence of many "solutions" is this: If only we could do this or that, then we could create an atmosphere in which human beings live in harmony. Solutions have taken various forms—attempts to alter basic institutions; proposals to bring affluence to the world; segregating, exiling, or killing people defined as outsiders to the community (e.g., Hitler's national policy of killing Jews and gypsies). These solutions suggest the power of visions of community.

Meanwhile, philosophers and writers wonder aloud whether there are any answers. Are twentieth-century people doomed to be eternally "waiting for Godot," in the phrase of playwright Samuel Beckett? Is there "no exit," as Jean-Paul Sartre implies?

Our purpose here is not to provide clear answers to the problems of human community, for there are none. Rather, we will present in a formal and systematic manner some issues that concern social bonds among people. Our hope is that such knowledge about community will be linked to acquaintance with the ties that bind so that we may make better choices, both in our personal lives and in our collective existence.

WHAT IS A COMMUNITY?

Like love, truth, and other abstract concepts, **community** has no agreed-upon meaning. In fact, in the discipline of sociology alone, there are at least ninety definitions of the word.

However, in general terms, a human community usually refers either to (1) a group sharing a physical space (e.g., residents of Chicago's Austin neighborhood), (2) a group sharing a common trait (e.g., a student or lesbian community), or (3) a group bound together by shared identity and common culture and typified by a high degree of **social cohesion** (e.g., the Tasaday of the Philippines). Often, this last group is called a "traditional community."

Territorially Based Communities

As noted above, a physical concentration of people—in a neighborhood, city, or nation—may be called a community. If asked, "What community are you from?" most of us would probably respond by naming a place—say, Chicago, the West Side, or Austin, depending on the context and the geographical knowledge of the questioner.

Here, we are not concerned with communities based only on the simple sharing of space. Rather, we focus on communities rooted in social relationships. In this context, community is based on a feeling of "we-ness," that is, a sense of shared identity and interdependence. Such a community may or may not share a physical territory.

Communities Based on Common Culture

Some groups share both a physical territory and a unified, cohesive social existence—the traditional community mentioned above. The Tasaday, for example, inhabit a common physical space. They also have strong positive feelings toward the group, wish to remain in the group, and accept the group's rules and goals.

However, many groups called communities today are not bound to a plot of land. A close-knit ethnic community, for example, can be widely dispersed. However, its members do share common origins and a common culture which bind them together and set them apart from others in the society.

Similarly, members of an occupational community do not inhabit a common territory. They can be spread throughout the world, and rarely do they share common origins. Yet certain occupational groups—lawyers, nurses, academics, and priests, to name a few—engage in activities that give rise to a shared culture, attitudes, and values in modern society.

Many consider a professional group (such as doctors) to be a community because it has the following characteristics:

1. Members are bound by a sense of shared identity.
2. Once in the profession, few leave.
3. Members share a common language (or jargon) which can be understood only partially by outsiders.
4. Members share common values.
5. In a social sense, members collectively reproduce the next generation.
6. Insiders are easily distinguished from outsiders in the professional community.
7. Requirements for membership are the same for all members.
8. The professional group has power over its members. (Goode, 1957)

This list stresses that a professional group is a community without a physical location. Still, it is often called a community because members share common identity, culture, and occupational goals.

Nonoccupational groups can also be considered communities if they meet the above criteria. Examples here include some religious, ethnic, and political groups, such as the Amana colony in Iowa, the Weatherpeople, and the Japanese-American community in San Francisco.

a

b

Fig. 5-1 TYPES OF COMMUNITIES. "Community" may refer to a place or group of people sharing a space, such as Chicago's Austin community. It can also mean a group which shares common values, culture, or traits but not a geographical location, such as an (*a*) occupational community. Another type, often called a "traditional community," refers to a group which shares both a common territory, culture, origins, and identity, such as (*b*) the Tasaday of the Philippines. (*a* Medical Illustrations Department, General Rose Hospital, Denver, Colorado. *b* © John Nance, Magnum)

Some social scientists (e.g., Kahler, 1957) distinguish between communities and collectivities. Communities derive from common *origins,* while collectivities are established on the basis of common *ends.* Using this distinction, occupational groups such as doctors, as well as other nonblood-related groups, would be considered collectivities, not communities.

A Sense of Community

A sense of belonging with others—a "weness"—typifies many traditional communities. But is this feeling—a sense of community—possible today? Many theorists argue that contemporary urban-industrial society is too large, too diverse, and too individualistic to promote a sense of community *except* in subcommunities (or collectivities) such as ethnic and occupational groups.

Before considering that possibility, let us examine forms of community in times past. We begin with what some scholars believe to be the most highly developed community in the Western world: the Athenian polis in ancient Greece.

The Athenian Polis of Ancient Greece

In the fifth century B.C., Greece was composed of a number of independent, economically self-sufficient, and self-governing political units called "poleis" (singular: "polis"). The word **polis** is ususally translated as "city-state," but this is a bad translation. The polis was not much like a modern nation-state, and it was much more than a city. For this reason, following the historian of the Greeks, H. D. F. Kitto, we use the Greek word, "polis."

By current population standards, a polis was small. Only three poleis—Athens, Syracuse, and Acragas—numbered more than 20,000 citizens. (*Note:* Not all inhabitants were granted citizenship. Slaves, who were foreigners, and other foreigners were not citizens. Further, women had no political rights. Thus, a citizenry of about 10,000 persons implies a total population of about 100,000.)

The small population of the polis is important in understanding its ethos. Greek philosophers insisted on this point. Plato wrote that the ideal polis should contain no more than 5,000 citizens (about 50,000 people). Aristotle maintained that the polis should not be too small or too large. He reasoned that it should be small enough so that all citizens could recognize one another on sight and be properly governed. But it should not be too small because it would not be economically self-sufficient. The idea of a metropolitan community numbering in the millions or a nation-state with over 200 million people, as in America today, would have seemed absurd to the ancient Greeks.

By contemporary standards, the physical scale of the polis was also small. Corinth, a commercial center, encompassed only 330 square miles. Sparta, covering 3,200 square miles, was considered enormous. To think in such small terms is difficult today. After all, the Los Angeles metropolitan area, covering 4,069 square miles, is larger than any ancient Greek polis. Ancient Greeks would not have liked living in a huge modern state like the United States. The Greeks were in contact with one such vast state, the Persian Empire, and they thought it suitable only for barbarians, not civilized people like themselves.

Why did the Greeks live under the small-scale polis system rather than consolidating into larger political units? Surely economic factors and geographical barriers (particularly mountains) contributed to maintaining the polis system; but the "real explanation," according to Kitto (1951:69), was the character of the Greeks: Fearing that differences in scale would become differences in kind, they chose to live in poleis.

A Communal Way of Life

Most citizens of a polis were farmers. Although agriculturalists, they preferred to live in a town or village, walk out to their fields, and spend any leisure time talking to fellow citizens in the public square.

To these ordinary citizens, the polis was a community where all issues of common concern were *public,* not private. Citizen participation was widespread; about 15 to 20 percent of the citizens in the Athenian polis served the community in some capacity each year, filling offices by lot and rotating administrative reponsibilites. Legislation took place in large popular assemblies. (Again, note that slaves and other foreigners were barred from public affairs. Further, women took no public role; they remained secluded in their homes, for Athens was a male-dominated community where men and women had separate spheres.)

From our vantage point today, it is hard to comprehend what the Athenian polis meant to ordinary Greek citizens, particularly in the Golden Age of Pericles (c. 490–429 B.C.). Depending on our political ideology, we see government either as a mechanism to prevent "the war of all against all" (the classical liberal approach based on Thomas Hobbes's philosophy); as a means of regulating who gets what when the market mechanism of supply and demand needs adjustment (the liberal approach); or as a weapon serving the interests of the powerful against the powerless (the radical approach). But to the Greeks, the polis represented a positive force. It was the only framework in which people could realize their human potential: intellectual, spiritual, and moral.

The democratic leader of the Athenian polis, Pericles, gives a clue to communal life in the polis in his famous Funeral Oration: "Each individual is interested not only in his own affairs but in the affairs of the polis as well. . . . We do not say that a man who takes no interest in politics is a man who minds his own business; we say that he has no business here at all."

Pericles's Funeral Oration and the Athenian Oath of Citizenship (see Fig. 5-2) indicate the public-spirited attitude of the Greeks. They were social animals, living in and through the polis. For the Greeks, the polis was a community and a way of life. It was an active agent, training the minds and characters of its citizenry. It was a living entity, and citizens were like members of a large extended family. As Kitto (1951:78) concludes, the Greek citizen was essentially an individualist in economic affairs. But in the rest of life, he was essentially communal: "Religion, art, games, and the discussion of things—all these were needs of life that could be fully satisfied only through the polis." This stands in stark contrast to current conceptions of self-fulfillment.

To summarize: The polis was built on a common cultural life. Its geographic area was compact, so that people identified with their locality, and its population was small enough so that citizens were personally known to one another. Unlike a city or nation-state in urban-industrial society, the polis was a self-sufficient entity with an ethos of public, not private, interest.

The Athenian polis was ancient Greece's crowning glory. Why, then, did it disappear as a way of life? Some accounts of the decline and fall of the polis system focus on the effect of trade and markets. According to economic anthropologist Karl Polanyi (1957), the Athenian polis under Pericles was governed by laws of economic reciprocity. The concept of

FROM THE OATH OF THE ATHENIAN CITY-STATE

WE WILL EVER STRIVE FOR THE IDEALS AND SACRED THINGS OF THE CITY, BOTH ALONE AND WITH MANY; WE WILL UNCEASINGLY SEEK TO QUICKEN THE SENSE OF PUBLIC DUTY; WE WILL REVERE AND OBEY THE CITY'S LAWS; WE WILL TRANSMIT THIS CITY NOT ONLY NOT LESS, BUT GREATER, BETTER AND MORE BEAUTIFUL THAN IT WAS TRANSMITTED TO US.

Fig. 5-2 ATHENIAN OATH OF CITIZENSHIP. Citizens pledged to transmit the polis's cultural heritage and to improve Athens as part of their civic duty. (Athenian oath as it appears at the Maxwell School of Citizenship and Public Affairs, Syracuse University. Reproduced by permission.)

profit hardly existed. Instead, economic exchanges were seen more as gift-giving than as trade; their chief function was to ensure social solidarity, not to redistribute wealth. This system of economic reciprocity faded with the emergence of a market economy (where prices are set by supply and demand) in the fifth century B.C. With market economy came new ideas—profit and individualism.

In Kitto's view, what destroyed the polis system was progress. The polis was suited for amateurs, not professionals or specialized experts. Indeed, the polis discouraged specialization and efficiency, for its ideal was participation: Every citizen could and should play a role in public affairs. To accomplish this, no role could be very difficult for an ordinary person to play. When life became more complex in the fourth century B.C., new experts were needed. Commerce had expanded on the Mediterranean, and Philip of Macedonia had introduced new military tactics in a war against the poleis. In short, the world was shrinking, and specialized skills—

military tactics and commercial skills in particular—were needed to meet the challenges. Athens responded by employing professional soldiers (mercenaries) instead of citizen-soldiers. This act denied the very ideal of citizen participation.

In addition, Athenian education changed. Under Pericles, education was free and available to all citizens; it was part of living in the polis. But to meet the new challenges in the fourth century B.C., education became specialized, and it was available only to those who could pay. Soon, divisions between the educated and uneducated appeared, and specialist experts separated from laypersons. At his educational academy, Socrates taught students that government should be left to experts instead of being decided by democratic vote and popular debate; these teachings—not the expression of unpopular opinions—may have led to his condemnation to death (see Stone, 1979).

These educational changes had wide-ranging effects. The educated of all poleis now had more in common with each other than with uneducated members of their own polis; this weakened the bonds of community. Further, the division between experts and laypersons destroyed the common knowledge base and culture upon which the polis was built.

Interestingly, it was at this time, the fourth century B.C., that the word **cosmopolis** was coined. It meant that people owed allegiance not to their own local community but to a larger group, the community of humankind. This new notion of cosmopolitanism, signaling the individual's connection to a wider community, helped to break down the traditional sense of community.

To conclude: As the educated became cosmopolitan in outlook, the ideal of the polis as a community waned. And as specialized experts in military and commercial affairs arose, the ideal of community gave way to the ideal of cosmopolitan life.

This brief account of the rise and fall of the polis, especially Athens, suggests that a sense of traditional community could not be sustained in the face of growing complexity and specialization. The preconditions for its existence—a simple, small-scale, self-sufficient, relatively unspecialized local way of life—gave way to a wider world and a more cosmopolitan outlook.

Now let us begin a more systematic examination of some issues touched upon in the history of the polis. For instance, does functional specialization necessarily lead to the breakdown of community? Can a sense of traditional community exist in a world shrunk to the point where a moon landing can be telecast via communications satellite to a global audience? Are individualism and loss of community inevitable companions of large-scale, complex society? We turn to classical urban scholars whose theoretical constructs deal with these very issues.

CLASSICAL URBAN THEORY

By the 1870s, Western Europe had experienced the effects of twin revolutions: the French Revolution and the Industrial Revolution. The giant broom of the twin revolutions was sweeping traditional community into the dustbin of history. The foundations of small-scale rural community—family, social hierarchy, church, relatively simple technology, property in land—were crumbling in the wake of industrialism, urbanism, and industrial capitalism. Great population shifts from countryside to city were in process, and England was on its way to becoming the first urban society in human history. Thus it is not surprising that at this time the idea of community became a dominant theme in European social thought.

Theorists living through the demise of traditional community formed differing judgments about the new urban-industrial-capitalist order. Tönnies, for one, romanticized the medieval small town as the home of the humane life and mourned the passing of traditional community. Marx, on the other hand, viewed the slow transformation from feudalism to industrial capitalism as a positive step, ending what he called "the idiocy of rural life." For Marx, the twin revolutions were liberating forces, freeing the political spirit and setting in motion the forces that would someday lead to a new basis for community—the solidarity of the working classes of the world.

The nineteenth-century theorists viewed the transformation of Europe in different ways, but they interpreted these changes in a similar fashion: as inevitable evolutionary developments from one form of social organization to another—from rural to urban, from simple to complex, from feudalism to capitalism, from small-scale to large-scale, from religious to secular. Hence, classical urban theory is based on polar contrasts between two forms of social organization and human personality.

Typologies of the Rural-to-Urban Shift

Theorists express these polar contrasts in the form of classification schemes called "typologies." As noted in Chapter 2, typologies are designed to be tentative models of the real world, not to correspond exactly to every observable case. A typology is composed of two or more **ideal types** that can be used to describe, compare, and test hypotheses, such as the rural and urban types of society.

Despite their unique features, typologies of the rural-to-urban shift share some common assumptions and characteristics. Most important is their evolutionary bias. The shift from rural life to city life is viewed as a unilinear, inevitable, and irreversible development. At one end of the evolutionary process lies simple rural life, and at the other end lies complex modern society. However, a continuum between the two poles is implied.

Let us take a closer look at some of the many rural-urban typologies, examining several classical nineteenth-century formulations and other more recent ones. We begin with the most well known: Tönnies's *Gemeinschaft-Gesellschaft* dichotomy.

Gemeinschaft and *Gesellschaft* (Tönnies)

Like other nineteenth-century theorists, Ferdinand Tönnies (1855–1936) based his typology on experience with changes in peasant communities in Western Europe. From that vantage point, he constructed a typology contrasting two forms of social organization: community and society. *Gemeinschaft* (community) lies at one end of the continuum, and *Gesellschaft* (society) lies at the other.

According to Tönnies, social life evolves in the following way: from family units to rural villages, to towns, to cities, to nations, and finally to cosmopolitan life. At the beginning stages of this evolutionary development lies *Gemeinschaft*, the traditional community that existed prior to the twin revolutions in Europe.

In *Gemeinschaft* social organization, people are bound together by common values, sacred traditions, and blood ties. They share a physical territory, common experience, and common thoughts. They are linked by a "reciprocal, binding sentiment." Kinship, land, neighborhood, and friendship are the cornerstones. These key elements are embodied in the family, the primary social unit.

By contrast, kinship, land, and friendship count little in *Gesellschaft*. In *Gesellschaft* (a form of social organization that accompanied the rise of industrialism, capitalism, and cities), there is a lack of close-knit family and friendship ties. Tönnies argues that in this urban-industrial capitalist society, human relations are based on contracts and laws, not

Fig. 5-3 *GEMEINSCHAFT* AND *GESELLSCHAFT.* (Richard Hedman)

binding sentiment. Attachment to land and neighborhood lose their meaning; money and credit become paramount concerns. Indeed, Tönnies, like his contemporary, Karl Marx, insists on the importance of the money economy in determining human interaction. For Tönnies, people in *Gesellschaft* measure all values, including self-worth, in terms of money. This cash nexus replaces community values based on traditional authority, binding sentiment, religious traditions, and kinship.

As described by Tönnies, *Gemeinschaft* is typified by small rural communities where people know one another and their place in the social system. In contrast, *Gesellschaft* is marked by large urban centers where people are strangers whose place in the social system can shift.

Individualism, not community interest, is the hallmark of *Gesellschaft*. Since no common morality exists in the heterogeneous city, people are free to calculate rationally what is in their own self-interest. *Saturday Night Fever* (1977) illustrates Tönnies's point. Both disco dancer Tony Manero (John Travolta) and his brother, a former priest, follow their own conscience in setting life goals. Neither is bound by family wishes, absolute moral values, or traditional authority. But in *Gemeinschaft*, Tönnies maintains, people do not base their actions on rational self-interest. Instead, they conform to accepted standards of behavior and share a common definition of right and wrong.

Why did *Gemeinschaft* evolve into *Gesellschaft?* For Tönnies, *Gesellschaft* arose with the growth of commerce and capitalism. It serves the interests of merchant-capitalists who trade commodities on the basis of contracts, not friendship or blood ties.

Fig. 5-4 BAMBERG, GERMANY, 1493. Medieval towns were romanticized by Tönnies as the source of the humane life. Bamberg's tall church spires, fortifications, and castle symbolize the feudal institutions whose strength waned with the passage of traditional community. (Hartmann Schedel, *Weltchronik* [Nuremberg, 1493])

How did Tönnies evaluate this movement from the simple rural community to the complex industrial city? He believed that the shift from *Gemeinschaft* to *Gesellschaft* meant an inevitable loss of community, a loss he tended to mourn with a sense of nostalgia. At the same time, he noted what he considered *Gesellschaft*'s positive aspects, particularly the rise of cities as cultural and scientific centers.

Mechanical and Organic Social Solidarity (Durkheim)

French sociologist Emile Durkheim (1858–1917) sees the rural-to-urban shift in terms of changes in social bonds among people or social solidarity. At the rural end of the continuum, people are mentally and morally homogeneous. In this form of social solidarity—**mechanical solidarity**—communities are not atomized.

At the other end of the continuum, the urban-industrial end, lies **organically solid** society. Here, the mental and moral similarities among people disappear, the collective conscience (shared beliefs, values, sentiments, and morality) weakens, and the **division of labor** stimulates individualism. People become highly differentiated according to their functional tasks.

To Durkheim ([1893] 1964), Western civilization was inevitably moving from mechanical to organic solidarity. That is, it was changing from a form of social organization based on a unity of thought, beliefs, sentiments, and manners to one based on a unity of heterogeneous individuals bound together by functionally interrelated tasks. For Durkheim, the prime force behind this evolution is the increasingly complex division of labor. In organically solid societies such as the United States, tasks are highly specialized. This

Table 5-1 Job Titles

What's Your Line?
Reptile keeper, spray-gun repairer, fun-house attendant, peanut-butter maker, experimental rocket-sled mechanic, comedy diver, accordian repairer, bowling alley detective, bank-note designer, astrologer, astronomer, snow-removing supervisor, bottle washer (Machine I), trombone-slide assembler, interpretive dancer, young-adult librarian, net-making supervisor, playground-equipment erector, press-box custodian.

SOURCE: U.S. Department of Labor, *Dictionary of Occupational Titles* (Washington, D.C.: U.S. Government Printing Office, 1977).

specialization is reflected in the Labor Department's *Dictionary of Occupational Titles,* which lists 1,371 pages of jobs known to the federal government, from artificial eye maker to zyglo inspector.

Both mechanically solid and organically solid societies, in Durkheim's view, are natural forms of social organization. Both are rooted in social unity; only the type of unity differs. The unity and homogeneity of rural society are replaced by a unity consisting of functional interdependence in industrial society. (Tönnies, in contrast, defines *Gemeinschaft* as a natural social form and *Gesellschaft* as artificial.)

What are the consequences of the evolution from rural, mechanically solid society to urban-industrial, organically solid society? Durkheim says that the collective conscience weakens as a society becomes more specialized and differentiated by function. Contracts and a belief in the individual replace the collective conscience. In urban-industrial society, moral order is upheld by contracts and restitutive law, not a common morality and repressive law.

To Durkheim, then, the two forms of social organization can be distinguished by their legal base: "Law reproduces the principal forms of social solidarity" ([1893] 1964:68). In mechanically solid society, the legal system represses offenses against the common morality or collective conscience; such offenses are symbolically repressed because they threaten the moral order. Retaliation and punishment are typical sanctions applied in mechanically solid society. But in organically solid society, few offenses are seen as threats to the entire moral order. In many cases, an offense is handled by making amends (restitution) to the injured party in the form of money.

Here is an example of the difference between repressive and restitutive legal systems. Suppose you are holding a gun that accidentally goes off, killing another person. Everyone agrees this was a freak accident. Would a court imprison or exile you? Not in organically solid society, for this action would not be considered a threat to morality. At worst, you could be judged negligent and ordered to pay restitution to the victim's survivors.

This same freak accident in mechanically solid society, however, could be punished in a repressive way. In *Things Fall Apart* ([1959] 1974), Nigerian novelist Chinua Achebe describes just such an incident. In the novel, the gun of an Ibo tribesman accidentally goes off, killing a sixteen-year-old boy. The punishment is seven years in exile, for "It was a crime against the earth goddess to kill a clansman, and a man who committed it must flee from the land" (117).

To summarize: Durkheim draws a polar distinction between two forms of social solidarity: mechanical and organic. The law, either repressive or restitutive, provides an index to a society's form of social solidarity.

In both forms, the division of labor functions to cement social bonds. In rural, mechanically solid society, the simple division of labor promotes a common morality (collective conscience); in urban, organically solid society, the complex division of labor promotes functional interdependence. As simple, homogeneous, rural society is transformed (by population growth, increased communication, and larger territory), the division of labor evolves toward higher and higher specialization of function.

If the complex division of labor malfunctions in urban-industrial society, Durkheim warned, it could not play its role of cementing social solidarity. For example, the division of labor can become so complex that people work at very specialized tasks, not knowing how their task fits into any larger whole. Under such conditions, people can experience feelings of anxiety and meaninglessness, not a sense of social solidarity. This point of view, as we shall see in Chapter 16, is especially relevant to contemporary job dissatisfaction.

Culture and Civilization (Spengler)

Oswald Spengler (1880–1936) was so unlike his predecessors in the typological tradition that the differences deserve comment. Spengler was an obscure high school teacher, not a respected scholar. But the book he wrote—translated as *The Decline of the West* ([1918] 1962)—had much more popular impact than the writings of Tönnies and Durkheim combined.

Spengler was not a social scientist. The label "agrarian mystic" comes closest to describing him. In *The Decline of the West,* Spengler celebrates the triumph of the will and intuition over reason and intellect, glorifying the notion of destiny and denigrating social science. This brand of mystic romanticism is echoed in Hitler's propaganda of the 1930s, particularly the Nazi film *The Triumph of the Will* (1936), which stresses the superiority of so-called Aryan community over heterogeneous society.

Spengler draws a fundamental contrast between country and city. Clearly, in his eyes the country is the home of all things bright and beautiful. He refers to rural, preindustrial life as the home of a living organic entity (culture). In contrast, the city is a dead mechanical shell, the home of civilization.

To express his evolutionary view of the shift from country to city, Spengler uses the metaphor of the seasons. In the spring of history, there are rural communities typified by intuition and unity. Then comes summer, the time of early urban stirrings. Religion becomes impoverished, mathematical and scientific thought expands, and rationality starts to replace mystical views of the universe. The autumn of a culture's history soon follows. Here is the "intelligence of the city," the height of intellectual creativity. And a cult of science, utility, and prosperity is not far behind; it follows in the winter season, that time of megalopolitan civilization and irreligious cosmopolitanism. It is in winter that civilization finally withers and dies.

Birth, growth, death, and rebirth. That, in Spengler's cyclical view of history, is the evolutionary sequence from culture to civilization, and back again to culture.

The central focus of Spengler's analysis is social psychological: the urban and rural personalities. In the preindustrial-rural community, Spengler writes, people interact on the basis of feelings. But in urban-industrial life, money becomes paramount; intellect takes over from intuition; and human interaction becomes shallow.

Urban Personality (Wirth)

Louis Wirth (1897–1952), a member of the Chicago school of sociology, was not at all

Fig. 5-5 URBANISM AS A WAY OF LIFE. Wirth says that a modern urbanite does not owe allegiance to a single group, but instead "acquires membership in widely divergent groups, each of which functions only with reference to a certain segment of his [or her] personality."

"The Military Order of the Louse is a veterans group, so-named because many servicemen got lice while riding in boxcars during World War I. The women's auxiliary, the Cootiettes, started in 1930. Our main activities are assisting veterans and keeping alive the spirit of fellowship; our allegiance is to the government of the United States of America." (Bill Owens)

attracted by Spengler's antiscientific mysticism. But he was vitally concerned with the social psychology of modern city dwellers. He asked, and answered, the question: Is there an urban personality?

In his still influential essay, "Urbanism as a Way of Life" (1938), Wirth argues that **urbanism**—patterns of social interaction and culture that result from the concentration of large numbers of people in small areas—affects the human personality. In his essay (see Box 5-1), Wirth implies a polar contrast between urban and rural personalities, and he theorizes that the way urbanites think and act is linked to the characteristics of modern cities.

More specifically, Wirth says that cities are large, dense settlements with heterogeneous populations. These three variables—large size, high density, and heterogeneity—promote a certain kind of emotional and mental response. Urbanites typically react by becoming sophisticated, rational, and relativistic. They become indifferent and seemingly uncaring toward one another because that is the only way they can protect themselves against "the personal claims and expectations of others." Human interaction becomes "impersonal, superficial, transitory, and segmental."

The lone individual counts for little in the modern city. Thus, to accomplish their goals, individuals with similar interests join together to form organizations. Unlike rural folk, city dwellers do not owe their total allegiance to any one group or community. A

Box 5-1

SIZE, DENSITY, AND HETEROGENEITY

"Urbanism as a Way of Life"

A Sociological Definition of the City

For sociological purposes a city may be defined as a relatively large, dense, and permanent settlement of socially heterogeneous individuals.

Size of the Population Aggregate

Ever since Aristotle's *Politics,* it has been recognized that increasing the number of inhabitants in a settlement beyond a certain limit will affect the relationships between them and the character of the city. Large numbers involve . . . a greater range of individual variation. Furthermore, the greater the number of individuals participating in a process of interaction, the greater is the *potential* differentiation between them. The personal traits, the occupations, the cultural life, and the ideas of the members of an urban community may, therefore, be expected to range between more widely separated poles than those of rural inhabitants.

That such variations should give rise to the spatial segregation of individuals according to color, ethnic heritage, economic and social status, tastes and preferences, may readily be inferred. The bonds of kinship, of neighborliness, and the sentiments arising out of living together for generations under a common folk tradition are likely to be absent or, at best, relatively weak in an aggregate the members of which have such diverse origins and backgrounds. Under such circumstances competition and formal control mechanisms furnish the substitutes for the bonds of solidarity that are relied upon to hold a folk society together.

Increase in the number of inhabitants of a community beyond a few hundred is bound to limit the possibility of each member of the community knowing all the others personally. . . . The increase in numbers . . . involves a changed character of the social relationship. . . .

Characteristically, urbanites meet one another in highly segmental roles. They are, to be sure, dependent upon more people for the satisfactions of their life-needs than are rural people and thus are associated with a great number of organized groups, but they are less dependent upon particular persons, and their dependence upon others is confined to a highly fractionalized aspect of the other's round of activity. This is essentially what is meant by saying that the city is characterized by secondary rather than primary contacts. The contacts of the city may indeed be face to face, but they are nevertheless impersonal, superficial, transitory, and segmental. The reserve, the indifference, and the blasé outlook which urbanites manifest in their relationships may thus be regarded as devices for immunizing themselves against the personal claims and expectations of others.

The superficiality, the anonymity, and the transitory character of urban social relations make intelligible, also, the sophistication and the rationality generally ascribed to city-dwellers. Our acquaintances tend to stand in a relationship of utility to us in the sense that the role which each one plays in our life is overwhelmingly regarded as a means for the achievement of our own ends. Whereas the individual gains, on the one hand, a certain degree of emancipation or freedom from the personal and emotional controls of intimate groups, he loses, on the other hand, the spontaneous self-expression, the morale, and the sense of participation that comes with living in an integrated society. This constitutes essentially the state of *anomie,* or the social void. . . .

The segmental character and utilitarian accent of interpersonal relations in the city find their institutional expression in the proliferation of specialized tasks which we see in their most developed form in the professions. The operations of the pecuniary nexus lead to predatory relationships which tend to obstruct the efficient function-

Box 5-1 *continued*)

ing of the social order unless checked by professional codes and occupational etiquette. The premium put upon utility and efficiency suggests the adaptability of the corporate device for the organization of enterprises in which individuals can engage only in groups. The advantage that the corporation has over the individual entrepreneur and the partnership in the urban-industrial world derives not only from the possibility it affords of centralizing the resources of thousands of individuals or from the legal privilege of limited liability and perpetual succession, but from the fact that the corporation has no soul. . . .

The dominance of the city over the surrounding hinterland becomes explicable in terms of the division of labor which urban life occasions and promotes. The extreme degree of interdependence and the unstable equilibrium of urban life are closely associated with the division of labor and the specialization of occupations. . . .

. . . Typically in the city, interests are made effective through representation. The individual counts for little, but the voice of the representative is heard with a deference roughly proportional to the numbers for whom he speaks. . . .

Density

An increase in numbers when area is held constant (i.e., an increase in density) tends to produce differentiation and specialization, since only in this way can the area support increased numbers. Density thus reinforced the effect of numbers in diversifying men and their activities and in increasing the complexity of the social structure. . . .

The different parts of the city acquire specialized functions, and the city consequently comes to resemble a mosaic of social worlds in which the transition from one to the other is abrupt. The juxtaposition of divergent personalities and modes of life tends to produce a relativistic perspective and a sense of toleration of differences which may be regarded as prerequisites for rationality and which lead toward the secularization of life.

The close living together and working together of individuals who have no sentimental and emotional ties foster a spirit of competition, aggrandizement, and mutual exploitation. Formal controls are instituted to counteract irresponsibility and potential disorder. . . . The clock and the traffic signal are symbolic of the basis of our social order in the urban world. Frequent close physical contact, coupled with great social distance, accentuates the reserve of unattached individuals toward one another and, unless compensated by other opportunities for response, gives rise to loneliness. The necessary frequent movement of great numbers of individuals in a congested habitat causes friction and irritation. Nervous tensions which derive from such personal frustrations are increased by the rapid tempo and the complicated technology under which life in dense areas must be lived.

Heterogeneity

The social interaction among such a variety of personality types in the urban milieu tends to break down the rigidity of caste lines and to complicate the class structure. . . . The heightened mobility of the individual . . . brings him toward the acceptance of instability and insecurity in the world at large as a norm. This fact helps to account too, for the sophistication and cosmopolitanism of the urbanite. No single group has the undivided allegiance of the individual. . . . The individual acquires membership in widely divergent groups, each of which functions only with reference to a certain segment of his personality. . . .

There is little opportunity for the individual to obtain a conception of the city as a whole or to survey his place in the total scheme. Consequently he finds it difficult to determine what is in his own "best interests" and to decide between the issues and leaders presented to him by the agencies of mass suggestion. Individuals who are thus detached from the organized bodies which integrate society comprise the fluid masses that make collective behavior in the urban community so unpredictable and hence so problematical.

Although the city . . . produces a highly differentiated population, it also exercises a leveling influence. . . . This leveling tendency inheres in part in the economic basis of the city. . . . Progressively as cities have developed upon a background of [mass production of standardized products for an impersonal market], the pecuniary nexus which implies the purchasability of services and things has displaced personal relations as the basis of association. Individuality under these circumstances must be replaced by categories. When large numbers have to make common use of facilities and institutions, those facilities and institutions must serve the needs of the average person rather than those of particular individuals . . . the cultural institutions, such as the schools, the movies, the radio, and the newspapers, by virtue of their mass clientele, must necessarily operate as leveling influences. The political process as it appears in urban life could not be understood unless one examined the mass appeals made through modern propaganda techniques. If the individual would participate at all in the social, political, and economic life of the city, he must subordinate some of his individuality to the demands of the larger community and in that measure immerse himself in mass movements. (Wirth, 1938:1–24. Copyright 1938 by the University of Chicago Press. Reprinted by permission.)

woman might simultaneously be a member of Save the Whales, a political party, a baseball team, a church-sponsored social group, and a labor union. Each group represents merely one part of the woman's total interests; none commands her undivided loyalty. Similarly, urbanites relate to one another on the basis of segmented roles—as teachers and students in a classroom, for example, rather than as total human beings who know each other's families, interests, concerns, and so forth.

Like Tönnies, Spengler, and Marx, Wirth insists on the importance of the money economy as a determinant of the urban personality. According to Wirth, the "pecuniary nexus" replaces personal relations as the basis for association in the city. Utility and efficiency replace emotion and intimacy. The result: depersonalization.

For Wirth, then, urbanism leads inevitably to specific forms of social action and personal behavior. For example, urbanites come into contact with too many people to interact in any but a superficial way. Wirth implies that the large, dense, heterogeneous city is such a powerful force in people's lives that they react to this entity in similar ways. That is, urbanites—regardless of race, color, creed, or social rank—react to their physical and social surroundings in a typically urban fashion.

Folk and Urban Societies (Redfield)

American anthropologist Robert Redfield shares Wirth's view that there is a typically urban personality. But Redfield is more interested in the rural end of the continuum, which he calls the "folk society."

In a small, preliterate, homogeneous folk society, Redfield (1947) argues, people treat nature personally. They do not make causal or scientific connections between events. Based on kinship ties and simple technology, a folk society (e.g., the Maya of Yucatan) has a strong sense of social solidarity. Moreover, Redfield argues, members of folk societies have no concept of profit or gain. In contrast, urban society is typified by an entirely different world view; it is secular, commercial, impersonal, and scientific.

Social Action Contexts (Weber)

Strictly speaking, the distinguished German sociologist Max Weber (1864–1920) is not in the rural-to-urban typological tradition. In fact, Weber ([1906] 1960:363) denies that a theorist can "speak collectively of the rural conditions of Russia, Ireland, Sicily, Hungary, and the Black Belt" in order to find a typically rural way of life. Then why is Weber included here? His typology of social action contexts is directly relevant to the typological tradition, especially the theoretical constructs dealing with urban personality.

Weber identifies four contexts in which social action occurs:

1. *Zweckrational* (expedient rationality)
   In this system of action, people consider the alternative means and ends at their disposal and choose the most expedient. Using means-ends rationality, an individual asks, "What's in it for me? Will this course of action serve my own best interests?"
2. *Wertrational*
   Here people choose among alternative ends, but they also hold absolute values which bar the selection of certain means. For instance, a practicing Catholic or Orthodox Jewish woman may not want any more children but finds herself pregnant; her absolute value of preserving life bars the possibility of abortion.
3. *Affectual*
   Here, means and ends become fused. This form of action is dominated by the individual's emotions, not rational calculation.
4. *Traditional*
   In this context, people react almost automatically to habitual stimuli, resulting in conformity to accepted behavior.

For Weber, the trend of modern bureaucratic life in the Western capitalist world is toward expedient rationality. Efficiency, profit, and self-interest replace traditional and affectual considerations. Here Weber echoes Tönnies and Durkheim.

Preindustrial and Industrial Cities (Sjoberg)

Contemporary American sociologist Gideon Sjoberg ([1960] 1965) is not, strictly speaking, in the rural-to-urban tradition either. His typology (detailed in Chapter 4) contrasts two city types: preindustrial and industrial. But Sjoberg's categories essentially deal with two types of societies, not cities: those his predecessors called rural and urban, mechanically solid and organically solid, and sacred and secular.

In Sjoberg's view, technology dictates social, political, and ecological organization. Taking energy sources (animate, such as people or animals, versus inanimate, such as steam or electricity) as his key variable, Sjoberg argues that extensive industrialization requires particular economic, social, and political institutions. An industrial city (dependent on inanimate energy sources) requires a centralized economic organization, a flexible kinship system, mass education, mass communication, and an achievement-oriented social class system. By contrast, a preindustrial city (dependent on animate energy sources) requires face-to-face communication, rigid social differentiation by age and sex, and informal social controls based on kinship, religion, and social rank.

How Useful are the Rural-Urban Typologies?

The late anthropologist Margaret Mead, noted for her outspoken wit as well as her scholarship, once gave this explanation for rural migration: "At least 50 percent of the human race doesn't want their mother-in-law within walking distance." Mead's remark may tell us as much about life in the countryside as the typologies do.

The typologies were constructed as tools for understanding the changes from rural-preindustrial to urban-industrial life. But they remain very limited tools for understanding. Essentially, four kinds of criticism can be leveled at the typologies. These deal with their major hypotheses, empirical evidence, analytical rigor, and contemporary relevance.

The rural-urban typologies have unique aspects, but they share a basic assumption: City and country are fundamentally different ways of life. In other words, the typologies take for granted that people think, feel, behave, and organize their activities differently in rural and urban cultures. (These differences, in general terms, are outlined in Table 5-2.) Further, the theoretical constructs assume that modern urban-industrial life requires or inevitably leads to particular forms of urban personality structure, social organization, and economic-political institutions.

One problem here is that researchers have not yet systematically tested these basic assumptions. In 1951, Louis Wirth warned social scientists not to mistake the "hypothetical characteristics attributed to the urban and rural modes of life for established facts." Wirth (in Hauser, 1967:506–7) added that the hypotheses embedded in the typologies have to be tested in the light of empirical evidence, and that this task had not yet been accomplished. Unfortunately, Wirth's criticism stands to the present day. No one has yet come forward with evidence to substantiate the major hypotheses embedded in the typologies.

Existing empirical evidence, however, does call into question the major hypotheses. The work of George M. Foster goes to the heart of the matter, questioning the assumption that urban and rural modes of life are fundamentally different. Anthropologist Foster (1965) finds many so-called urban personality traits in rural society. According to Foster, peasant societies have an "image of the limited good." That is, the good life is seen as finite and nonexpandable, and an individual can progress only at the expense of others. Cooperative behavior among peasants is perceived as dysfunctional to community stability. The result is that "extreme individualism is chosen over cooperation in preserving peasants' security," discouraging any changes in the status quo (Foster, 1965:310). Moreover, Foster finds that peasants typically express distrust of others, friendlessness, and suspicion of people outside the family. Such an orientation does not lead to the mechanical solidarity or sense of community that Durkheim and Tönnies envisioned. Rather, it leads to structural and psychological atomism.

Other researchers (e.g., Banfield and Banfield, 1958) support Foster's vision of preindustrial communities as fiercely competitive, uncooperative, and contentious. In light of such evidence, Tönnies's conception of *Gemeinschaft* seems a rather romantic vision of a past that never was.

If Foster and others find indifference and friendlessness in the countryside, other researchers find so-called rural personality traits in the city. The fieldwork of Oscar Lewis is illustrative. Anthropologist Lewis studied the "citification" of peasants in Mexico over a number of years. One such rural emigrant, Jesús Sanchez, had lived for over twenty years in a Mexico City slum tenement when Lewis interviewed him again, along with his four children. Their autobiographical

Table 5-2 Rural-to-Urban Typologies

	Preindustrial Rural Community	*Urban Industrial Society*
SPATIAL-GEOGRAPHIC	Cities organized around religious/public buildings, market centers. Symbols: church spires, forts, palaces. Urban places but no urban society. Close links to surrounding, immediate environment. Well-defined neighborhoods by ethnic/tribal group.	Cities organized around economic institutions, business/industry. Symbol: factory smokestacks. Urban society, dense settlements. Urban sprawl. Links to faraway places via communications and transport technology.
ECONOMIC	Nonmarket economy: barter, exchange, or money exchange at a simple level. Wealth measured in land (or cattle, etc.), not money. Agricultural base. Relatively self-sufficient communities. Cottage, handicraft industries. Simple division of labor. Relative self-sufficiency.	Market economy. Cash nexus. Wealth measured in money, capital. Heavy manufacturing base. Interdependence at regional, national, international levels. Complex division of labor. Functional interdependence.
SOCIOCULTURAL	Blood ties, extended family and kinship networks, neighborhood, friendship. Sense of community, belongingness. Face-to-face communication. Primary groups important. Tribal or ethnic cohesion. Homogeneity of culture, beliefs within tribal/ethnic group. Ascribed status.	Blood ties relatively unimportant, individual as primary unit. Segmented roles. Social mobility. Heterogeneity. Urban, urbane culture. Mass communication. Secondary groups important. Alienation, anomie. Achieved status.
POLITICAL	Traditional authority. Sacred traditions. Some experts (e.g., priests) with monopoly over knowledge, but generally widely shared knowledge base. Informal sanctions. Repressive law. Lack of contracts. Dominance by traditional religious/political elites. Family background, connections important.	Legal/rational authority. Secular traditions. Knowledge gap between experts and laypersons. Dominance by merchants, capitalists. Power elites. Occupations and professions among important interest groups. Bureaucracy. Restitutive law, contracts. Merit as principle of advancement rather than family background.

statements, recorded by Lewis in *The Children of Sanchez* (1961), show them to be living refutations of Wirth's urban personality type; they are not uncaring, utilitarian, or blasé.

The thrust of Lewis's research is that there is no such thing as a typically urban personality. He shows that city dwellers have different responses to city life. Indeed, Lewis (1967) argues that Wirth's key variables (large size, high density, and heterogeneity) are not the crucial determinants of the urban personality or urban social life. Lewis advocates studying the varied social areas or neighborhoods in a city, not the city as a whole, in order to understand the various urban personalities.

This brings up a related criticism of the typological tradition: its determinism. The typologies leave no room for varied cultural adaptations to urban-industrial life. Instead, the typologies assume that urbanization and industrialization are such powerful processes that they stamp out cultural and ideological differences.

Yet many examples show that differing value systems and cultural traditions do count heavily in people's adaptations to urban life. In addition to Oscar Lewis's research in Mexico, there are other examples of differential responses to urban life from other continents. In Uganda, for instance, middle-class Ganda tribespeople work in the capital city of Kampala, but they try to live in surrounding rural areas so that they can raise their own subsistence crops. This arrangement permits a strong continuity between rural and urban environments (Southall and Gutkind, 1957). In the sprawling, rapidly growing city of Bangkok, Thailand, to cite another example, traffic seems death-defying to foreigners. Since 1945, Bangkok's population has at least quintupled—to approximately 7 million people—and the streets are packed with people and noisy vehicles of all sorts. Despite this apparent chaos, Bangkok works efficiently and rather harmoniously. Thai architect/city planner Mr. Jumsai (in Kamm, 1978: 9) explains why: Bangkokites were once water people. For centuries they lived on canals, now filled in. But the people still live like water people. They drive their cars and trucks as they used to drive river boats, accommodating and yielding to drivers and pedestrians as they once did on the canals. According to Mr. Jumsai, "Water people adapt to the flow of the current. They go with the forces of nature, not against." This sense of accommodation pervades the social fabric of Bangkok, where overseas Chinese and other ethnic minorities live without apparent friction, unlike the inhabitants of so many cities in South Asia.

Last, there is the example of the Japanese-run factory. The factory has come to symbolize urban-industrial-capitalist life. In Western literature and social science, it has long stood for worker alienation and the loss of human feeling between employers and employees. But the Japanese factory does not fit this image; instead, it is like a family. According to some analysts, Japanese familylike factory relations reflect Japan's feudal past when landlords felt paternalistically responsible for their peasants. Others say that the concept of loyalty (to family, employer, etc.) pervades Japanese culture, including industrial relations.

These examples—Japanese familylike factories, Thai traffic patterns, and Ugandan residential patterns—suggest that we cannot make gross generalizations about *the* nature of city life or *the* personality of urbanites. In short, running a factory, beating the traffic, and living in crowded spaces are common features of urban-industrial life, but *the responses to these constants are different.* We think that *few, if any, personality or social characteristics are necessarily and invariably associated with urbanization and industrialization.*

Of course, we should not forget the Eastern European proverb: " 'For example' is no proof." That is, for every example of how culture mediates a group's adaptation to urban-industrial life, a determinist could respond, "Hey, just wait. It's only a matter of time. Eventually societies with similar economic systems will resemble each other (converge) in their basic institutional structures and world views." This view is called **convergence theory.**

To be even-handed, there is evidence pointing to convergence. For instance, cross-cultural data on occupational prestige rankings show that the same occupations rank high or low in social esteem throughout all urban-industrialized societies. (See Chapter 8 for more detail on this point.) Such data lead followers of Durkheim to reaffirm his sense of evolutionary development: Increases in the division of labor and the specialization of function inevitably lead to particular forms of social solidarity.

No matter which side of the convergence versus cultural adaptation debate one finds more convincing at the present time, there are other serious criticisms of the typologies. These concern their contemporary relevance and their analytical rigor.

First, their relevance in the contemporary world. Even remote rural villages today—whether in Nepal, Tanzania, or Mexico—hardly exist in isolation from the urban environment. Transistor radios, mass education, and international trade agreements provide direct links between countryside and city. Rural communities throughout the world are no longer self-sufficient islands. Instead, even remote villages exist within a world system of political economy.

So, if rural communities are tied to far-flung nations as well as to nearby cities, what rural-urban contrasts make sense today? Should we expect to find meaningful differences in people's attitudes and behavior depending on their rural or urban residence? Scholars disagree here too. One view, called the "massification thesis," holds that rural people in advanced industrial societies become indistinguishable from their city cousins because of mass media, mass education, and other influences which break down rural isolation and diffuse urban culture into the countryside. Another view is that appreciable rural-urban differences persist even in advanced industrial societies (see Glenn and Hill, 1978).

The contemporary relevance of the rural-urban typologies can be questioned on yet other grounds. The nineteenth-century typology builders assumed that European patterns of change would be universal. But the Western pattern—the nearly simultaneous rise of cities, industrialism, and capitalism—is not being repeated in much of the Third World. Hence, attitudes and behavior assumed to be associated with urbanization in Europe and America may not characterize Third World societies now undergoing urbanization.

This brings us to the problem of analytical rigor. The typology builders did not separate the key variables in their hypotheses on urbanization and social change. Which variable—urbanization, industrialization, or capitalism—supposedly leads inevitably, invariably, and necessarily to urbanism as a way of life? The typologies do not specify. Rather, they assume that these three processes go hand in hand. But individualism, to take just one supposed trait of the urban personality, may not be a necessary ingredient of urbanization per se. Individualism may not develop in an urban-industrial-*socialist* society. Moreover, if Foster's description of rural society and Kitto's account of the Greek polis are correct, individualism is not particularly an urban-industrial trait at all; it can exist in rural-agricultural communities too.

This is a serious criticism of the typologies: They make too much of the supposed differences between rural and urban traits to begin with. The typologies assume a fundamental contrast between modern urban personalities and traditional rural personalities. The assumption that modern urbanites have greater faith in science and technology than in religion for controlling events merits special attention in this regard. If that assumption is correct, how can we explain the mass suicide and murder of over 900 Americans who followed the command of their spiritual leader, Jim Jones, to die in Guyana? One explanation was offered by the well-known evangelist Billy Graham: "It was the work of Satan." This explanation and the events at the People's Temple in Jonestown occurred in 1978, not in the midst of preindustrial society. Thus, the differences between urban and rural personalities do not seem all that clear.

To conclude: We view the rural-urban typologies as limited tools for understanding the shift from rural-preindustrial to urban-industrial life. First, they have never been systematically tested. They remain *articles of faith* based more on historical imagination than on scientific research. Second, they are *deterministic.* The typological tradition comes out of a nineteenth-century Darwinian world view of unilinear evolution. It cannot account for significant differences within preindustrial communities or industrial societies. Third, the typologies are *ethnocentric.* They assume that what happened in Western Europe—particularly the hand-in-hand development of urbanization, industrialization, and capitalism—will happen universally. This has not been the case in much of the Third World. Fourth, they rest on a *dubious assumption:* that the transformation from rural-agricultural to urban-industrial life requires, or inevitably leads to, a radical change in the nature of human personality. To begin with, they make too much of the differences between city and country, between traditional community and modern society.

Instinctively, we may feel that the sense of community is not the same in the Athenian polis and the American metropolis. We sense that life in a tribal village and medieval London are somehow different. Of course, there are differences between everyday life in a polis and a metropolis. But it is dangerous to attribute the differences to urbanization alone. The effects of industrialization, cultural values and world-views, varied economic arrangements, and other variables have to be carefully unscrambled when assessing the rural-urban shift in various societies. So far, this has not been done. Instead, theorists have accomplished only what poet William Carlos Williams (1953:11) advised against:

> To make a start
> out of particulars
> and make them general, rolling
> up to the sum, by defective means.

ANOTHER LOOK

Looking back on the material presented in this chapter, one basic theme emerges: Theorists fundamentally disagree on the nature of urbanization and urbanism. Their disagreements are not rooted in their disciplinary backgrounds or their research methods. For example, anthropologists Robert Redfield and Oscar Lewis both studied the same Mexican village using fieldwork methods. They came to very different conclusions about the nature of rural life. Similarly, theorists do not agree on the nature of urban life. Disagreements do stem from differences in (1) levels of analysis and (2) theoretical orientations.

1. *Levels of analysis.* Tönnies, Durkheim, and Spengler are macro-level theorists interested in the broad sweep of change from rural to urban society. Hence, they focus on entire social systems in their analysis of urbanization and urbanism. Louis Wirth, investigating the urban personality, uses the entire city as his unit of analysis. Other theorists, notably Lewis, argue that neither entire social systems nor the city as a whole are proper units for studying social life or human personality. Lewis claims that large numbers, high density, and heterogeneity are not crucial determinants of either urban social life or the urban personality because both occur in smaller universes—families,

neighborhoods, and so on. Thus, Lewis advises using smaller units of analysis to study the urbanization process and urbanism. Using micro-level analysis, theorists often find many ways of life coexisting within the same city, not a single urban way of life.

2. *Theoretical orientations.* Both structural-functionalists and Marxist-oriented scholars pay little attention to cross-cultural differences in their analysis of modern urban life. They think that, in the long run, technological and economic imperatives will render cultural differences insignificant. This determinism is rejected by theorists who insist that values, cultural traditions, and particular historical conditions can influence social organization in important ways. Thus, structural-functionalists (e.g., followers of Durkheim) and Marxist-oriented theorists tend to view urbanization in the capitalist West as a single, unitary process with similar effects on human personality; others tend to stress the different forms and meanings that urbanization and urbanism have taken.

To integrate the insights from these opposing camps is impossible. No synthesis can occur given their strong division on such key issues as the nature of rural life or the effects of urbanization.

PROJECTS

1. **The division of labor.** Using historical materials and current U.S. Department of Labor data, compare and contrast the range of occupations in the Athenian polis, a medieval town, and a modern American city. Do your findings support Durkheim's dichotomy between a relatively simple division of labor in a mechanically solid society and a complex division of labor in an organically solid society?

2. **Urbanism as a way of life: The view from Hollywood.** Whether or not mass media productions reflect or create social reality is a much debated issue. Either way, we can assume that a mass medium is an important conveyor of social values and images.

In terms of images of urban life, we can assume that movies have influenced more people than Louis Wirth's classic essay. This leads to the following research question: Do commercially successful films reinforce or contradict Wirth's concept of urbanism as a single way of life? To investigate this question, view several films (examples: *Manhattan, Rocky, Taxi Driver, The Wanderers, Kramer vs. Kramer*) and analyze their content in terms of Wirth's notions of (a) the superficial, transitory character of urban social relations and (b) competition and formal control mechanisms as substitutes for bonds of kinship and common values.

SUGGESTIONS FOR FURTHER LEARNING

Because the concept of community is important in social science and humanistic fields, there are countless works that deal with the topic. These include empirical studies, theoretical works, first-hand accounts, and flights of fantasy. A good starting place is the discipline of sociology because the concept of community is a fundamental or "unit-idea" of sociological thought. The development of modern social thought on community is discussed by Robert A. Nisbet in *The Sociological Tradition* (New York: Basic Books, 1966). For a wide variety of views on community, including novelistic accounts, see David W. Minar and Scott Greer's reader with interpretations, *The Concept of Community* (Chicago: Aldine, 1969). This reader contains a section on "Politics and Community" with selections from Aristotle to Theodore H. White.

Classic works on community include Emile Durkheim, *The Division of Labor in Society* (New York: Free Press, [1893] 1964); Karl Marx, *Das Kapital* (New York: Modern Library, [1867] 1936); Claude-Henri de Saint-Simon, *On the Reorganization of European Society* (1814); Georg Simmel, *Philosophy of Money* (London: Routledge and Kegan Paul, [1900] 1978); Ferdinand Tönnies, *Com-*

munity and Society (New York: Harper & Row, [1887] 1963); and Auguste Comte, *The Positive Polity* (New York: Burt Franklin, [1851–1854] 1966). Essays of the German school (Weber, Simmel, Spengler) and the Chicago school (Park, Wirth, Redfield) appear in Richard Sennett's reader, *Classic Essays on the Culture of Cities* (New York: Appleton-Century-Crofts, 1969).

Day-to-day life in rural-preindustrial communities is perhaps best described by film makers, novelists, and other image makers. Among the most moving accounts of a traditional community is Ermanno Olmi's remarkable film *The Tree of Wooden Clogs* (1978). In telling the story of peasant life in Italy around the turn of the twentieth century, Olmi captures the ethos of *Gemeinschaft* and the ironies of its alleged social cohesion and bonds of friendship. Other excellent evocations of rural life can be found in historian Emmanuel Le Roy Ladurie's dramatic history of a town in southern France during the Inquisition, *Montaillou* (New York: Braziller, 1978); Camara Laye's *The African Child: Memories of a West African Childhood* (London: Fontana, 1962), and Robert Flaherty's pioneering documentary film of an Eskimo family, *Nanook of the North* (1922).

The shift from self-sufficient rural community to modern urban society is the theme of many nineteenth-century novels as well as later artistic works. A vivid account of the rural-to-urban shift is found in the novels of Honoré de Balzac, a conservative, aristocratic French writer who mourned the passing of traditional community and despised bourgeois capitalism. Orson Welles's film *The Magnificent Ambersons* (1942), based on a Booth Tarkington novel, depicts the impact of industrialization (particularly the automobile) on a small American town and the consequent changes in social structure. A film series produced by the American Universities Field Staff (1975) uses documentary evidence from five Third World cultures to portray the shift from traditional to modern society and the *Faces of Change.*

That observers disagree on the nature of the rural personality and rural life is clear from several recent studies. In his ethnographic autobiography, *The Horse of Pride: Life in a Breton Village* (New Haven: Yale University Press, 1978), Pierre Jakez-Hélias describes peasant life (which was dying as he grew up after World War I) as a triumph of the spirit. But historian Eugen Weber doubts whether the alleged simplicity of rural peasant life had much to offer. In Weber's *Peasants into Frenchmen: The Modernization of Rural France 1870–1914* (Stanford, Calif.: Stanford University Press, 1978), Weber notes that rural French folk willingly left the old ways behind. In terms of the American experience, Michael Lesy delves into the historical records of several Wisconsin counties in the late nineteenth century and finds a bleak way of life. His *Wisconsin Death Trip* (New York: Pantheon, 1973) paints a picture of rural mental illness, suicide, loneliness, and lack of community.

The psychological impact of urbanism is the subject of *The City and the Self* (1973), a film produced by Time-Life Multimedia. It explores the anonymity, aloofness, and indifference of urban life.

Concerning the nature of urbanization in the Third World, see sociologist Bryan Roberts's *Cities of Peasants* (Beverly Hills, Calif.: Sage, 1979). It traces the expansion of capitalism in the Third World and its impact on people in Third World cities; there is also a critical review of current notions about urbanization in developing countries.

The sense of being between two worlds—community and society—is hauntingly revealed in "The Long Walk of Fred Young," an episode on the Public Broadcasting System's *Nova* series (telecast Jan. 11, 1979). Fred Young is a Navajo who hunted barefoot as a child and works as a nuclear physicist as an adult.

KEY TERMS

Community A concept with numerous meanings, often used without precise definition. It can refer to a traditional community in the sense of *Gemeinschaft;* a group which shares nothing more than a territorial area; or a group which shares common values and culture without a common territorial area (e.g., an occupational group).

Convergence theory Macro-level social theory which predicts that over time advanced industrial societies will develop similar traits despite their cultural or ideological differences in order to fulfill similar functions.

Cosmopolis From the Greek, meaning "world city." A cosmopolitan person is one whose identification and involvement are with a larger social universe than the local community.

Division of labor Social differentiation within a society by task specialization or occupational role. This concept is central to both economic and sociological theory.

Ideal type A mental construct used as a heuristic device to describe, compare, and test hypotheses. An ideal type is not meant to correspond exactly to any particular case in the observable world; rather, it is designed as a tentative model. Examples: *Gemeinschaft, Gesellschaft.*

Mechanical and organic solidarity Durkheim's contrasting types of social solidarity. Mechanically solid societies are based on similar values, tradition, kinship, and a simple division of labor; organically solid societies are based on a complex division of labor requiring cooperation among heterogeneous people. Organic solidarity is so named because, in Durkheim's view, it is similar to the human body, in which specialized organs have to function interdependently if the entire organism is to survive.

Polis From the Greek, usually translated as "city-state." A self-sufficient, small-scale political unit. It was not much like a modern nation-state, and it was much more than a city.

Social cohesion Integrated group behavior resulting from social bonds or social forces cementing members together over time. To achieve it, group members accept the group's goals and standards of behavior.

Urbanism Patterns of social interaction and culture that result from the concentration of large numbers of people in small areas. The concept is also used to convey the idea that in advanced industrial societies, urban values, culture, and modes of social organization have spread even to rural areas.

REFERENCES

Achebe, Chinua
[1959]
1974 Things Fall Apart. Greenwich, Conn.: Fawcett.

Banfield, Edward and L. F. Banfield
1958 The Moral Basis of a Backward Society. New York: Free Press.

Durkheim, Emile
[1893]
1964 The Division of Labor in Society. New York: Free Press.

Foster, George
1965 "Peasant society and the image of limited good." American Anthropologist 67:293–315.

Glenn, Norval D. and Lester Hill, Jr.
1978 "Rural-urban differences in attitude and behavior in the United States." Pp. 12–20 in Jacqueline Scherer (ed.), Annual Editions. Guilford, Conn.: Dushkin.

Goode, William
1957 "Community within a community: the professions." American Sociological Review 23:194–200.

Hauser, Philip M.
1967 "Observations on the urban-folk and urban-rural dichotomies as forms of western ethnocentrism." Pp. 503–17 in Philip M. Hauser and Leo F. Schnore (eds.), The Study of Urbanization. New York: Wiley.

Kahler, Erich
1957 The Tower and the Abyss. New York: Braziller.

Kamm, Henry
1978 "Life in Bangkok: river tradition makes it work." New York Times (Nov. 19):9.

Kitto, H. D. F.
1951 The Greeks. Baltimore: Penguin.

Lewis, Oscar
1961 The Children of Sanchez. New York: Random House.
1967 "Further observations on the folk-urban continuum and urbanization with special reference to Mexico City." Pp. 491–503 in Philip M. Hauser and Leo F. Schnore (eds.), The Study of Urbanization. New York: Wiley.

Nance, John
1975 The Gentle Tasaday: A Stone Age People in the Philippine Rain Forest. New York: Harcourt Brace Jovanovich.

Polanyi, Karl, Harry W. Pearson, and Conrad M. Arensberg
1957 Trade and Market in the Early Empires: Economics in History and Theory. Glencoe, Ill.: Free Press.

Redfield,Robert
1947 "The folk society." American Journal of Sociology 52:293–308.

Sjoberg, Gideon
[1960]
1965 The Pre-Industrial City. New York: Free Press.

Southall, Aidan and Peter C. W. Gutkind
1957 Townsmen in the Making: Kampala and its Suburbs. Kampala, Uganda: East Africa Institute of Social Research.

Spengler, Oswald
[1918]
1962 The Decline of the West. New York: Knopf.

Stone, I. F.
1979 "I. F. Stone breaks the Socrates story." New York Times magazine (Apr. 8): 22+.

Tönnies, Ferdinand
[1887]
1963 Community and Society. New York: Harper & Row.

Weber, Max
[1906]
1960 "Capitalism and rural society in Germany." Pp. 363–85 in H. H. Gerth and C. Wright Mills (tr., eds.), From Max Weber. New York: Oxford University Press.

Williams, William Carlos
1953 Paterson. London: Peter Owen.

Wirth, Louis
1938 "Urbanism as a way of life." American Journal of Sociology 44:1–24.

Bill Owens

"The Masons is the oldest fraternal organization in the world. As a Mason you are never down and out. There is always a brother to help you."

CHAPTER 6 Communities Present and Future

All those lonely people . . . Strangers everywhere, going who-knows-where. Nowhere people. Lonely crowds, hearing only the sounds of silence. People who don't care about other people . . .

That is a popular image of life in the big city. As a friend from a small town in Texas wondered when she moved to a major **metropolis,** "Don't people here know we're all in the same cotton field together?"

Many popular images, including this one of lonely crowds in the metropolis, have some grounding in everyday experience. Yet this view of urbanites as isolated and unfeeling needs to be qualified. City dwellers aren't as disconnected from one another as the popular image would lead us to believe.

Also, the image of the rural, small-town past—where like-minded people cared deeply for one another in a well-ordered, stable community—is rather idyllic, existing more in theory than in reality. Still, that cozy, imagined world is compelling, especially for those of us who have lived in lonely crowds. How humane the ideal of traditional community seems: a way of life built on close social bonds, friendship, mutual caring, and personal security. But recall, too, the other face of traditional rural life. How many of us today would choose to submit to authority in the form of a mother-in-law or hereditary rulers? How many would want to spend our whole lives interacting mainly with blood relatives? As Margaret Mead implies, there is another and less attractive face of community: distrust of outsiders, lack of privacy, conformity to convention and authority, adherence to tradition. In addition, both social and geographic mobility are very limited. This feature seems especially unattractive for the majority of us who would have been unfortunate enough to be born serfs, slaves, and underlings rather than landlords, princesses, and rulers.

Many contemporary voices bemoan the loss of community and seek to reestablish it. Some advocate a wholesale rejection of Western technology and democratic tradition, substituting a religious way of life for so-called modernism. Russian exile Aleksandr Solzhenitsyn and Iran's Ayatollah Khomeini exemplify this approach. Others want to establish a sense of "we-ness" within advanced technological societies, looking to encounter groups, religious cults, or new settlements as vehicles for creating community. We will return to various types of community seekers after examining what is called, rightly or wrongly, metropolitan community.

SOCIAL CEMENT IN THE METROPOLIS

V. S. Naipaul, whose novels deal with Third World countries now emerging from a tribal or caste tradition into an uncertain modernity, says, "I feel no nostalgia for the miserable security of the old ways." For most people in modern society, "the miserable security of the old ways" is not even an option. Urbanism may not be a single way of life, as Wirth theorized, but it certainly does entail constant change, not the continuity of traditional community. Institutions, and traditions that once promoted a sense of personal security, however miserable, no longer fulfill that function for many urbanites. What, then, helps to bind contemporary urbanites together?

We get few clues from popular culture. In Woody Allen's movie *Manhattan* (1979), for instance, the main characters seem alone and adrift, dwarfed by New York City's skyline. The city itself is a major character in the film: the home of alienation and spiritual corruption as well as the hub of vitality and urbanity. But nowhere in the film do viewers get a sense of forces working to cement social bonds in urban-industrial society. There are no neighbors; no family or friends who can be counted on—always; no subcommunities, professional or ethnic, that provide support to the characters.

What movies like *Manhattan* do not, perhaps cannot, portray is a force that helps bind urbanites together: functional interdependence stemming from the complex division of labor. This interdependence is so abstract that it is difficult to show artistically.

Here is how functional interdependence works. Unless you limit travel to where your feet can take you, grow all your own food, entertain yourself without mass media, and buy nothing that must be paid for in money, you depend on countless people to sustain your daily existence. A brief list of goods and services suggests just how dependent on strangers we are: coal from Harlan County, Kentucky; bananas from Latin America; records from Nashville; newsprint from Canada; and a plumber from the Yellow Pages.

In urban-industrial society, people do not necessarily know one another. Nonetheless, they need one another. As Durkheim suggested in his model of organically solid society, the specialization of labor gives rise to functional interdependence.

Psychologically, we may not realize how much our daily activities are linked to other people's functions until our lives suffer disruption. A reduction in Mideast oil supplies or a strike of municipal employees remind us how much we depend on anonymous people.

Indeed, we are so functionally interdependent and specialized that we need one expert to find another expert. This is clear to anyone suffering from a rare illness. Finding a specialist to diagnose and treat the ailment requires the advice of other specialists. With the continuing expansion of knowledge and the "expertization" of almost everyone, we become increasingly dependent on the skill and good will of strangers throughout the world.

Measuring Functional Interdependence

Supplying a wide range of goods and services to residents of a geographical area requires a complex network of mutually sustaining activities. Measuring the extent of this network in spatial terms is one way of defining or delimiting a **metropolitan community** or **metropolitan area.**

The journey-to-work pattern between a city and its surrounding area is probably the most common measure of metropolitan community. According to Roderick D. McKenzie's classic book *The Metropolitan Community* (1933:84), the metropolitan area is "the territory in which the daily economic and social activities of the local population are carried on through a common system of institutions. It is essentially the commutation area of the central city." Here McKenzie implies that a metropolitan area is essentially an integrated *labor market,* measured by the number of people who live in the surrounding area and commute to the central city for work.

Another measure of interdependence between a city and its outlying areas is the extent of communication networks. For instance, how far away from San Jose, California, are San Jose newspapers read? At what geographical locations do people begin to read papers from San Francisco or other cities? Newspaper circulation areas, telephone calling areas, and TV viewing areas can indicate the extent of socioeconomic interdependence within a metropolitan area.

Standard Metropolitan Statistical Area (SMSA)

There is no one right way to measure the extent of a metropolitan area. What is important is that all concerned— scholars, government agencies, city planners, etc.—use the same measure. Otherwise, it is impossible to collect comparable data.

For this reason (to standardize the measurement of interdependence between a city and its surrounding area), the U.S. government developed the concept of a **Standard Metropolitan Statistical Area (SMSA).** As its name implies, the SMSA is not a political

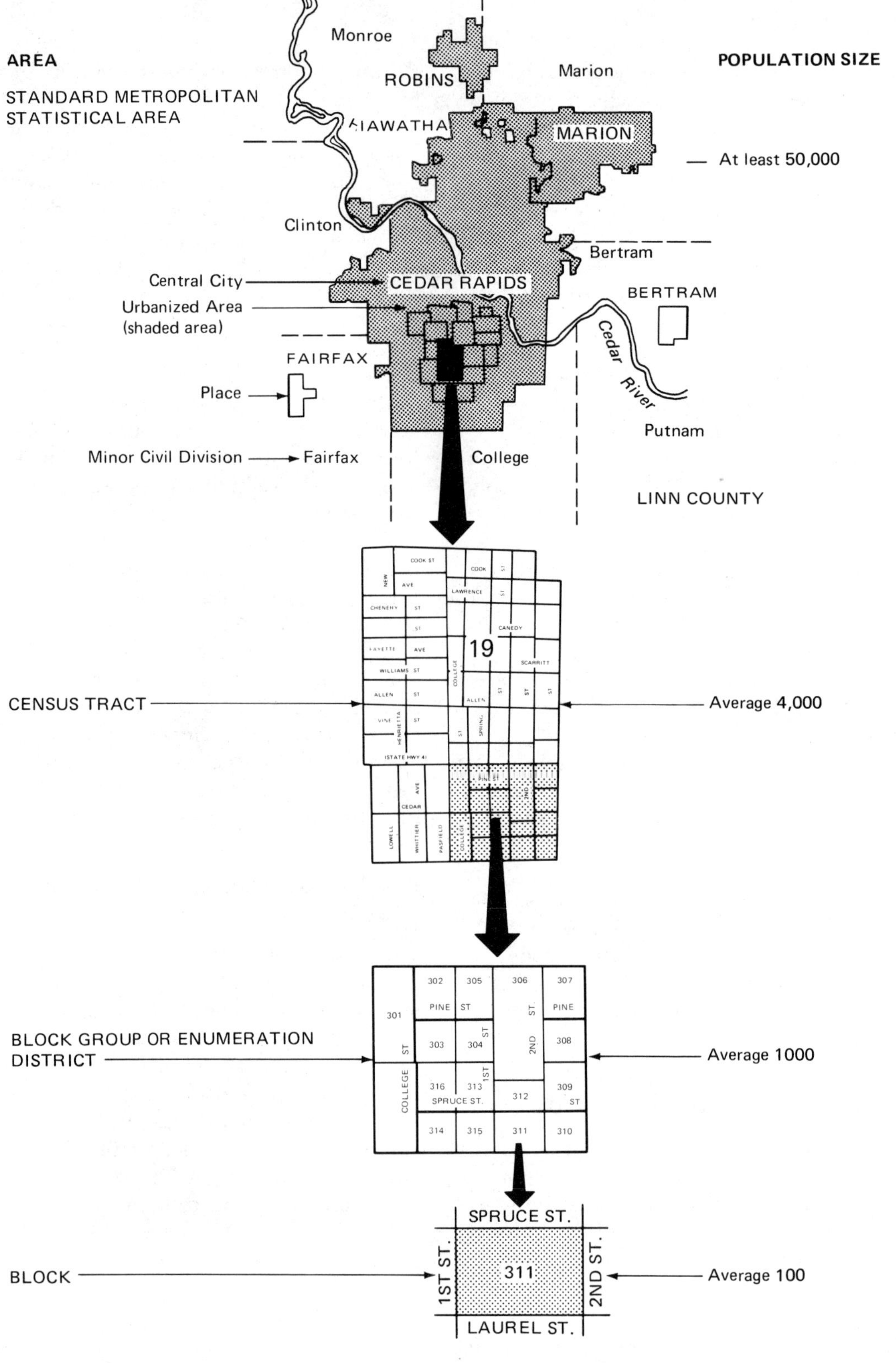
AREA
STANDARD METROPOLITAN STATISTICAL AREA
POPULATION SIZE
Monroe
ROBINS
Marion
MARION
At least 50,000
Clinton
Bertram
Central City
CEDAR RAPIDS
Urbanized Area (shaded area)
BERTRAM
FAIRFAX
Cedar River
Place
Putnam
Minor Civil Division
Fairfax
College
LINN COUNTY
19
CENSUS TRACT
Average 4,000
302
305
306
307
301
PINE
ST
303
304
2ND
308
316
313
1ST
309
SPRUCE ST.
312
COLLEGE
314
315
311
310
BLOCK GROUP OR ENUMERATION DISTRICT
Average 1000
SPRUCE ST.
1ST ST.
311
2ND ST.
LAUREL ST.
BLOCK
Average 100

unit; it is nothing more than a geostatistical creation.

First introduced in the 1950 census (in a slightly different form), the SMSA has been used widely by U.S. government agencies as a uniform area for data gathering, data analysis, and publication of statistics. Fig. 6-1 displays the component parts of an SMSA for which census data are available: SMSA, county, **central city,** urbanized area, place, minor civil division, **census tract,** block group or enumeration district, and block. Census data are also available for the United States as a whole, as well as for regions, states, and several more specialized statistical units.

Before describing the criteria used to define an SMSA, we should note how the U.S. Census Bureau defines and operationalizes some rather ambiguous terms, including "urban," "rural," and "central city." Here are some useful census definitions to keep in mind.

Urban places. Three different kinds of places are considered urban:

1. Any incorporated municipality with at least 2,500 people.
2. The densely settled urban fringe (often unincorporated areas).
3. An unincorporated place with at least 2,500 people located outside an urban fringe area.

Urbanized area. A subcategory of urban places. An urbanized area consists of a city with at least 50,000 people plus its adjoining urban fringe.

Rural places. All places not defined as urban. Rural places are subdivided into rural-farm and rural-nonfarm categories.

Central city. The central city is the SMSA's core—the city (or cities) around which an SMSA is formed. It must meet minimum population standards. Every place in the SMSA minus the central city is called the "outside central city."

These census categories do not solve all the problems of classification. For instance, a farming community of 3,000 people is classified as an "urban place," which can be misleading. But at least the categories are standard so that uniform data can be collected.

Now, back to the SMSA. Except in New England and Alaska, an SMSA is an *entire county or a group of contiguous counties which contain at least one central city having at least 50,000 inhabitants (or "twin cities" with a combined population of at least 50,000). Contiguous (adjoining) counties are included in an SMSA if they meet certain criteria of metropolitan character and socioeconomic integration with the central city. These criteria, outlined below, reveal that the SMSA is viewed essentially as an economic unit.* More specifically, it is defined in the same way that sociologist McKenzie defined the metropolitan area—as an integrated labor market. (An integrated labor market can be described as "the smallest area that is large enough to contain the workplaces of most of the people who reside in it, and the residences of most of the people who work in it." [Heilbrun, 1974:21])

Note that the entire county is the basic political unit of an SMSA, except in the New England states and Alaska. (For historical reasons, New England SMSAs are composed of cities and towns instead of counties. The

Fig. 6-1 COMPONENTS OF A STANDARD METROPOLITAN STATISTICAL AREA. An SMSA is an integrated economic and social unit with a large population center, the central city. This chart illustrates the hierarchical relationship among units within the SMSA for which U.S. Census Data is available. (Adapted from U.S. Bureau of the Census, *Census Geography* [October, 1978])

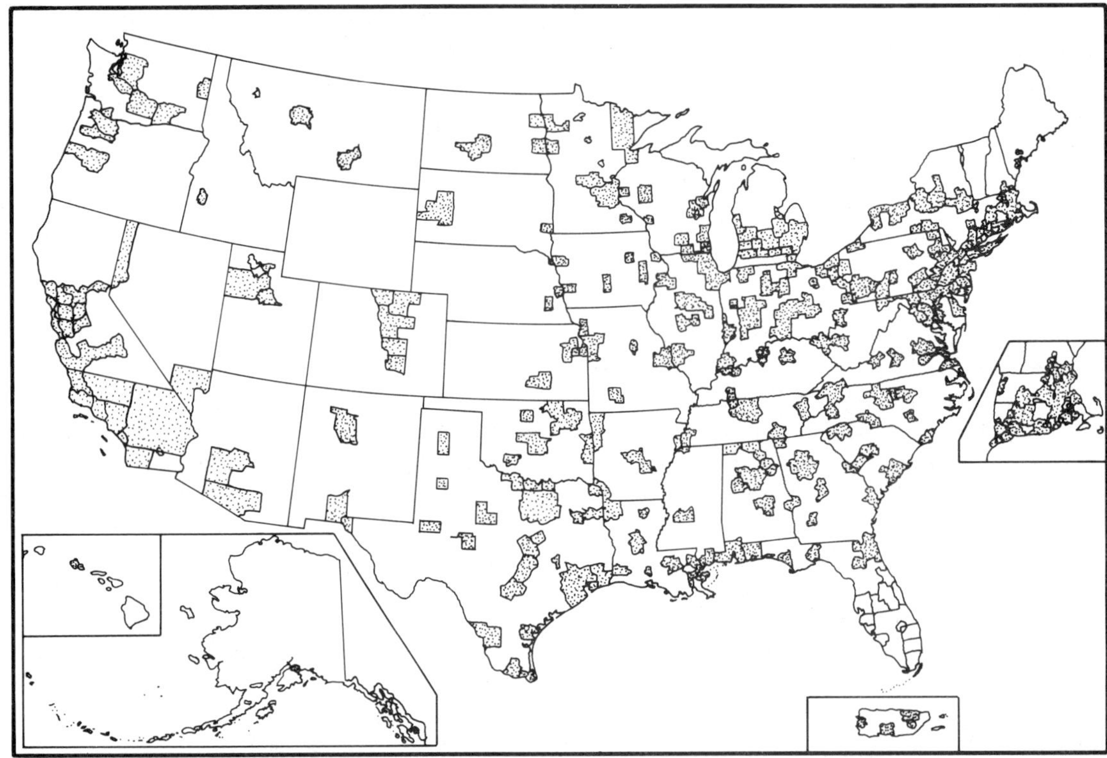

Fig. 6.2 SMSAs AS OF 1979. (U.S. Bureau of the Census)

minimum population standard for New England central cities is 75,000, not 50,000. In Alaska, there are no counties; census divisions are used for defining SMSAs.)

A county contiguous to the central city's county must meet several criteria of metropolitan character and integration to be included in an SMSA. First, at least 75 percent of the resident labor force in the contiguous county must do nonagricultural work. Second, at least 30 percent of the work force living in the contiguous county must work in the central city's county (this is McKenzie's "commutation area" definition), or the contiguous county must meet a series of other requirements based on commuting patterns, population density, population increase, and/or "urbanness." In other words, the Census Bureau uses the journey-to-work as a key indicator that the population around a central city forms a metropolitan system.

A metropolitan system, based on functional interdependence, does not stop at political boundaries. SMSAs can, and often do, cross state lines. Interstate SMSAs are common in the Northeast and Midwest, but they are rare in the Far West.

Also, metropolitan systems change over time; thus, so do SMSA boundaries. For instance, before 1963, Solano County, California, was included in the San Francisco-Oakland SMSA; in 1963, it became part of a newly created SMSA. This development reflects changing patterns of economic interdependence.

Over time, the number of SMSAs also changes. In the 1970 census there were 243 SMSAs in the United States and 4 in Puerto Rico, for a total of 247. By 1979 there were 284 SMSAs in the United States plus 4 in Puerto Rico, totaling 288.

Standard Consolidated Statistical Area (SCSA) or Megalopolis

When SMSAs themselves are "socially and economically closely related," these areas are combined into a supermetropolitan category by the Census Bureau. Such an area is called a **Standard Consolidated Statistical Area (SCSA).** Popularly, a metropolitan complex of this kind is often called a **megalopolis.**

An SCSA always includes *two or more contiguous SMSAs* which meet specific criteria of size, urban character, integration, and contiguity of urbanized areas. One of the constituent SMSAs must have a population of at least 1,000,000, and at least 75 percent of the population of each SMSA must be classified as urban. There are additional criteria concerning journey-to-work patterns between the two (or more) SMSAs and the sharing of the urbanized area around the central city.

In recent years, the number of supermetropolitan areas has increased. (In part, this reflects changes in the definition. Before 1976, such areas were called Standard Consolidated Areas, and there were only two—the metropolitan complexes around New York City and Chicago.) By 1977, there were thirteen SCSAs.

Changing Definitions

Starting in 1982, the U.S. Census Bureau will use new standards to define metropolitan areas. In brief, the most important changes are: (1) The SMSA will be replaced by the Metropolitan Statistical Area (MSA). Like the SMSA, the MSA is a large population nucleus together with adjacent areas that are highly integrated with that population nucleus. The definition of MSAs is made in terms of entire counties (except in New England). MSAs are classified into four levels based on total population size: Level A—1,000,000 inhabitants or more; Level B—250,000–1,000,000 inhabitants; Level C—100,000–250,000 inhabitants; Level D—100,000 inhabitants or less. (2) Subareas within Level A MSAs will be designated Primary Metropolitan Statistical Areas (PMSAs) if strong economic and social links exist within them. (3) Level A MSAs composed of two or more PMSAs will be designated a Consolidated Metropolitan Statistical Area (CMSA). The CMSA replaces the SCSA.

Where Are We Headed?

Will most Americans soon be living in a handful of giant SCSAs with 10 to 50 million inhabitants? Some observers think so. The late architect-planner Constantin Doxiades, for one, prophesied the coming of SCSA-like supercities. Others, however, foresee another future: a large-scale movement back to the countryside, to a new kind of rural society. These visionaries argue that new communications and transport technologies will radically change where people live and work in the postindustrial society. Instead of commuting to work, for instance, some will "communicate to work" (via computer and video systems). Others will commute from rural areas to faraway cities by very rapid transportation.

So, which is it—or are we headed in both directions?

True, we can't forecast the future with any certainty. However, we have no rational choice but to attempt to anticipate it. Before looking ahead to alternative futures—ranging from the new rural society and supercities to cities in the sky—let us first reexamine where we have been, this time focusing on major population shifts and the transformation of community life in the United States.

POPULATION SHIFTS

Looking back, we see how rapidly the United States was transformed from a collection of farms and small towns into a metropolitan nation. A few numbers will illustrate this shift from rural to urban and then to metropolitan life.

From Rural to Urban

In 1790, only 5.1 percent of the U.S. population lived in urban places. By 1850, this number had increased to only 15 percent.

The year 1920 was a landmark. For the first time in the nation's history, more Americans lived in urban centers than in rural areas. However, urban growth was uneven. Very large cities grew faster than smaller ones due to the centralization of industry there. This pattern of centralization of people and industry is important because it set the pattern of urban settlement from 1920 to 1970. Indeed, even after thirty years of regional decentralization, the pattern of centralization was still apparent in 1970: 45 percent of the nation's population lived on 15 percent of the land area in the continental forty-eight states. Further, this small core produced much more than its share of economic wealth and power. Those people living on 15 percent of the land generated 55 percent of the national income and "a far higher proportion of the higher levels of economic decision making" (Morrill, 1978:435). So, the pattern set by 1920 held in 1970: a significant degree of economic concentration in which the largest cities generated the greatest wealth.

From Urban to Suburban

The year 1920 also marked the start of another long-standing trend: the movement away from central cities. Just as the United States became an urban nation in 1920, suburbs started growing at a faster rate than central cities. By 1970, more people lived around U.S. cities than within them.

This major population shift—from central city to outside central city—has various names: "suburbanization," "metropolitanization," and "urban sprawl." Whatever it is called, it happened quickly. In fact, the transformation of America from an urban to a metropolitan or suburban nation took place in only fifty years (1920–1970), much faster than the rural-to-urban shift.

By 1970, the United States was a metropolitan nation. The majority of people—140 million, or 70 percent—lived within SMSAs. Perhaps more important, of this population, the majority (76 million) lived *outside* central cities.

Out-migration from central city to outside central city began in the nineteenth century. Streetcars and railroads made suburban areas more accessible to the well-to-do and socially prestigious groups. Suburban development did not boom, however, until after World War II. Between 1950 and 1970, suburbs grew from 30 million to 76 million residents. This massive population shift was encouraged by a host of federal government programs, from a $2-billion-a-year highway construction program to FHA and VA mortgage guarantees. Such federal support led to a suburban housing boom, permitting a mass exodus from central cities by white, middle-class, and some working-class Americans.

From Metropolitan Back to the Land?

One recent population shift is noteworthy because it reverses long-standing trends towards centralization and metropolitanization: the population boom in rural America. In the early 1970s, for the first time in this century, the nonmetropolitan growth rate exceeded the growth rate within SMSAs. More precisely, between 1970 and 1975, SMSAs gained population at the rate of 3.6 percent, while non-SMSAs grew at the rate of 6.3 percent. Entirely rural counties—not adjacent to SMSAs and having no urban places—were the fastest-growing areas in the early 1970s (Morrison, 1978).

Rural Oregon is one of these fast-growing areas. In fact, it became so popular in the early 1970s that Oregon's governor actively discouraged newcomers. As motorists crossed the state line from California, they were greeted with a highway sign inviting them to "enjoy your *visit*," with the implied plea, "but please don't settle down here."

Why are the rural areas becoming so attractive? Trying to find out, Moen and Martin (1978) asked people why they decided to move to rural Oregon when their company opened a plant there, or why they decided to stay in the San Francisco Bay Area. Their sample of people interviewed, while small and non-random, provides some clues to the new rural migration. Moen and Martin found that social bonds (involvement with family, friends, and community) were not important factors in the decision to move or stay. Two factors were important: economic bonds (involvement with career, spouse's work) and perceptions of the natural and cultural environment. Interestingly, urban amenities in the Bay Area, including sports, restaurants, and cultural events, did keep some from leaving. But for the movers, the natural environment was a big *pull* to the countryside. Also, the perceived urban disadvantages (crowding, traffic, noise, pollution, lack of personal safety) were a big *push* away from the metropolis. The movers to Oregon thought that such intangibles as a higher quality of life and peace of mind would be easier to obtain in rural Oregon than metropolitan California.

In other regions, rural persons are returning to their land and families. For example, waves of migrants are leaving Northern industrial cities for their ancestral homes in places like Corbin, Kentucky. With decentralization of employment, easier access to open space, more persons living on pensions, and the spread of retirement communities, many places once regarded as "nowhere" have now became "somewhere" (see Morrison, 1978).

From Frostbelt to Sunbelt

Another important population shift, starting about 1950, concerns interregional migration. Popularly, this shift is called the "yankee versus cowboy" phenomenon or the move from Frostbelt to Sunbelt.

Before 1950, people moved from the economically depressed Southern states to Northern industrial cities. In the 1950s, this pattern was reversed; population began flowing *to* the South—and the West.

By the 1970s, the broad band of Southern states from Florida to southern California called the "Sunbelt" took the lead in population growth. A sunnier climate had some impact, but more important were jobs and economic expansion. Private business decisions and federal government policies encouraged the massive migration. Gigantic post-World War II industries spread to the Deep South, Texas, southern California, and throughout the Sunbelt. Leading the list of new or expanded Sunbelt industries were oil

a

b

c

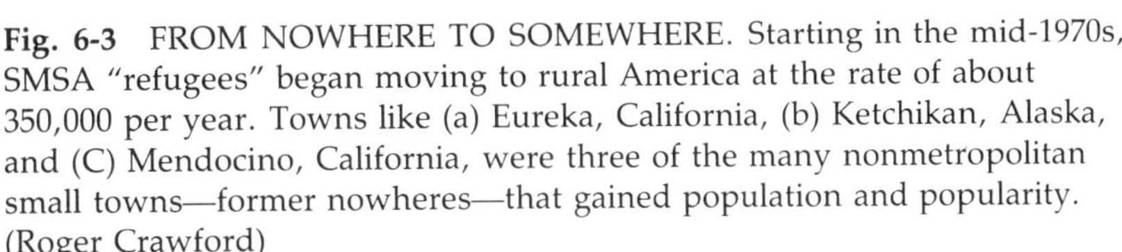

Fig. 6-3 FROM NOWHERE TO SOMEWHERE. Starting in the mid-1970s, SMSA "refugees" began moving to rural America at the rate of about 350,000 per year. Towns like (a) Eureka, California, (b) Ketchikan, Alaska, and (C) Mendocino, California, were three of the many nonmetropolitan small towns—former nowheres—that gained population and popularity. (Roger Crawford)

and gas extraction, electronics, agribusiness, aerospace, and defense-related production. After World War II, the federal government spent billions of dollars to provide infrastructure (highways, irrigation projects, etc.) to the Sunbelt and to support the newly established defense-related industries there.

Interpreting the Population Trends

The analysis of population shifts can provide clues to the changing patterns of economic well-being and political power in the nation's SMSAs and regions. It is a widely held opinion among urbanists that population and employment trends are good indicators of the economic health of an SMSA and a region. These trends can also be strong indicators of power shifts.

What do all these internal migrations—from Frostbelt to Sunbelt, urban to suburban, metropolitan both to rural and supermetropolitan—add up to? To begin with, they result in population and economic decline for many older Frostbelt SMSAs, particularly New York City and its metropolitan area. Long the nerve center of the nation, New York City has played a key control function in the nation's economy. With declines in population, employment, and investment, however, these control functions are being decentralized to the Sunbelt. A few corporate statistics suggest that New York City's importance is declining as the Sunbelt cities drain off population and capital. In 1970, 59 of the *Fortune* 500 companies were headquartered in the Sunbelt, compared with 83 in 1977.

This massive shift of population and capital from Frostbelt (especially New York City) to Sunbelt brings political consequences too. By the mid-1960s, the Sunbelt was playing a significant, perhaps decisive, role in national politics; it has controlled the Presidency since 1963 and much of Congress's inner workings. To many observers, this represents nothing less than a *power shift* (Sale, 1976) from the yankee Eastern establishment to the Sunbelt cowboys. Hence, in terms of interregional relations, shifts in population and resources mean a redistribution of political power and economic clout.

Several other population trends are noteworthy. First, the trend beginning in 1920—movement out of the central cities— continued, but it took a new turn in the 1970s. Entire SMSAs, not just their central cities, lost population. (Again, Frostbelt SMSAs were particularly hard hit.) This means that many suburban communities stopped growing or actually declined; suburbs on the edge of central cities tended to be the population losers. At the same time, nonmetropolitan areas grew—and at a faster rate than SMSAs. Thus, for the first time in the twentieth century, **counterurbanization** (*decreasing* size, density, and heterogeneity) was happening in the United States. Second, there was an opposite trend: the further concentration of population into denser areas.

Some of these trends are recent, particularly supermetropolitanization, counterurbanization, and decentralization to the Sunbelt. But one trend has remained constant since 1920: movement out of the central cities. Does this long-standing trend signal a search for community? Do suburbanites seek a sense of "weness" away from the urban core? Can New Towns and new rural areas create a sense of community? We now turn to such questions.

THE SEARCH FOR COMMUNITY

Millions of Americans voted with their cars between 1950 and 1970, moving from the urban core to the suburbs. This mass exodus from the central city meant that by 1970 more Americans lived around cities than within them.

What kind of people were these migrants? What kind of life did they lead once they got to the suburbs? A host of social critics thought they knew.

Diatribes Against "Suburbia"

Shortly after the mass exodus from central city to suburb began after World War II, social critics looked at "**suburbia**," and here is what they saw.

Boring couples with small children, spending Saturday picking crabgrass out of their lawns.

Ugly, poorly planned tract developments called Merry Meadows or Happy Acres, high-sounding names that masked cheap construction and dull lives.

A land of joiners and conformists.

Frenetic participation in meaningless activities.

And the unflattering portrait continues. *The Man in the Gray Flannel Suit* (1955) rushes off to catch his 6:43 A.M. commuter train, leaving his frustrated wife behind in *The Split Level Trap* (1960) with the children. After she tries to fix *The Crack in the Picture Window* (1956), she visits her neighbor for the morning kaffee klatsch. In a few hours, it's time to chauffeur the children to swimming lessons and then pick up her husband, *The Organization Man* (1956), at the train. The couple dines on a drab frozen dinner and rushes off to a Republican Club meeting. As they reach the *Point of No Return* (1949) on this day-in–day-out routine, the husband starts to drink too much and his wife quietly goes ga-ga.

That was the stereotype of the suburbs: a vast wasteland of sterility and sameness. This negative image dominated novels, films, and even so-called empirical studies in the 1950s.

With little empirical evidence but much venom, most of the supposed social science studies in the 1950s crucified the suburbs. John Keats's antisuburban study, *The Crack in the Picture Window* (1956), is exemplary. According to Keats, the Drones are typical of the spiritual malaise and materialism of suburbia. John and Mary Drone decorate their shoddily built, look-alike tract home in Rolling Knolls with plastic reproductions of high art. Further, the Drones live in a "jerry-built, homogenous, postwar Hell that destroys individualism":

> When all dwellings are the same shape, all dwellers are squeezed into the same shape. Thus, Mary Drone in Rolling Knolls was living much closer to 1984 than to 1934, for she dwelt in a vast communistic barracks. This communism, like any other, was made possible by the destruction of the individual. In this case, destruction began with obliteration of the individualistic house and self-sufficient neighborhood, and from there on, the creation of mass-produced human beings followed as the night the day. (Keats, 1956:61)

To Keats and numerous other critics, suburbia represented an antiutopia, a subtopia. It was the American nightmare, not the American dream. It symbolized middle-class mediocrity, conformity, political indifference, and meaningless participation.

Who were these critics who painted such a devastating picture of suburban life? Why did they attack with such venom? It is significant that the suburban image was the work of a small segment of Americans: urbane, upper-status white intellectuals. Overwhelmingly, the critics were well-educated WASP males; they lived either in the rural countryside or the major metropolitan centers, not in the suburbs.

These elite critics fall into two major categories, both tinged with romanticism. Some critics of suburbia looked backward, glorifying a rural past. Either they dreamed of recapturing Tönnies's vision of *Gemeinschaft* (people living in harmony with nature and one another in a tight-knit community) or they idealized Thomas Jefferson's American dream—a rural nation populated by self-sufficient, individualistic gentleman farmers. Jefferson thought that democratic traditions needed to be nourished in the soil of yeoman farmers' fields.

It is Jefferson's ideal that underlies the most influential attack on suburbia, William H. Whyte's best-seller, *The Organization Man* (1956). Whyte's analysis of "The New Suburbia: Organization Man at Home" is one of the few empirically grounded studies of the 1950s, and his treatment of suburban Park Forest, Illinois, is more even-handed than other critics' wholesale antisuburban tracts.

To Whyte, the young suburbanites of Park Forest, near Chicago, "have been recreating something of the tight-knit group of old." The community shows a great deal of "kindliness and fundamental decency" (1956:395). Yet, on balance, Whyte concludes that the group tyrannizes the individual:

> [Park Foresters] sense that by their immersion in the group they are frustrating other urges, yet they feel that responding to the group is a moral duty—and so they continue, hesitant and unsure, imprisoned in brotherhood. (404)

SUBURBIA: A PHOTOESSAY

"Fourteen years ago Dublin, California, was a crossroads on U.S. 50 and 21. The population was less than one thousand (most of them cows). Today Dublin is the crossroads of Interstate Highways 580 and 680 with a population of over twenty-five thousand people. We now have fifteen gas stations, six supermarkets, two department stores, and a K-Mart. And we're still growing." a

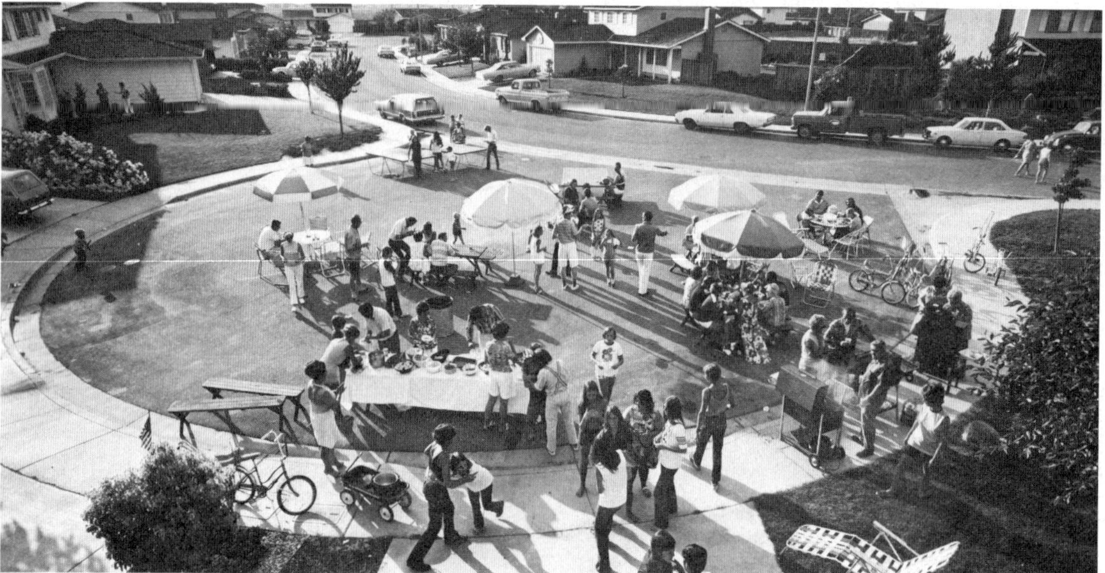

"This is our second annual Fourth of July block party. This year thirty-three families came for beer, barbequed chicken, corn on the cob, potato salad, green salad, macaroni salad, and watermelon. After eating and drinking we staged our parade and fireworks." b

c

"Because we live in the suburbs we don't eat too much Chinese food. It's not available in the supermarkets so on Saturday we eat hot dogs."

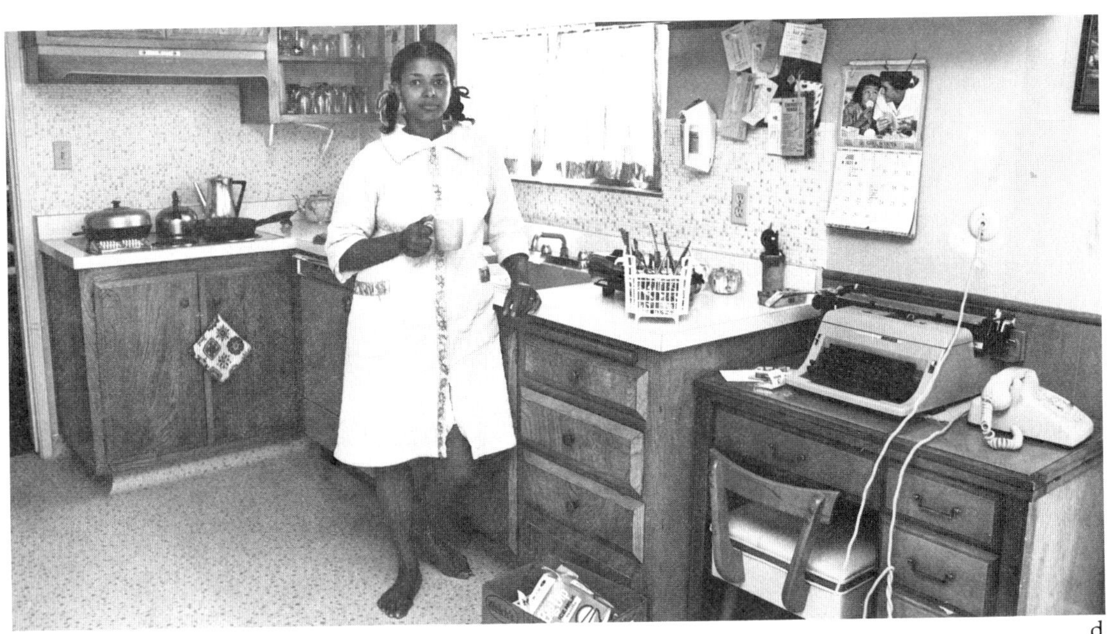

d

"I enjoy the suburbs. They provide Girl Scouts, PTA, Little League, and soccer for my kids. The thing I miss most is black cultural identity for my family. White, middle-class suburbia can't supply that. Here the biggest cultural happening has been the opening of two department stores."

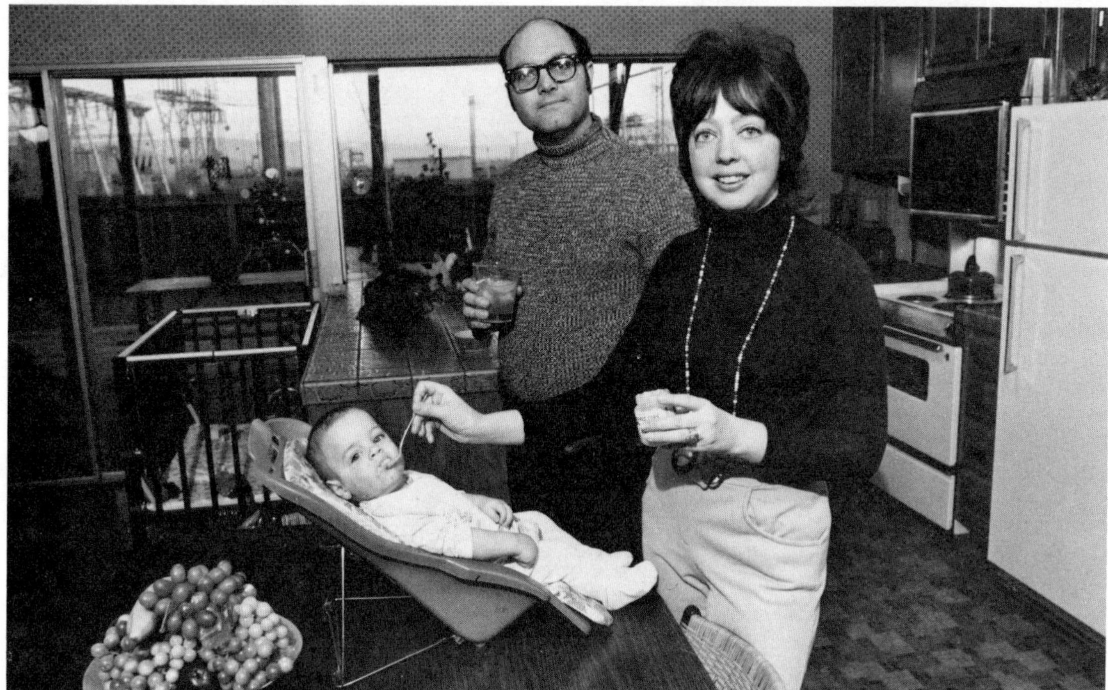

"We're really happy. Our kids are healthy, we eat good food, and we have a really nice home."

Fig. 6-4 SUBURBIA. (Bill Owens)

Whyte's verdict, then, is that the price of a tight-knit community is tyranny of the individual, a price too high to pay.

If Whyte looked back to self-sufficient communities, other critics of suburbia looked forward to an imagined urban future. In this romantic vision, cities would be centers of high culture, social order, and true sophistication. Contemporary cities, these critics bemoaned, were disorderly and barbaric.

To both kinds of romantics (the traditionalists and the futurists), suburbia was a dismal failure. Neither rural countryside nor city, the suburbs seemed to combine the worst features of both.

This antisuburban literature has a familiar ring, for the same themes run throughout American intellectual history. Indeed, the antisuburban diatribes of the 1950s echo the antiurban harangues of earlier times. And it is noteworthy that in both cases, members of the traditional WASP elite led the attack. They seem to have been reacting to an alien presence in their midst which threatened their most cherished American dreams.

Comparing the antisuburban diatribes with the antiurban attacks of the 1880s, we can see what fears these social critics shared. In the late nineteenth century, upper-status, well-educated WASPs worried that the immigrant "mobs" would destroy "their" cities and American cultural traditions, especially high culture. Such literary figures as novelist Henry James did not hide their disdain for the lower-class ethnics streaming into New York City. To James, they represented the first stage of "alienism." Patrician James also criticized the newly rich business tycoons, "the vulgar rich," for their bourgeois values. (He especially disliked the tycoons who made their fortunes in American cities and then deserted them for the "non-descript excrescences" of fashionable suburbs.) What James feared was the spread of both alien traditions and mass culture and bourgeois values. Similarly, Whyte and other antisuburban critics in the 1950s found fault with mass culture and bourgeois values, this time symbolized by a new mass migration: the move to the suburbs. But this time the "aliens" weren't lower-class ethnics; they were members of the white new middle class of corporate America.

To conclude: Lurking behind the 1950s critique of suburbia is the specter of Orwell's nightmare world of *1984,* where mass-produced people live in authoritarian **mass society.** Critics like Keats and Whyte feared that mass society, symbolized by suburbia, would destroy individualism. There is a certain irony here, for according to Durkheim, Tönnies, and others in the typological tradition, individualism can flourish *only* in urban-industrial society.

The Myth of Suburbia

When the dust started settling on the newly paved roads of tract developments, social scientists began to paint a more complex portrait of suburban life. Post-1950s studies show that life beyond the city limits is hardly a wasteland of drab conformity and dreary look-alike lives.

By the 1960s researchers had dropped the label "suburbia." It was, they inferred, a myth. Suburbs do not all look alike, nor do their inhabitants share a common lifestyle.

Instead of homogeneity, these later studies reveal a variety of suburban types. Economically, some suburbs are wealthy bedroom communities, while others are self-contained mini-cities. Some are industrial satellites located far from a central city; others shun any industry. Politically, Democrats also inhabit the urban fringe, despite the stereotype that the suburbs are Republican. Socioeconomically, upper-income older suburbs differ from middle-class newer settlements. For instance, *The Affluent Suburb* (Sternlieb et al., 1971) of Princeton, New Jersey, bears no resemblance to the *Working-Class Suburb* (Berger, [1960] 1971) of Milpitas, California. And in character, some suburbs do not seem suburban at all. A black suburb of St. Louis, for instance, resembles an urban ghetto neighborhood (Bollens, 1961), and an industrial suburb can have an urban character: a rather large, heterogeneous, high-density population.

In other words, the suburban landscape is diverse. So diverse that the label "suburbia" masks more than it reveals.

We can, however, construct a typology of suburbs that helps bring order to the diversity. Perhaps the most useful is one that distinguishes suburbs by their basic function: (1) *residential bedroom* suburbs, (2) *industrial-manufacturing* suburbs, and (3) *mixed* suburbs which combine features of the first two types. Empirical studies (e.g., Schnore, 1963) reveal systematic differences among the three types. Bedroom communities, for example, tend to have fewer nonwhite residents and higher family income levels than industrial or mixed suburbs. It should be noted that one type of suburb (say, a bedroom community) tends to retain its character over time, and that an individual suburb may be fairly homogeneous in its social-economic characteristics.

Diversity of suburban types can be illustrated by comparing two post-World War II tract suburbs: Milpitas, California, and Levittown, New Jersey. Sociological studies of these communities draw a different picture of suburban lifestyles than those produced by Whyte and Keats.

Working-class Suburb

Milpitas, California, a semirural community near San Jose, was transformed into a suburb of the mixed type in 1955. At that time, the Ford Motor Company closed its assembly plant in industrial Richmond (about fifty miles north in the Bay Area) and opened a new plant there. Virtually all the Ford auto workers moved with their new plant to Milpitas.

What happened to these urban auto workers when they moved to a suburb? That is the question asked by sociologist Bennett M. Berger, and he was surprised at the answers.

First, Berger made one basic assumption: Auto workers and their families would begin to change their attitudes, aspirations, and behavior as a result of the suburbanization process. This assumption, which pervaded the 1950s studies of the suburbs, turned out to be false. The earlier studies had predicted that suburban newcomers tend to switch politically from Democratic to Republican in trying to conform to their new surroundings. Further, antisuburban critics in the 1950s wrote that suburban residents were joiners, so Berger expected a burst of social and organizational activity in Milpitas. Initially, Berger also assumed that the auto workers, many of whom had purchased their first homes, would turn politically to the right, for homeownership is widely viewed as a conservative influence.

Yet, in 1957, after interviewing 100 Ford workers and their spouses, Berger found that in many important dimensions, the workers' lives and attitudes were apparently unaffected by their move from industrial city to suburb. As he documents in *Working-Class Suburb* ([1960] 1971), the workers did not become joiners. Instead, "Membership and activity in formal associations is rare: so is semiformal mutual visiting between couples" (92). Further, those who voted Democratic in industrial Richmond continued to vote Democratic in suburban Milpitas, even though they had since become homeowners.

In general, Berger concludes that working-class people do not take on the habits, attitudes, and aspirations of the middle class when they move to the suburbs. Later, when Berger's study was replicated by another researcher (Kaplan, 1965), his major findings were confirmed.

Levittown

Constructed by a single developer in the late 1950s, Levittown, New Jersey, is a bedroom suburb outside Philadelphia. (Residents later changed its name to Willingboro.) From the outside, it could have served as a model for Keats's dread "Rolling Knolls," home of the Drones. But from the inside, as Herbert Gans's monumental study of *The Levittowners* (1967) documents, the mainly working-class and lower-middle-class suburb does not fit the stereotype of suburbia.

Sociologist Gans lived in Levittown during its first years, gathering data as a participant-observer on the new suburb's way of life and politics. He found that the generally young residents were not marked by crushing conformity and dull homogeneity. What he did find, among other things, was that "By any yardstick one chooses, Levittowners treat their fellow residents more ethically and democratically than did their parents and grandparents. They also live a 'fuller' and 'richer' life" (1967:419).

Gans notes that there are no extremes in Levittown; most people are neither rich nor poor. Yet there is a range of occupations, mainly in the technical and service areas. In addition, people come from various ethnic backgrounds (Greek, Italian, WASP, Asian, and—after a court order—some blacks) and include Catholics, Protestants, and Jews.

Most Levittowners tend to see their homes as the center of their lives. But, Gans points out, they are much more "in the world" than their ethnic or WASP parents and grandparents were.

According to Gans, there is little evidence of what Whyte and others so feared: tyranny of the majority over the individual. Levittown neighbors may apply peer pressure to conform in minor ways (say, to keep the front lawn trimmed), but this does not lead to sameness of thought and action. Neighbors may imitate each other, but this often works to broaden life experience, as in the case of a man who discovered pizza at an Italian-American neighbor's house down the block.

In general, Gans (1967:417–420) finds that the young Levittowners are not like the portrait Whyte and Keats painted of suburbanites. Levittowners are not "apathetic conformists," "conspicuous consumers," "organization men," or "mass men." Nor are they like suburbanites who live in upper-middle-class bedroom communities. Instead, they have their own working-class culture which continues to flourish. According to Gans (149), the Levittowners "brought their cultures with them and the community they established thus only recreated old life styles and institutions on new soil." (See Box 6-1.)

What can be concluded from the studies of Milpitas and Levittown, and from studies of more affluent and less affluent suburbs such as Princeton, New Jersey, and East St. Louis? For one thing, *class* and *social rank* are still important factors in people's lives, whether in city or suburb. More broadly, the studies suggest that *suburbanism is no more a single way of life than is urbanism.* People in a city do not share common values, political views, or lifestyles, and neither do people beyond the city limits. Communities on the city's rim may share a label—suburb—but they don't share a way of life. One implication here concerns generalizations based on U.S. census categories: Gross generalizations based on the distinction between central city and outside central city can tell us little about how people feel, act, vote, or lead their everyday lives.

The studies also hint that neither suburbs nor cities are unified cohesive units, that is, communities. As Gans puts it (see Box 6-1), people did not move to Levittown in order to "revive" a sense of community; they came to carry on old ways of life in new houses. And, at least in Gans's view, social planners should not waste their time trying to re-create something that never existed in the first place: the cohesive community. Instead, says Gans, planners should focus on creating "improved living conditions in those aggregates to which we give the name 'community.' "

It is noteworthy that a generation has now passed since data were gathered for Gans's study of Levittown, Berger's study of Milpitas, and other trend-setting research on suburbs. Sequels—perhaps "Children of the Levittowners"—seem about due. Among other things, such sequels would indicate whether working-class culture still flourishes in some suburbs or whether it has been blurred and blended with middle-class lifestyles with the passage of time.

Neighborhoods as Communities

Gans's message is that suburbs are not unified, cohesive social units that deserve the

Box 6-1

THE ORIGINS OF A COMMUNITY

The Evolution of Levittown

Of all the decisions and factors that made a community out of strangers who purchased Levitt homes, the most important were, of course, the builder's. His decision to build another Levittown near Philadelphia, with houses in a \$12,000–\$15,000 price range, determined the age, class, and religious characteristics of the population, and these in turn influenced—perhaps determined—the informal and formal groups and institutions that developed in the community. Had he decided to build more expensive houses, a different kind of community would have resulted. . . .

The Nature of a New Community

Strictly speaking, what emerged in Levittown was the typical array of municipal bodies and individual associations which worked together when common interests were at stake, but competed most of the time. . . . These groups, taken together, were commonly thought to be "the community," mainly because their activities took place within the township limits and their jurisdictions began and ended there. . . .

Since most Levittowners did not participate actively in the so-called community organizations, the community that had been originated in their names was of minor importance in their lives. What involved them deeply was their house and the lot on which it stood, the adjacent neighbors and perhaps the block, friends elsewhere in Levittown, and the particular church or organization in which they were active. If one could measure "sense of community," it embraced only these, but not the community or even the neighborhood in which they had bought. Neighborhood boundaries had little meaning, for units of 1200 families were too large for face-to-face relations, and even the so-called neighborhood clubs usually recruited from only a block or two. . . .

By any traditional criteria, then, Levittown could not be considered a community. It was not an economic unit whose members were dependent on each other for their livelihood, and it was not a social unit for there was no reason or incentive for people to relate to each other as Levittowners on any regular or recurring basis. And Levittown was clearly not a symbolic unit, for the sense of community was weak. . . . Levittown . . . could best be defined as an administrative-political unit plus an aggregate of community-wide associations within a space. . . .

Indeed, just because Levittown was only a loose network of groups and institutions it was possible for these to develop quickly and in large numbers. Had the community been a cohesive social body, there would have been fewer groups, for the founding of additional ones would have signified an intrusion into a tight-knit social body. Conversely, not being a social body, Levittown needed to find groups, people, and symbols to make it appear as a body to other communities. . . . The attempts of the builder, and later, the township fathers to require stores and gas stations to adopt a uniform pseudo Colonial facade for their buildings was, likewise, an architectural means for creating a unity and cohesion that did not exist in the social system.

I do not mean to downgrade Levittown as a community, for my observations apply equally to all other communities, urban and suburban, and probably even to most communities of the past, including those now celebrated as cohesive units. . . . My argument here is not with Levittown, then, but with critics who seek to find a social unit in the community where none exists, and with romantic city planners, abetted by nostalgic social critics, who want to "revive" a sense of community that never was save in their imagination, instead of planning for the effective functioning of improved living conditions in those aggregates to which we give the name "community". . . .

Levittowners came not to build a new community but to move into a new house in which they could carry on old ways of family life, neighborhood relations, and civic activity. Perhaps the only new communities are utopian ones formed deliberately by people who have decided to alter their life according to a common plan, and such people would not have considered buying in Levittown. A few Levittowners came to start a new life or make significant changes in the old one, and some came with a fragile hope that somehow, a virginal community would avoid problems and conflicts of an established one. This hope was soon dashed by the necessities of the origin process. As one of the first arrivals recalled later: "I was so naive before I moved here. I didn't think there would be any juvenile delinquency; I thought only angels were moving in. It never occured to me that people are people no matter where you live." She put it well, for people being people, they brought their own cultures with them and the community they established thus only re-created old life styles and institutions on new soil. (Gans, 1967:chap. 7. Copyright © 1967 by Herbert J. Gans. Reprinted by permission of Pantheon Books, a Division of Random House, Inc., and the author.)

name "communities." If aggregates on the city's rim are not communities, can urban neighborhoods function as communities?

Gans's own study, conducted in Boston's West End, suggests that some city neighborhoods can function partially as communities. His research, reported in *The Urban Villagers* (1962), details the life of a low-income population of Italian-Americans. Gans found that the West Enders were like urban villagers, and that their way of life constituted a distinct working-class subculture. At the same time, Gans did not romanticize the West End:

> The West End was not a charming neighborhood of "noble peasants" living in an exotic fashion, resisting the mass-produced homogeneity of American culture and overflowing with a cohesive sense of community. (1962:16)

While not "overflowing with a cohesive sense of community," the West End urban villagers did live in a fairly homogeneous settlement that served to shield them from what Wirth termed "urbanism as a way of life"—social disorder, alienation, and anonymity. Other research, such as Oscar Lewis's study (1961) of the Sanchez family in Mexico City, also suggests that neighborhoods—especially low-income and ethnic settlements—provide social and cultural anchors for urbanites. In other words, neighborhoods can function as *Gemeinschaft-like* subcommunities within urban-industrial society.

How communitylike a neighborhood is depends on various characteristics of the residents. Most important are social rank, ethnicity, and family type. One research method used to determine neighborhood type is called "social area analysis" (detailed in Chapter 13); it uses these three key variables. Generally speaking, low-income and ethnic neighborhoods in the city tend to function more as subcommunities than do upper-income, heterogeneous neighborhoods.

Small Towns and the New Rural Society

> There is a need for intimate human relationships, for the security of settled home and associations, for spiritual unity, and for orderly transmission of the basic cultural inheritance. These the small community at its best can supply.
>
> (From the preface to the Town Plan, St. Johnsbury, Vermont)

The suburban dream apparently lost its glitter by the 1970s. According to several national attitude surveys, the majority of Americans, given a choice, would live in a small town—not a suburb (or a central city). Of course, attitudes are not always translated into action. In this case, however, unprecedented numbers of Americans acted on their preference for small-town rural life. This resulted in a counterurbanization movement that turned many "nowheres" into "somewheres." By the mid-1970s, nonmetropolitan counties were gaining about 350,000 migrants each year (Beale, 1975), who had moved to towns like Stump Creek, Pennsylvania, and Cave Junction, Oregon.

The brief history of one small town in-the-making hints at the ideals that sparked some SMSA refugees. (It also relates some of the problems they encountered.) In 1971, Chris Canfield, then a California business executive, started planning Cerro Gordo, a little town in the foothills of Oregon's Willamette Valley. Canfield was guided by a vision of a polis-like community: principles of self-sufficiency, democratic participation, and a communal way of life. But creating such a community in the midst of urban-industrial society has proved problematic. By 1978, the Cerro Gordo settlers were beset with fierce internal squabbles, struggles with the local planning commission, and financial troubles. As the first home took shape on the hillside, one settler commented, "The idyllic community . . . is on the other side of a lot of work and sacrifice, give-and-take, pride-swallowing and frustration" (in Robertson, 1978:129).

Census data do not reveal how many rural migrants are like the Cerro Gordoans, trying to create idyllic communities. Most likely, they represent a minority; most SMSA migrants probably move to established small towns in rural areas.

What is the attraction of small-town America? As noted earlier, people migrate from SMSAs to nonmetropolitan areas for a variety of reasons. Some are pushed there (by fear of unsafe cities, noise, etc.), and others are pulled there (by jobs or perceptions of a healthier environment). Here we focus on what appears to be a strong pull to the countryside for an unknown percentage of migrants: the search for community.

In an era of big cities, big bureaucracy, and big business, the ideal of a small community seems especially attractive. In the words of St. Johnsbury, Vermont's, Town Plan, the small community "at its best" can supply human needs for "intimate human relationships, . . . security . . . spiritual unity, and . . . orderly transmission of the basic cultural inheritance."

That some contemporary Americans seek the ideal of a small community is revealed in various attitude surveys. One such survey, conducted among 500 respondents in northeastern Connecticut, shows that the most desirable quality in a social living environment is to live near people one feels "comfortable with"; respondents felt that a small community can best fulfill that desire (Goldmark and Kraig, 1976:1–6).

Is it possible to promote a sense of community among rural residents without cutting them off from broader national issues? One proposal attempted to blend the small community with the larger society. Called the New Rural Society project (NRS), it began as the brainchild of the late Peter Goldmark in 1971. Goldmark, inventor of the LP phonograph record, envisioned communications technologies (teleconferencing, satellites, video, and so on) as instruments for upgrading life in rural communities. The communications revolution, Goldmark believed, would encourage business, people, and government to decentralize voluntarily. His federally funded NRS project proposed

"On our commune, everyone has to work. We chase off the freeloaders. The commune has to make money. It has to be a business, then it can grow. The government isn't going to take care of you. You have to band together to help each other."

Fig. 6-5 RURAL COMMUNE. (Bill Owens)

nationwide learning centers linked to local centers, offering continuing education for all and constant debate about current issues that affected local communities and the nation as a whole (Goldmark, 1976). In theory, NRS represents a way to encourage a wide spectrum of people to move to the countryside but not to separate themselves from those in cities; it would allow people to live near others they feel "comfortable with" without sacrificing a cosmopolitan outlook.

This brings us back to the two-sided face of community. To live near people one feels "comfortable with" usually means to live near people like oneself. To live in "spiritual unity" and "intimacy" has another side: parochialism and insularity. And to transmit "*the* basic cultural inheritance" implies that there is only one to pass on, not a variety of cultural heritages so characteristic of heterogeneous, urban-industrial society. In other words, the price of feeling a sense of "we-ness" and community with members of a small group is estrangement from people unlike those in the group.

True, many people in metropolitan areas

tend to live in subcommunities—neighborhoods, ethnic groups, occupational communities—and do not seek out meaningful contact with people unlike themselves. This can lead to psychological, if not physical, segregation within the metropolis. Yet the metropolitan environment does provide a setting for mingling with diverse people. It also presents opportunities for spreading new, perhaps unpopular, ideas and for learning from people unlike ourselves. Such an environment may not be comfortable or secure, but it can be growth-producing, both for individuals and for society as a whole.

To conclude: Reflecting on the various proposals for small communities within the urban society brings numerous questions of value and choice to mind. Is the pride of a small-town community (intimacy and security) worth the probable costs (e.g., odious distinctions between insiders and outsiders)? Will new communications technologies allow vast numbers of people to live in small communities but remain vitally connected to the larger society? Or will new communities, separate and unequal, be created in the countryside, leaving the less affluent trapped and abandoned in central cities?

Questions of democracy also arise. In a small community, the possibility of the majority's tyranny over the minority does loom large. There is also the problem of scale: "Democratic" decisions at the micro-level can be restrictive, even oppressive, to outsiders and harmful to the society as a whole. For instance, is it democratic if a group of 1,500 or 16,000 townspeople vote to prohibit people unlike themselves from moving there, thus assuring homogeneity?

There seem to be no easy answers to these questions. In fact, some believe we are doomed either to live without individual freedom and a broad outlook in local community or without close social bonds in cosmopolitan society. And as we now discuss, another proposed answer—New Towns—doesn't meet the dual challenge of creating communities that both (1) guarantee and encourage personal freedom and (2) provide intimacy and promote cohesive social bonds.

New Towns

Another approach to planning for community is to build an entire New Town from scratch—not a small community like Cerro Gordo, Oregon, but rather a town of at least 20,000 residents. Indeed, this approach became a movement in the United States.

In large measure, the so-called **New Town** (also called "New Communities") movement began partially as a response to the diatribes against the suburbs in the 1950s. Recall that critics called suburbia aesthetically ugly, environmentally wasteful, socially isolating, and functionally inefficient. Some planners thought that constructing New Towns would allow for urban growth without duplicating suburbia's assumed faults.

New Towns come in two varieties: those built solely by private developers and those assisted by government funds. There are no universally accepted standards for a New Town, but several elements for both varieties have emerged over the years: (1) sufficient size—planned for a target population of at least 20,000 on at least 2,000 acres; (2) development by a single developer to ensure coordinated management; (3) development that follows a master plan; (4) provision of various urban functions by reserving land for residential, public, industrial, and commercial uses; and (5) provision of different kinds of housing (owned, rented, apartments, single-family dwellings).

By 1974, 175 New Towns had been identified in the continental United States and Puerto Rico (Burby and Weiss, 1976:69).

Fig. 6-6 NEW TOWN. Reston, Virginia, is a nonfederally assisted New Town outside the nation's capital. (U.S. Department of Housing and Urban Development)

These include the private developments of Columbia, Maryland; Reston, Virginia; Irvine, California; and Lake Havasu City, Arizona. Among the few federally assisted New Towns actually built (before funds were cut off for the entire New Communities program) are the retirement colonies of Rossmoor Leisure World, California, and Sun City, Florida.

Who lives in these New Towns? Why do people go there, and why do they leave? How successful are these attempts to create whole new communities?

Differences among New Towns make any generalizations risky, but some commonalities do emerge. Based on data gathered in thirteen New Towns, Burby and Weiss (1976) found that residents tend to be young families with children. They have much higher family incomes (a median of $17,500 in 1972) and more formal education than the average family looking for housing in the same metropolitan area. (With few exceptions, privately developed New Towns have few housing opportunities for low-income families.) Furthermore, residents tend to be overwhelmingly white—about 97 percent.

People are attracted to New Towns for a variety of reasons, particularly the belief that they are "good places to raise children" and their proximity to natural environment (Burby and Weiss, 1976:19–20). People leave most frequently because they want a larger home or change employment.

In terms of governance and citizen participation, New Town residents seem to be no more involved in their communities than residents of conventional towns of the same size. Some critics argue that lack of citizen participation may have been built into the design by giving a single entrepreneur or development corporation monopolistic control.

In part, these New Towns—particularly the federally assisted ones—were created to improve the overall quality of life in the nation's cities and to prevent deterioration of the physical and social environment. But the Burby and Weiss evaluation shows them to be doing no better than conventional towns of the same size on a number of measures. Residents do not participate more in the community; nor are they more satisfied with their quality of life. Further, New Towns do not deliver urban services more efficiently than their conventional counterparts. As a proposed solution to urban growth and a method of building a sense of community, then, New Towns seem to fall short of their goals.

WHAT NEXT?

Space Age Cities

New Towns, suburbs, megalopoli, and small towns. These have been some responses to urban growth in the last thirty years. But what about the next thirty years? Here we move into a mind-boggling realm where proposals range from cities floating in space to cities below the earth and sea.

It may sound like science fiction or fantasy, but to former Princeton University physicist Gerard K. O'Neill and his fervent followers, there is a real possibility for creating permanent colonies in space that could house up to 10,000 people. According to O'Neill (1977), such space cities can be ready for habitation by the year 2000.

And what would life be like in orbiting cities? O'Neill seems to suggest that present patterns of social life will continue, simply transferred to a space colony. Yet data gathered in other closed, isolated environments, such as submarine crews, show that boredom and closed-in feelings are a common problem, producing conflict among members. So how can we expect merely to transfer earthly patterns of social organization to closed spaces in the sky?

While O'Neill touts *The High Frontiers: Human Colonies in Space* (1977), others look to a Jules Verne vision: cities beneath the sea. Jacques Cousteau and Edouard Albert, for instance, propose building an artificial island which would be a leisure town just off the coast of Monaco. The underwater section would house nightclubs and research labs; beaches and swimming pools would be at sea level; and apartments, entertainment places, and boutiques would rise above them. Others, like Hidezo Kobayashi, envision a marine civilization with underwater urban structures.

At present, cities below and above the earth are only a twinkle in the scientific eye. But who knows what the future holds? And even if they remain just a twinkle, the potentiality of such space age cities may spur our collective imagination to redesign earthbound settlements.

Fig. 6-7 WHAT'S NEXT? On the drawing board for future cities are some mind-stretching proposals, including a space habitat where 10,000 people would work and raise families in a wheellike structure orbiting the earth. (NASA)

To date, the wide range of proposed cities for the future—from earthly megastructures to marine structures—are architectural visions of the future (see Dahinden, 1972). They are exciting precisely because they are so unorthodox and mind-stretching. Nonetheless, they remain engineering and architectural answers to a host of socioeconomic and political issues.

On the socioeconomic side, there is no lack of visions about the urban future—or alternative futures. Whether writing science fiction, impassioned speeches, or scholarly tracts, most visionaries don't hide their values and hopes. Some prophets, inspired by utopian socialist experiments or anarchist dreams, foresee small communities based on voluntarism. Some see a new sense of community rooted in the overthrow of capitalism and the creation of a classless society. Others wish for a return to medieval traditional community: social hierarchy, the church, simple technology, and paternalistic rule. Meanwhile, liberals tend to avoid all-encompassing philosophies, focusing instead on specific policies for improvement, such as broad regional government.

Many of these visions are discussed elsewhere in more detail (see Chapters 10, 14, 16). Here, let us consider the unorthodox ideas of one contemporary thinker, William Irwin Thompson. Cultural historian Thompson (1978:90, 91, 183) speculates that the United States will pass from a postindustrial economy to what he calls a "metaindustrial" economy: a new planetary culture in which "40 per cent of the [U.S.] population becomes involved with food production" by the year 2000. He predicts that electronics and the miniaturization of technology, the decentralization of cities, and a profound transformation of individual consciousness "in a scientific return to animism" will foster "the creation of new metaindustrial villages and smaller, decentralized, symbiotic cities." In brief, Thompson paints a picture of an entirely new culture. A student of esoteric theology, Thompson looks forward to a future in which art, science, myth, and religion converge. The hope: a world polity "beyond the present materialistic civilization of warring industrial nation-states and exploited preindustrial societies (1978:183). Clearly, Thompson's prophetic vision doesn't fit into tidy ideological boxes.

Thompson and other prophets of a coming new age (e.g., Stavrianos, 1976) have relatively small followings at present. But that is not the point. Visionaries—whether scholars, poets, artists, or mystics—shake our most basic assumptions about what is and what ought to be. Essentially they are moralists, commenting on good and evil in the present while presenting alternatives for the future.

ANOTHER LOOK

For a change, theorists seem to agree on a basic point: Urban-industrial-capitalist society is too big, too specialized, and too heterogeneous to promote a sense of community except within smaller subcommunities. But on the question of what to do about this situation, if anything, consensus breaks down.

Differences in ideology and historical perspective are the basis of dissent over questions of modern community. Decentralists like Goldmark and Thompson think that communications technology permits a return to a smaller-scale, more humane village life without the parochialism of preindustrial communities. In this view, the global village is possible without reinventing what Marx called "the idiocy of rural life." Centralists, on the other hand, tend to be prourban. Those in the Marxist tradition look to the radical restructuring of economic and political institutions as the precondition for reconstituting a sense of community by abolishing inequality and oppression. Ultraconservatives argue that secular modern urbanites cannot handle freedom, democracy, and advanced technology; a return to benevolent, authoritarian, religious rule is one answer. Other conservatives wish for a Jeffersonian past. Meanwhile, numerous philosophers are skeptical that any form of human social organization—urban or rural—can encourage both personal freedom and intimate social bonds.

Theory aside, there seems to be a growing recognition in advanced technological societies that members of the global community share common concerns, perhaps a common fate. Since World War II, an understanding of the destructive power of technology (that crosses political borders) and the need for energy have alerted us to our interdependence, both nationally and internationally. This is reflected in language. "Afghanistanism" was once a term newspaper editors used to refer to the preference for stories about faraway, exotic places over hard-hitting, close-to-home news. That term disappeared almost overnight in December, 1979 when Soviet troops marched into Afghanistan. And no term has replaced it. Perhaps this signals the idea that no place on earth is now so remote as to deserve our ignorance or lack of concern.

PROJECTS

1. **The suburbs revisited.** A generation has passed since William H. Whyte's study of the new middle class suburb of Park Forest, Illinois, and Bennett Berger's study of the working-class suburb of Milpitas, California. What are these suburbs like today? Try to determine if they have retained their character—as described by Whyte and Berger—over time. Using U.S. census data (see, in particular, the *County and City Data Book* series), gather and analyze statistics on each suburb's residents and the type of facilities located there. In addition, compare and contrast Park Forest and Milpitas (suburbs of nearly equal population size) in terms of their rates of violent and property crimes known to police and the percentage of city government funds spent on police and fire protection.

2. **Neighborhoods as communities.** Do people in your city's neighborhoods feel a sense of community? Choose two neighborhoods and try to find out how residents perceive and feel about social relationships there. Construct a short questionnaire, including background questions on age and ethnicity, on the use of neighborhood facilities. Administer the questionnaire to residents, perhaps a nonrandom sample of twenty persons. Are there differences between respondents in the two neighborhoods concerning their social relationships? If so, why might this be?

SUGGESTIONS FOR FURTHER LEARNING

For an interpretation of the problems and prospects of American community life, see Maurice R. Stein, *The Eclipse of Community* (Princeton, N.J.: Princeton University Press, 1960). Sociologist Stein reviews theories of community and community studies and presents multidisciplinary perspectives on the nature of the modern community.

Studies of *Gemeinschaft*-like communities within urban-industrialized or industrializing societies include Charles Nordhoff's observations of utopian communities in nineteenth-century America, *The Communistic Societies of the United States* (New York: Dover [1875] 1966); Benjamin Zablocki's study of the Bruderhof, *The Joyful Community* (Baltimore, Md.: Penguin, 1971); Barbara Grizzuti Harrison's personal account and history of the Jehovah's Witnesses, *Visions of Glory* (New York: Simon & Schuster, 1978); and William M. Kephart's analysis of seven *Extraordinary Groups* (New York: St. Martin's, 1976), which include the Amish, the Father Divine movement, and modern communes.

For a strong argument that the small town in

America is not the polar opposite of urban society, but instead is permeated by the culture and politics of mass society, see Arthur J. Vidich and Joseph Bensman, *Small Town in Mass Society* (Princeton, N.J.: Princeton University Press [1958] 1968). Vidich acted as consultant for a two-part film produced by KPBS-TV, San Diego State University, that examines life in *Traditional Small Towns* (1977) and *Pleasure Domes and Money Mills* (1977).

That *Gemeinschaft*-like qualities exist within urban-industrial-capitalist societies is suggested by many observers from differing vantage points. Two motion pictures which focus on working-class Italian-American families, *Bloodbrothers* (1978) and *Saturday Night Fever* (1977), show kinship relations as emotionally suffocating and devastating to individual expression. From a different perspective, William H. Whyte depicts the loss of individualism to corporate values, both in managerial work and home life; see *The Organization Man* (New York: Simon & Schuster, 1956). In another vein, Michael Novak outlines the moral sensibilities and values of white ethnic subcultures that stress primary group relations and loyalties in *The Rise of the Unmeltable Ethnics* (New York: Macmillan, 1971).

Whether or not urbanism and suburbanism are single ways of life are research questions pursued by Oscar Lewis in "Further Observations on the Folk-Urban Continuum and Urbanization with Special Reference to Mexico City," (in Philip M. Hauser and Leo F. Schnore, *The Study of Urbanization* [New York: Wiley, 1967]); and by Herbert Gans in several books and articles, including *The Urban Villagers* (New York: Free Press, 1962) and *The Levittowners* (New York: Vintage, 1967). Different views of the suburbs can be seen in two photographic essays: Bill Owens's *Suburbia* (San Francisco: Straight Arrow Books, 1973), a visual anthropology of middle-class suburbanites in the San Francisco Bay Area; and Mary Lloyd Estrin's *To the Manor Born* (Boston: Little, Brown, 1979), a vision of upper-class, exclusive Lake Forest in suburban Chicago.

The malaise of urban and suburban life is a motif of much modern literature. Movies that portray the city as an alienating, lonely place are too numerous to mention. The fearful city is perhaps most chillingly portrayed in Ted Tetzlaff's *The Window* (1949). Malaise in white, middle-class bedroom suburbs is a theme in the novels of John Updike and *The Stories of John Cheever* (New York: Knopf, 1979). Philip Roth's story and film of the same name, *Goodbye Columbus* (1969), is a scathing indictment of what the 1950s writers called suburbia.

Visions of cities-to-be, from ancient times to the present, are presented in Robert Sheckley's heavily illustrated *Futuropolis* (New York: A & W Visual Library, 1978) and Helen Rosenau's architecturally oriented history, *The Ideal City* (New York: Harper & Row, 1972). For the ideas behind dreams that became realities, even if short-lived, see Albert Fried and Ronald Sanders, *Socialist Thought* (Garden City, N.Y.: Anchor, 1964), which contains writings by two utopian socialists, Charles Fourier and Robert Owen, the visionaries behind the nineteenth-century communities of Brook Farm and New Harmony, Indiana, respectively. For a controversial social engineering model of a modern community that some call Utopia, others call Dystopia, see B. F. Skinner's influential *Walden Two* (New York: Macmillan, 1948); the Twin Oaks communes are modeled after psychologist Skinner's fictional Walden Two community.

For much less ambitious projects to restructure communities in urban society, see Raymond J. Burby and Shirley F. Weiss's *New Communities U.S.A.* (Lexington, Mass.: Lexington Books, 1976), which evaluates the New Towns movement, and Carol Corden's comparative account of attempts by Great Britian and the United States to build New Towns, *Planned Cities* (Beverly Hills, Calif.: Sage, 1977). See also *New Towns and the Suburban Dream* (Port Washington, N.Y.: Kennikat, 1976), edited by Irving L. Allen.

For a case study of the psychological impact of New Towns, see Donald Klein's reader, *Psychology of the Planned Community* (New York: Human Sciences Press, 1977). It is mainly devoted to studies of Columbia, Maryland.

What kinds of human settlements will there be in the near future? The rural renaissance is the topic of Kevin F. McCarthy and Peter A. Morrison's *The Changing Demographic and Economic Structure of Nonmetropolitan Areas in the United States* (Santa Monica, Calif.: Rand, 1979). How nonmetropolitan residents evaluate their environment is the focus of *The Quality of Nonmetropolitan Living* (Ann Arbor, Mich.: Institute for Social Research, 1978) by Robert W. Marans and John D. Wellman.

On the distant or perhaps not-too-distant future of human settlements, see Nigel Calder's *Spaceships of the Mind* (New York: Viking, 1978), which discusses the ideas of Gerard O'Neill and others, including Freeman J. Dyson's sphere (proposed space cities that cluster around a star to make maximum use of energy).

The impact of new communications technology on restructuring communities, perhaps creating what Marshall McLuhan calls a "global village," is explored in *Electronic Meetings: Technical Alternatives and Social Choices* by Robert Johansen et al. (Reading, Mass.: Addison-Wesley, 1978). See also "The New Field of Urban Communications," particularly Melvin M. Webber's article, "Urbanization and Communications," and Mark L. Hinshaw's essay, "Wiring Megalopolis: Two Scenarios" in *Communications Technology and Social Policy* (New York: Wiley, 1973), edited by George Gerbner et al.

KEY TERMS

Census tract A small subdivision of a city or SMSA, devised by the U.S. Census Bureau to help tabulate and analyze census data. On the average, a tract contains 4,000 people.

Central city The population center of an SMSA, containing at least 50,000 people (or twin cities with a combined population of at least 50,000). This is not to be confused with the popular terms "center city" or "inner city."

Counterurbanization In an urbanized society, the process whereby the proportion of nonmetropolitan residents increases relative to the proportion of metropolitan residents, and cities become less dense, less heterogeneous, and smaller.

Mass society An imprecise term, used in the sense of *Gesellschaft.* Usually viewed as large-scale, urban-industrial society characterized by loss of traditional community ties, dependence on mass (instead of face-to-face) communications, and impersonal social relations.

Megalopolis A very large city that dominates a large surrounding area. From the Greek, meaning "great city."

Metropolis A big city that dominates the surrounding area economically, socially, and culturally. From the Greek, meaning "mother city."

Metropolitan community (area) A concentrated settlement of people in a densely populated territory which satisfies many daily needs through a network of interdependent relationships, mainly economic

New Towns In the United States, towns planned for at least 20,000 people, built solely by private developers or with government assistance, constructed from scratch according to a master plan.

Standard Consolidated Statistical Area (SCSA) U.S. Census Bureau term used to refer to regions comprising more than one SMSA which are closely related socially and economically. An SCSA always includes two or more contiguous SMSAs which meet specific criteria of size, urban character, integration, and contiguity of urbanized areas. One of the constituent SMSAs must have a population of at least 1,000,000, and at least 75 percent of the population of each SMSA must be classified as urban.

Standard Metropolitan Statistical Area (SMSA) As defined by the U.S. Census Bureau, a contiguous territorial unit economically and socially integrated around a central city (or twin cities) containing at least 50,000 people. The entire county in which the central city is located is always included in the SMSA. (In New England, cities and towns are used instead of counties.)

"Suburbia" Negative stereotype of the suburbs created by social critics in the 1950s, connoting ugliness, poor construction, middle-class mediocrity, and conformism.

REFERENCES

Beale, Calvin L.
1975 "The revival of population growth in nonmetropolitan America." ERS-605, Economic Development Division, Economic Research Service, U.S. Department of Agriculture, June.

Berger, Bennett
[1960]
1971 Working-Class Suburb. Berkeley, Calif.: University of California Press.

Bollens, John (ed.)
1961 Exploring the Metropolitan Community. Berkeley, Calif.: University of California Press.

Burby, Raymond J. and Shirley F. Weiss
1976 New Communities U.S.A. Lexington, Mass.: Lexington Books.

Dahinden, Justus
1972 Urban Structures for the Future. New York: Praeger.

Gans, Herbert
1962 The Urban Villagers. New York: Free Press.
1967 The Levittowners. New York: Random House.

Goldmark, Peter C. and Bonnie Kraig
1976 "Communications for survival." Stamford, Conn.: Goldmark Communication, Nov. 19.

Gordon, Richard E.
[1960]
1961 Split Level Trap. New York: Random House.

Heilbrun, James
1974 Urban Economics and Public Policy. New York: St. Martin's Press.

Kaplan, Samuel
1965 "The auto worker in suburbia: a replication of working-class suburb." Unpublished M.A. thesis. University of California, Berkeley, Department of Sociology.

Keats, John
1956 The Crack in the Picture Window. Boston: Houghton Mifflin.

Lewis, Oscar
1961 The Children of Sanchez. New York: Random House.

Marquand, John P.
1949 Point of No Return. Boston: Little, Brown.

McKenzie, Roderick D.
1933 The Metropolitan Community. New York: McGraw-Hill.

Moen, Elizabeth M. and Walter T. Martin
1978 "On moving out of the metropolis." Working Paper Number 13a. Presented at annual American Sociological Association meetings in San Francisco.

Morrill, Richard L.
1978 "Fundamental issues concerning future settlements in America." Pp. 431–40 in James W. Simmons and L. S. Bourne (eds.), Systems of Cities: Readings on Structure, Growth, and Policy. New York: Oxford University Press.

Morrison, Peter A.
1978 "The current demographic content of national growth and development." Pp. 473–79 in James W. Simmons and L. S. Bourne (eds.), Systems of Cities: Readings on Structure, Growth, and Policy. New York: Oxford University Press.

O'Neill, Gerard K.
1977 The High Frontier: Human Colonies in Space. New York: Morrow.

Orwell, George
1949 1984. New York: Harcourt, Brace.

Robertson, James and Carolyn Robertson
1978 The Small Towns Book. Garden City, N.Y.: Anchor.

Sale, Kirkpatrick
1976 Power Shift: The Rise of the Southern Rim and Its Challenge to the Eastern Establishment. New York: Vintage.

Schnore, Leo F.
1963 "The socio-economic status of cities and suburbs." American Sociological Review 28:76–85.

Stavrianos, L. S.
1976 The Promise of the Coming Dark Age. San Francisco: W.H. Freeman.

Sternlieb, George et al.
1971 The Affluent Suburb. New York: Dutton.

Thompson, William Irwin
1978 Darkness and Scattered Light. Garden City, N.Y.: Anchor.

Whyte, William H.
1956 The Organization Man. New York: Simon & Schuster.

Wilson, Sloan
1955 The Man in the Gray Flannel Suit. New York: Simon & Schuster.

Dorothea Lange

CHAPTER 7
Movin' On

Americans are always moving on.
It's an old Spanish custom gone astray,
A sort of English fever, I believe,
Or just a mere desire to take French leave,
I couldn't say. I couldn't really say.
But when the whistle blows, they go away.
Sometimes there never was a whistle
 blown,
But they don't care, for they can blow their
 own
Whistles of willow-stick and rabbit-bone,
Quail-calling through the rain
A dozen tunes but only one refrain,
"We don't know where we're going, but
we're on our way!"

(Stephen Vincent Benet, "Prelude" to *Western Star*)

Moving to the big city today is not necessarily a big deal. A rural Texan can go to Houston or San Diego without feeling totally cut off from family and familiar things. In mass society, institutions like McDonald's, Ma Bell, and the TV news are nationwide, and urban culture reaches into the backwoods. Only a tiny minority of rural Americans are unfamiliar with urban life, for "the cultural patterns of most of the supposedly rural areas of the United States today are clearly dominated by urban values, urban attitudes, and urban life-styles" (Palen, 1975: 7–8). There are notable exceptions, such as French-speaking Cajuns who live on the edge of Louisiana's bayous, preferring to hunt, fish, and brave the hardships of nature rather than live in cities. But few Americans moving to the city today would feel totally uprooted.

How different were the experiences of earlier generations of migrants! Imagine what Tevye the milkman in *Fiddler on the Roof* (1971) might have felt, uprooted from his Eastern European *shtetl* and rerooted in New York City. Or turn-of-the-century peasants, perhaps the Lombardy family portrayed in the remarkable film *The Tree of Wooden Clogs* (1978); how could they have adjusted to the rhythms of urban-industrial life?

MIGRANT EXPERIENCES

The Old Migration

Before the nineteenth century, English, Dutch, and other Western European settlers came to America to live on farms and build colonial cities. Blacks from Africa arrived shortly after the English settlement at Jamestown, Virginia, in 1619. But it was not until the era of rapid industrialization that massive immigration took place. From the 1840s to the 1910s, about 35 million Europeans fled their plots of land, villages, and *Gemeinschaft* communities to resettle in U.S. cities. They came from all over Europe—Sweden, Germany, Ireland, Southern and Eastern Europe. They came from Japan and China too, first to work on the railroads and perform hard labor.

Mainly peasants and rural folk, most immigrants were ill-prepared for urban life. They were the uprooted—from rural rhythms, traditional ways of life, and often family. Some were led to believe that they would find streets paved with gold in the New World. Instead, many met hostility and discrimination—or racism, in the case of the Japanese and Chinese.

"No Irish Need Apply" signs greeted Boston's Irish in the 1850s when they searched for work, and ethnic stereotypes were nearly universal. Old-stock Americans accused the "foreign element" of having "animal pleasures" and leading a "pigsty mode of life." Fear was often pervasive in the nineteenth century: fear of cheap immigrant labor; fear of "inferior races" overwhelming white Anglo-Saxon Protestant **(WASP)** culture; fear of Papism and international conspiracy; and fear of the unknown.

In 1882 the Chinese Exclusion Act effectively ended Chinese immigration. By the 1920s, all immigration to the United States was drastically curtailed by new restrictive legislation; the "immigrant hordes," as they were often called by critics, were shut out.

Internal Migration

In the 1920s, when immigration from abroad came to a halt, another large-scale migration began: an internal U.S. population shift. Once again the cities served as entry points for rural people—this time, black and white Americans.

In terms of numbers, the most significant internal movement was the migration of blacks out of the South and into Northern and Western cities. Between 1910 and 1970 over 6.5 million blacks left the South. Of those who remained, many also moved—from rural areas to cities. Today, the majority of U.S. blacks live in cities.

Since World War I, two kinds of forces have worked to move Americans from the countryside to the city: push and pull. Economic and natural forces (e.g., dust storms) pushed some off the land and pulled others into urban areas, more precisely, into what Burgess called the "zone of transition" (Zone II). Southern dirt farmers, displaced by mechanized agriculture or beset by constant pov-

Fig. 7-1 THE PROMISED LAND. Immigrant women and children arrive in New York City around 1907. (Museum of the City of New York)

erty, sought economic survival in cities. During the 1930s, Oklahoma whites (disparagingly called "Okies") moved westward when the Dust Bowl engulfed their land.

By World War II, large numbers of people were moving geographically, hoping to move up socially too. Southern blacks and rural whites were drawn to war-related industries in the North and West. Puerto Ricans moved to New York City seeking jobs. Hispanics in the Southwest came to Western cities. Today, most Hispanics, like most blacks, live in cities.

The New Migration

New waves of migrants appeared in the 1970s. On the one hand, there was an internal population shift. For the first time in U.S. history, more people were leaving cities and metropolitan areas than moving to them. On the other hand, world politics and changed immigration laws served to increase the number of overseas newcomers. In the 1970s, about 4.4 million immigrants entered the country, the largest number since 1900–1910, when a record 8.2 million persons arrived in the shadow of the Statue of Liberty's motto: "Give me your tired, your poor, your huddled masses yearning to be free."

Many immigrants in the 1970s were refugees. The plight of the "boat people" from Vietnam and other Indochinese nations—shunted from one port to another, at the mercy of pirates, typhoons, and politics—led

a

b

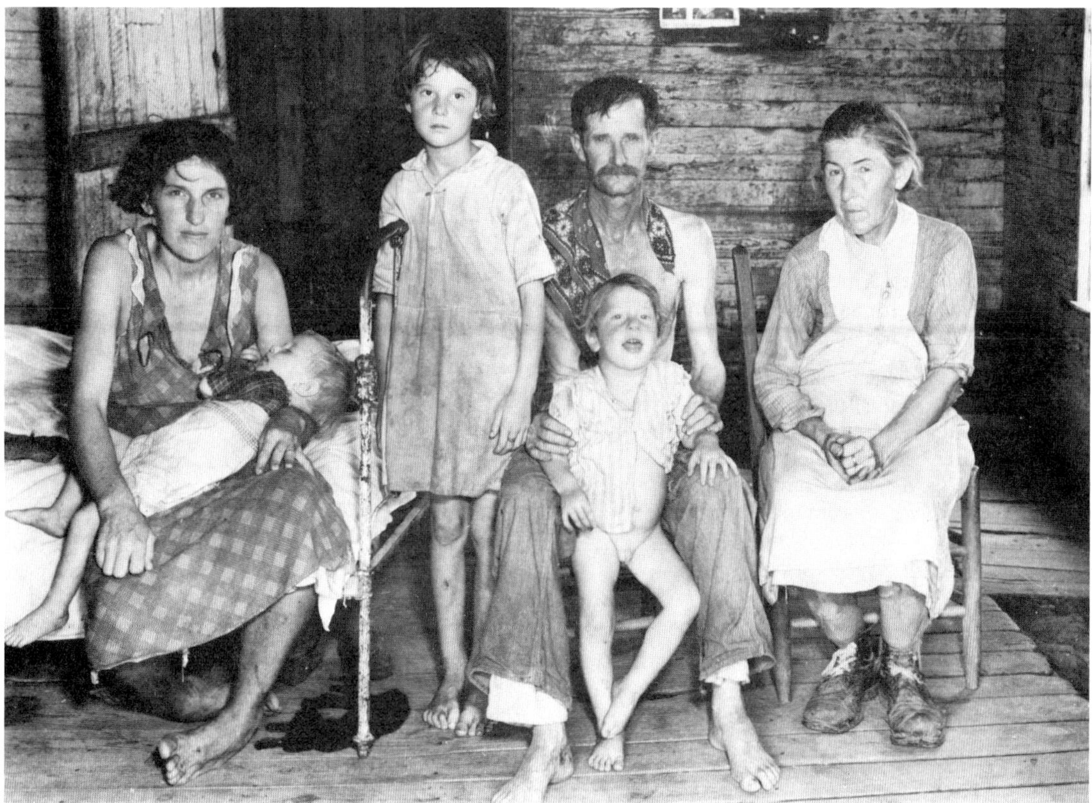

c

Fig. 7-2 THE PEOPLE LEFT BEHIND. Badlands, dust storms, and rural poverty pushed people off the land in the 1930s, and the hope of economic survival pulled many to the city. (*a*) Dust storm, Cimarron County, Oklahoma, 1936. (*b*) Rural poverty near Wadesboro, North Carolina, 1938. (*c*) Southern sharecropper family. (Library of Congress: *a* Arthur Rothstein; *b* Post Wolcott; *c* Walker Evans)

the federal government to make special provisions for their entry. In 1979–1980, about 200,000 boat people arrived from Asia, and thousands of Cuban refugees came shortly after.

If the national birthrate continues to decline, some predict that immigration will account for the total U.S. population increase after the year 2000 (Kirsch, 1978:35). Currently, more than 75 percent of all legal immigrants come from Latin America, mainly Mexico and Cuba, and Asia.

And if current trends continue, by 1990 California's population mix will be unique. Due to high birthrates among the Hispanic population and immigrants from overseas, **ethnic** and racial minorities will constitute a majority of the state's population. Further, by the mid-1980s, Hispanics, the nation's fastest-growing minority, will outnumber blacks and become the largest minority group. What this means for politics, culture, and everyday urban life is not clear. Much depends on the political leadership developed within the

Box 7-1

A POTPOURRI OF MIGRANT MEMORIES

The Uprooted

Dreams of America

Sitting in Plotzk or Kiev, what did future emigrants think life in America would mean? Mary Antin, an East European Jewish immigrant who arrived in 1889, gives us an inkling:

America was in everybody's mouth. Businessmen talked of it over their accounts; the market women made up their quarrels that they might discuss it from stall to stall . . . children played at emigrating; old folks shook their sage heads over the evening fire, and prophesied no good for those who braved the terrors of the sea . . . all talked of it, but scarcely anyone knew one true fact about this magic land. (Antin, 1899:11)

Stark Realities

Once here, "this magic land" turned into something else: sweat shops, tenements, and discouragement. Social reformer Jacob Riis describes a typical situation in New York City's seventh ward around 1900:

There were nine in the family: husband, wife, an aged grandmother, and six children; honest, hard-working Germans, scrupulously neat, but poor. All nine lived in two rooms, one about ten feet square that served as parlor, bedroom, and eating-room, the other a small hall-room made into a kitchen. . . . That day, the mother had thrown herself out of the window, and was carried up from the street dead. She was "discouraged," said some of the other women from the tenement. . . . (Riis, [1901] 1970:41)

From Dust Bowl to Peach Bowl

When the Dust Bowl hit during the Depression, some farmers in the Southwest traded their land for a Ford and headed west. They arrived in California hungry and broke, eating "tater stew so thin you could read a magazine right through it." Soon the Dust Bowl refugees were part of the Peach Bowl, wandering the open highways as migrant field labor.

The Dust Bowl refugees' plight has been celebrated in song and story. John Steinbeck's saga, *The Grapes of Wrath* ([1939] 1972) follows the Joad family to California, which did not turn out to be the promised land after all.

Seventh Heaven

At age sixteen, Malcolm X took a railroad job, mainly to visit Harlem. Here is how he remembers his first look at "This world . . . where I belonged":

Up and down along and between Lenox and Seventh and Eighth Avenues, Harlem was like some technicolor bazaar. . . . I combed not only the bright-light areas, but Harlem's residential areas from best to worst, from Sugar Hill up near the Polo Grounds, down to the slum blocks of old rat-trap apartment houses, just crawling with everything you could mention that was illegal and immoral. Dirt, garbage cans . . . drunks, dope addicts, beggars. Sleazy bars, store-front churches with gospels being shouted inside, "bargain" stores, hockshops, undertaking parlors. Greasy "home-cooking" restaurants, . . . barbershops advertising conk experts. Cadillacs, secondhand and new . . . Harlem was Seventh Heaven! (Haley and Malcolm X, [1964] 1966:74–76)

Forced Migration

During World War II, Japanese-Americans living on the West Coast were summarily herded into what were called "war relocation camps." This *haiku* by Sankuro Nagano reflects the irony of the internment camp experience in the land of "freedom":

Against the New Year sky,
Beyond the fence flutters
The Stars and Stripes.
(in Hosokawa, 1969:359)

Aztec heritage of migrations

After Guadalajara and Mexico City, Los Angeles is the largest Mexican city in the world. As the capital of La Raza, says Stan Steiner (1970:141),

Los Angeles "is to the Mexicans what Boston has been to the Irish and New York City has been to the Jews."

The heart of Los Angeles's Chicano population is the *barrio* (Spanish, originally meaning "neighborhood," later "native quarter" under colonial rulers). The barrio is a city within a city—a collection of urban villages, each with its own character, shrines, village patriarchs, gangs, and history.

Luis Valdez, the director of El Teatro Campesino of the California farm workers, says this about the history of Mexican migration:

> We are all migrants. We always have been. . . . La Raza has a tradition of migrations starting from the legend of the founding of Mexico. [The sun and war god of the Aztecs' ancestors forecast that if his people marched south they would establish a powerful kingdom.] In that march he prophesied that the children would age and the old would die, but their grandchildren would come to a great lake. In that lake they would find an eagle devouring a serpent, and on that spot they would begin to build a great nation. The nation was Aztec Mexico. . . . We put our old history on wheels of jalopies. Culture of the migrants! It is nothing but our Aztec heritage of migrations, mechanized. (in Steiner, 1970:130, 132)

various ethnic communities and their possible coalitions. Also important is the response of urban institutions and individuals.

Adjustments to Urban Life

Few generalizations can be made concerning migrants' responses to urban life. Some felt lost in the American city, overwhelmed with longing for the structure and order of rural life, whether in the Old Country or the American countryside. Others relished the fast tempo, the opportunities to get ahead, and the chance to break away from domineering mothers-in-law.

Such factors as ethnic background, religion, social class, and time of arrival in the U.S. city influenced how migrants responded to urban life. For instance, Eastern and Southern Europeans arriving before 1920 came at the "right" time. At least some of these uprooted rural folk, or their children, could begin at the bottom of the socioeconomic ladder and move up as the country grew economically and prospered. In other words, the American dream did in fact work for many of these early immigrant families. Starting in the slums and sweatshops pictured in Jacob Riis's 1901 photos, many children or grandchildren of the European immigrants moved up and out. But those who arrived in the city at a later date, especially Appalachian whites and Southern blacks, came at the "wrong" time. Social mobility has been more difficult in recent decades due to structural changes in the economy, technological innovation, and—in the case of blacks—institutionalized racism. Unskilled jobs, once the point of entry for moving up, now tend to be dead ends. Few, if any, janitors become corporate board members.

Blacks faced overwhelming obstacles. Their chances for economic advancement and social equality after 1920 were limited by segregation and discrimination, exclusion from many labor unions, and chronic injustice—all legal until the 1950s and 1960s. Desegregation laws, civil rights acts, and other public policies aimed at creating equal opportunities have not yet significantly improved the life chances of most blacks.

Blacks and Hispanics, the nation's largest minorities, remain disproportionately poor and outside the mainstream of the U.S. economy. Some scholars (e.g., Wilson, 1978) argue that the mass of black workers constitute a permanent underclass due to changes in the macroeconomic structure.

Fig. 7-3 GIVE ME YOUR TIRED, YOUR POOR . . . Historically, European immigrants came to the United States to escape famine, political oppression, landlessness, and religious persecution. This tradition continues in the twentieth century. Nazi Germany's most renowned emigrant, Albert Einstein, is shown here taking the oath of citizenship with his stepdaughter in a Trenton, New Jersey courtroom, Oct. 1, 1940. (Peter C. Marzio, National Archives)

Case Study: Irish Catholics and East European Jews

To illustrate the role that ethnicity and religion can play in immigrants' adjustment to urban America, let's look at two groups in New York City: Irish Catholics and East European Jews. The Irish started arriving after a potato famine in the Old Country during the 1840s. Waves of Russian, Romanian, and other East European Jews flocked to the New World after 1881; many were refugees, victims of pogroms like the one that struck Tevye's village in *Fiddler on the Roof.*

According to a descendant of Irish Catholic immigrants, Daniel Patrick Moynihan (in Glazer and Moynihan, 1963), the Irish brought from rural Ireland certain habits of mind that influenced their reaction to U.S. city life: experience in mass politics; suspicion of legal niceties; indifference to proprieties such as not stuffing ballot boxes; a capacity for political bureaucracy; a preference for informal over formal political institutions; and pride in taking orders from a chain of command (starting with an oligarchy of stern elders). These qualities, Moynihan says, were easily transferred from the Irish countryside to U.S. city politics. Eventually, they led to Irish control over machine politics from the early 1870s to the 1930s in New York City and elsewhere. However, this political power didn't lead to control in the private business sector or to a push for social change. According to Moynihan (in Glazer and Moynihan, 1963:229), "the Irish did not know what to do with power once they got it." Hence, they were "immensely successful" in politics, "but the very parochialism and bureaucracy that enabled them to succeed [there] prevented them from doing much with government" or using their political base to gain economic power.

The experience of the East European Jews was very different. Unlike the Irish in Ireland, East European Jews had long been a minority group within a larger hostile culture. While the Irish and many other immigrant groups came to America with one culture, "the Jews came with two, and frequently more than two cultures" (Sherman, 1965:122–123). Thus, the Jews didn't need to get used to minority group status, which sapped so much of the energy of other immigrant groups.

Further, the East European Jews had chosen a "loose pattern for their collective existence" (Howe, 1976), whereas the Irish community tended to be more clannish. Most immigrant Jews wanted to keep their separate cultural life. At the same time, they did not depend on their ethnic ties to enter American social and economic institutions; this they did on an individual basis.

While the Irish Catholics used their communal experience in the sphere of city politics, the East European Jews channeled their energies into the professions and business (although most first-generation immigrants were manual laborers and factory workers). The Jews had long been dependent on the sufferance of potential pogrom makers and Jew haters. Working for themselves—not joining the corporate bureaucracy—meant that they didn't have to depend on "the good will or personal reaction of a person who may not happen to like Jews. . . . The American Jew tries to avoid getting into a situation where discrimination may seriously affect him [or her]" (Glazer, 1958:140).

Other important ethnic differences also affected the response of the two groups to U.S. urban life. For one thing, by the turn of

Fig. 7-4 HESTER STREET. East European Jews lived on New York City's Lower East Side, the city's most densely populated area in the 1890s. One of the neighborhood's most crowded spots was Hester Street, where almost anything could be purchased from pushcarts and where new arrivals would line up, waiting for employers looking for cheap labor. (Library of Congress)

Fig. 7-5 AMERICAN DIET—ETHNIC POTPOURRI. (Peter Garfield)

the twentieth century, political dissent—especially socialism—had become a "vigorous strand within [Jewish] immigrant life" (Howe, 1976:287). For various reasons, this didn't happen in the Irish-American community. For another thing, the two groups developed into distinct subcultures based on world views, values, and religious doctrines. The East European Jewish subculture, as Glazer and Moynihan (1963:298) put it, is "secular in its attitudes, liberal in its outlook on sexual life and divorce, positive about science and social science," and passionate about education. Irish Catholics, by contrast, remain religious in their outlook, resist liberalized sexual mores, and strongly feel the "tension between moral values and modern science and technology" (298).

These differences show up in many areas, from choice of occupation to participation in civic activities. For instance, the Jews's positive attitude toward modern science is reflected in the fact that "new disciplines such as psychoanalysis, particularly in New York, are so largely staffed by Jews" (Glazer and Moynihan, 1963:298).

One might think that over the generations these differences become less important and that values of the two groups grow more alike. Not so, say Glazer and Moynihan. They argue that over the passing decades the values and attitudes of Irish Catholics and East European Jews have grown further apart.

Looking at five ethnic groups in New York City—the Irish, East European Jews, Puerto Ricans, Italians, and blacks—Glazer and Moynihan conclude that *race* and *ethnicity* are significant, often independent, variables affecting city life. In their estimation,

> Ethnicity is more than an influence on events; it is commonly the source of events. Social and political institutions do not merely respond to ethnic interests; a great number of institutions exist for the specific purpose of serving ethnic interests. (1963:310).

If this is true, whatever happened to the **melting pot?**

WHAT HAPPENED TO THE MELTING POT?

"These States," wrote poet Walt Whitman, "are the amplest poem. Here is not merely a nation, but a teeming nation of nations." A nation of nations—that was the vision: a great melting pot, a fusion of all immigrants into a new American. "Here," proclaimed naturalized American Jean de Crevecoeur in 1782, "individuals of all nations are melted into a new race of man." Thus, from the very beginning, America was viewed as a new nation—a nation unlike all others that would fuse people of different origins into one people.

But this ideal waned over the generations. When European Catholic and Jewish immigrants came in massive waves, many old-stock WASPs wondered whether the melting pot was possible—or desirable. By the 1880s and 1890s, several reactions to the immigrant tide had surfaced.

One reaction came from upper-crust WASPs: the founding of ancestral associations such as the Daughters of the American Revolution (DAR) in 1890. During the 1890s, some thirty-five hereditary, historical, and patriotic associations were formed as these old-stock WASPs searched for their roots (Baltzell, 1964).

Old-stock Americans also took direct action: trying to shut the floodgates. The American Protective Association (1886) and other groups aimed at restricting immigration were formed by those calling themselves "native Americans."

Liberal reformers had another approach: turning "them" into "us." Schools, military academies, sports clubs, and settlement houses became vehicles for **assimilation,** not **acculturation.** Their goals: to inculcate the "American way of life" and to "Americanize" the immigrants.

Another reaction was to deny that some immigrant groups were capable of being assimilated. The San Francisco School Board, for instance, declared in 1905 that it would segregate Japanese children to prevent white children from being "affected by association with pupils of the Mongolian race" (in Hosokawa, 1969:86).

By 1908, when Israel Zangwill's play *The Melting Pot* appeared on Broadway, the Chinese had already been barred from further immigration; the Japanese in California were officially classified as "aliens ineligible to citizenship"; blacks were segregated and denied civil rights; upper-class WASPs were busy finding their roots; and millions of Catholic and Jewish immigrants lived and died in unsanitary, overcrowded, oppressive urban slums. Still, Zangwill's play was a great success. It celebrated

> the great Melting Pot where all the races of Europe are melting and reforming! . . . The real American has not yet arrived. His is only in the Crucible. I tell you—he will be the fusion of all races, the coming superman. (1909:37–38)

Ethnic Consciousness and WASP Values

Today, the ideal of the melting pot has disappeared. In its place are **cultural pluralism** and ethnic consciousness. An upsurge in identification with ethnic roots is symbolized by such slogans as "Italian-American Power" and "Black Is Beautiful." It is also reflected in popular culture; among the cast of characters on prime-time TV in the 1970s were Kojak,

Fig. 7-6 AMERICANIZATION CLASS, 1919. Liberal reformers taught immigrants the "American way of life" and the English language. (Chicago Historical Society)

Columbo, Chico, the Jeffersons, Kaz, Banacek, the Romano family, and Paris—all identifiable ethnics.

In social science, the new ethnic consciousness is reflected in language. The groups once customarily called "minorities" (a word that refers more to the lack of a group's social power than its numbers) are now often called "subcultures" or "subcommunities"—that is, groups defining themselves as different from other groups and from the dominant culture in terms of world view and/or lifestyle.

Michael Novak, a spokesperson for the new ethnic consciousness and a descendant of Slovak immigrants, believes that white ethnics have been made to feel stupid, backward, and immoral by what he calls the WASP "superculture" in America. In *The Rise of the Unmeltable Ethnics* (1971:179, 180, 185), Novak describes and contrasts white ethnic working-class culture and WASP superculture, so-called because he feels it has tried to overwhelm and stamp out competing ways of life:

The WASP home cherishes good order, poise, soft voices, cleanliness . . . [such a home] offers culture shock to non-WASPs. Decorum and self-control. Tight emotions. . . . To the WASP, the direct flow of emotion is childish; his acculturation requires cognitive control. . . . The WASP way—the almost universal industrial way of the modern age—is to put a harsh rein upon the impulses of man's animal nature, . . . and to order him docilely *to produce.* It is a life geared to action, to "changing history," to progress.

Working-class white ethnic homes, Novak (1971:26) says, are just the opposite, and the people in them don't share WASP values or goals. Noise, family get-togethers, and emotionality typify white ethnic home life. And instead of seeking to change history, white ethnic males see the world as a tough, violent place where hard work, family discipline, and gradual self-development are the routes to moderate success. To the women, the world outside remains "mainly unchangeable."

Other observers agree that family and neighborhood are centers of working-class ethnic life. And some celebrate the vitality of such neighborhoods. Jane Jacobs (1961), for one, finds the ethnic neighborhood to be alive with activity, especially the sidewalks. She describes the "intricate sidewalk ballet" on her stretch of Hudson Street in New York City, a scene which not only animates the city but helps keep its residents safe:

When I get home after work, the ballet is reaching its crescendo. This is the time of roller skates and stilts and tricycles, and games in the lee of the stoop with bottletops and plastic cowboys; this is the time of bundles and packages, zig-zagging from the drug store back over to the butcher's; this is the time when teenagers, all dressed up, are pausing to ask if their slips show or their collars look right; this is the time when beautiful girls get out of MG's; this is the time when the fire engines go through; this is the time when anybody you know around Hudson Street will go by. (1961:52)

No one could mistake Jacobs's description of her ethnic neighborhood for a portrait of a middle-class WASP street scene.

One side note is of special interest here. Jacobs's description is a hymn to street life, stressing its humanity and vitality, its safety and orderliness. But other urbanists see the ethnic street scene in a different light. In his Pulitzer Prize–winning book *The Uprooted* (1952:155), historian Oscar Handlin comments that the active street life in nineteenth-century New York City is "evidence of the old home's disintegration. . . . Those children in earnest play at the corner—who controls them, to what discipline are they subject?" Thus, while Jacobs views the street as a ballet of social organization, Handlin sees it as an indicator of social *dis*organization in ethnic communities. Once again, what you see depends on how you look at it.

THE STEW POT

The persistence of ethnic communities, such as those described by Glazer and Moynihan, Novak, and Jacobs, suggests that America is a **stew pot,** not a melting pot. Some groups have remained aloof and unassimilated by choice, such as religious-based ethnic communities like the Pennsylvania Amish. But many groups had no choice: blacks, Chinese, Japanese, and Hispanics. For decades, they were victims of prejudice, discrimination, or racism.

Native Americans: The Unassimilated

Some groups have been assimilated more than others. In economic terms, native Americans have fared worst; they are the poorest ethnic group in the nation. The Navajo nation, presently the largest tribe, has a per capita income of about $1,000.

In social terms, official U.S. government

policy toward the first American has been assimilationist, but the policy has not worked: "Hardly any community or tribe has wholly disappeared since the end of the days of conquest by warfare, genocide, or disease" (Sturtevant, 1976:22). Forcibly removed from their ancestral homes, robbed of schooling in their tribal languages and sent off to Bureau of Indian Affairs schools, and overwhelmed by white migrants, native Americans still retain their distinctive cultures.

Officially, the federal government vowed to assimilate native Americans into the mainstream of American culture. Yet, they weren't granted citizenship until 1924.

The plight of the first Americans can be summed up as follows:

> All elements in the American population either decided to leave their native country (which implies some dissatisfaction and thus readiness to adjust to a new environment) or else were violently wrenched from their homes and sent into slavery across the ocean, leaving no choice but adjustment and assimilation. But Indians are not like this at all. They are members of societies that remained in their native country, where they were invaded, conquered, and overwhelmed by foreigners. (Sturtevant, 1976:22)

Blacks and Hispanics: Permanent Underclass?

Blacks from Africa first arrived in the English colonies in 1619. They were considered indentured servants who could work off their bonds after a period of time. This quickly changed, and by the mid-1600s, the black slave population in the South increased. Northerners in colonial America also held slaves, mainly as house servants and farm workers.

The forced migration of black Africans to the fields and cities of the colonies and the early migration of British and European settlers to North America were inextricably linked: "They were both undertaken primarily in the hope of securing a better life—for whites" (Greene, 1976:89).

From colonial days and the plantation South to the present, much has changed. Blacks now have citizenship and civil rights. Most live in urban areas, not rural places. And yet, as victims of long-standing racism and economic discrimination, consigned as a group to lower socioeconomic status, their fate has been questioned by many social scientists. William Julius Wilson's controversial and influential study *The Declining Significance of Race* (1978) argues that racial discrimination has created a huge black underclass, what others call a "proletariat." According to Wilson, a black sociologist at the University of Chicago, class is now more important than race in determining blacks' life chances. The mass of poor and poorly trained blacks, Wilson says, have little hope or chance of escaping poverty and low status.

Years earlier, Glazer and Moynihan came to the same conclusion. In 1963 they wrote that blacks and Puerto Ricans in New York City were a "submerged, exploited, and very possibly permanent proletariat" (1963: 299).

The notion that large groups of citizens may be *permanently* poor goes against the American grain. As De Toqueville long ago observed, Americans will endure poverty and even servitude, but not fixed class differences. In the past, different standards of life were made tolerable by the idea of equal opportunity for advancement. All were reassured that they too could move up socially and economically. This assumption has been at the heart of the liberal perspective. It is now questioned by neo-conservatives and radicals alike.

Making It: Japanese-Americans

While some ethnic groups never assimilated, others prospered. One group, Japanese-Americans, are a case in point—and a very special one. The Japanese have met with prejudice, discrimination, and racism—"the denial on racist grounds of the right to naturalization, the denial in the areas where they largely lived of the right to own land or enter certain professions, and eventually complete exclusion" (Hosokawa, 1969:xi). At the outbreak of World War II, about 100,000 Japanese-Americans living on the West Coast were evacuated from their homes and put behind barbed wire in "war relocation camps," a euphemism for concentration camps. Many of their businesses were taken over by whites, and their land was confiscated.

Yet, since the war, the Japanese-American community, a tiny minority group (less than one-half of 1 percent of the population), has prospered economically, escaped the ghetto, and managed to retain its distinctive culture. Traditional Japanese culture and values have much to do with it. First-generation Japanese-Americans *(Issei)* came from a culture in which "diligence in work, combined with simple frugality, had an almost religious imperative, similar to what has been called 'the Protestant ethic' in Western culture," and psychologically, the *Issei* carried with them an "achievement orientation" (Petersen in Hosokawa, 1969:495). Such values were transmitted from *Issei* to *Nisei* (the second generation in America) and to succeeding generations by strong family ties and culture.

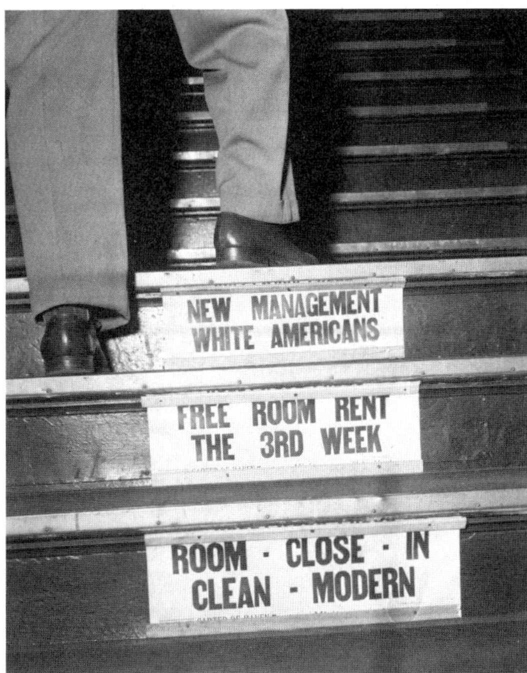

Fig. 7-7 NEW MANAGEMENT, WHITE AMERICANS. During World War II, Japanese-Americans on the West Coast were evacuated from their homes to relocation camps, and their businesses were taken over by whites. (National Archives)

Pride without Power

But for other groups, ethnic pride—rooted in a religious, national, and/or racial heritage—has not always been translated into social power or economic gains. The wide disparity between ethnic pride and relative lack of clout could be the stuff that dreams—or political coalitions—are built on. Alternatively, this gap could lead to social change—or social "disorder," depending on how you look at it.

Today, many forms of blatant discrimination are illegal. Nonetheless, social prejudice, fear, racism, and hate based on ethnic differences linger on. Antiethnic organizations, notably the Ku Klux Klan, remind us how deep the stream of hate runs in American society.

Cultural Pluralism

Few high school texts discuss the continuing importance of ethnicity in metropolitan America, particularly in politics. Neither do many influential scholarly works. For example, the already classic study of political *Participation in America* (Verba and Nie, 1972) makes only a single passing reference to ethnicity as a significant factor in levels of participation. In fact, few empirical studies even test the possibility that ethnic background may have an impact—independent of other factors, such as social class—on urban political participation. One of the rare studies that does test that possibility among six ethnic groups (Irish, blacks, Jews, Puerto Ricans, Cubans, and Dominicans) finds that ethnicity indeed has an independent impact on political attitudes, which affects participation (Nelson, 1979).

Why has ethnicity so often been neglected or downplayed as a force in sociopolitical life? There are several possible reasons. Perhaps it reflects a growing consensus among scholars that nonsocioeconomic factors, such as ethnicity, are not at the root of differences among social groups.

Alternatively, the neglect of ethnicity may reflect the power of the melting pot metaphor. In a nation considered democratic and modern, positions assigned at birth such as ethnic status are supposed to count for little. But this is just not the case. Persistent social,

Fig. 7-8 ETHNIC PLURALISM. Billboard in front of the Lower Manhattan Republican Club in 1950 shows the continuing importance of ethnicity in city politics. (Museum of the City of New York)

political, and economic inequalities still exist among ethnic groups, and our life chances are significantly influenced by the ethnic group into which we are born. This runs counter to democratic theory.

Although downplayed or ignored, ethnicity also has great impact on our personal as well as our social identity. It even affects our intimate relationships. A couple from different ethnic backgrounds, for instance, may have trouble communicating with each other. While they may go to a psychologist for help, their problem may not be psychological but rather cultural, tied to their ethnic modes of behaving and coping. Such ethnic cultural differences, say, between the cool WASP and the emotional ethnic, are not usually discussed openly, especially by people who consider themselves cosmopolitan.

Recognizing, even celebrating, ethnic differences brings back the enduring issue of community: insiders versus outsiders. As a *Newsweek* columnist phrased it, "You can't have the old enriching differences without some of the old prejudices" (Will, 1979:116). In other words, cultural pluralism wears two faces. One is proud and strong, giving a sense of special belonging to individuals and a rich variety to urban life. It gives the Dutch-Americans of Pella, Iowa (population 7,800), and the former residents of Boston's Italian-American West End a sense of community. But the other side is ugly, glowering with misunderstanding and hate. And it is in cities, which bring together heterogeneous individuals, where both faces of ethnic pluralism are so prominently displayed.

ANOTHER LOOK

Classical urban theory suggests that kinship and blood relations are key factors in the social organization of small-scale rural community called *Gemeinschaft* or mechanically solid society. Following the rural-urban typologies, then, it should come as no surprise that tribalism and ethnicity remain vitally important forces in developing countries today. In Afghanistan and Iran, for example, Pathan and Kurd tribes have led armed rebellions against central governments.

Classical urban theory also suggests that ethnic-based perspectives will give way to a more cosmopolitan outlook in urban-industrial society. But so far, at least, the two often coexist. Efforts to stamp out cultural differences based on ethnicity have failed miserably in many cases, both in the United States and other advanced technological societies. Whether in America, Canada, Europe, or Russia, many ethnic groups cling to their language and cultural traditions, sometimes in the face of official policies to obliterate them. Refusing to be melted into mass society, some, like the Basques in France and Spain, have turned to armed rebellion, while others, including the Scots, seek varying degrees of autonomy via legislative means.

Thus, blood ties and ethnic solidarity—cornerstones of traditional community—still play a key role in urban-industrial society. Indeed, Glazer and Moynihan argue that ethnicity is often a causal variable in metropolitan America, determining the fate of many social and political institutions. At a more subtle level, Novak shows that there are persistent differences in world view, cognitive style, and emotionality between white ethnics and WASPs in America.

Novak's observations are most interesting in light of classical urban theory, particularly Wirth's. Novak's distinction between the working-class white ethnic subculture and the WASP superculture parallels Wirth's dichotomy between rural and urban personality. That the rural personality (white ethnic subculture) has not disappeared within urban-industrial society lends support to

Wirth's critics, for it suggests that urbanism is not *a* way of life but rather ways of life. It also suggests that urbanization is not a single, universal, and universalizing process.

PROJECTS

1. **Ethnicity.** Determine the two largest ethnic groups in your community. For each one, find out when they first settled there, where they lived, what work they did, and what institutions they built (e.g., churches, private schools, clubs). Trace the changes over time from their arrival until today. Do members of each group cluster together in residential sections? What areas do they live in? What kinds of jobs do they hold now? Are their institutions still viable?

2. **Family history.** Use all available research tools—including oral histories with relatives, genealogy charts, library documents, archival materials, and family diaries—to establish your family's ethnic history and consciousness. When did they arrive here? Do members feel like part of the melting pot or the stew pot? What distinctive ethnic cultural traditions are retained by you or members of your family? Do most of your friends come from the same ethnic background? In what ways, if any, do you feel set apart from members of other ethnic groups?

SUGGESTIONS FOR FURTHER LEARNING

For an overview of the history of immigration to America and immigrants' lives once they settled in the country, see *A Nation of Nations: The People who Came to America as Seen Through Objects, Prints, and Photographs at the Smithsonian Institution* (New York: Harper & Row, 1976), edited by Peter C. Marzio of the Smithsonian Institution. This handsomely illustrated and designed volume contains short, readable, and frank essays by members of the Smithsonian staff, plus a useful bibliography.

Perhaps the most widely read book on the history of the mass migrations in the nineteenth century remains Oscar Handlin's *The Uprooted* (Boston: Little, Brown, 1952), a strong impressionistic account with relatively little empirical evidence. Handlin focuses on the loss of the Old World peasant community and the sense of alienation resulting in a new individualism. He makes few distinctions between differential adjustments to urban life among various European immigrant groups.

Scholarly study of the immigrant experience is greatly enhanced by a series of works published by Arno Press (New York). Multivolume series on the experience of Italian-Americans, the American Catholic tradition, the Puerto Rican experience, the Mexican-American and Chicano heritages, and the Chinese and Japanese in North America include literary chronicles as well as social science and personal accounts. Arno Press also publishes two series, called *The American Immigration Collection* (seventy-four books) and *The Reports of the Immigration Commission,* popularly known as the Dillingham Reports. This forty-one volume series, originally published between 1907 and 1910, provides fascinating clues to the legislation enacted between 1917 and 1924 which closed America's gates to immigrants. The Dillingham Reports presented what they felt to be scientific proof of the inferiority of Eastern and Southern Europeans.

Personal memoirs of immigrants include Mary Antin, *From Plotzk to Boston* (Boston: W.B. Clarke, 1899), and Thomas C. Wheeler (ed.), *The Immigrant Experience: The Anguish of Becoming American* (New York: Pelican, [1971] 1977). Selections include "A Chinese Evolution" by Jade Snow Wong; "Italians in Hell's Kitchen" by Mario Puzo; and "Norwegians on the Prairie" by Eugene Boe. In "Growing Up American" (*Society,* January/February 1977, pp. 64–71), sociologist Charles C. Moskos, Jr., recalls his Greek-American family and childhood in Chicago and Albuquerque, New Mexico.

The short film *Ellis Island* (1974) recaptures the arrival of Europeans in nineteenth-century America with old stills, interviews, and historical commentary. One effort to preserve the history and heritage of ethnic immigrants in the Boston area is a project under the direction of Carla B. Johnston which has produced a five-tape oral history, a film, and a book which stress the value of the rich ethnic mix of Somerville, Massachusetts.

The plight of rural migrants is told in the works of John Steinbeck, particularly *The Grapes of Wrath* (New York: Viking, [1939] 1972). The movie version of Steinbeck's novel of the Joad family, starring Henry Fonda, appeared in 1940. In his autobiographical account, *Black Boy* (New York: Signet, [1937] 1963), Richard Wright relates his hopes when heading north on a train for Chicago: "With ever watchful eyes and bearing scars, visible and invisible, I headed North, full of a hazy notion that life could be lived with dignity" (285). Wright's early memories of life in Mississippi include the escape from the home of an uncle who had just been lynched by a white mob.

Harlem on my Mind: Cultural Capital of Black America, 1900–1968 (New York: Random House, 1968) is a compilation of photos and news stories from the life and times of Harlem, including articles on the poetry of social protest in the 1920s, the lure of Northern industry to Southern blacks, and other aspects of urban black culture.

The new immigrant wave of the 1970s is the topic of *Society* magazine's September/October, 1977 issue. Various essays examine recent migrant experiences of East Indians, Koreans, Philippinos, and other ethnic groups. Michael J. Piore examines the rise of migration from Latin America and the Caribbean to the United States as well as the process that brought waves of European immigrants to America and blacks to Northern cities in *Birds of Passage* (New York: Cambridge University Press, 1979).

Numerous feature films capture aspects of immigrant and ethnic life. Franco Brusati's *Bread and Chocolate* (1974) is a poignant satire about an Italian immigrant in Switzerland who wants to assimilate so badly that he dyes his hair blond. *El Super* (1979) tells the story of a Cuban emigré working in New York City as a building superintendent. Co-directed by Leon Ichaso and Orlando Jimenez-Leal, it shows the vitality and despair of Cuban refugees in a cold, inhospitable climate and their adjustments to Manhattan. In *The Apprenticeship of Duddy Kravitz* (1974), actor Richard Dreyfus portrays Duddy's struggle to "make it" as a second-generation Jew in Montreal. Joan Silver's *Hester Street* (1975) gives a glimpse of Lower East Side life in New York City after the turn of the century.

For a discussion of melting pot versus "seething cauldron," see Peter I. Rose's edited anthology, *Nation of Nations: The Ethnic Experience and the Racial Crisis* (New York: Random House, 1972); among the contributors are James Baldwin, Vine Deloria, Jr., and Piri Thomas.

Among the many books concerning ethnicity cited in the chapter itself, one deserves special mention: Irving Howe's best-seller, *World of Our Fathers: The Journey of the East European Jews to America and the Life They Found and Made* (New York: Simon & Schuster, 1976). A scholarly portrait, it is also highly readable, a work of history and imagination which draws both on knowledge about and acquaintance with his subjects.

Michael Novak's magazine, *The Novak Report*, presents the latest developments in what he calls the "new ethnicity."

KEY TERMS

Acculturation A process by which one culture is modified through contact with another. Many subcultural differences are retained in the process.

Assimilation (1) The merging of dissimilar subcultures into one common culture or (2) the absorption of one group by another whereby the absorbed group loses its prior distinctiveness.

Cultural pluralism Heterogeneity within a society, where ethnic and other minority groups retain their cultural identity. Cultural pluralism results in a stew pot rather than a melting pot.

Ethnic Referring to a group with a sense of group identity different from other subgroups within a society. Ethnicity can be based on national, racial, or religious background.

Melting pot A process by which a unique American supposedly emerges from the blending together of immigrants with dissimilar backgrounds.

Stew pot Our term, showing rejection of the idea

that the United States is a true melting pot and implying that ethnic groups retain important social, economic, and/or cultural distinctions.

WASP Acronym for white Anglo-Saxon Protestant.

REFERENCES

Antin, Mary
1899 From Plotzk to Boston. Boston: W. B. Clarke.

Baltzell, E. Digby
1964 The Protestant Establishment: Aristocracy and Caste in America. New York: Random House.

Benet, Stephen Vincent
1943 Western Star. New York: Farrar & Rinehart.

Glazer, Nathan
1958 "The American Jew and the attainment of middle-class rank." Pp. 138–46 in Marshall Sklare (ed.), The Jews: Social Patterns of an American Group. Glencoe, Ill.: Free Press.

Glazer, Nathan and Daniel Patrick Moynihan
1963 Beyond the Melting Pot. Cambridge: MIT Press.

Greene, Jack P.
1976 " 'We the People'—the emergence of the American nation." Pp. 84–95 in Peter C. Marzio (ed.), A Nation of Nations: The People who Came to America as Seen Through Objects, Prints, and Photographs at the Smithsonian Institution. New York: Harper & Row.

Haley, Alex and Malcolm X
[1964]
1966 The Autobiography of Malcolm X. New York: Grove Press.

Handlin, Oscar
1952 The Uprooted. Boston: Little, Brown.

Hosokawa, Bill
1969 Nisei: The Quiet Americans. New York: Morrow.

Howe, Irving
1976 World of Our Fathers: The Journey of the East European Jews to America and the Life They Found and Made. New York: Simon & Schuster.

Jacobs, Jane
1961 The Death and Life of Great American Cities. New York: Vintage Books.

Kirsch, Jonathan
1978 "Chicano power." New West 3:35–40.

Marzio, Peter C. (ed.)
1976 A Nation of Nations: The People who Came to America as Seen Through Objects, Prints and Photographs at the Smithsonian Institution. New York: Harper & Row.

Nelson, Dale C.
1979 "Ethnicity and socioeconomic status as sources of participation: the case for ethnic political culture." American Political Science Review 73:1024–38.

Novak, Michael
1971 The Rise of the Unmeltable Ethnics. New York: Macmillan.

Palen, John
1975 The Urban World. New York: McGraw-Hill.

Riis, Jacob
[1901]
1970 How the Other Half Lives: Studies among the Tenements of New York. New York: Dover.

Sherman, C. Bezalel
1965 The Jew Within American Society: A Study in Ethnic Individuality. Detroit: Wayne State University Press.

Steinbeck, John
[1939]
1972 The Grapes of Wrath. New York: Viking.

Steiner, Stan
1970 La Raza: The Mexican Americans. New York: Harper.

Sturtevant, William C.
1976 "The first Americans." Pp. 4–23 in Peter C. Marzio (ed.), A Nation of Nations: The People who Came to America as Seen Through Objects, Prints, and Photographs at the Smithsonian Institution. New York: Harper & Row.

Verba, Sidney and Norman H. Nie
1972 Participation in America. New York: Harper & Row.

Will, George
1979 "Wagons in a circle." Newsweek (Sept. 17):116.

Wilson, William Julius
1978 The Declining Significance of Race: Blacks and Changing American Institutions. Chicago: University of Chicago Press.

Zangwill, Israel
1909 The Melting Pot: A Drama in 4 Acts. New York: Macmillan.

PART THREE
Rules of the Game

Douglas M. McWilliams

CHAPTER 8
Social Ladders

"All men are created equal." That's what American children learn in school.

As they grow up, they begin to realize that some people are more equal than others. Looking around town, they may notice that some people live in big houses on tree-lined streets while others inhabit shacks by the railroad tracks. On prime-time TV, they watch dramas in which people with badges of authority—police shields, white hospital coats, security clearance tags—wield power over those who don't. They may come across novelist F. Scott Fitzgerald's famous statement to Ernest Hemingway: "The very rich are different from you and me."

Before reaching voting age, most of us sense that—rhetoric and the Declaration of

Independence notwithstanding—all people are not born equal and don't grow up equal. Most of us sense these inequalities in America—between rich and poor, powerful and powerless, socially esteemed and socially shunned. But rarely do we examine the *social* bases of these differences. We haven't been taught to do so. Primary and secondary school textbooks rarely refer to inequalities that are linked to social factors. Hence, many Americans end up believing that existing disparities result from personal failure or bad luck.

Why is it that some Americans have more of the good things in life than others? How do social structural variables affect a person's life chances? This chapter explores these questions. It looks at the influence of class, status, power, sex, age, religion, race, and ethnicity on a person's place in the social hierarchy. First, it outlines two general theoretical approaches to equality and inequality: the perspectives of Karl Marx and Max Weber. Then it examines social hierarchies in urban America today.

This chapter, then, deals with the larger societal patterns that influence the games urbanites play. The next chapter focuses on the micro level of analysis: face-to-face social interaction. It concludes by demonstrating the utility of combining macro and micro perspectives to gain a more complete understanding of urban social organization.

TWO WAYS OF LOOKING AT SOCIAL STRATIFICATION: MARX AND WEBER

The topic of **social stratification** (the process by which individuals and groups rank each other in a social hierarchy; from the Latin *strata*, meaning "layers") has occupied social thinkers for thousands of years. Over the millennia, many explanations have been offered to justify a society's inequalities and to explain why some possess more valuables (money, prestige, material goods, knowledge, power) than others. In the case of India, inequalities between **castes** (rigid social divisions based on status ascribed at birth) are justified by Hindu scriptures linking one's present position in the social hierarchy to one's past lives. In other religious belief systems, one's current position on the social ladder is tied to faith, good works, or divine providence.

With the birth of modern social science in nineteenth-century Western Europe came new nonreligious explanations for social inequalities. As the German philosopher Hegel once wrote, "The owl of Minerva flies at dusk," meaning that wisdom appears at certain historical times: the approaching end of one era and the start of another. Two German social thinkers, Karl Marx and Max Weber, lived at such a historical moment. Both witnessed the rapid rise of industrial cities, the rural-to-urban shift, and the changing social relationships that industrialization and urbanization brought. Profoundly influenced by these changing times, first Marx, then Weber, formulated theories to describe and explain the bases of social stratification in different historical settings.

The models of Marx and Weber remain the leading theories of social stratification today. Often they are viewed as competing theoretical models. But in important ways, the two intellectual giants agreed. Indeed, Weber's model can be seen as an extension of Marx's model as well as an alternative to it.

Marx and the Concept of Class

[T]he "first and only" time her grandmother [the wealthy Mrs. Peabody, member of a distinguished upper-class New England family] ever slapped [her granddaughter Marietta Endicott Peabody Tree] was when, as a young girl, Marietta referred to an acquaintance as "very middle class." After the slap came these stern, grandmotherly words: "There are no classes in America—upper, lower, or middle. You are never to use that term again." (Birmingham, 1968:340)

Not long ago, Pulitzer Prize-winning journalist J. Anthony Lukas remarked that "America's dirty little secret is not sex. It is not power. Nor is it success. America's dirty little secret is class. It remains a secret even to some of its most cruelly treated victims." Noting a *New York Times* survey which found that one-quarter of all Americans don't consider themselves as belonging to any class at all, Lukas (1978:9) concluded, "To most of us, class is something only Germans with beards write about."

Most likely, Lukas was referring to one famous bearded German: Karl Marx. But he might have been noting another: Max Weber. Both Karl Marx (1818–1883) and Max Weber (1864–1920) insisted on the crucial importance of class in determining a society's system of individual rights and privileges. Both thought that one's class position was a key to one's life chances. Yet the name of Weber, a political liberal in his own time, is not well known to most Americans. In contrast, Marx is widely recognized, and to put it mildly, his ideas on social class have been unpopular among most Americans. At various times in U.S. history, even to be suspected of being a Marxist has spelled disaster for people in numerous walks of life. Some lost their jobs, their friends, even their lives (by suicide) for real or suspected adherence to Marxist theory. Woody Allen's film *The Front* (1976) dramatizes the plight of a Hollywood screenwriter blacklisted during the McCarthy era of the 1950s.

Why have Marx's ideas been considered alien, un-American, and dangerous? Why is the concept of class "America's dirty little secret"? What did Marx think brought about social and political inequalities? And why do his ideas still fascinate scholars and activists today, over 100 years after he sat in London's British Museum painstakingly working them out? Before we can begin to answer these questions, a little background on Marx's thought is called for.

As noted in Chapter 5, Marx was one of many European theorists who tried to make sense out of what was going on in his own time. Rural folk were streaming into the rising industrial cities in England to work in the expanding factory system. The nature and meaning of work were being transformed. To Marx, these changes (more fully discussed in Chapter 16) signaled a historical event that became central to his analysis of history: the emergence of a new class of people, a mass of urban workers who controlled neither their work process nor their working conditions. He called this class of urban propertyless workers the **proletariat.**

According to Marx, the proletariat was one of two major social divisions or classes to result from the development of capitalism. The other new class he called the **bourgeoisie:** urban-based propertied people who determined what the proletariat produced, how they produced it, and what wages they were paid.

To Marx, the development of medieval cities and mercantile capitalism in Western Europe were inextricably linked. Marx's choice of the word "bourgeoisie" denotes this linkage, for a "bourg" is literally a town; thus, a bourgeois is an urbanite.

Very briefly, Marx reasoned as follows. Both the proletariat and the bourgeoisie developed out of the transformation from feudal to capitalist society between the sixteenth and nineteenth centuries in Western Europe. As this historical shift proceeded, self-sufficient peasant economies died out. In

Fig. 8-1 KARL MARX AND MAX WEBER. (Marx, Radio Times Hulton Picture Library; Weber, Alfred Weber Institut fur Sozial und Staatswissenschaften der Universitat, Heidelberg, Germany)

their place arose city-based economies controlled by merchants and bankers, increasingly dependent on trade and commerce. The growth of mercantilist cities in medieval Europe, starting in the 1500s, marked the expropriation of rural people. According to Marx, the separation of the peasant from the soil was the basis of the whole capitalist process. As rural people were separated from the land and uprooted to work in urban manufacturing, they came under the domination of the bourgeoisie. Now the urban workers had no land, no wealth—nothing except their labor, which they sold to factory owners. Living at a subsistence level with no public welfare system or unions to represent them, workers had few bargaining chips against their employers. In this situation, capitalist factory owners could set the wage scale and working conditions to suit their own class interests—specifically, the maximization of profit. Inevitably, the class interests of the proletariat would conflict with those of the bourgeoisie; the owners of capital wanted to maximize profit, not the welfare of their workers.

Up to this point, Marx's analysis of history doesn't seem very controversial. Marx's contemporaries of varying ideologies described the process of social change (e.g., from *Gemeinschaft* to *Gesellschaft*) in much the same way that Marx viewed the shift from feudal to capitalist society. (That these descriptions of the rural-to-urban shift transcended ideology is indicated by a footnote to history: Marx's favorite novelist was a French conservative, Honoré de Balzac [1834], who mourned the passing of French aristocratic society but chronicled its demise in terms Marx thought brilliant.)

Marx did not invent the concept of class. It dates at least to ancient Rome, when people were ranked in six social divisions according to their wealth. Nor was Marx the first to recognize the existence of classes; many historians before him had used the concept. Then why are his ideas on social class considered un-American by so many?

First, Marx defined **class** in a way that linked economic control to social domination. Marx's logic was as follows. A person's social class is determined by his or her relationship to the **means of production** (e.g., land in feudal society, factories in industrial capitalism). Class depends on how much the individual owns or controls of the means of production. *Those who own or control the means of production in a society also control the social organization of production.* Thus, classes are not income groups. Class is much more than an economic position; it also denotes the social relations that grow out of the way a society organizes its economy (for example, private or collective ownership of the technology in use).

To a non-Marxist, "capital is just a thing (a machine, for example) or a sum of money. For a Marxist, that thing or that sum of money is only the facade for a social relation of domination: the machine has the mysterious power to compel people to obey 'its' rhythms, the money makes people dance to its tune" (Heilbroner, 1978:35). Under what Marx called the capitalist **mode of production** (the productive and social arrangements under capitalism, including the private ownership of the means of production), to be a capitalist or bourgeois ensures social as well as economic domination.

Secondly, Marx maintained that human history could be understood best as a continuing struggle among classes for domination and control over scarce resources. It is this idea—*inherent class conflict*—that has traditionally gone against the American grain. American ideology stresses the opposite idea: harmony among social classes. The assumption of class harmony is captured in a favorite saying by laissez-faire economists: "A rising tide lifts all boats," meaning that economic prosperity and growth help rich and poor alike.

Conventional widsom in the United States holds that the interests of workers are allied with the interests of business and industry, not antithetical. In the late 1970s some labor leaders, notably the head of the United Auto Workers, did speak of the "one-sided class war" (San Francisco *Chronicle*, 1978:12). But in a nation where one-quarter of the population rejects the concept of class as meaningful (and the majority of the rest see themselves as middle class), the notion of "class war" between haves and have-nots is not popular. Neither is Marx's idea that some are rich and powerful *because* others are poor and powerless.

Finally, what has seemed so alien about Marx's views are his predicted outcomes of the class struggle between bourgeoisie and proletariat, haves and have-nots. According to Marx, inherent contradictions within capitalism between the **forces of production** (the technology in use, for example) and the social **relations of production** (e.g., private ownership of the technology in use) would work themselves out in a dialectical process and lead to a new form of society. He believed that the proletariat would develop a subjective **class consciousness,** realizing that they share an objective class situation (long hours, little pay, no control over their work process, domination by another class). Ultimately, Marx thought, workers would act as a class to wrest control from the bourgeoisie. To Marx, this was inevitable: "the class struggle necessarily leads to the dictatorship of the proletariat" ([1852] 1977:341). He wrote in "The Communist Manifesto" in 1848, a year marked by revolutions in Europe:

> The essential condition for the existence, and for the sway of the bourgeois class, is the formation and augmentation of capital; the condition for capital is wage-labour. Wage labour rests exclusively on competition between the labourers. The advance of industry, whose involuntary promoter is the bourgeoisie, replaces the isolation of the labourers, due to competition, by their revolutionary combination, due to association. The development of Modern Industry, therefore, cuts from under its feet the very foundation on which the bourgeoisie produces and appropriates products.

Marx concluded that "What the bourgeoisie, therefore, produces, above all, is its own grave-diggers. Its fall and the victory of the proletariat are equally inevitable" ([1848] 1977:231).

Marx believed that capitalism's inevitable downfall and the equally inevitable rise of the proletariat to prominence would be only a transitional stage in human history. After some (unspecified) time, the dictatorship of the proletariat would lead to a new classless society. In this new socialist society, people would collectively decide their political and social being as well as their economic arrangements.

To conclude: Marx used one measure of social stratification: class. For Marx, class denotes social as well as economic domination (or dependence). His model of social stratification is like a pyramid where people are ranked on the basis of their ownership or lack of ownership of the productive means in their society. At the top of the pyramid are the bourgeoisie, a small number of people who control most of the society's wealth and power. In the middle of the pyramid are strata that Marx felt would eventually be eliminated by capitalistic advances (e.g., small business owners, termed small or "petty" bourgeoisie). The bottom layer of the pyramid broadens out to include the vast majority of people who have neither wealth nor power.

For Marx, power and wealth are two sides of the same coin under capitalism. Those who control the means of production control the society's social relations. Thus, the bourgeoisie controls not only the mechanical process of production but also the dominant ideas of the time and the governmental processes.

Marx's vision of a new society—based on equality instead of inequality of classes—has provided inspiration for revolutionary movements throughout the world. It has also provoked feelings of fear, distrust, hatred, and cynicism. In the United States, most Americans reject the notion of class struggle as the primary vehicle for social change.

Another reason that Marx's ideas have been unpopular in the United States is that to many people America represents the land of opportunity. In their minds, it is the place where a poor child can sell matchsticks on the corner, work hard, and climb the ladder to success, as in the Horatio Alger stories of the nineteenth century. That is the American dream—self-made men and women, rugged individualists. Horatio Alger's images of upward social mobility and an open class system have dominated American thought. Hence it is not surprising that at least 25 percent of the population consider themselves classless and that the vast majority of the remaining 75 percent see themselves as middle class, whether they are ditchdiggers or doctors. To a Marxist, the fact that so many Americans deny the existence of class indi-

Box 8-1

SOCIAL THEORIST AS POLITICAL PAMPHLETEER: "THE COMMUNIST MANIFESTO"

Section I: Bourgeois and Proletarians

The history of all hitherto existing society is the history of class struggle.

Freeman and slave, patrician and plebeian, lord and serf, guild-master and journeyman—in a word, oppressor and oppressed, stood in constant opposition to one another. . . .

The modern bourgeois society that has sprouted from the ruins of feudal society has not done away with class antagonisms. It has but established new conditions of oppression, new forms of struggle in place of the old ones.

Our epoch, the epoch of the bourgeoisie, possesses however, this distinctive feature: it has simplified the class antagonisms. Society as a whole is more and more splitting up into two great hostile camps, into two great classes directly facing each other: Bourgeoisie and Proletariat.

From the serfs of the Middle Ages sprang the chartered burghers of the earliest towns. From these burgesses the first elements of the bourgeoisie were developed.

The discovery of America, the rounding of the Cape, opened up fresh ground for the rising bourgeoisie. . . .

The feudal system of industry, under which industrial production was monopolized by closed guilds, now no longer sufficed for the growing wants of the new markets. The manufacturing system took its place. The guild-masters were pushed on one side by the manufacturing middle class; division of labour between the different corporate guilds vanished in the face of division of labour in each single workshop.

Meantime the markets kept ever growing, the demand ever rising. . . . The place of manufacture was taken by the giant, Modern Industry, the place of the industrial middle class, by industrial millionaires, the leaders of whole industrial armies, the modern bourgeois.

Modern industry has established the world-market, for which the discovery of America paved the way. This market has given an immense development to commerce, to navigation, to communication by land. This development has, in its turn, reacted on the extension of industry; and in proportion as industry, commerce, navigation, railways extended, in the same proportion the bourgeoisie developed, increased its capital, and pushed into the background every class handed down from the Middle Ages.

We see, therefore, how the modern bourgeoisie is itself the product of a long course of development, of a series of revolutions in the modes of production and of exchange.

Each step in the development of the bourgeoisie was accompanied by a corresponding political advance of that class. An oppressed class under the sway of the feudal nobility, an armed and self-governing association in the medieval commune; here independent urban republic (as in Italy and Germany), there taxable "third estate" of the monarchy (as in France) . . . , the bourgeoisie has at last, since the establishment of Modern Industry and of the world-market, conquered for itself, in the modern representative State, exclusive political sway. The executive of the modern State is but a committee for managing the common affairs of the whole bourgeoisie. . . . The bourgeoisie has subjected the country to the rule of the towns. It has created enormous cities, has greatly increased the urban population as compared with the rural, and has thus rescued a considerable part of the population from the idiocy of rural life. . . .

Modern industry has converted the little workshop of the patriarchal master into the great factory of the industrial capitalist. Masses of labourers, crowded into the factory, are organized like soldiers. As privates of the industrial army they are placed under the command of a perfect hierarchy of officers and sergeants. Not only are they slaves of the bourgeois class, and of the bourgeois State; they are daily and hourly enslaved by the machine, by the overlooker, and, above all, by the individual bourgeois manufacturer himself. (Marx in McLellan [ed.], 1977:222–227).

cates how powerful the wealthy few really are: They have succeeded in binding the weak by the chains of their own ideas.

A Marxist might accuse poor, powerless people who think they're middle class of living in self-deception (or, as Marx called it, **false consciousness**). In rebuttal, a non-Marxist might point to statistics showing a substantial amount of upward social mobility in America. According to government sources, for instance, about 20 percent of all men whose fathers had lower-class manual jobs had themselves achieved upper-echelon white-collar jobs (U.S. Bureau of the Census, 1977:522).

However one evaluates Marx's ideas, they are inescapable. Marxists and non-Marxists alike are still engaged in sorting out what he "really" meant and what application Marx's ideas have to the contemporary world. Critics and followers debate his political message of revolutionary action (is it applicable to post-industrial societies?); his assumptions about human psychology (can they account for people's drives to power? even under socialism, won't individuals try to reassert domination in the name of virtue, sex, or bureaucratic efficiency, if not wealth?); his consistency (is there an "early" Marx concerned with issues of alienation and a "late" Marx concerned with "laws" of capitalism?); and his views on history (is it wholly determined by structural factors, as he implies in some passages of his work, or is it dependent on the revolutionary consciousness of the proletariat, as he implies in other passages?). Contemporary Marxists don't agree among themselves on these points. Some Marxist intellectuals today even hold that the enemy is no longer capitalism but rather bureaucracy. They argue that bureaucracy—whether capitalist or socialist—is an instrument of domination and exploitation (Howard, 1978). As we shall soon see, this is not a new idea; Max Weber had the same notion.

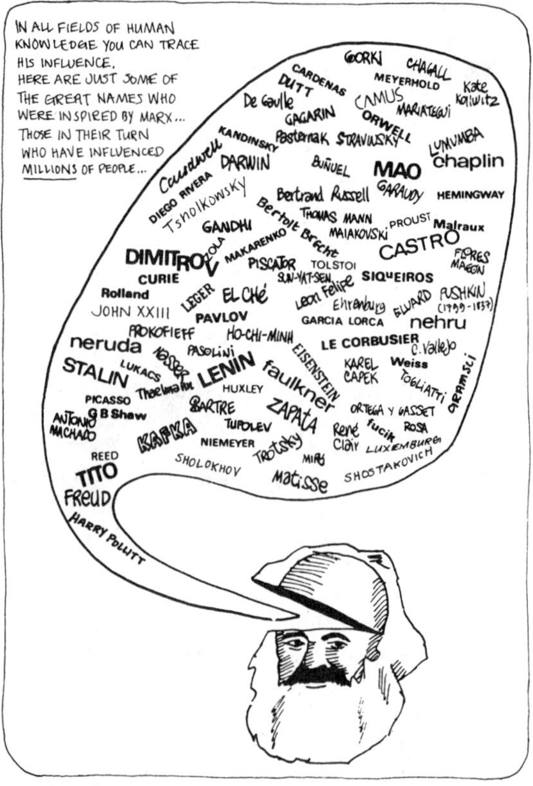

[illegible]8 MARX, THE INESCAPABLE (Rius, *Marx for Beginners* [New York: Pantheon, 1979], p. 35. English translation © 1976 by Richard Appiganesi. Originally published in English in Great Britain by Writers and Readers Publishing Cooperative. Reprinted by permission of Pantheon Books, a Division of Random House, Inc.)

If even those who consider themselves in the Marxist tradition question his ideas and view of human history, why do Marx's ideas continue to enthrall scholars, Marxist and non-Marxist alike? Economist Robert L. Heilbroner (1978:33) offers the following explanation: "The reason for the magnetism that Marx [still] exerts . . . is that Marx had the luck, combined of course with the genius, to be the first to discover a whole mode of inquiry that would forever belong to him. . . . I refer to Marx the inventor of critical social science, who 'critiqued' economics. . . . Marx invented a kind of social 'criticizing'—that is, subjecting the social universe to a particular sort of questioning."

According to Heilbroner, then, Marx continues to influence theorists "not because he is infallible" but rather because "he is unavoidable" for anyone who asks questions "about the nature of our thinking about society." "Sooner or later all such inquiries," Heilbroner says, "bring one to confront Marx's thought, and then one is compelled to adopt, confute, expand, escape from, or come to terms with the person who has defined the very task of critical social inquiry itself" (1978:33).

Weber's View of Social Stratification: Class, Status, Power

Max Weber was one of the most distinguished social inquirers who found Marx inescapable. He skillfully applied Marx's historical method, and his ideas on social stratification were influenced by Marx's previous work.

Weber did not refute Marx's notions on social stratification. Rather, he expanded on them. In fact, much of Weber's political sociology can be viewed as an attempt to "round out" Marx (Gerth and Mills, 1958:47).

Like Marx, Weber made capitalism a central theme in his scholarly work, calling it "the most fateful force in our modern life" (Weber, [1904–05] 1958:17). Weber viewed Western capitalism as unique because of its rational, bureaucratic form. That is, it is organized on the pursuit of profit by rational calculation; it uses rational techniques, such as the legal separation of personal property from corporate property; and it depends on bureaucratic organization. According to Weber, this particular Western form of capitalism—"rational bourgeois capitalism"—linked profit making with the bureaucratic organization of the economy and high technology.

Weber and Marx agreed on the paramount importance of capitalism in modern life. They did not, however, share the same interpretation of capitalist institutions. Specifically, Marx saw capitalism as irrational in terms of meeting human needs. Weber viewed capitalist institutions, especially bureaucracy, as the epitome of rationality and efficiency. In fact, it was this ever-increasing movement toward bureaucratic efficiency and rationality that struck Weber as problematic; while efficient, it would inevitably lead to the depersonalization of the individual.

Weber agrees with Marx that under capitalism there is a class struggle between haves and have-nots. But unlike Marx, he does not make class struggle the central dynamic of his work. Instead, the bureaucratization of everything, which went hand-in-hand with the development of capitalism in the West, is Weber's primary concern.

Weber felt that Marx did not go far enough. Agreeing with Marx that capitalism separates the peasant from the soil and the propertyless urban masses from the means of production, he extended the analysis. Bureaucratic organization separates all people from their labor—the scientist from the means of inquiry, the soldier from the means of violence, and the civil servant from the means of administration.

In brief, Marx and Weber had very different views of what was inevitable. To Marx, "the dictatorship of the proletariat" and socialism were inevitable. To Weber, only the "disenchanted garden" of rational calculation was inevitable, and it would bring the depersonalization of the individual through efficient bureaucratic management. Much more pessimistic than Marx, Weber commented that "For the time being, the dictatorship of the [corporate and government] official and not that of the worker is on the march" (in Gerth and Mills, 1958:50). Thus, while Marx looked forward to a socialist future in which people would control their work process and their lives, Weber felt that socialism (with its own bureaucracy) would be just another system for enslaving the individual.

Weber also felt that Marx's theory of history, with its emphasis on class struggle, was too one-dimensional. In his view, there were other important factors, especially the meanings that people brought to their situation.

Similarly, Weber felt that Marx's approach to social stratification was too simplified. For Weber, the economic order (class) was crucial to the social ranking process. But Weber contended that other institutional orders—the military, religious, political, legal, and so forth—were also important. All these institutional orders were interrelated, but they were also separate and distinct. In his essay "Class, Status, Party" ([1922] 1958), Weber identified three interrelated but distinct social orders which influence a person's social rank:

1. the economic order (class)
2. the prestige order (status)
3. the political order (power)

Class. Weber thought that those sharing the same position in the economic order (**class**) also share similar "life chances" or market position. They can expect similar opportunities for income, material goods, living conditions, and personal life experiences.

Researchers in the Weberian tradition usually determine class position by some measure of income and wealth. In contrast, Marxist researchers operationalize class in contemporary America on the basis of two criteria: (1) "whether or not the individual owns his or her own means of production" and (2) "whether or not the individual controls the labor power of others" (i.e., supervises people on the job) (Wright, 1978:1370).

Applying Weber's notion of class as shared life chances, what do we find? First, are the life chances of poor and rich Americans equal? Quite literally, they are not; the poor die younger. In addition, nonwhites die about five years younger than whites (U.S. Bureau of the Census, 1977:146, Chart 5/1).

In terms of housing, the poor—and especially poor blacks—are more likely than affluent people to live in substandard conditions. In 1974, about 42 percent of all blacks and about 28 percent of nonblacks with an annual income below $7,000 lived in households lacking some or all plumbing facilities. Meanwhile, less than 1 percent of whites and 2 percent of blacks earning $15,000 and over lived in similar conditions (U.S. Bureau of the Census, 1977:82, Chart 3/10).

The likelihood of being criminally victimized is also related to income level. The poor are more likely to be victims of personal crimes of violence than the rich. Conversely, the rich are more likely to be victims of theft than the poor (U.S. Bureau of the Census, 177:218).

Similarly, the poor pay more and get less in the marketplace. Numerous studies (e.g., Caplovitz, 1963) show that the poor often get shoddier merchandise and fewer groceries than the affluent for the same money. In terms of used cars, for instance, researchers found that people with annual incomes below $6,000 paid almost 10 percent more for an equivalent used car than those earning over $24,000 (*New York Times,* 1978:F 17).

Is this true of education too? Do rich and poor have unequal chances for higher education? This is an especially important question

Fig. 8-3 WEBER'S VIEW OF BUREAUCRACY: EFFICIENT BUT DEADLY. (Richard Hedman)

in the United States because higher education is viewed as the stepping stone to upward mobility. Government data on postsecondary schools show the following patterns: In 1974 about 65 percent of blacks and whites with family incomes of $18,000 or more were enrolled in institutions of higher learning. In the lowest family income category (below $3,000 annually), about 25 percent of whites and 30 percent of blacks were enrolled (U.S. Bureau of the Census, 1977:272, Chart 7/12). These data strongly suggest that, for better or worse, a person's chances for a higher education are directly tied to his or her economic position (class, in Weber's terms).

Using Marxist criteria of class (relationship to the means of production and supervisory responsibilities over others in the workplace), researchers also find inequalities based on class position. For instance, Wright (1978) shows that as a group, managers and supervisors get about $1,169 for each increment to education; income returns to workers with the same increments to education are much less—$655.

To conclude: Using either Weberian or Marxist measures of class, data reveal that in many areas, class position does make a difference in determining what a person can expect to get out of life in America.

Status. In Weber's view, the status order of prestige is related to the economic order (class) but separate from it. People who share the same position in the hierarchy of prestige share a similar lifestyle. They display similar symbols of consumption and respectability.

Taking some contemporary American examples, a high-prestige group might share the following kinds of symbols: knowledge of languages long dead, like Latin or Greek; subscriptions to *The New Yorker* or *The New York Review of Books;* refined tastes in modern art and French wine; classical record collections; tennis rackets; a TV set outside the living room; homes or apartments at a "good" address; membership in exclusive social clubs; and old-school ties to elite educational institutions. A lower-prestige group would share a different set of symbols: homes in tract developments; bowling balls; a knowledge of home repair skills; copies of *Family Circle* or *Reader's Digest;* a TV set in the living room; and ties to high school buddies.

In other words, different status groups live in different "taste cultures" (Gans, 1974). A shared taste culture gives people a sense of belonging to the same kind of community. And according to Weber, status groups *are* communities; people in similar status groups see themselves as having common interests

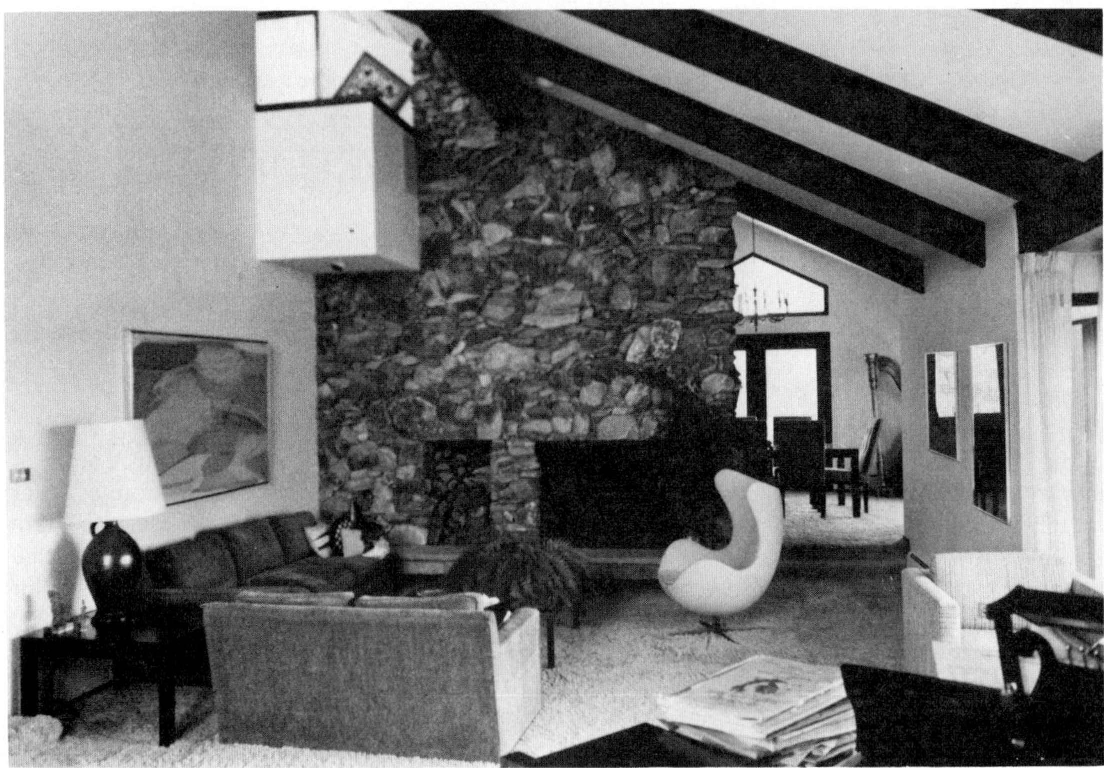

Fig. 8-4 WHO LIVES HERE? Not members of a lower-status group. The cathedral ceiling and stone fireplace; grand piano, oil painting in the living room, and harp in the dining room; lack of a visible TV set and understated elegance indicate that this is an architect-designed home (not part of a tract development) inhabited by professionals. (Richard J. Sanders)

and tastes. (On this point Weber and Marx differed. Marx felt that class members would recognize their common class interests. Weber thought that a person's objective economic position would not necessarily lead him or her to feel a sense of community with others who share that same position.)

Following Weber's analysis, then, we can predict the following. Members of similar status groups will tend to marry each other. Further, they will enjoy the same kinds of cultural events and display similar symbols of consumption.

Occupational groups, Weber noted, are also status groups. And in America, the work one does is probably the single best indicator of a person's relative prestige.

Many sociologists in the structural-functional tradition of Durkheim argue that the relative prestige of different occupations is essentially the same in all complex societies. Thus, in *Gesellschaft* societies, we should expect to find the same occupations at the top of the status ladder and the same occupations at the bottom. This is because all complex societies face similar "functional imperatives." To get these tasks accomplished, advanced technological societies organize themselves in similar ways.

Briefly, the structural-functional argument is as follows. Social differentiation "inherently implies stratification. Specialization of functions carries with it inherent differences in the control over scarce resources, which is the primary basis of stratification." These resources—skill, knowledge, authority, property—function together to "create differential power. . . . Thus, the division of labor creates a characteristic hierarchy of occupations with respect to power exercised" and "this power leads to special privilege" (Treiman, 1977:5). So, in this view, power, privilege, and prestige become intertwined. A study of occupational prestige worldwide (fifty-five countries) supports the view that there is indeed "a single, worldwide occupational prestige hierarchy" (Treiman, 1977:5–6).

What are some of the high-prestige and low-prestige occupations in the United States and other complex societies? At the top of the ladder are heads of state and other high government officials such as ambasadors; doctors; university professors; physicists; and mayors of large cities. At about the middle of the status ladder are the following occupations: professional athlete, advertising writer, TV cameraperson, and police officer. At the bottom of the ladder are garbage collectors, contract laborers, shoe shiners, and recipients of public assistance. According to an international survey, agricultural gatherer is the least socially esteemed occupation worldwide (Treiman, 1977:Appendix A).

These occupational prestige rankings suggest a connection between the status order (prestige), the political order (power), and the economic order (class) in a complex society. That is, occupations that are prestigious are often highly paid and socially powerful. Yet as Weber pointed out, this is not necessarily the case. His third dimension of social stratification—the power order—is related to, but separate from, class and status.

Table 8-1 Occupational Prestige Rankings in the United States

Occupational Title	*Prestige Score*
Member, President's cabinet	89
State governor	85
Department head, federal government	85
U.S. Supreme Court justice	84.5
Astronaut	80
Nuclear physicist	80
Physician	78
College professor	78
Mayor of a larger city	75
Priest	73
Department head, city government	70
Electrical engineer	69
City manager	66
Accountant for a large business	61
Computer programmer	51
Reporter on a daily newspaper	47
Local official of a labor union	41
Receptionist	39
Service station manager	37
Shipping clerk	29
Night watchman	22
Migrant worker	14
Cleaning woman in private home	13
Garbage collector	13

SOURCE: Adapted from Donald Treiman, *Occupational Prestige in Comparative Perspective*. Copyright © 1977 by Academic Press, 318–329. Reprinted by permission of Academic Press and the author.

Power. For Weber, a person's position in the **power** order is determined by the amount of control he or she has over politics and administration. This includes the exercise of formal and informal power. Elected officials and bureaucrats, for example, have formal power that goes with their office. Whoever becomes President of the United States or a member of the board of directors of AT&T has authority stemming from that position. As we will see in Chapter 11, power can also

Box 8-2

TWO APPROACHES TO SOCIAL STRATIFICATION

Dimensions of Stratification

Karl Marx	Max Weber
One dimension: class	*Three dimensions*
A person's relationship to the means of production determines how much wealth he or she will have and thus the lifestyle he or she will be able to afford. The class that owns or controls the means of production also controls the ideas in that society.	1. Class—shared life chances. 2. Status—shared lifestyle, social esteem, prestige. 3. Political power. Class, status, and power do not necessarily coincide. For example, members of political elites can be lower-class or low in social esteem.

Concept of Class

Karl Marx	Max Weber
A concept combining economic and social relations. A class is composed of individuals who share a common situation in terms of their relation to the ownership of the means of production. Classes are not income groups. Nor are classes occupational groupings (e.g., two people may both be engineers but one may be a propertyless employee and the other may be the owner of a large firm). In a capitalist system, there are *owners of capital* (bourgeoisie) who live off profits; *landowners* who live off rents; and *wage-laborers* (proletariat) who live off wages. Under capitalism, society is split into two great classes: bourgeoisie and proletariat. Class conflict is the key to understanding history.	Basically, an economic concept. A class is composed of people who share a common situation in terms of the market (what goods and services they can afford to buy) and similar life chances. Class divisions are based on property relations: property owners and the propertyless. Class struggles begin in an urban economy, where a credit market operates, and is developed by a small, powerful group (plutocracy).

be exercised informally—for example, behind the scenes by machine politicians or bank presidents.

To conclude: Weber outlined three dimensions by which people rank and socially differentiate one another: class, status, and power. Each represents a distinct social order, but they are functionally interrelated. In Weber's analysis, they don't necessarily coincide. Hence, a person may enjoy high status but wield little political power. Or a low-status person without property could conceivably have great political clout.

Weber did not make class the central dynamic of his work, although he recognized its importance in determining who gets what out of life. He felt that Marx's approach was too one-dimensional because noneconomic institutions are also important in determining where one fits in the social hierarchy.

Concept of Status

Marx didn't use this concept to differentiate people. He assumed that those with economic power also held social and political power in capitalist society. He also thought that under capitalism, ideas and culture were produced by the ruling class (the bourgeoisie) in its own interests.	Status is not necessarily determined by or linked to class. Both propertied and propertyless people may belong to the same status group. Those who share a similar status tend to share a similar lifestyle (e.g., belong to the same kinds of clubs, display similar symbols of their station in life). In modern society, occupation is the single best indicator of status group.

Using Marx or Weber: What Difference Does It Make?

Using Marx's unidimensional approach, a social scientist tends to find a rather cohesive elite holding economic (and thus political) power in a city or nation.	Using Weber's three-dimensional approach, a social scientist tends to find a more pluralistic and open system in which wealth, power, and prestige are unequally distributed.

STUDIES OF URBAN SOCIAL STRATIFICATION IN THE UNITED STATES

American social scientists generally adopt the Weberian approach when investigating how U.S. cities are socially stratified. But—and this is important—researchers in this tradition have not kept Weber's categories of class and status separate. Instead, they join class and status into a single concept: **socioeconomic status (SES)**. A person's SES is determined by a composite measure based on three variables: (1) income, (2) education, and (3) occupation. The rationale behind this composite measure is that the three variables tend to co-vary in complex societies, which means that high-skill occupations require a high level of education and are highly rewarded in terms of income.

What difference does it make if a researcher uses SES or separate measures of class and status? For one thing, SES ignores what Marx meant by class. It does not distinguish between owners and controllers of capital (including managers, large stockholders) and those who have little or no control over other people's work and social lives. For another thing, essentially SES is synonymous with prestige (the status order) *exclusively*. Consequently, studies that use SES as their indicator of social rank ignore what Weber originally meant: that class, status, and power (the three dimensions of stratification) are separate and distinct, although interrelated. And of course, using SES as an indicator of social stratification ignores class and the consequences of class. This is an ironic twist, for many American scholars who criticize Marx for being too one-dimensional turn out to be equally at fault. The difference is that most American scholars use status rather than class as their one dimension of social rank.

There are other problems with making status the only measure of social stratification. Most importantly, it assumes that status concerns are of paramount importance to everyone in America. Many studies (e.g., Chinoy, 1952; Stone and Form, 1953; Form and Stone, 1957) suggest that this is not the case. Blue-collar workers, for example, seem to be less interested in social respectability and prestige than in working conditions and monetary rewards; the opposite has been found in the case of white-collar workers. And the "back-to-the-land" movement in the 1970s of mainly white, well-educated sons and daughters of higher-prestige families may suggest that high status is not a primary concern of some (privileged) younger Americans. As Candice Bergen says in *T.R. Baskin* (1971), a film about a small-town girl coming to the big city, "I can't help thinking what everyone else wants is a bunch of crap." Or, alternatively, perhaps having a rural address and living in "voluntary simplicity" are merely new status symbols.

To conclude: SES is not a neutral research indicator. Using SES (rather than measures of status and class) as a filter through which to see the social system of American cities helps to perpetuate the notion that classes don't exist in America.

As we've noted so often, what you see depends on how you look at it. Remembering that *what is defined as empirical evidence depends on what researchers already believe,* let's review some leading studies on urban social stratification in America. We begin with an influential series of studies which established the pattern of research for future generations: the Yankee City series by social anthropologist W. Lloyd Warner and his associates.

Yankee City: Lifestyles in a New England Town

Beginning in 1930, W. Lloyd Warner and his research group studied the system of social ranking in a small New England town they called "Yankee City." (The actual city was Newburyport, Massachusetts, which then had a population of about 17,000.) To do this, Warner developed two techniques which set the research pattern for future researchers of urban social stratification. Both techniques were designed to measure what Warner called "social class." He defined social class as "two or more orders of people who are believed to be, and are accordingly ranked by the members of the community, in socially superior and inferior positions" ([1941] 1963:36). That's exactly what Weber meant by status. Thus, Warner's techniques to measure class actually measure status.

One of Warner's techniques to measure what he called class (and what we shall call status) is the method of Evaluated Participation (E.P.). Warner rated a person's E.P. by talking with others in the town and getting their estimates of that person's social rank. When people in Newburyport (and, subsequently, other towns) rated one another's status, they tended to base their estimates on such items as relative family standing in the community, what church the person belonged to, and club memberships.

The other technique used by Warner to investigate status is called the Index of Status Characteristics (I.S.C.). To obtain a person's I.S.C. rating, he used four variables: occupation, source of income, quality of house, and residential neighborhood. Warner constructed a score on an I.S.C. scale by weighting each variable and adding the weighted numbers. In the scaling procedure, occupation received the most weight and residential neighborhood the least.

Using these two techniques, Warner determined that Newburyport had six separate social strata (actually status groups), each with its own particular lifestyle. He identified the following strata and the percentages of townspeople in each: upper upper (1.4 percent); lower upper (1.6 percent); upper middle (10 percent); lower middle (28 percent); upper lower (33 percent); and lower lower (25 percent). Thus, most people in Yankee City were in the two lowest status groups (58 percent). Only a handful (3 percent) made up the top two layers.

Jonesville: A Typical Town, and How Its People Justify Inequality

Using the techniques of E.P. and I.S.C., Warner studied a small town near Chicago, dubbed "Jonesville" because it was considered to be a typical American community. Since it seemed to be representative, Warner used this town (actually Morris, Illinois) as a laboratory in which to look at status hierarchies in America.

What did Warner find in this typical American town? First, he found what he had found in Newburyport: six distinct status groups, each with its own particular lifestyle. Most people in Jonesville lived at the "Level of the Common Man," or what others term the "middle class." Above the Level of the Common Man is a layer divided into two parts and "crowned by an elite, and the one below [is] filled with a mixed old American and ethnic proletariat. . . . The highest crust is rewarded with deference; the lowest, often with ridicule, pity, or scorn" ([1949] 1964:23).

Second, Warner found that the status system of inequality in Jonesville (and by extension, America) operates according to two competing logics: "1) All men are equal and 2) Some men are superior in status, others inferior" ([1949] 1964:293). These two contradictory propositions support the following practices and beliefs which he found typified Jonesville:

1. People in Jonesville rank skilled jobs above less skilled jobs, clean jobs above dirty jobs.
2. Being a self-made person is good, but even better is to be born wealthy; "unearned income [e.g., investments] is better than earned wealth."
3. Wages, even if very low, are earned income and thus better than public aid; recipients of public welfare are the lowest on the social ladder.
4. Education is highly respected; people exposed to higher education are thought to be "superior."
5. People can move up or down the status ladder, principally by accumulating money and transforming it into socially approved symbols: educational advancement; marrying up; learning the proper social skills, such as speech patterns; and joining the right churches and clubs ([1949] 1964:294–96).

How can the acceptance of inequality in Jonesville be reconciled with the American ideal of equality? Warner says that the shared belief in the "American dream" (the idea that anyone who works hard can make it to the top) is the key. The American dream provides "the moral code which enforces the rules of social mobility by insisting that all able [people] who obey the rules of the game have 'the right' to climb" ([1949] 1964:297).

Furthermore, Warner sees the American dream as a very functional belief. Without it, "there would be little or no movement between the classes [status groups]." He concludes that there is no fixed social rank order in Jonesville—or American cities generally. Rather, there is a "system of open classes [again, status groups]" (297).

Clearly, this is one person's vision, filtered through particular ideological assumptions

Box 8-3

NOTHING SUCCEEDS LIKE ADDRESS: JONESVILLE, U.S.A.

Residential Neighborhoods

[In Jonesville, a small town about fifty miles from Chicago] the town's living space is sliced into three large layers. In the north, the railway cuts through, dividing the top and the middle, and in the south the waters of The Canal separate the thick middle from the thin, lower layer. In Jonesville, everyone knows that if you live north of the tracks or south of The Canal, you are on the wrong side of town. "North of the tracks" and "across The Canal" are symbolic terms, emblematic of low status. . . .

A glance at the map of Jonesville reveals that we were able to distinguish seventeen major and minor dwelling areas. Each was given an appropriate name and ranked according to its social reputation among the inhabitants of the town. The two major areas north of the tracks, Northwestern and Polish Town, are sometimes called Ixnay and Frogtown and a number of other derogatory terms. . . .

To rank the town's evaluation of these several dwelling areas, we used a seven-point scale, ranging from very good to very poor. Towpath ranked 7. . . .

Where You Live Identifies Who You Are

Residence and social status in Jonesville are so arranged that Top Circle (rated a 1), near the center of the city and identified as being superior

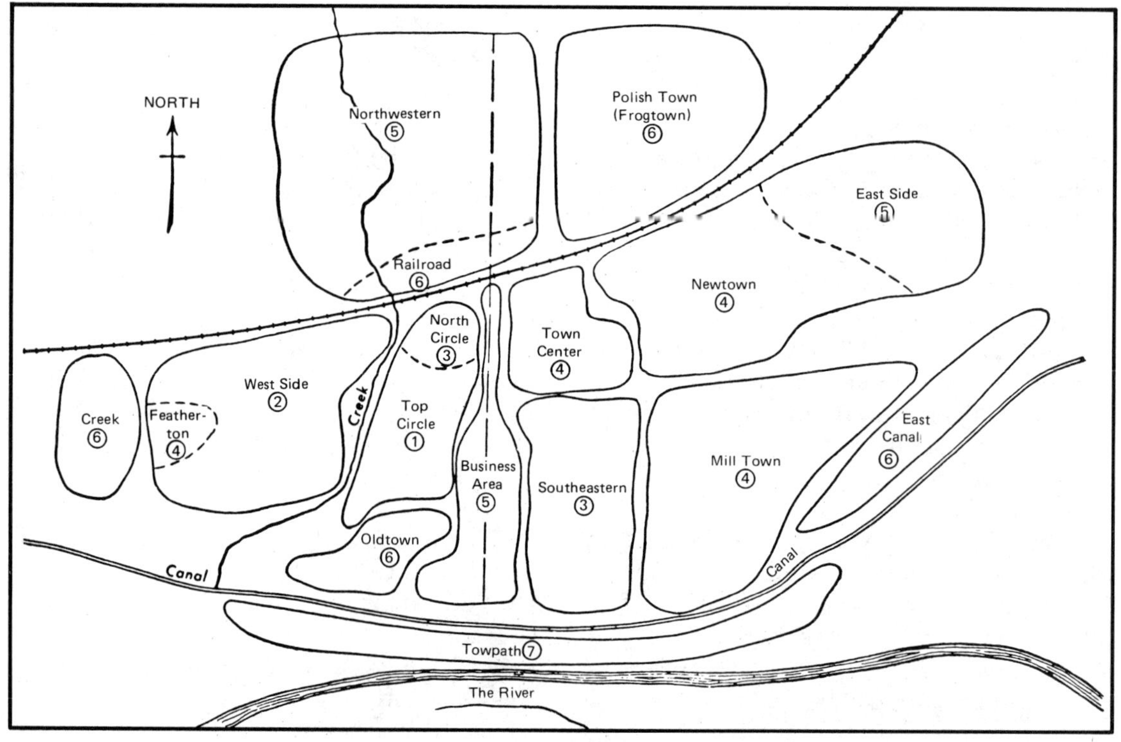

to the Common Man Level, blends into middle-class West Side (2) and into upper-lower-class districts.

. . . [E]ach man in Jonesville carries a working map of the city in his head . . . the map that is carried by him and those like him in other American communities is not merely one that could be constructed by compass and surveyor's instruments, since most of the people of Jonesville and America know that railways, canals, and interstate highways . . . are the boundaries which often separate common men from their social superiors and inferiors. Where a man lives in America's Jonesvilles helps label and grade him.

Houses as Status Symbols

The houses of Americans are valued by them not only as utilities but because they are outward symbols of the social status of those who occupy them. The houses of Jonesville were ranked according to their size and condition of repair. As could be expected, there is a close relationship between the rank of the house and the class of the person who lives in it, the higher classes occupying the fine houses, and the lowest, the poorest ones.

The fine houses and the shanties are distributed throughout the dwelling areas of Jonesville, not by chance but in accordance with the dictates of social class. [For instance] 82 percent of the houses in Top Circle belong to the two highest ranks and 82 percent of the families in Towpath live in houses ranked as sixth and seventh. (Warner and associates, [1949] 1964:35–43; subheads ours. Adapted and abridged from pp. 35–43 in *Democracy in Jonesville: A Study in Quality and Inequality* by W. Lloyd Warner and associates. Copyright, 1949, by Harper and Row, Publishers, Inc. Reprinted by permission.)

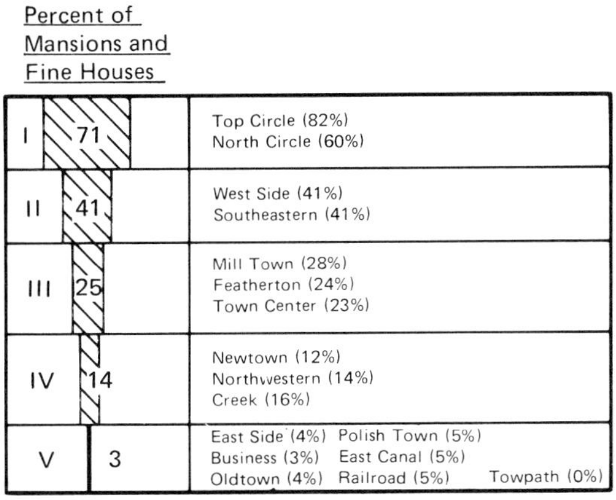

	Percent of Mansions and Fine Houses	
I	71	Top Circle (82%) North Circle (60%)
II	41	West Side (41%) Southeastern (41%)
III	25	Mill Town (28%) Featherton (24%) Town Center (23%)
IV	14	Newtown (12%) Northwestern (14%) Creek (16%)
V	3	East Side (4%) Polish Town (5%) Business (3%) East Canal (5%) Oldtown (4%) Railroad (5%) Towpath (0%)

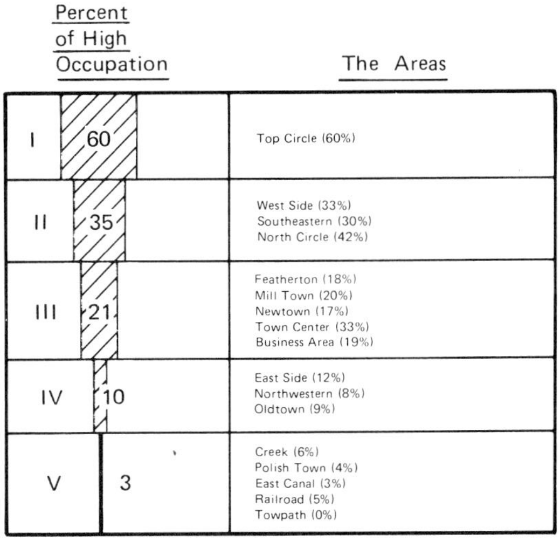

	Percent of High Occupation	The Areas
I	60	Top Circle (60%)
II	35	West Side (33%) Southeastern (30%) North Circle (42%)
III	21	Featherton (18%) Mill Town (20%) Newtown (17%) Town Center (33%) Business Area (19%)
IV	10	East Side (12%) Northwestern (8%) Oldtown (9%)
V	3	Creek (6%) Polish Town (4%) East Canal (3%) Railroad (5%) Towpath (0%)

and research techniques. Other researchers might (and did) paint a different community portrait of so-called typical American towns (see Thernstrom, 1966, for a different look at Yankee City). Writing about another typical town, called Middletown—in reality, Muncie, Indiana—the Lynds ([1929] 1956) found a fairly rigid class system in operation.

To conclude: The composite measure of SES, based on income, education, and occupation blurs Weber's distinctions. It also raises status to paramount importance and serves to perpetuate the notion that classes don't exist in the United States. This distortion of Weber's original meaning began with W. Lloyd Warner's influential series of urban studies, which set the pattern of research for future scholars. In their studies of Yankee City and Jonesville, Warner and his associates stated that they were studying class. In actuality, as we have noted, they studied what Weber meant by status. Warner found inequality in Yankee City and later in Jonesville. He also found that the American ideal of equality and the practice of inequality were rationalized by a deep-seated belief in the American dream of social mobility.

Kansas City: The Status System in a Metropolitan Area

Researchers may use more sophisticated measures than Warner's E.P. or I.S.C., but many remain just as one-dimensional in their approach to urban social stratification. A study of the Kansas City metropolitan area is illustrative. In *Social Status in the City* (1971), authors Coleman and Neugarten (trained by Warner) found five social classes (again, status groups): upper, upper middle, lower middle, working, and lower. In the Kansas City metropolitan area, only a handful—about twenty families—are at the top of the social ladder. On the lowest rung are most of the city's ethnic minorities and so-called hillbillies.

Studies of Particular Strata in the City

Warner and his associates looked at the entire social system in an American city. Other researchers have focused on a particular stratum. *Hard Living on Clay Street* (1973) by Joseph T. Howell is a notable example. It focuses on a white working-class neighborhood in Washington, D.C. Using participant-observation, Howell paints a portrait of two distinct types of blue-collar families: "hard living" and "settled" families, all migrants from the South.

Howell notes that the hard living families cope with everyday life in one way, the settled families in another. Generally, the lifestyle of the hard living families is characterized by heavy drinking, marital instability, tough and profane manners, political alienation, strong individualism, rootlessness, and a present time orientation (263–64). Meanwhile, the settled families attend church regularly, have roots in the community, stay away from liquor, hold politically conservative ideas, have refined manners, and are concerned with their reputations. In the settled families' eyes, the hard living folk are "white trash." In popular terms, the difference between the two groups is often expressed by the following dichotomy: the "respectable" poor (settled) and the "disreputable" poor (hard living).

Howell's study raises several issues pertinent to our discussion of status and class. First, it suggests that two different status groups live side by side. The settled and hard living families, both in the same economic position, do not share a set of symbols, attitudes, or values. Thus, Howell may call his research a study of a working-class neighborhood, but he is really dealing with two status groups residing as neighbors.

Table 8-2 Status Hierarchy in Kansas City

	Upper	*Upper Middle*	*Lower Middle*	*Working*	*Lower*
Median family income (1954)	$34,000	$11,900	$6,300	$4,300	$2,600
Self-employed	74%	34%	16%	10%	0%
College degree	66	41	6	0	0
Church preference or affiliation					
Protestant	74	72	78	77	62
Catholic*	13	15	18	22	38
Jewish†	13	13	4	1	0

*Catholics constituted 20 percent of the white population.

†Jews represented only 3 percent of the city's population.

SOURCE: Adapted from Richard P. Coleman and Bernice L. Neugarten, *Social Status in the City* (San Francisco: Jossey-Bass, 1971), Table 2, pp. 72–79. Copyright © 1971 by Jossey-Bass. Reprinted by permission of Jossey-Bass.

Second, Howell's portrait of blue-collar families suggests that people in the same objective economic situation don't necessarily react in similar ways. To a Marxist, the reaction of the settled families might indicate false consciousness—about their "real" class situation. To a follower of Warner, however, the settled families' more cautious and refined lifestyle shows the power of belief in the American dream. Many children from settled families went to college; no children of the hard living families did so, and most didn't even finish high school. The settled families, concerned with what others thought of them and with social respectability (status concerns), were indeed more upwardly mobile than the hard living families. As we discuss in the following chapter, the same *objective* situation (in this case, being part of the urban working class or proletariat) can be interpreted *subjectively* in different ways, and people's interpretation of their situation influences their behavior.

Finally, although Howell doesn't suggest it, his study indicates that class is a more significant variable than race in explaining urban social behavior. In many important ways, the hard living folks on Clay Street resemble black streetcorner men observed across town hanging out at *Tally's Corner* (Liebow, 1967). (This thorny issue is examined in the next section.)

Many researchers, like Howell, have analyzed the lifestyles or life chances of poor whites or blacks uprooted from the South and rerooted in Northern cities (e.g., Liebow, 1967; Gitlin and Hollander, 1970). Others have investigated the other end of the social ladder: the rich, prestigious, and/or powerful. One such account is *Philadelphia Gentlemen* (Baltzell, 1958). This study found two strata or layers of elites in Philadelphia: the social aristocracy, at the very top of the social ladder, and the achieving elite, just below. Together, these two strata made up Philadelphia's upper class. While there was no single lifestyle among this class (in both Marx's and Weber's sense of the term), their associations promoted a sense of class solidarity. For example, they tended to belong to the same highly esteemed social clubs, to have inherited wealth, and to have prestigious occupations (or be married to those who did). While not completely homogeneous, Philadelphia's upper class contained no blacks and just a sprinkling of people with Southern European or Jewish backgrounds; otherwise, it was mainly WASP.

The finding that Philadelphia's upper class is almost exclusively WASP raises some complicated issues. For instance, to what extent do race, ethnicity, and religion affect a person's life chances? Is race or class background a better predictor of a person's position on the social ladder? Are some cities more egalitarian than others? What role does local culture play in determining a person's lifestyle? These are not easy questions to answer. Few researchers have asked questions in this way. Consequently, little data are available. Further, the data that do exist lend themselves to varying interpretations. With these methodological and ideological problems clearly in mind, we now examine the effects of several variables on a person's social rank: race, religion, sex, and age.

OTHER VARIABLES INFLUENCING SOCIAL RANK

American reseachers have focused on status as the key dimension of social stratification. Where do such factors as race and ethnicity, religion, sex, and age fit into this model? How are they related to class, power, and status? As suggested above, the answers are far from clear-cut.

Race and Religion

As American cities go, Salt Lake City, Utah, is most unusual. Settled by Mormons in the nineteenth century, the city, the SMSA, and the state of Utah are dominated by Mormon influence. Perhaps in no other U.S. city are the lines between church and state less clear. Estimates of Mormon influence differ, but the church itself says that 60 percent of Salt Lake City's and 70 percent of Utah's population are Mormons. The church is a major landowner and media controller, owning two TV stations, eleven radio stations, two universities, hotels, and much more (Ivins, 1978:49).

In 1974 Felix McGowan migrated to Salt Lake City(SMSA population in 1970: 557,757; 2 percent black). Growing up as one of a handful of blacks in a small Texas town, McGowan, a non-Mormon, was no stranger to racial discrimination. Some time after he moved to Utah to launch the state's Equal Employment Opportunity Program, he told the press, "As a black, I honestly don't believe there is any place I can go in this Mormon society. If I move up, it will be only as a token thing, and in order to do so I would have to sell myself, to adopt to some extent a religious point of view. Let's face it, the government here is controlled by the religion" (in Ivins, 1978:49).

McGowan says that his young son has also been affected by racial discrimination: "He came home every day crying because the other kids called him a nigger. He had good teachers, he did well in the public schools, but he was constantly being told, one way and another, that he was inferior" (in Ivins, 1978:49).

Blacks disagree on the degree of Mormon racism. One man defined it as blatant: "Look around. No black firemen, no blacks in the Sheriff's department, no city, state or county black division heads. . . . What's subtle?" A black professor, on the other hand, says that racism in Utah "isn't blatant—it's just assumed" (in Ivins, 1978:49).

In 1978 the Mormon church changed its religious doctrine, ending the ban on male blacks in the priesthood. (Being a member of the priesthood, previously closed to males of black African ancestry—and still closed to all women—is a prerequisite in the religion for attaining a higher position in Heaven. This belief effectively assigns blacks and women to a separate and lower Heaven.) The lifting of the ban on male blacks in the priesthood, many observers felt, would have wide impact in Salt Lake City and Utah, especially in the area of employment practices.

Salt Lake City represents an extreme case. Few modern U.S. cities of its size are so dominated by a single religious group, especially a church that traditionally assigned blacks to a lower status in Heaven, as well as on earth. In few other U.S. cities today do one's chances for high status and political power appear to be so closely linked with one's religion and race.

In most other U.S. cities, the effects of race, religion, and ethnicity on a person's life chances or lifestyle are more difficult to assess and disentangle. Religious and ethnic discrimination is often subtle and hard to measure. How does a researcher gather data on prestigious clubs that refuse admittance to blacks, Jews, or Catholics? How many marriages take place between ethnic group members and WASPs? How often do people in supervisory positions select people from similar ethnic or religious backgrounds when they have a heterogeneous field to choose from? Evidence is scarce.

There is also little evidence about the relative influence of ethnicity and religion on status or class. To what degree does ethnicity or religion divide members of the same status group? For instance, do high-prestige Catholics have more social contacts with lower-prestige Catholics or with high-prestige Protestants? Few studies deal with these issues. The few that do suggest that ethnicity plays a "large role in restricting intimate social relationships not only to members of one's own status level or social class, but to members of one's own ethnic group" (Gordon, 1978:261).

In contrast to the paucity of data on many of the above questions, there is abundant information that blacks in U.S. cities have different—and unequal—life chances, lifestyles, and power. The Kerner Commission summarized the mountain of data succintly in 1968: "Our nation is moving toward two societies, one black, one white—separate and unequal." More than a decade later, the number of black elected officials and the educational level of blacks had increased dramatically. Yet poverty for the mass of blacks had spread, not abated. Big city ghettoes didn't disappear. Unemployment among blacks doubled in the 1968–1978 period. And so on.

These facts are undisputed. But how are we to interpret them? The traditional interpretation has been that racial discrimination is the key factor in limiting blacks to low-prestige and low-paid work. This interpretation is now under heavy attack. The scholarly work of William Julius Wilson, a University of Chicago sociologist, is indicative of this changing interpretation.

When Wilson published the book *Power, Racism and Privilege* in 1973, he paid little attention to class. By 1978, he had changed his mind. In *The Declining Significance of Race* (1978:150), Wilson argued that "class has become more important than race in determining black life-chances in the modern industrial period." Wilson's argument is essentially this: Economic and technological change (the rapid growth of the corporate and government sectors, for instance) has led to a segmented labor market. This has served to solidify class differences between (1) a huge black underclass (created originally by discrimination and oppression) which is poor and poorly trained and (2) a much smaller group of well-educated, affluent, and privileged blacks who are experiencing many job opportunities. These economic divisions among blacks are widening with time. One implication of Wilson's work is that the poor underclass—whether they live on Clay Street or hang out at Tally's Corner—shares a common fate. This fate is based on their class position, whether white or black.

Wilson's study is bound to stimulate other scholars. Perhaps the complicated issues concerning the relative importance of race, ethnicity, religion, and class in determining an American urbanite's life chances, lifestyle, and power will be a major research topic in this decade. Hopefully, this will be the case, for much work on these complex and ideologically loaded issues is sorely needed.

Sex and Age

Abundant statistical information testifies to the increasing participation of women in the labor force, declining fertility rates, and many other topics. However, little attention has been paid to women in social stratification studies. This is so for several reasons. Until quite recently, women were considered as appendages of their husbands; they were assumed to adopt the status and privileges of the men they married. With singlehood or divorce and full-time paid work becoming a way of life for more and more women, this assumption is changing. Also, social scientists themselves didn't pay attention to the variable of sex. In most cases, studies of urban social stratification ignored women. In others, theorists treated women as a lower-status group, not recognizing differences among subgroups. Thus, much research and theory are needed on sexual stratification and differential life chances for men and women.

The theoretical work that remains to be done centers on the economic, social, and political inequalities between men and women and how these inequalities are perpetuated or diminished. One sociologist working on sexual stratification argues that "women's degree of control (relative to the men of their group) over the means and fruits of production is the most important predictor of how well female status and life opportunities compare to those of the males of their group . . . [in sixty-one preindustrial societies] economic power was overwhelmingly the most important predictor of women's life options" (Blumberg, 1978:vi, 31).

Sexual stratification transcends economic systems. In the Soviet Union, the majority of women work at low-paid blue-collar jobs; women professionals tend to be stuck at the lowest levels in their fields. In Israeli collective agricultural settlements (kibbutzim), the pioneer women started as equals, but even in this socialist milieu there is sexual inequality. Why sexual inequality exists in the kibbutz—founded on the ideals of a small classless society with economic, social, and political equality for all members—is a matter of some debate. But the point here is that sexual stratification exists and is a continuing feature of modern societies, whether they are capitalist, socialist, or combine the features of both. In other words, sexism is an international and intereconomic phenomenon.

Ageism, on the other hand, appears to be most prevalent in societies which define human value in terms of economic productive capacity. That is, the more a society believes that "you are what you do," the more the very old and the very young (the economically unproductive) will tend to be devalued.

In the United States, the specter of the old age home haunts many, who see themselves being relegated to the sidelines. Even in

Japan, where family obligations traditionally meant taking care of one's parents, many older people face the twilight years bathed in darkness. Japanese moviemaker Yasujiro Ozu sensitively portrays the plight of an old couple whose children see them as a burden in *Tokyo Story* (1953).

Not hired because they're "too old" or forced to retire, stripped of social roles that give meaning to their lives, and often pushed aside, the old may be called "senior citizens," but they're often treated as less than equal citizens. As the life expectancy in advanced industrial countries continues to increase, what will happen to people in their not-so-golden years?

Young people also receive unequal treatment. In some cases, American customs or laws presumed to protect children have served to deny them civil rights. In other cases (for example, widespread exclusion from juries), young adults face discrimination.

The specific consequences of age stratification for young and old include economic discrimination, age stereotyping, and territorial segregation (Johnson and Kamara, 1977–1978). In other words, old and young share a common plight.

ANOTHER LOOK

Scholars and citizens agree that inequality exists. But why it exists—and the role of sex, race, class, status, access to power, ethnicity, and religion in maintaining or perpetuating inequality—is a matter of continuing controversy.

At the urban level, how a researcher goes about studying inequalities among individuals or groups has less to do with disciplinary background than ideology. And what the researcher finds—an open system characterized by social mobility or a more rigid system of small, exclusive elites and social immobility—depends mainly on the theoretical orientation of the study. Those using the concept of status tend to find an open system; those using the concept of class tend to emphasize the rigidity of the social hierarchy. A subtle and immeasurable influence on researchers may also be present: fear—of change in the basic nature of the society and the economy. After all, why should we expect urbanists to be free from values about equality?

Those desiring to reduce inequality don't agree on how to do it. Programs of equal opportunity have been the liberals' mainstay, together with tax policies and public assistance. Marx had another solution—the creation of a classless society. Weber held out little hope of any solution, believing that even under socialism people would be oppressed and depersonalized by a common enemy: bureaucratic organization. Others have pointed to the rise of a new class, not predicted by Marx: scientists and technicians, intellectuals and professionals. This new class, it is often argued (e.g., Gouldner, 1979), shares a more important form of capital than money—culture—and it is increasingly gaining power and demanding autonomy. And, the argument continues, this new class will reject the social hierarchy.

Meanwhile, researchers have failed to disentangle the factors that influence collective inequalities, including sex, race, ethnicity, class, religion, and age. Ethnic and sexual stratification have been particularly neglected as independent factors that help determine who gets what out of life.

PROJECTS

1. **Attitudes on class.** To investigate how some people in your community view the social struc-

ture and their place in it, construct a questionnaire and administer it at various sites in the community. You might ask the following kinds of questions: Do classes exist in America? How do you define yourself (upper class, upper middle, middle, lower middle, working class)? Does everyone in the United States have an equal chance to lead a long life and to get a good job? The questionnaire should be short but include background information on each respondent, including occupation or job title. When examining responses, see how many respondents list themselves as middle class; how many of these are in the U.S. census categories of professional or managerial workers? What attitudes do your respondents hold toward class?

2. **Social status.** Replicate Warner's study of the distribution of housing in Jonesville in your community. Where are the fine houses located? Where do people with high-status occupations live? Is there a concentration of high-status homes in a particular neighborhood or neighborhoods?

SUGGESTIONS FOR FURTHER LEARNING

For an introduction to Karl Marx's thought, including his views on capitalism and social stratification, see Robert C. Tucker, *The Marx-Engels Reader* (New York: Norton, 1972), or David McLellan (ed.), *Karl Marx: Selected Writings* (New York: Oxford University Press, 1977). Both contain helpful commentaries.

For an introduction to Max Weber's thought, including the essay "Class, Status, Party," see Hans H. Gerth and C. Wrights Mills (eds.), *From Max Weber: Essays in Sociology* (New York: Oxford University Press, 1958). The editors' introduction compares Weber and Marx.

For a comparison of Marx, Durkheim, and Weber's thought, see Anthony Giddens, *Capitalism and Modern Social Theory* (London: Cambridge University Press, 1971). This book, not for beginners, contains an excellent chapter on "Fundamental concepts of sociology" which considers Weber's notions of class, status, and party. A secondary source which presents Marxian and Weberian concepts of social stratification is David A. Karp et al., *Being Urban: A Social Psychological View of City Life* (Lexington, Mass.: D.C. Heath, 1977). It also offers another view of social stratification: a symbolic interactionist perspective, emphasizing the instabilities in status arrangements and the ambiguities involved in placing people on a particular rung of the social ladder.

American economist Thorstein Veblen detailed the lifestyles of various status groups in *The Theory of the Leisure Class* (New York: Macmillan, 1899) and popularized the term "conspicuous consumption." Veblen, who taught for a time at the University of Chicago, was concerned, as Weber was, with the growth of rationality in modern life. Veblen advocated a society run by scientists and engineers (technocrats) instead of businesspeople. Another economist, John R. Commons, had ideas which paralleled those of Weber. In *Institutional Economics: Its Place in Political Economy* (New York: Macmillan, 1934) and *The Economics of Collective Action* (New York: Macmillan, 1950), he deals with various forms of power—moral, economic, and physical—and shows how they are linked together in property relationships.

A board game designed and produced by political scientist Bertell Ollman is called "Class Struggle." Paralleling Marx's views on class, it pits capitalists against workers. Other game players include small-business people, students, and professionals.

Literature dealing with various issues of social stratification is wide and varied. It ranges from the classic American dream tales of upward social mobility by Horatio Alger, including *Ragged Dick and Mark, the Match Boy,* reprinted in 1962 (New York: Crowell-Collier), and John P. Marquand's portrait of upper-class life in Boston, *The Late George Apley* (Fort Lee, N.J.: Little, 1937), to Jack London's socialist outrage, expressed in his story of class oppression, *The Iron Heel* (New York: Macmillan, 1907). The effects of race on life chances are vividly portrayed in Claude Brown's autobiographical account, *Manchild in the Promised Land* (New York: Signet, 1965), and the novels of Ralph Ellison, Richard Wright, and James Baldwin. Ellison's *Invisible Man* (New York: Signet,

1953) listens to records of Louis Armstrong playing and singing "What Did I Do to Be so Black and Blue?" sitting in his Harlem basement with 1,369 lights—to convince himself that he really exists in a world where people refuse to see him.

The recent outpouring of literature on sexual stratification includes Alix Kates Shulman's *Burning Questions* (New York: Knopf, 1978), a novel which has the heroine reading the Lynds's study of *Middletown* and leaping "over the horizon into historical consciousness . . . over the rim into self-consciousness."

Numerous films and video productions, from varying ideological points of view, deal with the themes of class and status. A feature-length classic from the Marxist perspective is Henry Bieberman's *Salt of the Earth* (1953). Bieberman, one of the "Hollywood Ten" producers blacklisted during the McCarthy era, weaves together themes of class, ethnic, and sexual oppression around the incident of a miners' strike in the Southwest. More recently, Richard Broadman's documentary, *Mission Hill and the Miracle of Boston* (1979), depicts urban renewal in Boston as a class struggle—with the capitalists destroying neighborhoods and winning the battle. Fritz Lang's classic silent film *Metropolis* (1927) presents a different ideological message: that workers (representing the "hands") and their bosses (representing the "head") each have a distinct place in society, but that to work smoothly together, both should be joined by human feeling or "heart"; the film can be interpreted as a defense of rigid social stratification under capitalism. On the other hand, Stanley Kramer's Western *High Noon* (1952) can be interpreted as presenting a contrary message. Critic Pauline Kael called *High Noon* a kind of civics lesson in which the frontier Western town represents a "microcosm of the evils of capitalist society." (See Pauline Kael, *Kiss Kiss Bang Bang* [New York: Bantam, 1969], p. 349.)

Among the many films that treat topics of racial and ethnic stratification are Arthur Penn's *Little Big Man* (1970), which attacks the American treatment of native Americans, and Robert Mulligan's *To Kill a Mockingbird* (1962), which deals with small-town prejudice against blacks.

Ageism and the loss of roles in old age are sensitively portrayed in Japanese director Yasujiro Ozu's *Tokyo Story* (1953). It also shows that stratification by age and isolation of older people are international phenomena.

Several TV productions are noteworthy in depicting themes of differential life chances and lifestyles. The Masterpiece Theatre series on the Public Broadcasting Service (PBS), *Upstairs, Downstairs,* shows two lifestyles within an English family's home: the "upstairs" upper-class family and the "downstairs" lower-class servants. A PBS miniseries telecast in 1978, *The Best of Families,* portrays the lifestyles of three New York families in the late nineteenth century: an Irish-American lower-class family, an upwardly mobile professional family, and an upper-class family of railroad-stock magnates.

Themes of class, status, and power are also found on the walls of city buildings and in the works of distinguished photographers, many of whom worked for the federal government's Works Progress Administration in the 1930s. One social commentary on the role of railroad barons is painted on the walls of buildings in Revelstoke, British Columbia, Canada; the murals satirize the entrepreneurs who helped construct the town.

KEY TERMS

Bourgeoisie Literally, "people who live in towns or cities" (bourgs). In Marx's analysis of social stratification, the bourgeoisie is the class that owns the means of production and thus controls the social relations of production under capitalism. The class opposing the bourgeoisie is the proletariat.

Castes Rigid social divisions based on status ascribed at birth. A caste system is typified by lack of social mobility; it is a closed class system. The classic example is traditional India where Brahmins constitute the highest caste and the Harijans (Untouchables) constitute the lowest caste.

Class As used by Karl Marx, class position in the social hierarchy is determined by one's relationship to the means of production (ownership or nonownership). As used by Max Weber, class is determined by one's market position. A group of people who share a similar relationship to the means of production (Marx) or market position (Weber) are members of the same class.

Class consciousness Sense of belonging to and identifying with a particular social class. This awareness is accompanied by a sense of solidarity with other individuals in the same class and the feeling that one's own interests are tied to the position of the class as a whole.

False consciousness In Marxist analysis, the sense of belonging to or identifying with a social class to which one does not belong objectively.

Forces of production In Marxist analysis, the technological, economic, and knowledge base of a society. It is one component of the mode of production (together with the social relations of production).

Means of production In Marxist analysis, land in a feudal society, and factories in an industrial capitalist society. Marxists maintain that the dominant class in a society is the one which owns or controls the means of production.

Mode of production To Marx, this consists of (1) the forces of production and (2) the social relations of production. Together, these two components shape a society.

Power In Weber's analysis, one dimension of social stratification which can be independent of the economic and prestige orders. Power is the ability to force others, even if they resist, to carry out your policies. The political order consists of administrative-bureaucratic and elected positions in the corporate and governmental spheres.

Proletariat Marx's term for the urban propertyless workers who, he felt, stood in opposition to the owners of the means of production (the bourgeoisie) in industrial capitalist society.

Relations of production In Marxist analysis, how people involved in production relate to each other and to the surplus that they collectively produce. Under capitalism, the social relations of production are the relations between the people who produce the surplus (workers) and those who decide how it should be appropriated (capitalists).

Social stratification The process by which individuals and groups rank each other socially and differentiate each other in a hierarchy. From the Latin, *strata* ("layers"; singular: stratum). Caste and class societies are socially stratified.

Socioeconomic status (SES) A composite measure based on income, education, and occupation that combines class and status to determine a person's or group's place on the social ladder.

Status One of Weber's three dimensions for ranking members of a society. Status is based on the prestige or social esteem that others in the society accord a person. It is a position in the social structure that, according to Weber, carries with it a certain lifestyle.

REFERENCES

Baltzell, E. Digby
1958 Philadelphia Gentlemen: The Making of a National Upper Class. New York: Free Press.

Balzac, Honoré de
[1834]
1946 Père Goriot and Eugenie Grandet. New York: Random House.

Birmingham, Stephen
1968 The Right People: A Portrait of the American Social Establishment. Boston: Little, Brown.

Blumberg, Rae Lesser
1978 Stratification: Socioeconomic and Sexual Inequality. Dubuque, Iowa: Wm. C. Brown.

Caplovitz, David
1963 The Poor Pay More: Consumer Practices of Low-Income Families. New York: Free Press.

Chinoy, Eli
1952 "The tradition of opportunity and the aspirations of automobile workers." American Journal of Sociology 57:453–59.

Coleman, Richard P. and Bernice L. Neugarten
1971 Social Status in the City. San Francisco: Jossey-Bass.

Form, William H. and Gregory P. Stone
1957 "Urbanism, anonymity and status symbolism." American Journal of Sociology 62:504–14.

Gans, Herbert
1974 Popular Culture and High Culture. New York: Basic Books.

Gerth, Hans H. and C. Wright Mills (eds., tr.)
1958 From Max Weber: Essays in Sociology. New York: Oxford University Press.

Gitlin, Todd and Nanci Hollander
1970 Uptown: Poor Whites in Chicago. New York: Harper & Row.

Gordon, Milton M.
1978 Human Nature, Class, and Ethnicity. New York: Oxford University Press.

Gouldner, Alvin W.
1979 The Future of Intellectuals and the Rise of the New Class. New York: Seabury.

Heilbroner, Robert L.
1978 "Inescapable Marx." New York Review of Books (June 29):33–7.

Howard, Dick
1978 The Marxian Legacy. New York: Dutton.

Howell, Joseph T.
1973 Hard Living on Clay Street: Portraits of Blue Collar Families. Garden City, N.Y.: Anchor Doubleday.

Ivins, Molly
1978 "Mormon action on blacks promises impact on Utah." New York Times (June 18):1 ff.

Johnson, Gregory and J. Lawrence Kamara
1977–
1978 "Growing up and growing old: the politics of age exclusion." Journal of Aging and Human Development 8:99–110.

Liebow, Elliot
1967 Tally's Corner: A Study of Negro Streetcorner Men. Boston: Little, Brown.

Lukas, J. Anthony
1978 Book Review, Chance and Circumstance. New York Times Book Review (June 11):9 ff.

Lynd, Robert S. and Helen Merrell Lynd
[1929]
1956 Middletown. New York: Harcourt Brace & World.

McLellan, David (ed.)
1977 Karl Marx: Selected Writings. New York: Oxford University Press.

New York Times
1978 "Used cars: the poor get poorer." New York Times (June 18):F 17.

San Francisco Chronicle
1978 "UAW chief calls Carter ineffective." San Francisco Chronicle (July 20):12.

Stone, Gregory P. and William H. Form
1953 "Instabilities in status: the problem of hierarchy in the community study of status arrangements." American Sociological Review 18:149–62.

Thernstrom Stephan
1966 " 'Yankee City' revisited: the perils of historical naivete." American Sociological Review 30:234–42.

Treiman, Donald J.
1977 Occupational Prestige in Comparative Perspective. New York: Academic Press.

Warner, W. Lloyd and associates
[1941]
1963 Yankee City. New Haven, Conn.: Yale University Press. One volume, abridged ed.

[1949]
1964 Democracy in Jonesville: A Study in Quality and Inequality. New York: Harper Torchbooks.

Weber, Max
[1922]
1958 "Class, status, party." Pp. 180–95 in Hans H. Gerth and C. Wright Mills (eds., tr.), From Max Weber: Essays in Sociology. New York: Oxford University Press.
[1904–05]
1958 The Protestant Ethic and the Spirit of Capitalism. New York: Scribner's.

Wilson, William Julius
1973 Power, Racism and Privilege. New York: Macmillan.
1978 The Declining Significance of Race: Blacks and Changing American Institutions. Chicago: University of Chicago Press.

Wright, Erik Olin
1978 "Race, class and income inequality." American Journal of Sociology 83:1368–97.

U.S. Bureau of the Census
1977 Social Indicators 1976. Washington, D.C.: U.S. Government Printing Office (December).

Walker Evans

CHAPTER 9 Discovering the Rules

Pedestrians push their way pell-mell through a busy intersection. Subway riders grab the first empty seat they see. Bar patrons sit in a quiet corner to avoid conversation. Or so it may seem at first glance. But appearances are often deceiving, especially in the case of face-to-face encounters with urban strangers.

This chapter looks behind some of those appearances. It focuses on everyday, routine activities of urban life—walking down a busy street in the CBD, riding public transportation, meeting people in a bar. Looking closely at such ordinary activities is not easy, precisely because they are so ordinary. We tend to take them for granted and not subject them to analysis. After all, what adult in America thinks twice about the proper way to ride a subway or walk down a city street? We know how to accomplish these tasks without thinking! In other words, these actions seem natural.

Here we treat these natural behaviors as curious and problematic indeed. It is as if we are visitors in a strange, exotic country, prepared to suffer culture shock from exposure to a totally unfamiliar way of life. But geographically, we don't have to move anywhere. Instead, we'll be "traveling" along familiar city streets and perhaps making some startling discoveries.

Our aim is to illuminate *how* routine social interaction takes place and *why* it happens as it does. As a guide on this mystery tour of the familiar, we will draw upon the insights of sociologists, social psychologists, and anthropologists.

TAKING A FRESH LOOK AT THE FAMILIAR

In studying urban **social interaction,** we are mostly studying ourselves—our friends and families, our work mates and fellow students—or groups of people about whom we have already formed some opinion. For this reason, it is harder to examine ourselves with detachment than it is to study a foreign culture; we hold fewer preconceived notions and moral judgments about proper or improper behavior patterns in faraway lands. Suspending these assumptions long enough to see our own culture objectively is difficult. That is one reason why anthropologists have tended to scrutinize other cultures, not their own. It is also one reason why foreigners have provided some of the most astute observations about American culture.

Although it is difficult, taking a fresh look at familiar surroundings can be enlightening and often amusing. Anthropologist Horace Miner (1956), for example, examined his own society using a trained eye and tongue in cheek, with insightful and humorous results (see Box 9-1). How many of us could so dispassionately record our own rites, such as the "ritual fasts to make fat people thin and ceremonial feasts to make thin people fat"? It takes discipline and perhaps a good sense of humor to look at ourselves as if *we* are the curious beings.

Pedestrian Behavior

Since that is our mission—to look closely at the everyday activities of people in urban places—let's begin with an impressive but usually unnoticed feature of city life: the large numbers of total strangers that urbanites encounter daily. Standing on a busy streetcorner in San Francisco's CBD, for instance, one of our students counted 4,000 passersby within one hour. On one midtown Manhattan block in New York City, some 38,000 pedestrians pass by on an average weekday (Whyte, 1974).

It is also impressive that pedestrians move in and around the CBD smoothly, with few scuffles or other incidents. But we take this for granted. Does anyone applaud the fact that pedestrians actually reach their destination without knocking each other down or holding up traffic? No, we just expect it.

We also expect that when we step off a busy streetcorner, we'll reach the other side of the street without mishap. Upon reflection, however, crossing a busy street is no small accomplishment. Three or four hundred strangers may be marching toward you; armies of unknown people are edging up from behind, all walking at different speeds; cars may be careening into your path; broken glass or dog excrement may be lying in wait. In this potentially dangerous battlefield, crossing the street now seems like a high-risk venture, not a routine activity.

Why is it, then, that crossing the street is such a commonplace event? Because we

Box 9-1

BODY RITUAL AMONG THE NACIREMA

. . . [The Nacirema] are a North American group living in the territory between the Canadian Cree, the Yaqui and Tarahumare of Mexico, and the Carib and Arawak of the Antilles. . . . According to Nacirema mythology, their nation was originated by a culture hero, Notgnihsaw, who is otherwise known for two great feats of strength—the throwing of a piece of wampum across the river Pa-To-Mac and the chopping down of a cherry tree in which the Spirit of Truth resided.

Nacirema culture is characterized by a highly developed market economy that has evolved in a rich natural habitat. While much of the people's time is devoted to economic pursuits, a large part of the fruits of these labors and a considerable portion of the day are spent in ritual activity. The focus of this activity is the human body, the appearance and health of which loom as a dominant concern in the ethos of the people.

. . . The fundamental belief underlying the whole system appears to be that the human body is ugly, and that its natural tendency is to debility and disease. Incarcerated in such a body, man's only hope is to avert these characteristics through the use of the powerful influences of ritual and ceremony. Every household has one or more shrines devoted to this purpose. The more powerful individuals in the society have several shrines in their houses, and, in fact, the opulence of a house is often referred to in terms of the number of such ritual centers it possesses.

. . . While each family has at least one such shrine, the rituals associated with it are not family ceremonies but are private and secret. The rites are normally only discussed with children, and then only during the period when they are being initiated into these mysteries. I was able, however, to establish sufficient rapport with the natives to examine these shrines and to have the rituals described to me.

The focal point of the shrine is a box or chest, which is built into the wall. In this chest are kept the many charms and magical potions without which no native believes he could live. These preparations are secured from a variety of specialized practitioners. The most powerful of these are the medicine men, whose assistance must be rewarded with substantial gifts. . . . The medicine men . . . decide what the ingredients [of curative potions] should be and then write them down in an ancient and secret language. This writing is understood only by the medicine men and by the herbalists who, for another gift, provide the required charm.

. . . In the hierarchy of magical practitioners, and below the medicine men in prestige, are specialists whose designation is best translated "holy-mouth-men." The Nacirema have an almost pathological horror of, and fascination with, the mouth, the condition of which is believed to have a supernatural influence on all social relationships. Were it not for the rituals of the mouth, they believe that their teeth would fall out, their gums bleed, their jaws shrink, their friends desert them, and their lovers reject them.

. . . In conclusion, mention must be made of certain practices that . . . depend upon the pervasive aversion to the natural body and its functions. There are ritual fasts to make fat people thin and ceremonial feasts to make thin people fat. Still other rites are used to make women's breasts larger if they are small, and smaller if they are large. General dissatisfaction with breast shape is symbolized in the fact that the ideal form is virtually outside the range of human variation. A few women afflicted with almost inhuman hypermammary development are so idolized that they make a handsome living by simply going from village to village and permitting the natives to stare at them for a fee.

. . . Our review of the ritual life of the Nacirema has certainly shown them to be a magic-ridden people. It is hard to understand how they have managed to exist so long under the burdens they have imposed upon themselves. (Miner, 1956:503–7. Reproduced by permission of the American Anthropological Association from the *American Anthropologist, 58* (3), 1956, and the author. Copyright 1956 by the American Anthropological Association.)

expect that other pedestrians will follow the "rules of the game" and be competent game players. Like so many everyday activities, street crossing is governed by rules that are widely shared within any culture. These culturally shared rules (**norms**) are often implicit and hidden, but they exist nonetheless. If they didn't, the simple act of crossing a busy street would be impossible.

In the United States, most children learn explicit rules for being good pedestrians: "cross on the green, wait on the red," "look both ways before crossing," "keep your head up," and "watch out for open manhole covers." Other rules are not made explicit. For example, how many of us are aware that we follow definite walking patterns? Pedestrians can take any path to get across a busy street—but they don't. Looking at films of people walking down a midtown Manhattan street one block from Times Square, Michael Wolff (1973) found several interesting walking patterns, including the following:

1. In low-density pedestrian traffic, walkers detour from their original path to avoid bumping into another person; after the other person passes, the walkers return to their original path.
2. In high-density pedestrian traffic, there's no room to step completely around an oncoming walker. Thus, to accommodate people coming in the opposite direction, pedestrians use a range of almost imperceptible actions. One maneuver, used especially to avoid bumping into members of the same sex, is the "step-and-slide" (Wolff, 1973:39). Here, a person slightly angles the body, turns the shoulder, and takes a tiny side step.

Now, what happens if a person is a bad or incompetent pedestrian? Usually, dirty looks or sharp words follow. If, for example, a person doesn't execute the step-and-slide maneuver in dense traffic and thus jostles another pedestrian, the jostled party might say something like, "Whatsamatter, ya blind?" Such comments suggest that the jostler violated the rules of the game.

To discover people's expectations about routine activities, like walking down the street, researchers try deliberately to break the rules of the game. That's the way Wolff gathered his data. He designed an experiment which aimed at purposefully disrupting routine behaviors. For instance, his experimenters would stay on a straight-line collision course with an oncoming pedestrian. Cameras hidden from view recorded the surprised and shocked reactions of the oncoming pedestrians to this unexpected behavior.

What Wolff concluded from the experiment in New York City is that cooperation, not competition ("Each person for himself"), is the general rule shared by pedestrians. They expect that others will look around and notice who is coming toward them. And they expect that other pedestrians will cooperate "in avoiding contact and inconvenience to the other: Each pedestrian is responsible for recognizing cues . . . that are signals for cooperation and special consideration (for example, old age) . . . and behaving accordingly" (Wolff, 1973:40).

It turns out, then, that appearances are deceiving; few pedestrians push pell-mell through a busy intersection. Instead, they avoid collision courses, estimate what moves and countermoves to take, and monitor the immediate environment for special problems. And all within a fraction of a second! (Despite this efficiency, people themselves have been neglected by transportation researchers. In part, this may reflect the problem of taking the familiar for granted. At any rate, while the federal government and private companies spend millions of dollars for research on

Fig. 9-1 WHY DON'T THEY KNOCK EACH OTHER DOWN? The rule of pedestrian behavior is cooperation, not competition. (Brack Brown)

transportation, there are few studies of this low-technology transport: feet.)

Among the few studies of pedestrian behavior that do exist, there is a gem: William H. Whyte's comparative study, "New York and Tokyo: A Study in Crowding" (1978). Part of a larger comparative research project on street life in large urban complexes, Whyte's report deals with the pedestrian environments of two of the world's largest cities: how they differ, what common denominators exist. Despite the cultural and physical differences between the two cities, Whyte concluded that New York and Tokyo pedestrians act a great deal alike.

For example, Whyte discovered the following:

1. New Yorkers and Tokyoites are highly skilled pedestrians. "They make very efficient use of space" and "navigate adroitly."

2. Both walk fast. Whyte notes that people in big cities walk faster than people in smaller cities, and this holds true worldwide. The reason is unclear. One social psychologist (Milgram, 1970) thinks that the fast pace in very large cities is related to "stimulus overload," a bombardment of stimuli which apparently encourages people to speed up to seek relief. Others (e.g., Cranz, 1978) maintain that the stimulus overload encourages people in very large cities to walk faster so that they can take advantage of more events and stimuli that the city offers.

3. Both are very cooperative in their behav-

ior toward other pedestrians. While both New Yorkers and Tokyoites give "impressive performances" to avoid collisions, Whyte notes that "Tokyo's pedestrians are in a class by themselves." The scene that Whyte paints of *apparent* chaos at a major subway station in Tokyo is instructive:

> By all accepted density standards [Shinjuku subway station] is a manifest impossibility. It is really a complex of stations and separate lines, confusing in its layout, inter-connected with an intricate set of corridors, walkways, escalators, cul de sacs. Its concourses are a mass of cross-flows, obstructed by knots of people waiting for other people, teenagers, vendors, people saying goodbye. Even at off-peak times one has to look sharply to find a clear path; at the rush hours, when the pedestrian traffic reaches an intensity unmatched anywhere, the scene appears chaotic.
>
> But it isn't. Somehow, people sort themselves out and for all the density the pedestrian speeds remain quite high; indeed, it is at rush hour that one sees the most running. By rights, people should be bumping into each other all over the place. They don't seem to . . . . [Furthermore, it seemed that] a good many of the pedestrians were rather stimulated by the challenge, and perhaps a bit pleased with themselves. (Whyte, 1978: 8–9)

If we think inductively, these micro observations and impressions by Whyte and Wolff suggest certain hypotheses about the nature of city life:

Hypothesis #1: *Crowding in one's immediate physical presence significantly affects how one behaves.*

This hypothesis is all the more interesting because the effects are not in the expected direction. That is, it is widely believed that crowding is bad for people, that it can debilitate them psychologically. Yet, pedestrians in crowded situations seem to cooperate and, as Whyte's impressions of Tokyo suggest, even to enjoy themselves. Further, in crowded situations such as rush hour traffic, urbanites don't seem nearly as indifferent to the needs of others as Wirth implies they should be in "Urbanism as a Way of Life" (1938).

Hypothesis #2 *Mutual trust—not distrust—is the norm in urban public places.*

That trust, not distrust, is the norm is indicated by people's reactions to violations of trust (for example, following a collision course while walking down the street): surprise and disbelief. If distrust were the norm, pickpockets could not operate on a busy street. Pedestrians would clutch their valuables. If bumped into, they would assume an evil intent (instead of incompetence) and call for police or civilian assistance in apprehending the jostler.

These hypotheses (which grew out of observing behavior on city streets) fit into a larger theoretical framework in which to understand routine social interaction. According to the eminent Canadian-born sociologist Erving Goffman (1971:5), pedestrian traffic codes constitute one of many sets of ground rules that "provide the normative bases of public order." This means that social order in a crowded city can be maintained only if people don't aggress against each other. Rules (norms) help people to adjust to each other's behavior and know what to expect of each other. This allows undisrupted interaction between people who have never met.

To conclude: Here are two discoveries (or more precisely, hypotheses) we have made on this short trip down city streets:

1. Routine interaction in public places embodies unspoken but widely shared understandings or rules; these rules are not usually brought to conscious awareness by members of the culture. If someone violates the rules, others react with disbelief or disapproval.
2. Shared social understandings are the

basis of public order. Without such rules or norms, other people's actions would be unpredictable and thus frightening or threatening; people would hardly be confident that their own routine goals (like walking to the store) could be reached. If the cement of public order—mutual trust—crumbled, a city would be a battlefield where every stranger constitutes a potential threat.

Subway Behavior

On American city streets, it is a common understanding that pedestrians will keep their heads up, scan the environment, and adjust their behavior according to the needs of others. Do the same rules apply below the city streets, on subways?

Just as in the case of walking on the city streets, most of us are unaware that there are rules for riding public transportation—until somebody violates them. That is, riding a bus or subway is such a routine activity that we take it for granted. As ethnomethodologist Harold Garfinkel, a distinguished observer of routine, everyday events, puts it, familiar settings (like subways) are full of " 'seen but unnoticed,' expected background features" (1967:36).

Again our task is to bring these background features into the foreground; our approach, as before, is to treat the familiar as unusual and problematic. In this way we are like **ethnographers**, social scientists who study a community's culture by participant-observation. Our job is to decode the verbal and nonverbal messages that people send each other and to describe behavior appropriate to the situation (e.g., riding a subway).

Appropriate behavior is culturally relative. (See the discussion of proxemics in Chapter 14.) That is, in the same context, what is appropriate behavior in one culture may be out of place in another. Take, for instance, train behavior. Traveling by train (third class) through Greece, one could expect some variation on the following scene: passengers sharing whatever food and wine they have with strangers in their compartment; babies nursing at their mothers' breasts; chickens squeezed in the compartment and noisily peeping; smugglers trying to peddle their wares; and people sleeping amid the commotion. This is not what Americans expect to find when they board Amtrak. If they did, they might wonder where Allen Funt's *Candid Camera* crew was hiding or call the police. Whatever their reaction, the Greek train scene (where people are open to social interaction) would violate American expectations. On U.S. trains, one expects to be casually noticed by other passengers but left alone.

The same is true of American subways. Subway riders expect to be treated with what Erving Goffman calls **civil inattention.** To be civilly inattentive, "one gives to another enough visual notice to demonstrate that one appreciates that the other is present (and that one admits openly to having seen him), while at the next moment withdrawing one's attention from him so as to express that he does not constitute a target of special curiosity or design" (Goffman, 1963:84).

Civil inattention takes various forms. Researchers who conducted participant-observation in Boston and New York City subways (see Box 9-2) found that some riders bury their heads in a newspaper. Others stare into space, look straight ahead without expression, or daydream.

Under certain circumstances, the general rule of civil inattention on subways can be suspended. Subway riders may smile or show openness to others they consider nonthreatening. This category includes children and matronly, middle-aged housewives. That middle-aged women—who look like

Box 9-2

SUBWAY BEHAVIOR

Subway behavior is regulated by certain societal rules and regulations that serve to protect personal rights and to sustain proper social distance between unacquainted people who are temporarily placed together in unfocused and focused interaction. This trivial occasion gives rise to many rules pertaining to larger social gatherings, particularly those focusing on a specific issue. For this reason, we can study the larger problems of social order by focusing on these small units, these interludes of everyday life. Subway riding demonstrates, for example, the ways in which we generally afford "civil inattention" to others in one's immediate presence and, in turn, the others' acceptance of complete absorption in "subordinate" involvements by ourselves. Despite this closeness of contact and the mutual vulnerability of the passengers, little focused interaction occurs, few people are accosted, and few friendships arise. How these things *do not take place* is the problem for discussion here.

The rules [of subway behavior] . . . can be best discovered and confirmed by examining and even committing infractions and improprieties against the socially accepted behavior of riders. The conclusions drawn in this essay are based on actual observations of behavior in the Boston and New York City subways.

. . . In most cases, the people entering a subway car do not have similar focuses of activity, because their usual activities have been temporarily suspended and their main involvement is passively riding to their destinations—hardly a demanding task for someone who knows the way. . . . Indeed, one way in which competence in the role of rider is exhibited is to sit with closed eyes or actually go to sleep and then jump up at the precise moment the train comes to the stop where one wants to get off.

. . . When a person enters a car in which there are many empty seats in various places, two conflicting considerations may influence that person's selection of a seat, both of which are aimed at reducing the threat of exposure and accessibility to others, particularly if the rider is a woman. The first consideration concerns the newcomer's discomfort at being "on stage" in front of other riders . . . ; he feels compelled to take the nearest vacant seat so that he can discreetly slip in among the mass of seated passengers. . . . Unlike the model who walks down an aisle . . . at a fashion show, the subway rider is giving a nonshow, communicating to others that he does not wish to be communicated with.

A second consideration of the newcomer in the subway car concerns whom he will sit beside or between. . . . Newcomers usually look for seated people who appear self-contained, that is, who are sitting squarely in their seats and either directing their attention to newspapers or books or concealing any interest in their surroundings with blank faces. When choosing among different but equally involved riders, people tend to sit down next to others of the same sex. The least desirable people chosen as "seatmates" seem to be older, shabbily dressed people and people apparently lacking in self-control, sprawled in their seats. . . .

When seated, people usually assume inconspicuous behavior—sitting squarely, at first turning neither left nor right, and maintaining expressionless faces. Faces are often immediately buried in newspapers and books . . . ; sometimes passengers may be indulging in various forms of autoinvolvements, especially daydreaming. People without books or papers . . . may begin to stare at fellow passengers, alternating fleeting or blank stares with an innocent staring off into space. These stares and glances at fellows are quite restricted and concealed . . . ; they are the behavior components of what Goffman (1963:84) has called "civil inattention." . . .

. . . Some people are more open to interaction than others, usually because of the innocuous qualities that we can attribute to them. Middle-aged housewives of matronly build, who are neat in appearance and are usually carrying shopping bundles, are one such type. . . . They can demonstrate by word as well as appearance that they are no threat to anyone.

Another interesting exception to the civil inattention rule is found in the behavior that riders display when young children are present . . . the child's stare is often greeted by a smile rather than a sign of discomfort; the passenger, by smiling, shows that he is not threatened by this violation of face-to-face interaction and even returns the openness shown him.

. . . These rules of close, face-to-face interaction enable people to avoid unnecessary encounters and to hide their emotions. In urban environments, where so much interaction or potential interaction takes place, this may be a necessity in order to get through the day and limit the moral claims that every other might make upon you. (Levine, Vinson, and Wood, 1973:208–12.

housewives—constitute no threat is a revealing insight into our culture.

Civil inattention also comes into play when choosing a seat mate in the subway car. People do tend to grab the first empty seat they see. But there is another consideration, especially for women: Which potential seat mate looks the least threatening? People look for self-contained persons who show civil inattention. When choosing among equally self-contained and civilly inattentive persons, riders tend to sit down next to members of their own sex. This observation qualifies the first impression that subway riders sit in the nearest vacant seat. It also raises fascinating questions about trust levels between the sexes.

What purposes does civil inattention serve? Civil inattention is one device urbanites use "for immunizing themselves against the personal claims and expectations of others" (Wirth [1938] 1969:153). It may also serve as a mechanism of social control, keeping potentially dangerous situations from happening. When strangers aren't sure of each other's intentions, civil inattention helps to promote privacy and to maintain public order. In other words, the rule of civil inattention functions to "protect personal rights and to sustain proper social distance between unacquainted people who are temporarily placed together" (Levine et al, 1973; see Box 9-2).

Bar Behavior

Within any culture, proper social distance varies with the social context. In America, strangers keep their distance on subways. But they don't in a bar. The bar is one setting where the proper social distance is considerably less than in a subway.

In a bar, the general rule of civil inattention is suspended. Whereas idle glances on a subway show that a person is closed to social interaction, researchers have found that the same kinds of glances in a bar demonstrate a person's openness. In a bar, almost no patrons bury their heads in a newspaper or book. But if they do, this gesture can serve to open conversation, not close off the possibility as in a subway. As Sherri Cavan observed while researching her ethnography of bar behavior, *Liquor License:*

> A middle-aged woman was sitting by herself, thumbing through a large book of Steinberg cartoons. A man sitting at the other end of the bar came over, asked her what she was looking at and then joined her. ([1966] 1973:144)

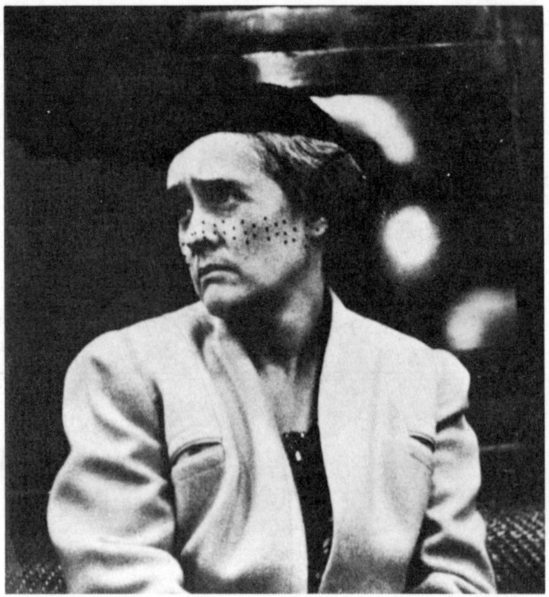

Fig. 9-2 CIVIL INATTENTION IN THE NEW YORK CITY SUBWAY. Distinguished photographer Walker Evans captures the vacant faces associated with proper behavior on public transport. (*Many Are Called* by Walker Evans, introduction by James Agee. Copyright © 1966 by Walker Evans. Reprinted by permission of Houghton Mifflin Company.)

In other words, what might ensure civil inattention in the subway or other settings can be an overture for social interaction in a bar.

If a person enters a tavern alone and wishes to remain alone, he or she will usually sit at the bar, not an empty table, and will sit in a particular way. According to Cavan, the solitary drinker—who is not open to social interaction—shows the intention to stay closed off by minimizing the physical space he or she occupies. Typically, a man will "sit with his forearms either resting on the edge of the bar, or flat on the bar before him, his upper torso hunched slightly forward over the bar, with all of his drinking accoutrements (drink, cigarettes, change, ashtray, and the like) contained within the area before him" ([1966] 1973:144–45). This posture serves to protect the solitary drinker from eye contact with others (one signal of openness in a bar).

To conclude: When people enter a bar they are expected to be sociable, not civilly inattentive. If they don't want to be sociable, they have to send body language signals for privacy (in subways, it's the opposite; people have to send signals for openness). But the solitary drinker is the exception in a bar, for "sociability is the most general rule in the public drinking place. Although the bar is typically populated primarily by strangers, interaction is available to all those who choose to enter" (Cavan, [1966] 1973:143).

Why is it that in most urban public settings, civil inattention serves to limit contact among strangers while sociability is the norm in bars? Cavan thinks this norm is associated with the idea that bars aren't really serious places. Instead, they are considered a setting for a time out from life's important concerns. Thus, she argues, what might seem threatening or dangerous in a more serious place appears nonthreatening in a bar (Cavan, [1966] 1973:154).

EVERYDAY GAMES AND DRAMAS

Looking at people in various urban public places—streets, subways, bars—it is clear that the rules of the game (norms) and the roles people play (e.g., bar patron, subway rider, pedestrian) help to structure individual behavior, perceptions, even emotions. But to what extent? How much freedom do urbanites have to change the rules of the game? To create new roles in the drama of everyday life? Or to play old roles in a new way? Here, social theorists disagree.

Whose Games Do We Play?

Thus far, in Part 3, we have drawn connections between what people do and what society expects them to do. We noted that whether in a bar or on city streets, people usually follow rules that they didn't construct, although they may be unaware that rules even exist. We also discussed the impact of macro social structure on individual behavior, particularly noting the effect of class and status on people's actions. For example, various community studies show that what appear on the surface to be personal choices—what part of town one lives in, what style of house one chooses—are heavily influenced by one's social rank in the community.

Most sociologists and anthropologists agree that social structure (including norms, roles, and social rank) shapes individual identity and behavior. But they debate the

Fig. 9-3 BAR SOCIABILITY. The general rule among urban strangers—civil inattention—is suspended in a public drinking place and is replaced by sociability. (© 1978 John Pearson)

degree to which people have freedom to invent new games or play by their own rules.

Theorists who focus on the larger patterns of social structure (**macro-level social analysis)** tend to stress the degree to which people follow society's rules. Marxists, for example, maintain that a person's class and class interests are most important in determining attitudes and behavior. Marx thought that what people produce and how they produce it determines a society's norms, morality, ideology, and individual consciousness: "Life is not determined by consciousness, but consciousness by life" (Marx, [1859] 1977:164).

Non-Marxists also point to the great impact of social structural variables on individual behavior. For example, Peter L. Berger (1963) writes that even in the most private games people play—courtship and marriage—the couple doesn't invent the game "or any part of it." The rituals (from dating to meeting the family, from holding hands to making love) are socially set. The couple merely decides that they will play the game with each other and not with other possible partners. Sociologist Berger says that Americans may believe that love is an "irresistible emotion that strikes where it will." Yet, upon deeper investigation, it turns out that "the lightning shaft of Cupid seems to be guided rather strongly within very definite channels of class, income, education, racial and religious background" (1963:35). In other words, macro theorists of varying orientations point to the *determining* role that social structure plays in molding individual actions and thoughts.

Micro-level social analysis, on the other hand, tends to stress the freedom individuals have to negotiate the rules and improvise new acts. Symbolic interactionists, for example, do not deny that people act within the framework of their society and its rules, but these social psychologists maintain that "human beings are active in shaping their own behavior. Such structural features as social roles, social classes, and the like [do] set conditions for human behavior and interaction, but do not cause or fully determine the behavior and interaction" (Manis and Meltzer, 1978:7). Symbolic interactionists see individual behavior as part of a complex process in which people are constantly modifying their own actions in relation to other people's behavior and their interpretations of what's happening. In this view, people are not programmed, mindless robots. Instead, people themselves give meaning to situations and act accordingly; "the features (structures) of society are maintained and changed by the *actions* of people, and are not autonomous, or self-regulating . . . . Human behavior is an elaborate process of interpreting, choosing, and rejecting possible lines of action. This process cannot be understood in terms of mechanical responses to external stimuli" (Manis and Meltzer, 1978:7,8).

Other social theorists interested in micro processes also stress the active role people play in molding their own behavior. Whatever their theoretical orientation (e.g., **symbolic interactionism, ethnomethodology)**, most micro theorists emphasize two points: (1) people have choices in how to act and (2) people bring different meanings to the same event. Hence, they argue, we must try to understand other people's meanings (that is, the actors' subjective point of view) if we are to understand their behavior.

This debate over how much freedom people have to make up their own rules is essentially one of degree, not of kind. Both macro and micro theorists acknowledge that social structure and social organization provide the framework in which people act and give meaning to events. The difference is that macro theorists tend to see people as prisoners of society's rules, whereas micro theorists tend to focus on people's ability to push back (or build anew) the prison walls. (*Note:* The simple micro-macro distinction can't capture the variety of approaches to the study of society. For instance, Max Weber examined the development of meaning at the macro level, and commentators on Erving Goffman's work suggest that his micro studies are essentially analyses of social structure.)

Before discussing how micro and macro levels of analylsis can be combined to study urban behavior, we turn to several useful concepts developed by micro theorists. These concepts—**the definition of the situation** and **the presentation of self**—deal with the same basic point: that social interaction, customs, and beliefs are often problematic.

"The Definition of the Situation" (W. I. Thomas)

Reality, like beauty, exists in the eye of the beholder. The same object or event can have different meanings for different people, and "the degree of difference will produce comparable differences in behavior" (McHugh, 1968:8). That is the essence of social psychologist W. I. Thomas's classic statement on the subjective quality of reality: "If men [and women] define situations as real they are real in their consequences" (1928:572).

Thomas's statement points out that there are *multiple* realities, not just one reality. Perhaps this is most evident when cross-cultural social interaction takes place. For instance, as detailed in Chapter 14, North Americans who converse at a distance of about 12 inches are considered cold and distant by Latins; Latins who hold head-to-head conversations are considered pushy and aggressive by North Americans. The potential consequences: misunderstanding, discomfort, even prejudice or fist fights.

Here are two examples of multiple realities and their potential consequences within the same culture. Example one: George wines and dines Donna at the fanciest restaurant in town for weeks. She likes him and fantasizes about marrying him. Then George tells her, "I love you." Before Donna reacts to these ambiguous words, she must decide what they mean to him. She asks herself, "Is his concept of love the same as mine? Is he just giving me a line? Will his love smother me? How many others does he love?" And so on. How Donna reacts to George's declaration of love (from planning a wedding to saying farewell) depends on what meanings she thinks George attaches to it.

Example two: In the early 1970s, a civil rights group in Syracuse, New York, showed two photographs to a group of white, suburban, middle-class church members. In each photo, a male teenager, dressed casually, was running down the street. There was only one significant difference between the two teens: one was black, the other white. Respondents in this experiment were asked to describe what each teenager in the photos was doing. The range of responses was as follows, in order of times mentioned:

White Teen Running Down Street	*Black Teen* Running Down Street
1. Good samaritan, running to help a needy person (perhaps a car-accident victim)	1. Thief, running from police or making a fast getaway
2. Hurt child, running home for help	2. Looter during an urban riot, running toward a a store to rob it
3. Jogger or Little Leaguer, out for exercise	3. Curious spectator, running to watch a fire or an accident

When presented with the profile of their responses, the church members were shocked. For in large measure, they did share a common definition of the situation—in this case, one they themselves labeled racist. Yet, a few in the group did not attribute negative (indeed, criminal) meanings to the black teenager's behavior. Why did a minority of the group attribute normal behavior (curious spectator) to the black's gesture of running? An interesting research question. But that was not the experimenters' concern. Their concern focused on the potential real-life consequences of the majority's shared understanding: racist stereotypes that can bring psychological—and physical—harm to blacks. Their goal: to change the majority's definition of the situation.

From the symbolic interactionist point of view, these examples—words of love, gestures of running—show that stimuli have no inherent meaning. By themselves, words, gestures, symbols, and objects are meaningless; only people make them meaningful. Symbolic interactionists do not claim that people are free to attribute any meaning at all to an event or a symbol. To the contrary, they emphasize that meanings are socially derived through interaction. Hence, in America, people share the assumption that a star-spangled cloth flying at half-mast on a long pole means that someone important has died. If they see a woman in a long white dress with a veil, they assume she is being married.

What, then, is the special relevance of this social psychological concept—the definition of the situation—to urban life? It helps to explain why social order in the modern metropolis is so much more fragile than in traditional rural communities. When groups and individuals share a common definition of the situation, the basis for social order exists. Shared understandings of what is normal, proper, and good behavior characterize *Gemeinschaft* communities. In contrast, *Gesellschaft* societies are typified by heterogeneous populations with plural belief systems. For instance, Americans have different definitions of the situation concerning the supernatural and paranormal (see Table 9-1).

It is in the modern metropolis that people are unlikely to share the same definition of the situation and, consequently, are unlikely to react similarly to the same event or stimulus. This situation lends itself to social disruption and conflict.

Let's apply this fairly abstract point to a practical problem: what to teach in a public high school. Imagine that you are a member of a neighborhood group in Oakland, California; the group is concerned with what teenagers are learning in social studies courses. Besides yourself, the following neighborhood people show up at the first meeting to discuss what should be taught: astrologers and astrophysicists; gays and straights; Chinese-Americans, whites (WASPs and ethnics), Chicanos, blacks, native Americans, and Pakistani Americans; housewives and women executives; est graduates and Moonies; welfare recipients, car mechanics, lawyers, and a self-proclaimed hedonist; Marxist community

Table 9-1 Multiple Realities
Nationwide poll question: "Which of the following do you believe in? UFOs, angels, devils, astrology, ghosts, and/or witches?"

	Percentage expressing belief in
57%	UFOs
54%	Angels
39%	Devils
29%	Astrology
11%	Ghosts
10%	Witches

SOURCE: Gallup Poll, "Surprising Number of Americans Believe in Paranormal Phenomena" (Princeton, N.J.: Gallup Organization, June 15, 1978). Copyright © 1978 by Gallup Poll. Reprinted by permission.

organizers, tax protesters, John Birch society and ACLU members; advocates of appropriate technology, environmentalists, and an oil refinery executive; and atheists, Protestants, Catholics, Jews, Muslims, and Hindus.

Given this diversity, conflicts over what to teach surface immediately. The astrologer insists that students be taught that the position of the stars governs their lives. "Hooey," shouts the astrophysicist, advocating instruction in scientific methods to measure social phenomena. Some Chicanos want a bilingual program; others don't. A Marxist community organizer claims that the social science text ignores the key variable in American life—social class—while the John Birch member thinks it is laced with anticapitalist propaganda. The environmentalist dislikes the text because it advocates unlimited growth, and the oil company executive says that "kids should learn that without growth, there is no more prosperity." Meanwhile, the car mechanic worries that her child can't even spell the word "environment." A feminist castigates the text for its sexist neglect of women in U.S. history, but a lawyer thinks the book gives a realistic assessment of American history. The gays question how the subject of marriage is treated in class. And so it goes.

Given these varied social backgrounds, concerns, ideologies, and stocks of knowledge, it seems a miracle that any collective action can take place. Yet it usually does. How? *How is social order possible in a milieu of multiple realities?* Emile Durkheim, the ninteenth-century sociologist, answered this important question by taking for granted that people conform to society's rules because they were taught to do so as children and because they benefit from assuming that others will also conform. Durkheim's stance is a structural-functional one, emphasizing the process by which people internalize norms and conform to them.

But other theorists have different answers. Philosopher Alfred Schutz (1967) argues that (1) individuals in the same culture share the belief that they can put themselves in one another's shoes and understand how another person could view their behavior; this allows for the development of empathy and understanding; and (2) this empathy and understanding allows people to transcend their personal experience and exchange perspectives through social interaction. Through the exchange of perspectives, Schutz thinks, people can question the rules they learned as children. Thus, they can help make or unmake the rules which create social order.

Erving Goffman (1959) might answer the question "How is social order possible?" in the following way. People hold different definitions of the situation, but they still have working agreements which help maintain order. This "working consensus," as Goffman calls it, may conceal wide disagreements among participants in any social interaction. But the working consensus is like a contract that states: If you support my act, I'll support yours; and if we cooperate, we'll all get our everyday tasks accomplished. Thus, when people enter the physical presence of others, they take each other's behavior into account (even if no verbal communication occurs). They constantly modify their own behavior in order to act properly in a given situation. Acting properly reduces vulnerability, risk, and embarrassment. It is also less time-consuming than making up the rules from scratch every time people interact. In this way, social order is upheld.

We now turn to Goffman's ideas on how people try to impose their definitions of reality on others. He contends that we present ourselves in certain ways, trying to control or manage the impressions others have of us.

"The Presentation of Self" (Erving Goffman)

Erving Goffman explores "the little interactions that are forgotten about as soon as they occur." He microscopically examines "the little salutations, compliments and apologies" (for example, smiles and "I'm sorry") that "serious students of society never collect." He finds "empty" gestures "perhaps the fullest of all." In short, his domain is "the slop of social life."

Goffman's examples of "the slop of social life" are taken mainly from urban society, but he is not usually classified as an urbanist. And rarely are his micro studies mentioned in the context of urban studies. This is unfortunate, perhaps one casualty of the dubious distinction between things urban and otherwise.

Goffman has been labeled "the Kafka of our time" because, like the great Czech writer, he "communicates so vividly the horror and anguish—as well as some of the absurd comedy—of everyday life" (Berman, 1972:1). His world, like Kafka's, is peopled with ordinary individuals—clerks, bureaucrats, shoppers—doing ordinary things. But in Goffman's hands, this ordinary world becomes extraordinary and complex.

In Goffman's vision, just getting through the day—standing in a bus line, greeting friends and acknowledging strangers, entering a repair store, and engaging in similar routine activity—is full of ritual, perhaps magic. In his view, this ritual process is worth exploring because it reveals the fragility and complexity of social behavior, particularly urban behavior

Esentially, Goffman's vision is a theatrical one. He presents the everyday world as a theatre in which we all act out **roles** and give performances in ongoing plays. His imagery is drawn from the stage. Hence, a person (in its first dictionary meaning, from *persona*) is a mask. Brief encounters in urban places are treated as masked rituals. Individuals are always "on" (as in "on stage"), performing and creating their roles. This theatrical model of social behavior recalls Shakespeare: "All the world's a stage and all the men and women merely players."

To Goffman, when we play roles and interpret other people's performances on the stage of everyday life, we wear masks or ritual faces. Our ritual faces aren't who we "really" are—but who we "really" are doesn't much matter. What does matter is the image we want the audience (observers) to have of our performance. Our masks allow us to manipulate our appearances and save face before others. That is what we do, according to Goffman, hundreds of times each day; we have an unspoken understanding with our audience whereby all of us role players agree to conduct ourselves to maintain our own face and the faces of other participants in the scene. Thus, for Goffman, most routine social interaction in urban settings is nothing more than the effort to control the impression we make on others ("impression management"). We manage these impressions to keep up appearances and win acceptance from the audience. We want our audiences to accept our appearance—our performance—because it is on the basis of our appearance (and inferences about it) that they will react to us.

How we present ourselves, Goffman maintains, depends on the impression we want to make on a particular audience. We choose a role from our repertoire of identities; we put on one of our many faces, depending on our intent and our audience. Thus, we don't play the same part in front of all our audiences—family, strangers, colleagues, etc.—because "urban life would become unbearably sticky for some if every contact between two individuals entailed a sharing of personal trials, worries, and secrets. Thus if a man wants to be served a restful dinner, he may seek the service of a waitress rather than a wife" (1959:49).

How do we present ourselves in urban public or semipublic places? In ways that will appear proper to those around us, Goffman says. This serves to avert real or potential danger and embarrassment and get the results we want.

If, however, a person feels that things aren't normal—that "something is up"—he or she may put on a performance to conceal the sense that something is wrong. Sometimes these acts can be pathetic: "Witness the vain and painful effort of someone sitting beside an obstreperous drunk on public transportation; witness the effort of the individual to act as if the drunk were either not there or not a special point of concern, in either case not something to cause his seatmate to appear to be anything but a person in a situation in which all appearances are normal and nothing is up" (Goffman, 1971:271).

For women in American cities, ordinary walking may entail a "put-on," a performance designed to show that nothing is up. For instance, as a woman walks past a group of men on their lunch hour sitting on the pavement watching the world (and especially women) go by,

> . . . her face becomes contorted into a grimace of self-control and fake unawareness; her walk and carriage become stiff and dehumanized. No matter what they say to her, it will be unbearable. She knows that they will not physically assault her or hurt her . . . . What they will do is impinge on her. They will use her body with their eyes . . . . They will make her ridiculous, or grotesquely sexual, or hideously ugly. Above all, they will make her feel like a thing. (Tax in Goffman, 1971:272)

In this urban world of strangers, then, the woman walking down the street is not what she appears to be; she is trying as best she can to avoid embarrassment by managing the impressions that her audience has of her.

Such everyday encounters—a woman walking by an audience that may not support her act, a man trying to maintain a normal appearance while sitting next to a potentially disruptive drunk, people averting their eyes from each other on subways—are Goffman's primary focus. More precisely, he is concerned with how these social encounters are structured. And Goffman (1959:254) thinks that the most significant factor in this pattern of social interaction is "the maintenance of a single definition of the situation . . . expressed . . . and sustained in the face of a multitude of potential disruptions."

At this point, we return to some shared definitions of the situation—those working agreements, usually unspoken, that hold in a milieu of multiple realities—urban society.

WALKING THE TIGHTROPE

Minimizing Involvement, Maximizing Social Order

Urban society presents a Janus-like face: freedom and anarchy. One side offers freedom for individuals to choose among alternative realities. The other portends danger: that the social order will break down from conflict over what's proper or right (normative conflict). That urbanites do take collective action and are not in constant conflict with each other suggests that some rules or norms, some shared definitions of the situation, still hold in this milieu of multiple realities. Throughout this chapter, we have seen indications that such norms exist. On the city streets, for instance, pedestrians cooperate so that they can all reach their destinations.

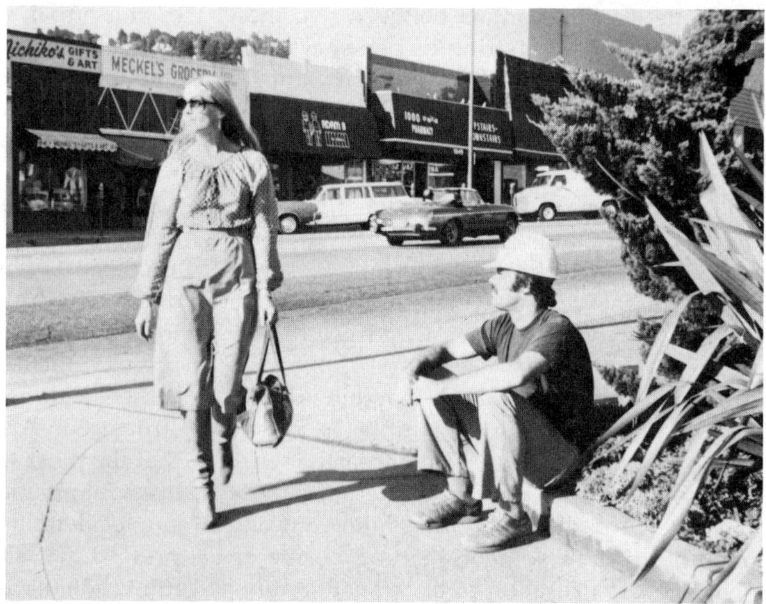

Fig. 9-4 URBAN PERFORMANCE. Ordinary walking down the street may be a put-on, designed to avoid embarrassment and control the audience's impressions. (E. Barbara Phillips)

Below city streets, people appear civilly inattentive while they ride the subway.

But here again, the implications are two-sided. The very norms which protect personal privacy and limit involvement with strangers (for example, civil inattention) also promote the indifference so often attributed to urbanites. "I didn't want to get involved" is a common reason given by people who walk away from fellow human beings in trouble in urban public places. Yet the norm of noninvolvement may be highly situational. According to a study of *The Unresponsive Bystander* (Latané and Darley, 1970), urbanites are less likely to intervene in emergency situations if a crowd is nearby. Latané and Darley suggest that in a crowd, each individual assumes that someone else will take responsibility. Thus, what appears to be indifference is really something else: a "diffusion of responsibility." This argument again points to numbers as a variable in urban social behavior. Further, it calls into question Wirth's notion that urbanites are indifferent, blasé and uncaring.

To conclude: Urbanites seem to walk a tightrope. On the one hand, to get through the day, they cooperate with strangers. On the other, they maintain distance from them. Norms of behavior in public places provide guidelines on the proper degree of intimacy or noninvolvement (not the specific behaviors) expected there. According to one hypothesis, "urbanites seek to *minimize involvement* and to *maximize social order*" (Karp et al., 1977:110). In this view, urbanites share a common understanding, a common definition of the situation, that permits routine social interaction to take place. That is, they agree to cooperate to the extent that daily public life can go on. At the same time, they agree to protect their personal space by limiting the intensity of their involvement with strangers.

The "mini-max" hypothesis suggests that the quality of urban social behavior can best be understood by combining seemingly opposite ideas: "intimate anonymity," "public privacy," and "involved indifference." These descriptions seem schizoid. Yet they indicate the precarious balancing act that urbanites perform many times daily.

CONSTRUCTING SOCIAL REALITY

Some norms of public behavior, such as civil inattention, seem to work to everyone's benefit. But this doesn't mean that all such rules are so mutually beneficial. A question posed by Erving Goffman focuses on this point.

In *Relations in Public* (1971:288), Goffman comments that people's immediate surroundings—their homes and offices, for example—are viewed as their possessions, as part of their "fixed territory." People assume that these fixed territories will be free of danger, like a safe haven, for "the individual's sense of privacy, control and self-respect is tied to the dominion he exerts over his fixed territories." Now, what happens when someone's fixed territory is damaged by people who don't share the same standards of care? That is what occurred to the president of Columbia University, Grayson Kirk, when 150 student demonstrators occupied his office for six days in 1969. When Kirk returned to his office, he found cigarette butts and orange peels covering his rug, plus other remnants of the occupation. Looking around at this sight, he turned to reporters and asked, "My God, how could human beings do a thing like this?" But Goffman asks other questions: "The great sociological question, of course, is not how could it be that human beings would do a thing like this, but rather how is it that human beings do this sort of thing so rarely. How come persons in authority have been so overwhelmingly successful in conning those beneath them?" (1971:88n.)

With these questions, Goffman hints that we can't really understand how the rules work without looking at both the *process* (micro focus) and the *structure* (macro focus) of social interaction. That is, people may be active agents in creating new performances, but they create them within a cultural, political, and historical context.

The Public Definition of Reality

In urban society—characterized by multiple realities—competing individuals and groups are constantly struggling to transform their own definition of reality into the public definiton of reality: a world of ready-made, taken-for-granted meanings, attitudes, feelings, and thoughts. As the student demonstrators' behavior indicates, this ready-made world of meanings is neither unchanging nor unchangeable. Meanings are open to constant negotiation and reinterpretation. At the same time, there are also widely shared assumptions about how social interaction *should* take place at a particular historical moment. These shared assumptions (definitions of reality) are not simply there; they are generated by social processes and molded by power relations, class structures, and other social structural features.

We don't all have an equal chance of getting others to accept our definition of reality: "He who has the bigger stick has a better chance of imposing his definitions of reality" (Berger and Luckmann, 1967:109).

Now we turn to a discussion of black streetcorner men, one group of Americans who don't have big sticks (power, authority, wealth, high status, control over or access to mass media). Consequently, they have less chance of imposing their definitions of reality on other groups. In telling their story, Elliot Liebow demonstrates the power of applying both micro and macro levels of analysis to the study of urban social behavior.

Table 9-2 Widely Shared Definitions of Reality

Economic Sector
Owners of manufacturing firms have the right to decide what product to make and how much to pay their workers (with a minimum wage floor).
Competition is a good thing.

Political Sector
Government and politics are so complicated that most Americans can't understand what's going on.

Aesthetic Sector
Men and women who weigh 350 pounds are not physically attractive.

Social Sector
Having a large family—ten children—is a strain on the parents and a burden on society.

COMBINING MICRO AND MACRO ANALYSIS TO STUDY URBAN BEHAVIOR

Case Study: *Tally's Corner*

Anthropologist Liebow recorded the daily, routine activities of twenty-four black men who hung out around a corner, *Tally's Corner*, near a carry-out restaurant in Washington, D.C. He talked with them on the street and accompanied them to their haunts: their homes, pool halls, neighborhood stores, and sometimes courtrooms. Liebow was an outsider for many reasons (race, religion, occupation, residence, manner of speech), but he participated in their lives as well as observing them. (Indeed, he reports that his marginality was disadvantageous in some ways but partially offset by the fact that "as an outsider, I was not a competitor" [1967:251]). His data are drawn from observing the actions of the men—unskilled construction workers, busboys, menial workers, and unemployed, from their early twenties to their mid-forties.

A casual observer might think that the streetcorner men are hanging out because they're lazy, irresponsible, seeking instant gratification, or present-time oriented. They are wrong, says Liebow. And here is how he came to this conclusion.

To understand why the men hang out on the streetcorner, why they work at the jobs they do—or quit—and why they hold the attitudes they do, Liebow moved from the micro-level (the streetcorner) to analyze larger social patterns that shape their lives (macro level). In so doing, he demonstrates that the men's jobs and self-concepts are molded by their place in the class and status system.

To begin with, the jobs the streetcorner men could get—parking attendant, janitor, counterman, stock clerk, and the like—are generally dead ends. What janitor ends up at a white-collar job in the building he cleans? More importantly, all available work is low-paid and low-status. Liebow notes that neither society nor the streetcorner man who performs these jobs thinks they're worth doing and worth doing well:

> Both employee and employer are contemptuous of the job. The employee shows his contempt by his reluctance to accept it or keep it, the employer by paying less than is required to support a family. (Liebow, 1967:58)

Thus, these men are trapped in work that offers no prestige, little money, no chance for advancement or interesting opportunities, and little else. More prestigious work is closed to them. They lack the education (most went to inferior schools), and they don't have a network of friends and contacts that upper-middle-class people routinely develop by going to the right schools. Finally, they belong to a minority group, one that has experienced racial discrimination in employment and opportunities for training in highly paid trades.

In short, these are men without a future. And they know it.

Not having a future affects even the most intimate sphere of their lives: relationships with friends and lovers. Given the streetcorner men's structural situation, "friendship is easily uprooted by the tug of economic or psychological self-interest or by external forces acting against it." Friendships are very meaningful to the streetcorner men, but they are often threatened by routine crises that more affluent people don't face constantly.

Only by looking at the ways social structure impinges on the streetcorner men's lives, Liebow implies, can we make sense of their seeming refusal to work (detailed in Box 16-2) and their treatment of friends and lovers. Liebow concludes that the key factor in these men's lives is not psychological but rather social structural: the inability to earn a living and support their families. Behind their attitude toward their work and themselves is society's evaluation that they are worthless.

If Liebow had stopped his analysis at the micro level of face-to-face interaction on the streetcorner, he could not have made the connections between personality and social structure. Nor could he have shown so powerfully that the way these men define their situations grows out of the values, sentiments, and opportunities provided by the larger society.

ANOTHER LOOK

Being urban involves playing games and following rules we didn't create. Yet, as the symbolic interactionists emphasize, urbanites can break the rules or help create new ones.

Of course, breaking the rules means taking risks. These risks can be minor or life-endangering. To break the unspoken rule of sociability in a bar by slighting a stranger may earn a person nothing more than a dirty look. But who knows? Perhaps this anonymous person believes himself to be the Devil and responds with a stab of his pocket knife. Similarly, college students who stage a live-in at the president's office may risk jail, expulsion from school, or long-term surveillance as "troublemakers."

The other side of this coin is that rule-breaking behavior (deviance from norms) can lead to new definitions of reality and social change. In the students' case, their actions could contribute to a general reconsideration of the proper relationship between students and authority figures.

People seem to accept injustice as long as they think it is inevitable or grant it moral authority. India's untouchables, for instance, have accepted their low status because they assume they are being punished for acts committed in previous reincarnations (see Moore, 1978). If, however, people think that an injustice is unnatural, they often rise up against it. Once again, this illustrates W. I. Thomas's dictum and demonstrates the link between beliefs and social action.

Most of the time, most of us don't break the rules. The rules provide comfort and security. They serve to reduce potential risk, physical or psychic. This is especially true in urban public life. Urbanites are surrounded by people whom they know nothing about—where they are coming from or where they are going, literally and figuratively. It's easier to conform, and we expect others to do the same.

This is what many general rules—civil inattention, for instance—are all about: risk avoidance. Indeed, much of urban public behavior can be understood as attempts to avoid risk. This stands in contrast to everyday encounters in rural, small-scale societies. In the Greek polis, citizens knew each other on sight. There was no wide diversity in their definitions of the situation. They could reasonably predict one another's behavior. In this milieu, urban public life could thrive.

Can urban public life survive, let alone thrive, today in postindustrial society? That seems to be *the* question. Have we put such a high premium on maintaining social order and personal privacy that we avoid the promise of city life: new experiences, learning from people unlike ourselves? Will those who can possibly afford it retreat to private spaces (the home with its room-size TV and communications system), well protected from the risky arena of urban streets and gatherings? Or can we create a new urban public life that offers growth opportunities for all?

Many observers hope so, and numerous visionaries think they know the way to enrich city life. Their solutions depend mainly on their ideologies and their levels of analysis: radical changes in the rules of the game, or transforming lower-class individuals into middle-class citizens, or decentralizing public institutions and promoting community control (see Sennett, 1970).

However we might evaluate these proposals to enrich urban public life, one point is clear. The way people interact at the face-to-face level cannot be divorced from larger patterns of social structure. Micro meets macro, intersecting at the carry-out streetcorner and every other urban public place.

PROJECTS

1. **Classroom behavior, micro level.** Few students subject what goes on in the classroom to objective analysis because it is such a routine, familiar activity. That is the goal of this project: to analyze the rules of the classroom game. Observe three classes with different teachers and examine such features as the following: Who sits where? Who initiates discussion? What do people wear? What are they talking about? What is the manner and style of speech used (vocabulary, tone, loudness)? Who negotiates possible disagreements? What happens if some disruption occurs? On the basis of your preliminary observations, formulate at least two hypotheses about classroom behavior.

Now, do a second round of observations—this time, testing your hypotheses. If, for instance, you posit that teachers tend to pay more attention to students sitting near them than students farther away (e.g., in the back of a large classroom), count the number of times eye contact is maintained with each group as well as other indicators of attentiveness (e.g., responsiveness to questions from each group). If you hypothesize that female students are more likely to speak up in class than male students if the teacher is female, then compare and contrast the number of times women speak in various classes taught by males and females. Depending on your hypotheses, you may want to note indicators of restlessness (coughs, slouched body posture), lack of interest in the class (side conversations, newspaper reading, falling asleep), or control mechanisms (assigned seat arrangements, attendance taking, etc.). Reexamining your data, what general rules for classroom behavior do you find?

2. **Classroom behavior, macro level.** The purpose of this project is to reexamine data collected in Project 1 in light of larger social contexts. For example, do the class size, teaching format, and interpersonal dynamics of the class reflect power and status patterns of the larger society? Do the age, sex, race, and academic rank of the professor

seem to affect students' response or teachers' style? Is the classroom a setting for democratic participation or a training ground for hierarchical organization? What authority relationships do students take for granted?

3. **Breaking the rules: making the background expectancies inoperative.** Urbanites generally display trust—not distrust—to strangers. Test the existence of this norm by the following experiment: Board a city bus and ask the driver if this bus passes a certain street that you want. After receiving an answer, ask again, "Does it *really* pass this street?" Continue this line of questioning (for example, "Are you sure?"). What is the bus driver's reaction? (And your own?)

4. **Presentation of self.** Think about a social occasion that you attended recently (say, a party) at which there were people previously unknown to you. How did you present yourself? What clothes did you wear? What information did you reveal about yourself to these strangers? What impressions did you want them to have of you? How did you go about managing these impressions? Finally, in your terms, was it a successful performance?

SUGGESTIONS FOR FURTHER LEARNING

For an introductory primer on how to conduct qualitative field work, John Lofland's *Analyzing Social Settings* (Belmont, Calif.: Wadsworth, 1971) offers detailed instructions on intensive interviewing, participant-observation, and analysis of data. Norman K. Denzin's *The Research Act: A Theoretical Introduction to Sociological Methods* (Chicago: Aldine, 1970) and George McCall and J. L. Simmons's *Issues in Participant Observation: A Text and Reader* (Reading, Mass.: Addison-Wesley, 1969) treat such issues as limits and advantages of fieldwork, drawing implications from qualitative data, and the various roles of a participant-observer. For a first-person account of doing fieldwork, see the methodology section of Elliot Liebow's *Tally's Corner.*

Micro studies in urban social interaction include several works by Erving Goffman. See especially the "weird but brilliant light," as one reviewer called it, that he sheds on "normal appearances" in *Relations in Public: Microstudies of the Public Order* (New York: Basic Books, 1971).

For a look at how "public privacy" is constructed, see Laud Humphrey's study of homosexual males' behavior in public bathrooms, *Tearoom Trade* (Chicago: Aldine, 1970), and David Karp's study of people in pornographic bookstores and movie theatres, "Hiding in Pornographic Bookstores: A Reconsideration of the Nature of Urban Anonymity," in *Urban Life and Culture* (now renamed *Urban Life*) (January, 1973:427–51). Works by Robert Sommer and Edward Hall discuss the spatial dimensions of constructing public privacy (see Chapter 14).

Various studies—on pedestrian behavior, poolroom behavior, subway behavior, etc.—are colected in *People in Places: The Sociology of the Familiar* (New York: Praeger, 1973), edited by Arnold Birenbaum and Edward Sagarin. The introduction to the essays is especially useful; it weaves together the concerns of symbolic interactionists with the concerns of such theorists as Freud, Marx, and Weber.

For a look at the ways in which people present themselves in public places, see Lyn Lofland's article on waiting behavior, "In the Presence of Strangers: A Study of Behavior in Public Settings" (Ann Arbor, Mich.: University of Michigan's Center for Research on Social Organization, 1966).

Akira Kurosawa's great enigmatic film *Rashomon* (1951) gives an acquaintance with multiple realities. This Japanese film (later copied in Hollywood, with an American setting) portrays a double crime, variously interpreted by three participants and a witness. What *really* happened? Kurosawa doesn't say.

Various visions of urban encounters are found in art. Faceless strangers and civilly inattentive subway riders are found in Saul Steinberg's drawings; Franz Kafka's story of "The Metamorphosis" (of Gregor Samsa from a clerk to a gigantic insect) deals with the alienation and anonymity of urban life. Movies of the 1970s often presented a vision of mean city streets. This mood is exemplified in *Taxi Driver* (1976), directed by Martin Scorcese. An angry cabbie, embittered by what he sees of human cruelty in New York City, buys a gun and begins to kill the crooks and pimps he despises. On the other hand, movies like Paul Mazursky's *An Unmarried Woman* (1978) depict the big city as a place where strangers can connect and partake of a rich cultural heritage.

The classic primary work on combining macro and micro approaches to the study of urban social interaction is Elliot Liebow's *Tally's Corner: A Study of Negro Streetcorner Men* (Boston: Little, Brown, 1967). A secondary analysis of micro studies, written from a symbolic interactionist perspective, is David A. Karp et al., *Being Urban: A Social Psychological View of City Life* (Lexington, Mass.: D.C. Heath, 1977).

In *Scenes* (Beverly Hills, Calif.: Sage, 1977), John Irwin describes various lifestyles in modern cities (e.g., the surfing scene, fern bars, the dope scene) with an emphasis on everyday life as a series of theatrical performances. See, in particular, his discussion of "hanging out" as an urban scene.

KEY TERMS

Civil inattention Erving Goffman's term, referring to a general rule (norm) of urban social interaction. It occurs when "one gives to another enough visual notice to demonstrate that one appreciates that the other is present (and that one admits openly to having seen him), while at the next moment withdrawing one's attention from him so as to express that he does not constitute a target of special curiosity or design."

Definition of the situation W. I. Thomas's term, referring to the idea that objective reality is less important than people's subjective interpretation of events, objects, action. His famous statement—"If men define situations as real they are real in their consequences"—suggests that the same action or event can hold various meanings for various people, and that people will respond differently to the same action or event depending on the meaning they attach to it.

Ethnography A study of a group of people or community using fieldwork methods (participant-observation, in-depth interviewing) to describe the behavior and attitudes of the people under study. Ethnographers focus on actors' subjective meanings and definitions of the situation.

Ethnomethodology A movement or "school" in sociology led by Harold Garfinkel. Ethnomethodologists (from the Greek: *ethno*—"people," *meth*—"a way of doing things") study the unspoken, tacit rules and agreements that govern ordinary, everyday activities. Often, their method is to break the rules, making background expectancies inoperative, to understand commonsense knowledge.

Macro-level social analysis Analysis of social structural features (class structure, discrimination patterns, educational institutions, etc.) which mold an entire society.

Micro-level social analysis Analysis of interpersonal processes which mold everyday social interaction.

Norms Rules of the game; standards of right and wrong behavior that are shared within a group or society. Norms change over time, and vary from culture to culture.

Presentation of self Erving Goffman's term, referring to the self-conscious attempt a person makes to control the impressions that other people have of her or him.

Role The performance of expected rights, obligations, and behaviors associated with a person's status. To "play a role" is to act according to expected, preestablished behavior patterns. Role is inseparable from status, for status is a collection of rights and duties, and role is the performance of those rights and duties.

Social interaction (face-to-face) Encounters that happen any time two or more people come into each other's physical presence, thereby exerting reciprocal influence on each other's behavior. Verbal communication is not necessary for social interaction to take place.

Symbolic interactionism A theoretical perspective within the discipline of sociology which focuses on micro-level processes of social interaction. Symbolic interactionists pay special attention to the meanings people attach to events and behavior and the ways in which they communicate meanings (via words, gestures, and other symbols).

REFERENCES

Berger, Peter L.
1963 Invitation to Sociology: A Humanistic Perspective. Garden City, N.Y.: Anchor.

Berger, Peter L. and Thomas Luckmann
1967 The Social Construction of Reality. Garden City, N.Y.: Anchor.

Berman, Marshall
1972 Book review of Erving Goffman Relations in Public. The New York Times, Section 7, (February 27):1–18.

Cavan, Sherri
[1966]
1973 "Bar sociability." Pp. 143–54 in Arnold Birenbaum and Edward Sagarin (eds.), People in Places: The Sociology of the Familiar. New York: Praeger.

Cranz, Galen
1978 Personal interview, June 29. Berkeley, Cal.

Garfinkel, Harold
1967 Studies in Ethnomethodology. Englewood Cliffs, N.J.: Prentice-Hall.

Goffman, Erving
1959 The Presentation of Self in Everyday Life. Garden City, N.Y.: Anchor.
1963 Behavior in Public Places. New York: Free Press.
1971 Relations in Public: Microstudies of the Public Order. New York: Basic Books.

Karp, David A., Gregory P. Stone, and William C. Yoels
1977 Being Urban: A Social Psychological View of City Life. Lexington, Mass.: D.C. Heath.

Latané, Bibb and John Darley
1970 The Unresponsive Bystander: Why Doesn't He Help? New York: Appleton-Century-Crofts.

Levine, Janey, Ann Vinson, and Deborah Wood
1973 "Subway behavior." Pp. 208–16 in Arnold Birenbaum and Edward Sagarin (eds.), People in Places: The Sociology of the Familiar. New York: Praeger.

Liebow, Elliot
1967 Tally's Corner: A Study of Negro Streetcorner Men. Boston: Little, Brown.

Manis, Jerome G. and Bernard N. Meltzer
1978 Symbolic Interaction: A Reader in Social Psychology. Boston: Allyn & Bacon.

Marx, Karl
[1859]
1977 The German Ideology. Pp. 159–91 in David McLellan (ed.), Karl Marx: Selected Writings. New York: Oxford University Press.

McHugh, Peter
1968 Defining the Situation. New York: Bobbs-Merrill.

Milgram, Stanley
1970 "The experience of living in cities." Science 167:1461–68.

Miner, Horace
1956 "Body ritual among the Nacirema." American Anthropologist 58:503–7.

Moore, Barrington, Jr.
1978 Injustice: The Social Bases of Obedience and Revolt. New York: Pantheon.

Schutz, Alfred
1967 Collected Papers, ed. Maurice Natanson. The Hague: Martinus Mijhoff.

Sennett, Richard
1970 The Uses of Disorder: Personal Identity and City Life. New York: Knopf.

Thomas, William I. and Dorothy Swaine Thomas
1928 The Child in America. New York: Knopf.

Whyte, William H.
1974 "The best street life in the world." New York Magazine 15:26–33.

Whyte, William H., assisted by Margaret Bemiss
1978 "New York and Tokyo: a study in crowding." Pp. 1–18 in Hidetoshi Kato (ed.), A

Comparative Study of Street Life. Tokyo: Research Institute for Oriental Cultures, Gukushuin University.

Wirth, Louis
[1938]
1969 "Urbanism as a way of life." Pp. 143–164 in Richard Sennett (ed.), Classic Essays on the Culture of Cities. New York: Appleton-Century-Crofts.

Wolff, Michael
1973 "Notes on the behavior of pedestrians." Pp. 35–48 in Arnold Birenbaum and Edward Sagarin (eds.), People in Places: The Sociology of the Familiar. New York: Praeger.

PART FOUR
Who Runs This Town?

Bill Owens

Leonard Freed, Magnum

CHAPTER 10 The Skeleton of Power

"Who runs this town?"

That sounds like a simple question, but it's deceptive. And as with most questions worth asking, serious observers answer in different ways.

Political scientists, lawyers, and public administrators often approach this question by examining a city's legal structure. This is because, as President Franklin D. Roosevelt once said, "structure *is* government." Knowing what cities and city officials can do legally is vital to understanding who runs any town.

But legal structures reveal only part of the story. Understanding the networks of informal power and influence may be equally important, perhaps more important, in figuring out who holds power and has the ability to get things done. For instance, Chicago's city charter contains no mention of party bosses or ethnic voting blocs. Nor does it refer to the influence of private corporations and other interest groups on public policy. Yet, these are key actors in that city's politics. Thus, both formal and informal power structures need to be examined before any conclusions are reached about who runs this town.

This chapter looks at the legal and institutional framework of local government. It investigates such questions as: How are cities legally organized? What power and formal authority do city officials have? How do cities interact with other units of government in the U.S. federal system? The next chapter deals with the other aspect of power: extralegal structures. It examines informal networks of power and influence.

First, a word about the name of the game—power. Like love, truth, beauty, and other abstract concepts, power can be defined in a hundred ways. Here, power means the ability to force an individual or group to do something, even if they resist. Ultimately, power is rooted in the threat of force or the actual use of coercion. Power can be distinguished from authority and influence. By authority, we mean legitimate power—power used in such a way that people see it as legitimate. By influence, we mean informal power, sometimes based on persuasion rather than coercion or the threat of coercion.

We begin with an overview of governmental power and authority. In particular, we examine the role that citizens think government *should* play in their lives.

THE SCOPE OF GOVERNMENT

"That government which governs least governs best." Jefferson's saying reflects the deep distrust many Americans feel toward government at any level, no matter who runs it. Fear of excessive government and centralized, faraway authority is a recurrent theme in U.S. history, rooted in the Jeffersonian ideals of liberty and small government.

Government's Limited Scope

For ideological reasons, the scope of government in the United States is smaller and weaker than that of any other major country in the world today. In France, England, and Sweden, for instance, government is expected to regulate the extent and nature of physical growth and to oversee the general health and welfare of its citizenry. But in the United States, the dominant ideology assigns as much responsibility as possible to the private rather than the public sector.

The scope of the public sector at all levels—federal, state, and local—increased dramatically in this century as America changed from a country of farms and small towns to a metropolitan nation. Yet, governments still operate in a climate generally hostile to them. And since Watergate, an atmosphere of public cynicism prevails. Trust in government at all levels has been steadily declining since the 1960s. This mood is captured in a news columnist's comment about Congress: "The crime rate in Congress is probably higher than in downtown Detroit" (Newfield in Bogart, 1980:5).

In the last decade, numerous groups have attacked big government and big spending. They have called for measures aimed at limiting or reducing the scope and cost of government. These proposals include government's deregulating private business, limiting government spending, and reducing the number of government employees. Some observers view this package of proposals as a move to reprivatize American life. Some see it as evidence of a resurgence of laissez-faire doctrines. Others contend that it represents a revolt (mainly by white middle-class people) against governmental redistribution of income or social benefits to minorities and the poor. However these most recent attacks on big government and big spending are interpreted, they are as traditionally American as baked beans and hominy grits.

Public-Private Sector Relationships

Even in spheres where American government is expected to act (either as problem-solver, distributor of resources and benefits, or regulator), it is assumed that public policy will be made in conjunction with private group interests. Often private interests play a significant, even dominant, role in *public* decision making. At the local level, for example, real estate brokers and large land developers have a significant impact on zoning decisions, and private business influences urban redevelopment plans. Similarly, professional organizations, unions, and corporate officials are generally consulted on policies affecting their interests. Often such groups initiate policy proposals.

The political philosophy that underlies these public-private sector relations is rooted in classical liberalism and pluralist democracy. The dominant ideology holds that government reflects the individual citizen's wishes through group representation, and that government does not serve any one group's interest more than another's. Hence, under the theory of pluralism or interest group democracy, government should act as a broker, balancing private interests.

The Proper Role of Local Government

The dominant American ideology holds that local government should act as a forum in which competing private interests negotiate and come to an accommodation that serves the entire community's interest. In this view, government is supposed to be a facilitator of private economic activity, not an obstacle. Thus, private enterprise expects local government to set the stage for their activities by providing infrastructure (such as streets and sewers), maintaining police and fire protection, supporting a good business climate, and regulating certain activities to prevent chaos and quackery (e.g., land use regulations, public health standards).

To protect their citizens' welfare and to prevent untrammeled competition, local governments today have varying degrees of authority to intervene and regulate private business—by granting health permits to restaurants, construction permits to builders, and so forth. Clearly the granting or withholding of such benefits can mean economic life or death to private entrepreneurs. Given these economic stakes, we could predict that local politics cannot be separated from economics. This close connection between political power and potential profit should be kept in mind when analyzing who runs any town.

To conclude: Urban governments provide a number of services and goods, ranging from well-maintained roads to legal entitlements to make money. Various groups are concerned when their interests are at stake, whether they involve getting sewer hookups for a suburban housing development or a neighborhood day-care center. Local government is at the center of competing demands for its scarce resources. It can't fund all the projects proposed. It can't award more than one contract to build a new school or give everyone a license to operate a taxi. In this milieu, there are bound to be conflicts of interest, opportunities for corruption, and attempts to manipulate or persuade the public via the mass media.

One final note: Local communities don't answer the normative question "what *should* government do?" in the same way. Some communities expect—and expect to pay for—only minimal public services. Others demand a higher level of services and more of them. Thus, the local political environment is a key factor in analyzing the scope of local government. The following typology of political environments classifies cities according to the level and kind of activity their citizens expect and authorize:

1. *Cities that promote economic growth.* Governmental policies encourage business growth and expansion.
2. *Cities that create and foster pleasant living conditions.* Governmental policies encourage the provision of services which add comfort and beauty to the community, such as well-maintained parks, recreation centers, and streets without potholes.
3. *Cities that provide only minimal or caretaker services.* Governmental policies discourage the increased role of the public sector in the community.
4. *Cities that mediate among diverse interests.* Governmental policies seek to juggle and balance conflicting interests (Williams and Adrian, 1963).

Population size and mix influence the local political environment. So does the level of tax resources available to the community. For instance, relatively homogeneous, residential, upper-status suburbs do not need to promote economic growth or mediate among conflicting interests. Large, heterogeneous cities, on the other hand, often seek to juggle conflicting interests.

CITIES AS CREATURES OF THEIR STATE

In the United States, cities are entirely creatures of their state governments. This stems from a decision made by the republic's founding fathers; they made no mention of cities in the U.S. Constitution. Instead, they granted the states the right to create or not to create all local jurisdictions, including cities.

When the states did create cities, they kept legal power over them. Hence, it is the fifty state legislatures that decide how city governments are structured.

General Law Cities and Charter Cities

States grant legal powers to their creatures—the cities—in two different ways. Some states establish the general powers of city governments in state law; these are called **general law** cities. Other states spell out the powers of a city in a charter approved by the legislature; these are called **charter cities.**

Charters granted to cities by their states vary in content, but most describe the form, composition, powers, and limitations of city officials. To illustrate, a city charter might state that the City Council will be elected every four years; have one representative from each of ten districts; and have authority over personnel, zoning, parks, and budgeting.

An important variation is the home rule charter. Under **home rule** provisions in a state constitution, the precise definition of city powers is left up to the city voters, within limits set by the state constitution. About 75 percent of large U.S. cities operate under home rule provisions. About half of the states provide for home rule within their state constitutions, and about a dozen more allow home rule through legislation (Goodman, 1980:51).

Dillon's Rule

When a legal question arises concerning the extent of power granted by a state to a city, the courts have traditionally ruled against cities. In other words, the courts narrowly construe city powers. This narrow construction of city powers is based on **Dillon's rule,** named for Iowa State Judge John F. Dillon, who published a leading treatise on municipal law (see Box 10-1).

What difference does it make if states legally control cities and if the courts narrowly interpret city powers? A great deal. Dillon's rule means that "a city cannot operate a peanut stand at the city zoo without first getting the state legislature to pass an enabling law, unless, perchance, the city's charter or some previously enacted law unmistakably covers the sale of peanuts" (Banfield and Wilson, 1963:65).

Because cities can do only what state legislatures expressly permit them to do (or what is "fairly implied" or "indispensable"), city charters often describe city powers in painstaking detail. Here is one illustration from the former city charter of Nashville, Tennessee:

> In the event any regular member of the Fire Department above the rank of pipeman or ladderman, shall be temporarily absent from his duties without pay, because of illness or disability the chief of the Fire Department, subject to the approval of the Mayor, shall designate any regular member of the Fire Department from a lower rank to perform the duties of such member during his absence. . . . (Banfield and Wilson, 1963:65)

Even under home rule charters (whereby cities can amend charters without going back to the legislature), cities are far from independent entities. They are still bound by the law of their state. And the state is omnipotent. In a 1923 case involving the city of Trenton and the state of New Jersey, the U.S. Supreme Court ruled that a state has the legal power to eliminate cities altogether, even against the will of the city's residents (see Box 10-2).

State Legislatures and City Interests

Clearly, the posture of a state legislature is important to the cities of that state. Unfortunately for cities, state legislatures have generally adopted negative stances toward their cities—boxing them in with narrow grants of legal power and voting new power grudgingly.

Box 10-1

WHAT CAN A CITY DO?

Dillon's Rule

It is a general and undisputed proposition of law that a municipal corporation possesses and can exercise the following powers, and no others: First, those granted in express words; second, those necessarily or fairly implied in or incident to the powers expressly granted; third, those essential to the accomplishment of the declared objects and purposes of the corporation—not simply convenient, but indispensable. Any fair, reasonable, substantial doubt concerning the existence of power is resolved by the courts against the corporation, and the power is denied. (Dillon, 1911:Vol. 1, sec. 237. Copyright © 1911 by Little, Brown Co. Reprinted by permission.)

Box 10-2

CITIES AS POLITICAL SUBDIVISIONS OF THE STATE

The city is a political subdivision of the state, created as a convenient agency for the exercise of such of the governmental powers of the state as may be entrusted to it. . . . The State, therefore, at its pleasure may modify or withdraw all such powers, . . . expand or contract the territorial area, unite the whole or a part of it with another municipality, repeal the charter and destroy the corporation. All this may be done, conditionally or unconditionally, with or without the consent of the citizens, or even against their will. (From U.S. Supreme Court in *Trenton* v. *New Jersey,* 262 U.S. 182, 185–186 [1923])

City politicians have felt victimized by their state legislatures for a long time. This is clear from Tammany Hall (New York City) boss George Washington Plunkitt's colorful complaint in the late nineteenth century:

> [New York City] is ruled entirely by the legislators at Albany. . . . The hayseeds [who run the Albany state legislature] think we [in New York City] are . . . sort of wards of the State, who don't know how to look after ourselves. . . . The hayseeds will look at you as if you were a child. . . . (in Riordan, [1906] 1963:21–22)

Plunkitt, a Democratic Party machine boss (whose life and times are featured in the next chapter), was hardly a neutral observer of the scene in the late 1800s. Yet he rightly identified a long-standing problem for cities: a state legislature dominated by rural, and usually antiurban, interests.

Demographics help to explain why state legislatures have traditionally represented antiurban interests. Historically, rural residents outnumbered urbanites. Not until 1920 did more than 50 percent of the U.S. population live in urban areas. By 1960, almost 70 percent of the population was urban, but about one-third of the states still had very large proportions of their population in rural areas. Further, before 1962 most state legislatures did not have the one-person–one-vote rule. Usually state legislative districts were drawn so that rural voters could elect more than their proportional share of representatives. For example, before 1962 only 11 percent of Californians (mainly from rural areas) could elect a majority of members of the California State Senate (Murphy and Rehfuss, 1976:28–49). Beginning with a landmark Supreme Court case in 1962, *Baker v. Carr,* an ongoing process of reapportionment has been underway. This court decision required one-person–one-vote, and it has led to a redrawing of electoral district lines so that the population in all legislative districts is substantially equal.

Since **reapportionment** in 1962, rural domination of state legislatures has generally been reduced. Legislatures have become more responsive to the needs of cities—less so, however, than one might have expected. Again, demographics helps to explain why. By 1970, 31.4 percent of the U.S. population lived in central cities; 31.4 percent lived in rural areas or nonmetropolitan small communities; and 37.2 percent lived within SMSAs but outside central cities. Roughly, then, the 1970 population was one-third urban, one-third suburban, and one-third rural or small town, with a slight suburban dominance.

The irony is this: State legislatures were reapportioned to assure one-person–one-vote at the very time when population was shifting to the suburbs. Thus, reapportionment generally did not significantly benefit big cities. It did benefit suburbs and hurt rural areas (Lehne, 1972).

In the case of New York City, for instance, the city's seats in the State Assembly remained almost constant after reapportionment. Meanwhile, the suburbs of New York City gained ten seats and the rural areas lost eighteen. City-suburban coalitions formed around some issues, to the mutual benefit of cities and suburbs and to the detriment of rural areas. Highway expenditures reflect this new coalition; those expenditures benefiting New York City and its suburbs increased after reapportionment. But more often, a new suburban-rural coalition emerged, replacing the historic rural, antiurban coalition. This new antiurban coalition continues to vote against legislation designed to meet big city problems. Welfare is a case in point. In New York State, suburbs contain fewer welfare recipients than New York City. Reapportionment served to stiffen rural-suburban resistance to increased welfare benefits which would have gone to residents of New York City.

To conclude: U.S. cities are creatures of state law. States can grant or take away powers from cities at will. State legislatures spell out city powers in general laws or charters. In some states, cities are granted considerable discretion to determine their own structures and powers under home rule charters, but even home rule cities are far from independent. Furthermore, cities have been under the domination of state legislatures, historically controlled by rural interests and antiurban attitudes. Demographic shifts and reapportionment reduced rural domination. But ironically, suburbs—not cities—gained the most influence and power from these changes.

FORMS OF CITY GOVERNMENT

As suggested, the first step in understanding how cities work is to clarify the city-state relationship. The second step entails understanding how a city's internal government is structured.

Getting something done in a city takes know-how and know-who. Who has the authority to condemn an unsafe building? What bureaucrat can grant a permit to hold a rally in the park? Can the mayor fire the school superintendent who has ordered the closing of the high school for his own birthday? Knowing whom to go to and how to get something done begins with an understanding of a city's governmental form.

Most city governments fall into one of three categories: the **mayor-council form,** the **council-manager form,** and the **commission form.** Large U.S. cities generally have a mayor-council form. Some smaller cities also follow this model. However, many smaller and medium-size communities, particularly metropolitan suburbs that grew up in this century, have a city council-manager form. Here a city manager, appointed by the **city council** and accountable to that legislative body, plays a key leadership role, and the elected mayor is less important. Finally, some cities have a commission form of government in which elected commissioners act collectively as the city council and individually as heads of city departments.

Mayor-Council Form

The mayor-council form is the most common form of city government in the United States. It is also the predominant form in large cities. The organization chart in Fig. 10-1 shows that under this form of government, mayors typically have appointment power—that is, they can appoint department heads. They do not have this power in council-manager cities. The organization chart also shows that the mayor and city council are elected independently. The mayor's independent elected

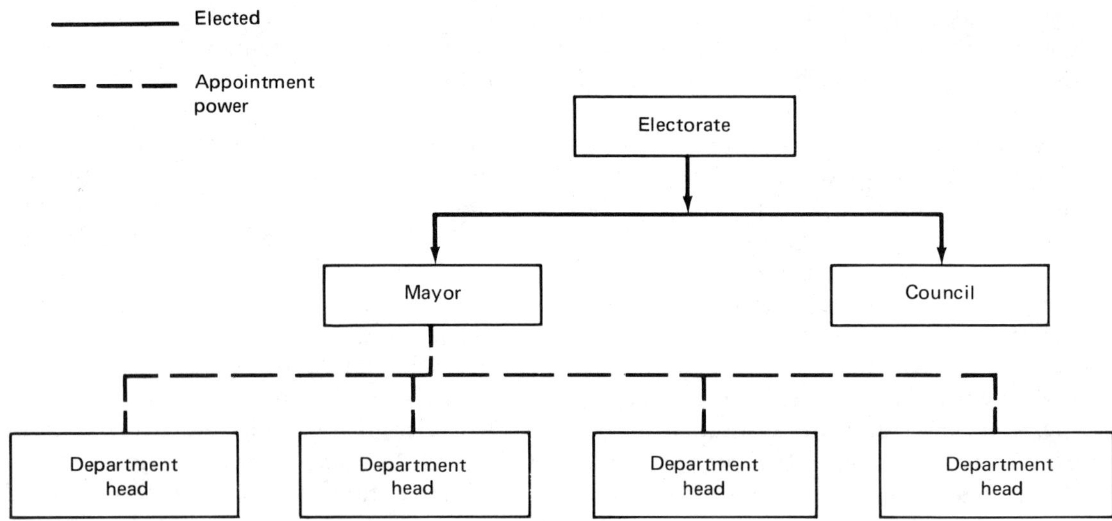

Fig. 10-1 THE MAYOR-COUNCIL FORM OF GOVERNMENT.

status and significant appointment power indicate that under the mayor-council form, mayors have important executive powers. Other factors, not revealed on the organization chart, contribute to the mayor's role as executive leader. These may include the ability to intervene directly in the conduct of city government operations, to veto the city budget, and to initiate legislation.

Council-Manager Form

Consider Fig. 10-2. The fact that the mayor is in a box, somewhere off in left field, is a significant feature of the council-manager form of government. Under this form, which is common in many medium-size American communities, the mayor has much less power and authority than in a mayor-council government.

The important actor in this fairly recent form of government is the **city manager**, appointed by the city council, as Fig. 10-2 indicates. Usually the manager serves at the pleasure of the elected city council and can be removed at any time if a majority of councillors so decide. The city manager, in turn, typically has the power to hire and fire heads of city departments. He or she is also responsible for preparing the city budget, developing policy recommendations for the council's action, and overseeing city government.

In many cities, the city manager draws a bigger salary than the mayor or council members (who may be part-time or amateur administrators). Further, the city manager has a larger personal staff and more control over the flow of information than the mayor or councillors. This combination of professional expertise and access to and control over information gives city managers informal power beyond what is revealed in organization charts.

Commission Form

Under the commission form of government, voters elect a relatively small number of commissioners, who play a dual role as legislators and executives. Commissioners approve legislation and also head the city's departments.

The commission form was introduced in Galveston, Texas, following a flood in 1900 which "left both the city and its finances underwater" (Abrams, 1971:57). Today, no U.S. city with a population over 500,000 operates under this form—for good reasons. As Fig. 10-3 shows, there is no strong executive leader. Power is exercised collectively by the city commissioners—the parks commissioner, police commissioner, and so on. Historically, this ideal of collective leadership has resulted in a lack of coordination and government by amateurs.

To conclude: Few cities today use the commission form; the mayor-council structure predominates in the largest cities; and council-manager governments are most commonly found in medium-size cities and suburbs. This pattern is shown in Table 10-1. However, this table doesn't reveal why the council-manager form is so attractive to medium-size communities and so unattractive to large cities. To understand this, some background is necessary.

The city manager plan was initiated in Staunton, Virginia, in 1908. It spread slowly throughout the nation up to the 1940s. After World War II, the council-manager form became widespread in medium-size communities, especially upper-income, white suburbs. Generally speaking, these suburbanites

Fig. 10-2 THE COUNCIL-MANAGER FORM OF GOVERNMENT.

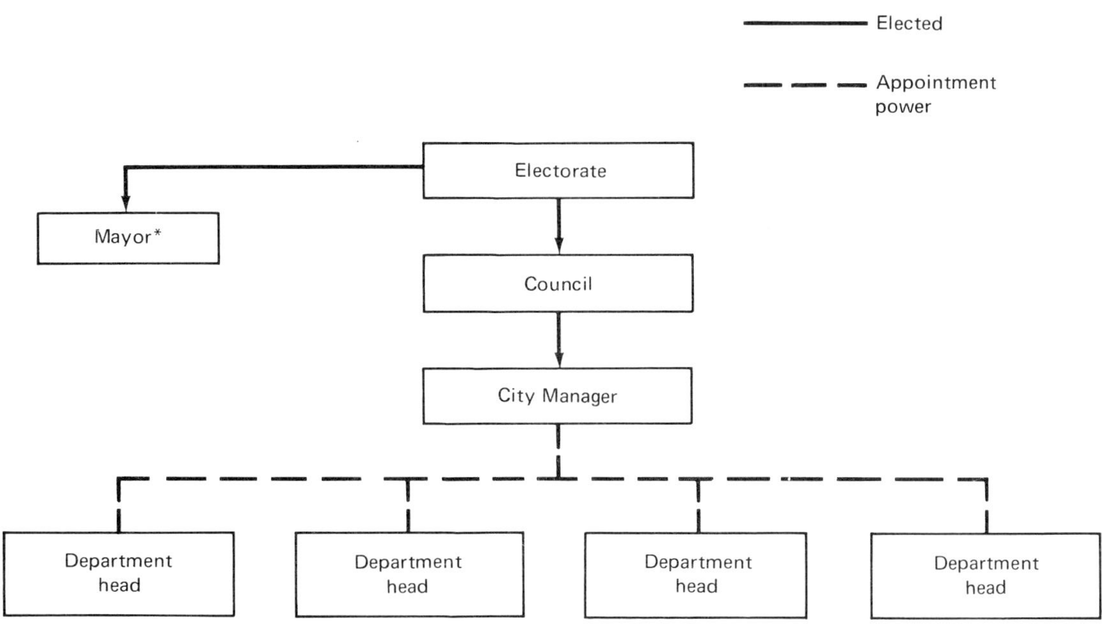

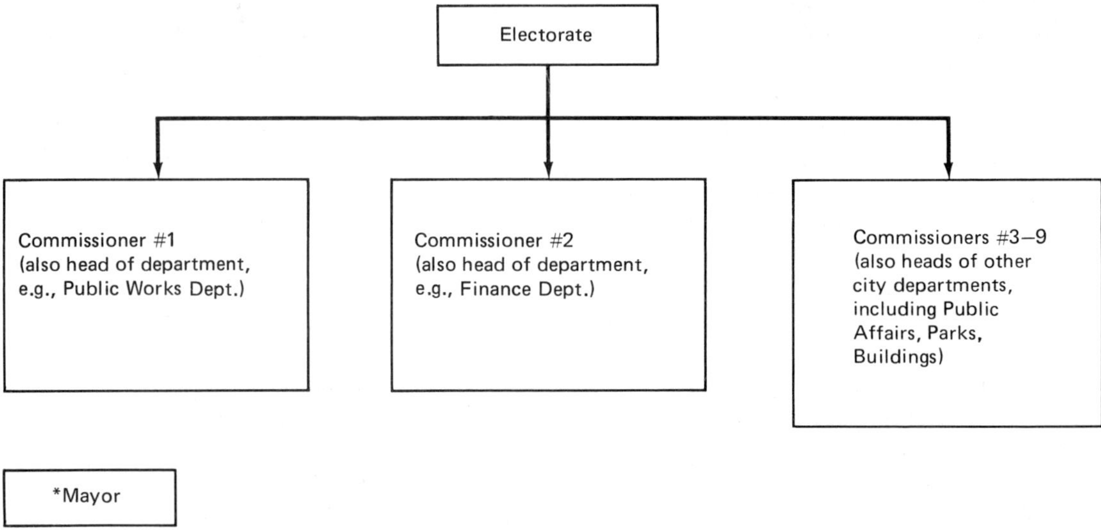

Fig. 10-3 THE COMMISSION FORM OF GOVERNMENT.

thought that the council-manager form would ensure professional, businesslike government and guard against something defined as inefficient, unprofessional, and corrupt: big city politics. According to two long-time observers of governmental structure, council-manager governments seem best suited to "relatively homogeneous white-collar communities where the political representation of diverse interests is not an important factor" (Bollens and Schmandt, 1970:116). In other words, ordinarily we shouldn't expect to find a city manager running a city composed of various ethnic groups and a significant blue-collar population. Typically, mayors operate in cities that mediate among diverse interests (type 4 in the typology on p. 258).

ORGANIZATION OF CITY GOVERNMENTS

Mayors, Strong or Weak

In cities with mayor-council governments, the **Mayor** is popularly considered to be the head of city government, the responsible official with whom the local buck stops. But as the song says, "It ain't necessarily so." Often a mayor is powerless to improve bus service, create jobs for the unemployed, or reorganize the delivery of city services. The following exchange before a congressional committee between Senator Abraham Ribicoff (D.-Conn.) and then mayor of Los Angeles, Sam Yorty, is instructive:

Senator Ribicoff:
As I listened to your testimony, Mayor Yorty, I made some notes. This morning you have really waived authority and responsibility in the following areas: schools, welfare, transportation, employment, health, and housing, which leaves you as head of a city with a ceremonial function, police, and recreation.

Mayor Yorty:
That is right, and fire.

Senator Ribicoff:
And fire.

Mayor Yorty:
Yes.

TABLE 10-1 Frequency of Government Forms

		Form of Government (No. and %)				*Type of City (No. and %)*		
Population Group	*All Cities*	*Mayor-Council*	*Council-Manager*	*Commission*	*Town Meeting*[a]	*Central*	*Suburb*	*Independent*
Over 1,000,000	6	6 (100)	—	—	—	6 (100)	—	—
500,000 to 1,000,000	20	15 (75)	5 (25)	—	—	20 (100)	—	—
250,000 to 499,999	30	13 (43)	14 (47)	3 (10)	—	30 (100)	—	—
100,000 to 249,999	98	38 (39)	31 (52)	9 (9)	—	80 (82)	18 (18)	—
50,000 to 99,999	256	93 (36)	145 (57)	13 (5)	5 (2)	124 (48)	132 (52)	—
25,000 to 49,999	520	170 (33)	293 (56)	39 (8)	18 (3)	80 (15)	297 (57)	143 (28)
10,000 to 24,999	1,360	585 (43)	620 (46)	55 (4)	100 (7)	21 (1)	854 (63)	485 (36)
5,000 to 9,999	1,550	881 (57)	530 (34)	43 (3)	95 (6)	—	841 (54)	709 (46)
2,500 to 4,999	2,090	1,451 (69)	451 (22)	54 (3)	134 (6)	—	909 (43)	1,181 (57)
Total, all cities over 2,500	5,930	3,252 (54)	2,109 (36)	218 (4)	353 (6)	361 (6)	3,051 (51)	2,518 (43)

[a]Includes representative town meeting, a democratic form of local government found particularly in New England.

SOURCE: International City Managers' Association, *The Municipal Year Book* (Washington, D.C.: 1978), table 3, p. xiii. Reprinted by permission of the International Management Association.

Senator Ribicoff:
Collecting sewage?
Mayor Yorty:
Sanitation; that is right.
Senator Ribicoff:
In other words, basically you lack jurisdiction, authority, responsibility for what makes a city move?
Mayor Yorty:
That is exactly it. (U.S. Senate Hearings, 1966–67:774).

In this exchange, Senator Ribicoff seems to blame Mayor Yorty for "waiving" responsibility. But in fact, Yorty never had the responsibility. In Los Angeles, as in many cities, mayors have limited powers, making them weak chief executives. Under the weak mayor-council arrangement, the city council or independent administrative boards dominate city decision making. Further, mayors (either strong or weak) have no authority to control many independent units of government within their political boundaries (e.g., school districts), as we shall soon see.

In weak mayor governments, administrative boards or commissions exercise power independently of the mayor (who typically appoints members and can remove them). This arrangement serves to broaden the base of political participation. Indeed, city boards are often appointed with a keen eye on local power blocs. In San Francisco, for example, members of appointed boards reflect the city's ethnic and cultural pluralism. They are composed of a mix of blacks, whites, Hispanics, single parents, labor unionists, real estate brokers, gays, environmentalists, and so forth.

Hyperpluralism and Government by Bureaucrats

A weak mayor form of government is attractive to many citizens because it can lead to government *responsive* to diverse interest

Box 10-3

WHAT MAKES A MAYOR STRONG OR WEAK

Legal Structure

Strong

1. Mayor-council plan, which grants the mayor the following powers in the city charter:
   a. A four-year term of office with possible reelection for many terms
   b. Power to appoint and remove city commissioners and/or department heads at will
   c. Power over the city budget (e.g., the right to submit an executive budget or have veto power over items in the budget)

Weak

1. Council-manager or commission form of government, with only a ceremonial role for the mayor
2. Mayor-council plan, in which the city charter limits the mayor's power in the following kinds of ways:
   a. A short term of office (e.g., two years)
   b. Commissioners and department heads not subject to the mayor's authority (e.g., commissioners appointed by the city council, agency heads protected by civil service)
   c. Little or no authority over budget matters

Local Government Context

Strong

1. State constitution and/or general laws, and/or city charter provisions do not significantly limit city authority
2. City performs many important local government functions

Weak

1. State constitution and/or general law and/or city charter provisions limit city authority significantly
2. Other layers of government (county, special districts, etc.) perform many important local government functions

Personal Power and Influence

Strong

1. An effective political organization (e.g., a well-oiled political machine)
2. Strong support from powerful local interests, such as the financial/business community or labor

Weak

1. A weak or substantially nonexistent political organization
2. Lack of support from powerful local interests

groups. But does it lead to *responsible* government? No, say many political scientists. Frederick Wirt makes a strong case for the idea that its costs outweigh its benefits. Political scientist Wirt (1972:114) argues that the price paid for decentralized, fractionated power in a pluralistic city is an inability to formulate and implement long-range public policy:

When successful policy outcome rests necessarily upon the agreement of so many disparate private groups and public authorities, the power of one component to block any action is magnified. Over time, consequently, only minor policy adjustments are possible.

According to Wirt, the result of so many disparate actors playing the political game is **hyperpluralism.** Having too many (hyper) different decision points and too many groups with veto power (pluralism) paralyzes public policymaking. The result, Wirt says, is *non-decisionmaking*.

In the absence of strong executive leadership and the presence of disparate competing factions, who runs a heterogeneous U.S. city? According to Wirt, the bureaucrats take over. He claims that the result is a "government by clerks": long-staying, professional civil servants who were never elected and thus can't be recalled. They may be regulated by professional norms of service and efficiency, but they're not accountable to the citizenry. The growing strength of municipal unions further erodes city executives' power and authority. Max Weber (Chapters 8 and 16) predicted what some call "the bureaucratic phenomenon"—the rise and expansion of rational but fearsome bureaucratic administration and politics.

Many studies of big city politics tend to find decisionmaking there hopelessly fractionated (e.g., Sayre and Kaufman, 1960). Indeed, some wonder if there are any solutions to unresponsive bureaucracies, proliferating and competing interest groups, and weak control over public employees and management structures. The title of one study of city politics sums up this viewpoint: *The Ungovernable City* (Yates, 1977).

To conclude: The formal structure of government limits leadership. Weak mayors have a hard time providing executive leadership and gathering resources to meet urban needs. Even strong mayors, who have more authority to meet some urban needs, can't control many key policy areas that have impact on the quality of life in their cities. Nonetheless, mayors—weak or strong—bear the brunt of public dismay when trouble occurs. As New York City's former mayor, John V. Lindsay, bemoaned:

> . . . the Board of Education and its empire [which I am not authorized to control] cannot continue to travel in its own orbit. . . . No matter how many asbestos walls are put between me and the Board of Education, at the end I get the blame if there's trouble. . . . (in Hentoff, [1967] 1969:162)

Given their limited legal power, weak mayors must use informal powers to push through their programs. These include the power to persuade, the support of public opinion, and, in some cases, the influence that comes from controlling a well-oiled political machine. Box 10-3 outlines some factors that make a mayor weak or strong.

THE CONTEXT OF LOCAL GOVERNMENT

We have hinted at one reason why mayors are unable to govern effectively: They can't control other units of government. Both strong and weak mayors operate in the context of a fragmented metropolis.

Fragmentation of the Metropolis

"God must have loved cities" because "He made so many of them." So comments a political scientist on the enormous number of local governments in the United States (Schultze, 1974:229). As Table 10-2 shows, in 1972 there were 22,185 local governmental units in the nation's SMSAs, with an average of 86 per SMSA. To further complicate matters, local government is organized in a crazy quilt pattern of separate and often overlapping types of local government.

To unravel the intricacies of this crazy quilt, some basic vocabulary is necessary. **Municipality** is the U.S. Census Bureau term for

TABLE 10-2 Number of Local Governments in SMSAs

Class of Local Governments	*No. in SMSAs (1972)*	*% of SMSAs (Total)*
All local governments	22,185	100.0
Special districts	8,054	36.2
Municipalities (e.g., cities)	5,467	24.6
School districts	4,758	21.4
Towns and townships	3,462	15.6
Counties	444	2.0

SOURCE: U.S. Bureau of the Census, *Census of Governments, 1972, Governmental Organization* (Washington, D.C.: U.S. Government Printing Office, 1973), Vol. 1, p. 10.

general-purpose units of local government. Cities are general-purpose governments—that is, they undertake a variety of functions and provide a range of services. Hence, by definition, cities are municipalities. Towns, townships, and boroughs are also municipalities. Other units of local government—separate from municipalities—include school districts, other special districts, and counties. "Fragmentation," "proliferation," and "Balkanization" are terms often used to refer to this pattern of local government.

This is the way the crazy quilt of local government is patterned within an SMSA: Cities and other municipalities lie within the boundaries of a county. Within city boundaries (and often extending beyond them) are school districts and various other special districts that are independent of the city. Each unit of government—county, city, special district, school district—is a separate legal entity. This is important for analyzing how local government operates.

Special Districts

Special districts are the most widespread type of local government, and their number keeps growing. They are set up to serve either a single purpose, such as sewage treatment, or several purposes, such as sewage and water provision.

Directors of special districts are not accountable to city or county government officials because special districts are totally separate legal entities. Their boundaries do not necessarily conform to those of any other local government unit. Often they overlap the boundaries of the city and each other.

The existence of independent, overlapping special districts can create problems for the coordination of public services. Fig. 10-4 illustrates this problem. It shows an unincorporated area of Portland, Oregon, in which eleven separate special districts provide various services to area residents. None of the boundaries of these special districts are contiguous. Some residents live within the borders of one district but just outside the borders of another. Each of the eleven districts has its own governing body, totally separate from all other local government units. Uncoordinated services can result if sewer district supervisors use Plan A for digging ditches while water district supervisors use Plan B for supplying water.

Many states have attempted to limit the proliferation of special districts and to consolidate existing ones. These efforts have met with only limited success.

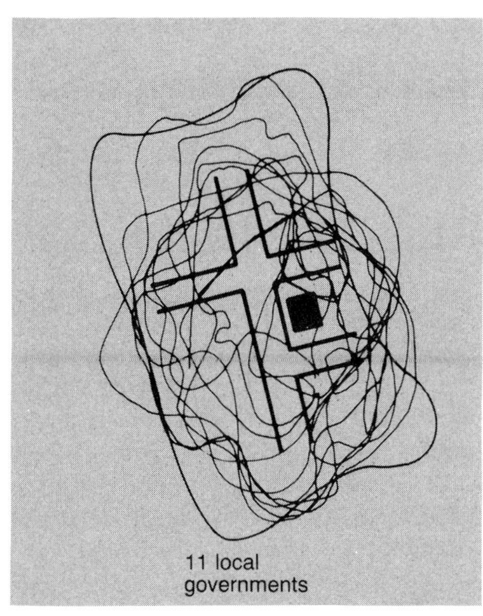

Fig. 10-4 OVERLAPPING SPECIAL DISTRICTS. The location of special district boundaries in one unincorporated portion of Portland, Oregon, 1967. (From John C. Bollens and Henry J. Schmandt, *The Metropolis,* 3rd ed., New York, Harper & Row, 1975, p. 47. Based on information from the Portland Metropolitan Study Commission. Reprinted by permission of John C. Bollens.)

Why are special districts so popular? The main reason is that special districts are separate from other local governments and thus are not subject to their debt limits. Special districts can issue bonds or borrow money after other local governments have reached the legal limits of their borrowing authority. For example, residents who want more sewers in a city which has already reached its debt limit might form an independent sewer district. The new special district could sell bonds to finance the sewer construction, unrestricted by the city debt limit. Also, districts can be drawn around a functional area regardless of local government boundaries. A mosquito abatement district may cover the swampy part of three cities.

Counties (including Urban Counties)

Historically, the **county** has proved to be a very stable unit of government; its boundaries have generally remained unchanged for decades. For this reason, the county is used by the U.S. Census Bureau as the basic unit of the SMSA and the new MSA.

In rural areas where there are no incorporated cities, county government acts as the general-purpose local government; typically, it regulates land use, licenses businesses, and provides police and fire protection. In urban areas, cities usually take over the basic general-purpose local government functions for their residents. In urban areas, counties serve as the general-purpose local government only for the unincorporated territory which lies within them. Counties also may provide some services to the residents of cities within their boundaries. For example, frequently the county operates libraries within both cities and unincorporated areas.

In recent times, a new spatial-demographic entity has emerged: the **urban county.** This term is used in various ways. It may refer to either (1) a county which has assumed comprehensive authority over governmental functions, as in the case of Dade County, Florida (Miami's county); (2) any county with a large, dense population, giving it the characteristics of a city; or (3) a county which meets specified population size and legal power requirements to be eligible for federal community development block grant funds.

Type 1 urban counties may perform a variety of services for county residents, including those traditionally delivered by municipalities: police, garbage collection, health services, roads and highways, libraries, jails, planning, and sewage disposal (see U.S. ACIR, 1972). Many cities within the boundaries of type 2 urban counties contract with the county to provide one or more public service. Type 3 urban counties receive federal funds to undertake community development activities on a coordinated basis.

Urban counties will probably become increasingly important. Recognizing this, some states have passed legislation which treats urban counties essentially as cities. By 1975, thirteen states permitted counties to adopt home rule charters. These charters grant counties the authority to perform all functions that cities in those states can perform (Murphy and Rehfuss, 1976:149–50).

The State's Role in Urban Affairs

Apart from their formal legal power, states exert power and authority over cities in many ways. For example, state programs operate within a city's boundaries, and cities may have little or no influence on these programs. Highway construction is illustrative. A state-funded highway can dramatically affect local land use, industrial location, and housing. Yet those cities through which it passes have no voice in determining its route.

The level of state involvement with urban issues varies widely. Some states have taken an active role, creating new institutions to deal with their cities. The most ambitious effort of this sort is New Jersey's Department of Community Affairs, started in 1967. By 1977, the state agency's $70.4 million budget went to numerous urban programs, from housing and community development to crime prevention (New Jersey Department of Community Affairs, 1977). New York State took a different tack, setting up the Urban Development Corporation (UDC), a state-level agency handling large-scale redevelopment activities. The UDC sponsored over 100 residential housing programs, primarily for low-income tenants. But beset with financial troubles, the UDC defaulted on its debts in the mid-1970s and remains debt-ridden, facing an uncertain future.

To conclude: City governments are only one of several units of local government. Counties, school districts, and other special districts also exist, often performing city-like functions. In SMSAs, there is a crazy quilt of fragmented and overlapping municipalities, counties, school districts, and other special districts. Some states (such as New Jersey) also play a significant role in local affairs.

Areawide Planning Efforts

In theory, the variety and vast array of decentralized local governments assures citizens a democratic voice in matters that directly affect their lives. In practice, however, things are quite different.

For one thing, voters have little or no control over the most widespread of all local governments: the special district. Critics charge that supervisors of special districts often put special interests (particularly private business) or technical concerns above the public interest. Theodore W. Kheel, for one, argues that the Port Authority of New York and New Jersey (a multistate special district) is dominated by the interests of its corporate bondholders. In effect, Kheel says, the Port Authority serves the rich and is indifferent to the needs of people in the New York City area (Kheel, [1969] 1971:443–49).

For another thing, many local issues—particularly land use and economic growth policies—have areawide effects. If City A permits a large chemical factory to locate there, nearby cities can be affected (by pollution, new transport patterns, etc.). But the affected cities have no say in the matter. Thus, the crazy-quilt pattern of fragmented local government appears to give metropolitan residents the worst of both worlds: little democratic control and lack of coordinated policies.

Pushed largely by federal government requirements or incentives, most SMSAs have established some kind of metropolitanwide planning organization. These organizations, called either a **council of governments (COG)** or an **areawide planning organization (APO)**, are strictly voluntary and advisory. Local governments are not legally required to follow their recommendations. Consequently, COGs operate on good will. The enthusiasm of participating governments to nurture a COG varies greatly from one SMSA to another.

COGs themselves vary enormously, depending on the size of the region, the staff's skill in developing acceptance among member governments, and member governments' attitudes toward them. A large COG, such as the Association of Bay Area Governments (ABAG) in northern California, employs almost 100 professional staffers and engages in numerous planning activities involving land use, "fair share" housing, water quality, and airport location. In addition, it provides research studies for the region and acts as an information clearinghouse.

Do COGs represent the wave of the future for interlocal cooperation and areawide coordination? Or are COGs doomed to be little more than intergovernmental talk shows where views are expressed but nothing much happens? The evidence is not yet in. There are some indications, however, that when serious conflicts occur, some member governments will simply pull out or threaten to do so. Their future depends a great deal on (1) the development of metropolitan "diplomats" who can forge new metropolitanwide alliances, (2) the backing of the federal government, and (3) citizens' response to the COGs' emerging role.

CHANGING GOVERNMENTAL STRUCTURES

Broad Regional Government?

Even if COGs do develop into effective areawide mechanisms, are they enough? Many analysts think not. "By the time we have achieved metropolitan government of some sort," says one observer of metropolitan growth, "we will long since have desperately needed regional governmental bodies to deal with the structure and development of urban regions" (Pickard, 1977). In a report to a federal commission, this same analyst, Jerome P. Pickard, predicts that by the year 2000, over 80 percent of the U.S. population will live in twenty-eight urban regions—concentrated, large, continuous zones of relatively high density. The present fragmentation of local government will be unable to handle these "huge webs of urbanization."

In essence, Pickard is predicting that the concept of the city will soon be obsolete. He then asks, how can effective decisions be made and rational policies be achieved for entire urban regions, for megalopolitan communities that are politically fragmented, socially atomized, and economically complex? His answer: broad regional government.

Broad regional government may be a rational response to governmental fragmentation. However, it doesn't appear to be politically acceptable, at least for the near future. Indeed, American citizens are calling for less, not more—and more remote—government. How, then, will public services be delivered to metropolitan and megalopolitan residents? Most likely, by muddling through. Thus far, public services have been provided via a combination of traditional responses, minor adaptations, and innovative experiments.

Traditional Responses and Minor Adaptations

On the more traditional side, residents of the urban fringe (unincorporated areas near a municipality which have urban service needs) are getting such urban services as police and fire protection in various ways: (1) by **incorporation,** thus creating a new municipality; (2) by contracting with the county or a nearby municipality for services; (3) by **annexation;** and (4) by forming special districts. Each of these techniques has its own problems and prospects.

Incorporation creates yet another local government, thereby adding to local fragmentation. Contracting for services allows urban fringe residents to keep their highly valued rural environment, but at whose expense? Some observers feel that under contracting arrangements city residents pay more than their fair share because residents of unincorporated areas don't pay for large capital investments (jails, firehouses, etc.) or for training city employees. The problem of coordinating special districts has already been noted. Recall also that the number of special districts has grown enormously since the 1950s, resulting in even more fragmentation of the metropolis.

Annexation is the only traditional response that doesn't lead to an increased number of local governments. Annexation results in political integration rather than metropolitan government. However, since it requires boundary changes, annexation is not feasible in many SMSAs, where most land is already incorporated into municipalities.

To cope with disputes over annexation, incorporation, and special district formation, some states have set up boundary commissions. So far, they have helped somewhat to check the further proliferation of local governments, but they have had little success in reforming the existing crazy quilt of local governments in the metropolis.

Innovative Experiments

On the more innovative side, the most ambitious proposals—broad regional government and a single, unified metropolitan government (called a "one-tier" or "one-level" government)—are just plans on a drawing board. But four models of structural change are currently in operation.

To date, the most ambitious effort at structural change is Toronto, Canada's federated or consolidated metropolitan government. Toronto established a "two-tier" **federation** in 1953. It consists of a single, areawide government as the first tier and the preexisting local governments as the second tier. The newly created metropolitanwide first tier, called the Municipality of Metropolitan Toronto or "Metro," is governed by representatives from the preexisting governments: Toronto's municipal government plus twelve suburban governments. Metro has jurisdiction over the entire metropolitan area, which includes 1.2 million inhabitants living in a 241-square-mile area. Metro has powers over many important urban functions: property assessment, water supply, sewage disposal, mass transit, health services, welfare, administration of justice, arterial roads, parks, public housing, redevelopment, and planning. Under Toronto's two-tier plan, some functions were retained by local governments while others were shared with Metro. For instance, Metro maintains reservoirs and pumping stations, but the second tier of local governments handles the distribution of water to their residents.

Short of federation, there is another model of structural change: the comprehensive urban county plan. Operating in Dade County (Miami), Florida, since 1957, a two-tier government gives the county government a powerful and integrating role over an area of 2,054 square miles and twenty-seven municipalities. Among its functions, the comprehensive urban county government is authorized to promote the entire area's economy, own and operate mass transit systems, construct expressways, provide uniform health and welfare services, and maintain central records and communication for fire and police protection.

City-county consolidation is another technique. It is a one-government, not a two-tier, approach. Usually this type of governmental re-organization consists of the total or substantial merging of the county government with the largest city (or all municipalities) within its boundaries. Since World War II, there have been four major city-county consolidations: Baton Rouge and East Baton Rouge Parish (the parish is Louisiana's equivalent of the county) in 1947; Nashville-Davidson County, Tennessee (1962); Jacksonville-Duval County, Florida (1967); and Indianapolis-Marion County, Indiana (1969).

A more moderate type of institutional change is the formation of metropolitanwide special districts, either single- or multi-purpose in nature. Currently, about 125 such metropolitanwide special districts are in operation, mostly within larger SMSAs. The Port Authority of New York and New Jersey is such a special district, one that crosses state as well as municipal boundaries.

Are these innovations success stories or not? Opinions differ widely. Most observers think that Toronto's two-tier government has made substantial strides toward rational policymaking for the metropolis. The evaluations of Dade County's comprehensive urban county plan are more mixed. One assessment points to considerable instability between the new urban county government and preexisting municipal governments, plus continuing fiscal and administrative problems. On the other hand, two political scientists conclude that the Dade County two-tier arrangement appears to be "generally improving" over time, growing toward "greater maturity" (Bollens and Schmandt, 1975:280–81).

City-county consolidations face great opposition, usually from outlying residents, who must approve the consolidation by popular vote, but sometimes from central city residents, who also must approve the change. As for the most moderate structural reform, the metropolitanwide special district, it has made significant gains in dealing with pressing metropolitan needs but is limited to one or a few functions. Further, like special districts that are not metropolitanwide, it is criticized for its nonaccountability to the people it serves.

On balance, it appears that the current crazy quilt of local government is being patched up with bits and pieces. There is no whole new cloth.

Why have efforts to reform local government structure met with so little success? First, many interest groups correctly perceive that major structural changes would not be in their narrowly defined self-interest. Suburbanites, for example, tend to oppose any reform that links their future to the fiscal and political problems of their nearby city. Black leaders often oppose metropolitanwide government because they could lose their recently won power in some central cities. Northern Democrats tend to resist metropolitanwide government because Republicans form a numerical majority in the SMSA as a whole but not in the central city. Secondly, structural reform is hard to sell to voters. By contrast, metropolitanwide special districts can be established either without a popular vote or by state law requiring a popular majority in the entire area. Federation, comprehensive urban counties, and city-county consolidations usually require popular majorities in all the municipalities involved, a very difficult consensus to obtain.

To conclude: Scholars don't agree on how metropolitan politics should be structured. One group, the centralists or consolidationists, claims that there are too many local governmental units to provide efficient, effective, and responsible government. Their solutions: centralized metropolitan or even broad regional government. Another group holds that government is not decentralized enough to provide responsive government. Their solutions: community control or neighborhood government. Finally, still another group thinks that the present system works well and is highly desirable because it allows citizens to maximize their choices in the consumption of public goods (e.g., through choice in housing location). This group has no proposed solutions because it doesn't define fragmentation as a problem.

Whatever scholars propose about metropolitan politics, citizens dispose in the end. And proposed reforms of any sort inspire yawns or fear—fear of more bureaucracy, more expense, less control, or changes in the balance of local power. Thus, in the near future, the chances of reshaping local government seem dim.

THE FEDERAL ROLE IN URBAN AFFAIRS

As detailed above, local governments in the United States have rarely undertaken major institutional changes. Yet, even without governmental reorganization at the local level, significant shifts in local programs and policies have occurred in the last two generations. The most important external force in redirecting local government policy has been the federal government. Federal agency officials have pushed (critics say forced) cities to rethink their programs with a variety of incentives and penalties.

Expansion of Federal Involvement in U.S. Life

Since the 1930s, the federal government has been playing a larger role in U.S. life. The expansion of federal involvement in the economic and social life of the country has significantly affected metropolitan politics, both directly and indirectly. This means that the question "Who runs this town?" can't be answered without reference to the federal government.

It was during the Great Depression of the 1930s that the role of the federal government in American life began to grow. Amid the bread lines and competing ideologies of the time (ranging from radical proposals to redistribute wealth and power, technocratic manifestos to let scientists and engineers run government, and hate campaigns blaming blacks and Jews for economic distress, to demagogic appeals for fascist-type rule), President Franklin D. Roosevelt's New Deal administration moved decisively to maintain social order and economic security. (Radical critics say that it worked to save capitalism; conservative critics, to end capitalism.) Millions of Americans, assumed to be "temporarily poor" during the Depression, were provided with some form of social security through New Deal programs. Many functions once handled privately (by family, churches, charities, etc.) or not at all were assumed by the federal government.

Subsequently, during World War II and

after, the federal role kept growing. The "temporarily poor" didn't disappear, and the national interest of a world power was translated into the need for defense industries located throughout the country and efficient transport links. Soon federal funds flowed into and around the nation's small towns as well as big cities. Meanwhile, modern technology and corporate business organization also expanded significantly,and the Springdales of the nation—small towns and hamlets—found themselves in the midst of a mass society (Vidich and Bensman, [1958] 1971). As a result, decisions made in faraway federal agencies and corporate headquarters affected the lives of Americans in cities and rural areas, whether they realized it or not.

Federal policies don't have to be labeled "urban" to affect urban life. Indeed, many federal programs not so designated have changed the fabric of the metropolis as much as, or more so than, funds earmarked for cities. Let's take a look at two such programs: housing and transportation.

How Federal Policy Affects Urban Housing and Transportation

Housing Beginning with the New Deal, the federal government has pursued policies intended to strengthen financial institutions that provide mortgage money for housing, particularly single-family detached housing. For instance, the Federal Housing Administration (FHA) was created in the midst of the Depression, when millions of homeowners were defaulting on mortgage payments because they were out of work, housing construction was at a virtual standstill, and banks were going bankrupt. The FHA was established to provide mortgage insurance to protect lenders (banks) against the risk of default on long-term, low-down-payment mortgage loans. The FHA contributed to a gradual recovery of the home finance industry during the 1930s, and then it spurred the massive post-World War II suburban housing boom. Other federal housing credit institutions (e.g., the Federal National Mortgage Association, called Fannie Mae) helped to create a national secondary mortgage market so that housing construction funds can flow freely into growth areas.

What impact did these federal housing policies have on cities and suburbs? An enormous impact. By stimulating suburban growth, federal programs underwrote the exodus of white middle-class residents from central cities. In so doing, they helped to cement metropolitanwide housing patterns of economic and racial segregation.

Transportation Similarly, billions of dollars poured into highway construction by Congress after World War II had a broad impact on the metropolis. The new interstate highway system, funded 90 percent with federal monies, allowed commercial and industrial enterprises to move out of their central city locations and relocate in the suburbs. These location decisions by private business contributed to the erosion of the central city's tax base and to its financial stagnation.

To conclude: Whether intended or not, national policies not specifically urban have helped to change the shape and character of cities since World War II. In particular, federal policies opened up the suburbs, spurred regional growth in Sunbelt cities where new defense-related industries were generously supported, and provided the infrastructure (roads, airports) for private business to serve a national mass market. Cities, legal creatures of the state, increasingly became economically and socially tied to the national political economy.

Federal Urban Programs

In recent decades, the number of federal programs aimed specifically at the metropolis has risen dramatically. So have funding levels. Not surprisingly, so have the size and number of federal agencies which implement urban-oriented programs.

One cabinet-level agency, the Department of Housing and Urban Development (HUD), was established by the administration of President Lyndon B. Johnson in 1965 specifically to address urban needs. A year later, the Department of Transportation (DOT) was set up, increasing the national government's already active role in financing urban transit. Other cabinet-level departments expanded their urban programs. And new programs, including the controversial War on Poverty, channeled funds directly to cities or urban community groups.

At present, the federal government is heavily involved in a wide range of urban programs, from child nutrition and law enforcement to community development. Cities lobby intensely for programs (Farkas, 1971), through both nationwide organizations and individual lobbyists. And the stakes are high. Federal outlays to state and local government quadrupled between 1969 and 1979 to $85 billion, much of it being spent in cities (U.S. OMB, 1978:175).

States versus Cities versus Community Control: The Battle for Federal Urban Funds

Who would control federal funds targeted to urban areas? This was a key issue in the 1960s and 1970s. The main contenders in the struggle for control were the states, the cities, and citizens' groups. A brief look at the War on Poverty shows why control was—and remains—an issue worth fighting for, and how the way in which federal funds are distributed affects who gets what benefits.

When the War on Poverty was launched in the mid-1960s, substantial funding from the federal Office of Economic Opportunity (OEO) was funneled directly to neighborhood and community groups, bypassing both the states and the cities. For a while, some community groups felt they could design and implement programs of their own choice. When some community-controlled Community Action Programs (CAPs) used federal OEO money in ways not envisioned—or desired—by members of Congress and mayors (e.g., demonstrating at city halls and state capitols, setting up cooperatives, demanding changes in urban "removal" programs), angry mayors and governors reasserted control over antipoverty funds.

In practical terms, then, control over federal aid is politically as well as economically important. Federal funds directed to cities, bypassing statehouses, increase the power of local officials and decrease the power of governors. Funds channeled directly to citizens' groups in the community decrease the influence of local elected officials. In other words, the balance of power between states, cities, and citizens' groups can shift dramatically as a result of federal urban policy.

Understanding the politics of money, cities in the 1970s supported changes in the federal grant-giving system. In general, cities wanted fewer or no strings attached to federal assistance, thus minimizing federal control over local programs. **General revenue sharing,** passed by Congress in 1972, is one of several federal grant programs that channels money directly to cities, giving local officials discretion over how it should be spent.

Determinants of Federal Urban Policy

Whether or not there is a single federal urban policy is debatable. Most observers say there are numerous policies that affect cities but no unified policy.

Observers do agree that the level of federal support to cities is not constant. What determines the level of support? Political scientists point to the party composition of Congress as an important factor.

In Washington, D.C., a joke has been told for decades: "Democrats spend a lot of money and so do Republicans. The difference is that Republicans feel guilty about it." This may be true of military spending, but it doesn't hold for urban aid. Congressional voting studies show that Democrats, particularly Northern Democrats, have been more disposed to granting federal aid to cities than Republicans. Between 1945 and 1974, for example, 75 percent of Democratic Senators and 38 percent of Republicans supported urban legislation; so did 76 percent of Democratic House members—but only 28 percent of Republicans (Caraley, 1977:147). Northern Democrats in Congress voted in favor of pro-urban bills 94 percent of the time. Thus, while the national mood and many complex factors are involved, who controls Congress—Democrats or Republicans—is a major determinant of how much money is spent on cities.

What of the future? Much turns on the national mood and demographics. Over time, more congressional districts have become suburban. To date, a clear suburban bloc has not stabilized in the House of Representatives. If one does, federal urban policies will surely reflect this development—to the detriment of cities and the benefit of suburbs.

THE QUESTION RECONSIDERED: WHO RUNS THIS TOWN?

Federal regulations, state laws, areawide planning suggestions, special district decisions, county legislation, neighborhood requests. This list suggests that cities are not masters of their own fate. Instead, they are just one layer of government operating within a web of government—some call it a marble cake—of overlapping and intersecting layers.

To attain one's political goals, knowledge of the formal structures of government is essential. Knowing who's in charge in this governmental maze—who to blame, where to go for an authorization, where to protest a decision—is the first step in getting something done in city politics.

Here is a case study of one citizens' group that successfully worked its way through the maze of political structures. It highlights the necessity of appreciating the complexities of government's formal organization. Also, it shows that any meaningful response to the question "who runs this town?" must take into account the web of government reaching from Washington, D.C., to the neighborhood day-care center.

Case Study: What Bananas Learned about the Formal Structure of Government

The sign over a small building in Berkeley, California, reads BANANAS. No fruit is for sale there. Instead, on the front porch lie ice-cream containers, fabric remnants, and wood scraps, all ingredients for children's play projects.

Inside the building, organized chaos prevails. A dozen women are answering phones and giving information about day care as actively as stockbrokers tell their clients about hot prospects. Parents and children stream in and out of the information area. A social service worker answers the "Warm Line," a precrisis counseling service for parents with day-care needs.

What's going on here? The name says it all:

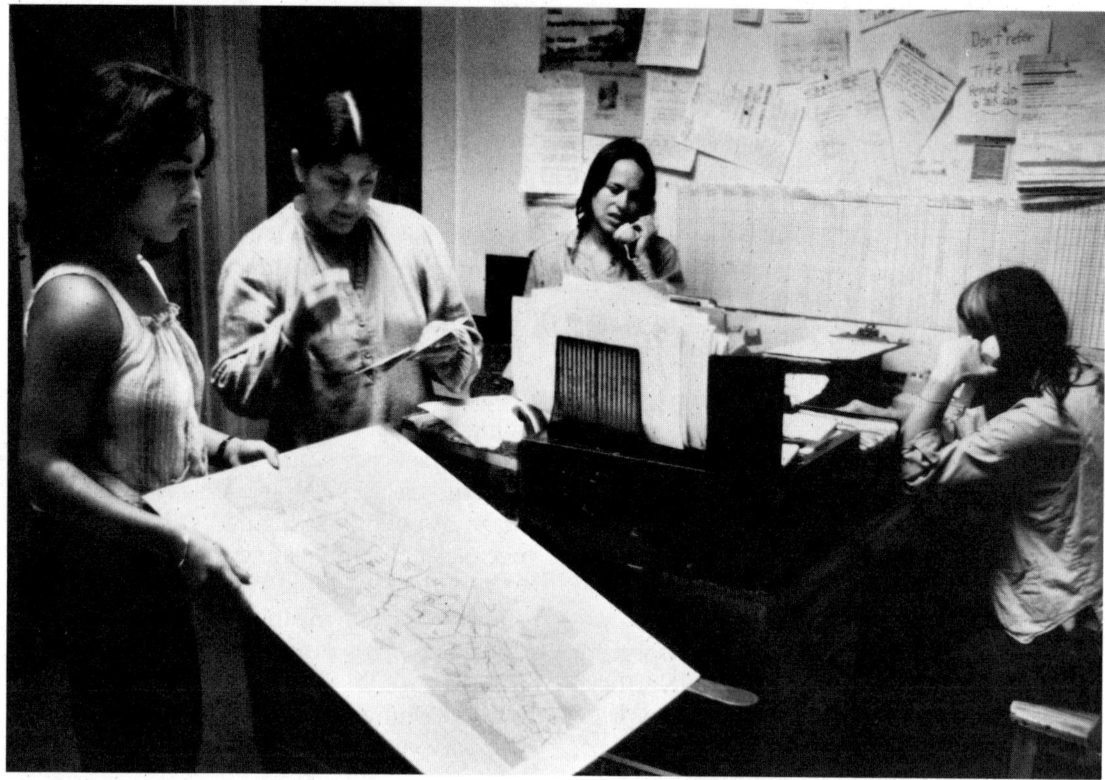

Fig. 10-5 BANANAS. This Berkeley, California, group of women learned its way around governmental structures. After years of hard work, it got what it wanted. (Cathy Cade)

Bananas, a multipurpose community service, helps to prevent parents from "going bananas" by providing various kinds of assistance with their preschool children.

Bananas didn't happen overnight. It grew out of years of frustration, organizing, and political struggle. Staff members learned by personal experience. Their first lesson was how to deal with and through governmental structures. To a significant degree, Bananas exists today because it learned this lesson.

In 1972, a small group of women—Bananas—became concerned that Berkeley had no place where parents could get information and help to set up play groups for preschool children. This nonhierarchically structured group had no money or community support, but they did have energy and commitment to their cause. They began to organize information assistance to parents, children, and daycare providers. After four years of hard work, they began to deal with city officials, trying to get government support for their activities.

In the process, they discovered whom to approach ("know-who") to get their project moving. Here are some of the lessons they learned.

1. *Find out who makes the decisions in city government.* Berkeley has a council-manager

form of government. The city manager has the final word under this system, and negotiations for funding were carried on directly with him. Bananas didn't deal with the mayor.The specific budget recommendation ($18,477 in 1978) came from the city manager, since his office prepares the city budget.

2. *Find out what the city is authorized to fund.* There is no prohibition in Berkeley against using taxpayers' money for day-care activities. If there were, Bananas would have had to seek funding elsewhere.

3. *Find out what government agencies have an interest in the activity (and how they relate to city government).* Berkeley, like other towns, exists in a web of governments. Bananas had to learn the structure regarding child care. At the level closest to home is the Berkeley Unified School District, a special district run by an elected School Board. The Board, not accountable to city government, was often in disagreement with city officials. Since the school district provides child care for about 1,000 preschool children in the schools, they are an interested party to other day-care activities in the community. Bananas dealt with the School Board, not the Berkeley city council, to coordinate information and referral activities.

Bananas also dealt with another interested party: the Berkeley Parks and Recreation Department. This city department administered a voucher system, paying low-income and working mothers a stipend for day care. Bananas staff members worked with the Parks and Recreation Department on a daily basis to refer voucher recipients to appropriate day-care centers.

Yet another interested party was the county. Alameda County, in which Berkeley is located, was operating day-care-related programs. The county Social Services Department administered a federal program giving child-care vouchers to eligible recipients. When Bananas felt that the county was not taking full advantage of the voucher program, they pressed for wider benefits. To accomplish this, they went to the County Board of Supervisors, not the Berkeley city council.

Bananas also dealt with a state-mandated Regional Center for child care, a clearinghouse agency for so-called special-need children. To provide clear guidance to parents, Bananas had to go to this regional planning organization for information.

Then there is the state of California. It, too, is involved in child care by subsidizing certain types of day care for handicapped children and other children with special needs. Bananas learned about the direct aid the state could provide to their clients.

Indirectly, through the county programs, Bananas was involved with federal funding. They also found out that the Department of Health, Education and Welfare (now two cabinet-level departments) provides direct funding to a few special day-care operations.

So, who runs this town? Bananas moved through the governmental maze to find out. At the level of formal structure, they discovered—often the hard way—that power and authority in their area of concern, child care, were shared by different layers of government and several city bureaucracies.

Eventually, Bananas got what it wanted, but not before it learned how informal networks of power operate. That is a theme we pick up in Chapter 12.

ANOTHER LOOK

Citizens and scholars from various disciplines agree that the role of government at all levels has increased dramatically during their lifetimes. They disagree on whether this is desirable, necessary, or inevitable in mass society.

Concerning local government, American traditions have favored fragmented authority and power. While many political scientists (particularly liberals) describe the current crazy quilt of local government as irrational and inefficient, voters have not been willing to support major structural change. Meanwhile, some analysts say that even major structural change at the SMSA level isn't enough. Only broad regional government will be able to deal with urban service needs of the near future.

While scholarly debate over local government structures continues, citizens have been initiating ideas of their own. In several states, notably California, there have been a series of successful proposals aimed at limiting state and local spending and hence local programs. At the same time, federal involvement in local programs continues apace. This presents a basic contradiction for those seeking community control, those seeking small government, and those seeking to get government "off their backs." With limited state and local spending, either local citizens will get fewer or lower levels of urban services or the federal government will most likely step in to fill the service vacuum. If urbanites are unwilling to accept fewer or lower levels of services and the federal government moves into the breach, this further erodes the ideals of local control and small government. How this contradiction—between ideals of localism and taxpayers' growing resistance to funding local programs—is resolved or at least handled is an issue worth watching in the 1980s.

PROJECTS

1. **City government.** Determine the legal structure of the city in which you live or one nearby. Is it a general law or charter city? If a charter city, is it a home rule charter city? Next, determine the form of the city government: mayor-council, council-manager, or commission. What are the major commissions, boards, departments, and agencies of the city?

2. **Local government context.** Examine the various layers of government, of which your city (or a nearby one) is just one. For instance, what kind and how many special districts lie within the city? What are significant state and federal involvements in the city?

SUGGESTIONS FOR FURTHER LEARNING

For an extensive treatment of the formal structure of city governments, see Demetrios Caraley's text, *City Governments and Urban Problems* (Englewood Cliffs, N.J.: Prentice-Hall, 1977). See also Charles R. Adrian and Charles Press, *Governing Urban America*, 5th ed. (New York: McGraw-Hill, 1977).

Edward Banfield and James Q. Wilson's classic on the topic, *City Politics* (New York: Vintage, 1963), is dated, but it contains a clear and readable explanation of state-city relations and formal city structure. For a clear text organized around public policy issues, see Robert L. Lineberry and Ira Sharkansky, *Urban Politics and Public Policy*, 3rd ed. (New York: Harper & Row, 1978).

Bryan T. Downes, *Politics, Change, and the Urban Crisis* (North Scituate, Mass.: Duxbury, 1976); John J. Harrigan, *Political Change in the Metropolis* (Boston: Little, Brown, 1976); and Alan Shank and Ralph W. Conant, *Urban Perspectives: Politics and Policies* (Boston: Holbrook, 1976) refer to and draw implications from the formal structure of city government.

Anthologies containing readings relevant to the formal structure of local government include Edward C. Banfield (ed.), *Urban Government*, 2d ed. (New York: Free Press, 1969); Alan Shank, *Political Power and the Urban Crisis*, 3d ed. (Boston: Holbrook, 1976); and Stephen M. David and Paul E. Peterson, *Urban Politics and Public Policy: The City in Crisis* (New York: Praeger, 1976).

Kenneth Fox examines *Better City Government: Innovation in American Urban Politics, 1850–1937*

(Philadelphia: Temple University Press, 1977), noting in particular the history of the idea that strong city governments might be a good response to urban needs.

City Governments in Action (Trumbull Studio Productions, 1967) is a brief (11 minutes) color film which explains the basic forms of city government and the duties of city officials. The film provides examples of departmental functions in and out of city hall. A film, produced by the International City Managers Association, describes metropolitan fragmentation and the growth in complexity of local government: *Tommorrow's Government Today* (International Film Bureau, 1964). The film stresses the need for trained and skilled local government personnel (a main concern of the ICMA). Another basic film is *City Government in the United States* (BFA Educational Media, 1976), which describes the various forms of government structure and their advantages and disadvantages.

KEY TERMS

Areawide Planning Organization (APO) See Council of Governments.

Annexation The addition of territory to a unit of government. Annexation usually involves a city's adding adjacent land to meet the problems of metropolitan expansion.

Charter The basic law of a local governmental unit that defines its powers, responsibilities, and organization. State constitutional or statutory provisions specify the conditions under which charters will be granted.

Charter city A city whose powers are defined by a charter from the state. Distinguished from a general law city.

City council The policymaking and, in some instances, administrative board of a city. City councils are typically unicameral bodies, usually composed of five or seven members. The structure and powers of city councils vary with the form of city government.

City manager A professional city administrator, appointed by the city council, in a council-manager form of government; the chief executive officer of the council-manager city.

Commission form of government A form of city government in which both legislative and executive powers are exercised by commissioners. Not to be confused with a *city commission.* Features of the commission form of government include (1) the concentration of legislative and executive power in a small group of commissioners elected at large on a nonpartisan ballot; (2) the collective responsibility of the commission to pass ordinances and control city finances; (3) the individual responsibility of each commissioner to head a city department, such as public works, finance, or public safety; and (4) the selection of a mayor from among the commissioners, effectively reducing that office to one of largely ceremonial functions.

Council-manager form of government A form of city government in which the city council appoints a professional administrator, the city manager, to act as the chief executive. With variations from city to city, the essentials of this plan are (1) a small council of five or seven members elected at large on a nonpartisan ballot, with power to make policy and hire and fire the manager; (2) a professionally trained manager, with authority to hire and fire subordinates, who is responsible to the council for efficient administration of the city; and (3) a mayor chosen separately or from within the council, but with no executive functions.

Council of Governments (COG) A voluntary organization of municipalities and counties concerned with areawide problems in a metropolitan area.

County A major local government subdivision of the state. Counties may perform a variety of local government functions, including provision of welfare and social services, administration of libraries, and repair and maintenance of roads. Counties are typically governed by boards of supervisors or county commissioners. In rural areas, counties usually act as the general-purpose local government. In urban areas, they act as the general-purpose government for unincorporated territory and provide some services to residents of both unincorporated and incorporated areas within them.

Dillon's rule A rule enunciated by Iowa Judge John F. Dillion, a nineteenth-century authority on municipal corporations, stating that a municipal corporation (such as a city) can exercise only those powers expressly granted to it by state law, those necessarily implied by the granted powers, and those essential for the purposes of the organization. If any doubt exists, it is to be resolved against the local unit in favor of the state.

Federation An approach to municipal governmental reorganization that assigns areawide functions to an areawide or metropolitan government and leaves local functions to existing municipalities. For example, Toronto's "Metro" government.

General law city A city created pursuant to the general law of the state in which it is located rather than under a charter.

General revenue sharing An approach to the transfer of federal funds to lower levels of government—states and general-purpose local governments. Under general revenue sharing, states and local governments may use federal monies as they decide; there are no strings attached. This contrasts to program-related monies.

Home rule Power vested in a local government, such as a city, to draft or change its charter and manage its own affairs, subject to the state constitution and general law of the state. Under home rule, state legislative interference in local affairs is limited.

Hyperpluralism The belief of some political scientists that city governments suffer from too many (hyper) private groups and public authorities playing the political game, which results in the paralysis of urban policymaking and the consequent bureaucratic takeover of political functions.

Incorporation The formation of a new city from previously unincorporated territory. State law specifies how new cities are to be incorporated.

Mayor The titular head of city government. The degree of a mayor's legal authority varies. In mayor-council governments, there are strong and weak mayors. In a council-manager government, the city manager runs the day-to-day city affairs.

Mayor-council form of government A form of city government in which the mayor is elected to serve as the executive officer of the city and an elected council serves as the legislative body.

Municipality The U.S. Census Bureau term for general-purpose units of local government other than counties. Municipalities include cities, towns and townships, and boroughs.

Reapportionment Redrawing of legislative district lines so that representation in elected government bodies is proportional to the actual population. In 1962 the U.S. Supreme Court ruled in *Baker* v. *Carr* that representation had to be on a one-person–one-vote basis.

Special district An independent unit of local government established to provide one or more limited functions, such as water. Special districts are usually created to meet problems that transcend local government boundaries or to bypass taxation and debt restrictions imposed upon local units of government by state law.

Urban county (1) A county with responsibility for providing urban services for incorporated or unincorporated areas within its borders or (2) a county where there is a substantial and densely settled population, giving it the character of a city or (3) a county which meets specific criteria enabling it to receive certain federal funds.

REFERENCES

Abrams, Charles
1971 The Language of Cities. New York: Viking.

Banfield, Edward C. and James Q. Wilson
1963 City Politics. New York: Vintage.

Bogart, Beth
1980 "Corruption is in the system." In These Times (February 20–26):5.

Bollens, John C. and Henry J. Schmandt
1970 The Metropolis, 2nd ed. New York: Harper & Row.
1975 The Metropolis, 3rd ed. New York: Harper & Row.

Caraley, Demetrios
1977 City Government and Urban Problems. Englewood Cliffs, N.J.: Prentice-Hall.

Dillon, John F.
1911 Commentaries on the Law of Municipal Corporations, 5th ed. Vol. 1, sec. 237. Boston: Little, Brown.

Farkas, Suzanne
1971 Urban Lobbying. New York: New York University Press.

Hentoff, Nat
[1967]
1969 "A mayor speaks on the bureaucracy." Pp. 161–65 in Leonard I. Ruchelman (ed.), Big City Mayors. Bloomington: Indiana University Press.

Kheel, Theodore W.
[1969]
1971 "The Port Authority strangles New York." Pp. 443–49 in David M. Gordon (ed.), Problems in Political Economy: An Urban Perspective. Lexington, Mass.: D.C. Heath.

Lehne, Richard
1972 Reapportionment in the New York State Legislature: Impact and Issues. New York: Municipal League.

Murphy, Thomas P. and John Rehfuss
1976 Urban Politics in the Suburban Era. Homewood, Ill.: Dorsey Press.

New Jersey Department of Community Affairs
1977 Annual Report. Trenton, N.J.: New Jersey Department of Community Affairs.

Pickard, Jerome P.
1977 Report to the Federal Commission on Population Growth and the American Future. Washington, D.C.

Riordan, William L.
[1906]
1963 Plunkitt of Tammany Hall. New York: Dutton.

Sayre, Wallace and Herbert Kaufman
1960 Governing New York City: Politics in the Metropolis. New York: Russell Sage.

Schultze, William A.
1974 Urban and Community Politics. North Scituate, Mass.: Duxbury Press.

U.S. Advisory Commission on Intergovernmental Relations (ACIR)
1972 Profile of County Government. Washington, D.C.: U.S. Government Printing Office.

U.S. Office of Management and Budget (OMB)
1978 Special Analyses of the Budget of the United States Fiscal Year 1979. Washington, D.C.: U.S. Government Printing Office.

U.S. Senate
1966–
1967 Federal Role in Urban Affairs. Hearings Before the Subcommittee on Executive Reorganization of the Committee on Governmental Operations, 89th and 90th Congress, 2nd Session.

Vidich, Arthur J. and Joseph Bensman
[1958]
1971 Small Town in Mass Society: Class, Power and Religion in a Rural Community. Princeton, N.J.: Princeton University Press.

Williams, Oliver P. and Charles R. Adrian
1963 Four Cities: A Comparative Study in Policy Making. Philadelphia: University of Pennsylvania Press.

Wirt, Frederick M.
1971 "The politics of hyperpluralism." Pp. 101–25 in Howard S. Becker (ed.), Culture and Civility in San Francisco. New Brunswick, N.J.: Transaction.

Yates, Douglas
1977 The Ungovernable City. Cambridge, Mass.: MIT Press.

Thomas Nast

CHAPTER 11
Bosses, Boodlers, and Reformers

Urban politics is a drama. It is played out against a backdrop of legal, institutional structures. A tidy organization chart would show these structures in a series of boxes: the mayor or city manager, followed by the city council and department heads, boxed in at the center of a mosaic of governments from Washington, D.C., down to the local Board of Education.

But what the organization chart doesn't show lies at the heart of the drama—patterns of influence. The two are inseparable. Formal structure is the skeleton of politics, and informal structures breathe life into the body politic. Getting something done in a city, whether having an ordinance passed or starting a gov-

Fig. 11-1 ORGANIZATION CHART. Charts only show how formal structures operate. They can't reveal how informal influences affect city politics. (© 1976 Richard Hedman)

ernment-funded program, requires acquaintance with structures of influence as well as knowledge about government.

Systems of influence today can best be understood in a historical context, first by looking back to a time when city bosses and machine politics ran most of the nation's cities. Over time, most of these old-style machines ran out of steam, but new-style machines are alive and well today. This chapter traces these changes in local politics and suggests reasons for the changes. It begins with a discussion of an uniquely American institution: the city political machine. For decades, bosses and their machines provided the power and energy to get things done.

THE CITY POLITICAL MACHINE

Beginning after the Civil War, virtually all U.S. cities at one time or another were dominated by a political machine. In some cities, machines rose and fell in a few years, succeeded by other machines or reform governments. In others, a machine retained power for generations. Today, with some notable exceptions such as Chicago, only fragments of the great old machines remain. So-called reform governments have replaced most of them, and new forms of coalition politics have arisen. As one writer puts it, "One gets a sense of the excitement of the paleontologist in searching through the fossils of American party machines" (Schultze, 1974:177).

Yet, the old machine, which generally ran out of steam, is a political model that has present-day applications. In many large and small U.S. cities, politics is organized on a machinelike basis or has surviving elements of party machinery. For instance, many cities have ward-size bosses who act like the old machine bosses.

A colorful cast of characters revved up the old machines and kept them oiled: men like cigar-chomping Tammany leader George Washington Plunkitt in New York City and Chicago's Richard J. Daley, a man of many malapropisms. Another set of actors and actresses helped to smash the machines: reformers or, as the bosses called them, "goo-goos."

A Bunch of Crooks or Friend of the Poor?

In the 1870s, political satirist Thomas Nast drew devastating cartoons depicting New York City's Boss Tweed and his Tammany Hall (the Democratic Party machine) Ring of machine operatives. One cartoon (at the beginning of this chapter) shows the Tweed Ring feasting on the corpse of New York City, strewn with the bones of law, liberty, justice, and the city treasury. Standing on a cliff crumbling in a political storm, the Tammany "vultures" intone, "Let us prey."

Nast's cartoons helped to fix one image of machine bosses that persists in the American mind: corrupt, incompetent characters concerned primarily with taking money from the public treasury to feather their own nests. But there is also a contradictory image that remains in the American imagination: the city machine as friend—even family—to the poor and powerless, particularly lower-class white ethnics. This vision can be found in much popular literature which romanticizes the boss. In Edwin O'Connor's novel *The Last Hurrah* (1956), for instance, Boston's Mayor Jim Curley is portrayed as the warm-hearted protector of the city's Irish in the late nineteenth century.

Which image more nearly approximates the reality? Before deciding, let's look at how machines work, what services old machines provided, and what forces led to their general extinction.

How City Machines Work

Whether past or present, city machines are highly structured, hierarchical organizations with no pretense to an individualistic mentality. In fact, party discipline and organizational loyalty fuel the machine.

Controlling votes is the name of the machine game. The machine is goal-oriented, and its goal is getting nominees elected to public office. It is organized to achieve this goal. A cadre of loyal party workers (and a core of voters) is held together by a mixture of material rewards and psychic benefits, including personal recognition, jobs, and a sense of community. This loyal cadre is part of a highly disciplined party hierarchy headed by a single executive or board of directors (Greenstein, 1964).

Typically, the hierarchically structured machine has a bottom rung in charge of mobilizing the votes of a single **precinct** (the basic unit of voting and party organization in the United States). Machine precinct captains are responsible to **ward** captains or bosses. At the top is a central committee composed of ward bosses and the central boss. A sense of loyalty, trust, and discipline bind the lower and upper levels together.

At the street level, where voters deal with machine operatives, contacts are face-to-face and unbureaucratic. This lack of red tape and bureaucratic rigidity were appealing features to immigrants in the nineteenth and twentieth centuries. These newcomers feared or could not understand City Hall, settlement houses, and private charities that were supposed to be tending to their needs. Tammany Hall leader George Washington Plunkitt boasted that he could get clothing and temporary shelter to fire victims in his New York City ward very quickly—before they froze to death—while the city and private organizations could not.

In dealing with constitutents, machines are informal. But internally, they run like an army or a business. Here is a British scholar's comment about late-nineteenth-century city machines:

> An army led by a council seldom conquers: it must have a commander-in-chief, who settles disputes, decides in emergencies, inspires fear or attachment. The head of [the machine]is such a commander. He dispenses places, rewards the loyal, punishes the mutinous, concocts schemes, negotiates treaties. He generally avoids publicity, preferring the substance to the pomp of power. . . . He is a Boss. (Bryce, 1889, Vol. II:109)

Sitting "like a spider, hidden in the midst of his web," the Boss recalls another publicity-shy figure: the Godfather. The fictional Don Corleone in *The Godfather* (Puzo, [1969] 1973) is a commander-in-chief, running an organization resembling an old-style machine.

Once in control of a city, a machine fueled its engine in numerous ways. (1) It gained control of patronage jobs. Chicago's Mayor Daley (head of the Cook County Democratic machine) personally controlled at least 25,000 jobs. (2) It decided who got city contracts, often padded to permit healthy profits for machine supporters. For example, Boss Tom Pendergast of Kansas City ran three businesses that relied on city contracts, including a wholesale liquor firm which sold to retail outlets that stood to lose their liquor licenses if they didn't buy supplies from his firm (Gist and Fava, 1974:457). (3) It gave insiders a chance to speculate in real estate by profiting from advance tips on city action (see Box 11-1). (4) It granted special favors (e.g., zoning variances) for a bribe to the machine. (5) It got kickbacks from recipients of city contracts. And (6) sometimes it got pocket money from blackmail of persons threatened with criminal prosecution by machine-controlled city attorneys.

To conclude: The city machine is an informal structure of influence and power that never appears in a city's charter or organization chart. It is an organization that mobilizes votes and distributes the benefits of office to supporters. Internally, the city machine is held together by trust and discipline. It combines rational goals with brotherly loyalty. Like an army or a business, it is based on strict discipline and hierarchy. But machines deal with their constituents in a nonbureaucratic, personal manner. Its power and influence in the city are based on the services it provides.

What Services Machines Provide(d)

Getting some help with the rent or a job down at City Hall. Maybe some graft, what Plunkitt called "honest graft," or otherwise. These don't seem to be big benefits to get from a city machine. Yet, when all the thousands of small favors and economic assists are totaled, they add up to a major urban social service: an informal welfare system.

It is important to remember that city machines rose to prominence in the nineteenth century as hundreds of thousands of European immigrants, mostly poor and unskilled, poured into the nation's cities. These immigrants had few support networks. Family members and friends were frequently left behind in the old country. Private charities and churches were ill-equipped to deal with all the immigrants' daily needs, and there were almost no government welfare programs. In this context, the old machine functioned as a personal deliverer of services, without layers of bureaucracy.

Like family, the machine could be counted on. It could bail you out of jail, get you a job when work was hard to find, supply you with free railroad passes, remember you with

BOX 11-1

HOW THE MACHINE WORKED

"Practical" Advice From George Washington Plunkitt, Tammany Hall Politician

On controlling votes

There's only one way to hold a district; you must study human nature and act accordin'. You can't study human nature in books. . . . If you have been to college, so much the worse for you. . . . To learn real human nature, you have to go among the people, see them and be seen. I know every man, woman, and child in the Fifteenth District, except them that's been born this summer—and I know some of them, too. I know what they like and what they don't like, what they are strong at and what they are weak in, and I reach them by approachin' at their right side. . . .

For instance, here's how I gather in the young men. I hear of a young feller that's proud of his voice. . . . I ask him to come around to Washington Hall and join our Glee Club. He comes and sings, and he's a follower of Plunkitt for life.

What tells in holdin' your grip on your district is to go right down among the poor families and help them in the different ways they need help. I've got a regular system for this. If there's a fire in Ninth, Tenth, or Eleventh Avenue, for example, any hour of the day or night, I'm usually there with some of my election district captains as soon as the fire-engines. If a family is burned out I don't ask whether they are Republicans or Democrats, and I don't refer them to the Charity Organization Society, which would investigate their case in a month or two and decide they were worthy of help about the time they are dead from starvation. I just get quarters for them, buy clothes for them . . . and fix them up till they get things runnin' again.

Another thing. I can always get a job for a deservin' man. I make it a point to keep on the track of jobs, and it seldom happens that I don't have a few up my sleeve ready for use.

On "honest graft"

There's an honest graft, and I'm an example of how it works. I might sum up the whole thing by sayin': I seen my opportunities and I took 'em.

Just let me explain by examples. My party's [the Democrats] in power in the city, and it's goin' to undertake a lot of public improvements. Well, I'm tipped off, say, that they're going to lay out a new park at a certain place. I see my opportunity and I take it. I go to that place and I buy up all the land I can in the neighborhood. . . . Ain't it perfectly honest to charge a good price and make a profit on my investment and foresight? Of course, it is. Well, that's honest graft. (in Riordan, [1906] 1963:3–4, 91–92; subheads ours. First published 1963 by E.P. Dutton and Co., Inc. and reprinted with their permission. All rights reserved.)

a gift for your wedding, and generally help you when you needed help. And at Christmas time, there was food. Chicago's renowned social reformer and Hull House director, Jane Addams, records that the alderman from her ward, Johnny Powers, the famed "Prince of Boodlers" (grafters), personally delivered ten tons of turkeys and ducks, shaking each voter's hand as he greeted "Merry Christmas" (Addams, [1898] 1972:14).

The old machine also served as a vehicle of economic assimilation for immigrants. This kind of assimilation promoted upward mobility, but it allowed white ethnic immigrants to keep their ethnic identities. Indeed, city machines fostered ethnic identity, not cultural assimilation. This is ironic, for even opponents of machine corruption thought that at least machines were doing something "good": ladling the immigrants into the melting pot (see Stead, 1894). But to the contrary, machines encouraged the stew pot. They used "ingenious techniques for capitalizing upon ethnic and racial heterogeneity" (Lowi, 1968:v). One technique involved settlement patterns. In Chicago, for example, the Irish tended to reside on the South Side. This housing pattern was encouraged by the machine, for the Irish could then be controlled by a ward boss of their own ethnic background and also become a voting bloc.

To most people living in a city's ward, machine politics meant ethnic politics. And ethnic politics provided a way to climb the economic ladder for white ethnics, who were generally barred by class and ethnic prejudice from advancing through jobs in commerce and industry.

The career of George Washington Plunkitt, long-time Tammany boss in New York City, shows how the machine provided opportunities for at least a few lower-class white ethnic males. Plunkitt started out as a butcher's assistant in a working-class Irish ward. He rose through the ranks of the Tammany machine, becoming the master of "honest graft."

Now, let's take a look at two well-oiled, efficient machines. Operating almost 100 years apart, the Tweed Ring controlled New York City from 1866 to 1871, and the Daley machine controlled Chicago politics from 1955 until Daley's death in 1976–and beyond. These brief case studies give a flavor of the bosses and the forces which promoted them.

Case Study: New York City's Tweed Ring, 1866–1871

Most often, political scientists point to Tammany Hall boss William Tweed and his Tweed Ring as exemplars of corrupt machine rule (e.g., Mandelbaum, 1965; Callow, 1966). Some assert that Tweed (who never ran for mayor) and his Ring (the Mayor, City Controller, some aldermen, numerous operatives) stole as much as $200,000,000 from the public treasury in five years.

Tweed was a huge man with uncouth manners, and he spent money conspicuously. Since he had been a man of modest means before rising through Tammany's ranks, he was often attacked as a vulgar crook, a plunderer. Cartoonist Thomas Nast was a particularly effective and vicious assailant, depicting Tweed as a vulture.

There is little doubt that Tweed was corrupt. It is also true that New York City's debt rose rapidly under Tweed, about $31 million in two years. And construction projects sponsored by Tweed were scandalously expensive.

But before passing judgment on Tweed, consider his social context and the sources of contemporary criticism. First, many of Tweed's critics came from educated and wealthy WASP backgrounds. Thomas Nast is a case in point. In his cartoons, Nast often depicted lower-class Irish as apes. He was distressed to see power in "his" city pass into the hands of people he considered ill-mannered and unpolished: Irish Catholic immigrants, mainly poor and uneducated. It is noteworthy that Nast did not use his poison pencil to caricature WASP robber barons like John Jacob Astor, who enjoyed warm working relationships with the bosses and who were hardly paragons of virtue. Indeed, the robber barons' unscrupulous wealth-getting techniques—stock manipulation, price fixing, false advertising—and profits from political corruption made the taking of public boodle pale by comparison. Thus, Nast's attacks on Tweed's Ring seem to be based more on class, ethnic, and religious

Fig. 11-2 BOSS WILLIAM TWEED OF NEW YORK. Caricature by Thomas Nast and a contemporary photograph. (Photograph from the collection of Leo Hershkowitz.)

bias than on righteous indignation against corruption per se.

Second, it isn't clear that the Tweed Ring was really a machine at all. The standard interpretation of the machine (e.g., Mandelbaum, 1965) depicts it as a tight-knit organization run on greed and personal gain, with little regard for the public interest. Those who interpret the machine in this way, seeing it essentially as a system of organized bribery operating without a sense of the public good, point to the Tweed Ring's ability to dominate virtually every aspect of New York City's political life. But another, alternative view of the Tweed Ring holds that tight-knit machines didn't emerge until much later in the nineteenth century, when business entrepreneurs needed stable city governments to provide the proper climate for long-term business investments. (Shefter, 1976).

Whether or not it was a tight-knit machine, the Tweed Ring did have substantial impact on New York City, then undergoing rapid change. It pressed a range of school, hospital, and public works projects; obtained reforms to protect city teachers' job security; and established much-needed public baths (Hershkowitz, 1978:348). The Ring provided jobs for lower-class laborers before government employment or unemployment programs existed. It changed the bias of the New York City Parks Commission, which had previously concentrated funds in Central Park to benefit upper-class residents, and diverted funds to smaller parks that met the needs of lower-class immigrants. It secured a new city charter in 1871 that centralized city government and reduced governmental fragmentation (and, not incidentally, made the machine's work easier). This charter reform represented a more efficient way of reviewing budgets than the former structure, in which each city department presented an independent budget to the state legislature.

Finally, Tweed, who died in jail a broken man in 1878, may have been much maligned by history. Recent scholarship suggests that the extent of the Tweed Ring's corruption was far less than previously believed (Hershkowitz, 1978).

Thus, the ledger sheet shows that Tweed and his Ring were both a bunch of crooks and a friend to the poor. It was something else too: *a friend of the rich*—especially the rising class of entrepreneurs, whose fortunes grew during the post-Civil War period of rapid industrialization and urbanization. The Tweed Ring didn't challenge the fundamental interests of the new entrepreneurs. Nast and other aristocrats may have hated Tweed and his lower-class ilk, but the machine bosses weren't antibusiness. Nor were they radical in their politics. Tweed's Ring worked comfortably and often closely with the robber barons. In fact, when Tweed was being prosecuted in 1871 for corruption, John Jacob Astor and five other millionaires signed an affadavit attesting to Tweed's good character, swearing that he never stole a cent from the New York City treasury. Financier Jay Gould (who once boasted that he could hire one-half of the working class to kill the other half) paid Tweed's $1 million bail.

Case Study: The Daley Machine in Chicago, 1955–1976 (and Beyond)

People called Richard J. Daley many names: *king maker* (for his support of John F. Kennedy for President in 1960); *fascist pig* (for his role at the Democratic National Convention in 1968); *a damn good mayor* (even the beacon of Republican sentiments, the *Chicago Tribune,* supported his later mayoral campaigns); and simply *Boss.* Observers dispute the wisdom of his policies, but they agree that Mayor Daley had clout. And Daley's clout, extending far beyond Chicago,

Fig. 11-3 MAYOR RICHARD DALEY OF CHICAGO. Caricature by David Levine and an official photograph. (Drawing by David Levine. Reprinted with permission from *New York Review of Books* Copyright © 1968. NYREV, Inc.; Photo: Office of the Mayor, City of Chicago)

was based on his leadership and control of the Cook County (Chicago) Democratic Party machine, the nation's last full-blown old-style machine.

In many ways, Daley resembled the bosses of the nineteenth century more than most of his urban contemporaries, so-called reform mayors like New York City's John V. Lindsay. Like so many Chicago machine politicians before him, Daley came from a lower-class, Irish immigrant family. He grew up in the Bridgeport section of Chicago, an Irish-American neighborhood, and he never moved away. A devoutly religious and old-fashioned family man, Daley didn't try to be refined or polished. Chicagoans delighted in his malapropisms (for instance, "Together we must rise to ever higher and higher platitudes"). Yet despite his rough edges, Harvard-educated presidential nominees and corporate business executives paid him court at City Hall. The reason: He had clout, power and influence based in a well-oiled machine.

Daley didn't create Chicago's machine. It grew out of the economic crisis of the 1930s (Gosnell, [1937] 1968:8). The machine was consolidated during the 1930s and 1940s but weakened by Daley's predecessor. In the 1950s, at a time when machines in New York City and other places withered away, Daley refueled the machine by making adaptations and promoting internal reforms.

Under Daley's leadership, the day-to-day activities of Chicago's ward bosses remained much as they had been for decades. A ward boss's typical evening consisted of the following types of work: talking to a black building manager seeking a reduction in the $20-per-month rodent extermination charge in his building; listening to two precinct captains who were asking for forty-two garbage cans; counseling a female computer programmer who thought she was being mistreated by her supervisor; and speaking to a Polish-American truck driver who was looking for work. In each case, the ward boss said that he would see what he could do (Rakove, 1975:122).

As central boss, Daley spent part of each work day in similar activities. One observer reports that

> By two o'clock [Daley]'s back behind his desk and working. One of his visitors will be a city official unique to Chicago city government: the director of patronage. He brings a list of all new city employees for the day. The list isn't limited to the key employees, the professional people. All new employees are there—down to the window washer, the ditch digger, the garbage collector. After each person's name will be an extract of his background, the job, and most important his political sponsor. Nobody goes to work for the city, and that includes governmental bodies that are not directly under the mayor, without Daley's knowing about it. (Royko, 1971:23)

Daley wanted to see every name on the list because the individual became much more than an employee: "he joins the political Machine, part of the army numbering in the thousands who will help win elections. They damn well better, or they won't keep their jobs" (Royko, 1971:23).

What drove Daley and his ward bosses to devote so much time and energy to people's personal problems? To larger issues affecting city life? For many, the motive was payoffs and jobs. Daley himself was never accused of enriching himself at the public trough, but relatives and friends were found on the city payroll. For others, there were some of the same motives that impel people in other walks of life: ego satisfaction, power, success. But not fame—for most ward bosses remain unknown to the public. Nor ideology—Chicago's machine operatives are essentially pragmatists, not ideologues. They may share many concerns of the liberal wing of the Democratic Party, but they don't seek to implement a particular political platform. Instead, they seek to win elections, provide services, and act as power brokers between conflicting ethnic and interest groups. One ward boss summarized his philosophy as follows: "Don't make no waves" and "Don't back no losers" (Neistein in Rakove, 1975:11).

In terms of substantive policies, the Daley machine encouraged large-scale business in the city. For example, to sweeten the pot for the giant Sears corporation, seeking to build a headquarters, the city agreed to pay more than $1 million to relocate sewer lines for the proposed building (O'Connor, 1975:139). The Sears building, now the world's tallest, is only one of many built during Daley's rule. Daley's record on housing construction, however, is another and controversial story. Daley's machine effectively blocked dispersal of low-income, racially integrated housing. This led to an even higher concentration of blacks in virtually segregated neighborhoods. Chicago remains the North's most racially segregated city to this day.

In terms of internal organization, the Daley machine adjusted to the city's changing ethnic composition, in particular to the increase in black and Hispanic communities. Widening the patronage net from old-line ethnic group supporters, the Daley machine reached political accommodation with the late William Dawson, a member of Congress who ran a tight-knit black sub-machine on Chicago's South Side. As one political scientist and Daley insider summarizes:

> The machine co-opts those emerging leaders in the Black and Spanish-speaking communities who are willing to cooperate; reallocates perquisites and prerogatives to the Blacks and the Spanish-speaking, taking them from ethnic groups such as the Jews and Germans, who do not support the machine as loyally as their fathers did; and ostracizes or punishes those aspiring Black politicians who will not cooperate. (Rakove, 1975:16)

Whether the machine that Daley left behind will have the clout to punish dissidents is an open question. Indeed, so is the tight-knit machine's continued existence in Chicago.

Why Machines Rise

Muckraking journalist Lincoln Steffens once asked a New York City boss, "Why must there be a boss, when we've got a Mayor and a council . . ." The boss broke in, "That's why. It's because there's a mayor *and* a council *and* judges *and* a hundred other men to deal with" (Steffens, 1931:187).

Sociologist Robert Merton ([1958] 1968) offers a more theoretical approach to the reasons behind the machine's existence, one from the structural-functional perspective. Merton holds that a persistent social structure must perform some positive functions inadequately fulfilled by other structures or else it would cease to exist. He argues that machines fulfill latent functions unmet by other institutions, including the following: humanized and personalized welfare for the poor; direct and centralized contact for big business interests; jobs and social mobility for ethnic newcomers and others who cannot move up socioeconomically in business and industry; and protection for various illegal activities run by those excluded from legal opportunity structures. In brief, it serves the needs of the poor and certain interest groups, especially corporate business.

Conflict-oriented theorists hold a different view of machines. They agree that machines provided services to the poor—and wealthy entrepreneurs—but they argue that these needs could have been met in other more radical ways. According to this perspective, the Tammany Hall machine in the nineteenth century was a conservative force, preying on the poor and helping to preserve the structure of poverty inherent in capitalist enterprise (Knauss, 1972). That is, the machine diffused or coopted the energies of the lower class—which, in European countries, was calling for revolutionary answers to poverty, not some help with the rent. In this view, the Daley machine is comparable to a colonial empire, ruling white ethnic groups by a combination of divide-and-rule tactics and relegating most Irish-Americans as well as black and Spanish-speaking people to the position of the "submerged majority" (Knauss, 1972:90).

These two interpretations do not stand in total contradiction. Rather, their emphases differ. So do their taken-for-granted assumptions about the nature of politics in the U.S. Both note the machine's latent functions but disagree on who really benefited from their rule.

Why Machines Fall

The logical extension of the structural-functionalist argument on the rise of machines is this: Machines fall when they no longer serve needed functions or when other institutions evolve to fulfill the same functions. Thus, according to this analytic framework, machines have gradually withered away because of long-term macro-level changes affecting cities. The following reasons are usually advanced for the old machine's widespread demise in the twentieth century:

1. *The scope of government increased.* Fewer people depended on city machines for favors and rewards as government began supplying welfare services. Also, party machines couldn't offer as many goodies when various reforms took hold (e.g., the rise of a civil service, merit-based bureaucracy which cut into patronage jobs).
2. *Competing institutions (besides government) grew in strength.* Labor unions and single-issue groups gained influence and power at the expense of political parties and their machines.
3. *Business interests no longer found the machine useful.* As the scope of the federal government expanded in the twentieth century, and as corporate business expanded its operations throughout the nation's cities, big business could deal with the centralized federal regulatory commissions (such as the Interstate Commerce Commission), many of which they helped to establish. At the city level, some local business leaders were in the forefront of government reform, realizing that good government reformers would sponsor policies in their interests (e.g., efficient government) and that the bosses had become a liability to them.

To conclude: Old-style machines withered away because of macro-level changes in American society that affected cities: the growth of big government, which supplied social services, and the expansion of big business, which wanted to deal with centralized control at the federal level. The machine's unique functions were gradually taken over by rival institutions. In most cities, old machines were replaced by newer, more streamlined models of government.

LOCAL GOVERNMENT REFORM

Long-term societal changes in U.S. life, especially the growth of corporate business and the expanded role of the federal government, were accompanied by vigorous municipal reform efforts which contributed to the fall of machines. It is unlikely that reformers could have smashed city machines on the strength of their ideas alone, but the combination of historical forces undermining the machine and articulate, organized reformers desiring its demise led to a reform agenda.

So-called good government reformers, or "goo-goos," emerged in the latter part of the nineteenth century as a response to machine politics, immigration, industrialism, and rapid urbanization. The successes and failures of these reformers explain much of the variation in local government forms today. For example, before the reform movement, virtually all local governments had a mayor-council form. The widespread council-manager form in medium-size and smaller communities today is a direct outgrowth of the goo-goos' efforts.

The Goo-Goos: A Disparate Lot

Leaders in the movement to reform municipal government, a movement dating roughly from the 1890s through the Progressive Era to 1917, had motives as mixed as their backgrounds. Some were like college-educated Jane Addams, a settlement house worker distressed by urban poverty and social isolation in the city. Addams viewed reform as one way to get city government to meet the desperate needs of the people who came to her Hull House in Chicago. There were muckraking journalists too, like Lincoln Steffens, who exposed *The Shame of the Cities* (1904); they sought to control urban crime, graft, vice, and political corruption. There were professors of political science and public administration, who wanted to extend administrative norms of behavior (rationality and efficiency) to the political sector, particularly to the executive branch; they supplied a stream of efficiency-oriented proposals to reform-minded commissions (Schick, 1973–1974:14). And there were other academics, including sociologists at the University of Chicago, who wanted to re-create the conditions of a small-town community within the metropolis and to stem what they considered social "disorganization."

What groups provided the good government movement with its principal strength and fundamental purpose—middle-class reformers, professionals, or business groups? This is a subject of lively debate among scholars (cf. Brownell and Stickle, 1973; Kennedy, 1971; Stave, 1972).

Since the words and thoughts of the reformers are preserved in their writings, it's possible to get a sense of what they believed they were doing. But many scholars advise going beyond the reformers' words and focusing instead on the practice of reform to get a better perspective on the movement and the reformers' purposes. Historian Samuel P. Hays (1964) notes that the reformers described themselves as just plain folks interested in morality, rationality, and efficiency in city government. But, Hays claims, this was hardly the case. According to Hays, most reformers were WASPs from upper-income business or professional backgrounds (see Box 11-2).

In Hays's view, the disparate lot of reformers had a rather self-serving purpose which united them, whether they were conscious of it or not: the centralization of decision making. Doing business at the ward level was simply not what the business and professional people wanted; their world was cosmopolitan, not based in their neighborhood community.

Furthermore, Hays contends, the reformers' manifest goal—government by trained professionals—meant that nonprofessionals would be shut out of city government. In effect, this meant that minorities, immigrants, and members of the lower class would be excluded from city politics. In other words, the latent function of the reform thrust for businesslike, efficient government was to consolidate power in the hands of upper-middle and upper-class WASP elites.

Thrusts of the Reform Movement

The municipal reform movement had several interconnected thrusts. First, it attempted to make machine government difficult or impossible. Second, it tried to make elected officials more accountable to voters. Third, it sought to make government less political and more businesslike. Fourth, it tried to stamp out industrial disorder and movements considered dangerous and anti-American. Each thrust led to a set of specific measures.

To make machine politics more difficult, reformers supported *direct primaries* (in which voters, not the machine bosses, select candidates); *nonpartisan elections;* and *citywide, at-large elections* (rather than ward or district elections, which, in theory, increased the clout of ward bosses). To make local government officials more responsive to citizen demands, reformers pushed the **initiative, referendum,** and **recall** —measures aimed at giving citizens more direct say either in

BOX 11–2

WHO WERE THE REFORMERS AND WHAT DID THEY WANT?

The Politics of Municipal Reform

. . . Reformers [in the Progressive Era, roughly 1904–1917] loudly proclaimed a new structure of municipal government as more moral, more rational and more efficient, and because it was so, self-evidently more desirable. But precisely because of this emphasis, there seemed to be no need to analyze the political forces behind change. . . . Consequently historians have rarely tried to determine precisely who the municipal reformers were or what they did, but instead have relied on reform ideology as an accurate description of reform practice.

The reform ideology . . . appears in classic form in Lincoln Steffens' *Shame of the Cities*. The urban political struggle of the Progressive Era, so the argument goes, involved a conflict between public impulses for "good government" against a corrupt alliance of "machine politicians" and "special interests."

. . . The prevailing view [is] . . . that reform in general and municipal reform in particular—sprang from a distinctively middle-class movement. . . . The weakness of the "middle-class" theory of reform stems from the fact that it rests primarily upon ideological evidence, not on a thoroughgoing description of political practice. . . .

Available evidence indicates that the source of support for reform in municipal government did not come from the lower or middle classes, but from the upper class. The leading business groups in each city and professional men closely allied with them initiated and dominated municipal movements. . . . [Much evidence shows] that the business community, represented largely by chambers of commerce, was the overwhelming force behind both commission and city-manager movements.

Dominant elements of the business community played a prominent role in another crucial aspect of municipal reform: the Municipal Research Bureau movement. Especially in the larger cities, where they had less success in shaping the structure of government, reformers established centers to conduct research in municipal affairs as a springboard for influence. The first such organization, the Bureau of Municipal Research of New York City, was founded in 1906; it was financed largely through the efforts of Andrew Carnegie and John D. Rockefeller.

. . . Although reformers used the ideology of popular government, they in no sense meant that all segments of society should be involved equally in municipal decision-making. They meant that their concept of the city's welfare would be best achieved if the business community controlled city government.

. . . Prior to the reforms of the Progressive Era city government consisted primarily of confederations of local wards. . . . These particularistic interests were the focus of a decentralized political life. City councilmen were local leaders. They spoke for their local areas . . . pre-reform officials spoke for their constituencies, inevitably their own wards which had elected them, rather than for other sections or groups of the city.

The ward system of government especially gave representation in city affairs to lower- and middle-class groups. Most elected ward officials were from these groups, and they, in turn, constituted the major opposition to reforms in municipal government.

. . . This decentralized system of urban growth and the institutions which arose from it reformers now opposed. Social, professional, and economic life had developed not only in the local wards in a small community context, but also on a larger scale had become highly integrated and organized, giving rise to a superstructure of social organization which lay far above that of ward life and which was sharply divorced from it in both personal contacts and perspective.

By the late nineteenth century, those involved in these larger institutions found that the decentralized system of political life limited their larger objectives. *The movement for reform in municipal government, therefore, constituted an attempt by upper-class, advanced professional, and large business groups to take formal political power from the previously dominant lower- and middle-class elements so that they might advance their own conceptions of desirable public policy. These two groups came from entirely different urban worlds, and the political system fashioned by one was no longer acceptable to the other.* [emphasis added]

The drama of reform lay in the competition for supremacy between two systems of decision-making. One system, based upon ward representation and growing out of the practices and ideas of representative government, involved wide latitude for the expression of grass-roots impulses and their involvement in the political process. The other grew out of the rationalization of life which came with science and technology, in which decisions arose from expert analysis and flowed from fewer and smaller centers outward to the rest of society.

. . . the Progressive Era witnessed rapid strides towards a more centralized system. . . . It involved a tendency for the decision-making processes inherent in science and technology to prevail over those inherent in representative government. (Hays, 1964:157–69. Copyright © 1964 by *Pacific Northwest Quarterly*. Reprinted by permission of Pacific Northwest Quarterly and the author.)

proposing and deciding on legislation or in removing officials thought to be insensitive or corrupt.

To take politics out of government and make it more efficient, the reformers sponsored measures to change the form of local government and to professionalize government. To separate politics from administration, they pushed the *council-manager form* of government. To take the "spoils" out of office, they wanted *civil service merit examinations* for local government service. This would not only cut patronage possibilities, it would also provide job security for bureaucrats who couldn't be dismissed when a new faction got control of city hall. To increase the efficiency of city government, they supported *professional education* in public administration and city planning.

Finally, reformers founded a number of private institutions aimed at "Americanizing" the children of immigrants. These included settlement houses, the YMCA, and the Playground Association of America. Reformers also used the public schools to inculcate values of patriotism, obedience, and duty. It was in the 1880s, for instance, that saluting the flag was introduced into grammar schools (Tyack, 1974). These reform efforts at citizenship training and patriotism grew out of mixed motives: humanitarianism and/or an urge to turn "them" into "us," thus preserving the dominant WASP culture in the face of immigrant non-Protestant religious beliefs and Southern and Eastern European cultural traditions.

That many reformers acted from ethnic prejudice and class interests is suggested in the comments of Andrew D. White, a Progressive reformer, and the first president of Cornell University, in 1890:

The work of a city being the creation and control of the city property, it should logically be managed as a piece of property by those who have created it, who have a title to it, or a real substantial part in it [and not by] a crowd of illiterate peasants, freshly raked in from the Irish bogs, or Bohemian mines, or Italian robber nests. . . . (in Banfield and Wilson, 1963:153)

What White and many other Progressive reformers sought to prevent was a city ruled by a "proletariat mob" (in Banfield, 1961:213). They also wanted to prevent the rise of "anti-Americanisms," particularly socialism, anarchism, and syndicalism.

It is an interesting and almost forgotten fact that one "ism"—municipal socialism—was a serious competitor to the reform movement. Between 1900 and the start of World War II, Milwaukee, Wisconsin, Berkeley, California, and other cities elected socialists to the city council or the mayoralty. The Industrial Workers of the World (the Wobblies, see Chapter 1) also presented radical alternatives to good government reform measures (Stave, 1975).

To conclude: Beginning at the end of the nineteenth century and gathering momentum in the early twentieth, a disparate lot of reformers—ranging from settlement house workers and journalists to professors of public administration and business people—called for reforms in city politics. Their major goals: (1) to make machine politics difficult or impossible; (2) to make elected officials more accountable to voters; and (3) to make government more businesslike and less political. This group of reformers, mainly members of the new middle and upper classes (professionals and expansionists from business, labor, and agriculture) wanted to adapt the new urban-industrial society to meet their own needs. They chose government reform to do it. In place of the personalized, ward-level, somewhat representative government under the machine, they urged efficiency-minded, professional, centralized city government. One latent function of their reform agenda was to wrest control of the nation's cities from those they considered unprofessional and uncouth: lower-class ethnics.

How Successful Were the Reformers?

Many structural changes desired by the good government reformers were instituted in American cities, particularly medium-size and smaller cities. For instance, the council-manager form of government is a direct outcome of the goo-goos' efforts. But reformers never completely gained control over city governments, and the larger, more heterogeneous cities were especially difficult for reformers to reshape.

At this point, we should ask: What difference did reform make in the actual day-to-day operations and policies of city governments? Scholars are not in total agreement here. One well-regarded study points out that, in general, the more a city government was reformed, the less responsive it became to the needs of different racial and income group constituencies in the city (Lineberry and Fowler, 1967). Another study of urban politics argues that the machine controlled and manipulated the lower-class vote, but the reformers reduced and trivialized it (Greenstone and Peterson, 1973). Most assessments conclude that good government reform led to lower voter turnouts, less diversity in the class and ethnic composition of city government, and less responsive and representative government (Hawkins, 1971: 93–99).

Only the most naive goo-goos thought that municipal reform would end patterns of influence, and indeed it has not. Even in completely reformed governments, trained professionals do not develop value-neutral policies without regard to their political consequences.

MACHINES: AN UPDATE

With notable exceptions like Chicago, the old machines were broken by a combination of the goo-goos' reform efforts and macro-societal factors such as the rise of rival institutions. But fragments of the machines remain. In many cities, a hundred little amenities of life can depend on the clout of ward-level bosses: how many times a week garbage is collected, who gets a new construction job, or how bright the street lights shine. Especially in cities with large ethnic voting blocs, including Philadelphia, Boston, Tucson, and Baltimore, machine-style politics at the ward level continues to be an important force.

In short, good government reform didn't completely do away with time-honored patronage jobs or other benefits that politicians can dispense to supporters. Despite civil service merit exams, nonpartisan elections, and other reforms, who you know—or who you can get to—still counts in city politics.

One modern development is noteworthy: the new machine. The new machine derives its power base from nonelected office: the city's bureaucratic administration. It doesn't depend on loyal ward bosses or city councillors who deliver votes or give out turkeys at Christmas.

Robert Moses, New-style Boss

The new machine and how it works are best exemplified by one man and the empire he built: Robert Moses's New York City. A lifelong bureaucrat and appointed official, Moses never served as mayor of the nation's largest city. Yet it was Moses—not the mayors, city planners, professorial consultants, or Democratic Party heads—who shaped modern New York City's total urban environment. From the 1930s to the late 1960s, Moses molded a city and its sprawling suburbs. And his influence didn't stop there. "In the twentieth century, the influence of Robert Moses on the cities of America was greater than that of any other person" (Mumford in Caro, 1975:12).

How Moses, hardly a household name, built his empire and used his power to shape a city in his own vision is a tale well told by Robert A. Caro in *The Power Broker: Robert Moses and the Fall of New York* (1975). The following quick study of Moses is based on Caro's Pulitzer Prize-winning book.

Robert Moses started his long career in 1909, during the era of municipal reform. A passionate idealist with imagination, iron will, determination, arrogance, and dreams, he worked for the good government organization in New York City as a specialist in civil service reorganization. He argued for the idea that jobs and promotions should be awarded on the basis of merit, not patronage. He spent the years 1914–1918 in the administration of New York City's reforming mayor: one year devising a public personnel system and another three years fighting to get it adopted. He battled with the city's appropriations unit, the Board of Estimate, which was "dominated by one of the most corrupt political machines the United States had ever known" (1975:4), to replace patronage with civil service. By 1918, Moses had made such a nuisance of himself that Tammany Hall decided to crush him—and it did. Caro (1975:5) reports that at the age of thirty, with his civil service personnel system papers being used as scrap paper, "Robert Moses, Phi Beta Kappa at Yale, honors man at Oxford, lover of the Good, the True and the Beautiful, was out of work and, with a wife and two small daughters to support, was standing on a line

Fig. 11-4 ROBERT MOSES, THE POWER BROKER. Operating behind the scenes, Moses shaped most of the development of highways, bridges, parks, beaches, and related infrastructure for the New York City area as well as massive redevelopment projects and housing construction. (Photo by Arnold Newman, courtesy of Robert Moses)

in the Cleveland, Ohio, City Hall, applying for a minor muncipal job."

According to Caro, Robert Moses spent the rest of his life using that same iron will, determination, and imagination in another way: to amass power. He wanted power to transform his ideas into reality. And Moses was successful.

Moses sat atop an empire built on the bureaucracies of New York City parks, urban renewal, and highway programs. The immensity of his power and his empire is suggested by a few statistics: Since 1931, seven bridges linking the island boroughs of New York were built; "Robert Moses built every one of those bridges." Between 1945 and 1958, the New York City Housing Authority built 1,082 buildings; "no site for public housing was selected and no brick of a public housing project [was] laid without his approval." Moses built every superhighway in New York City except one. He built Shea Stadium and decided what factories, stores, and tenements would be torn down for urban renewal. He was the dominant force behind two enormous private housing developments in Manhattan and the Bronx.

More importantly, for over thirty years, Moses was responsible for establishing the priorities of what got built in the New York metropolitan region. This had a vast impact on "not only the physical but also the social fabric of the cities, on the quality of life their inhabitants led" (Caro, 1975:7–8).

How did Robert Moses become America's greatest builder—of roads, parks, hospitals, schools, urban renewal sites, even sewers (whose design and site he approved)? He used an institution still in its infancy when he came to it in the 1930s: the public authority. Public authorities supposedly are entities outside governmental bureaucracies. Their members are appointed for long terms which, in theory, insulate them from politics. They were institutions thought to be not only outside but above politics. But under Moses, public authorities—the Triborough Bridge Authority, New York's Housing Authority, Parks Authority, and so forth—were political machines "oiled by the lubricant of political machines: money. Their wealth enabled Moses to make himself not only a political boss but a boss who in his particular bailiwick—public works—was able to exert a power that few political bosses in the more conventional mold ever attain" (Caro, 1975:17).

To conclude: Robert Moses was a political boss, new style. He became the chief behind-the-scenes mover and shaker in city and metropolitan politics by deciding where public works were located. He became New York's "ward boss of the inner circle" without campaigning for votes or dealing with ward bosses. Using the public authorities as his power base, he became "the locus of corruption in New York City" (although personally, he was honest in financial matters). Giving out retainers, fees, contracts, and commissions (for public relations, insurance, labor unions, building contracts), Moses succeeded in replacing graft with legal benefits.

ANOTHER LOOK

America made a unique contribution to urban politics: the city machine. In general, theorists agree that the machine was a product of its times, rising in an era of rapid industrialization and urbanization and falling in an era of national expansion. But theorists disagree on the costs and benefits of this institution, which was based on networks of influence and power rather than legitimate authority. Disagreements center on who benefited most, and the answers depend on the scholar's theoretical orientation. Social scientists who stress the idea of harmony in the social system (structural-functionalists) say that the city machine served the needs of various social groups, and when it could no longer serve these needs, it sputtered out. But conflict theorists have a different interpretation. They say that the old machines served the interests of the rising class of business people more than it served the poor, and it ran out of steam when the business interests found new and better ways to serve their needs. Further, conflict-oriented scholars argue that the city machines served an important latent function: By providing some benefits to a few ethnics, they diverted the lower classes from seeking more radical alternatives to their plight.

The good government reform movement is also variously interpreted. Some scholars see the movement as a progressive step toward efficiency and rationality in local government. Others view it as a power grab by professionals and entrepreneurs to control the cities, preventing the "unwashed proletarian mob" from taking power.

On one point scholars agree, whatever their theoretical orientation, discipline, or political ideology: No type of structural reform has succeeded in doing away with informal networks of influence. Neo-conservatives like Pat Moynihan and Nathan Glazer point to whole bureaucracies in New York City's reform government that exist mainly to serve ethnic interests. In an update to *Beyond the Melting Pot* (1979:ix), they write that "Ethnicity and race dominate the city, more than ever seemed possible in 1963." Liberal scholars often point to the widening net of influence (as the next chapter details), and radicals tend to focus on behind-the-scenes dealings by elites that influence city policymaking. Once again, while they agree that informal networks count in city politics, they disagree on how these networks operate and who they benefit most. That is the subject to which we now turn.

PROJECTS

1. **Biography of a boss.** Select a famous cityboss from material in the Suggestions for Further Learning and do a biographical sketch of him. When did he flourish? What social and economic context set the stage for his reign? What was his ethnic identity, his power base? Can you determine the sources of his money and power? With what concrete activities is the boss associated? What finally happened to him? Relate the *facts* of the boss's life to some of the *theoretical material* in this chapter on how machines worked and the functions they served.

2. **Modern machines.** The shadow of old machines lives on in more subtle forms today. One area in which machinelike structures are likely to exist is the delivery of social services to low-income groups. Test this hypothesis for a community near you by examining the local Community Service Agency (CSA) and/or Concentrated Employment Training Act (CETA) program or some other social service program delivery system. Can you identify a strong bosslike figure or figures in the program who dominate decision making (e.g., who is hired and where grant monies go)? Is there an ethnic basis of power in the system? What latent and manifest functions do the program(s) serve?

3. **Reformers.** Examine the local political reform movement in one city. Examine political histories to determine what group(s) were active in charter revision or other political reform activities. What groups are currently active in local government reform? Determine the social bases of the groups—past and present—and their agendas. What do they say about their own motives? Are there alternative explanations for their political behavior?

SUGGESTIONS FOR FURTHER LEARNING

A number of books provide portraits of urban bosses and the way they operated. Harold Zinc's *City Bosses in the United States* (Durham, N.C.: Duke University Press, 1930) remains a classic in this genre.

Bruce M. Stave's *Urban Bosses, Machines, and Progressive Reformers* (Lexington, Mass.: D.C. Heath, 1972) has selections by contemporary observers, both criticizing the bosses (e.g., Jane Addams, Lincoln Steffens) and defending them (George Washington Plunkitt). It also contains case study materials and classic political science and sociological interpretations (e.g., the works of Samuel Hays and of Robert Merton). Alexander B. Callow, Jr.'s *City Bosses in America* (New York: Oxford University Press, 1976) contains similar material.

William L. Riordan's *Plunkitt of Tammany Hall* (New York: Dutton, [1906] 1963) contains the personal reflections of a Tammany Hall politician from the time of Boss Tweed through the end of the nineteenth century.

A standard negative interpretation of Boss Tweed and the Tweed Ring can be found in Seymour Mandelbaum, *Boss Tweed's New York* (New York: Wiley, 1965). Mandelbaum makes extensive use of contemporary materials from Tweed's rivals, including the *New York Times's* revelations about financial irregularities in constructing the New York county court house. In contrast, Leo Hershkowitz in *Tweed's New York* (Garden City, N.Y.: Anchor, 1978) depicts Tweed as a victim of the older New York City elite, which disliked him as much for his involvement with Catholic (largely Irish) voters and politicians as for his graft. Hershkowitz draws on recently found financial records of New York City and much other original scholarship for his provocative (but not entirely convincing) thesis that Tweed was only moderately crooked.

Cartoons by Thomas Nast caricaturing Tweed and the Tweed Ring are contained in Morton Keller, *The Art and Politics of Thomas Nast* (New York: Oxford University Press, 1968).

A novel which romanticizes the political machine is Edwin O'Connor's *The Last Hurrah* (Boston: Little, Brown, 1956).

Mayor Richard J. Daley and his machine are best described in Milton Rakove, *Don't Make No Waves . . . Don't Back No Losers* (Bloomington: Indiana University Press, 1975). Rakove, a political scientist who spent years as a participant-observer of the Chicago machine, shows how the machine was organized, what values its members held, and what it did. His book contains case study material describing the actual interactions between ward politicians and their constituents. It does not particularly praise Daley, but it does not condemn him. Critical journalistic treatments of the Daley machine include Len O'Connor's *Clout* (New York: Avon, 1975), Mike Royko's *Boss* (New York: Signet, 1971), and Eugene Kennedy's *Himself: The Life and Times of Mayor Richard J. Daley* (New York: Viking, 1978).

Robert A. Caro's *The Power Broker: Robert Moses and the Fall of New York* (New York: Vintage Books, 1975) is a massive (1200+ page) dissection of how Robert Moses masterminded much of the physical development in New York City—bridges, beaches, parks, housing projects, and such colossal developments as the UN building and Rockefeller Center. In telling Moses's story, Caro provides unparalleled insight into the way in which political power at the local level operates.

One of Frank Capra's social-message films, the classic *Mr. Smith Goes to Washington* (1939), depicts a back-room political boss and businessman at the federal level, Jim Taylor (head of the Taylor machine in the U.S. Senate), being countered, somewhat unsuccessfully, by a righteous and moral opponent. Movie critic Robert Sklar comments in *Movie-Made America* (New York: Random House, 1975:211) that "once Capra's heroes begin their open struggles with wealth and power, they find themselves unable to triumph by asserting their strength and involving their alliances. [The political bosses] are simply too wealthy and powerful."

KEY TERMS

Direct primary Selection of candidates to run in an election by direct vote of the electorate, rather than selection by a party committee or other back-room method.

Initiative An electoral device by which interested citizens can propose legislation through petitions signed by a specified number of registered voters (usually 5–15 percent). The initiative process bypasses local elected officials. If passed, an initiative becomes law without being considered by the governing body of the city.

Machine A political organization to mobilize votes and distribute the benefits of office to its members.

Precinct The basic unit of political party organization in the United States. Cities and counties are divided into precinct polling districts, each containing from 200 to 1,000 voters.

Recall A provision permitting removal of elected officials before the expiration of their terms if the electorate so votes in a special recall election. It was introduced by reformers as a device to increase the accountability of local elected officials.

Referendum An electoral device which permits citizens to decide directly upon proposed legislation. A proposed bill is placed on the ballot and voted on directly by the electorate. Their decision is binding on the local governing body of the jurisdiction in which the referendum took place.

Ward The political division of a city for purposes of electing members to the city council (or board of aldermen). In cities where there are district elections, each ward elects one representative to the local governing body of the city.

REFERENCES

Addams, Jane
[1898]
1972 "Why the ward boss rules." Pp. 10–15 in Bruce M. Stave (ed.), Urban Bosses, Machines, and Progressive Reformers. Lexington, Mass: D.C. Heath.

Banfield, Edward C.
1961 Urban Government. New York: Free Press.

Banfield, Edward C. and James Q. Wilson
1963 City Politics. New York: Vintage.

Brownell, Blaine A. and Warren E. Stickle (eds.)
1973 Bosses and Reformers: Urban Politics in America, 1880–1920. Boston: Houghton Mifflin.

Bryce, James
1889 The American Commonwealth. New York: Macmillan.

Callow, Alexander B., Jr.
1966 The Tweed Ring. New York: Oxford University Press.

Caro, Robert A.
1975 The Power Broker: Robert Moses and the Fall of New York. New York: Vintage.

Gist, Noel P. and Sylvia Fleis Fava
1974 Urban Society. New York: Thomas Y. Crowell.

Glazer, Nathan and Daniel Patrick Moynihan
1979 Beyond the Melting Pot: The Negroes, Puerto Ricans, Jews, Italians, and Irish of New York City, 2nd ed. Cambridge, Mass.: MIT Press.

Gosnell, Harold F.
[1937]
1968 Machine Politics: Chicago Model. Chicago: University of Chicago Press.

Greenstein, Fred I.
1964 "The changing pattern of urban party politics." Annals of the American Academy of Political and Social Science 353:1–13.

Greenstone, J. David and Paul E. Peterson
1973 Race and Authority in Urban Politics: Community Participation and the War on Poverty.New York: Russell Sage.

Hawkins, Brett
1971 Politics and Urban Policies. Indianapolis: Bobbs-Merrill.

Hays, Samuel P.
1964 "The politics of reform in municipal government in the Progressive era." Pacific Northwest Quarterly 55: 157–69.

Hershkowitz, Leo
1978 Tweed's New York. Garden City, N.Y.: Anchor.

Kennedy, David (ed.)
1971 Progressivism: The Critical Issues. Boston: Little, Brown.

Knauss, Peter R.
1972 Chicago: A One-Party State. Champaign, Ill.: Stirpes.

Lineberry, Robert P. and Edmond P. Fowler
1967 "Reformism and public policies in American cities." American Political Science Review 3, 61:701–16.

Lowi, Theodore J.
1968 "Foreward to the second edition: Gosnell's Chicago revisited via Lindsay's New York." Pp. v–xviii in Harold F. Gosnell, Machine Politics: Chicago Model. Chicago: University of Chicago Press.

Mandelbaum, Seymour
1965 Boss Tweed's New York. New York: Wiley.

Merton, Robert
[1958]
1968 "Manifest and latent functions." Pp. 73–138 in Robert Merton, Social Theory and Social Structure. New York: Free Press.

O'Connor, Edwin
1956 The Last Hurrah. Boston: Little, Brown.

O'Connor, Len
1975 Clout. New York: Avon.

Puzo, Mario
[1969]
1973 The Godfather. New York: Fawcett World.

Rakove, Milton
1975 Don't Make No Waves . . . Don't Back No Losers. Bloomington: Indiana University Press.

Riordan, William L.
[1906]
1963 Plunkitt of Tammany Hall. New York: Dutton.

Royko, Mike
1971 Boss. New York: Signet.

Schultze, William A.
1974 Urban and Community Politics. North Scituate, Mass.: Duxbury.

Shefter, Martin
1976 "The emergence of the political machine: an alternative view." Pp. 14–44 in Willis D. Hawley et al. (eds.), Theoretical Perspectives in Urban Politics. Englewood Cliffs, N.J.: Prentice-Hall.

Shick, Allen
1973–
1974 "Coming apart in public administration." Maxwell Review 10, 2:13–24.

Stave, Bruce M. (ed.)
1972 Urban Bosses, Machines, and Progressive Reformers. Lexington, Mass.: D.C. Heath.
1975 Socialism and the Cities. Port Washington, N.Y.: Kennikat.

Stead, W.T.
1894 If Christ Came to Chicago: A Plea for the Union of All Who Love in the Service of All Who Suffer. Chicago: Laird & Lee.

Steffens, Lincoln
1904 The Shame of the Cities. New York: P. Smith.
1931 The Autobiography of Lincoln Steffens. New York: Harcourt Brace.

Tyack, David
1974 The One Best System: A History of American Urban Education. Cambridge, Mass.: Harvard University Press.

Bill Owens

CHAPTER 12 Getting Things Done

If Boss Tweed were alive today, he would find an expanded political arena. Typically, old-style machines were based on coalitions of white ethnic immigrants, business interests, and boodlers. Today, the range of political players is much broader. On the local political scene are such additional groups as Third World ethnics, municipal employee unions, gays, feminists, and a host of single-issue interests (tax revolters, environmentalists, nude beach proponents, advocates for the disabled, historic preservationists, and so forth).

In this crowded scene, how do groups find

each other, let alone work together, for mutual benefit? What shapes and forms do coalition politics take today? How can ordinary citizens participate in public decision making? And what impact are these varied new players having on community power relations? We now turn to these questions.

After a brief discussion of coalition politics, we illustrate how coalitions are built with a case study of an urban renewal project. Then we examine conflicting perspectives on community power relations and citizen politics. Finally, we return to Bananas, the Berkeley women's group, to see what they learned about getting things done by using their political resources.

COALITION POLITICS

Past or present, people representing varied interest groups in the city join together in alliances, trying to secure benefits that local government can dispense. What contractor will get the bid for a new building? Which neighborhood will get the building? What kind of services will be dispensed there? Which people— and whose—will get the jobs created by the new building? Such specific concerns are often the objects of intense political struggle, fought out in the arena of coalition politics. In this arena, several rules of the game are commonly understood: "you help me and I'll help you" and "politics makes strange bedfellows."

In Tweed's New York City, political battles were fought over which neighborhoods got public baths, what jobs went to the Irish or other ethnic groups, and who got the lucrative contract to plaster the new courthouse. Graft and ethnic politics played a major role in determining who got what from the city treasury. Today, ethnic politics remains a key factor and graft has not been eliminated, even in the most reformed governments. But now groups and individuals also seek a bigger share of the legal benefits available from municipal government. And single-issue groups seek government's help in furthering their aims, whether it be no smoking in local stores or setting up a women's health center.

From Tweed's day to the present, the players and issues may have changed,but the game remains the same. Whether old machine, reform government, or issue-oriented politics in a reform context, groups compete for scarce resources by organizing coalitions. These coalitions are informal; they have no formal standing in the city's legal structure.

Case Study: The Fight Over Yerba Buena Center

One battle in San Francisco over who got what—and what share—of public resources will illustrate the nature of coalition politics. This battle is meticulously described in one of the best available case studies of city decision making, *Yerba Buena: Land Grab and Community Resistance in San Francisco* (1973) by city planner Chester Hartman. Hartman's book, the basis of the following study, details the complex nature of coalition building and the stakes involved in the bitter contest over land use.

Yerba Buena is an eighty-acre parcel of land adjacent to San Francisco's CBD. In Burgess's model, it is part of the Zone-in-Transition. It was the focus of an intense political struggle in the late 1960s and 1970s, for it was the proposed site of a comprehensive redevelopment program.

Once, Yerba Buena had thrived. After the San Francisco earthquake in 1906, the Southern Pacific railroad located its main terminal there, bringing with it a cluster of luxury hotels, warehouses, and light manufacturing plants.

But by the mid-1960s, Yerba Buena was in decline. As Chapter 13 describes in detail, macro-societal trends changed the face of the city. Manufacturing activity declined; white-collar work increased; new technologies made the railroad obsolete for many purposes; and the composition of the city population was changing. These economic and demographic forces took their toll on Yerba Buena. By the 1960s, most of its warehouses had been abandoned for new ones near the port, airport, or suburban locations. Manufacturing had declined. Few goods and people came into the city by train. The residential population of the area consisted of elderly, single, lower-class men and a mixture of ethnic families. Most residents were poor, without power or prestige. They lived in the old luxury hotels, which had long since become residential hotels, offering cheap accomodations in very faded elegance. Many residents were clients of welfare and social service agencies.

Change for the area seemed inevitable. But what kind? And in whose interests?

One answer was aggressively pursued by the local government agency responsible for urban renewal and redevelopment, the San Francisco Redevelopment Agency (SFRA), and a coalition of interest groups it helped to put together. This constellation of interests proposed a convention center complex—the Yerba Buena Center. Their plan included a convention center, tourist hotels, sports arena, office buildings, and parking garage. It was to be a joint venture of private and public resources. The SFRA would clear the lands; the city and private developers would build the center; city bonds would underwrite some publicly owned parts of the center.

Private business groups formed the backbone of the coaltion put together by the SFRA. Who were they? Why did they support it? Traditional political stakes were involved: economic gain, jobs, and a variety of other benefits.

First, private economic gain. Several long-established local business groups viewed the proposed Yerba Buena Center as a boon. The San Francisco Convention and Visitors' Bureau was in the forefront of the pro-Yerba Buena forces. Composed of tourist-oriented businesses, the bureau wanted a convention complex for obvious reasons. Visiting conventioneers would eat in their restaurants, patronize their clubs and bars, purchase tickets in their travel agencies, and buy "I Got My Crabs at Fisherman's Wharf" T-shirts in their stores. Likewise, the local Hotel Owners' Association envisioned conventioneers packing their hotels. The Chamber of Commerce shared these visions and thought a convention center would be generally good for business. These pro-Yerba Buena Center commercial interests did not stand idly by or just make rhetorical statements about the benefits to the city from such a project. They funded studies "proving" how much San Francisco would benefit from the proposed center; lobbied elected city officials to give necessary approvals; and actively intervened in project planning.

Second, jobs. The proposed construction of a massive new physical complex was attractive to the building trades unions, and they joined the pro-Yerba Buena coalition for this reason. At times, when the project was stalled, they mobilized support in the form of street demonstrations.

Third, a host of other benefits. Different versions of the Yerba Buena plan reflected efforts to woo a wide range of other interest groups. An Italian cultural center was proposed by the city's Italian-American mayor to get support from San Francisco's influential Italian-American community. A civic light opera center was added to the plan in an attempt to appeal to the local social elite, who wanted such a cultural facility. Plans for parking garages were expanded and shifted closer to a nearby department store; a high-level executive of the store served as head of the Redevelopment Commission (the appointed body in charge of the Redevelopment Agency) and as a member of the corporate board which would run the parking garages.

In short, a pro-Yerba Buena Center coalition came together around self-interest. Members of the alliance sought different resources and benefits: money, jobs, cultural facilities, and other perquisites for themselves. They didn't define this as selfish or narrow. In their thinking, what they wanted for themselves made a good, livable city.

This pro-Yerba Buena Center coalition had enought clout to move ahead with the project. The local mass media added their influence in the form of editorials and news stories, stressing the benefits to the city as a whole from a convention site. By 1966, the San Francisco Redevelopment Agency had obtained a federal grant to acquire land, relocate the residential occupants, and demolish buildings.

Then a reaction set in. Neighborhood residents, mostly poor and elderly, fought to stop what they saw as a land grab. Some residents, seasoned in the labor struggles of the 1930s, established an organization called Tenants and Owners in Opposition to Redevelopment (TOOR) to represent and protect neighborhood interests. TOOR demonstrated against the proposed convention center, appealed to the city government to stop it, and filed a lawsuit to block the project. In their view, the Yerba Buena Center would destroy the neighborhood they had long called home. If development did take place, they demanded fair treatment: construction of subsidized housing they could afford, located in the same neighborhood or nearby; social services and open space; and a voice in planning how their future neighborhood would be built.

When it started, TOOR hardly seemed a threat. It had little clout, especially against the well-staffed pro-convention center coalition. About all it did have, according to grizzled ex-labor leader George Wolff who led TOOR, was a sense of injustice: "It was a good beef." Armed with "a good beef," neighborhood residents fought hard to preserve their turf. But alone, without allies, a sense of moral outrage and injustice was a weak weapon.

TOOR, staffed by several politically astute radicals who lived in the neighborhood and representing a group of ethnically diverse poor and elderly persons, initially found an ally in a very different group: environmentalists. These people (mainly young professionals who lived far from Yerba Buena) opposed the project on ecological and aesthetic grounds. They feared that high-rise buildings in Yerba Buena would destroy the city's low-density land use and offbeat charm. They didn't want more cars to come into the city and add to air pollution. Housing and social services—the Yerba Buena residents' main concern— was not the environmentalists' key issue. But since both the environmentalists and TOOR wanted to stop the Yerba Buena project, they made common cause.

This improbable coalition between the poor and elderly and the affluent and young was joined at one point by another group: disgruntled taxpayers. The proposed Yerba Buena project was going to be very expensive, and a portion of the development was to be financed by city-backed bonds. City officials, with rosy projections, told taxpayers that the bonds would be paid off at no cost to the city. But the taxpayers' group feared that the convention center could be a financial dis-

Fig. 12-1 REDEVELOPMENT—FOR WHAT? FOR WHOM? These were concerns underlying the struggle between competing coalitions for or against San Francisco's proposed Yerba Buena Center. (Michael Schwartz)

aster and that the city would have to raise property taxes in order to repay its bonds. Moreover, the taxpayers' group resented the fact that the city had not submitted the bond issue to voter approval. They felt that this was illegal as well as immoral. So, another temporary alliance was struck with the neighborhood residents by yet another group that opposed the convention center (some taxpayers)—but for very different reasons. Eventually the original pro-Yerba Buena coalition found itself under attack on several fronts. Sued in federal court for illegal displacement of the residents, vilified before officials of the Department of Housing and Urban Development, and lambasted at City Hall, they came to a standstill. For a while.

Then a complex deal was struck between the city and TOOR. Essentially, TOOR obtained funding for housing projects in exchange for an end to litigation. Thereafter, TOOR sided with the city against its former allies, the environmentalists and fiscal opponents of the convention center.

What was the eventual outcome of the struggle? As is so frequently the case in politics, neither TOOR and its sometime allies nor its opponents totally won or lost. The pro-Yerba Buena Center coalition won to the extent that the major outlines of its proposal were kept intact. However, TOOR won significant accomodations. New, low-rent housing units had been built by the late 1970s, including Wolff House (named for TOOR's leader, who died during the struggle), which now houses former residents of the Yerba Buena area. Relocation benefits and social services were improved too.

TOOR's sometime allies got the city to undertake environmental impact analyses, scale down the size of the parking garages, and increase the amount of public open space in the project area. And the taxpayers' group won in the sense that it persuaded the city to reduce the amount of the bond issue and hence the city's potential fiscal liability.

This case study illustrates some important points about urban politics. First, informal power arrangements are the key to understanding how things get done. Nothing in the city charter of San Francisco or any other city deals with the role that private interest groups or citizens' action associations play in policymaking. Yet such groups are leading actors in the process of policy formation. Nor does the city charter or the organization chart of city government indicate the relative influence of neighborhood residents versus opposing groups or the possibility of increasing that influence by coalition building. These are matters of informal power and influence.

Second, the Yerba Buena struggle illustrates that in U.S. cities, by and large, it is private interests that mold the plans of proposed projects. Government units, such as redevelopment agencies, act as power brokers to resolve conflicts among competing private groups.

Third, successful political outcomes can result from effective coalition-building efforts. In most cases, rather strange political actors can find themselves making common cause. In Yerba Buena, for a time, labor unions and business interests joined forces to promote the proposed convention center; the elderly poor, led by neighborhood radicals, were aligned for a while with liberal socially esteemed environmentalists and fiscal conservatives. This array of forces on either side came together on a single issue; it was not a broad-based coalition of a multi-issue nature, which is much more difficult to put together or sustain.

Finally, the Yerba Buena case shows that in politics, few things happen overnight. Participation in coalition politics can lead to anxiety for people with short time lines, low frustration levels, and a distaste for conflict. Moving a project forward or trying to stop it takes patience, wits, organizational talent, energy, imagination, and perseverence. Often it also takes money, access to the mass media, endless strategy meetings, and hard bargaining. Some players in the game of politics command more resources than others by virtue of their social and economic position, their personal characteristics, and their occupational role. While players don't start with equal resources, even the most organized and powerful groups (in the Yerba Buena case, economic elites and government officials) sometimes reach political accommodation with less powerful groups having fewer resources.

The Yerba Buena struggle leads us to consider broader questions about the nature of power in the urban community. We now turn to this complex and ideologically loaded issue.

COMMUNITY POWER

According to most civics texts, local decision-making is a broadly participatory effort in which almost everyone has a chance to express strongly held views and in which consensus emerges, reflecting the public interest. The Yerba Buena case study suggests that this conventional textbook version of how decisions are made is rather idealized. How can we better understand the local decision-making process? What theoretical framework best fits the actual practice? Researchers have been investigating these questions for decades, and they don't agree.

Community power research in America began with a few participant-observer studies in the 1920s and 1930s, after the reform movement had gained a foothold in many large and small U.S. cities. The most influential work of this period was produced by Robert S. and Helen M. Lynd, professors of sociology and social philosophy. Their landmark studies of *Middletown* ([1929] 1956) and *Middletown in Transition* (1937) traced the day-to-day life of a typical small Midwestern urban community (Muncie, Indiana, never identified by name by the Lynds). In Middletown, the Lynds found that government was "enmeshed in undercover intrigue and personalities" (1937:322) that operated mainly behind the scenes. The Lynds concluded that voters were apathetic and that "experts" (doctors, intelligence testers, etc.) were starting to displace the authority of the judicial system. Further, according to the Lynds, government in Middletown was becoming an "adjunct to the city's dominant interests," particularly business (1937: Chap. 24).

After World War II, community power research attracted numerous investigators, mainly those working in the sociological and social anthropological traditions. Later, starting in the 1960s, a new spate of studies appeared, largely in response to those in the 1950s. These studies, mainly conducted by political scientists, challenged both the methodologies and the findings of the earlier studies. More recently, community power research has changed its focus—to a comparative analysis. Let's now look at the ways these community power researchers answer the question "Who runs this town?" We pay special attention to two competing models of community power: the **elitist** and **pluralist models.**

The Elitist Model

"Who runs this town?" According to Floyd Hunter, a relatively small and cohesive economic elite. Many sociologists (e.g., Baltzell, 1958; Lowry, 1965) agree. Hunter's seminal study of *Community Power Structure* ([1953] 1963) found that in "Regional City" (Atlanta, Georgia), a rather small group of rich and/or socially prestigious local influentials controlled the city's decision making. These influentials, Hunter says, shared similar values and weren't, for the most part, accountable to the public.

How did Hunter arrive at his conclusions? To identify Regional City's influentials, Hunter used the method of **reputational analysis.** First, he compiled a long list of people who might exercise power in Atlanta. From various sources, Hunter constructed a preliminary list of 175 names. Second, he selected a panel of people to judge the names on the list; these judges were balanced in terms of ethnicity, religion, age, occupation, and sex. Those people receiving top ratings from the judges left Hunter with a short list of 40 names. Finally, he conducted personal interviews with all those on the short list

Fig. 12-2 ELITIST MODEL. Floyd Hunter argues that a small elite makes virtually all the important decisions in urban politics. (Richard Hedman)

accessible to him (27 persons), asking them to identify the most influential people in the city. From their replies, Hunter reached this conclusion: The community power structure of Atlanta was dominated by top executives in banking, finance, commerce, and insurance. There were also some lawyers, industry executives, and socially prominent persons, but they were far fewer in number. Interestingly, the smallest number of influentials came from the sectors of government and labor (see Table 12-1).

After establishing that Atlanta was run by a small group of business and professional people, Hunter explored the interaction among these elites. Here he used another research technique: **sociometry**, a method for studying small group interaction—who interacts with whom. By tracing what committees the top 40 participated in, on what corporate boards they sat, and to what social clubs they belonged, Hunter concluded that the most influential people in Atlanta interacted very closely. Fig. 12-3, a sociogram, depicts one aspect of this close interaction: interlocking directorates of corporate leaders. This sociogram shows graphically what one of Hunter's interviewees stated in words:

> . . . there are "crowds" in Regional City—several of them—that pretty well make the big decisions. There is the crowd I belong to (the Homer Chemical crowd); then there is the First State Bank crowd, the Regional Gas crowd, the Mercantile crowd, the Growers Bank crowd, and the like. (in Hunter, [1953] 1963:77)

These "crowds," according to people Hunter interviewed, were primarily responsible for making fundamental city decisions, such as the decision to undertake urban renewal in the downtown area. These decisions were made by informal consensus of the economic elites. Formal government decision makers, including the mayor, were only peripheral actors until the stage of implementation was reached.

In general, subsequent studies of community power which use Hunter's reputational method have come to the same conclusion: The elitist model most closely approximates the reality of community power and decision making.

The implications of Hunter's research were upsetting to those who saw city political processes (and American politics in general) as a participatory process that promoted the public interest rather than narrow private interests. Hunter's model—that elites ran the city of Atlanta and largely determined the fate of over 300,000 inhabitants (the population when he studied it)—led to more studies of community power and a competing model: the pluralist model.

The Pluralist Model

"Who runs this town?" According to a Yale political scientist's influential study, published in 1961, community power is not held by a small, cohesive economic elite. Rather, power is shared among different local elites. Investigating *Who Governs?* (1961) in New Haven, Connecticut (population then 150,000), Robert Dahl found that power in the city is broadly diffused. Decision makers in one issue area, such as education, weren't influential in another, such as urban redevelopment. Thus, Dahl concluded that pluralist democracy works at the urban level.

How did Dahl arrive at his findings? To identify community influentials, he employed **decision analysis**: observation and analysis of a political system (also termed "issue" or "event analysis"). This technique focuses on the actual decision-making process. Dahl chose three key local areas—education, urban redevelopment, and nominations for political office—and looked at decisions in each issue area made over a

Table 12-1 Policymakers in Hunter's Regional City

Type of Occupation	*Number of Leaders*	*Positions Held*
Commercial	11	President (4); chairperson of board (3); general manager (1); executive manager (1); managing editor (1)
Banking, finance, insurance	7	President (5); vice-president (1); executive vice-president (1)
Professional	6	Attorney (5); dentist (1)
Manufacturing and industry	5	Chairperson of board (3); president (2)
Leisure and socially prominent persons	5	Social leader ("high society") (5)
Government	4	Mayor (1); school superintendent (2); county treasurer (1)
Labor	2	Union president (2)

SOURCE: Adapted from Floyd Hunter, *Community Power Structure* (New York: Anchor, 1963), Table 4, p. 75.

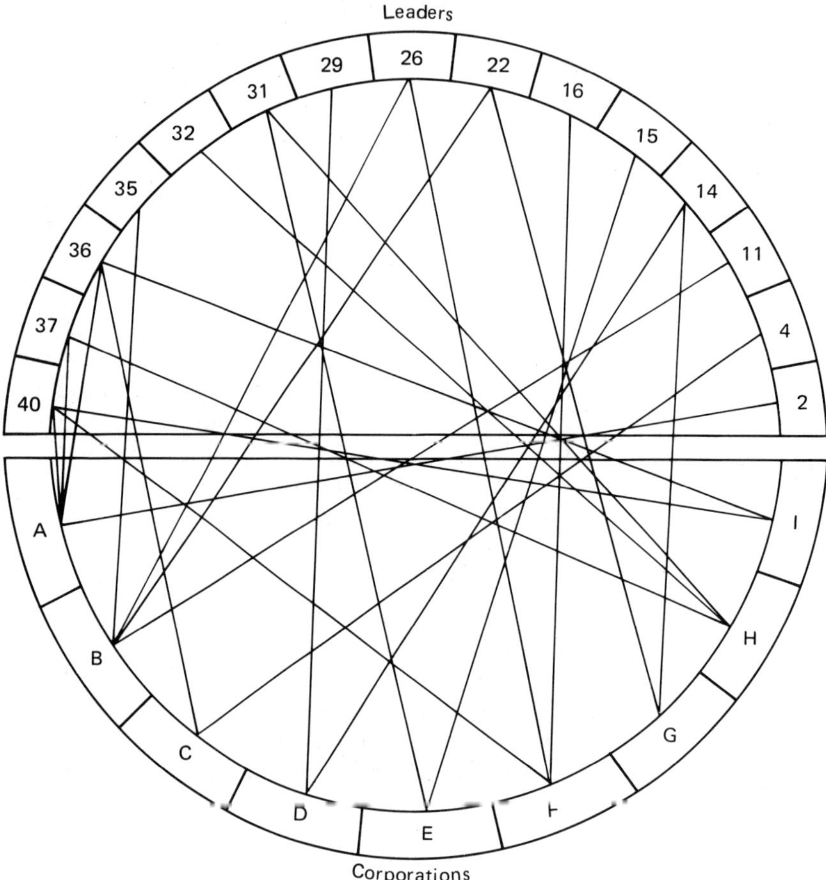

Fig. 12-3 INTERLOCKING DIRECTORATES IN REGIONAL CITY. In this sociogram, the top half of the circle identifies individual community influentials by number; the bottom half identifies Atlanta corporations by letter. The lines show the connections between the top 40 influentials and their corporations. For instance, Person 11 (bank vice-president) sits on the board of directors of Corporation B together with Persons 22, 26, and 35 (the head of a manufacturing company, the president of a chemical company, and the executive vice-president of another bank). (Floyd Hunter, *Community Power Structure* [New York: Anchor, 1963], p. 76. Copyright © 1953 by The University of North Carolina Press. Reprinted by permission.)

period of about a decade. From interviews with participants in the decisions, news accounts, written records, and observations, Dahl determined who initiated successful proposals or who successfully vetoed someone else's policy alternative. Then Dahl judged that those with the greatest proportion of successes in making public policy were the most influential leaders in New Haven.

Dahl determined that leadership in New Haven was more specialized than Hunter had found in Regional City. In Hunter's Atlanta, there was a set of interlocking relationships between a small financial-commercial elite which was influential in essentially *all* major decisions. That is, the banker or manufacturer who had a major say in redevelopment decisions also influenced education and party nomination decisions. By contrast, in New Haven, Dahl found a *specialization of influence:* "With few exceptions any particular individual exerts a significant amount of direct influence in no more than one of the three issue areas studied" (1961:181). Thus, he deduced that New Haven was not monolithic in its power sturcture. Rather, it was pluralistic. Diverse groups, each with its own sphere of influence, ran New Haven.

Dahl also found diversity among the leaders. They came from various class, white ethnic, and religious backgrounds. (Dahl didn't describe their race; presumably all were white.) No one stratum of society, he argued, produced leaders in different issue areas.

Yet Dahl did not claim that groups in New Haven shared power equally. Still, in his view, "New Haven [was] a republic of un-

Fig. 12-4 THE PLURALIST MODEL. Pluralists argue that urban politics is characterized by the representation of various interests in the community, not the domination of a cohesive elite. (© 1976 Richard Hedman)

Table 12-2 Specialized Leadership in Dahl's New Haven

Number of Actors Successful	*Redevelopment*	*Party Nominations*		*Public Education*	*Including Duplications*
		Democratic	*Republican*		
One time	19	0	4	7	30
Two or three times	5	2	2	8	17
Four or more times	2	2	3	1	8
Total	26	4	9	16	55

SOURCE: Robert Dahl, *Who Governs?* (New Haven: Yale University Press, 1961), Table 14.1, p. 181.

equal citizens—but for all that a republic" (1961:220).

The Debate Between Elitists and Pluralists

Dahl and Hunter disagreed on the role and degree of involvement of the business community in local government. For Dahl, professional politicians determined government decisions, while business executives and professionals made their mark in civic organizations. For Hunter, a commercial-financial elite informally set basic policy, later implemented by government officials.

Both Hunter and Dahl are trained social scientists, committed to scientific rigor, accuracy, and honesty. How, then, could they arrive at such different conclusions about who runs this town?

One possibility is that the towns themselves are different, and that their findings reflect significant variations between Atlanta and New Haven. However, this explanation falls apart in light of subsequent restudies of the two towns. On the one hand, a restudy of New Haven found that a big business ruling elite is in control (Domhoff, 1977). On the other hand, a restudy of Atlanta found that a series of competing coalitions exists (Jennings, 1964). Evidently, the power structures of Atlanta and New Haven aren't as different as scholars' perceptions of them.

In other words, what you see depends on how you look at it. Here are the bases for the researchers' disagreements:

1. *Differences in disciplinary perspectives.* Hunter was trained in sociology and anthropology; he emphasized social structure and social class in his analysis of community power. Instead of giving weight to the formal machinery of government, he focused on informal social networks ("crowds"). In fact, he argued that formal decision makers were brought into policymaking only *after* the real decisions had been made in the private sector. In contrast, political scientist Dahl emphasized the importance of formal government structure. He did not take a close look at extragovernmental decisionmaking. Consequently, official position (e.g., mayor) plays a much more important part in Dahl's analysis of power structures than in Hunter's work.

2. *Differences in research methods.* The elitist-pluralist debate has centered largely on this issue. Hunter's critics charge that his reputational method leads to the identification of a relatively small economic elite. Critics say that if you ask "who are the top leaders in

this town?", you will find that there is a small, cohesive leadership. In addition, critics charge that Hunter confuses the reputation for power with the substance of power. The fact that knowledgeable people think an individual exercises power is not proof; it is only hearsay evidence. Thus, Hunter and those who hold an elitist model of power are accused of lack of rigor in their methods of research.

By the same token, Dahl's critics charge that decision (or event) analysis is misleading; it leads to the identification of a pattern of broader participation in decision making than actually exists. Critics of pluralism argue that Dahl's decision analysis neglects a whole dimension of power: the ability to keep issues out of the decision-making arena altogether (Bachrach and Baratz, 1962). For example, a study that defines the issue as the decision makers did might conclude that, in the 1940s, the major issue in a Southern town was fluoridation of the water supply—that is what decision makers there might have said. Of course, this would overlook the fact that schools in that town were entirely segregated or that racial discrimination existed; these were not issues for the local policymakers. In other words, decision analysis can't investigate *nondecisions,* those that never reach the public stage (e.g., the decision to keep schools segregated). Further, Dahl's critics say that his choice of decisions to investigate—political nominations, public education, and urban redevelopment—narrowed the field of political activity and neglected broader *private sector* decisions. Finally, critics point out that Dahl gave little specific information on the decisions he studied, so that readers must take his conclusions on faith.

It is noteworthy that subsequent community power studies using Hunter's reputational technique tend to find elitist patterns of local power, while studies using Dahl's decision analysis tend to find pluralist patterns of local power. This suggests an implicit bias in the research techniques.

3. *Differences in theoretical orientation.* Hunter assumes that inherent conflict exists between social classes, that the interests of the few (the "crowds" of economic elites) run counter to the interests of the many. It follows, then, that the elites rule in their own interest, *against* the interests of the citizenry. Hunter rejects the notion that government is neutral, a mere negotiator among interest groups representing a wide spectrum of the population. By contrast, in *Who Governs?,* Dahl takes social stability for granted. Consequently, he does not explore the measures which assure social continuity (e.g., lack of information, threat of coercion). Conflict-oriented theorists criticize Dahl and pluralists generally for assuming that a political consensus exists and that this consensus works to everyone's benefit. This assumption of social harmony, critics say, prevents pluralists from studying how and in whose interests this alleged consensus is maintained. On the other hand, pluralists attack Hunter and conflict-oriented theorists generally for looking for conflict based on social class differences and therefore finding it.

4. *Differences in levels of analysis.* Hunter did discuss his influentials' ties to the federal government and foreign interests, but both Hunter and Dahl focused on the city level. Thus their differences cannot be accounted for by the level of analysis they used. Indeed, both scholars have been criticized for restricting their discussion of community power to the micro level. In his restudy of New Haven, Domhoff (1977) argues that community power in that city cannot be understood if it is not placed in a macro-political context. Domhoff believes that a national network for urban policy planning exists, and that New

Haven's suburban ruling class (which Dahl thought had withdrawn from city politics) has become part of this national network, dominating the politics and culture of the central city via decision making at the national level. Similarly, sociologists Vidich and Bensman insist that community politics cannot be understood except in the context of national life. In their study of a *Small Town in Mass Society* ([1958] 1971:320), Vidich and Bensman wrote that "Almost all aspects of [small-town life in upstate New York] were controlled by external forces over which [townspeople] had little control; the idea of democratic self-determination had no basis in fact." As we shall see in a case study of Caliente, a small town in the Western desert (Chapter 15), life-and-death community decisions are often made in places far from the community.

5. *Differences in political ideology*. Both Dahl and Hunter found relatively small numbers of people participating in community decision making. In both cases, the top leadership represented about 1/100th of the city's population. Also, they agreed that the top leaders work with a second level of minor decision makers (Dahl called them "subleaders" and Hunter called them the "understructure"), but that a very small group effectively made major decisions. Thus, their findings do not seem too different. The major difference between Hunter and Dahl lies in the interpretation of their data. And their interpretations stem from normative assumptions about how democracy *should work*.

Hunter implied that something was rotten in Atlanta; local government practice didn't live up to democratic ideals. In his view, it is not proper for a small economic elite to make decisions, for he assumes that the interests of elites are not the interests of the citizenry as a whole. Hunter found that most people are apathetic about politics because they're not consulted about decisions which affect their lives ([1953] 1963:239). Further, he found that people disadvantaged by the status quo are not an articulate group and can't make their demands known. However, Hunter didn't accept the elitist community power structure as inevitable or legitimate. He offered proposals, based on his community organization background, to bring about wider participation in local politics and to make pluralism really work.

Dahl, on the other hand, was more pessimistic when he wrote his New Haven study. He thought that the masses should not be full participants in the political process because they are the "apolitical clay" of the system (1961:227). He believed that it was better for this inert mass of clay to remain inert. People—including scholars—change their minds over the years. (Dahl has since become a member of the Democratic Socialist Organizing Committee, an organization committed to ideals closer to Hunter's proposals than to interest-group pluralism.) But in the 1950s, Dahl thought that democracy's health is best preserved by depending on the competence and standards of political elites. For this reason, some observers claim that "pluralism" is misnamed; it should be called "democratic elitism" (Bachrach, 1967).

Some critics suggest that by putting his stamp of approval on New Haven's power structure, Dahl was guilty of "ideological spleen" (Phillips, 1971–1972:85). That is, he wrote off the mass of citizens without examining why they're apathetic or ill-informed. Others charge that Hunter was too optimistic about the common people ever being full participants in the political process.

Interestingly, liberal social scientists tend to look at cities and see pluralistic power structures; radical social scientists tend to see elitist systems of power. Similarly, decentralists tend to view community power as highly concentrated; centralists tend to see a dispersion of power.

To conclude: The study of community power has attracted a variety of scholars, including those who are not often considered urbanists (e.g., Dahl and Hunter, the Lynds, and W. Lloyd Warner before them). Why? The microcosm of the city provides a testing ground for democratic theory in general. Perhaps this is the key to understanding the debate between elitists and pluralists.

Scholars engaged in the continuing debate over the nature of community power are dealing with an age-old normative question: "Who *should* govern?" Pluralists find that current decision makers—professionals, experts, members of the well-educated upper middle class, and a few lower-status people—run things in a rational, efficient, and evenhanded manner. Their rule ensures social order. Critics of pluralism, on the contrary, find that local decision makers are members of elite groups who make decisions with their own interests in mind, interests that conflict with those denied access to policymaking, particularly lower-class and lower-status people. Hunter and those using the elitist model are far less concerned with questions of efficiency and rationality in government than the pluralists; the elitists stress issues of equality and equal representation of everyone's interests. Between these two perspectives lies a chasm of difference.

Comparative Community Power Research

The debate between elitists and pluralists has not been settled. Meanwhile, some suggest revising the research question. Instead of asking, "who runs this town?" or "who governs?" an alternative question is put forward: "who governs, where, when, and with what effects?" (Clark, 1968).

This question has served as a guide for comparative studies of community power. Such studies seek to go beyond the single-city, case study approach. Their aim: to develop a general model explaining differences among cities and their power structures.

Comparative analyses of community power seek to uncover structural characteristics differentiating one community from another. Their eventual aim is to explain variations among community power structures. Factors that comparative theorists identify as influencing community power include population size, degree of heterogeneity, and attitudes toward political participation (see Box 12-1 for details).

New Directions in Community Power Research

In recent times, there have been some new approaches to studying community power. One new direction emphasizes the relationship between the type of community power structure and the public policy outputs that result from each type. Another less new but still innovative idea is to replicate a study of a representative American town over time. The so-called Middletown III project, started in 1976, promises to describe social changes in Muncie since the Lynds studied it in the 1920s and restudied it in the 1930s, thereby avoiding the "customary bad method of examining the present and guessing about the past" (Caplow, 1980:50).

CITIZEN POLITICS

Citizen Participation

Studies of community power—whether pluralist, elitist, or comparative—do not find great numbers of local citizens participating in decision making. In fact, both Hunter and

Box 12-1

FACTORS AFFECTING COMMUNITY POWER STRUCTURES

	Pluralist	*Elitist*
Population size	Large	Small
Economic system	Diversified	Monolithic
Degree of industrialization	High	Low
Strength of labor unions	Strong	Weak
Proportion of absentee business owners	Large	Small
Social composition	Heterogeneous	Homogeneous
Community and (particularly) elite attitudes toward political participation and political equality	Pro	Con
Number of secondary associations (civic organizations, social clubs, ethnic and religious organizations, etc.)	Many	Few
Partisanship in local government	Partisan	Nonpartisan
Kind of local political institutions	Nonreform	Reform
Competition among elements of the power structure	Presence of competition	Absence of competition

(Adapted from Lineberry and Sharkansky, 1971:159–61).

Dahl found tiny minorities of the population playing the game of city politics.

Pluralists assume that these actors, while small in number, represent a diversity of groups and interests. Further, they assume that political leaders don't serve the interests of one group more than another. Pluralists point to the following individuals or groups as participants in the political process, either formally or informally: (1) government officials, elected and appointed; (2) government bureaucrats; (3) business executives and business-oriented organizations (e.g., Chamber of Commerce); (4) organized labor; (5) political parties; and (6) special-interest groups and single-issue groups (e.g., Association for the Education of the Mentally Retarded, local garden club, Right to Life organization).

Radical critics of pluralism reject the idea that the power of the local garden club or the association for the mentally retarded can be equated with the power of corporate institutions. They say that, for example, to equate the PTA with Mobil or IBM is to ignore the message of George Orwell's *Animal Farm* (1954): "All animals are equal. . .but some are more equal than others."

Starting in the mid-1960s (amid the Watts,

California, race riots and other urban conflagrations), a number of activists and political theorists have been trying to change the rules of the political game. Their goal: to make the less equal a bit more equal, to bring new players into the arena of politics. More specifically, they have sought to broaden the structures of influence and power to include those who Dahl and Hunter agreed didn't participate in local policymaking: the poor and near-poor, the powerless, racial minorities, and the socially unesteemed. What they called for was **citizen participation.**

But exactly who should participate? What forms should political participation take? How much power should this long-excluded group have in making public policy? What would the stirring slogan "Power to the People" mean in practice? These questions stirred controversy and fear in the 1960s. Since that time, the focus of citizen participation has shifted, suggesting what is at stake when there is a proposed change in the political rules. Here is a brief description of events and movements that had an impact on urban politics.

In the early 1960s, the civil rights movement had mobilized large numbers of blacks, many of whom had never before voted, let alone participated in more active forms of public policymaking. In large measure, these new political players came from lower-class backgrounds and had lifestyles that differed from those of traditional decision makers. How these new players would use their potential for political power was a question in many people's minds.

In 1964 Congress passed the War on Poverty program put forward by President Lyndon B. Johnson. Then the debate over how "the people" would exercise their power heated up, for no one could predict how newly politicized blacks and others long excluded from the political process would use their resources. Under the War on Poverty program, the federal government mandated a rather vague provision for the "maximum feasible participation of the poor" in community action programs ("maxfeas" for short). This meant that poor people were supposed to participate in the planning and execution of community action programs. However, members of Congress and mayors alike had few hints that "maxfeas" would be taken seriously. When there was a surge of energy and militant action by the poor in many cities, traditional political actors were taken by surprise. And they were not happy. Some local officials developed ingenious methods of dealing with citizen participants, especially militant ones. Often they sent out what Tom Wolfe (1971) calls the "flak-catchers," low-level bureaucrats whose job entailed calming the militants down and catching their flak (see Box 12-2). Meanwhile, when the new political participants tried to secure social changes in their own interests, they were called a host of names, including "uncouth" and "un-American."

The exact intent of Congress in mandating "maxfeas" is not clear. But one thing is clear: Congress did not intend that opportunity extended to the poor and powerless should upset the traditional balance of power at the urban level. Members of Congress complained, threatening to veto funds for the War on Poverty. Democratic mayors complained to the national Democratic administration, threatening to do something if funds weren't redirected away from community groups and funneled back to city hall.

By the late 1960s, the War on Poverty had been reduced to a holding action. Vietnam gripped the nation and the federal purse; some activists switched from antipoverty to antiwar efforts, and critics raged against the program. Mayors and members of Congress had been stung by the unintended conse-

Box 12-2

AN IRREVERENT LOOK AT THE POVERTY PROGRAM

"Mau-Mauing the Flak Catchers"

The poverty office [in San Francisco] was on the first floor and had a big anteroom; only it's almost bare, nothing in it but a lot of wooden chairs. It looks like a union hall minus the spittoons. . . . It's like they want to impress the poor that they don't have leather-top desks. . . . All our money goes to you. . . .

So the [thirty-five black, Chicano, Filipino and Samoan] young aces from the Mission [a poor, ethnically mixed neighborhood] come trooping in, and they want to see the head man. The word comes out that the No. 1 man is out of town, but the No. 2 man is coming out to talk to the people.

This man comes out. . . .

"Have a seat, gentlemen," he says, and he motions toward the wooden chairs.

But he doesn't have to open his mouth. All you have to do is look at him and you get the picture. The man's a lifer. He's stone civil service. He has it all down from the wheatcolor Hush Puppies to the wash'n'dry semi-tab-collar shortsleeved white shirt. . . .

He pulls up one of the wooden chairs and sits down on it. . . .

"I'm sorry that Mr. Johnson isn't here today," he says, "but he's not in the city. He's back in Washington meeting some important project deadlines. He's very concerned, and he would want to meet with you people if he were here. . . ."

"Now I'm here to try to answer any questions I can," he says, "but you have to understand that I'm only speaking as an individual, and so naturally none of my comments are binding, but I'll answer any questions I can, and if I can't answer them, I'll do what I can to get the answers for you."

And then it dawns on you, and you wonder why it took so long for you to realize it. This man is the flak catcher. His job is to catch the flak for the No. 1 man. . . .

Everybody knows the scene is a shuck, but you can't just walk out and leave. . . . So . . . might as well get into the number. . . .

One of the Chicanos starts it off by asking the straight question, which is about how many summer jobs the Mission [community] groups are going to get. This is the opening phase, the straight-face phase, in the art of mau-mauing. . . .

"Well," says the Flak Catcher—and he gives it a twist of the head and a fling of the hand and the ingratiating smile—"It's hard for me to answer that the way I'd like to answer it. . . . But I can tell you this. At this point I see no reason why our project allocation should be any less, if all we're looking at is the urban-factor numbers for this area, because that should remain the same. . . ."

It goes on like this for a while. He keeps saying things like, "I don't know the answer to that right now, but I'll do everything I can to find out." . . .

So one of the bloods says, "Man why do you sit there shining us with this bureaucratic rhetoric, when you said yourself that ain't nothing you say that means a goddam thing?"

Ba-ram-ba-ram-ba-ram-ba-ram—a bunch of the aces start banging on the floor in union. It sounds like they have sledge hammers. . . .

"Well," says the Flak Catcher, "I can't promise you jobs if the jobs aren't available yet"—and then he looks up as if for the first time he is really focusing on the thirty-five ghetto hot dogs he is now facing. . . . They look *bad*. . . .

The Flak Catcher is still staring at them, and his shit-eating grin is getting worse. . . .

"Man," says the blood, "if you don't know nothing and you can't do nothing and you can't say nothing, why don't you tell your boss what we want!"

. . . "As I've already told you, he's in Washington trying to meet the deadlines for *your* projects!"

. . . "Shit, pick up the telephone, man!. . . . We coming back here in the morning and we gonna *watch* you call the man!"

. . . Of course, the next day nobody shows up

at the poverty office to make sure the sucker makes the telephone call. Somehow it always seems to happen that way. Nobody ever follows it up. You can get everything together once, for the demonstration, for the confrontation, to go downtown and mau-mau, for the fun, for the big show . . . but nobody ever follows it up.

. . . And then later on you think about it and you say, "What really happened that day? Well, another flak catcher lost his manhood, that's what happened." Hmmmmmmm . . . like maybe the bureaucracy isn't so dumb after all. . . . All they did was sacrifice one flak catcher, and they've got hundreds, thousands. . . . They've got replaceable parts.

. . . The poverty program not only encouraged mau-mauing, it practically *demanded* it. . . . To get a job in the post office, you filled out forms and took the civil-service exam. To get into the poverty scene, you did some mau-mauing. If you could make the flak catchers lose control of the muscles around their mouths, if you could bring fear into their faces, your application was approved. (Wolfe, 1971:130–49). Reprinted with the permission of Farrar, Straus & Giroux, Inc., from *Radical Chic & Mau-Mauing the Flak Catchers* by Thomas Wolfe. Copyright © 1970 by Thomas Wolfe.

quences of the "maxfeas" provision for citizen participation. Even the War on Poverty's sponsor, President Johnson, accused the program of being run by "sociologists and kooks." And the omnipresent Daniel Patrick Moynihan, wearing his professorial hat, argued that "maxfeas" was based on *Maximum Feasible Misunderstanding* (1969). The political backlash against "too much participation" by "the wrong kinds of people" served to emasculate the antipoverty program, and President Richard M. Nixon dismantled it during the early 1970s. (Several War on Poverty programs, however, remain in existence, notably the Legal Services Corporation; they are either administered by cabinet-level agencies or run independently.)

Even today, there is no agreement on the meaning of participation or too much participation. For some citizens, participation in politics is a spectator activity: voting, putting a bumper sticker on the car, or talking back to the TV newscaster. For others, it is more involving: writing a letter to the editor, giving money to a political candidate, joining a group with political goals. And for the relatively few, participation means stepping into the political arena: running for political office, organizing a citizen's group, lobbying government officials, advising policymakers, soliciting funds for a political party, or sponsoring an initiative or recall campaign.

Federal legislation calling for local citizen participation may have been an attempt to reach the grass roots. (The War on Poverty was only one of several federal programs in the 1960s calling for citizen participation.) Alternatively, it may have been a way of managing potential conflict in the cities, never really intended to go beyond the "grass tops."

Sherry Arnstein (1969) suggests that citizen participation is like a ladder; the bottom rungs only look like forms of participatory democracy. In her view, many forms of so-called citizen participation are deceptive illusions, designed to manipulate people or give them a chance to blow off steam. For example, suppose that a city's urban renewal agency decides to raze twenty units of low-cost housing so that a nearby hospital can use the space for expansion. At the same time, the city agency gets a Citizen's Advisory Committee to rubber-stamp the project, thus legitimizing the agency's prior decision. By manipulating the advisory group into thinking it helped to make the decision, the city can muffle complaints from the soon-to-be-homeless poor tenants. In other cases, tenants of public housing projects are brought together for cleanup campaigns, thereby diverting attention from such issues as the project's deteriorating facilities or lack of security.

On higher rungs of the participation ladder, citizen involvement may mean closing the knowledge gap between citizens and "experts." This is important, for information and access to information are key tools in decision making. Most often, access to information is monopolized by those who hold power. Or it may involve consulting people (via attitude surveys) or placating citizens. For instance, saving two or three units of low-income housing in the way of hospital expansion may placate the community, but it doesn't mean that the poor are partners in decision making.

At the top rungs of the ladder, the political have-nots either share in community power or control local institutions, such as schools or neighborhood centers.

Looking back, people who were involved in the 1960s attempts at citizen participation have mixed feelings. Some feel that it was a time of exciting experiments in social change that didn't last long. But they also wonder whether it was a cruel hoax, perpetuating political and economic inequality under the guise of equal opportunity.

Table 12-3 A Ladder of Citizen Participation

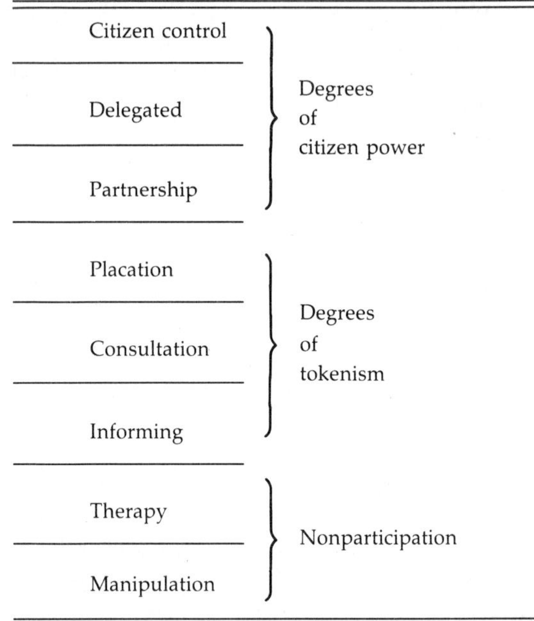

Rung	Category
Citizen control	Degrees of citizen power
Delegated	
Partnership	
Placation	Degrees of tokenism
Consultation	
Informing	
Therapy	Nonparticipation
Manipulation	

SOURCE: Sherry Arnstein, "A Ladder of Citizen Participation," *Journal of the American Institute of Planners* (July, 1969):217. Reprinted by permission of the Journal of the American Institute of Planners and the author.

Advocacy Planning

Direct citizen participation in local decision making is only one approach to broadening the structures of influence and power. Some professionals thought they could contribute to making pluralism work in another way: **advocacy planning.** Leaders of this movement, started in the late 1960s, argued that American city planning leaves out concerns of diverse groups either by accident or on purpose. They suggested providing technically skilled advocates (lawyers, architects, city planners) to represent the poor and powerless, traditionally excluded from the planning process. They thought that if low-income groups, blacks, single parents, and others each had advocate planners pressing their particular needs and interests, city planning would be more responsible to all segments of the pluralist community. Following this logic, dozens of advocacy planning centers sprang up throughout the nation in the 1960s. But by the late 1970s, advocacy planning had gone the way of citizen participation. Few practicing advocate planners remain. There are notable exceptions, many of whom are associated with "The Planners Network," facilitated by Chester Hartman (author of *Yerba Buena,* cited earlier in this chapter).

Advocacy planning was not universally well received, particularly by radical theorists. Asking "Whom does the advocate planner serve?" one critic answered, essentially, not the poor and powerless (Piven, [1970] 1975). In this view, advocacy planning merely diverts attention from important issues, focusing instead on technical details. In this way, it is argued, the interests of those who already hold power are served and the poor remain dependent on professionals.

The Politics of Turmoil

From advocacy to mass action and protests—that is what Richard A. Cloward and his colleague Frances Fox Piven (1975) see as methods with the potential to bring about social change in the interests of the poor. Cloward and Piven believe that mass disruption—not voting, bargaining, or running for political office—is the best strategy for the have-nots to gain community power.

But Cloward and Piven qualify their judgment, warning that militancy could lead to repression or even worse conditions for the poor if the timing is wrong. The 1960s were a "right time," in their view, for various macrostructural reasons (e.g., a national consciousness of poverty).

To conclude: New forms and techniques for the expression of citizen views have emerged in the last twenty years. These range from mass action (demonstrations, riots) to class action (lawsuits). Using one or more of these techniques, new players have entered the local political arena. Various subcommunities have been organized around their interests, forming a host of groups ranging from the Italian-American Anti-Defamation League and the National Welfare Rights Organization to Taxpayers for Property Tax Relief. Rarely were these new game players greeted with enthusiasm or grace by traditional community decision makers. In some cases, repression, threats, even murder accompanied the struggle for citizen politics. On the other hand, so did political accommodation. Voting rights were made secure for blacks through grass roots organizing. Legal rights for welfare clients were established via class action lawsuits. Women ran for political office in communities throughout the nation. Day-care centers were funded by cities in response to demands from community groups like Bananas. And so on.

GETTING SOMETHING DONE

Picket the mayor's office, bring a lawsuit in federal court, lobby the bureaucrats, convince the Chamber of Commerce, get professional planners to make plans, mau-mau the flak catchers, organize, build a coalition, riot, ask the ward boss. As we have just seen, these are some methods urbanites have used in the game of local politics to get what they want.

What methods work best? That depends on the particular circumstances—there is no easy or single answer. Moreover, the methods people use to reach their political goals depend on who they think runs the town. Those who side with Hunter in the community power debate might think that talking to bureaucrats in order to get their proposal enacted is a waste of time. Those who side with Dahl might lobby the functional experts on a particular issue.

To change the distribution of local governmental resources, most groups in America have worked within the existing political system, either by lobbying, organizing, bringing lawsuits, or finding—and pushing—the levers of power. This brings us back to Bananas, the day-care service group we encountered in Chapter 10.

Case Study Continued: How Bananas Learned Who Runs this Town and Got Some Things Done

Any group trying to reach its political goals has to understand the rules of the game. Bananas had to learn about formal government structure before they knew whom to approach. That learning process was accompanied by some important lessons in the structure of influence too.

Here is a summary of what Bananas learned about the nature of influence in its home town.

Political lesson 1. The city machine (or at least its shadow) lives on, even in the most reformed governments. Not the Tweed Ring of yesteryear, nor a Daley-like version—but a shadow model. In Berkeley, California (population about 115,000), there is a shadow machine which includes elected officials in the city of Berkeley, the neighboring city of Oakland, the county government, the State Assembly, and the U.S. House of Representatives. That is, a group of Democratic party politicians—ranging from the city and county to the state and national levels—works closely together on issues of common concern. Congressperson Ronald Dellums (Dem.-Calif.) is an influential member of this group, often referred to locally as "the Dellums machine."

The so-called Dellums machine doesn't look much like an old machine. It lacks strict discipline and hierarchical structure. Its goal is not spoils; its members press a particular political agenda and share a common ideological perspective. But it does work to mobilize votes and dispense benefits.

Over the course of several years, as Bananas provided services welcomed by the community and built credibility, they found that they could work with members of the Dellums machine. And Bananas found that things got done when Dellums called a State Assemblyman, who in turn talked to a Berkeley City Council member and a County Supervisor about space for a day-care center. In the past, Bananas had asked, written memos, talked, demonstrated, and lobbied. Now it took only a few phone calls from the right people to bring action. According to Bananas member Arlyce Curry (1978), the group could never have gotten funding from the city of Berkeley or accomplished many of its goals without the backing of the Dellums machine.

Political lesson 2. In local government, there is usually more than one coalition; a group trying to obtain something can work with several coalitions. As in many cities, Berkeley politics has various coalitions. Aside from the Dellums group, there is the Berkeley Democratic Club (a group of more middle-of-the-road liberals than members of the Dellums machine). Bananas didn't deal with the Democratic Club for several years. But as this group gained more seats on the City Council (and the Dellums-supported group lost seats), Bananas found that it had to work with another ally.

Political lesson 3. Ethnicity and race are important factors in city politics; compromise among different ethnic groups often entails conflict. Today, Bananas is a multiracial group. But it began as a mainly white group which splintered from a biracial day-care organization. The split between blacks and whites centered on jobs and services: who would work at the day-care centers and which community (black or white) would receive more services. For some time, tempers ran high as the black-dominated group charged racism, and Bananas's staff accused them of racial power plays. Meanwhile, the black-dominated group received city funds for day care and Bananas didn't. As Bananas appealed to a broader constituency and became known as a resource for other day-care groups (including a Chicano group which Bananas helped to obtain city space), it gained credibility. Finally, after five years of grass roots organizing, a new Berkeley city manager, himself a black, decided to mediate between the black and white groups. After about six months of negotiations, the city's day-care budget was split, half going to the black-dominated group and half to Bananas. Later, Bananas expanded its membership and became a multiracial group.

Political lesson 4. Never underestimate the power of good will and mutual aid. Bananas alone was weaker than Bananas supported by a range of community interests: single parents, feminists, day-care center operators, and community service agencies.

In short, Bananas learned the facts of community political life by personal experience. Members of the group spent years of hard work learning how to accomplish their goals. Understanding the informal power structure was a major element in their eventual success.

ANOTHER LOOK

Urban politics, using either peaceful methods of compromise and negotiation, back-room deals, or more militant techniques of confrontation, is a process that determines who gets what from the public purse. The history of U.S. cities shows that both formal and informal power structures are used and manipulated by people seeking public resources.

The way groups play the political game depends on how they think it works. And the way scholars describe the structure of community power depends on their research methods, political ideology, level of analysis, theoretical orientation, and intellectual discipline. The debate between pluralists and elitists illustrates once again that what you see depends on how you look at it.

It is also noteworthy that scholars do agree on one point: The number of people involved in making key decisions affecting a city's distribution of resources is very few, relatively speaking. Is this good or bad? Here scholars disagree. Some fear hyperpluralism and the consequent government by bureaucrats or paralysis of policymaking. Others are more frightened by the notion that small elites control the quality of urban life. Still others suggest that the issue is essentially false, for the whole idea of local control is mere illusion anyway; key decisions affecting cities are no longer made there, for the growth of big business and big government has changed the nature of politics. In this view, significant decisions with political impact—where a new company will locate and pay taxes, how much federal aid the city will get, and so on—are made far away from the city, with little citizen participation.

What can concerned citizens do to make an impact in city politics? Again, the answers to this question depend on how the problem is defined. In the last decade or so, the solutions have ranged from citizen initiatives to cut taxes and attempts at organizing around single issues to efforts at forming broad-based decentralist groups which seek to increase community control over resources. And then there are those who have fled big cities, either to nonmetropolitan small towns or idealistic communities like Cerro Gordo, Oregon. Or to survival outposts like those in rural California where small groups, outfitted with a year's supply of canned food and an armory of guns, wait for the total collapse of the cities. These too are solutions to urban problems of powerlessness, apparently pursued mainly by those who were not traditionally excluded from the political process: highly trained, upper-status whites. Does this mean that in American cities today, even the powerful feel powerless? If so, can we expect a revolt of the professionals? New coalitions between strange political bedfellows, perhaps capitalist communalists and utopian socialists? Changes in formal structure that would recognize the diversity of interest groups in a heterogeneous society? Or the appearance of a savior on a white horse, offering easy answers to difficult questions? So many questions, so few sure indicators.

PROJECTS

1. **Community power.** Do a reputational study of power in your community. The simplest form might consist of having professors at your college or university list the most influential people in the community. More time-consuming and more valuable studies would involve surveys of several different types of "knowledgeables" and/or use of an expert panel with follow-up interviews, asking those who score high on the list to identify powerful actors in the community.

2. **Community power.** Do a decisional study in your community. A simple approach would be to analyze who participated in two or more issues, based on newspaper coverage of the issues. Content analysis of news articles could be supplemented by one or more of the techniques used by Dahl: interviews, direct observation (e.g., attending sessions of formal decision-making bodies), and examination of historical records.

SUGGESTIONS FOR FURTHER LEARNING

For a case study of coalition politics, see Chester Hartman, *Yerba Buena: Land Grab and Community Resistance in San Francisco* (San Francisco: Glide, 1973). City planner Hartman provides details on a complex battle between downtown groups and neighborhood residents over a large-scale redevelopment project.

The classic statement of the elitist model of community power is Floyd Hunter's *Community Power Structure* (New York: Anchor, [1953] 1963). The classic opposing statement from the pluralist perspective is Robert Dahl's *Who Governs?* (New Haven: Yale University Press, 1961). Comparative community power studies are collected in an anthology by Terry Clark, *Community Structure and Decision Making* (San Francisco: Chandler, 1968), a book for advanced students. A thorough annotated bibliography of the community power literature through 1972 is James H. Svara and Willis D. Hawley, *The Study of Community Power: A Bibliographic Review* (Santa Barbara, Calif.: ABC-Clio, 1972).

For case studies of community power in the pluralist tradition, see Roscoe Martin et al., *Decisions in Syracuse: A Metropolitan Action Study* (Bloomington: Indiana University Press, 1961); Linton C. Freeman, *Patterns of Local Community Leadership* (Indianapolis: Bobbs-Merrill, 1968); and Wallace S. Sayre and Herbert Kaufman, *Governing New York City* (New York: Russell Sage, 1960). For case studies in the elitist tradition, see Ritchie P. Lowry's study of "Micro City" (Chico, California), *Who's Running This Town?* (New York: Harper & Row, 1965); August E. Hollingshead's study of Morris, Illinois (studied also by W. Lloyd Warner and named "Jonesville"), *Elmstown's Youth* (New York: Wiley, 1949); and C. Wright Mills's study of a Midwestern city of 60,000 people, "The Middle Classes in Middle-Sized Cities" in the *American Sociological Review* (11: 520–29).

For an examination of the influence of external factors on small-town political life, see Don Martindale and R. Galen Hanson, *Small Town and the Nation: The Conflict of Local and Translocal Forces* (Westport, Conn.: Greenwood, 1969), and Roland J. Pellegrin and Charles Coates's study of Baton Rouge, Louisiana (called "Big Town" in the study), "Absentee-Owned Corporations and Community Power Structure" in the *American Journal of Sociology* (61:413–19).

In *Political Influence* (New York: Free Press,

1961), political scientist Edward C. Banfield presents what he calls "a new theory of urban politics," focusing on Chicago's political "realities."

"New Directions in Power Structure Research" is the theme of a special issue of *The Insurgent Sociologist,* edited by G. William Domhoff (Ann Arbor, Mich., 1979).

Sherry Arnstein describes the experience of citizen participation in the federal Model Cities program and develops her model of participation in "A Ladder of Citizen Participation" in *Journal of the American Institute of Planners* (35,4:16–24).

Daniel Patrick Moynihan attacks the concept of "maximum feasible participation" in *Maximum Feasible Misunderstanding* (New York: Free Press, 1969), arguing that federal policymakers had no clear theory of what they meant by the phrase, and that in practice, "maxfeas" was a disaster.

A tongue-in-cheek work of New Journalism satirizing community participation and the antipoverty programs is Tom Wolfe's "Mau-Mauing the Flak Catchers" in *Radical Chic and Mau-Mauing the Flak Catchers* (New York: Bantam, 1971), which describes how San Francisco poverty groups (black, Chicano, and Samoan) confront minor government officials in a ritualized manner in order to rip off poverty program money.

The classic statement of advocacy planning is Paul Davidoff's 1965 article, "Advocacy and Pluralism in Planning," in *Journal of the American Institute of Planners* (31,4:332–37). Davidoff argues in favor of a system in which disparate community interests would be represented by advocate planners. An incisive critique of advocacy planning from an explicitly radical perspective is Frances Fox Piven, "Whom Does the Advocate Planner Serve?" in *Social Policy* (May/June, 1970) and reprinted in Richard A. Cloward and Frances Fox Piven, *The Politics of Turmoil* (New York: Vintage, [1970] 1975). Piven argues that naive advocate planners who get community groups involved in "planning" actually do them a disservice. This diverts them from the more important mass disruptive actions they might take. Poor people's problems, Piven argues, involve political power—not devising technically better plans.

Informal local government processes are examined in *How Things Get Done* (NET, 1964) and *Citizen Harold* (National Film Board of Canada, 1972). The former describes coalition politics and local government processes; the latter, bureaucracy and change in city hall in a Canadian setting. Two films on citizen participation taking an extremely positive view of the future of the now-defunct Model Cities program are *Cities in Quest of Tomorrow* (National Audiovisual Center, 1970) and *The Process Works* (National Audiovisual Center, 1971).

KEY TERMS

Advocacy planning A means by which professionals (city planners, lawyers, etc.) offer technical assistance to those claiming that their interests are inadequately represented or hurt by official government bodies.

Citizen participation The concept of trying to actively involve a wide range of citizens affected by government programs in their design and implementation.

Decision analysis A research technique, associated with Robert Dahl, used to gain an understanding of how a political system works. It involves the observation and analysis of decision making and actors involved in making decisions. The decision analyst attempts to find out who made important decisions and how they were made by observing events directly, analyzing historical records, and interviewing participants in the decision (e.g., urban renewal project sites).

Elitist model of community power A model, associated with Floyd Hunter, that describes urban politics as dominated by a relatively small, cohesive elite, primarily from the private business sphere.

Pluralist model of community power A model, associated with Robert Dahl, that describes urban politics as pluralistic in terms of the individuals or groups represented in decision making, with no one dominant group.

Reputational analysis A research technique, associated with Floyd Hunter, used to gain an understanding of how a political system works. It involves surveying the opinions of knowledgeable persons in the community about who makes key decisions.

Sociometry The study of the network of relationships among members of a group. The patterns of interaction in a group can be presented diagrammatically, using a sociogram.

REFERENCES

Arnstein, Sherry
1969 "A ladder of citizen participation." Journal of the American Institute of Planners 35,4:216–24.

Bachrach, Peter
1967 The Theory of Democratic Elitism: A Critique. Boston: Little, Brown.

Bachrach, Peter and Morton S. Baratz
1962 "The two faces of power." American Political Science Review 56:947–52.

Baltzell, E. Digby
1958 Philadelphia Gentlemen. Glencoe, Ill.: Free Press.

Caplow, Theodore
1980 "Middletown fifty years after." Contemporary Sociology 9:46–50.

Clark, Terry
1968 Community Structure and Decision Making: Comparative Analyses. San Francisco: Chandler.

Cloward, Richard A. and Frances Fox Piven
1975 The Politics of Turmoil. New York: Vintage.

Curry, Arlyce
1978 Personal interview. Berkeley, Calif., July 21.

Dahl, Robert
1961 Who Governs? Democracy and Power in an American City. New Haven: Yale University Press.

Domhoff, G. William
1977 Who Really Rules? New Haven and Community Power Reexamined. New Brunswick, N.J.: Transaction.

Hartman, Chester
1973 Yerba Buena: Land Grab and Community Resistance in San Francisco. San Francisco: Glide.

Hunter, Floyd
[1953]
1963 Community Power Structure: A Study of Decision Makers. New York: Anchor.

Jennings, M. Kent
1964 Community Influentials: The Elites of Atlanta. Glencoe, Ill.: Free Press.

Lineberry, Robert L. and Ira Sharkansky
1971 Urban Politics and Public Policy, 2d ed. New York: Harper & Row.

Lowry, Ritchie
1965 Who's Running This Town? Community Leadership and Social Change. New York: Harper & Row.

Lynd, Robert S. and Helen M. Lynd
[1929]
1956 Middletown. New York: Harcourt Brace & World.
1937 Middletown in Transition. New York: Harcourt Brace & World.

Moynihan, Daniel Patrick
1969 Maximum Feasible Misunderstanding. New York: Free Press.

Orwell, George
1954 Animal Farm. New York: Harcourt Brace & World.

Phillips, E. Barbara
1971–
1972 "You've repossessed my bootstraps, so brother, can you spare a dime?: the liberal paradigm of political economy in theory and practice." Maxwell Review 8: 59–95.

Piven, Frances Fox
[1970]
1975 "Whom does the advocate planner serve?"

Pp. 43–53 in Richard A. Cloward and Frances Fox Piven, The Politics of Turmoil. New York: Vintage.

Vidich, Arthur and Joseph Bensman
[1958]
1971 Small Town in Mass Society: Class, Power, and Religion in a Rural Community. Garden City, N.Y.: Doubleday.

Wolfe, Tom
1971 "Mau-mauing the flak catchers." Pp. 117–84 in Tom Wolfe, Radical Chic and Mau-Mauing the Flak Catchers. New York: Bantam.

PART FIVE
Space and Place

Allan Jacobs

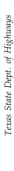

Texas State Dept. of Highways

CHAPTER 13
City Form and Space

For the tourist, a city proudly presents its unique face—its French Quarter, Fisherman's Wharf, Eiffel Tower, or Bronx Zoo (but not its South Bronx). Often there's a special tour bus with oversize windows so that visitors can admire the local landmarks.

Urban geographers may be interested in these unique features of a city, asking how and why they happen to be there. In addition, they would look for patterns in city form and space. Hiking around a city, an urban geographer might notice the following kinds of spatial features:

1. Residences of affluent and poor people, segregated in different neighborhoods.
2. A CBD with its higher concentration of skyscrapers than in suburban fringe areas.
3. Shops selling specialized items, such as sheet music for the harpsichord or Makonde wood carvings from East Africa, located in nonresidential areas.
4. Children's playgrounds, located outside the CBD.

These observations can be used to generate statements of relationship (hypotheses) about city form and space. One hypothesis is the following: People and activities are not randomly distributed throughout a city or metropolitan area; particular spatial patterns exist which are influenced by economic and social forces.

Measuring these nonrandom spatial patterns and theorizing about why they take the forms they do have been largely the domain of geographers. Yet, as is so often the case in urban scholarship, disciplinary boundaries are blurred. Among the disciplines and subfields concerned with city space are economic geography, cultural geography, political science, sociology, history, anthropology, archeology, and city planning.

This chapter draws on those disciplines and subfields to describe, explain, and predict the existence of particular spatial patterns both among and within cities. We begin with a discussion of the **system of cities**—how cities are arranged *in relation to each other*. Then we examine the **internal structure of the city**—how spatial patterns are arranged *within* modern U.S. cities.

THE SYSTEM OF CITIES

Cities are of different sizes and types, and they serve different needs. People living in a small rural community can buy some essentials (milk, gasoline) locally. But they would have to travel to a larger town for more specialized goods and services. To find a store that has a large selection of wallpaper, for instance, they would have to go to a nearby medium-size town. And if they were interested in seeing an opera, they'd have to go to a much larger city.

At each level of city size, then, there is likely to be a different degree of specialization in terms of the goods and services available. The general rule is this: The larger the *population* of the city (not the physical size), the more varied the available commodities and services. In brief, a *hierarchy* or *system of cities* exists.

Fig. 13-1 illustrates this systematic arrangement of cities. It shows how different cities in one region, the upper Midwest, provide different types of services. The very smallest cities (the shortest column on the diagram) have minimum convenience facilities—eating places, banks, hardware store, drug store, and gas stations. They may also contain some other functions—any two of several functions, such as a fish store or garage. The next category of city—a full-convenience city—contains all the above plus some other functions, such as a furniture store and laundry. The largest city(s) in the region—a primary wholesale/retail city—has a full array of functions, from the most unspecialized (grocery stores) to very specialized (wholesale bulk oil stores).

In this urban hierarchy or system of cities, there are many more smaller cities and hamlets—with few available goods and services—than larger urban places. These

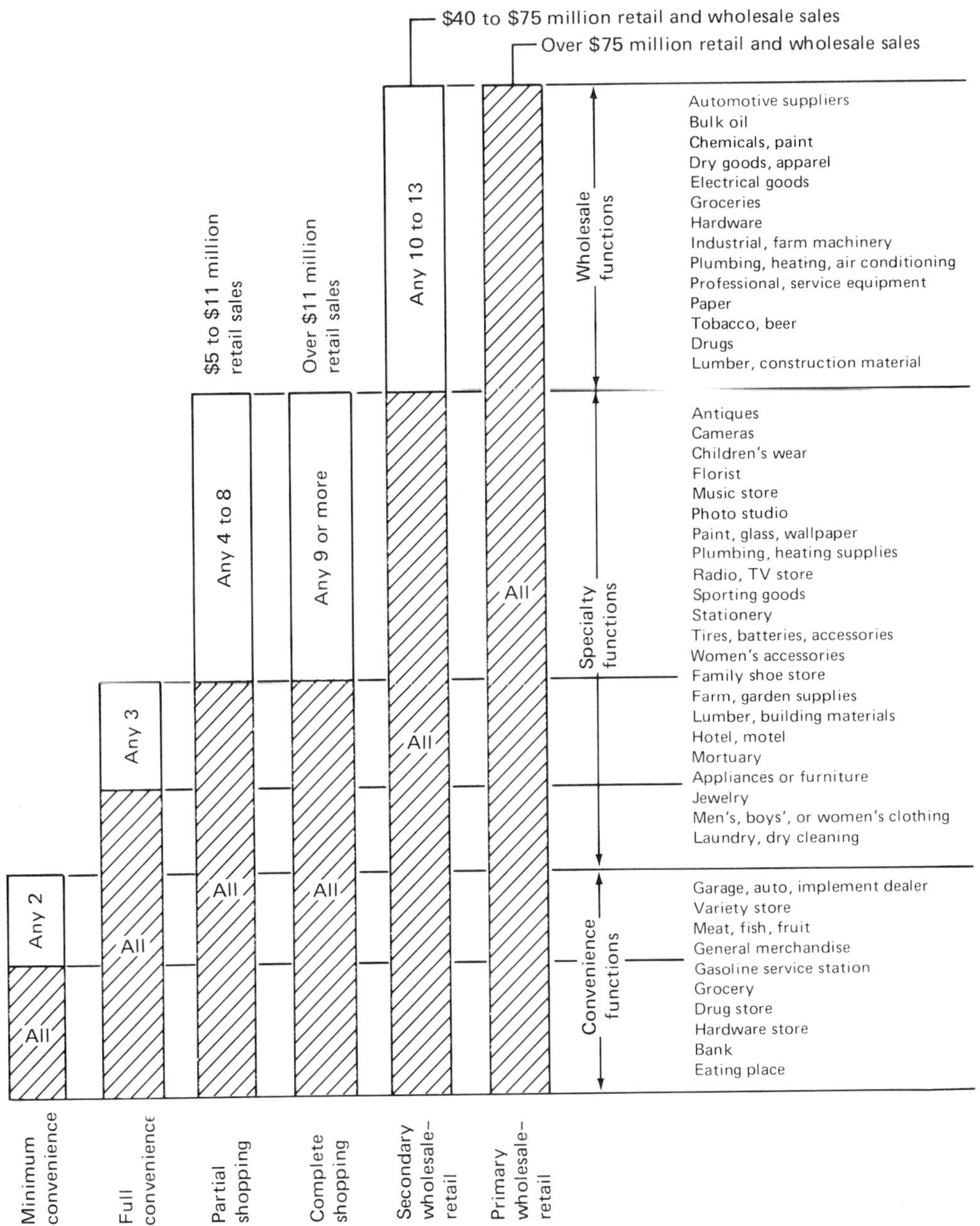

Fig. 13-1 GOODS TRADED IN CITIES AT DIFFERENT LEVELS IN THE HIERARCHY. (John R. Borchert, "The Urbanization of the Upper Midwest," *Upper Midwest Economic Study,* Urban Report No. 2 [Minneapolis, February 1963], Figure 4, p. 12. Reprinted by permission of John R. Borchert.)

unspecialized small communities are also the most widely distributed throughout a geographical region. In the upper Midwest, for instance, small communities with a restaurant (but no jewelry store) are numerous and widely distributed throughout the region. There are many fewer partial shopping cities with jewelry stores and some other specialty functions. And there are very few large cities with wholesale bulk oil and other highly specialized stores. These larger cities are centrally located in the region, providing goods and services to the surrounding area.

Central Place Theory

These centrally located cities—central places—have been a focus of urban geography since the early 1930s. At that time German geographer Walter Christaller developed what is called **central place theory**. Since Christaller's seminal work, urban geographers have expanded on his insights.

Central place theory attempts to demonstrate a relationship between the number, importance, and distance of cities from one another within a geographical area or region. It deals with two key variables: city *importance* (roughly measured by population size) and *distance* to other cities and urban communities.

Christaller's theory of central places (cities) is as follows. Using deductive reasoning, Christaller argued that a central place would provide goods and services to people living in a surrounding region, commonly referred to as a "hinterland." He thought that a hierarchy of goods and services would be available (ranging from the lowest to the highest order of services available), depending on the importance or population size of the city. Central places of the lowest order (small towns) would serve only a nearby area. Central places of a higher order (larger towns and cities) would serve a roughly circular area covering a larger surrounding region; this region might contain several lower-order central places. Finally, a large, region-serving city would serve a roughly circular area around it which might contain many other lower-order central places.

But there is a problem. If each city serves a surrounding area which is *circular* in shape, some communities would fall between the boundaries of the circles and not be served by any central place. Moving the circles together solves the problem of underservice but creates a new one: overlaps, thus overservice. To correct for these problems of underservice or overservice, Christaller theorized that the area surrounding central places would not be circular. Instead, the area would be shaped like a hexagon—which fills the complete area, leaving no unserved spaces (as in Fig. 13-2).

According to central place theory, small towns and cities (providing the most basic goods and services) will serve small hexagonal regions. It follows logically that the largest city in the region (the one with the opera house) would serve the largest hexagonal area and be centrally located in terms of its region.

One way to understand central place theory is to recall an old cliché: "cities can't exist if residents do nothing but take in each other's laundry." In other words, there must be economic interaction and exchange between a city and the world outside if the city is to stay viable.

Central place theory conceives of cities as part of a regional landscape, not as self-sufficient economic entities. Various commodities and services must be exchanged. Some items or information will be "exported" from the city, such as banking services or manufactured goods. These will be exchanged for food, wood, and other things that the city

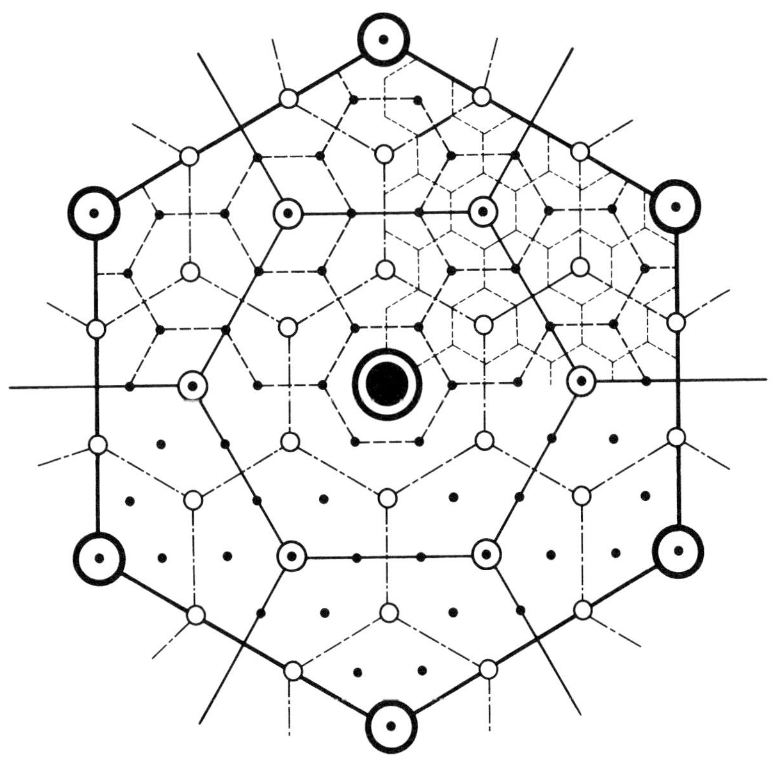

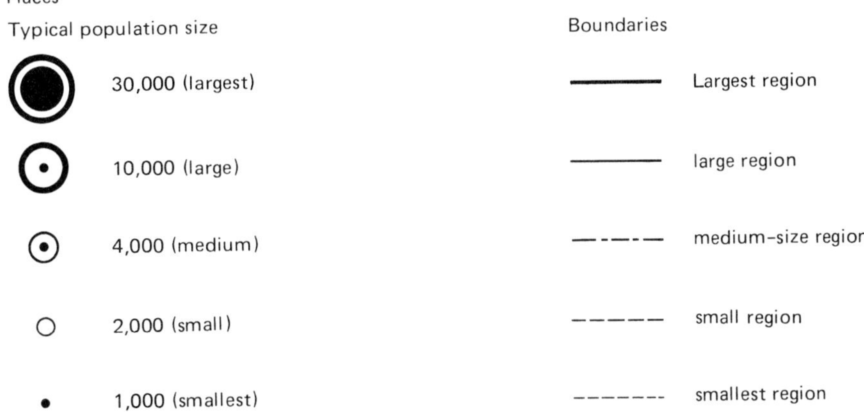

Fig. 13-2 MARKETING REGIONS IN A SYSTEM OF CENTRAL PLACES. According to Walter Christaller, the largest central place in the region illustrated (population size: 30,000) is the most important marketing center for a large hexagonal region around it. Progressively smaller central places lie at the center of a system of smaller hexagonal marketing regions within the main marketing region. (Walter Christaller, *Central Places in Southern Germany* [Englewood Cliffs, N.J.: Prentice-Hall, 1966], p. 66. Copyright © 1933 by Gustav Fisher Verlag Jena. Reprinted by permission.)

"imports." This simple import-export model holds for twentieth-century supercities just as it did for urban specks in a rural world some 5,000 years ago.

Central place theorists use two measures to determine the level of economic interchange between a city and its outside world. These measures are hinterland and range.

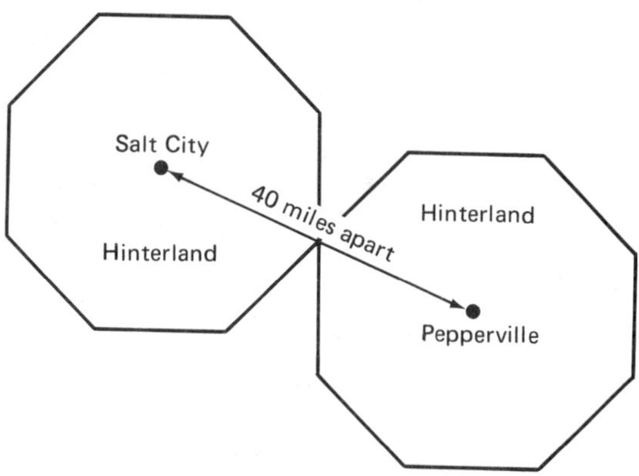

Fig. 13-3 HINTERLANDS OF TWO HYPOTHETICAL CITIES. Dots show the location of two central places (Salt City and Pepperville); outside lines show the extent of the hinterland.

Hinterland

As noted, a city (central place) provides a number of goods and services for its surrounding area. That area is commonly called the city's **hinterland.** In other words, hinterland refers to a city's sphere of influence.

Imagine, for example, two cities—Salt City and Pepperville—located on flat land, each with one daily newspaper. People in Salt City read their daily, the *Eagle,* and residents of Pepperville read their paper, the *Daily Planet*. But which paper will outlying rural people read? Those around Salt City will be most interested in the news, supermarket ads, and entertainment of their central place, Salt City. So, the *Eagle* would be the dominant newspaper in a roughly hexagonal area around Salt City. The *Daily Planet* would dominate Pepperville's hinterland for the same reasons.

The boundaries for a city's hinterland depend on the particular activity in question. A hinterland as measured by newspaper readership will undoubtedly be larger in area than a hinterland as measured by bakery deliveries. For each of these activities (newspaper readership, bakery deliveries, bank deposits, grocery shopping, commuting to work, etc.), a researcher could empirically determine the spatial extent of a city's hinterland.

Fig. 13-4 shows different ways of measuring the extent of the Mobile, Alabama, hinterland. The hinterland as determined by retail trade is quite small because people tend to shop near their homes. The hinterland as measured by newspaper readership is rather large.

Knowing the extent of a city's hinterland is useful for various planning purposes. Newspapers, for instance, want to include news and advertisements of interest to readers in their entire market area. Transportation planners need to know the outer limits of the hinterland in order to best serve all potential users.

It is interesting to note that both Walter Christaller and Robert E. Park thought that metropolitan influence could be measured by communication patterns. In Christaller's case, he conducted empirical research on the location of telephones in southern Germany. Sociologist Park believed that newspaper circulation would be a good indicator of the extent of a city's hinterland.

Christaller ([1933] 1966) noted that *geo-*

graphical distance is not really important in measuring the hinterland. What is important is *economic* distance. Here Christaller recognized that the real world was much more complicated than his simple, symmetrical model of hexagonal service areas. The real world has all sorts of factors—topographical (e.g., mountains, lakes) and sociopolitical (e.g., territorial boundaries between nations)—which could alter the hexagonal patterns of exchange between a central place and its hinterland. Thus, he advocated using economic distance as a measure of hinterland, for it takes into account diverse variables, including the costs of travel and shipping.

Range

Range may be conceptualized as the area from which persons travel to the central place

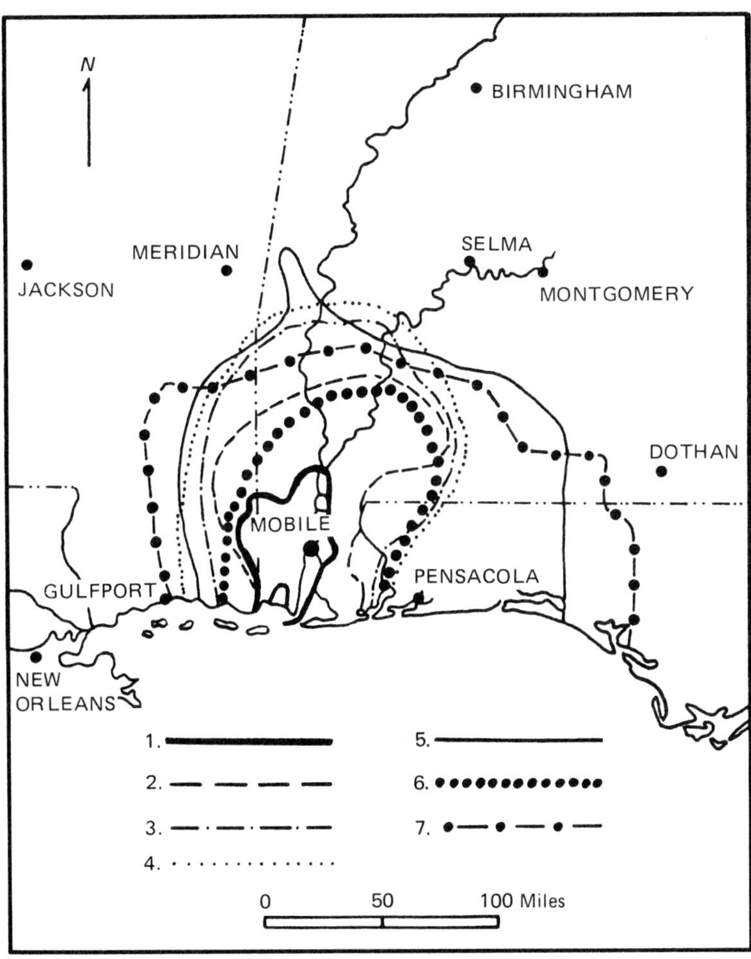

Fig. 13-4 SERVICE AREAS OF MOBILE, ALABAMA. In addition to (1) the boundary of the area within which 60 percent or more of the retail business is done in Mobile, the map shows the areas within which Mobile services 50 percent or more of the (2) wholesale grocery, (3) wholesale meat, (4) wholesale produce, and (5) wholesale drug business. Two newspaper boundaries are shown: the first (6) enclosing the area within which Mobile newspapers have 50 percent or more of the out-of-town circulation and the second (7) enclosing the area within which Mobile newspapers have at least 15 to 20 percent of the out-of-town circulation. (Edward L. Ullman, "Mobile: Industrial Seaport and Trade Center" [Chicago: University of Chicago, 1943], Fig. 7. Copyright 1943 by the University of Chicago, Dept. of Geography. Reprinted by permission.)

to purchase a service or merchandise (such as a baseball game or gasoline) offered there. A range has a *lower* and an *upper* limit. The lower limit of the range is the radius that encloses the minimum number of consumers necessary to provide a sales volume adequate for the good to be supplied; this number is also referred to as the *threshold*. For example, a baker would have to have enough customers near enough to buy bread before opening a bakery. The area in which these customers live is the *lower* limit of a range. The *upper* limit of the range is defined as the maximum distance from which people will come to the central place to purchase the good. For example, if bread costs fifty cents a loaf, the full cost of bread plus other costs (transportation expenses, lost work time) for someone next door to the bakery would be fifty cents. For someone a block away, the cost might be five cents more. Thus the cost of bread to that person would be fifty-five cents. At a certain point—the upper limit of a range—the cost of traveling to the bakery becomes too high. At this point, a potential customer will either purchase bread elsewhere, do without it, or substitute something for it, perhaps crackers.

To conclude: Christaller's classic theory of a system of cities, central place theory, is based on the idea that a central place (a city or urban community) serves a hexagonally shaped hinterland surrounding it. Small cities fit into a hierarchy in which larger cities serve larger hexagonal areas, encompassing some smaller towns and cities. Each city is functionally tied to its surrounding area. The extent of the hinterland varies for different products and services exchanged. The range also depends on the product in question; generally, people are unwilling to travel great distances for essential goods, and thus they are more widely distributed over regional space. The lower and upper limits of a range determine what goods and services will be available in a central place.

Does Central Place Theory Really Work?

Social science theories and models aim to explain and/or predict something. How useful is Christaller's model in explaining or predicting the number, size, and spacing of cities within a region?

Christaller's theory works best under the conditions that his model assumes: flat land areas with a uniformly distributed population and a relatively unspecialized economy. Thus, in places like parts of Iowa, the Canadian province of Saskatchewan, and Snohomish County in Washington state, where these conditions exist, there is an observable hierarchy of cities (Berry and Garrison, 1958; Berry, Barnum, and Tennant, 1962; Hodge, 1965). In Snohomish County, for example, central places can be arranged in three categories according to the presence of urban functions: hamlets, villages, and towns.

Of course, Snohomish County has a much simpler economy than Cook County, Illinois, or other nonagricultural areas. So, the question is this: Does central place theory accurately describe current spatial patterns in regions with nonagricultural, advanced economies? Geographer Allen Pred (1977) thinks not.

Pred points out that city systems in advanced economies like the United States are quite different from those in southern Germany in the 1930s, where Christaller conducted his research. One big difference is that the American economy today is dominated by very large firms, and this trend continues apace. Between 1960 and 1973, the number of domestic and foreign jobs controlled by the 500 largest U.S. corporations grew more than 68 percent—to a total of 15.5

million jobs (Pred, 1977:99). Most of these corporations, Pred observes, are multilocational, carrying on their activities in more than one place.

A map that Pred developed shows the location of jobs controlled by business organizations located in the San Francisco-Oakland-San Jose megalopolitan complex (see Fig. 13-5). In all, multilocational business firms in the Bay Area control jobs in 234 other metropolitan centers in the United States and Canada.

It is clear from Pred's map that many people working in one part of the nation are occupationally tied to some remote headquarters. Safeway Stores, for example, has its headquarters in the San Francisco Bay Area, but it is a national chain, employing people in hundreds of localities from Anchorage, Alaska, to Little Rock, Arkansas, and Washington, D.C.

Pred offers additional empirical evidence which calls into question Christaller's model of a system of cities. According to Christaller's model, it could be predicted that the very largest city in a system of cities—in the United States, New York City—would contain the headquarters of the nation's largest business corporations. Yet Pred found that only one-quarter of the 500 largest U.S. corporations were headquartered in New York City. Indeed, many of the top 500 were located in relatively small communities. Pred concludes that in an economic world of multilocational business enterprises (which make location decisions on the basis of many complex factors), central place theory tells only part of the story.

Pred's findings have important policy consequences. Many regional planners, trying to improve the economic situation of depressed areas such as Appalachia, assume that a large-scale investment in a city will primarily benefit that city and its nearby hinterland. This seems logical enough: Build a large factory in a depressed city, and most of the "secondary benefits" will occur nearby. Not necessarily, says Pred. Given the multilocational interdependencies of the modern corporation, a new microwave oven factory in Wheeling, West Virginia, will provide jobs in that Appalachian city, but the nonlocal growth impact of the new factory is likely to be felt in far-flung cities. The new factory in Wheeling can create openings in the Houston headquarters for junior management executives and jobs in San Diego for blue-collar workers who make oven parts.

Despite their serious differences over how the system of cities works, Christaller's model and Pred's critique of that model share a common assumption: functional interdependence. Or, to paraphrase poet John Donne, no city is an island. That is, cities and their hinterlands are interdependent in terms of economic functions. Christaller, of course, assumed that hinterlands would depend essentially on a nearby central place. Pred, in effect, reconceptualizes the notion of hinterland, suggesting that the nation—indeed the world—can be a central place's hinterland.

Classifying Cities by Function

The same assumption—functional interdependence—is also basic to another way of examining the system of cities. This approach, in the typological tradition of theory building, uses the *principal function* performed by a city as its key variable for classifying city types. It recognizes that some cities serve as central places while others specialize in one kind of activity, such as recreation or mining.

Since the early 1940s, geographers have constructed a series of typologies designed to classify cities according to their dominant function (cf. Murphy, 1974:101–24; Yeates

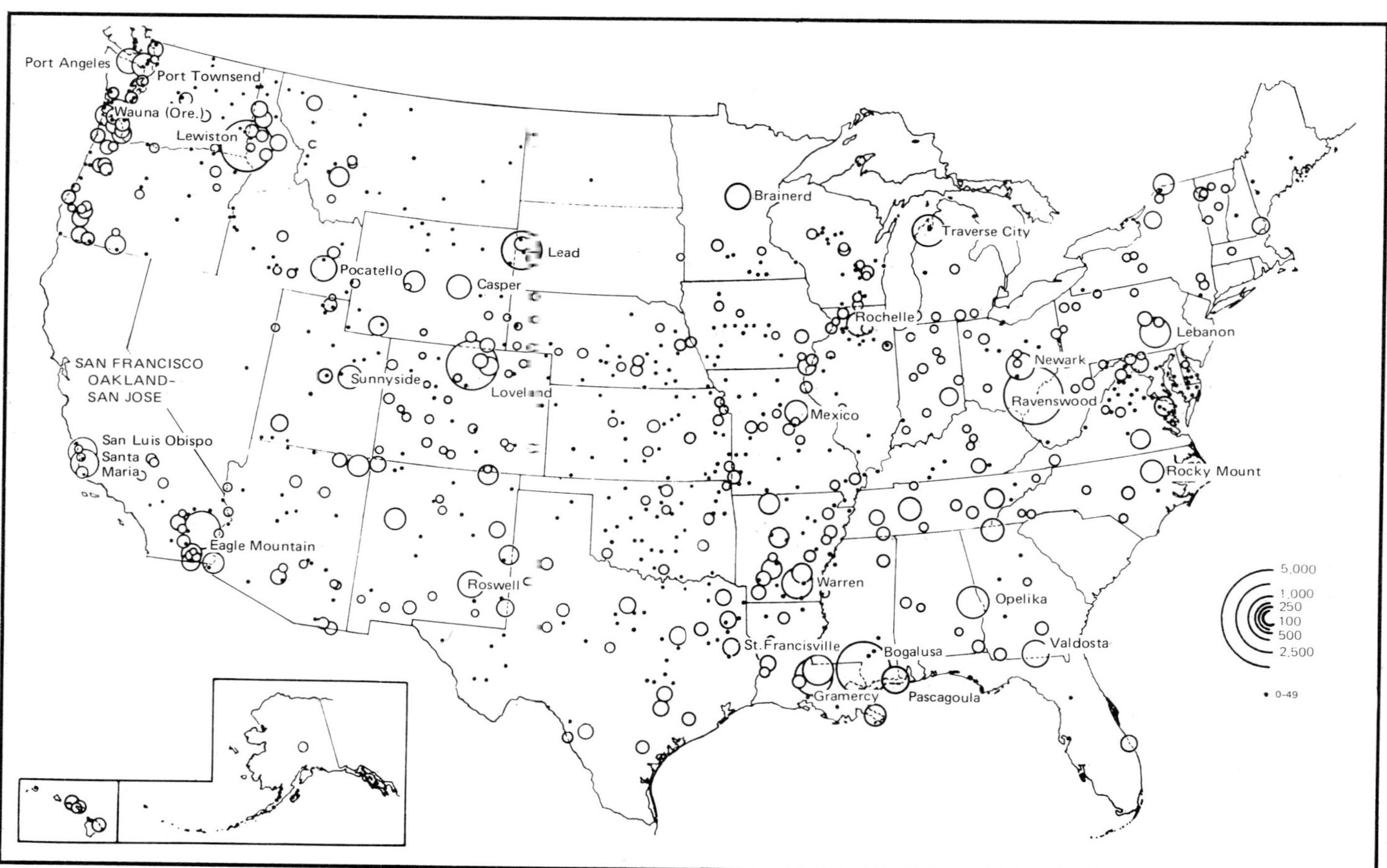

Fig. 13-5 JOBS LOCATED IN ONE GEOGRAPHICAL AREA ARE OFTEN CONTROLLED FROM A DIFFERENT GEOGRAPHICAL AREA. Allen Pred's map shows where multilocational business organizations, headquartered in the San Francisco-Oakland-San Jose metropolitan complex, control jobs outside the surrounding area or hinterland. (Allen Pred, *City Systems in Advanced Economies* [New York: Wiley, 1977], p. 142. Copyright © 1977 by John Wiley and Sons. Reprinted by permission of the publisher and the author.)

and Garner, 1976:153–78). While the various typologies may not use the same categories or the same methods to derive them, they share a common goal: to group together cities which are most functionally alike.

Two geographers, Chauncy Harris and Edward Ullman, pioneered the effort to classify cities by function. In 1945 (p. 7) they wrote that "The support of cities as suppliers of urban services for the earth can be summarized in three categories, each of which presents a factor of urban causation":

1. *Cities as central places* (performing comprehensive services for a surrounding area; these cities tend to be evenly spaced throughout the region).
2. *Transport cities* (performing "break-of-bulk" services; these cities tend to be arranged in linear patterns along rail lines and at seacoasts).
3. *Specialized function cities* (performing one service, such as mining or recreation, for large areas).

Harris and Ullman did not think that a city would be exclusively engaged in only one of the three functions. Rather, they reasoned, most cities would represent a combination, and the relative importance of each factor would vary from city to city. New York City, for instance, is a principal center for wholesaling and retailing (central place type); a great port (transport type); and a manufacturing center (specialized function type).

Harris also developed a more complex classification scheme using eight functional categories. Fig. 13-6 illustrates the geographical distribution in the United States of these eight city types.

Another typology was developed in the early 1960s and used by the International City Managers Association (ICMA). The ICMA's typology (1963) uses fourteen categories of city type, detailing the criteria for each type. For instance, for a city to be classified as a *manufacturing type*, 50 percent of the jobs there would have to be in manufacturing and less than 30 percent in retail trade.

The ICMA classification scheme is somewhat more refined than its predecessors. But all these typologies recognize the same fact: Almost no cities are exclusively engaged in any one function.

Although these typology constructers recognized that their simple schemes could not compare hundreds of such multifunction cities in terms of hundreds of variables, they couldn't do much about it. However, thanks to computer technology and new analytic techniques called "multivariate analysis," it is now possible to compare patterns of functions between cities in terms of numerous variables. It is noteworthy that the leader in multivariate classification of American cities has been Brian J.L. Berry (1972), who many years earlier conducted the tests of central place theory in Snohomish County, Washington, and Iowa.

To conclude: Central place theory and functional classification of cities do not conflict with each other: they examine closely related phenomena from slightly different angles. Central place theory uses categories developed by Christaller to examine what functions a city performs for its hinterland and in relation to other cities in a system of cities. The threshold and range of central places are key concerns. Much of central place theory seeks to answer the question: What type of function will occur in a city of a given size? Functional classification schemes do not use Christaller's concepts, such as threshold and range. They draw upon U.S. census data, necessarily in the categories used by the census, and they seek to provide a snapshot picture of what is going on in the city: how many people are engaged in what kinds of

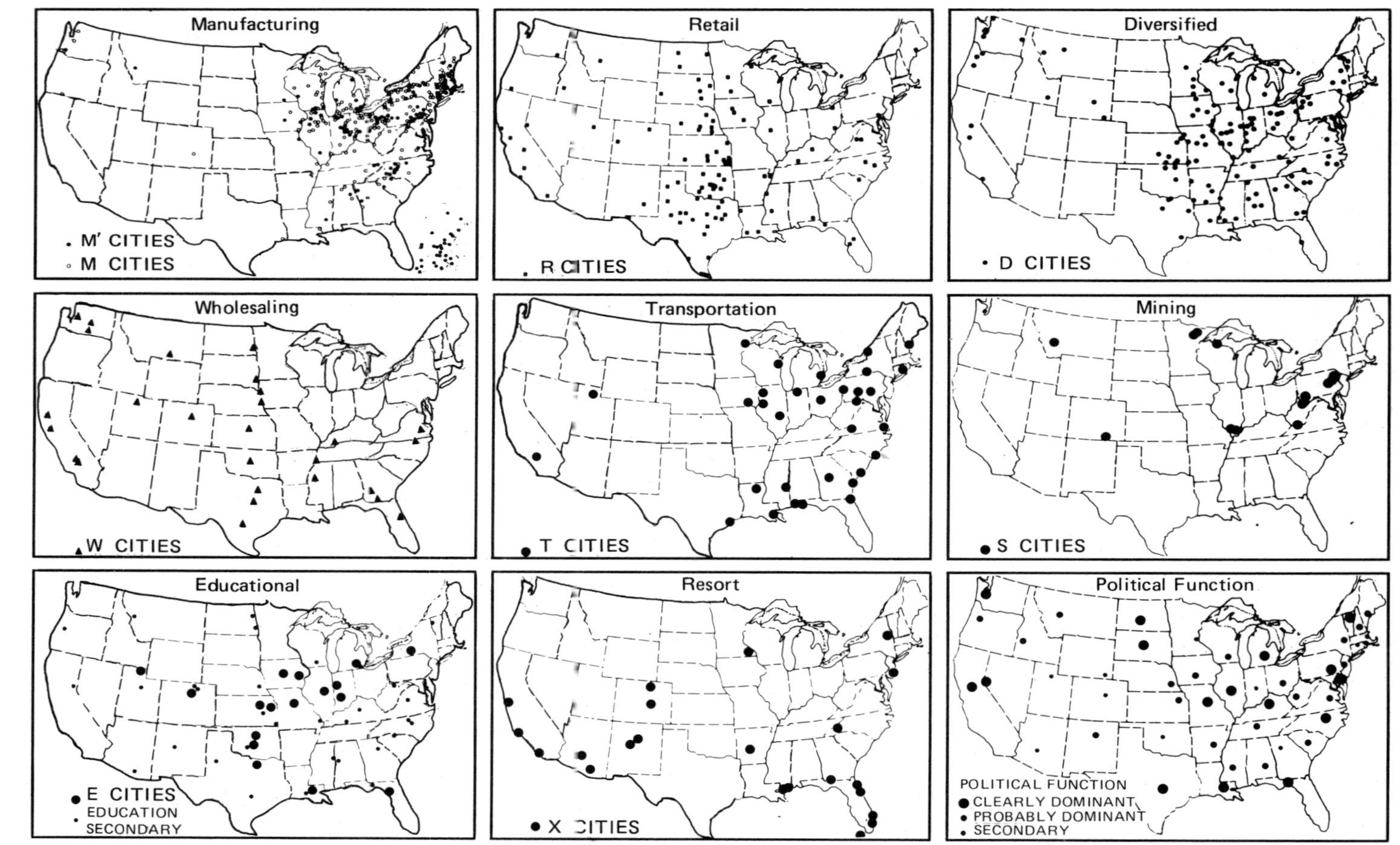

Fig. 13-6 DISTRIBUTION OF FUNCTIONAL TYPES OF CITIES. (Chauncy Harris, "A Functional Classification of Cities in the United States," *Geographical Review* 33:86–99. Copyright 1943 by the Geographical Review. Reprinted by permission of the publisher and the author.)

Table 13-1 Classes and Definitions of Different Functional Types of Cities as Defined by the ICMA, 1963

Mm Manufacturing: 50% or more of aggregate employment is in manufacturing, and less than 30% is in retail trade.

M Industrial: 50% or more of aggregate employment is in manufacturing, and over 30% is in retail trade.

Mr Diversified-manufacturing: employment in manufacturing is greater than retail employment, but less than 50% of aggregate employment.

Rm Diversified-retailing: greater employment in retailing than in manufacturing, but manufacturing is at least 20% of aggregate employment.

Rr Retailing: retail employment is greater than manufacturing or any other component of aggregate employment, and manufacturing is less than 20% of aggregate employment.

W Wholesaling: employment in wholesale trade is at least 25% of aggregate employment.

S Service: employment in selected services is at least 30% of aggregate employment, but the city does not qualify for any other category.

Other: [Definitions of Mining, Transportation, Resort, Government and Armed Forces, Professional, Hospital, and Education cities are included.]

Note: Total number of persons employed in manufacturing, retail trade, wholesale trade, and selected services is referred to as "aggregate employment."

SOURCE: Victor Jones, Richard L. Forestall, and Andrew Collver, "Economic and Social Characteristics of Urban Places," *The Municipal Yearbook, 1963* (Chicago: International City Managers Association, 1963), pp. 85–157. Reprinted by permission of The International City Management Association, Washington, D.C., and Victor Jones.

activities? The last two generations of urban geographers have worked with theory from both traditions.

Moving from the system of cities approach, we now examine the spatial patterns *within* cities. The key question here is, "how are cities internally structured?"

THE INTERNAL STRUCTURE OF CITIES

Fancy houses, skyscrapers, public housing, factories and warehouses, ball parks: what part of town are they in? As we hypothesized at the beginning of this chapter, they are not located just anywhere—by chance—in city space.

To determine exactly where they are located requires empirical investigation. It means going out and observing what facilities do or do not exist in different locations.

In our effort to understand how people and their various activities are distributed over space, we now have a great deal of help. During the last fifty years, sociologists, geographers, and economists have collected data and constructed models which attempt to describe and explain general patterns of urban spatial structure. We now turn to the three classic models of the internal organization of a city: the concentric zone model, the sectoral model, and the multiple nucleii model.

Concentric Zone Model (Ernest W. Burgess)

University of Chicago sociologist Ernest W. Burgess pioneered the systematic study of the city's internal structure. In the 1920s, he developed a model of internal city structure and urban growth: the so-called Burgess **concentric zone model** or hypothesis. This model remains important today—and controversial.

The concentric zone model grew out of Burgess's fascination with a remarkable city at a remarkable time. In the early part of this century, Chicago—the laboratory for the **Chicago school of sociology**—was a city in transition. The population change in the city over a very short period of time was noteworthy. In 1880 the emerging metropolis had about half a million inhabitants. Ten years later, the population had more than doubled.

Chicago was (and remains) a city of great ethnic diversity. By 1920 there were large communities of Czechs, Italians, Eastern European Jews, Swedes, Germans, Irish, Italians, Lithuanians, Poles, and increasing numbers of blacks (4.1 percent of the population at that time).

The Windy City resembled a vast collection of urban villages, each having its own churches, social clubs, politicians, newspapers, welfare stations, schools, and restaurants. Alongside this ethnic diversity was prejudice, especially against the newer immigrants from Southern and Eastern Europe, and a desire to residentially segregate the foreign stock.

As Chicago's population increased, these urban villages or enclaves (enclosed territories) grew, contracted, or shifted. Burgess was impressed with the great differences between various city neighborhoods and tried to make sense of the *spatial patterns* and *cultural life* in these communities. He speculated that there was a pattern to the way these neighborhoods grew or shifted, just as there was in plant and animal communities (Park, Burgess, and McKenzie, 1925:47–62).

This theoretical framework—that cities, like plant and animal communities, have a characteristic organization and develop territorially as a result of competition for space—is called **urban ecology** or, more broadly, human ecology.

Urban ecologists are concerned with the study of the spatial distribution of people and institutions in cities. This distinctive perspective originated with members of the Chicago school, particularly Robert Park and Ernest W. Burgess, and it is continued today by urban ecologists such as geographer Brian J.L. Berry and sociologist John Kasarda (Berry and Kasarda, 1977). Key concepts in this perspective include competition for a place in urban space, residential segregation, invasion, and succession. Implicit hypotheses in urban ecology include the following: (1) cultural changes in a city are correlated and reflected in changes in spatial, territorial organization, and (2) there is an intimate relationship between the social and moral order in a city and physical space, between physical distance and social distance, and between residential proximity and social equality. Urban ecologists investigate the interrelationships between physical space and the social order at three levels: neighborhood, city, and region.

Working from the perspective of urban ecology, Burgess developed and refined a zonal model. The city can be conceived as a series of concentric circular zones of typical combinations of land use (see Fig. 13-7). This model was derived from empirical research through inductive reasoning processes. Yet, as noted in Chapter 3, Burgess worked from a theoretical framework (urban ecology), so that the concentric zone model is a product

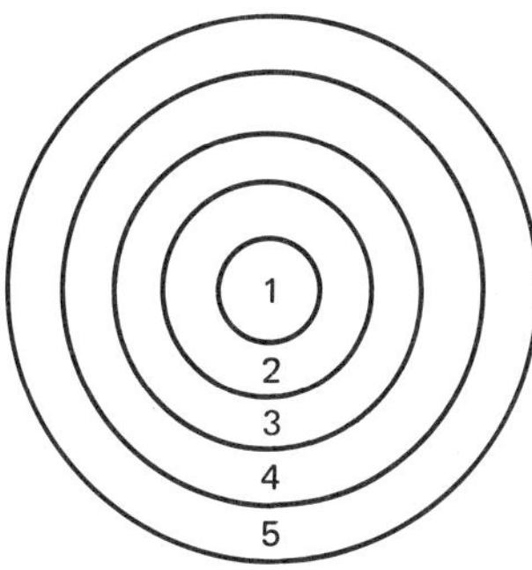

Fig. 13-7 BURGESS'S CONCENTRIC ZONE MODEL OF THE U.S. CITY. 1 = CBD. 2 = Wholesale and light manufacturing; lower-class residential. 3 = Working-class residential. 4 = Middle-class residential. 5 =Commuter's zone.

of both inductive and deductive reasoning processes.

Here is what Burgess says about his model: "In the growth of the city we have differentiated the series of concentric zones which is one way of indicating as the city expands outward from its center, how each successive zone tends to encroach upon the further outlying zones" (Burgess and Bogue, 1964: 11).

Burgess saw the city as containing five successive zones. Zone I is the center of business and civic life. Zone II surrounds Zone I; it is the Zone-in-Transition where "areas of residential deterioration caused by the encroaching of business and industry from Zone I" are found. It is a district of rooming houses, slums, and artists' colonies. Zone III contains duplexes or two-family housing where immigrants and second-generation families (the children of immigrants) live. Zone IV houses "small businessmen, professional people, clerks, and salesmen" who live in apartments and shop at neighborhood shopping centers. Zone V consists of a ring of bedroom suburbs (Burgess, [1923] 1925:114–23).

This zonal model doesn't just describe spatial patterns; it contains an implicit hypothesis on the relationship of urban space to social order. Burgess thought that *physical location* and people's *social background* are connected in city space. Taking one example—family type—Burgess noted that Zone I (the CBD) is mostly a "homeless men's region"; Zone II is "the habitat of the emancipated family"; Zone III is "the natural soil of the patriarchal family transplanted from Europe"; Zone IV provides "the favorable environment for the equalitarian family"; and Zone V is "without question the domain of the [female-centered] family" (Burgess, [1923] 1925:114–23).

What, then, is the relationship between physical location and social background? The model postulates an inverse relationship between central location and an urbanite's socioeconomic status (SES). That is, the higher up on the social ladder, the farther the person lives from Zone I. Thus, the zonal model hypothesizes that *where people live depends on their position on the social ladder.*

If this hypothesis is correct, we should be able to predict changes in urban residence patterns. For one thing, we should expect a relationship between social mobility and physical space. Thus, we could predict that *as people move up the social ladder, they move out from the city center.* Many urban ecology studies conducted in the 1920s showed that this was indeed the case. Immigrant groups first settled in Zone II, the Zone-in-Transition, and moved to outlying zones as they moved up socioeconomically. Then other new migrants to the city would replace the groups that moved up—and out. Such was the succession of residential movements in the city.

A classic illustration of succession is the textile mill towns of nineteenth-century Massachusetts. First the English, then the Irish after them, then the Czechs and Middle Europeans, and finally Italians, Poles, and other Southern and Eastern European immigrants resided near the CBD. Over the generations, as each group moved up the SES ladder (say, from unskilled worker to skilled laborer to first-line supervisor and perhaps to manager), it moved its residence farther out. As one group moved up and out, its homes were sold or rented to a group below them on the social ladder. And thus the various groups succeeded one another on the same plots of ground.

The zonal model contains another hypothesis that concerns urban growth. It postulates that cities and towns tend to expand radially from their CBD.

All the hypotheses contained in the zonal model grow out of one basic assumption: that *economic competition* is the chief organizing agent of human communities. Darwin thought that competition in the struggle for existence is the key variable in the organization of animal communities. Burgess thought that economic competition played a similar role in human affairs, and that it would be expressed in terms of a struggle over space.

According to Burgess, people and business activities tend to be separated into rather homogeneous subareas of a city, and this segregation into so-called natural areas is part of the competition for space. That is, these homogeneous natural areas are not planned but result from the workings of the self-regulating economic market (Adam Smith's "invisible hand" mentioned in Chapter 3).

To Burgess, then, market forces are the key determinants of a city's internal structure. On this point, most urban land economists and urban geographers agreed with Burgess.

On other points, however, urban geographers and urban land economists disagreed with Burgess's model and developed different models of city structure. The two most important competing models are Hoyt's sectoral model and Harris and Ullman's multiple nuclei model.

Sectoral Model (Homer Hoyt)

Homer Hoyt, a real estate economist, worked for the Federal Housing Administration (FHA) during the 1930s. The FHA was searching for ways to understand the dynamics of residential change in order to guide policymakers in determining which neighborhoods were safe investment risks. Accordingly, Hoyt (1939) examined the residential patterns of a large number of cities and changes they had undergone over time.

As Hoyt organized data on 142 cities, he observed spatial patterns which didn't fit Burgess's concentric zone model. Hoyt's main criticisms of the Burgess model, based on the collected data, were as follows:

1. The retail shopping center, *not* the financial center, is the central point in most cities.
2. The wholesale and light manufacturing zone adjoins the central business district but does *not* encircle it.
3. Heavy industry tends to follow river valleys and river fronts, bays or deep tidal basins, or outer belts. New transportation technology is the key factor here, for it is no longer necessary for industry to locate in a concentric pattern close to the center of the city.
4. Working-class people tend to locate near industry. However, as factories *do not* form a concentric circle around the CBD, neither do the workers' homes.
5. High-rent areas *do not* form a complete circle around the outer edge of the city.
6. Commuter housing takes the form of scattered isolated communities; it is *not* a zone at all (Hoyt, 1939:17–23).

Hoyt's data did more than conflict with and partly invalidate Burgess's hypothesis. They suggested an alternative model of internal city structure: a **sectoral model** of the U.S. city. This model, pictured in Fig. 13-8, describes American cities as organized in *wedges of activity moving outward from the city center,* particularly along railroad lines, roads, trolley tracks, and other transportation corridors.

Hoyt found that the rent structure of housing also tended to be organized by sectors, not zones. Thus, rents along a transport line moving out from the center of the city were often similar. A high-rent wedge might start near the center of the city and follow an exclusive boulevard out to the city edge. A low-rent wedge might follow the railroad corridor.

Since Hoyt developed his sectoral model in the 1930s, many empirical studies have suported his basic thesis of sectoral growth along radial transport lines. But the controversy regarding the nature of the internal structure of cities did not end with Hoyt.

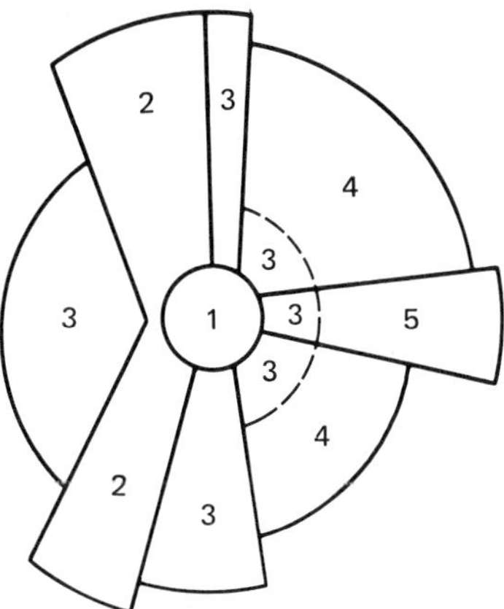

Fig. 13-8 HOYT'S SECTORAL MODEL OF THE U.S. CITY. 1 = CBD. 2 = Wholesale and light manufacturing. 3 = Lower-class residential. 4 = Middle-class residential. 5 = Upper-class residential. (Adapted from Chauncy Harris and Edward L. Ullman, "The Nature of Cities," *Annals of the American Academy of Political and Social Science* 242: Fig. 5, p. 13. Copyright by American Academy of Political and Social Science, 1945. Reprinted by permission of the publisher and Chauncy Harris.)

Multiple Nuclei Model (Chauncy Harris and Edward L. Ullman)

Geographers Chauncy Harris and Edward L. Ullman (1945) developed another model of urban form and growth which departs significantly from both the concentric zone and sectoral models. The two geographers based their so-called **multiple nuclei** theory on the idea that cities develop not one but many nuclei (centers) of activity.

According to Harris and Ullman, four factors cause the development of multiple nuclei: (1) certain activities need specialized facilities (e.g., a port needs a waterfront); (2) similar activities tend to cluster together (e.g., financial institutions group together on Wall Street in New York); (3) some unlike activities are not compatible (e.g., an auto assembly plant and an entertainment district would not be good neighbors); and (4) certain activities cannot compete financially for the most desirable sites (e.g., lower-class housing and warehousing cannot afford to locate in high-rent districts).

In most large American cities, the following districts have developed around nuclei: (1) Central Business District, (2) wholesale and light manufacturing district, (3) heavy industrial district, and (4) residential district(s). Minor nuclei also form around cultural centers, parks, outlying business districts, and small industrial centers. Or a university might form a nucleus for a quasi-independent community. The important point is that

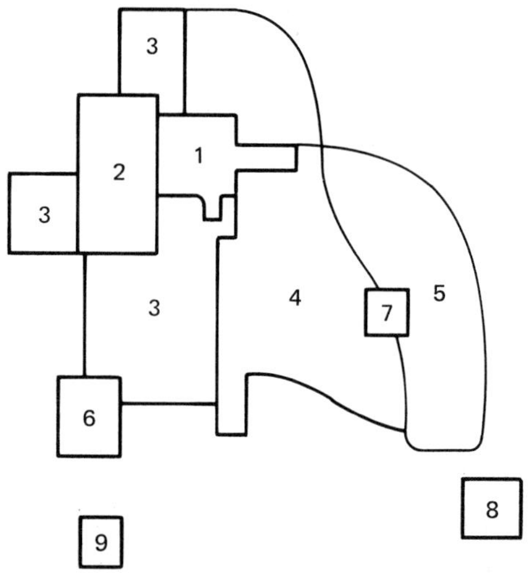

Fig. 13-9 HARRIS AND ULLMAN'S MULTIPLE NUCLEI MODEL OF THE U.S. CITY. 1 = CBD. 2 = Wholesale and light manufacturing. 3 = Lower-class residential. 4 = Middle-class residential. 5 = Upper-class residential. 6 = Heavy manufacturing. 7 = Outlying business district. 8 = Dormitory suburb. 9 = Industrial suburb. (Adapted from Chauncy Harris and Edward L. Ullman, "The Nature of Cities," *Annals of the American Academy of Political and Social Science* 242: Fig. 5, p. 13. Copyright by American Academy of Political and Social Science. Reprinted by permission of the publisher and Chauncy Harris.)

the different areas need not conform to either zonal or sectoral patterns.

To conclude: The classic models of urban form and growth shed light on recurring patterns in the physical organization of cities. But they have come under heavy criticism for several reasons. Some critics wonder if *any* general model is possible, for no city is so neatly organized that it totally fits some theoretical model. Physical features such as hills and lakes serve to distort expected spatial patterns. Further, critics suggest that human nonrational variables can influence spatial patterns. And some critics maintain that the classic models were developed at a particular point in history—the industrial era—and are not well suited to explain urban growth in a postindustrial age.

We now turn to some critiques of the classic models. We start with Walter Firey's explicit critique of Burgess, Hoyt, and Harris and Ullman's models. Then we examine an approach to studying urban growth and differentiation which implies a critique of the classic models: social area analysis. Finally, we look at new analytic techniques for describing and generalizing about urban space.

Firey's Critique: The Classic Models Are Too Deterministic

One important critic of the classic models, Walter Firey (1947), argues that city land use patterns are not based purely on deterministic, economic considerations. Firey claims that such nonrational factors as sentiment and symbolism influence city shape.

Looking around Boston, Firey noted that actual land use didn't fit the patterns predicted by any of the classic models. For instance, old churches and the Boston Common (a public park) are located on very expensive land and low-density eighteenth-century redbrick buildings stand on Beacon Hill, a high-status, high-rent residential district. If the models were correct, none of these should have been standing; they would have been torn down to make way for higher-density uses in the economic competition for space.

Firey concluded that the classic models couldn't account for noneconomic considerations: people's sentimental attachment to urban landmarks, whether their existence made economic sense or not. He rejected several notions inherent in the classic models: (1) that physical space can be divorced from cultural values; (2) that land use blindly follows some sort of Darwinian economic imperative; and (3) that people passively accept whatever the market dictates. Many recent events offer support for Firey's views. Consider, for example, the "save Grand Central Station" movement in New York City and numerous instances where historical preservation societies have saved buildings from the wrecker's ball.

To correct for the economic determinism of the human ecologists' classic models, Firey called for an approach he termed "cultural ecology." This approach, in contrast to urban ecology, would take into account specific cultural and historical factors influencing a city's land use patterns.

Social Area Analysis: A Method of Investigating Urban Growth and Differentiation

While Firey found fault with the classic models for leaving out cultural variables, others criticize Burgess, Hoyt, and Harris and Ullman for neglecting *societal* variables. These critics point out that the classic models treat the city as if it were an island, adrift from its larger society and a unique form of social organization.

One approach—social area analysis—attempts to look at city form and space as a product of societal forces. Social area analysis (technically, the term refers to a *method* of investigation developed by sociologists Eshref Shevky and Wendell Bell) starts from a basic premise: Urban growth and differentiation result from changes in the organization of society.

Shevky and Bell (1955) identify the *increasing scale and complexity of society* as the major determinant of urban growth and differentiation. They argue that the trend toward social differentiation associated with this increasing scale and complexity (e.g., changes in occupational skills from blue-collar to white-collar and changes in productive activity from agricultural and manufacturing to services) would lead to spatial differentiation in cities. Specifically, they argue that groups in society tend to segregate themselves on the basis of *social rank, family type,* and *ethnicity and race.* Shevky and Bell measure social rank by an index of occupation and education; family type by several measures, including type of residence, age of children, and wife's status in the labor force; and ethnicity/race by the proportion of blacks and other segregated populations in the census tract.

According to social area analysis, *as a city becomes more complex and heterogeneous, areas within the city become more homogeneous* (in terms of social rank, family status, and ethnicity). One study of the Chicago metropolitan area using Shevky and Bell's basic approach found this generally to be the case. Chicagoans do live among people like themselves in terms of class, race, ethnicity, and point in the life cycle (Rees, 1970).

Few disagree with the underlying premise of social area analysis—that changes in the socioeconomic organization of society have spatial effects. But the Shevky-Bell model has been questioned on both theoretical and empirical grounds. Specifically, critic Janet L. Abu-Lughod (1969) found that one of its measures of change—social rank—accounts for most of the variation in city structure, and that another measure—family type—is culture-bound and inapplicable to other social systems, such as Egypt. Other critics say that the model uses such a small number of variables to construct the three measures of change (seven in all) that it can't accurately describe the population characteristics of urbanites.

Computer-based Models of Urban Structure

Thanks to computer technology and sophisticated analytic techniques, researchers have recently met the objection that social area analysis uses too few variables; many variables can now be built into a factor analysis.

But a word of caution is appropriate here.

Complex data analyses with hundreds of variables can be very useful in measuring urban growth and describing empirical reality. But they don't necessarily lead to the construction of more useful theories to *explain* the sociospatial structure of a city. No computer-based model of city structure has yet gained wide acceptance.

WHERE PEOPLE LIVE

For all their problems, the classic models do give a general sense of land use in the American industrial city. But they can't describe the specifics. For instance, they are not useful for predicting precisely where in a city or metropolitan area a particular social group will settle.

Many empirical studies do provide such detailed information. Some use social area analysis (or its sophisticated descendant, factorial ecology) to pinpoint who lives where in terms of social rank, race/ethnicity, and family type. Others use a variety of methods to examine patterns of housing segregation by race or age. We now turn to some of these studies.

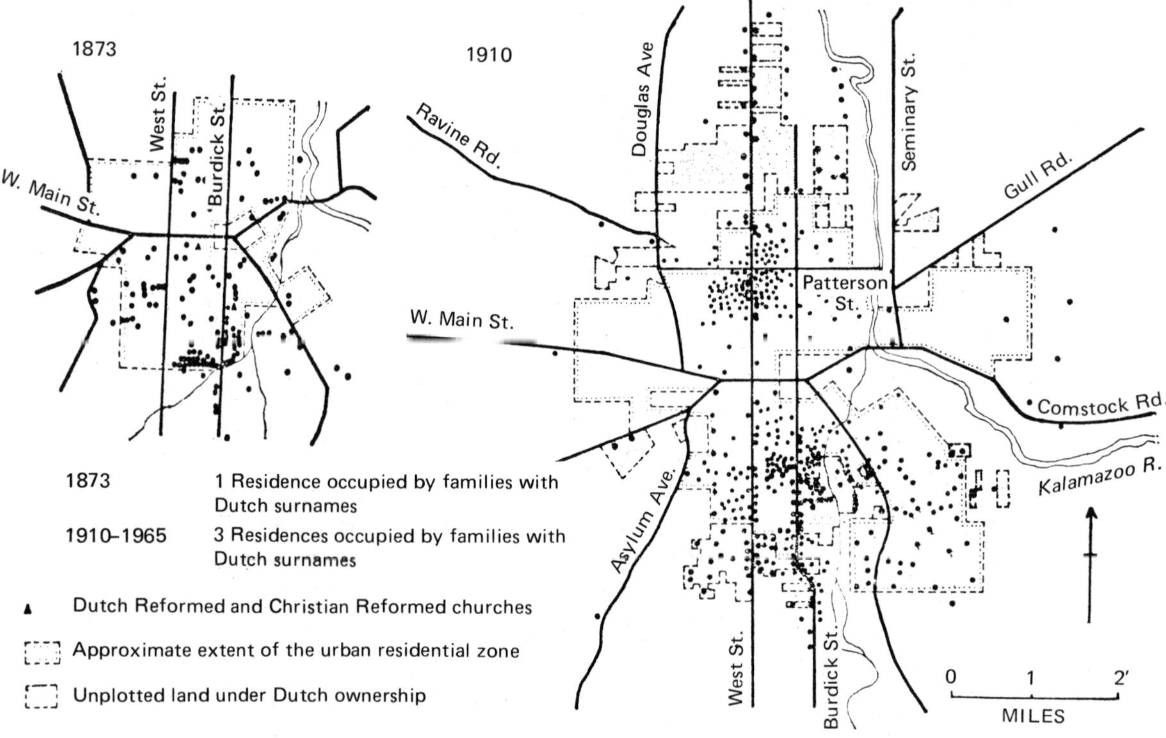

Fig. 13-10 THE CHANGING DISTRIBUTION OF DUTCH HOUSEHOLDS IN KALAMAZOO, MICHIGAN, 1873 and 1965. (John Jakle and J. A. Wheeler, "The Dutch and Kalamazoo, Michigan: A Study of Spatial Barriers to Acculturation," *Tijdschrift Voor Economische en Sociale Geografie* [Royal Dutch Geographical Society: Leyden, Netherlands, 1969], p. 251. Reprinted by permission of TESG and the authors.)

How Race and Ethnicity Affect Housing Patterns

Stewpot America. That image better captures the situation of many American migrants to the city, both from overseas and the rural countryside, than the metaphor of the melting pot. As noted in Chapter 7, some groups did melt into the dominant culture; others were partially assimilated; some rejected the dominant culture altogether as a matter of choice; and still others were hardly affected.

One way of measuring the degree to which an ethnic or racial group has blended into the dominant culture is to examine that group's housing pattern over time. Housing patterns—segregation or dispersion, for example—are not the only measure of **assimi-**

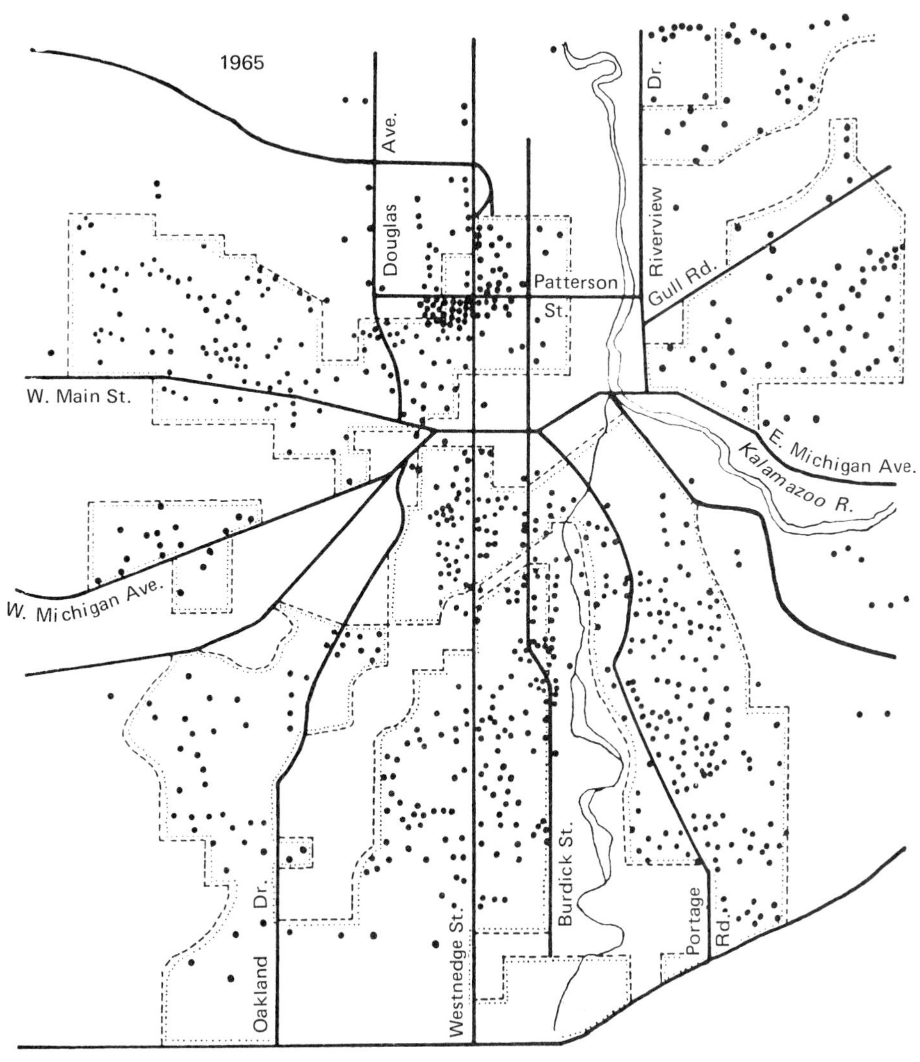

lation. But often they indicate larger patterns of social mobility or acceptance.

Consider the contrast between the housing patterns of Dutch immigrants and their families in Kalamazoo, Michigan, and black migrants to Chicago over a period of time. As Fig.13-10 shows, families with Dutch surnames spread throughout Kalamazoo between 1873 and 1965. They did not stay grouped together in one area.

Contrast the Dutch pattern of housing dispersion in Kalamazoo to the black pattern of housing segregation and concentration in Chicago, shown in Fig. 13-11. Dutch immigrants in Kalamazoo dispersed as they moved up the socioeconomic ladder and became Americanized. There was no residential area of the city from which they were systematically excluded. Conversely, Chicago's blacks were systematically excluded from some sections of the city and did not, as a group, climb the socioeconomic ladder. Thus, in 1970, Chicago's blacks remained highly segregated and concentrated in a small **ghetto** area near the center of the city. Moreover, this pattern extended to metropolitan Chicago. As of 1970, almost one-half of Chicago's suburbs with more than 2,500 inhabitants had no black residents; only two had more than 50 black residents. What we have here, then, is a metropolitanwide pattern: the segregation and concentration of blacks (Berry and Kasarda, 1977:21–52).

In fact, this pattern of black exclusion from suburbs is nationwide. As of 1977, America's suburbs remained about 94 percent white.

Is this continuing pattern of black housing segregation and concentration purely a matter of racial discrimination? Some observers think so. In the case of Chicago, Mayor Richard J. Daley believed it was "right and just to avoid the encroachment of blacks into established [white] ethnic neighborhoods. . . . Blacks, he thought, brought with them social problems of all kinds. . . . [T]hey didn't keep their yards clean, and the neighborhoods went to hell and that kind of thing" (Erlichman in Scheer, 1979:8).

But most observers think it is much more complicated, involving issues of social rank as well as race. For Berry and Kasarda (1977:22), the key to understanding the virtual isolation of metropolitan Chicago's blacks is neighborhood status:

> Since blacks as a group are considered of lower status by many whites and, in large concentrations, are associated with residentially undesirable areas, the arrival of large numbers of blacks reduces a neighborhood's rank in residential status hierarchy for whites. . . . Because neighborhood status is so affected by racial change, areas that attract large concentrations of blacks are typically unable to retain white residents. . . .

Berry and Kasarda's empirical findings in Chicago support what researchers found in other U.S. cities: if whites can possibly afford to do it, they will live with those of their own social rank and race. For those familiar with the Burgess model and the premises of social area analysis, this should come as no surprise. Both hypothesize that in a heterogeneous urban society, people will sort themselves out by social background variables. Burgess and Park thought this sorting-out process happened in an unplanned fashion, creating natural areas. And before the Great Depression, they charted the shift of ethnic neighborhoods in Chicago, using the terms **invasion** and **succession** to describe some of the sorting and sifting.

Since the University of Chicago researchers first used these terms to describe residential urban change, studies in Chicago and elsewhere have documented the process. They tend to find a period of "penetration" in which a few minority group families buy into a residential area. This period is followed by

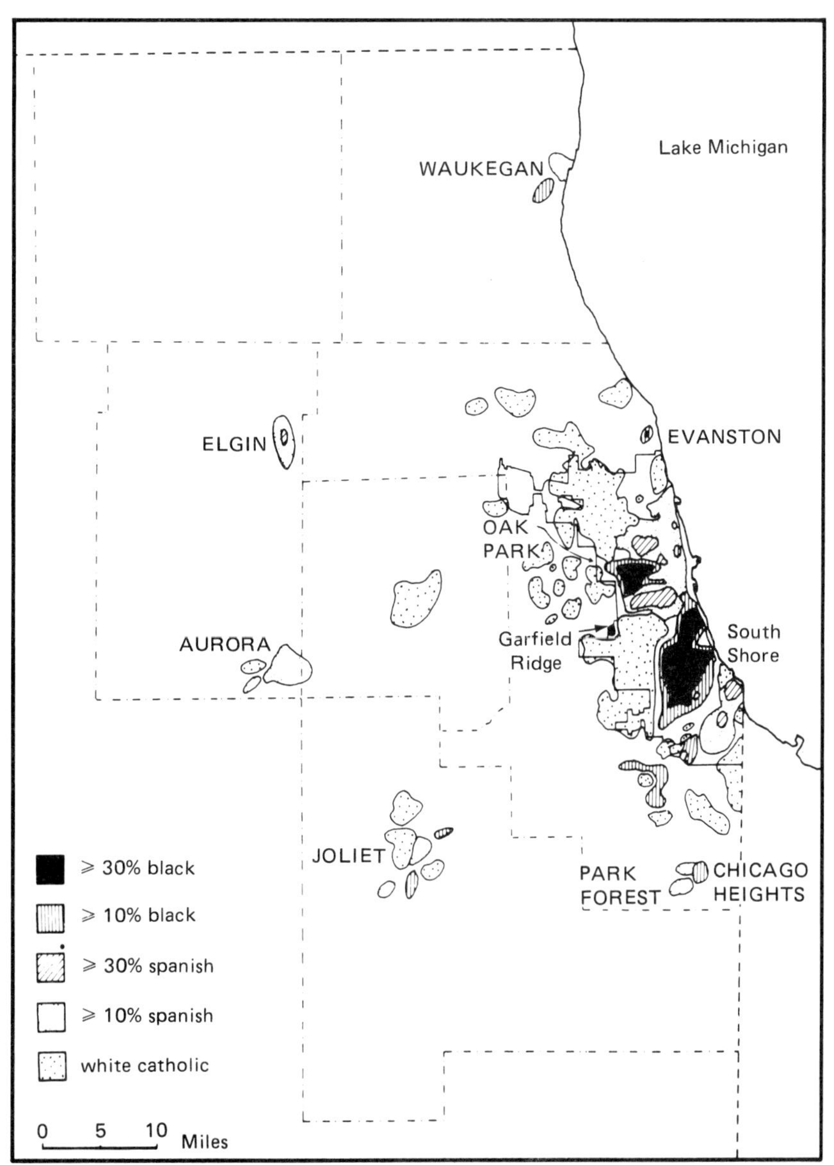

Fig. 13-11 BLACK, WHITE CATHOLIC, AND SPANISH-SPEAKING CONCENTRATIONS IN THE CHICAGO METROPOLITAN REGION IN 1970. (Brian J. L. Berry and John D. Kasarda, *Contemporary Urban Ecology* [New York: Macmillan, 1977], p. 30. Copyright © 1977, Macmillan Publishing Co., Inc. Reprinted by permission of the publisher and the authors.)

the "invasion" in which a substantial number of their group follows.

The process of neighborhood invasion is sometimes accompanied by block-busting, a tactic practiced by unscrupulous real estate speculators. In a typical block-busting situation, the speculator comes into a white neighborhood and warns residents that "they" (nonwhites) are going to move in very quickly. White residents are led to believe that their property values will drop sharply as the area becomes "undesirable." These scare tactics may stimulate panic selling at artificially low prices. Then the block-buster can purchase the houses cheaply and resell them to minority buyers at inflated prices.

How Age Affects Housing Patterns

Just as people sort themselves out by social rank, family status, and race/ethnicity, so do they group themselves by age. At different points in their life cycle, individuals may seek out different residential locations. For instance, as one woman goes through life, she may reside in a swinging singles area near the heart of the city, later move to a suburban house to raise children and commute to work, and, after the children grow up, move to a city apartment.

Understanding the population characteristics of neighborhoods in terms of age (and family structure) is essential to informed policymaking. It would make no sense to locate day-care centers in the heart of a retirement colony or playgrounds where there are no children.

The population pyramid is a convenient device for presenting information about a community's age composition. Fig. 13–12 shows pyramids for two different kinds of communities in terms of age. Pyramid A is top-heavy, illustrating that most neighborhood residents are middle-aged or older. Pyramid B bulges out at the bottom, revealing the relatively large number of children in the neighborhood.

Pyramid-type diagrams can be used to display various characteristics of a population, including sex, income, family composition, occupation, and marital status. Interestingly, new categories (added in the 1980 decennial U.S. census) will permit more refined data analysis and pyramid building. Of special interest is a category added under household living arrangements and family styles: partner/roommates—unrelated adults of the opposite sex, unmarried, sharing two-person households.

Population pyramids are useful for looking at a given population at one moment in time, say, 1980. But they are static in nature; they don't reveal how the population characteristics of a community may change over time. For this kind of data analysis, a dynamic study is required. The uses of a dynamic study can be illustrated by examining an important trend occurring in many American cities today: gentrification.

Gentrification

A dynamic study of a neighborhood located in Burgess's Zone III might show the following breakdown by social rank over time: 1970—90 percent working class, 5 percent middle class, 5 percent upper-middle class; 1975—70 percent working class, 5 percent middle class, 25 percent upper-middle class; 1980—40 percent working class; 10 percent middle class, and 50 percent upper-middle class. These data indicate that the neighborhood is undergoing **gentrification** (from the English "gentry," the class immediately below the nobility). That is, people of higher class and status over the decade invaded

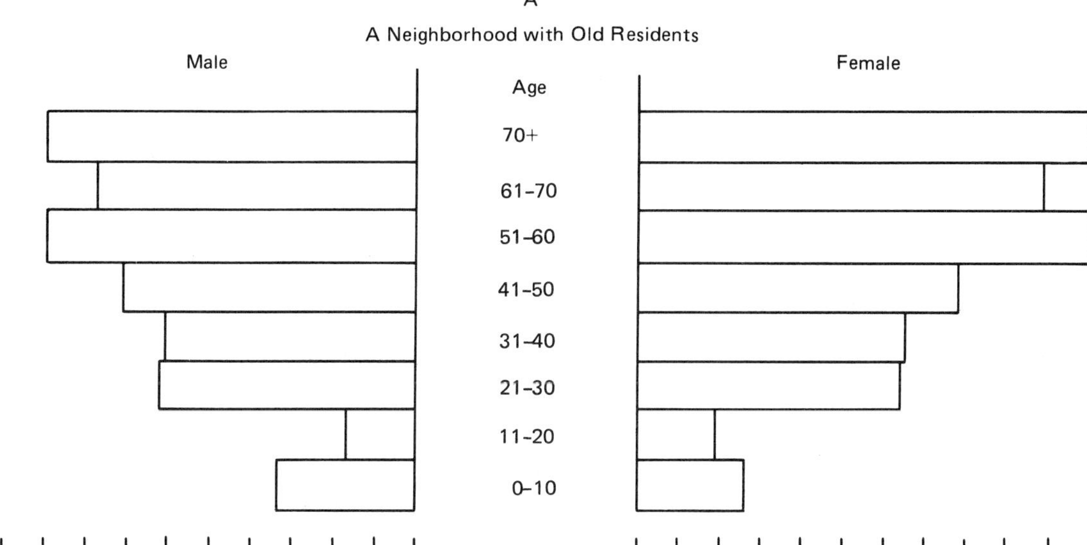

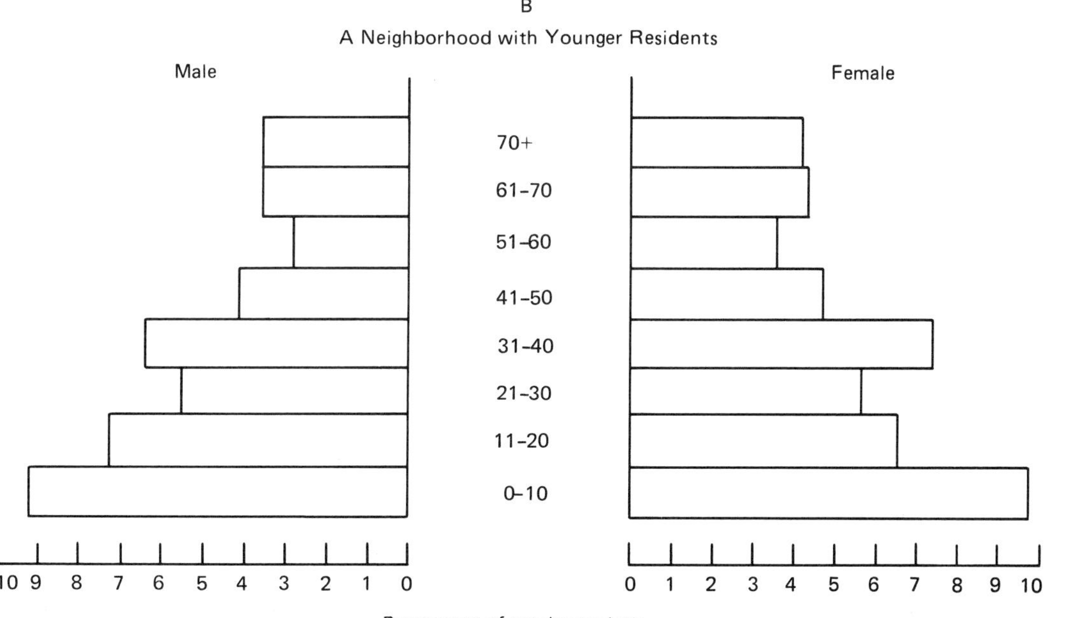

Fig. 13-12 POPULATION PYRAMIDS OF TWO NEIGHBORHOODS WITH DIFFERING AGE STRUCTURES, DISAGGREGATED BY SEX.

a working-class area, renovating existing homes.

Gentrification is occurring in many American cities that have charming inner-city houses. In Washington, D.C., for instance, the now fashionable and expensive Georgetown section was primarily a lower-status area until World War II. More recently, parts of Capitol Hill and the Adams-Morgan area have been undergoing gentrification.

Some observers of the American city applaud this development. They say that gentrification is bringing back the white middle and upper-middle classes to the city. But an important question remains: where will those gentrified out of their homes go? Dynamic studies can chart neighborhood change, but they can't provide policy direction. Whether gentrification should be slowed down or speeded up via public policy is a normative issue, not a question that can be answered by looking at data.

Up to this point, we have treated housing patterns as if they exist in isolation from other human activities. Now we will examine patterns of industrial and commercial activity in a city which influence housing and so many other land uses.

ECONOMIC ACTIVITIES IN METROPOLITAN SPACE

After streets and roads (which consume the largest amount of a city's space), housing is usually the most widespread land use. Commercial and industrial activities take up far less space, about 10 percent combined (Murphy, 1974:311, 379). Although economic activities don't take up much room, relatively speaking, they greatly influence what kinds of housing exist in a city (rooming houses, mansions, slums, etc.) and what kinds of people live there.

Central Business District (CBD)

The downtown or **central business district (CBD)** is the key commercial area inside most modern U.S. cities. This area is much more than a physical place. It is a symbol of a city's cultural vitality as well as its economic well-being. It may evoke numerous images: skyscrapers, hustle-bustle, street musicians, high fashion, litter, big department stores, and/or empty streets after the offices close.

Following Walter Firey's remarks about people's sentimental attachment to landmarks, we could hypothesize that a rundown CBD has subtle psychological effects on urbanites. But beyond these difficult-to-measure effects, the CBD serves basic economic functions. Its major functions are (1) the retail selling of goods and services for profit and (2) the performance of office and financial activities for a city and its hinterland.

As in central place theory, exchange plays a key role in understanding the importance of the CBD in America. Exchange of goods, services, and information requires social interaction, and intensely developed areas like the CBD permit convenient face-to-face interaction. For example, tens of thousands of corporate and financial workers are concentrated in a small physical area on New York City's Wall Street.

How can a CBD be precisely defined and delimited? The U.S. *Census of Retail Trade* (1976:Introduction) provides some guidelines. This U.S. Census Bureau publication characterizes the CBD as "an area of very high land valuation; an area characterized by a high concentration of retail businesses, offices, theatres, hotels, and 'service' businesses; and an area of high traffic flow." Ordinarily, the CBD follows existing census tract boundaries, consisting of one or more whole census tracts.

To more precisely delimit CBDs, urban

Fig. 13-13 CHICAGO'S LATE MAYOR, RICHARD J. DALEY, SURVEYS HIS CITY'S CBD. In large measure, Daley was responsible for reviving the Windy City's CBD in an age of increasing decentralization of commerce and industry. Under his aegis, Sears built the world's tallest building on the CBD's fringe. (© 1966 Chicago Tribune)

geographers have mapped and measured a variety of things: building heights, traffic flows, employment in retail trade, land values, and residents' perceptions of the CBD (Murphy, 1974:347–52). Such studies find that land values peak close to the center of the CBD. They also show that land uses within the CBD change as distance from this point of peak land value increases. For example, the proportion of land devoted to retailing declines as one moves out from the point of highest land value.

Land uses vary in vertical space too. Moving upward from the ground floor of buildings in the CBD through successive stories, offices increase while retailing declines (Murphy and Vance, 1954a, 1954b).

Over the years, the CBD has changed as technology and the economy have evolved. Since the Second World War, white-collar and service industries have gained in importance as the United States moved from an industrial to a postindustrial economy. Retail sales activities in the CBD have declined as suburbs drew downtown department store customers out of cities; the big stores tended to decentralize rather than expand in the CBD. Further, new communications technologies—computers, telephone conferencing, electronic storage of data—made it possible to communicate quickly without face-to-face interaction. All these changes meant that firms which once clustered in the CBD became free to move to the urban fringe or even rural areas. Thus, a large insurance company can now locate in a suburban area and interact with customers, claimants, and companies by phone instead of face-to-face; it can store its data anywhere and retrieve them instead of storing them in some downtown central place.

To conclude: The CBD is a high-rent district with relatively few residential units but with a heavy concentration of people flowing through on foot and in vehicles. It is typified by certain kinds of activities: offices, retail sales, hotels, cultural events, and services. But with suburban development, new technologies, and the shift from an industrial to a postindustrial economy, the CBD has suffered declines in some of its traditional functions, particularly retail sales. White-collar and service activities have become increasingly important, however, and some observers even predict a renaissance for many of the nation's CBDs due to spiraling energy costs.

Decentralization of Commercial Activities

Retail stores, restaurants, hotels, and other commercial and service activities have never been exclusively located in the CBD. In the post-World War II years, commercial activities have been increasingly located in other parts of the city or outside the central city.

MRCs. Most SMSAs have several **major retail centers (MRCs)**. Fig. 13-14 shows that the Akron, Ohio, SMSA contains sixteen MRCs in addition to the CBD, itself an MRC. Some are located in the city; many more are found on the city's fringes. Most are located along major transportation corridors. Akron's pattern is typical of the distribution of MRCs in SMSAs.

Newer MRCs are often one-stop shopping centers, replete with drug and department stores, pizza parlors, a movie house, and specialty shops. Many of these are suburban shopping malls. The man who pioneered their design in the early 1940s, architect Victor Gruen, included public cultural facilities as well as retail stores in his original plans. Developers perverted his plans, and later Gruen denied he was the father of the "malling of America."

Model of Commercial Structure. According to geographer Brian J.L. Berry (1963), the modern U.S. city's commercial structure consists of four basic components: (1) a hierarchy of business centers, (2) highway-oriented ribbons, (3) urban arterial developments, and (4) specialized function centers. The hierarchy of business centers starts with streetcorner developments and ends with the metropolitan-serving CBD. Highway-oriented ribbons are natural developments along transportation strips such as gas stations and motels. Urban arterial commerce includes lumber stores that need good access to urban customers but avoid high-rent districts like the CBD. Specialized function areas include used-car lots or doctors' office buildings, which tend to cluster together.

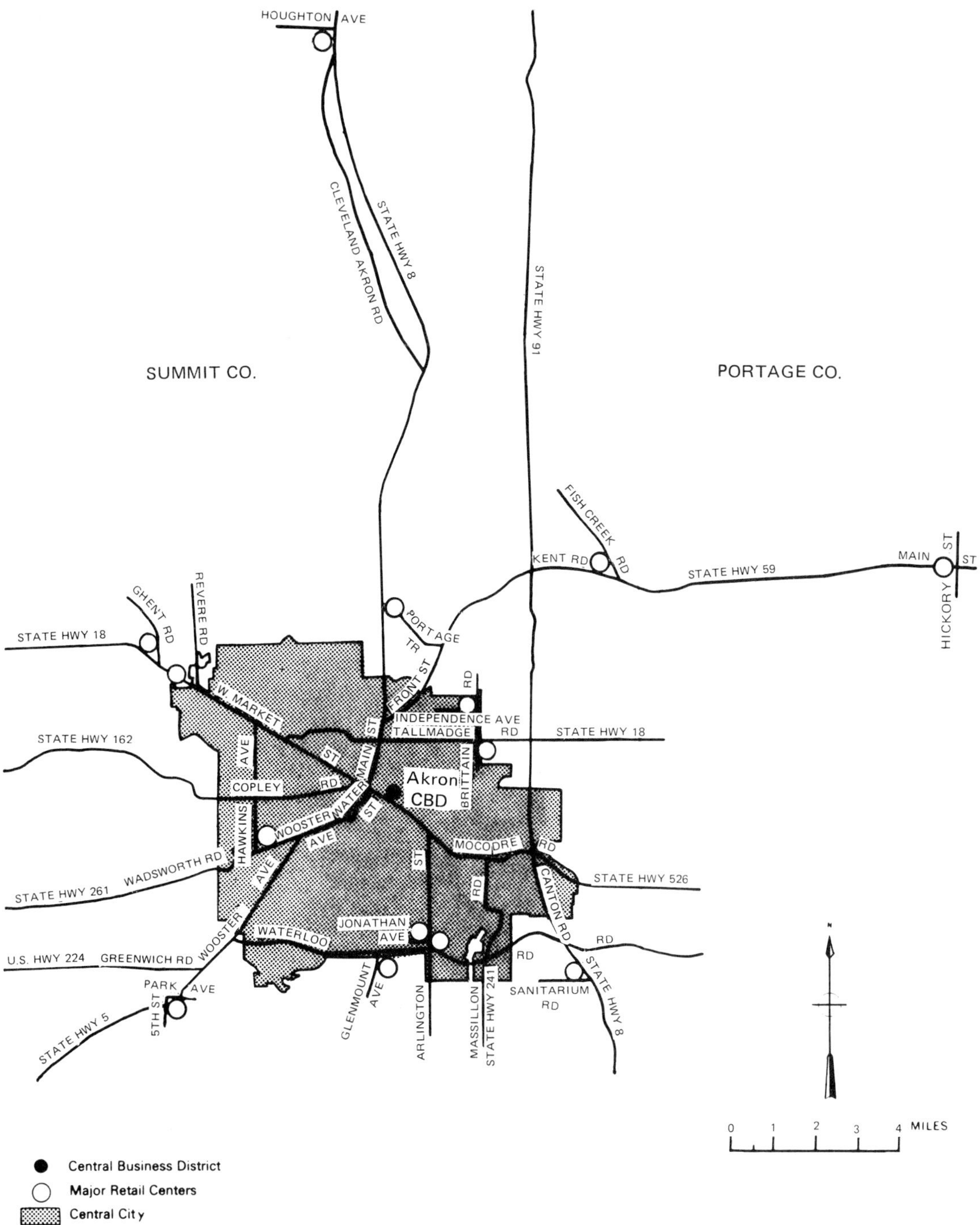

Fig. 13-14 MAJOR RETAIL CENTERS (MRCs) OF AKRON, OHIO. (U.S. Bureau of the Census, *Census of Retail Trade: 1972, Vol. 3, Major Retail Center Statistics* [Washington, D.C.: U.S. Government Printing Office, 1976], Part 3, 36-6)

Manufacturing

Manufacturing consists of (1) transforming raw materials into new products and (2) assembling component parts into new products, such as cars or TV sets. This transformation usually takes place in an urban plant, factory, or mill.

Indeed, the "dark satanic mill" and factory smokestack once symbolized the economic lifeblood of the city. That was in the nineteenth and early twentieth centuries. Now, in the postindustrial economy, manufacturing in the United States is declining relative to the service and information sectors.

Still, manufacturing remains a significant urban activity in some parts of the United States. Older Frostbelt cities tend to have the highest proportion of their work force in manufacturing. Significant concentrations of manufacturing cities are found in the Piedmont region of the Southeast too. And since the Second World War, manufacturing activity has been moving to the Sunbelt.

Some kinds of manufacturing are more heavily concentrated in cities and SMSAs than others. For instance, virtually all printing and publishing takes place within SMSAs, but only a small percentage (about 20 percent) of lumber and wood manufacturing is located within SMSAs (Northam, 1975:291).

The kinds of companies that locate in SMSAs have important economic implications. As Chapter 15 details, the industry mix of an SMSA is a prime determinant of the area's economic health.

How does a firm decide where to locate a new factory? Typically, a large national or multinational company first decides on a country, a region within the country, the type of area (urban, suburban, or rural) within the region, and finally, a specific site.

In making the regional decision, a firm considers macro-level factors: the availability of labor and raw materials as well as transport costs. Once the regional decision is made, a firm decides what type of area best suits its needs. No two kinds of plants will have precisely the same needs. Printers, for instance, need a site near the CBD, whereas a sawmill in the CBD makes no economic sense. A useful way to think about location decision at the area level is to imagine a manufacturing firm buffeted by two opposing forces: centrifugal forces pushing it away from an inner-city location and centripetal forces pulling it toward the same location. Box 13-1 summarizes these forces affecting industrial site location.

Once a firm decides what region and area best meet its particular needs, it will comparison shop for sites within acceptable areas. At this point, micro-level considerations become important: does this site have a good sewer system and other facilities?

Ultimately, some combination of forces will exert enough push or pull for the industry to make a location decision. And increasingly, centrifugal forces—those pushing industry away from central locations are proving stronger than centripetal ones.

There is one other important factor in industrial location: the state of technology. The pattern of manufacturing location is historically linked to the technology available at a particular time. Older manufacturing areas such as Lowell, Massachusetts, were located near energy sources (rivers, waterfalls) and transport facilities (canals, harbors, rivers). With the development of railroads in the nineteenth century, firms tended to locate their plants in relation to rail lines. With the development of a comprehensive national highway system in the post-World War II era, plants are now situated along highways in outlying industrial parks and/or centrally located redevelopment areas.

To conclude: Planners didn't consciously

Box 13-1

WHAT MAKES INDUSTRIES LOCATE INSIDE OR OUTSIDE OF CITIES?

Centrifugal Forces in Industrial Location

1. **Topography.** (For example, hilly cities have little land for industrial sites.)
2. **Late industrialization.** Built-up cities may have little land for factories.
3. **Manufacturing type.** Refineries, steel mills, meat-packing plants, etc., may create nuisances if located in the city.
4. **Nonfocused transportation.** A harbor front, navigable river, canal, belt railway, or modern highway facilities may provide advantages for industries to spread out.
5. **Building type.** Some factories need a large space for one-story manufacturing or warehousing buildings.
6. **Zoning.** Zoning ordinances of the central city may fail to set aside enough land or large enough parcels of land for manufacturing.
7. **High land values in central cities.** Firms may avoid high cost.
8. **Labor force.** A cheap (nonunionized) rural or suburban labor force may tempt industry away from cities.
9. **Annexation.** Where annexation of adjacent land is impossible, firms may be located outside the corporate limits of a city.
10. **Tax laws.** If city property taxes are high, there is an incentive for firms to avoid locating there.

Centripetal Forces in Industrial Location

1. **Topography.** (For example, a city surrounded by swamps may keep industry in the city. Or the city may provide a port.)
2. **Early industrialization.** Cities founded as centers for industry may have centralized manufacturing amenities.
3. **Manufacturing type.** Factories needing water, sewage, gas, electrical, and fire services find that they are best (or only) available from the city.
4. **Focused transportation.** Where transportation is good in the city but poor outside it, firms may cluster in the city.
5. **Building type.** Some industries expand by taking over old buildings. Such developments result in centralized manufacturing.
6. **Zoning.** Early adoption of zoning with liberal provisions has favored centralization in some cities.
7. **Unsuitable land in the suburbs.** Some suburban land is cheap because it is not really suitable for manufacturing.
8. **Labor force.** Cheap labor from slum areas at the edge of the CBD may tempt some firms to locate near the city center.
9. **Annexation.** Where annexation laws are liberal, new industries may be built on land annexed to a city.
10. **Tax laws.** If city property taxes are low or special tax deals are made, industry may be lured to the city. (Adapted from Kitagawa and Bogue, 1955:121–23). Reprinted by permission of Scripps Foundation for Research in Population Problems.

decide to put a big department store in the CBD or a lumber yard on an urban artery. In the United States, economic activities developed spatially in an unplanned manner. Nonetheless, economic activities are not randomly distributed throughout metropolitan space. To the contrary, particular spatial patterns exist. These patterns are primarily influenced by economic logic and the state of technology.

ANOTHER LOOK

"Have economic logic. Will travel." That could be the motto for theorists concerned with the shape of urban space since the nineteenth century. Economic assumptions underlie theories of urban form and space, and they cross-cut disciplines and political ideologies.

Central place theorists use economic logic to deduce that there is a system of cities, a functionally interdependent urban hierarchy. Theorists who classify cities by function also assume economic interdependence. Durkheim (Chapter 5) does the same. The U.S. government bases its definition of the SMSA on the notion of an integrated labor market (Chapter 6). Urban ecologists build a theoretical framework around the idea that human communities develop spatially as a result of economic competition, and that industrial cities are structured internally by market forces.

Even critiques of central place theory and the classic models assign a major role to economic forces in shaping the modern city. Allen Pred's critique of central place theory doesn't refute its basic assumptions. Instead, Pred updates Christaller's theory to fit advanced technological, capitalist economies. Pred suggests that a city's hinterland in the postindustrial era doesn't stop at hexagonally shaped borders but often extends past regional, even national, boundaries. In Walter Firey's critique of Burgess, Hoyt, and Harris and Ullman's models of city structure, economic factors are not denied. In effect, Firey says that people do not live by the exchange of bread alone, and that noneconomic factors such as sentiment and symbolism should be added to the models. And even those like Lewis Mumford (Chapter 4), who think that religion and art can, and indeed have, historically determined human settlement patterns, say that unrestricted economic competition has shaped the modern U.S. city.

Thus, theorists from many disciplines agree that macro-level economic factors have influenced, even determined, the shape and form of urban-industrial space. But they do not agree on whether or not this unplanned growth and development of modern cities has been good or bad for people who live in them. That is, the theorists of urban form *describe* the same processes affecting urban spatial growth and differentiation but *prescribe* varied solutions for changing the modern metropolis. This situation should sound familiar, for nineteenth century theorists (Marx, Tönnies, Durkheim) described the rural-to-urban shift in similar ways. But they too prescribed different solutions to what they viewed as the ill effects accompanying that shift.

The design of new cities, of course, depends on what people think is wrong with the old ones. In part, the next chapter deals with this issue. It also suggests how micro-level factors affect urban space and how micro- and macro-level forces together shape urban space.

PROJECTS

1. **Ranges and hinterlands.** Review the material in this chapter describing hinterland and range. Select a number of industries located in the largest

city of the nearest SMSA. Companies which retail perishable goods (e.g., bakeries and dairies), provide a good for local consumption (e.g., newspapers), or retail general consumer goods likely to be used within the SMSA (e.g., hardware or lumber stores) are best for this exercise. Obtain the name and phone number of key personnel in the office of the director, billing department, planning and statistical office, or other appropriate part of the company who would probably be familiar with the geographical area of company sales. This personnel information is available in a standard reference volume, *Contacts Influential* (San Francisco and Lincoln, Nebraska: Contacts Influential International, annual), available in the reference section of most libraries. From the people selected, attempt to determine where the good is sold.

Map as clearly as possible the range of the various companies using, for example, different colored lines or acetate overlays. Based on the ranges established, draw an approximate line marking the hinterland of the city. How do your findings square with classic theory?

2. **Functional classification of cities.** Select five cities that have a population of over 50,000 and which also appear to have different economic functions. Determine the precise number of persons employed in each city from the *Area Statistics* volume of the U.S. Census Bureau as follows:

a. *Manufacturing* from the *U.S. Census of Manufactures*
b. *Retailing* from the *U.S. Census of Retail Trade*
c. *Service work* from the *U.S. Census of Selected Service Industries*
d. *Wholesale Trade* from the *U.S. Census of Wholesale Trade*

Figures from these four sources will provide a reasonably complete picture of city employment. The sum of the figures from the four sources may be considered "aggregate employment" for purposes of this project. Refer to the definitions of functional city types in Table 13-1. Using the definitions which appear there, classify the five cities you are examining as either manufacturing, industrial, retailing, wholesaling, service, or other functional types of cities.

3. **Commercial structure of cities.** On a map of your community, identify (with different colored pins or dots) four types of commercial areas as follows:

a. An "isolated convenience store." (A small, family-owned grocery store is ideal. Laundries, local restaurants, cafes, drugstores, and barbershops will do.)
b. A store, salesroom, or professional building in a "specialized area." (A new or used auto sales lot or company is ideal. Furniture, entertainment, printing, or medical establishments in a cluster of like activities will do.)
c. A business which is located along a "highway oriented ribbon." (A drive-in food stand along a highway is ideal. Gasoline stations, motels, ice cream parlors, and fruit and vegetable stands will do.)
d. A store which is a part of a "regional shopping center."

This project works well with a team of students, each of whom may study one area. Alternatively, one student can visit all four.

For each area, interview ten people. Determine: (a) where the person started from (lives); (b) whether other shopping stops are part of his or her trip. If so, find out how many and where they are located; (c) the approximate value of any purchase they have made or intend to make [give people the option of not responding to this question].

To display the responses to item (a), put a colored pin at the point where each person began her or his trip, with a piece of colored yarn running to the business establishment. The information for (b) can be displayed by drawing a square with a colored dot at its center for each type of business and plotting the number and approximate location of other stops for each interviewee by dots in a different color connected by a line showing the route followed. The information for (c) can be arrayed in tabular form.

4. **Age-sex pyramids.** Review Fig. 13-12 and the discussion of age-sex pyramids. Obtain the volume *U.S. Census of Population and Housing*, which contains census tract information for your commnity. Skimming the age characeristics in the city,

select one census tract which has a high concentration of older residents and one which has a high concentration of young children. If any other census tracts stand out as having unusually nonuniform distributions of population by age or sex, you may want to include them also.

Construct age-sex pyramids for each census tract similar to those in Fig. 13-12. Construct some plausible hypotheses about the areas based on the census data alone. For example, if the data show many young families with children, you may hypothesize that the area will contain a high concentration of modestly priced apartment houses.

Visit the two census tracts. Do your observations seem to support your hypotheses?

SUGGESTIONS FOR FURTHER LEARNING

Two comprehensive introductory textbooks on urban geography are Ray M. Northam, *Urban Geography* (New York: Wiley, 1975), and Maurice Yeates and Barry Garner, *The North American City*, 2d. ed. (New York: Harper & Row, 1976), both of which cover material on the system of cities, internal structure of cities, urban residential patterns, and commercial and industrial location. Both books are somewhat broader than pure urban geography texts, introducing material which might be classified as historical, economic, or sociological.

Raymond E. Murphy's *The American City*, 2d ed. (New York: McGraw-Hill, 1974) is more technical, with carefully referenced material and precise use of terminology. Much of the material discusses work done in the 1950s, 1940s, and earlier, and the conceptual framework rests heavily upon the typological tradition and city classification tradition rather than more modern work.

Three urban geography books by foreign authors are less focused on contemporary American issues. Welsh geographer Harold Carter's *The Study of Urban Geography*, 2d ed. (New York: Wiley, 1976) is a scholarly and theoretical book which draws heavily upon British examples. James H. Johnson, *Urban Geography* (New York: Pergamon, 1972), also by a British author, covers essentially the same material as the Northam and Yeates and Garner books, but with fewer references to American material. J. Beaujeu-Garnier and G. Chabot's *Urban Geography* (New York: Wiley, 1967) combines general descriptions of cities in different regions of the world and a functional classification approach which is removed from both American examples and theory.

David Herbert, *Urban Geography* (New York: Praeger, 1973), focuses on urban social geography. It touches on some of the material described in this chapter but emphasizes residential patterns and social geography, compresses discussion of theoretical material on the internal structure of cities and city systems, and treats some topics, such as manufacturing location, only in passing.

A textbook which combines material from urban geography with psychological and sociological material on perception and human behavior is John Jakle, Stanley Brunn, and Curtis Roseman, *Human Spatial Behavior* (North Scituate, Mass.: Duxbury Press, 1976).

The ecological approach to urban spatial analysis is explored in Brian J. L. Berry and John D. Kasarda, *Contemporary Urban Ecology* (New York: Macmillan, 1977), which both summarizes the recent literature on many aspects of urban form and space and reports the authors' substantial original contributions. An anthology of articles from the ecological perspective is Kent P. Schwirian, *Comparative Urban Structure* (Lexington, Mass.: D.C. Heath, 1974). This volume contains a number of the classic statements on both the system of cities and the internal structure of cities, as well as a range of contemporary factorial ecology studies. Its contents are somewhat more comprehensive than the subtitle, *Studies in the Ecology of Cities*, suggests.

Key writings on the internal structure of the city through 1971 are collected in Larry S. Bourne (ed.), *The Internal Structure of the City* (New York: Oxford University Press, 1971). This anthology also deals with other topics in urban studies including urban imagery, policy issues, and futurism.

Key writings on the system of cities and the urban hierarchy are collected in Larry S. Bourne and James W. Simmons (eds.), *Systems of Cities* (New York: Oxford University Press, 1978). This anthology also contains writings which cover other aspects of urban studies, as well as materials on current policy dilemmas.

Studies of urban residential structure are synthesized in R. J. Johnson, *Urban Residential Patterns* (New York: Praeger, 1972), a comprehensive volume which surveys the entire literature to the date of publication. Another volume which focuses specifically on the important issue of black residential patterns (with some material on spatial aspects of black commercial and other nonresidential activities) is Robert T. Ernst and Lawrence Hugg (eds.), *Black America: Geographic Perspectives* (Garden City, N.Y.: Doubleday, 1976).

Films on city form and space include *Faces of the City* (Australian Information Bureau, 1971), which describes the internal structure of the city; *Cities: How They Grow* (Encyclopaedia Britannica, 1953), which describes the nature of the system of cities; and *Geography of Survival* (Sterling Associates, 1972), which deals with city-hinterland and city-rural issues.

KEY TERMS

Assimilation The process by which different cultures (or individuals, or groups representing different cultures) are merged into a homogeneous unit. The most frequent and important instances of assimilation occur when a dominant group absorbs a weaker group.

Central Business District (CBD) An American term indicating the heart of the city; commonly referred to as "downtown." The U.S. Census Bureau defines the CBD as an area of very high land valuation; characterized by a high concentration of retail businesses, offices, theaters, hotels, and service businesses; and marked by high traffic flow.

Central place theory Economic geographer Walter Christaller's theory (1933), which holds that a hierarchy of central places (cities) would evolve to serve surrounding hinterlands. The smallest central places, offering a limited range of goods and services, would serve relatively small, hexagonal-shaped areas, while the largest central place in a region would have a wide range of goods and services available and a much larger hinterland containing many smaller and intermediate central places.

Chicago school of sociology A school of thought developed at the University of Chicago which attained its greatest prestige in the late 1920s and early 1930s. Sociologists Ernest W. Burgess, Robert E. Park, and Louis Wirth were leading members of the school. The urban ecology perspective developed by the Chicago school shaped subsequent thinking about cities.

Concentric zone model A model of the internal structure of the city, developed by Chicago school sociologist Ernest W. Burgess in the 1920s which conceptualized cities as organized in a series of concentric zones radiating out from the city center. Each zone tended to have a different population type and set of land uses and functions. Ethnic groups, according to Burgess, initially tended to settle close to the center of the city and gradually moved out toward the periphery as they became assimilated.

Gentrification The process whereby members of a higher-income group move into a neighborhood occupied by lower-income persons. When this occurs, the neighborhood will be physically improved but many of the former residents displaced.

Ghetto A section of a city, often rundown and/or overcrowded, inhabited chiefly by a minority group that is effectively barred from living in other communities because of prejudice or economic barriers.

Hinterland The area which is adjacent to and dependent upon an urban center. The term once referred to the back-country or the area in back of the coastal region. Today the term is used to refer to the urban sphere of influence. The hinterland of a metropolis may consist of the area of commutation or trade area.

Internal structure of the city The location, arrangement, and interrelationships between social and physical elements within a city.

Invasion and **succession.** Terms which describe the process of social change in cities. These terms fit into a theoretical model which sees successive social groups competing for and succeeding one another in a given physical area. *Invasion* describes the entrance into an area of a new class or group and the resulting displacement of certain other classes or groups of existing residents. The process may, however, involve an amalgamation of the invasion types with resident types. *Succession* describes the order, in a series of territorial occupations, as one group in an area is forced out or replaced by another.

Major retail center (MRC) A U.S. Census Bureau term for those concentrations of retail stores (located in an SMSA) having at least $5 million in retail sales and at least ten retail establishments, one of which is classified as a department store. MRCs include planned suburban shopping centers and older neighborhood developments which meet the above prerequisites.

Manufacture To transform a substance into a new product. Assembly of component parts is also considered manufacturing if the new product is not a building (a structure or other fixed improvement).

Multiple nuclei model A model of the internal structure of the city developed by geographers Chauncy Harris and Edward L. Ullman. In their view, a city has more than one nucleus. Thus, not only the CBD, but also a port, university, or industrial area, may act as the center around which activities are organized.

Range A term in central place theory referring to the zone or tributary area around a central place from which persons travel to the center to purchase the good (service or merchandise) offered at that place. Theoretically, the upper limit of this range is the maximum possible radius of sales. The lower limit of the range is the radius that encloses the minimum number of consumers necessary to provide a sales volume adequate for the good to be supplied profitably from the central place.

Sectoral model A model of urban growth developed by real estate economist Homer Hoyt in the 1930s. The theory holds that classes of land use tend to be arranged in wedge-shaped sectors radiating from the CBD along major transportation corridors.

System of cities A term used to describe how cities of different sizes and functional types are interdependent and economically interrelated in systematic ways. The literature on system of cities describes the specialization of functions among cities and how they interact and interconnect.

Threshold A concept in central place theory which describes the minimum population which will support an urban function.

Urban ecology The study of the spatial distribution of people and institutions in cities from a distinctive perspective, originated by members of the Chicago school of sociology (particularly Ernest W. Burgess and Robert E. Park) and continued by contemporary urban ecologists.

REFERENCES

Abu-Lughod, Janet L.
1969 "Testing the theory of social area analysis: the ecology of Cairo, Egypt." American Sociological Review 34:198–212.

Berry, Brian J. L.
1963 "Commercial structure and commercial blight." Research Paper No. 85, University of Chicago, Department of Geography research series. Chicago: University of Chicago.
1972 City Classification Handbook. New York: Wiley.

Berry, Brian J. L. and William L. Garrison
1958 "The functional bases of the central place hierarchy." Economic Geography 34:145–54.

Berry, Brian J. L., Gardiner Barnum, and Robert J. Tennant
1962 "Retail location and consumer behavior." Papers and Proceedings of the Regional Science Association 9:65–106.

Berry, Brian J. L. and John D. Kasarda
1977 Contemporary Urban Ecology. New York: Macmillan.

Burgess, Ernest W.
[1923]
1925 "Growth of the city." Pp. 47–62 in Robert E. Park, Ernest W. Burgess, and Roderick McKenzie, The City. Chicago: University of Chicago Press.

Burgess, Ernest W. and Donald J. Bogue (eds.)
1964 Contributions to Urban Sociology. Chicago: University of Chicago Press.

Christaller, Walter
[1933]
1966 Central Places in Southern Germany. Tr., C. W. Baskin. Englewood Cliffs, N.J.: Prentice-Hall.

Firey, Walter
1947 Land Use in Central Boston. Cambridge, Mass.: Harvard University Press.

Harris, Chauncy
1943 "A functional classification of cities in the United States." Geographical Review 33:86–99.

Harris, Chauncy and Edward L. Ullman
1945 "The nature of cities." Annals of the American Academy of Political and Social Science 242: 7–17.

Hodge, Gerald
1965 "The prediction of trade center viability in the Great Plains." Regional Science Association, Papers and Proceedings 57:87–118.

Hoyt, Homer
1939 The Structure and Growth of Residential Neighborhoods in American Cities. Washington, D.C.: Federal Housing Administration.

International City Managers Association (ICMA)
1963 Municipal Year Book. Washington, D.C.: ICMA.

Jakle, John and J.A. Wheeler
[1969]
1972 "The Dutch and Kalamazoo, Michigan: a study of spatial barriers to acculturation." Tijdschrift Voor Economische en Sociale Geografie 60:249–54.

Jones, Victor, Richard L. Forestall, and Andrew Collver
1963 "Economic and social characteristics of urban places." Pp. 85–157 in The Municipal Year Book: 1963. Chicago: International City Managers Association.

Kitagawa, E. M. and D. J. Bogue
1955 Suburbanization of Manufacturing Activity Within Standard Metropolitan Statistical Areas. Oxford, Ohio: Scripps Foundation.

Murphy, Raymond E.
1954 The Central Business District. Chicago: Aldine.
1974 The American City: An Urban Geography, 2d ed. New York: McGraw-Hill.

Murphy, Raymond E. and James E. Vance, Jr.
1954a "A comparative study of nine central business districts." Economic Geography 30:301–36.
1954b "Delimiting the CBD." Economic Geography 30:189–222.

Northam, Ray M.
1975 Urban Geography. New York: Wiley.

Park, Robert E., Ernest W. Burgess, and Roderick McKenzie
1925 The City. Chicago: University of Chicago Press.

Pred, Allen
1977 City Systems in Advanced Economies. New York: Wiley.

Rees, Philip H.
1970 "The factorial ecology of Chicago: a case study." Pp. 319–94 in Brian J. L. Berry and

Frank E. Horton (eds.), Geographic Perspectives in Urban Systems. Englewood Cliffs, N.J.: Prentice-Hall.

Scheer, Robert
1979 "Ehrlichman talks about Nixon." San Francisco Chronicle (May 30):8.

Shevky, Eshref and Wendell Bell
1955 Social Area Analysis. Berkeley and Los Angeles: University of California Press.

U.S. Bureau of the Census
1976 Census of Retail Trade, 1972. Vol. 2: Area Statistics. Washington, D.C.: U.S. Government Printing Office.

Yeates, Maurice and Barry Garner
1976 The North American City, 2d ed. New York: Harper & Row.

Stephen Hender

CHAPTER 14
A Sense of Place

How important is a sense of place? Important enough for politicians to evoke it. When Senator Ted Kennedy kicked off his presidential campaign in 1979, he spoke at Boston's historic Faneuil Hall. This setting evoked American heroes, past glories, and revolutionary events. Identification with place, as good speechwriters know, can have a subtle impact on voters.

Physical settings can have mind-boggling effects as well. Consider the case of Carlos Castaneda. As an anthropology graduate student at UCLA, Castaneda set out to do fieldwork among the Yaqui Indians. Once there, he became drawn into the mystical reality of his informant, a sorcerer named Don Juan. At one point, Don Juan suggested that he find his "own spot" on the floor of the cabin where they were staying. Puzzled, Castaneda tried to respond to this strange request. "I had to feel all the possible spots," Castaneda reports in his field notes. "I covered the whole floor. . . . I deliberately tried to 'feel' differences between places." As he continued, Castenada "saw" two spots on the floor that appeared to glow and shimmer. When he approached one spot, he felt nauseous and afraid; the other one made him feel exhausted. Later, he heard Don Juan talking and laughing above his head and woke up. "You have found the spot," Don Juan told him (Casteneda, 1968:29–30, 34).

Castaneda's extraordinary experience illustrates two themes that run throughout this chapter: (1) the sense of place can have a powerful, even magical, impact on us—often at the unconscious level, and (2) people perceive and attach meaning to physical space in various ways. These themes complement a macro-level theme of Chapter 13, namely, that city form and space reflect a society's economic and social structure.

This chapter, then, is about how people perceive and use space. It begins with a discussion of general perception and spatial perception. Next, it examines views about the effects of physical environment on human behavior. Then it moves to close encounters in space: What happens if a man tries to invade a woman's personal space, or if outsiders enter your turf? After reviewing the findings of environmental psychology—a subdiscipline devoted to the study of behavior/environment—the chapter considers the principles that architects, landscape architects, urban designers, and planners use to shape urban space. Lastly, it turns to dreams: grand dreams of creating new cities.

PERCEPTION: FILTERING REALITY

We have seen that one person's reality is another's fantasy. People in the same city have different cognitive maps (Chapter 2). Radicals, liberals, and conservatives can look at the political economy and see very different realities (Chapter 3).

Fig. 14-1 indicates why people disagree on what's real. It shows that perceptual data are processed through three reality filters: cultural, social, and psychological. It implies that the way we filter perceptual data determines how we construct "objective" reality.

Cultural Filters

Reflecting on how culture transforms physical reality—what is *there*—into experienced reality, American anthropologist Dorothy Lee (1959:1) says:

> . . . the universe as I know it or imagine it in the Western world is different from the universe of the Tikopia, in Polynesia. It follows . . . that I feel differently about what I see. As I look out of my window now, I see trees, some of which I like to be there, and some of which I intend to cut down . . . the Dakota Black Elk Indian, however, saw trees as having rights to the land, equal to his own.

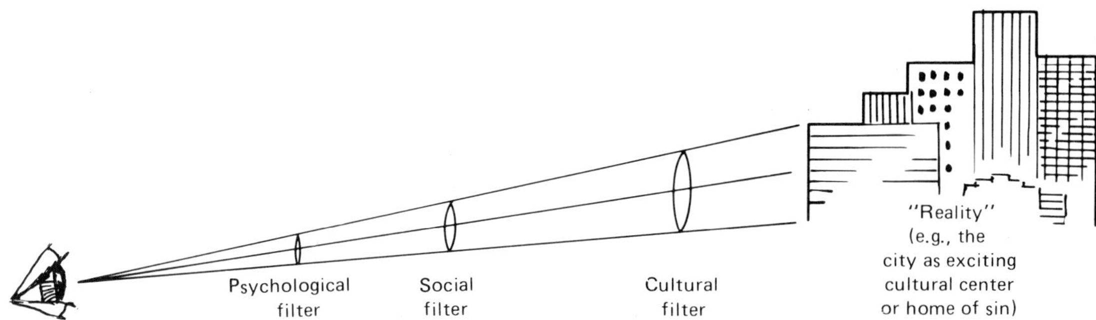

Fig. 14-1 THREE FILTERS OF REALITY. Sense data pass through cultural, social, and psychological filters before becoming "objective" reality in our minds.

Lee also notes that we perceive our behavior within the conceptual framework of our own culture:

> When I throw a ball, do I perform an aggressive causal act, as my culture predisposes me to believe? Or does the ball leave my hand, as the Greenland Eskimo puts it, or do I merely actualize the ball's potential to move, as the Navaho would have it? (1959:2)

Others suggest that what we see (and feel) depends on what language we speak. According to the Sapir-Whorf hypothesis, named for the two anthropologists who developed it, language does much more than reflect culture; it molds our world view and thoughts. In this view, people's conception of reality is significantly determined by the categories available to them in their language. For instance, Hopi Indians have no tenses in their language, nor do they have nouns for times or days. The Sapir-Whorf hypothesis suggests that, as a result, Hopis see the world in terms of dynamic, ever-changing motion. By contrast, English speakers see the world in terms of linear progression; for them, seconds, hours, and years mark the "reality" of time passing by. English speakers also tend to see events as having a beginning, middle, and end; they define things as past, present, or future. This way of viewing the world is foreign to a Hopi speaker.

Language and other elements of culture (including the objects we produce and the beliefs we hold) provide the context in which people perceive reality. Within that broad cultural context, there are often subcultural meanings too. For instance, gyrating wildly on a disco dance floor may be perceived as harmless fun by some, perhaps most, Americans, but not by members of a religious community which equates dancing with evil.

Who is to say which cultural or subcultural reality is true? Or, as anthropologist Lee (1959:2) asks, "Are they all true, all different facets of the same truth?"

Social Filters

Within the cultural context, social identity also helps to shape the reality people perceive. Consider, for example, a common scene of pedestrians and shoppers along Chicago's opulent "Magnificent Mile" at Christmas time. The *meanings* observers attach to this bustling scene—and what they actually *see*—can differ with social background. All a child might see in this morass of sense data are the stuffed toys in the store windows. A journalist might focus on an unusual or paradoxical event, perhaps a bag lady sifting through the garbage amid the affluence. Meanwhile, the bag lady sees none of this affluence as she searches through the garbage containers for something to eat.

It follows that what we see and how we distort features of the urban environment are conditioned by who we are. Sociologists of knowledge and social psychologists are among those who study possible patterns of distortion based on social location and social affiliation. One classic study, "They Saw a Game" (Hastorf and Cantril, 1954), documents the importance of the perceivers' social and academic affiliations in the selective perception of a college football game. Surveying fans of both teams, researchers found that they actually saw very different games.

Psychological Filters

Lastly, we filter information through our own particular needs, memories, feelings, past experiences, and present concerns. Thus, a starving Cambodian might focus on food scraps lying on the ground, whereas a well-fed Congressperson touring refugee camps might not notice them.

Psychoanalysts also point to the role that fantasies, myths, and long-forgotten experiences play in perceiving reality. How these operate is a matter of debate, but it is generally acknowledged that the unconscious mind can have powerful effects on a person's thoughts and acts. Sigmund Freud first became aware of the power of the unconscious in 1882; later he called this "psychic reality."

To conclude: How we construct reality depends partially on chance—the culture into which we're born and raised and the language we speak; partially on our social location and identity; and partially on our psychic history and present concerns. Thus, what our senses pick up from the environment and translate into "objective reality" constitutes a highly selective process of perception.

PERCEIVING THE BUILT ENVIRONMENT

Billboards, tombstones, buildings, highways, and everything else people construct form the **built environment.** The built environment serves both functional and symbolic purposes. For instance, an apartment building at a "good address" is more than a shelter; it is a symbol of the residents' status. As an essayist of metropolitan life puts it, "Nothing succeeds like address" (Lebowitz, [1974] 1978).

Architecture as Symbolic Politics

Buildings offer clues to the values of the people who built them. Political scientist Harold Lasswell (1979) argues that many American buildings reflect one of the society's central concerns: power. In Lasswell's view, architecture makes a political statement, expressing the values of a society's dominant elites.

Architecture speaks in different voices, depending on who's listening. When an angry mob destroyed the U.S. Embassy building in Pakistan's capital of Islamabad in 1979, it was not commenting on the artistic merit of a widely acclaimed architectural triumph. Rather, the mob attacked a building-as-symbol of power.

If political change occurs in a society, meanings attached to buildings can also change. For example, before the Chinese revolution in 1949, pagodalike buildings in Beijing's Forbidden City symbolized the grace and power of China's ruling dynasties.

Fig. 14-2 FORTRESS AMERICA. The massive, fortresslike Pentagon in suburban Washington, D.C., symbolizes U.S. military might. (U.S. Army photograph)

Today, the same buildings represent the former rulers' exploitation of the peasants' resources and labor.

Las Vegas, Nevada

Sometimes the built environment sends messages that are far from subtle. Such is the case of Las Vegas, Nevada, a gambling and pleasure spot supreme. In the words of Tom Wolfe (1977:7), Las Vegas is "the only town in the world whose skyline is made up neither of buildings, like New York, nor of trees, like Wilbraham, Massachusetts, but signs." Indeed, Las Vegas buildings are little more than concrete sheds with neon signs, including a restaurant shaped like a duck—which is actually one huge sign. Architect Robert Venturi and his colleagues ([1972] 1977) call this "duck and shed" architecture. They say that these extreme forms of advertisement are functional to the local economy.

a

Fig. 14-3 HOW BUILDINGS SPEAK TO US. "Our architecture reflects us, as truly as a mirror," said Louis Sullivan, the inventor of the skyscraper. As objects, buildings can represent the values of a culture—in tall church spires, factory smokestacks, or skyscrapers. Buildings send different messages to different audiences too. (*a*) Once part of the Forbidden City in Beijing, this former temple, a symbol of grace and imperial power under China's former rulers, is now a people's museum. (*b*) Downtown Chicago with its steely majesty and industrial power, combined with a curlique bit of fantasy, a parking garage.
(*a*, *b* © Galen Cranz)

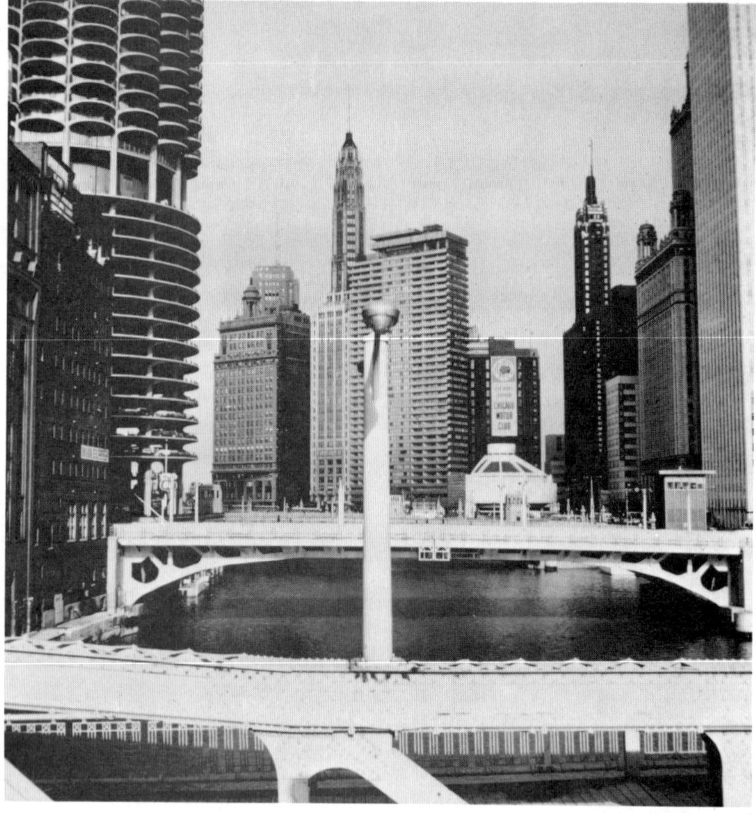

b

Box 14-1

SIGNS, SEX, AND SHOW BUSINESS

The Las Vegas Story

Las Vegas is the only town in the world whose skyline is made up neither of buildings, like New York, nor of trees, like Wilbraham, Massachusetts, but signs. One can look at Las Vegas from a mile away on Route 91 and see no buildings, no trees, only signs. But such signs! They tower. They revolve, they oscillate, they soar in shapes before which the existing vocabulary of art history is helpless. I can only attempt to supply names—Boomerang Modern, Palette Curvilinear, Flash Gordon Ming-Alert Spiral, McDonald's Hamburger Parabola, Mint Casino Elliptical, Miami Beach Kidney. Las Vegas' sign makers work so far out beyond the frontiers of conventional studio art that they have no names themselves for the forms they create. Vaughan Cannon, one of those tall, blond Westerners, the builders of places like Las Vegas and Los Angeles, whose eyes seem to have been bleached by the sun, is in the back shop of the Young Electric Sign Company out on East Charleston Boulevard with Herman Boernge, one of his designers, looking at the model they have prepared for the Lucky Strike Casino sign, and Cannon points to where the sign's two great curving faces meet to form a narrow vertical face and says:

"Well, here we are again—what do we call that?"

"I don't know," says Boernge. "It's sort of a nose effect. Call it a nose."

Okay, a nose, but it rises sixteen stories high above a two-story building. In Las Vegas no farseeing entrepreneur buys a sign to fit a building he owns. He rebuilds the building to support the biggest sign he can get up the money for and, if necessary, changes the name. . . . In the Young Electric Sign Co. era signs have become the architecture of Las Vegas. . . . Men like Boernge, Kermit Wayne, Ben Mitchem and Jack Larsen, formerly an artist for Walt Disney, are the designer-sculptor geniuses of Las Vegas, but their motifs have been carried faithfully throughout the town by lesser men, for gasoline stations, motels, funeral parlors, churches, public buildings, flophouses and sauna baths.

Then there is a stimulus that is both visual and sexual—the Las Vegas buttocks décolletage. This is a form of sexually provocative dress seen more and more in the United States, but avoided like Broadway message-embroidered ("Kiss Me, I'm Cold") underwear in the fashion pages, so that the euphemisms have not been established and I have no choice but clinical terms. To achieve buttocks décolletage a woman wears bikini-style shorts that cut across the round fatty masses of the buttocks rather than cupping them from below, so that the outer-lower edges of these fatty masses, or "cheeks," are exposed. I am in the cocktail lounge of the Hacienda Hotel, talking to managing director Dick Taylor about the great success his place has had in attracting family and tour groups, and all around me the waitresses are bobbing on their high heels, bare legs and décolletage-bare backsides, set off by pelvis-length lingerie of an uncertain denomination. I stare, but I am new here. . . . On the streets of Las Vegas, not only the show girls, of which the town has about two hundred fifty, bona fide, in residence, but girls of every sort, including, especially, Las Vegas' little high-school buds, who adorn what locals seeking roots in the sand call "our city of churches and schools," have taken up the chic of wearing buttocks décolletage step-ins under flesh-tight slacks. with the outline of the undergarment showing through fashionably. (Wolfe, 1977:7–8). Copyright © 1963, 1964, 1965 by Thomas K. Wolfe, Jr. Copyright © 1963, 1964, 1965 by New York Herald Tribune, Inc. Reprinted by permission of Farrar, Straus and Giroux, Inc.

The Learning from Las Vegas Studio, Yale University.

That is, Las Vegas depends on persuading transient consumers to stop and spend money. In addition, the unlikely blend of architectural styles at gambling casino-hotels like Caesar's Palace—Italian Renaissance, neoclassic, modern, and early Christian tomb—are very functional, for they appeal to the fantasies of a diverse clientele.

In Las Vegas, the built environment doesn't let you forget where you are. No one familiar with U.S. urban culture could mistake its pleasure domes for a center of manufacturing or high finance. Las Vegas has a distinctive sense of place.

Most U.S. cities are far less distinctive—or bizarre, depending on your taste. Nonetheless, people feel a sense of place wherever they live. They invest the natural and built environment with meaning and sentiment.

DOES ENVIRONMENT DETERMINE BEHAVIOR?

Will youngsters growing up amid the tall signs and desert sands of Las Vegas be significantly different from others raised in snowy, tree-lined Wilbraham, Massachusetts? Do bad housing conditions produce bad people?

The extent to which the natural and built environment affects behavior is a question of persistent debate. One view maintains that environment determines behavior. At the very least, it states, the natural and built environments play a key role in determining behavior. Britain's Lord Manny Shinwell speaks eloquently for this point of view—**environmental determinism**—in describing his own background. Born in 1884 (and interviewed by R. W. Apple in 1979, at age ninety-five), Shinwell grew up in Glasgow, Scotland's, notoriously squalid Gorbals slum, where people "lived in three-story tenements, with one lavatory on each landing for three families. Filthy black smoke poured in when you opened the windows. There was every opportunity to become a criminal, and even the best of us emerged from it as hardened agitators and rebels."

Shinwell did not become a criminal. But he did emerge as an agitator and rebel of sorts. A school dropout at age eleven, he read voraciously, got out of the Gorbals, went on to play a leading role in the nationalization of England's coal mines, and become a combative orator in the British Parliament for forty-eight years.

Shinwell's story raises difficult questions. Was it the filthy smoke pouring in and the crowding or was it the poverty and social conditions in the Gorbals that influenced residents' behavior? This is hard to sort out, for bad physical conditions often go hand-in-hand with low income and low status. If a teenager living in a deteriorated tenement commits robbery or murder, we can't conclude that the physical environment determined such behavior. After all, not all people who live in the same physical environment, like the Gorbals, become criminals. This fact supports critics of physical environmental determinism. Critics argue that cultural and psychological variables have more influence on behavior than does physical environment. This dilemma of interpretation can be illustrated by examining one notoriously bad physical environment: the Pruitt-Igoe public housing project in St. Louis, Missouri.

Case Study: Pruitt-Igoe

Before its demolition in 1974, Pruitt-Igoe symbolized the worst kind of urban environment. The massive project covered 57 acres and contained 33 slab construction buildings, each with 2,762 apartments on 11 stories. It was designed originally to house about 10,000 people, whites living in the Igoe

Fig. 14-4 PRUITT-IGOE HOUSING PROJECT. St. Louis, Missouri's, vast low-income residential complex came to symbolize bad design and social disaster. Built in 1954, it was demolished just twenty years later by the U.S. Department of Housing and Urban Development. (U.S. Department of Housing and Urban Development)

portion and blacks living in the Pruitt portion. A Supreme Court decision barred this racial segregation, and the project became racially integrated.

When Pruitt-Igoe opened in 1954, it won praise as an exciting advance in low-income housing. A decade later, it was the subject of worried commission reports as a social disaster area. By the mid-1960s, it was occupied entirely by poor blacks, mainly on welfare and disproportionately living in large, female-headed households. By the early 1970s, federal officials gave up on Pruitt-Igoe. The entire project was dynamited and totally demolished in 1974.

Reviewing the sad history of Pruitt-Igoe, an environmental determinist would have a ready explanation for its failure: bad physical design. Pruitt-Igoe was very large and very densely settled. Each high-rise was identical to the next. The project had virtually no open space, elevators that stopped only on some floors, easily broken windows, and other poor design features. To a physical determinist, social disaster was predictable, for the project design spelled trouble.

In contrast, a critic of physical determinism would point out that physical design was the least of the problems at Pruitt-Igoe. In a housing project with large numbers of poor children, juvenile delinquency and vandalism could be anticipated no matter how well designed it was. Further, as long as tenants were unemployed, without ownership rights in their residence, and conscious of their "bad address," hopelessness and hostility could be expected.

Who's right? One perceptive commentator argues that there is no right answer in the debate about environmental determinism because it is based on faulty assumptions. Galen Cranz, a sociologist of spatial behavior at Berkeley's School of Architecture, believes that both environmental determinists and their critics are on the wrong track. Cranz says that there is a reciprocal relationship between the built environment and human behavior. The built environment affects behavior but, at the same time, it reflects broader social, economic, and political forces. In her view, people receive messages about the social meaning of their world from many sources—verbal, nonverbal, and environmental. Usually these varied sources transmit similar messages, only in different symbolic forms. Cranz calls this "redundancy."

Applying the redundancy concept to the Pruitt-Igoe case, we would note how verbal, nonverbal, and environmental sources sent the same message to poor black residents: You are inferior beings. This message was reinforced in subtle and not-so-subtle ways—waiting in line for welfare checks, being subjected to police surveillance and discriminated against in jobs, and so forth. Residents could hardly avoid knowing that the larger society devalued them as low-status, low-income black persons, for the message was all around them. In the mass media of the 1950s and early 1960s, for instance, few blacks appeared in any role; those visible few were most often cast as bad people or losers. So, Pruitt-Igoe's prisonlike physical design merely confirmed the larger society's negative attitude toward them. Over and over, in various forms, the message of inferiority went out. Redundancy.

Perhaps Winston Churchill had the final word. When he reopened the House of Commons after World War II, he said: "We shape our buildings and then they shape us."

EXPERIENCING PERSONAL SPACE

How people experience space depends on their reality filters and the kind of space they occupy. Here we focus on two types of occupied space, personal and social.

A leading environmental psychologist, Robert Sommer (1969:viii), uses the term **personal space** in two ways: to describe (1) "the emotionally charged zone around each person, sometimes described as a soap bubble or aura, which helps to regulate the spacing of individuals" and (2) "the processes by which people mark out and personalize the spaces they inhabit." Personal spaces are those we consider ours.

Personal Space as Protective Bubble

We treat our bodies and that invisible bubble surrounding our bodies as the most private, inviolate territory. It is ours; we own it. All societies have rules about touching the bodies or invading the body territories of others. In the United States, for instance, "affectionate bodily contact is almost completely taboo among men" (Parsons, 1951: 189).

What happens if another person tries to break our bubble by invading it? That depends. We may withdraw and move away; we may get hostile; we may do nothing. Researchers find that one key variable in people's reactions to the invasion of personal space is sex. Conducting experiments on Los Angeles beaches, researchers found that men can routinely invade women's personal space, but the reverse is not acceptable. The researchers offer two different explanations: (1) women are simply more sociable than men or (2) women can't prevent their space from being invaded because, in general, their social status is lower than that of men (Skolnick et al., 1977:307–16).

How big is a person's bubble? That depends too. Bubble sizes vary from culture to

Fig. 14-5 IMMEDIATE PHYSICAL ENVIRONMENT. People tend to see their personal space, home base, and home range as inviolate territories or "defensible space." (J. D. Porteous, "An Organizing Model of Territoriality in an Urban Setting," in *Environment and Behavior: Planning and Everyday Urban Life* [Reading, Mass.: Addison-Wesley, 1977], p. 29. Copyright © 1977 by J. Douglas Porteous. Reprinted by permission.)

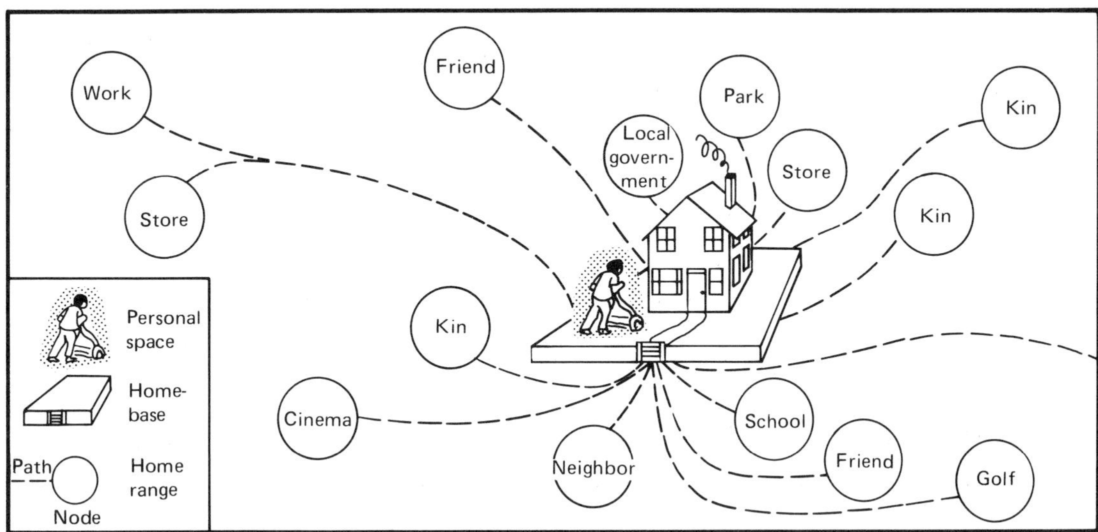

culture. Not knowing this could lead to misunderstanding, even trouble. That is one reason why U.S. embassy officials receive training in what anthropologist Edward T. Hall (1959) calls **proxemics**: the study of how people in different cultures use intimate space, particularly for social interaction such as conversation.

Hall, a pioneer in the study of personal space, illustrates why proxemics is important for cross-cultural understanding: "In Latin America the interaction distance is much less than it is in the United States. Indeed, people cannot talk comfortably with one another unless they are very close to the distance that evokes either sexual or hostile feelings in the North American." The result, Hall (1959:164) says, is that "when they move close, we withdraw and back away. As a consequence they think we are distant or cold, withdrawn and unfriendly. We, on the other hand, are constantly accusing them of breathing down our necks, crowding us, and spraying our faces."

Nonverbal communication may be equally misunderstood. Hall (1966) recounts a personal experience that illustrates the point. While waiting for a friend in an empty hotel lobby in Washington, D.C., Hall seated himself in a solitary chair. He expected any stranger to leave him alone. Yet, a stranger entered the lobby and stood so close to Hall that he could hear him breathe. Hall moved slightly to signal his annoyance with body language. The stranger only moved closer. But Hall would not abandon his post. He thought, "Why should I move? I was here first." Moments later, a group arrived to join his "tormentor." It was then that Hall realized, from gestures and language, that the stranger was an Arab. Later, Hall described the scene to an Arab colleague, who helped him understand what had happened. "In Arab thought I had no rights whatsoever by virtue of occupying a given spot; neither my place nor my body was inviolate! For the Arab, there is no such thing as an intrusion in public. Public means public."

The size of a person's inviolate sphere of privacy varies with the surroundings, the social importance of the person, and other characteristics such as age. Each culture has implicit rules about the proper spatial distance in particular situations. In America, a person who invades another's body territory—even for a specific purpose, such as asking directions—usually acknowledges the intrusion by saying, "Excuse me."

Personalizing Our Space: Home Territories

Home territories are "areas where the regular participants have a relative freedom of behavior and a sense of intimacy and control over the area" (Lyman and Scott, [1967] 1970:92). They are spaces in which we feel safe and comfortable. Home territories consist of home base (the home and its immediate surroundings) and home range (places where a person feels safe and a sense of belonging).

"Home," writes an urban designer, "is a haven in the turbulent seas of life. It embodies the familiar, it is the place we feel most comfortable in, where we know better than anywhere else what will happen. Home is bound up with our identity. We instinctively rise to its defense when it is attacked or threatened" (Appleyard, 1978b:1). Or as the English say, "A man's home is his castle."

Meanings attached to home pass through cultural, social, and psychological filters. In the United States, the meaning of home base varies with social class and status. Two research studies illustrate these differences. A study of Pruitt-Igoe found that the most important function of home to tenants was house-as-safe-haven (Rainwater, 1966). The study suggests that lower-class, low-status tenants lived in a world of perceived threat: crime and vandalism, health hazards, verbal abuse, and so on. To them, home represented a retreat. By contrast, to upper-class, high-status groups, home also symbolizes their social position. Striving young executives in the San Francisco Bay Area frequently choose mock-colonial homes which conspicuously display their stability and wealth; more established professionals tend to choose less showy and better designed homes (Werthman, 1965).

Living spaces are more than devices for sending messages to others about who we are or wish to be. Homes are also symbols of the way we perceive ourselves. According to architect Claire Cooper (1976:36), "The furniture we install, the way we arrange it, the pictures we hang, the plants we buy and tend are expressions of ourselves, all are messages about ourselves that we want to convey back to ourselves." She calls this "house-as-symbol of self."

Through their homes, people often tell themselves one thing, outsiders another. In most American homes, for instance, the living room doesn't look lived in. There are no cookie jars, coats lying around, or papers strewn about. If guests are expected, it is usually the living room that is cleaned up, while unkempt bedrooms or other private spaces are left as is. In France, upper-status families often have a special room for entertaining—the parlor—whose perfect appearance usually contrasts to the messier private spaces. Similarly, Japanese-American families in northern California often present a conventional image to their neighbors by their front yard landscaping; for their own enjoyment, they use a rear, hidden-from-view Japanese garden (Appleyard, 1978a).

Beyond home base lies home range, that area in which a person feels a sense of belonging or perhaps ownership. As we note in the next section, public territories (social space) are often converted into the home range of individuals or social groups.

The extent of a person's home range varies with age, social standing and background, and personal disposition. Children tend to have the narrowest home ranges. Very young children may perceive a one-block area around home as home range. For older children, home range is often equated with their neighborhood.

For some adults, too, home range consists of little more than their neighborhoods. This is often the case with immigrants who arrive in large cities speaking no English. One of our students says that his mother lives and works in San Francisco's Chinatown, and she has not been outside that neighborhood since she arrived some forty years ago from China. This suggests that residents of ethnic neighborhoods have a stronger sense of home range than residents of more heterogeneous neighborhoods.

For other adults, the office is an all-important part of home territory. Under certain conditions, a person can invest his or her office with the symbolic meaning of home base—inviolate territory and safe haven. The most dramatic example of office-as-safe-haven is a government's embassy building. Traditionally and by international accord, any government's embassy anywhere in the world is considered inviolate territory; an embassy building symbolizes the honor and security of a nation. Thus, in 1979 when the U.S. Embassy in Teheran, Iran, was invaded and hostages were taken in an unprecedented action, many Americans reacted as if their own homes had been threatened.

The drama of Teheran and the little everyday dramas of feeling uncomfortable when someone moves "too close" indicate that we invest physical space with symbolic meaning, and that these meanings can have a powerful

(The Lawen Group)

Fig. 14-6 HOUSE-AS-SYMBOL. This newspaper ad is selling more than just shelter. It is marketing a house as a symbol of status and self-identity.

impact on our feelings and actions. This impact may be intensified when territorial encroachment occurs.

EXPERIENCING SOCIAL SPACE

Social space consists of public territories which, officially at least, offer equal access to all. Individuals generally feel that they do not control the use of social space, although they have free access to it. As discussed more fully in Chapter 9, Americans tend to maximize their privacy and minimize their involvement with strangers in social space.

Colonizing Social Space: The Case of Boston

Officially, streets, public beaches and parks, and other public territories are open to all. In practice, these social spaces often become colonized or expropriated into some group's home territory. At that point, the invisible borders of this private "turf" may be defended against invaders. "Streets are most vulnerable to colonizing in this manner" and "streets become unofficial home areas to all those groups who require relatively secluded yet open space in which to pursue their interests or maintain their identities" (Lyman and Scott, [1967] 1970:95).

Sometimes the transformation of public territory into turf reflects a strong sense of community. If so, rigid divisions between insiders and outsiders can occur, resulting in hostility or territorial terror. This is the case in Boston. "The tourist who makes a wrong turn," says a Boston news reporter, "can find himself in another Boston—a city of 'turf,' of neighborhoods to avoid, of hostile graffiti. This Boston . . . is a place where . . . race affects the places blacks can drive, work and play" (Husock, 1979:32–34). In Boston, blacks generally avoid the city's beaches, located in South Boston (a poor, white, Irish neighborhood and the scene of beachfront confrontations). In fact, blacks avoid South Boston altogether. A black minister phrased it as follows: "You don't drive through South Boston, you don't use their beaches, you're taking your life in your hands if you do" (in Husock, 1979:90).

There are less dramatic examples of the impact of a sense of place on people's behavior. In most cities, for example, sidewalk panhandlers stake out a territory and colonize it, discouraging spatial invasion by "respectable types" with their frightening looks.

Streets

Most urbanites use social space daily because they walk or ride down city streets. After observing street behavior in New York City and Tokyo, William H. Whyte (1978:14–16) concludes that people like somewhat crowded streets. This observation flies in the face of assumptions made by many planners and architects who, in Whyte's view, "overscale" and design megastructures which bury streets in underground concourses or put streets "up in the air in glass-enclosed walkways." According to Whyte, the result is the loss of the vital friction of social space, a loss of activity and liveliness.

To conclude: Whether human territoriality is genetically programmed or culturally learned is a matter of much debate, particularly among sociobiologists and sociologists. In either case, people do display a sense of territoriality. Human ecologists from Park and Burgess (1925) to Amos H. Hawley (1950) use the concept of territoriality in their analysis of urban communities, paying particular attention to territorial invasion of one ethnic group by another. In recent years, social scientists have paid increasing attention to personal as well as social space, focusing on their symbolic meanings to individuals and social groups. This current focus—on the symbolic uses of space, on the meanings people attach to home territories and public territories—can be viewed as an implicit critique of the classic models of urban space. The work of Sommer, Hall, Appleyard, and Whyte, among others, suggests that nonrational, noneconomic factors influence people's perception and use of space. Shades of Walter Firey!

Policy Implications

What are some policy implications that follow from these insights about human spatial behavior? Psychologist Robert Sommer (1969) argues that an understanding of how people perceive and use space is fundamental to intelligent design of the built environment. His studies of various intimate and public environments—from homes for the elderly to the Los Angeles airport—suggest that even very minor rearrangements of things in space can affect people's behavior. For instance, Sommer visited a hospital where the chairs were arranged in such a way as to make cleaning the floors easy but conversation among patients impossible. A slight shift of the furniture gave patients a chance to converse freely.

Sommer's ideas about space have particular significance for those persons displaced from their home base and home range: people who live in total institutions, such as hospitals and jails. Institutionalized people have little control over their personal space. The psychological implications of feeling powerless to control one's immediate environment are suggested in the following account of a schizophrenic as she neared recovery in a hospital:

> To the stupefaction of the nurse, for the first time I dared to handle the chairs and change the arrangement of the furniture. What unknown joy to have an influence on things; to do with them what I liked. . . . (in Sommer, 1969:83)

Increasingly, design professionals are drawing on the work of Sommer and other students of the environment in order to better shape the spaces in which we live, work, and play. Design professionals are also becoming aware that what is important to them, such as subtle nuances in building design, may be relatively unimportant to people who have to use those spaces. For instance, a user study of a low-income housing project found that tenants would have preferred better maintenance service and less subtle architecture. And they would have preferred larger kitchens—the typical social gathering place for residents—and smaller living rooms (Cooper, 1975).

In many other cases, however, there is a wide gap between what planners think people need and what people want. William Whyte's caustic comments about the planned disappearance of lively streets suggest this gap. Other defenders of the lively street, particularly Jane Jacobs (1961), have a large popular following, but to date, their impact on planning and public policy is limited.

ENVIRONMENTAL PSYCHOLOGY

Environmental psychology deals with the relationships between human behavior and the physical environment, both natural and built. Theorists and researchers in this subdiscipline commonly are trained as psychologists, but other behavioral scientists call themselves environmental psychologists as well. Researchers tend to focus on rather limited kinds of human behavior, particularly people's perception of the environment and the environment's impact on their actions and emotional states.

Key Concepts and Research Thrusts

Environmental psychologists have no single model for studying behavior/environment relationships. They work from mechanistic models, cognitive models, or behavioral models (Heimstra and McFarling, 1978:7–8). But researchers do share a common vocabulary, including the following concepts (see Ittelson et al., 1974):

perception—how people perceive or become aware of their environment
cognition—how people assign meaning to the world around them and make sense out of their environment
personal space—(1) the moving bubble around our bodies and (2) the process of personalizing immediate space
privacy—freedom from the presence or demands of others
crowding, overcrowding—a large number of persons gathered closely together in limited space
sensory adaptation—how people adapt to the environment, particularly under conditions of stress or sensory overload
territoriality—how people identify, possess, feel safe in, and/or defend space
dominance behavior—how people react in situations of inequality

Long before researchers called themselves environmental psychologists, they conducted behavior/environment studies. Such studies followed no plan but rather "proceeded in fits and starts depending upon local interest and the availability of funds" (Sommer, 1969:8). Over the years, large corporations funded basic research on people's reactions to temperature, light, color, and sound. They also supported applied research, including studies of light intensity in factories, carpeting in hospitals, and background music in offices. One landmark in applied research, funded by plumbing suppliers, is the work of Alexander Kira and his Cornell colleagues, *The Bathroom: Criteria for Design* ([1966] 1976). Such an eight-year study may evoke snickers from the uninitiated (or perhaps the Golden Fleece Award from Senator William Proxmire, had it been federally funded), but Kira's findings have serious implications for environmental design. For example, Kira's work shows that most standard bathroom equipment is difficult for the disabled and elderly to use with ease. This leads to a sense of helplessness and frustration. The implication here is that redesign of basic household equipment could decrease their feelings of powerlessness.

One particularly important area of applied research concerns institutional settings, such as hospitals, offices, schools, and college dorms. Sommer's research, mentioned earlier, suggests that institutional decisions about space are often made with little knowledge of user behavior. Environmental studies can make clear the impacts of various alternatives—open or partitioned offices, secluded or centrally located nurses' stations, movable or stationary school desks—on people's emotional states and patterns of social interaction.

We should remember, however, a basic point sometimes downplayed or overlooked by environmental psychologists: *Spatial arrangements reflect power arrangements.* This means that user needs and institutional needs may stand in direct conflict. How space is arranged may reflect the needs of people in charge to maintain control or to provide services efficiently rather than humanely. For instance, schoolchildren may prefer to have moveable rather than stationary desks. But teachers may find the constant rearrangement of their pupils disconcerting. Similarly, secluded nurses' stations in hospitals may isolate nurses from each other, patients, and visitors. This arrangement may be considered functional in the minds of hospital administrators, for it makes "time-wasting" chit-chat difficult. Even minor rearrangements of space, then, may entail changes in the structures of power and authority.

Rats, Chickens, and People

"It is interesting," says Robert Sommer (1969:12), "that more is known about animal than about human spatial behavior." Much research has been done on the way animals adapt to shared space. We know, for instance, a great deal about the connections between the crowding of rats and their disoriented behavior, about the crowding of chickens and their decreased egg laying, about the territoriality of captive animals and their strengthened dominance orders. Laboratory animals do react to crowded conditions by competing for space and by developing certain pathologies. But what about the human animal? How do high density and crowding affect us? And what about people in captive spaces, like total institutions—do they develop a stronger sense of territoriality?

Michelson (1976) has reviewed studies of crowding in various environments, including prisoner-of-war camps, slave ships, densely populated cities such as Hong Kong, and housing units with more than 1.01 persons per room (the U.S. Census Bureau's definition of "overcrowded"). He finds their conclusions ambiguous and mixed. The basic problem is that crowding tends to go hand-in-hand with other factors, such as powerlessness and low status. If, for instance, POWs are psychologically disoriented, how can it be shown that crowding is the key variable leading to their disorientation? Perhaps other factors—isolation from the familiar, lack of control over space, etc.—may be more important than density.

Indeed, some studies suggest that crowding is less important for people than other conditions. Baldassare (1979) concludes that crowding has no measurable impact on residential well-being and minimal effects on social interaction. Baldassare thinks that most humans can avoid "social overload" by organizing their activities and space. Yet, those who lack the social power to control their space—the disabled, the poor, and children, for instance—may be more affected by residential crowding. Another study finds that schoolchildren in Toronto who live in crowded housing units learn less well than those who don't. However, further analysis suggests that the presence or absence of someone in the room is a key factor in the child's learning, not crowding per se (Michelson, 1976:158).

Concerning territoriality, one important study suggests that caged people do react like caged animals. We refer to a study of schizophrenic patients on a psychiatric ward by psychologists. They found that territoriality was important in the patients' behavior. For instance, patients who exhibited a strong sense of territoriality were more likely to win in confrontations with other patients which occurred within their territory. Territoriality helped to define the social hierarchy of the ward (Esser et al., 1970).

To conclude: Behavior/environment studies are problematic for several reasons. In most cases, people are not captive animals like laboratory rats; leaping from conclusions about rats or chickens to the way humans react is unjustified. Further, the notion that persons in authority (such as hospital administrators and office managers) are unaware of

Fig. 14-7 A GOOD FIT? (Richard Hedman)

user needs may be naive. Ken Kesey's portrayal of Big Nurse in *One Flew Over the Cuckoo's Nest* (1962) illustrates the point. Consciously or unconsciously, Big Nurse manipulated mental patients by exercising control over their space. True, patients may have felt more comfortable, secure, and powerful in other kinds of spaces. However, it does not follow that Big Nurse or other authority figures will modify spatial arrangements under their control on the basis of behavior/environment research findings. Their need to maintain authority may conflict with people's need to control their space. And like so much else in urban life, those with power, authority, or high status have more ability to control their space than those without these resources.

This brings us to a more thorough exploration of the design of urban spaces. What assumptions or theories underlie the thinking of those who shape the spaces we live in: building architects, landscape architects, planners, interior decorators, and other design professionals?

SHAPING URBAN SPACE

Design Principles

When men and women receive their degree in architecture from Harvard University, they rise at the graduation ceremonies and a university official pronounces them qualified "to shape the space in which we live." This pronouncement makes design professionals sound like value-free technicians, which of course they are not.

Those deemed qualified to shape urban space—architects, licensed interior decora-

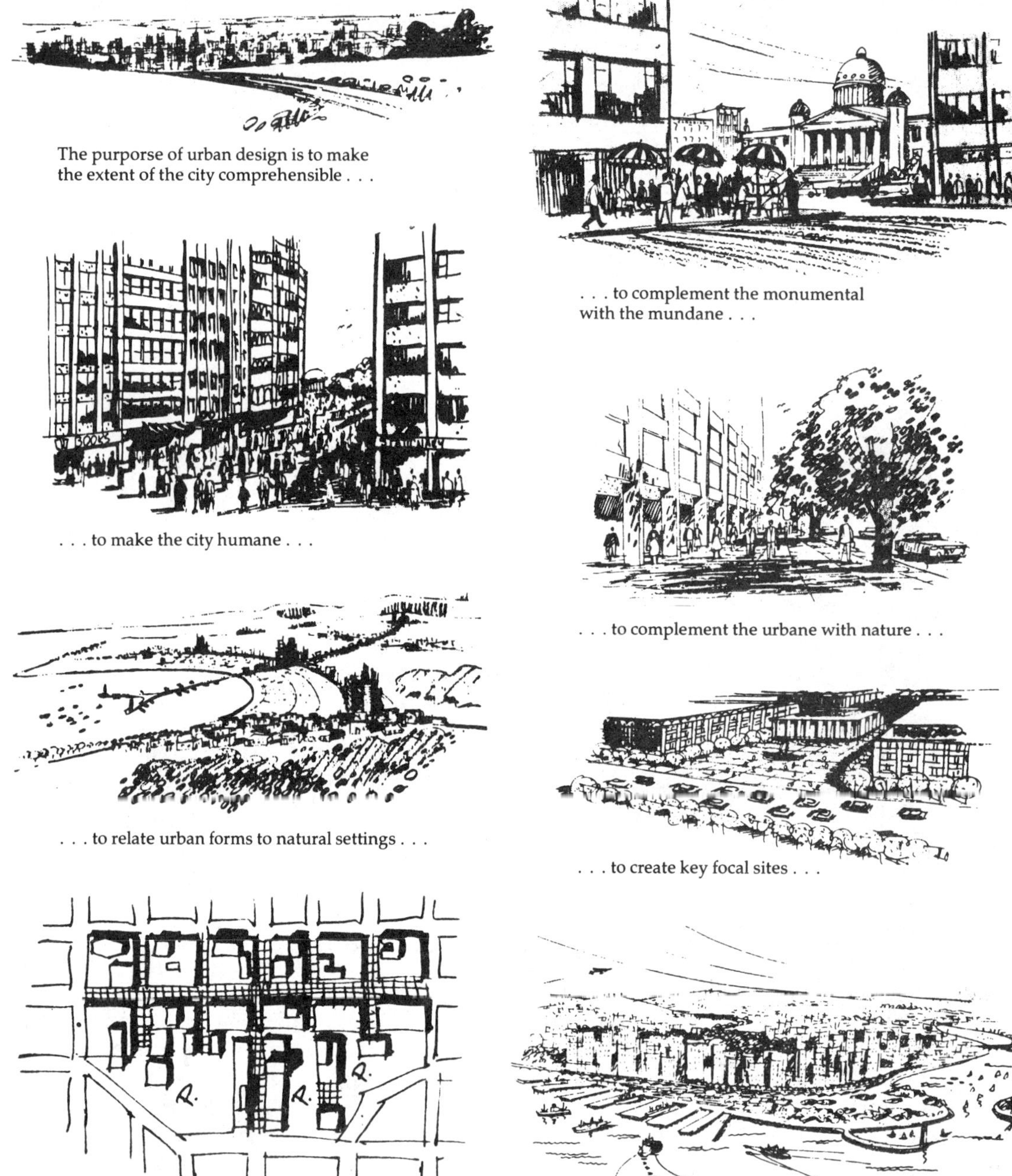

The purporse of urban design is to make the extent of the city comprehensible . . .
. . . to complement the monumental with the mundane . . .
. . . to make the city humane . . .
. . . to complement the urbane with nature . . .
. . . to relate urban forms to natural settings . . .
. . . to create key focal sites . . .
. . . to weave new centers into the urban fabric . . .
. . . and to make the city a harbor of diversity.

Fig. 14-8 PURPOSES OF URBAN DESIGN. (Paul D. Spreirigen, *Urban Design: The Architecture of Towns and Cities* [New York: McGraw-Hill, 1965], pp. 68–69. Copyright © 1965 by McGraw-Hill, Inc. Used with permission of the publisher and the author.)

tors, planners, and other design professionals—learn to think in a certain way about the physical world. This way of thinking is called "design."

What is design? According to architect-designer Christopher Alexander (1964:1), design is "the process of inventing physical things which display new physical order, organization, form in response to function." In his early theoretical work, *Notes on the Synthesis of Form* (1964:15), Alexander states that "Every design problem begins with an effort to achieve fitness between two entities: the form in question and its context." However, a physical form is part of a whole ensemble of components, and a design objective (e.g., using the most appropriate material for each part of a building) may conflict with another design principle (e.g., using uniform materials for an entire project). Achieving "fitness" between form and context is particularly difficult when the context is obscure. This is the case when architects and planners try to design an entire new city.

What constitutes a good fit between form and context? According to Alexander, that's hard to define. Perhaps it is easier to see what constitutes a bad fit. For instance, we know there is a bad fit if a see-saw in a children's playground is designed with dangerously sharp edges.

Of course, design questions involve value judgments. Most importantly, whose values will be served? Consider, for example, the eight purposes of urban design outlined in Fig. 14-8. "To make the city humane" seems a noble purpose, but what does it actually mean? To urban designers (who are usually trained as architects initially but who concentrate on large-scale design issues), it may mean the razing of a densely settled area they consider a slum. This may seem inhumane, however, to residents of a densely settled neighborhood who happen to like it there. Such was the case with Boston's West End, as Herbert Gans fully describes in *The Urban Villagers* (1962).

In other words, designing urban spaces is not a value-neutral process. Perhaps it was the growing awareness of this fact that led Christopher Alexander to depart from his original scientific-rational approach to design and to embark on a new course, one that rejects many established design principles and does not pretend to be value-free.

Modern city planning and urban design, Alexander maintains, are based on an unfortunate model—the city as a tree: a rigid, abstract structure that lacks complexity and contains no overlapping structures. He argues that "It is this lack of structural complexity, characteristic of trees, which is crippling our conceptions of the city" ([1965] 1978:382). In his view, a city is not a tree; a city should be designed with ambiguity, overlap, and multiplicity of aspect.

In 1977 Alexander and his colleagues at Berkeley's Center for Environmental Structure published a seminal work on city design calling for a new way of designing for complex social systems. They have developed what they call *A Pattern Language* (Alexander et al., 1977). The "language" consists of some 250 elements which the authors think should be considered in the design process. Alexander and his colleagues don't pretend to be value-free. Instead, they call for a participatory, process-oriented, dynamic structuring of symbolic and functional patterns in environmental design. Here is a small sampling of their design principles:

On home and work

The artificial separation of house and work creates intolerable rifts in people's inner lives. . . . Concentration and segregation of work leads to dead neighborhoods. (1977:52)

On communal space

Give every institution and social group a place

where people can eat together [because] without communal eating, no human group can hold together. (pp. 699, 697)

On institutional scale
To make the political control of local functions real, establish a small town hall for each community of 7000, and even for each neighborhood. (p. 240)

On access to ideas and services
Allow the growth of shop-size spaces around the local town hall, and any other appropriate community building. Front these shops on a busy path, and lease them for a minimum rent to ad hoc community groups for political work, trial services, research, and advocate groups. No ideological restrictions. (p. 244)

On the importance of multipurpose, communal places
Somewhere in the community [create] at least one big place where a few hundred people can gather, with beer and wine, music, and perhaps a half-dozen activities, so that people are continuously criss-crossing from one to another. (p. 446)

This sampling reveals that Alexander and his colleagues represent a new attitude to architecture and planning—an alternative to mainstream ideas and practices that stress functional order and the separation of contexts within city space. Clearly, Alexander is a decentralist, trying to mold the physical environment to meet what he considers human needs for small-scale community and activity. He is also an integrator, trying to bring together in space those various activities that people enjoy or need for survival.

Alexander's ideas are controversial, particularly his insistence on what might be called messy order, such as criss-crossing functions in space. *A Pattern Language* is sending ripples through many architectural and design schools. Still, it hasn't had much impact on the built environment. Given the radical restructuring of social life that it implies, this is not surprising.

Designing an attractive, functional city is the goal of many a planner or designer, even if few get the chance. Architects, on the other hand, design buildings. What are their goals? According to one architect, "We try to design buildings that are orderly, economical, and pleasing" (McLaughlin, 1962; see also Box 14-2). Of course, what is orderly, economical, or pleasing depends on one's taste and values. To architect-designer Christopher Alexander, treelike order in a building or city is deadly. Large-scale environments, which might be economical, bring high social costs in the long run. And aesthetic pleasure, Alexander would argue, comes not from having everything in its separate place but rather from interlacing varied human activities.

To conclude: Most design professionals do not make explicit the values underlying their work. Christopher Alexander is an exception to that rule. He makes numerous unsubstantiated statements about the nature of human beings (e.g., "All people have the instinct to decorate their surroundings" [1977:1147]). Yet he does not hide his ideology. He stresses the need for community and communalism, the need for people to create and re-create their own environments, and the need to learn from various aspects of the city. He likes small, family-owned grocery stores, cafes where urbanites can watch the world go by, and elevated places as city landmarks. Most of all, he wants to enrich the city by breaking it into "a vast mosaic of small and different subcultures, each with its own spatial territory, and each with the power to create its own distinct life style . . . so that each person has access to the full variety of life styles in the subcultures near his [or her] own" (1977:50).

Alexander's vision of decentralized subcommunities is not widely shared in the design professions. Nor is it economically

Box 14-2

HOW ARCHITECTS THINK, WHAT ARCHITECTS DO

Two Days in the Work Life of an Architect

Monday

It has been a good weekend; busy, filled with all sorts of things. I never have to decide whether I am practicing architecture or doing what I want to do—the two are synonymous. . . .

One thing I have to do, and that is to think a lot about what I am designing. On Friday night I was discouraged about the shopping center we have begun in the drafting room. It isn't right yet. This morning . . . I realized that our drawings are getting ahead of our thinking. We need more information about how the buildings will be used, more analysis of the problems we are trying to solve. The sponsor will be in at ten, and we shall do some probing together.

I stuck my head into the drafting room when I arrived at the office. About half of our staff of ten were clustered around one table. Joe, who is job captain for the shopping center project, had been doing some pondering too. I got into the discussion. Joe will be with me in the meeting with the sponsor, and we agreed on the additional information needed for the program. . . .

The telephone rang; it was a client who had been to see his new house over the weekend; the house has just been roofed in. The client thinks something isn't like the drawings. I explain that it has only been roughed in, and when finished will be just what the drawings show.

. . . I arrived home with three current magazines, a draft of a specification, and a book on contemporary architecture in Brazil, all under my arm. My daughter lifted the book on Brazil and wanted to know why my buildings aren't as exciting as those of the Brazilians. Architecture, young lady, is usually exciting in the process, but we aim to solve problems, create order and satisfactions.

Friday

[The morning is filled with meetings and phone calls.]

My partner and I save Friday for lunch together. We need a chance to talk quietly, away from the interruptions of the office. Today we went over the jobs we are doing: their status now and our plans for carrying them through. There was some inevitable consideration of finances, and then we discussed in broad terms the kind of work we do and hope to do.

I suppose our practice might be characterized as typical of many over the country, although there is so much variety in what we do that nothing of itself seems typical. Most of the projects that come to us relate to the everyday lives of people, and we try to design buildings that are orderly, economical, and pleasing. But there are opportunities to reach for values beyond these; our society is not a level one. And it undoubtedly is wrong to say that any job should be accepted as routine, though some inevitably become so.

For ourselves, there is constant satisfaction in seeing built what we have thought, felt, and sometimes dreamed about, bringing a sense of fulfillment that can be deep and lasting when we have done well. At times, too, there are satisfactions that come with contributing to the lives of individuals and the community. My partner shared with me at lunch the kick he got when the mother of several children told him: "The children are learning far more rapidly and well in that new school you designed. They are much happier than in their old building, and your school has given a new look to the neighborhood." (Adapted from McLaughlin, 1962:182–95). Copyright © 1962 by Robert W. McLaughlin. Reprinted with permission of Macmillan Publishing Co., Inc., and the author.

probable, if current dominant values don't change. But his ideas may have an important impact on the postindustrial cities of America. And his explicit ideology is a refreshing antidote to the false value-free rhetoric of so many design professionals.

Designing the Natural Environment

"Landscape" and "architecture" may seem contradictory, but together they reflect the goal of landscape architecture: to shape the natural environment just as the architect molds the built environment. Frederick Law Olmsted, the profession's pioneer, coined the term "landscape architecture" in 1858.

Olmsted, the developer of Central Park in New York City, had specific ideas about parks. He wanted to keep rural nature in a close relationship to the industrial cities growing up in post-Civil War America. This would relieve the anxiety of urban life, Olmsted thought. Parks would also strengthen the sense of community within large cities. Where else, he asked, could over 50,000 people come together "with an evident glee in the prospect of coming together, all classes represented . . . each individual adding by his mere presence to the pleasure of all others . . . ?" (in Glaab and Brown, 1976:234).

Olmsted's influence stretched from New York City's Central Park and the boulevards of Chicago to San Francisco's Golden Gate Park. He inspired a park and boulevard movement in the late nineteenth century, and he provided the ideology for reshaping the industrial city.

Assessments of Olmsted's work vary. According to two urban historians, Olmsted was more instrumental than anyone else in terms of reshaping "for the better the way in which American cities were to grow" (Glaab and Brown, 1976:233). Critics, on the other hand, argue that Olmsted and the designers and planners he inspired were antiurban and aristocratic in their approach to parks. Their aesthetically pleasing grand getaways from soot and noise, it is argued, did nothing to relieve the urban anxiety rooted in poverty and social conflict.

However Olmsted's work is judged, he left an indelible stamp on the natural environment of American cities. Indeed, one could reasonably claim that the natural and built environment of U.S. cities today is, to a significant degree, the handiwork of two impassioned men: Olmsted, who developed Central Park in the nineteenth century, and master builder Robert Moses, who controlled Central Park (and much else) in the mid-twentieth century. (Refer to Chapter 11 on Moses.) It is interesting to note that neither was an elected political official.

Today, landscape architects rarely have a chance to reshape huge pieces of urban space or to impose their ideologies on an entire city, let alone a nation. Instead, most do the following kinds of work: landscape planning and assessment (e.g., evaluating the suitability of land for a new national park); site planning (e.g., analyzing a proposed hospital site to assess the fit between the form of the natural environment and the building); and/or landscape design (i.e., super gardening—selecting plants and materials).

Landscape architects (almost named "rural embellishers" by Olmsted) are not the only professionals concerned with the natural environment. Increasingly, urban designers and city planners are becoming conscious of natural settings, devoting attention to working with, rather than against, nature. Ian McHarg is a leading advocate of "design with nature."

According to McHarg ([1969] 1971:31), designers generally neglect the natural environment in their decisions, say, about highways: "In highway design, the problem is reduced to the simplest and most commonplace terms: traffic, volume, design speed, capacity, pavements, structures, horizontal and vertical alignment." These considerations, McHarg adds, are then filtered through a purely economic cost-benefit model, driving out noneconomic values such as damage to wildlife.

McHarg believes that noneconomic values can be served in the planning process, thus ending what he calls planners' "institutionalized myopia." McHarg's ideas have already made an impact. His major contribution: increasing the range of considerations for decision making, particularly in the realm of major public works projects.

THE IMAGE OF THE CITY

Making the City Observable

Urban designers try to make the city observable. What does that mean? "Making the city observable," says one urban designer, "means making the plethora of public information public" (Wurman, 1971:8). It means making clear visually the patterns of the city.

Prof. Kevin Lynch of MIT has developed specific ideas about the visual image of the city. Lynch (1960) classifies the contents of a city's image which are associated with physical forms into five main elements: paths, edges, nodes, districts, and landmarks. In Lynch's scheme, *paths* are the channels along which an observer moves: streets, transit lines, railroads, canals. *Edges* are linear breaks in the continuity of the city: shores, walls, railroad cuts, edges of development. *Districts* are the medium-to-large sections of the city having some common identifiable character which an observer may mentally enter "inside of." *Nodes* are strategic spots in a city: intensive foci to and from which people travel. *Landmarks* are reference points which the observer does not enter.

Fig. 14-9 LYNCH'S ELEMENTS OF THE CITY IMAGE. (Paul D. Spreirigen, *Urban Design: The Architecture of Towns and Cities* [New York: McGraw-Hill, 1965], pp. 50–51. Copyright © 1965 by the American Institute of Architects. Reprinted by permission.)

One of Lynch's main interests is the **imageability** of a city: that quality of the urban landscape that evokes a strong image in anyone who observes it. Imageability is "that shape, color, or arrangement which facilitates the making of vividly identified, powerfully structured, highly useful mental images of the environment" (Lynch, 1960:9). Lynch is concerned with a city's imageability, or heightened visibility, because he found in his research that people feel most comfortable in city space when they can recognize visually its overall patterns.

Lynch's work has influenced urban designers throughout the world. The design of Venezuela's city of Ciudad Guyana, for example, was inspired by his ideas.

The View from the Road

Roads and streets take up most of the U.S. city's space. For that reason alone, they are worth special attention. In addition, "Public streets are the primary determinants of the form of the city . . . the routes, and the physical environment along them, are the initial and dominant experience of the city for all people" (Wurman, 1971:35).

Roadwatching can be, perhaps should be, a delight. In fact, Kevin Lynch and his colleagues (1964) say that the highway is a work of art. Hence, they want to make each journey an artistic experience for drivers and passengers. How? By designing highways that give people a sense of the rhythm and continuity of the road.

To give highway engineers a better idea of what alternative views from the road would be, Lynch's colleague, Donald Appleyard, constructed an urban simulator at Berkeley in which a tiny camera moves through a large wooden model. The resulting films show, in advance, what people would see along each proposed highway site.

Imagine how a mundane drive through town would be transformed if accompanied by Lynch and Appleyard. Instead of tuning out the environment and tuning in the eight-track stereo, we might hear a running commentary on the sequence illustrated in Fig. 14-10:

> The market is very close on the right and on the same level. The bustle of people and the crates of vegetables can almost be felt. . . . The road just in time curves quickly to the left to avoid the obstacles. . . . After a slight curve, daylight appears at the end of the tunnel. We rise to the open air and continue up to the sky, flattening out at the third-story level, feeling free in the air. . . . (Appleyard et al., 1964:68)

To conclude: Apparently, people have a need to recognize and make coherent patterns out of their physical surroundings. To Kevin Lynch, it is the job of the city planner and urban designer to make the city's image more recognizable, vivid, and memorable to the city dweller. Clear images, Lynch believes, give people emotional satisfaction, an easy framework for communication, and personal security. To architect designer Christopher Alexander, coherent patterns of environmental structure are also crucial, but he would design them in a more complex, subtle way: via overlapping and criss-crossing functions in space. Both design theorists emphasize the social and psychological impact of urban forms on city dwellers' well-being.

GRAND DESIGNERS

A city can be considered an art form—a special art form that reflects the builders' belief system and values. Villages constructed by the Dogon tribe in Mali, West Africa, reveal the imprint of their values and cosmology. The tribe feels indissolubly connected with the cosmos and its timeless rhythms, and the physical layout of the

Dogon village reflects this belief. Each building stands in a particular relation to the sun, and the granary building (symbol of the world system) is constructed with invariant male-female parts (Griaule, 1965). A Dogon community is a work of artistic symmetry and cosmic vision; it is a symbolic representation of the tribal universe. Similarly, the ancient city of Babylon was more than a city; it was a vision of heaven on earth.

Heaven on earth—or at least a better society—has been a perennial interest of philosophers, artists, and city planners. Often, the ideal city transcends the dominant ideas of the society that produced it. Like artists, visionary planners suggest solutions to problems only dimly understood in their own time. Thus in the twelfth century, European visionaries designed cities of God on earth amid war and strife. In the nineteenth century, utopian socialists designed classless communities amid the evolution of industrial capitalism.

Here we focus on only a few grand designers. This brief survey is intended to indicate the range of visions and the sources from which they sprang: patriotism, profit and philanthropy, paternalism, pure aesthetics, ideology, religious ardor, and utopian dreams.

Pierre L'Enfant's Washington, D.C.

Major Charles Pierre L'Enfant was a grand designer inspired by the vision of America as

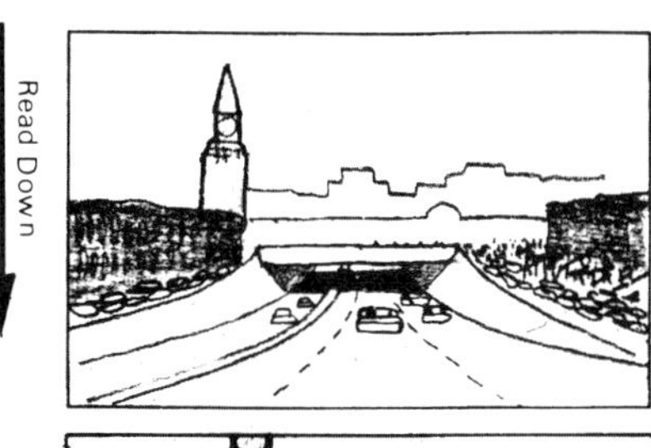

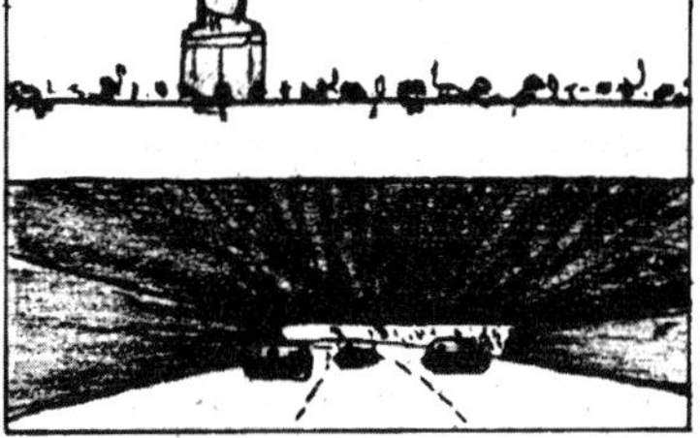

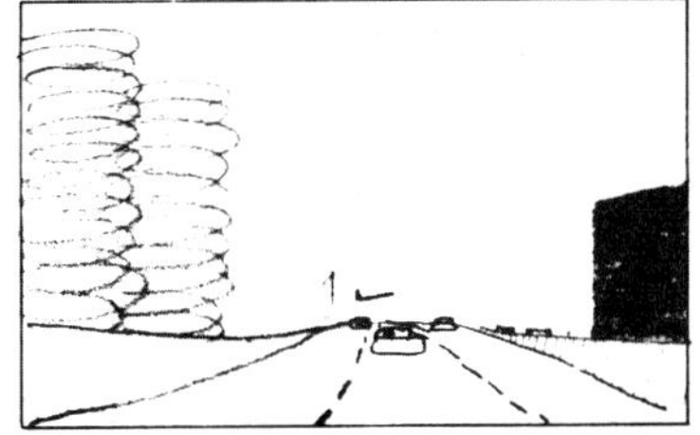

Fig. 14-10 VIEWS FROM THE ROAD. Six sketched film frames showing what drivers would see along a highway site. Urban designer Donald Appleyard uses such films to help decision makers decide between alternative highway routes. (Donald Appleyard, Kevin Lynch, and John Myer, *The View from the Road* [Cambridge, Mass.: M.I.T. Press, 1964], p. 81. Copyright © 1974 by The M.I.T. Press. Reprinted by permission of The M.I.T. Press and the author.)

The thriving City of Eden as it appeared on Paper *The thriving City of Eden as it appeared in Fact*

Fig. 14-11 NEW EDEN? Charles Dickens poked fun at American grand designers in his novel *Martin Chuzzlewit*, based on his visit to Cicero, Illinois. These drawings, from his novel, show the gap between the best-laid plans and the reality.

a new society. L'Enfant, a young French infantryman, came to America to fight in the Revolutionary War.

For several years after the Revolutionary War, the new national government moved from place to place, debating alternative sites for the nation's capital. Badly divided, Congress finally decided on a new location on the Potomac River, and George Washington himself rode along the wild and swampy eighty-mile general location, choosing the precise site where Washington, D.C., now stands. Meanwhile, L'Enfant was instructed to do general survey work on the new site. Interpreting this charge very liberally, he plunged ahead, with remarkable results.

On one design point, L'Enfant was adamant. The new capital was not to be a gridiron city with parallel streets running at right angles to one another. While practical, the gridiron lacked the grandeur L'Enfant thought appropriate to a capital city. Thomas Jefferson, a designer as well as philosopher and future president, approached L'Enfant with his own proposal: a checkerboard city with alternate squares left in open space. L'Enfant responded that such a grid concept was "tiresome and insipid." L'Enfant won.

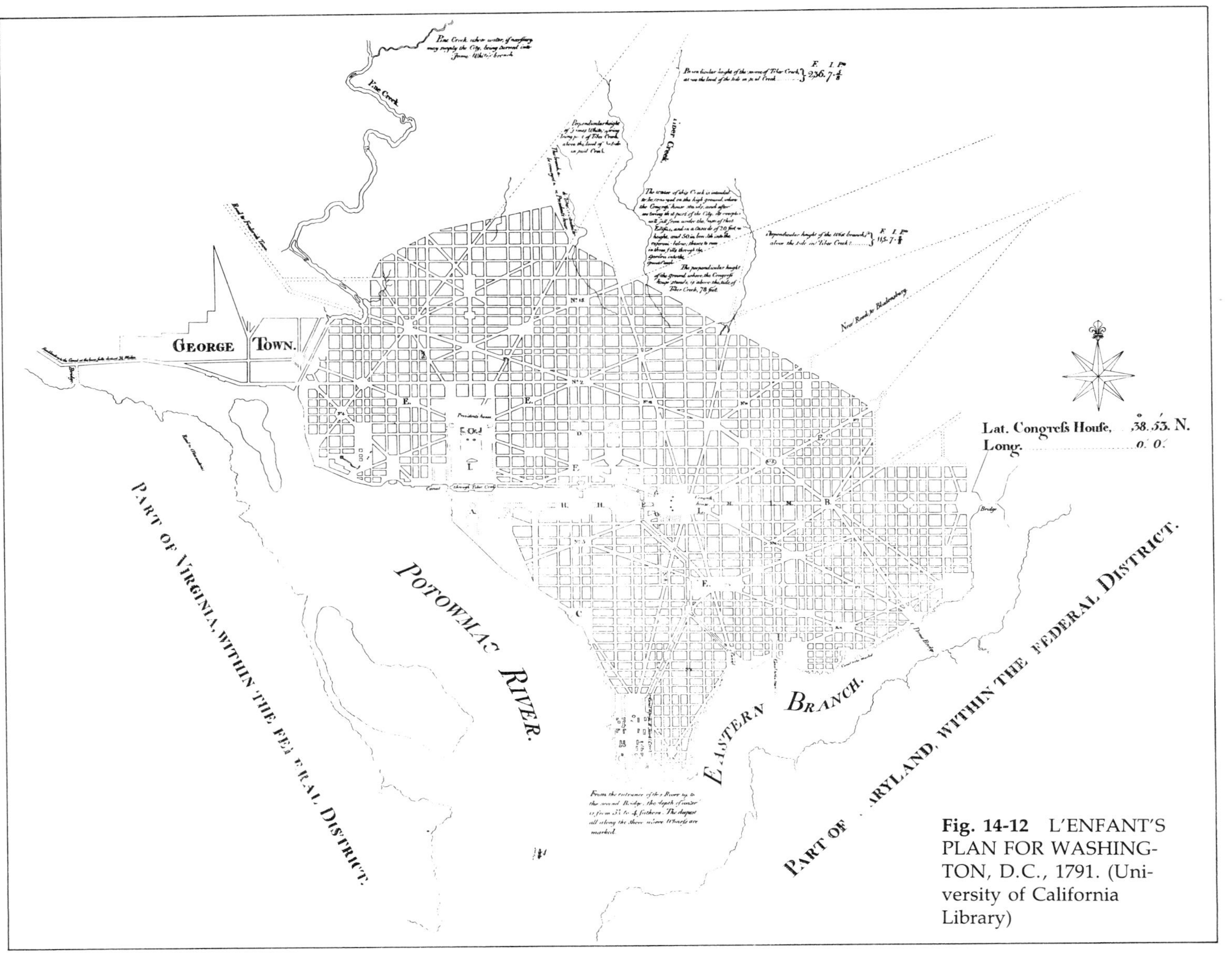

Fig. 14-12 L'ENFANT'S PLAN FOR WASHINGTON, D.C., 1791. (University of California Library)

Still today, Washington reflects L'Enfant's grand design. There is a wheellike arrangement of streets running off a central spoke; long malls with vistas; broad diagonal avenues bearing the names of the original thirteen colonies; and major public buildings arranged in a federal triangle.

Utopian Visionaries

In America, utopian visions existed from the very beginning. Indeed, to some, America itself was utopia: the New World, a chance to create paradise on earth. The names of colonial towns—New Haven, Connecticut, and New Hope, Pennsylvania, to name only two—convey this idealism.

Early utopians were inspired by religious visions. Generally, they set up small, intentional communities. Most often they were Protestant separatists breaking away from established sects, such as the United Society of Believers, popularly called the Shakers. The oldest communistic society in the United States, the Shakers set up a parent community in 1792 at Mount Lebanon on the border of Massachusetts and Connecticut.

In the nineteenth century, religiously inspired utopian communities flourished from Oneida, New York, to the frontier of the Midwest. But there was also a new development: the growth of secular utopian visions. Some became translated from paper blueprints into actuality. One of the most famous is Robert Owen's experiment at New Harmony, Indiana.

Owen, a rich industrialist turned utopian entrepreneur, came to the United States from Scotland in the 1820s to "introduce an entire new system of society" which would "remove all causes for contest between individuals." Utopian socialist Owen (like his French contemporary, Fourier) believed that large cities around industrial areas were unhealthy, and the best alternative was a small, self-sufficient community. In such a community Owen hoped to promote a noncompetitive, wholesome way of life based on socialism and education.

Owen designed an architectural model of his ideal community: a square-shaped arrangement which would contain between 800 and 1,200 people. Inside the square were to be public buildings, while families would live on three sides and children over three years of age would live on the fourth side. Outside the square were to be manufacturing facilities, stables, farm buildings, and agricultural land.

The design plan of New Harmony was never realized. Instead, Owen and his followers moved into a village formerly occupied by another utopian sect. The hopes for New Harmony were not realized either. The dream of utopian socialism was quickly shattered by internal dissent.

Still, the failure of New Harmony did little to dampen the spirits of other communitarian experiments in the mid-1800s. Dozens of other communities, both religious and secular, were established. One of the longest-lived was John Humphrey Noyes's community of radical Protestants in Oneida, New York. Their imposing Mansion House still stands, and descendants of the original Oneida community still conduct tours, explaining to visitors how the system worked. Of special interest, guides say, is the Oneida community's theory and practice of communism in human relationships as well as material goods (via "complex marriage" and the dissolution of the nuclear family).

Company Towns: Lowell, Massachusetts, and Pullman, Illinois

New Harmony and Oneida exemplify the search for a radically new and better social order through communitarian socialist ideals. Planned manufacturing towns were inspired by different motives: profit, paternalism, and/or reform in the interest of softening class antagonism.

Lowell, Massachusetts, is the most famous example of early planned manufacturing towns. Built by Frances Cabot Lowell in the early nineteenth century, it was the model for dozens of other New England mill towns.

Realizing that he would need abundant cheap labor to run his water-powered textile mills, Lowell set out to attract workers, mainly New England farm girls, to his town. And disturbed at the horrific social conditions in English factory towns that he had visited, Lowell set out to improve the workers' lot. The result: Lowell, Massachusetts, a planned town. It was laid out physically to fit the social order Lowell envisioned. Textile mills lined the river, flanked by a canal. Between them was housing for America's first female labor force—boarding houses operated much like convents (see Chapter 16). A main road linked the manufacturing and housing areas to other urban activities.

About a half-century later, cities privately built by industrialists reached their zenith in Pullman, Illinois. George M. Pullman, the railroad sleeping car magnate, decided to consolidate his manufacturing activities and housing for his workers at a 4,000-acre site about twelve miles south of Chicago. Designed by an architect and a landscape engineer, the town of Pullman was meant to be a model industrial community. When it went into operation in 1881, the town presented a strong contrast to the crowded, unsanitary tenements inside industrial cities. There were neat row houses, a shopping center, an elegant theatre, a hotel, church, and school, and a host of cultural institutions (not including bars or brothels). By the early 1890s, the population reached about 12,000 Pullman workers and their families—living in Pullman-owned homes.

Why did George Pullman build such a town? In part, he had a great deal of imagination; he was an environmental determinist of sorts and thought that miserable urban conditions led to workers' "costly vices." And in part, he hoped his planned community "would soften the bitter antagonism which wage earners often felt toward their employers, and would enable him to attract a stable and highly competent labor force; it would also earn 6 per cent on the money invested in it" (Glaab and Brown, 1976:237).

Did the town serve Pullman's ends? No. Paternalism or "benevolent, well-wishing feudalism," as it was often called in its own day, went against American democratic ideals. Labor violence, culminating in the Pullman strike of 1894, showed that workers' hostility toward their benevolent boss was not softened by decent housing or terraced front yards. Shortly after the strike, an Illinois court ruled that Pullman's company had no legal right to run the town. Eventually, Pullman got rid of the town, and it was annexed to Chicago.

Lowell and Pullman are striking examples of company towns with pretensions to design excellence. But they are part of a broader pattern. Similar experiments, much less grand in scale, include Kohler, Wisconsin (plumbing fixtures); Hershey, Pennsylvania (candy bars); and Gary, Indiana (steel).

The City Beautiful Movement

Ironically, at the very time that Pullman's feudal dream of industrial community south of Chicago was being smashed by labor violence, events in the Windy City were to have a greater impact on the future of urban America. Chicago—the symbol of the rising industrial city—was chosen to host the 400th anniversary celebration of Columbus's discovery of America. This World's Fair of 1893–1894 (called the Columbian Exposition) marked the beginning of great interest in city planning and landscape architecture.

The Columbian Exposition was not just a typical fair; it was a brand new city. Working from a design by Frederick Law Olmsted, Chicago architect-planner Daniel H. Burnham supervised the construction of what came to be called the "White City" (see Fig. 1-5). This monumental group of buildings, constructed on a plan, was set in an environment of green open space, grand boulevards, and an artificial lagoon on Chicago's South Side. By the time the fair closed in 1894, about 27 million people had attended. What they saw, in the words of one historian of American city planning, was

> . . . An enthralling amalgam of classic Greece, imperial Rome, Renaissance Italy, and Bourbon Paris, as impossible in the midwest as a gleaming iceberg would be in the Gulf of Mexico, yet somehow expressive of the boastfulness, the pretensions, the cultural dependence, the explosive energy, and the ingenious optimism of industrial America. . . . The millions gaped and admired and almost disbelieved that so much beauty and splendor had sprung up in Chicago, city of grain and lumber and meat, city of railroads and smoke and grime . . . the brilliant image of symmetrical edifices, colossal statues, and stupendous domes burned in memory long after the summer pilgrims had returned to their lackluster commercial cities, dreary mill towns, and homely prairie villages. (Scott, 1969:33)

After the Columbian Exposition, civic beautification organizations sprang up in many cities, and the City Beautiful movement took hold. "Make no little plans," Burnham advised in 1912, for "they have no magic to stir men's blood. Make big plans; aim high in hope and work."

While the near-evangelical fervor of Burnham and his followers didn't lead to the total reshaping of American cities, his bold vision did have impact. Still today, touches of City Beautiful architecture and landscaping can be found throughout the United States, from Omaha and Buffalo to St. Louis, Seattle, and San Francisco. Perhaps even more importantly, Burnham and Olmsted's White City and Burnham's subsequent plan for Chicago's urban growth in 1909 signaled a new era: the growing acceptance of city planning as a legitimate tool for urban industrial America.

Ebenezer Howard's Garden City

Visionary Ebenezer Howard (1898) combined socialist principles with romantic ideals to propose a new kind of planned community: the garden city. In the English reformer's vision, the best of countryside and city could be combined by building small, rather self-sufficient communities limited to about 30,000 people, surrounded by permanent green belts. Around the turn of the twentieth century, Howard proposed that London be surrounded with cooperative communities where slum dwellers and people of all income groups would live and collectively own the land. The aim of these new towns was to motivate London slum dwellers to willingly resettle—without being forcibly displaced, as urban renewal in the United States has so often done—and to provide standard housing as well as to "save" London by providing new parks, sewers, and so forth.

When two garden cities were actually built in England, planners throughout the world became interested. Garden cities became fashionable in the United States after 1910. But many, like Forest Hills Gardens, New York (financed by the Russell Sage Foundation and designed by Frederick Law Olmsted, Jr.), became bedroom communities for affluent commuters, not cooperatively owned communities for all income groups, as Howard had proposed.

The garden city movement in the United States attracted noted urbanists, including Lewis Mumford. Yet, Howard's ideas for stemming the slums and sprawl of industrial cities did not progress very far in the United States, given its traditions of private enterprise.

The Ideal City, Soviet Style

Despite Daniel Burnham's memorable phrase, big plans have never really stirred American blood—at least, not enough to totally rebuild or redesign cities. Instead, city planning has proceeded piecemeal.

Private master builders—the Levitts of Levittown, for instance—and a few public builders (headed by the master builder of them all, Robert Moses in New York City) did change the face of the metropolis in the twentieth century, but such efforts followed no overall plan. Why? Some observers point to deep-rooted American traditions of localism and the fear of federal government intervention as destructive of democratic ideals. This view is expressed by Wisconsin's Governor Lee Dreyfus: "The federal government should defend the shore, deliver the mail, and stay the hell out of my life" (in Ingalls, 1979:3).

Soviet observers of the American scene have a different explanation. A group of architect-planners at Moscow University claim that American cities grew in an unplanned way as a direct result of monopoly capitalism. This group says that the Soviets are trying to overcome the "accidental character of city growth" in the Soviet Union and to create new urban environments as "part of a unified plan for the national economy" (Gutnov et al., 1970:5–6). This national, integrated approach to urban planning stands in direct contrast to the American piecemeal tradition.

Given the opportunity to shape a national urban policy, what would the Moscow University group do with it? First, it rejects American theories and practice of city planning—or unplanning. For instance, it rejects the megalopolis, Western architectural revivals (such as City Beautiful architecture), and the restoration of the countryside inside the city (such as Olmsted's work). Secondly, this group proposes an ideal communist city, or more precisely, a new design concept called the New Unit of Settlement (NUS). The NUS is to be a self-regulating unit of about 100,000 persons which incorporates city and countryside. It is to fulfill what the planners define as the city's essential purpose: "to be an organic community."

The Moscow group starts from the assumption that "the mode of production, being the sum of productive forces and relations of production, influences the spatial and temporal organization of the environment, not in a direct or mechanical way, but in an indirect one—through the specific kinds of relationship dominant in a given society" (Gutnov et al., 1970:23–25). Thus "primitive society," they say (1970:24), is characterized by environmental structures based on a social system of kinship with houses branched around families, while in feudalism "the closed circle of relationships within each class isolates classes from each other (the lords in their castles . . . the serfs in their fields and villages, the merchants and artisans in their towns)." Wanting to avoid what they define as environmental structures influenced by monopoly capitalism ("spontaneous functional dissolution of the large city"), they propose a spatio-temporal structure that reflects communist life: the NUS.

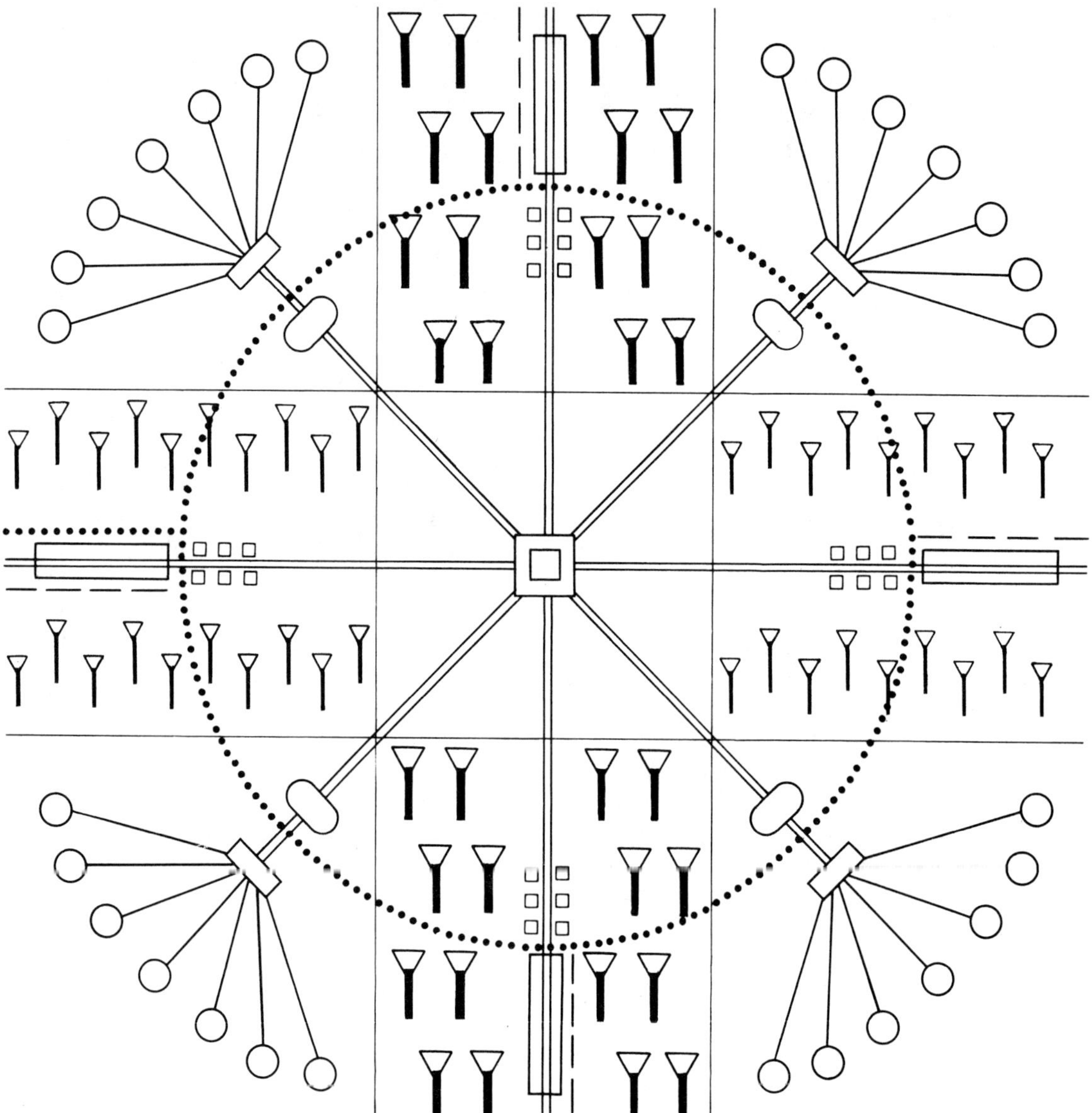

Fig. 14-13 NEW UNIT OF SETTLEMENT (NUS). This plan shows the basic structure of the ideal communist city as designed by a group of architect-planners at Moscow University. The NUS is located in an urban zone. Sectors are planned as spokes around the community center. Residential sectors (separate from industrial sectors) are linked by rapid transport, and cars circulate on a beltway. (Alexei Gutnov et al., *The Ideal Communist City* [New York: Braziller, 1970], p. 118. Reprinted by permission of the publisher, George Braziller, Inc., 1968. All rights reserved.)

Basically, the NUS is a treelike structure with sectors arranged on a circular plan (see Fig. 14-13). It is designed along the following principles: equal mobility for all (housing sectors are equidistant from the center); pedestrian scale (people can walk to the center); green belts linking residential sectors; and a system of public transport linking residential sectors to nearby industrial complexes.

Several NUSs would be "rationally distributed" within an urban zone. At the center of the entire urbanized area, composed of several urban zones, would be central institutions coordinating and directing economic, sociocultural, and scientific activities.

What is so distinct about this group's vision is not their rejection of the megalopolis or their distaste for architectural revivals; nor is it their stress on rational planning. Many U.S. planners share these values. Rather, it is the communist planners' emphasis on centralized institutions to coordinate and direct a broad range of activities within urban regions that distinguishes their vision of ideal cities.

Megastructures or Ministructures?

The tradition of grand design is alive and well in America today. The range of innovative ideas—from satellites in the sky to underwater structures—is suggested in Chapter 6. Here we examine the ideas of one visionary, architect-planner Paolo Soleri. Then we look at one criticism of Soleri's work which, incidentally, could also be applied to the Soviet NUS visionaries: For all their futurism, they are reinventing not the wheel, but the tree.

Soleri (1969) advocates a new kind of city for the future. Soleri's dream is not easy to describe in words; linear, analytical thought is not his forte. Perhaps the best way to understand his vision is by looking at the plans for a Soleri-designed community, which he calls an **arcology:** the blend of architecture and ecology. An arcology is intended to place people in megastructures, making the land available for agriculture, work, and leisure.

In terms of design, Soleri's arcologies have one surface but many levels. Most extend below the ground and high in the air. They range from a massive arcology holding a half-million residents on less than two square miles of land to an offshore community anchored to the continental shelf.

Despite their massive scale, Soleri says that his arcologies are "about miniaturization": creating a more intimate and less wasteful form of human spatial organization. The large spaces of the arcologies would be divided into large and small spaces to give inhabitants a sense of human scale.

Soleri and some of his followers have begun construction of an arcology for about 3,000 inhabitants at a remote desert site about seventy miles north of Phoenix, Arizona. Named Arcosanti, it is a prototype of futurist Soleri's vision.

Like most visionaries, Soleri has devoted followers—and vocal detractors. One of the most interesting critiques of his work (and one that could be applied equally to the Moscow group's NUS concept) comes from Christopher Alexander. He finds the organic shapes of Soleri's futuristic cities to be organized on the old principle of the tree, complete with its rigid structure. Alexander rejects the city-as-tree plan as artificial. More importantly, Alexander makes a connection between city form and human personality. In his view, cities rigidly structured like trees help to create rigid, disciplined people. The city-as-tree may have been suitable for ancient Roman military camps because discipline and order were the values of those in charge. But the tree is not suitable for modern, pluralistic societies. In other words,

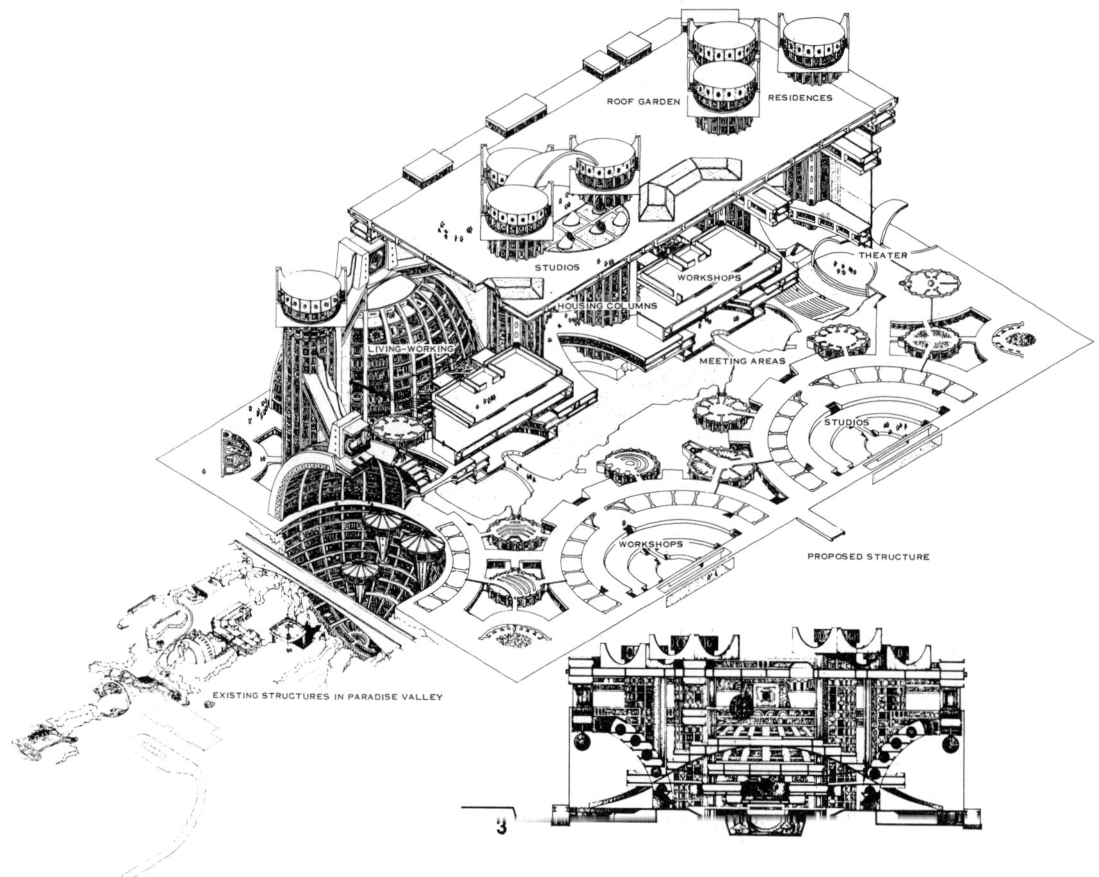

Fig. 14-14 ARCOSANTI. Visionary Paolo Soleri is supervising work on the construction of this arcology in Arizona. (Paolo Soleri, *Arcology: The City in the Image of Man* [Cambridge, Mass.: MIT Press, 1969], p. 112. Copyright © 1969 by The M.I.T. Press. Reprinted by permission of The M.I.T. Press and Carolyn Soleri.)

Alexander finds a bad fit between treelike cities and democratic contexts.

ANOTHER LOOK

Whatever grand designers dream up, people will undoubtedly continue to personalize their space. A spot of color here, a sentimental remembrance there, status symbols and territorial markings all around.

Still, no matter how creative we are in trying to control and personalize our space, we are limited by the larger social context. People who want to live in large communal groups, for example, can't do so if the housing stock is composed of small apartments. Social facts constrain individual action. Once again, micro meets macro. The way people perceive, use, and interpret their environment is linked to their social-cultural being.

Theorists disagree on this: How much does the built environment influence human behavior? Does physical environment merely reflect, or can it also create, social reality? Social scientist Harold Lasswell views architecture as a symbolic expression of a society's dominant values. So do design theorists Alexander and the Moscow group, among others. But these design theorists go a step further; they want to create new physical forms in order to create new social patterns. Thus, despite their deep ideological differences, decentralist Alexander and the Moscow centralists share a basic assumption: that city form and space not only reflect values but also shape human action. In their view, a new society cannot be constructed on the cornerstones of old buildings. In fact, many visionaries share that idea.

Sociologists of the Chicago school (Park, Burgess) had a different perspective. As sociologists, they didn't focus on the design of buildings, but they did insist on the interrelationship of spatial forms and social processes, notably economic competition. Moreover, Park and Burgess were interested in reforming the industrial city, not remaking it. Their hope: to improve the physical environment in order to decrease what they considered "social disorganization." A strong emphasis on determinism, whether physical (Alexander) or socioeconomic (Park and Burgess), underlies much of this thought.

Meanwhile, other theorists implicitly reject physical determinism and the idea that bad physical environments produce social disorganization. Herbert Gans's work is illustrative. Gans says (see Chapter 6) that living in what others might call a slum—such as Boston's West End—does not lead to social disorganization. Nor does moving to and living in suburban Levittown change people's behavior. Creating new buildings, even new institutions at the community level, had little impact on how Levittowners acted or felt.

In other words, the extent to which space and place influence or mold behavior remains controversial. As on many other key issues, theorists do not share a common vision.

PROJECTS

1. **Personal space.** How large are people's protective bubbles? Test their bubble size by breaking them—that is, invading their space. Be sure to choose a range of people whose space you can invade: older and younger, authority figures, family and friends, men and women. At what distance do these various people seem to feel uncomfortable when you engage in a conversation?

2. **Uses of social space.** Observe how people use space. For example, select a social space, such as a park, and identify users and their behavior. Are there any instances of expropriation or personalizing of social space?

3. **City planning.** What is the general design of the community in which you live? Is it what Christopher Alexander would call a tree? Or are there subtle, complex, overlapping functions in space?

4. **Utopia.** Design a city (in physical terms) that would reflect your own particular notion of a social-political-economic ideal way to live. Include the location of major institutions, living quarters, and basic economic activities.

SUGGESTIONS FOR FURTHER LEARNING

Many classics in the field of personal and social space are noted in the chapter itself, including the works of Robert Sommer on *Personal Space* and Edward T. Hall's studies of proxemics. To these should be added, in our view, the collected works of Erving Goffman, particularly *Relations in Public* (New York: Basic Books, 1971); *Encounters* (Indianapolis: Bobbs-Merrill, 1961); and *Asylums* (Garden City, N.Y.: Doubleday, 1961).

For a general overview of human spatial behavior from a sociological perspective, see William H. Michelson, *Man and His Urban Environment* (Reading, Mass.: Addison-Wesley, 1976); this volume contains a critique of the human ecology approach to space as well as a review of the literature of crowding, density, and the influence of social class on environment. Also for a brief discussion with a useful typology of spatial territories (public, home, interactional, and body), see Stanford M. Lyman and Marvin B. Scott, "Territoriality: A Neglected Sociological Dimension," *Social Problems* 15(1967):236–48. This article contains a section on the reactions of people who are systematically denied free territories, including body adornment and reorganization of psychic space (via drugs).

For a general overview of human spatial behavior from the perspective of social geography, see John A. Jakle et al., *Human Spatial Behavior* (North Scituate, Mass.: Duxbury, 1976). William H. Ittelson et al. present *An Introduction to Environmental Psychology* (New York: Holt, Rinehart and Winston, 1974).

In *Humanscape: Environments for People* (North Scituate, Mass.: Duxbury, 1978), editors Stephen Kaplan and Rachel Kaplan present a broad range of articles, including sociobiologist Edward O. Wilson's "Density and Aggressive Behavior" and architect-designer Christopher Alexander's "A City Is Not a Tree." Of particular interest in the collection is "The Experience of Living in Cities" by Stanley Milgram. He argues that large numbers, density, and heterogeneity of the city are experienced by individuals as social "overloads" which lead to "adaptive mechanisms"; the "ultimate adaptation" is total disregard of the needs and interests of strangers.

The symbolism of physical settings concerns a wide range of scholars. For instance, the distinguished professor of the history of religions, Mircea Eliade, discusses the religious meaning of dwellings, which he sees not only as "machines for living" but as "the universe that man constructs for himself by imitating the paradigmatic creation of the gods, the cosmogony" in his essay, "The World, the City, the House" in *Occultism, Witchcraft and Cultural Fashions* (Chicago: University of Chicago Press, 1975). In "Rethinking Closets, Kitchens, and Other Forgotten Spaces" in *Ms.* (December, 1977), architects Susanna Torre, Cynthia Rock, and Gwendolyn Wright look at the relationship between women's domestic space and traditional family roles. In *The Signature of Power* (New Brunswick, N.J.: Transaction, 1979), Harold Lasswell discusses the political symbolism of architecture. *Court House*, edited by Richard Pare (New York: Horizon, 1978), contains more than 300 images of U.S. courthouses, reconstructing American life from the era of log cabins to today's more flamboyant structures.

For a user study of space, see Claire Cooper, *Easter Hill Village* (New York: Free Press, 1975). She finds that people living in a small public housing project and its architects have different ideas about what people need and want.

The evocation of a sense of place is commonly the forte of visual and literary artists. In the film *Northern Lights* (1979), directors John Hanson and Rob Nilsson vividly evoke a particular time and place: the landscape of desolate Dakota farmland around 1915 as Norwegian homesteaders struggle to collectively win out against powerful interest groups (bankers, Eastern grain dealers, and railroad tycoons). A film by Andrew David, *Stony Island* (1979), captures the look and feel of a tough South Side Chicago neighborhood. *Blue in Chicago* (New York: Harper & Row, 1978) is a series of stories by Bette Howland, including one that describes Chicago as not a city but "just the raw materials for a city" and Lake Michigan as a "big dirty bathtub." David Plante's novel, *The Family* (New York: Farrar, Straus & Giroux, 1978), is concerned with space and place, both real and imagined, in Providence, Rhode Island. Mordecai Richler's stories of St. Urbain Street in Montreal are collected in *The Street* (Toronto and Montreal: McClelland and Stewart, 1969). In *Look Homeward,*

Angel (New York: Scribner's, 1929) novelist Thomas Wolfe exalts Asheville, North Carolina, while Sinclair Lewis satirizes small-town American life in *Babbitt* (New York: Harcourt Brace, 1949).

While the strong point of artists, a sense of place is sometimes evoked by social scientists and historians. See, in particular, Jane Jacobs's description of New York City's Hudson Street in *The Death and Life of Great American Cities* (New York: Vintage, 1961) and Alan Trachtenberg's *Brooklyn Bridge: Fact and Symbol* (Chicago: Phoenix, [1965] 1979), which is accompanied by Walker Evans's photographs. In *Paris: A Century of Change 1897–1978* (New Haven: Yale University Press, 1979), architectural historian Norma Evenson traces changes in the City of Light as it outgrew its horse and carriage heritage. No ordinary tour, *The City Observed: New York* (New York: Vintage, 1979) by Paul Goldberger is a witty look at civic architecture.

For keen observations of street life as well as a novelistic account of what design professionals do, see Hungarian author George Konrad's *The City Builder* (New York: Harcourt Brace Jovanovich, 1977). It is the story of an architect-city planner in an East European city for whom city planning represents a way to prevent chaos.

For accounts of home territories and defensible space, see Oscar Newman, *Defensible Space* (New York: Macmillan, 1972); Kenneth E. Read, *Other Voices: The Style of a Male Homosexual Tavern* (Chicago: Phoenix, 1980); and Sherri Cavan, *Liquor License* (Chicago: Aldine, 1966).

The symbolism of home base, home range, and social spaces can be seen in Claude Fregnac and Wayne Andrews, *The Great Houses of Paris* (New York: Vendome, 1979); David Hicks, *Living with Design* (New York: William Morrow, 1979); and Paul Hirshorn and Steven Izenour's account of *White Towers* (Cambridge, Mass.: MIT Press, 1979), the fast-food hamburger chain.

For studies of American city planners, architects, and landscape architects, see Thomas S. Hines, *Burnham of Chicago: Architect and Planner* (Chicago: Phoenix, 1979), a series of books on Thomas Jefferson's architecture by the University of Virginia Press; Michael Laurie, *An Introduction to Landscape Architecture* (New York: Elsevier, 1975); John W. Reps, *The Making of Urban America: A History of City Planning in the Unites States* (Princeton, N.J.: Princeton University Press, 1965); John Coolidge, *Mill and Mansion: A Study of Architecture and Society in Lowell, Massachusetts* (New York: Columbia University Press, 1942), and William H. Wilson, *The City Beautiful Movement in Kansas City* (Columbia, Mo.: University of Missouri Press, 1964). For a closer look at the plans for Alaska's new capital site, see David Littlejohn, "A Tale of New Cities," *New West* (April 24, 1978).

For normative judgments on what cities can and should be in terms of vitality and humaneness, see architect John Field's film, *Cities for People* (1974), which lauds human-scale cities with a distinctive sense of place (San Antonio, Savannah, San Francisco), and Arthur Mokin's *The City at the End of the Century* (Arthur Mokin Productions, New York City, n.d.), which is a hymn to New York City. Ian McHarg's views on designing with nature are presented in *Multiply and Subdue the Earth* (NET, 1969).

Some utopian visions—and attempts to actualize them in the United States—are detailed in Charles Nordhoff, *The Communistic Societies of the United States* (New York: Dover, [1875] 1966); he includes a variety of religious and secular groups, including the Oneida community, the Amana Society, and noncommunistic colonies of Anaheim, California, and Vineland, New Jersey. In *Communes in the Counter Culture* (New York: William Morrow, 1972), Keith Melville traces the modern communes' roots and connections to older utopian visions. For Pullman's concept of a better society, see Stanley Buder, *Pullman: An Experiment in Industrial Order and Community Planning 1880–1930* (New York: Norton, [1945] 1962).

For an update on New Harmony, Indiana, see architecture critic Ada Louise Huxtable, "A Radical New Addition for Mid-America" (New York *Times*, Sept. 30, 1979, Sec. 2). She focuses on a handsome new building in Owens's dream town and its fit with the town's historic past.

In the film *City Limits* (National Film Board of Canada, 1971), best-selling author Jane Jacobs sparkles with insight on how city space might be used humanely. Jacobs is a critic of sterile, functional city planning. She likes the creative disorder of older neighborhoods, active streets, and well-used odds and ends of city space.

KEY TERMS

Arcology Architect Paolo Soleri's term, blending elements of architecture and ecology, to describe compact, self-contained futuristic cities, which he compares with the design of great ocean liners. Soleri's arcologies range from small projects like Arcosanti, an experimental community actually under construction in Arizona, to megastructures to replace New York City.

Built environment As distinguished from the natural environment, it is everything that people have constructed.

Environmental determinism The view that the built environment plays a determining, or at least crucial, role in shaping human behavior.

Imageability Kevin Lynch's term describing the degree to which a city is visually legible or evokes a strong image in any observer's mind.

Personal space As used by Robert Sommer, both the bubble around each person and the processes by which people demarcate and personalize the spaces they inhabit.

Proxemics The study of how people in various cultures use space, especially for social interaction.

REFERENCES

Alexander, Christopher
1964 Notes on the Synthesis of Form. Cambridge, Mass.: Harvard University Press.
[1965]
1978 "A city is not a tree." Pp. 377–402 in Stephen Kaplan and Rachel Kaplan (eds.), Humanscape: Environments for People. North Scituate, Mass.: Duxbury.

Alexander, Christopher et al.
1977 A Pattern Language: Towns, Buildings, Construction. New York: Oxford University Press.

Apple, R. W., Jr.
1979 "Britain's notable nonagenarians." New York Times Magazine (November 11): 50+.

Appleyard, Donald
1978a "Environment as symbolic action." Working paper. Berkeley: Institute for Urban and Regional Development.
1978b "Home." Working paper. Berkeley: Institute for Urban and Regional Development.

Appleyard, Donald, Kevin Lynch, and John Myer
1964 The View From the Road. Cambridge: MIT Press.

Baldassare, Mark
1979 Residential Crowding in America. Berkeley: University of California Press.

Castaneda, Carlos
1968 The Teachings of Don Juan: A Yaqui Way of Knowledge. New York: Pocket Books.

Cooper, Claire
1975 Easter Hill Village. New York: Free Press.
1976 "The house as symbol of self." Pp. 435–49 in Harold M. Proshansky et al., Environmental Psychology. New York: Holt, Rinehart & Winston.

Cranz, Galen
n.d. "Double talk: redundancy as a way of conceptualizing the relationship between humans and their environment." Unpublished manuscript.

Esser, A. H., et al.
1970 "Interactional hierarchies and power structure in a psychiatric ward: ethological studies of dominance in a total institution." Pp. 25–61 in S. J. Hutt and C. Hutt (eds.), Behavioural Studies in Psychiatry. Oxford: Pergamon Press.

Gans, Herbert
1962 The Urban Villagers. New York: Free Press.

Glaab, Charles N. and A. Theodore Brown
1976 A History of Urban America, 2d ed. New York: Macmillan.

Griaule, Marcel
1965 Conversations with Ogotemmeli. London: Oxford University Press.

Gutnov, Alexei, et al.
1970 The Ideal Communist City. New York: Braziller.

Hall, Edward T.
1959 The Silent Language. Garden City, N.Y.: Doubleday.
1966 The Hidden Dimension. Garden City, N.Y.: Doubleday.

Hastorf, Albert H. and Hadley Cantril
1954 "They saw a game: a case study." Journal of Abnormal and Social Psychology 49:129–34.

Hawley, Amos H.
1950 Human Ecology, A Theory of Community Structures. New York: Ronald Press.

Heimstra, Norman W. and Leslie H. McFarling
1978 Environmental Psychology, 2d ed. Monterey, Calif.: Brooks/Cole.

Howard, Ebenezer
1898 Tomorrow: A Peaceful Path to Real Reform. London: S. Sonnenschein.

Husock, Howard
1979 "Boston the problem that won't go away." New York Times Magazine (November 25): 32+.

Ingalls, Zoë
1979 "The chancellor as governor: 'he's no longer an education man.' " The Chronicle of Higher Education (November 19):3–4.

Ittelson, William H., et al.
1974 An Introduction to Environmental Psychology. New York: Holt, Rinehart & Winston.

Jacobs, Jane
1961 The Death and Life of Great American Cities. New York: Vintage.

Kesey, Ken
1962 One Flew Over the Cuckoo's Nest. New York: Viking.

Kira, Alexander
[1966]
1976 The Bathroom: Criteria for Design. New York: Viking.

Lasswell, Harold
1979 The Signature of Power. New Brunswick, N.J.: Transaction.

Lebowitz, Fran
[1974]
1978 Metropolitan Life. New York: Fawcett Crest.

Lee, Dorothy
1959 Freedom and Culture. Englewood Cliffs, N.J.: Prentice-Hall.

Lyman, Stanford M. and Marvin B. Scott
[1967]
1970 "Territoriality: a neglected sociological dimension." Pp. 88–109 in Stanford M. Lyman and Marvin B. Scott, A Sociology of the Absurd. Pacific Palisades, Calif.: Goodyear.

Lynch, Kevin
1960 The Image of the City. Cambridge: MIT Press.

McHarg, Ian
[1969]
1971 Design with Nature. Garden City, N.Y.: Doubleday/Natural History.

McLaughlin, Robert W.
1962 Architecture: Creating Man's Environment. New York: Macmillan.

Michelson, William H.
1976 Man and His Urban Environment. Reading, Mass.: Addison-Wesley.

Park, Robert E., Ernest W. Burgess, and R. D. McKenzie
1925 The City. Chicago: University of Chicago Press.

Parsons, Talcott
1951 The Social System. New York: Free Press.

Rainwater, Lee
1966 "Fear and the house-as-haven in the lower

class." Journal of the American Institute of Planners 32:23–31.

Scott, Mellier
1969 American City Planning. Berkeley: University of California Press.

Skolnick, Paul, et al.
1977 "Do you speak to strangers? a study of invasions of personal space." European Journal of Social Psychology 7:307–16.

Soleri, Paolo
1969 Arcology: The City in the Image of Man. Cambridge, Mass.: MIT Press.

Sommer, Robert
1969 Personal Space. Englewood Cliffs, N.J.: Prentice-Hall.

Spreiregen, Paul D.
1965 Urban Design: The Architecture of Towns and Cities. New York: McGraw-Hill.

Venturi, Robert, et al.
[1972]
1977 Learning from Las Vegas. Cambridge, Mass.: MIT Press.

Werthman, Carl
1965 Planning and Purchase Decision. Berkeley: Center for Planning and Development Research.

Whyte, William H.
1978 "New York and Tokyo: a study in crowding." Pp. 1–18 in Hidetoshi Kato (ed.), A Comparative Study of Street Life: Tokyo, Manila, New York. Tokyo: Research Institute for Oriental Cultures, Gakushuin University.

Wolfe, Tom
1977 The Kandy-Kolored Tangerine-Flake Streamline Baby. New York: Bantam.

Wurman, Richard Saul
1971 Making the City Observable. Minneapolis and Cambridge, Mass.: Walker Art Center and MIT Press.

PART SIX
Paying Their Way

Bill Owens

WPA mural by John N. Ballator

CHAPTER 15 Producing, Consuming, Exchanging

"The fate of cities," observes sociologist Herbert Gans (1979:102), "is determined by the economic health of their labor markets, tax bases, and the effectiveness of state and Federal support programs." If correct, this means that economic functions are the heart of the matter: the basic life-and-death-determining system of urban existence.

Most local government officials agree with Gans. Nearly 90 percent of city officials in every region of the country and in communities of every size who responded to a National League of Cities poll in 1979 were more worried about the economy than about crime or other social issues (Associated Press, 1980:22). In general, the local officials are concerned about economic decline—coping with a future that promises less, not more.

Most social theorists also agree with Gans. Whatever their ideological differences, theorists have ranked economic activities high on their list of factors that influence, perhaps determine, the fate of cities. Historically, ancient Greek philosophers insisted that the polis should not be too small because it would risk losing its self-sufficient economy. More recently, economics has been the pivot of much urban theory. Recall, for example, the debate over the earliest cities. Economic assumptions underlie both the Childe thesis and the trade thesis of Jane Jacobs. In both cases, it is assumed that what people produce and exchange are prime determinants of human settlement patterns. Christaller's central place theory also rests on economic logic: The spatial distribution of cities within an urban hierarchy is determined by the exchange and production of goods and services. Burgess's concentric zone hypothesis rests on another economic assumption, namely, that economic competition is the key determinant of land use. Sociologist Roderick McKenzie's definition of a metropolitan area and the U.S. government's SMSA concept grow out of economic reasoning too. Both use the integrated labor market as the leading indicator of interdependence within a geographical area.

Surprisingly, the list of urban theorists just mentioned—Gans, Burgess, Christaller, Childe, Jacobs, McKenzie—contains no urban economists. This is because the subfield of urban economics is a mere infant. Economists didn't "discover" the city or the SMSA as a proper unit of analysis until this generation. The first urban economics text appeared in 1965. Since that time, numerous economists have turned their attention to the metropolis. But the fact remains that much of what is known about local economies—their labor markets, land use and growth, residential and industrial location—is based on the theories and research of noneconomists using economic assumptions.

This chapter is about basic economic functions. It pays special attention to the single most important factor in the growth or decline of metropolitan economies: the state of the national economic health.

We begin with a basic vocabulary of political economy. Of course, economists don't agree among themselves any more than other social scientists do. Thus, what's basic to one kind of economic analysis is peripheral to another or rejected altogether. Consider, for example, the concept of the market of supply and demand. The self-regulating market mechanism is central to classical liberal economics. Most introductory textbooks look at the world through the filter of the competitive market. Yet many economists reject this basic assumption about how the world works. Even some influential modern liberals view the market mechanism with suspicion. John Kenneth Galbraith (1968, 1979), for instance, argues that supply and demand no longer work to regulate the economy. In general, Galbraith (1968) says, business corporations manipulate the market to suit their own needs. In particular, the "free market" doesn't work at all to regulate oil prices. According to Galbraith (1979:3), the OPEC oil cartel has proved "inconveniently resistant to free market doctrine."

Other voices, from some unexpected areas, echo Galbraith's words. We might predict that Marxist economists would repudiate the market mechanism, and indeed they do. They argue that the American economy (and its subsystems of urban economies) are best understood in the framework of monopoly capitalism, not the competitive market system. But we might be surprised to find that even some conservatives question free market theory. Respected scholar Charles Lindblom, a professor of politics and economics at

Yale who is considered a conservative, stirred great controversy in the late 1970s with his book *Politics and Markets* (1978). There he maintains that the emergence of large private corporations renders market doctrine obsolete. Essentially, Lindblom concurs with Galbraith; markets are necessarily manipulated by big business corporations in order to ensure economic stability and growth.

Meanwhile, market doctrine continues to enjoy widespread support among U.S. economic researchers. And introductory economics texts in the mainstream, like Paul Samuelson's *Economics*, contend that the market mechanism still works generally to answer the questions of who gets what and what goods are produced.

This shows, once again, that what you see depends on how you look at it. With this in mind, we turn to some important concepts that political economists use to explain how the world works. First, we define concepts in the mainstream of U.S. economic analysis. Then we describe several concepts that are central to an alternative way of understanding political economy: Marxist theory. Like other theoretical perspectives, Marxist political economy can be accepted or rejected. But it should at least be understood, especially since the Marxist vision presents a worldwide challenge to free market economies.

POLITICAL ECONOMY: A BEGINNING VOCABULARY

Supply, Demand, Price, and the Market Mechanism

"You can make even a parrot into a learned political economist—all he must learn are the two words 'Supply' and 'Demand.' " So says an anonymous pundit of a market economy (in Samuelson, 1964:56). Indeed, these twin concepts—**supply** and **demand**—provide the cornerstones of classical economics, that body of thought associated with Adam Smith ([1776] 1970) and carried forward today by such theorists as Milton Friedman.

The logic of supply and demand is as follows. In a market or "free enterprise" economy, the supply of a particular good, such as automobiles, is assumed to be related to consumer demand. Why produce a car if no one will buy one? (An advertising campaign might, of course, persuade the public that it *needs* a car or a second car, thus stimulating demand for the product.)

Demand for a product implies that consumers both want and will pay for it. Let's take car buying as an example of how supply and demand work. The number of cars that will be produced, the logic goes, depends on their cost. A demand curve shows how many cars will be purchased at different price levels. Fig. 15-1 shows that at $4,000 the demand for a new car will be very great indeed (assuming there is gas to power it). As the **price** rises to $8,000, the demand falls. The demand curve shows that the lower the price, the greater the demand. The demand curve slopes downward. This indicates the inverse relationship between the price of a good and the quantity of that good demanded by consumers. Economists often call this the "law of downward-sloping demand."

Now, let's look at the supply side. How many cars will be produced at different prices? This information can be charted with a supply curve. Suppose, for example, that new cars are selling for $3,000. At that price, manufacturers do not want to supply *any* cars to the market, for they can't make a profit; they would lose money. Car manufacturers would produce something else that yielded a higher profit. But they would be willing to produce about 5 million cars if the price was $4,000. As the price keeps rising, manufacturers are willing to supply increasing num-

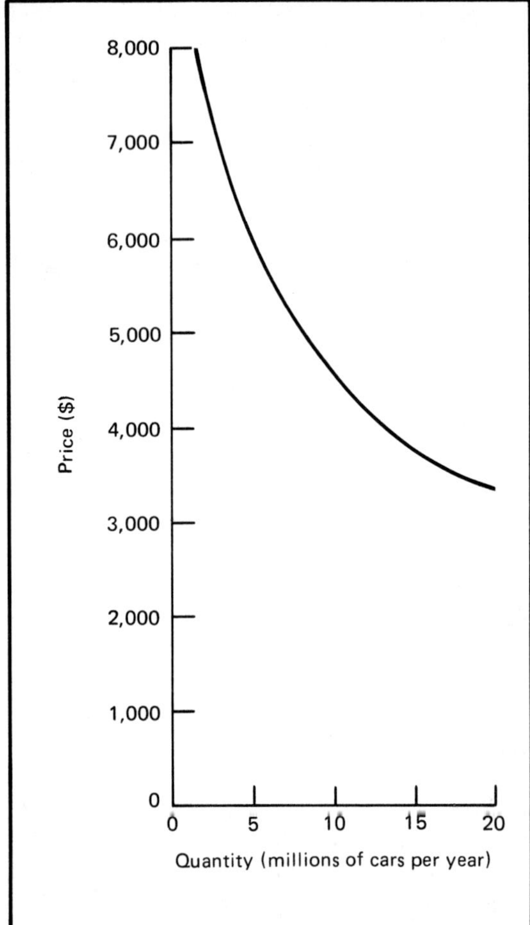

Fig. 15-1 DEMAND CURVE. This curve for cars slopes downward, indicating that as price increases, demand decreases.

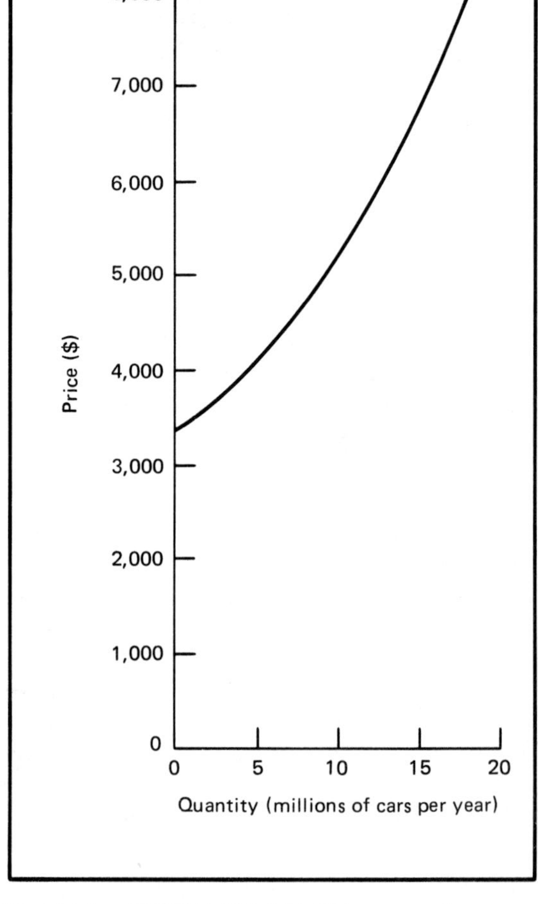

Fig. 15-2 SUPPLY CURVE. This curve shows that the higher the price of cars, the more will be supplied to the market.

bers of cars, as the supply curve in Fig. 15-2 shows. This supply curve indicates that the higher the price, the more cars will roll off the assembly lines.

At some point, classical economic theory continues, a point of equilibrium between supply and demand will be reached. That is, there will be a price that satisfies both consumers and producers. In the case of cars, this equilibrium point can be found by putting the demand and supply curves together and noting the point at which they intersect. In the example here (Fig. 15-3), the point of intersection is at a little less than $5,000. This represents the equilibrium price. Above that price, the theory states, there will tend to be a surplus of cars on the market and hence a downward pressure on the price. Below the equilibrium price, there will tend to be a shortage of cars and hence an upward pressure on the price. According to Samuelson (1964:63), the equilibrium price is the only price that can last for any length of time. This is because the equilibrium price "is that at which the amount willingly supplied and the amount willingly demanded are equal."

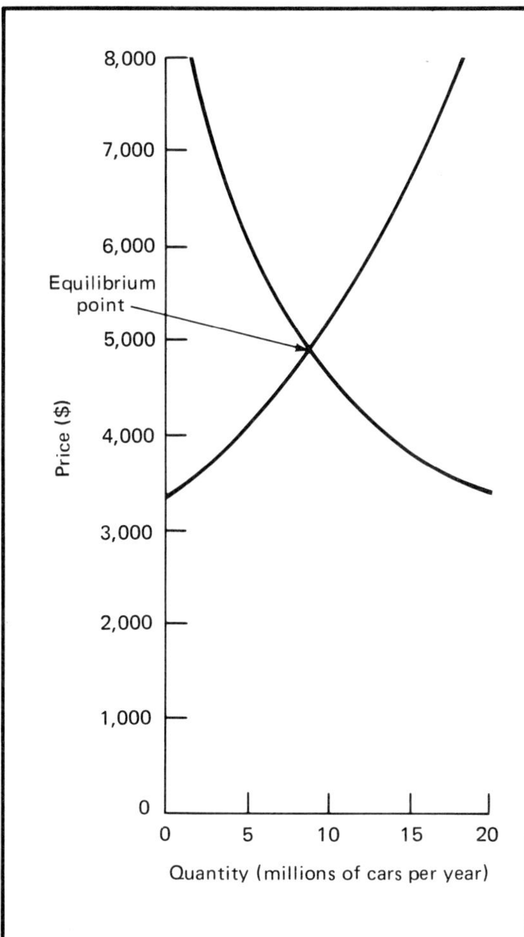

Fig. 15-3 EQUILIBRIUM PRICE. The point at which the supply curve intersects with the demand curve is called the equilibrium price or point. This is the point at which the amount of a product produced and the amount demanded are the same.

Profit

A basic assumption underlies the above discussion of supply and demand. It is this: Suppliers attempt to maximize their **profit** while consumers attempt to maximize their well-being (utility).

What exactly is profit? According to Samuelson (1964:181), profit is what "you have left over from the sale of product (your oranges, apples, bread, and manicures) *after* you have paid the other factor costs" (wages, interest, rent).

Firms pursue different strategies to maximize profit. They may hire cheaper labor, employ more efficient managers, increase advertising, buy less expensive raw materials, expand markets, and so forth. Or they may relocate to areas, at home or abroad, where taxes are lower.

Is profit the only goal of private business firms? Here economists disagree. Some argue that business has a social responsibility to the community in which it operates. Nonsense, retorts the dean of economic conservatives, Milton Friedman. He says that the "Social Responsibility of Business is to Increase Its Profits" (1970)—nothing else. Other economists, such as Lindblom and Galbraith, contend that modern corporations seek stability and growth as well as profit.

Utility

Do individuals and households also try to maximize their gain? Yes, according to free market doctrine. Indeed, the assumption of the "rational, self-interested economic individual" (maximizing utility or well-being) is a key psychological assumption underlying classical liberal economics. As detailed in

Chapter 3, liberal philosophers and political economists base their view of how the world works on this vision of human nature.

Recently, however, this basic assumption has come under attack. For instance, Harvey Leibenstein argues in his book *Beyond Economic Man: A New Framework for Microeconomics* (1976) that market doctrine is wrong; people don't follow the model of rationality attributed to them.

Despite such criticism, the model of rational economic behavior underlies conservative and liberal thought. Meanwhile, Marxists have a different perspective. They tend to emphasize the deception (via advertising, mass media, political rhetoric, etc.) used by dominant elites to control and confound members of the working class, making it difficult for them to even know what's in their best interest.

Externalities

When something is produced—chemicals, apple cider, color TV sets—the production process can have external effects. These effects may benefit or penalize innocent bystanders. For example, if a chemical plant dumps waste into a river, the waste contaminates the river for everyone. This is called a "negative externality." On the other hand, a "positive externality" can bring social benefits to members of the community. A new Metro station in Washington, D.C., may give an economic boost to surrounding shops or the bees from a flower nursery may pollinate the neighbors' gardens—all without cost to the neighbors.

Even the most rational, self-interested person may not be able to calculate the effect of **externalities.** What, for instance, is the effect of oil refineries' discharging tons of pollutants into the air? Residents of suburban San Francisco claim that one negative externality of their nearby refineries is a much higher than average rate of cancer. Or consider the case of gambling in Atlantic City, New Jersey. The majority of urbanites there, including one pastor of a downtown church, voted for casino gambling in the 1970s. They reasoned that new hotels and gambling would bring jobs and an economic boost to the city's lagging economy. However, many have since changed their minds. Gambling brought an influx of prostitutes and purse snatchers to the downtown area. One result: a sharp decline in membership and attendance at central city churches. According to the downtown pastor (in Janson, 1979:20), worshippers fear getting harassed or mugged. In addition, churchgoers must travel through the debris of hotel construction to get to church, and once there, must pay higher parking fees. The pastor now says that the negative externalities outweigh the positive ones: "If I were now living in another city and gambling were proposed as a solution to economic problems, I'd say 'Drop dead.' "

Externalities, either positive or negative, are not distributed according to any equitable scheme. Factory smoke may pollute one part of the urban landscape and not another. The benefits or costs of externalities are often randomly distributed.

Equity

Equity refers to the fair or just allocation of something. What's considered fair, of course, is a matter of perspective. Consider the case of the gasoline shortage or high energy costs. Pure market theorists think it fair to allocate available gas and home heating fuel by the price system. Those who can afford the product will pay the higher price; others will make substitutions or do without. Liberals think this unfair, preferring some kind of

a

b

Fig. 15-4 EXTERNALITIES. (*a*) In 1867, Chatanooga, Tennessee, was partially inundated because farmers upstream failed to take flood control measures. (*b*) Chatanooga in 1967; the city benefited from government-sponsored dams built for agricultural and energy purposes. (*a,b* Tennessee Valley Authority) rationing system. Thus, what's fair or equitable is filtered through a larger framework of justice, a normative theory.

Efficiency

Economic **efficiency** is usually measured by cost per unit of production. If the Whiz Gas Range Company produces two stoves at a cost of $150 while the Flamethrower Company produces two comparable stoves at a cost of $75, then Flamethrower is considered twice as efficient as Whiz.

Efficiency is not always easy to measure. Ms. Gruff, a secretary, may type 100 words per minute, but her brusque manner discourages clients from coming to call on her boss. Mr. Smiley, on the other hand, is a slower typist, but his friendly manner attracts potential customers. Who's more efficient? How can this be measured? This problem of measuring efficiency becomes exacerbated as the United States moves into the postindustrial economy. More and more people will be working in service and information sectors of the economy, where efficiency is no longer a matter of producing cheaper stoves. How can a public school teacher's or public administrator's efficiency be measured when profit is not a goal and social benefit is hard to gauge with precision?

Many factors affect efficiency: the state of technology; cost of raw materials; availability, skill, and cost of labor and management; location; access to transport, and so forth. Later in this chapter, we'll focus on one of these factors, industrial location, noting its importance for efficient and thus profitable production.

AN ALTERNATIVE VOCABULARY

Marxist social scientists reject both the liberal and conservative perspectives on how the political economy should and does work. Marxists argue that consumer sovereignty is a sham and that the public good can't result from each individual's pursuit of self-interest.

Here we focus on several concepts that are central to the Marxist critique of the market mechanism and competitive capitalism: capital, surplus value, and monopoly capitalism. This brief discussion will indicate why Marxist analyses of the U.S. national economy and urban economies are so at odds with orthodox studies. It should also shed some light on how others in the world see us, since the Marxist model of political economy is the norm—not the competing alternative—in many nations today.

Capital

To a non-Marxist like Paul Samuelson (1964:46), **capital** is "elaborate machinery, large-scale factories and plants, and stores and stocks of finished and unfinished materials." The U.S. economy, Samuelson adds, "receives the name 'capitalism' because this capital, or 'wealth,' is primarily the private property of somebody—the capitalist."

To a Marxist, capital is not just a thing, like machines. It is much more. It is a social relation. Marxists think that the means of production in society, like machines, become capital when "they have been monopolized by a certain sector of society and used by that class to produce surplus value—that is, the income of the capitalist class (generally, profits, interest, and rent) that comes from the exploitation of another class" (Gurley, 1975:32). Thus, for Marxists, capital is more than the means of production in society; it is the way in which these means are used. In this way, Marxist thought links economics to politics and social order. **Capitalism** is not only an *economic* system based on private property; it is also a *political* and *social* system based on the domination and exploitation by capitalists of nonpropertied workers.

Surplus Value

Business firms make a profit because they are efficient and compete successfully in the marketplace. Often, firms buy something (raw materials), fashion it into a manufactured good, and resell it for profit. Or they exchange goods for profit. Or they increase prices, which provides profits. That is how free market theorists explain profitability. Marxists have a different explanation.

To a Marxist, a key source of profit in capitalist economies derives from **surplus value.** What is surplus value and when does it arise? Marx's concept of surplus value may be explained in this way:

> Surplus value arises when a capitalist purchases labor-power (the capacity for labor) at its value, employs the labor-power in a work process that he controls, and then appropriates the commodities produced. Surplus value is the difference between the net value of these commodities and the value of labor-power itself. (Gurley, 1975:33)

In this view, the secret of profit is human labor-power: "A worker sells his labor-power—his mental and physical capabilities—to a capitalist for its value, and the capitalist uses the labor-power to obtain commodities which have a value higher than that of the labor power purchased" (Gurley, 1975:33). In a word, profit results from the exploitation of labor in the production sphere.

Monopoly Capitalism

In nineteenth-century Great Britain and America, the characteristic economic unit was the small firm. Typically, many textile firms (like Lowell's factory in Massachusetts) or bakeries would each produce a small share of the total product available in the marketplace. Such firms often faced stiff competition from one another. This situation typified competitive capitalism.

Marxist scholars emphasize how much this situation has changed since the nineteenth century. The typical economic unit today, Paul Baran and Paul Sweezy (1966:6) write, is "a large-scale enterprise producing a significant share of the output of an industry, or even several industries, and able to control its prices, the volume of production, and the types and amounts of its investments." In other words, they contend, the *typical* economic unit in capitalist countries now has the attributes of a monopoly.

In their essay on *Monopoly Capital* (1966), Baran and Sweezy focus on one major theme: the ways in which profit or *surplus*—"the difference between what a society produces and the costs of producing it"—is generated and absorbed under monopoly capitalism. (Note: Marxist theorists don't equate profit and surplus. However, one form of profit, in their view, results from the private appropriation of "surplus value.") They stress the critical role that technological innovation played in the development of a system composed of giant corporations which maximize profit and accumulate capital: **monopoly capitalism.** These corporate giants, Baran and Sweezy argue, are price makers: "they can and do choose what prices to charge for their products" (p. 57). Price makers ban price cutting to reduce competition and remove "the dangerous uncertainties from the rationalized pursuit of maximum profits" (p. 59). Often this takes the form of cartels that regulate prices and output. Or it can take the form of tacit collusion among business firms. In either case, the result, they claim, is clear: Competitive capitalism has faded away, replaced by monopoly capitalism. And they argue that the capitalist state (e.g., the U.S. government) actually functions to strengthen monopoly and regularize its operations.

The implications of Baran and Sweezy's critique of market doctrine are wide-ranging. For example, they contend that the Great Depression of the 1930s was not "the Great Exception" but rather the "normal outcome of the workings of the American economic system" (p. 240). They also claim that "the purpose of United States military aid to underdeveloped countries is to keep them in the American empire if they are already there and to bring them in if they are not—and in any case to insure that there are no further defections from the 'free world' " (p.204).

Without explicating their tightly reasoned and complex analysis of capitalist crises and monopoly capitalism, let us focus here on one issue of special relevance to urban America: automobilization. Writing on the history of monopoly capitalism, Baran and Sweezy (pp. 244–45) pose an interesting question: Why did the second wave of automobile production in the United States occur *after* World War II and not in the 1930s, when it would have led to a needed economic boom? After all, the technology existed to produce cars and to get the depressed economy moving again. And people presumably needed more cars (and the suburban homes to which cars provided access) as much in the 1930s as in the 1940s. "The answer," they say, "is that in 1937 people did not have the required purchasing and borrowing power to get things started, while after 1945 they did. . . . We have here a classic case of quantity turning into quality." What they mean is that the suburban boom generated a snowball effect, making shopping centers and other facilities either necessary or profitable. But even with these powerful stimuli and with defense spending increases, Baran and Sweezy (p. 246) say, unemployment grew. Their conclusion: "Surely, an economy in which unemployment grows even during the expansion phase of the business cycle is in deep trouble. . . . Developments which in a rational society would make possible a great advance toward abundance for all, under monopoly capitalism constitute a threat to the very livelihood of an ever growing proportion of the working people" (p.248).

To conclude: The view that economic life is inseparable from political and cultural life is a key assumption of Marxist thought. To Marx, at any historical time, people have a certain level of productive capacity. This capacity depends on the technology available to them (machines, tools, etc.), the natural environment (fertile or infertile land, water, etc.), and their own knowledge and skills. These Marx calls the "material forces of production." Marx believed that the material forces of production determine how people survive economically (for instance, in nomadic food gathering or industrial production). And, Marx thought, the material forces of production determine how people socially relate to one another in the process of producing and exchanging things and ideas (for instance, as master and slave, as capitalist and worker). Marx called these production and exchange relationships the "social relations of production." Together, the material forces of production and the social relations of production (the economic base of society) mold what Marx called the "superstructure": the way people think; their legal systems; their political and religious institutions; and their world views. In brief, Marx held that the dominant ideas and institutions of any society are determined by people's material being.

Conservative and liberal thought do not make such necessary and inevitable links between economics and social-political life.

Yet most social scientists—whatever their ideological perspective—agree that the way people organize themselves economically and the productive forces available to them have a great impact on their lives.

This applies to cities too. As two non-Marxist urbanists put it, "What is not always recognized is the fact that economic forces are prime determinants of the ecological and physical structures of cities. Directly or indirectly, these factors influence the pattern of living as well as the social and governmental institutions of metropolitan complexes. Changes in the mode of production or of economic organization inevitably find reflection in metropolitan life" (Bollens and Schmandt, 1970:72). Given the importance of economic structure, we now move to a closer examination of the productive patterns of U.S. metropolitan areas.

THE ECONOMY OF URBAN AREAS

Cities and SMSAs in the National Economy

No city is an island. This truism is especially applicable to the analysis of urban economies. To a significant degree, the United States is a single economic unit—not a nation of separate towns and cities. Corner bakeries no longer supply the bulk of bread for sandwiches in small-town America or big cities; national and regional corporations do. In other words, the nation—and often, other nations—is the hinterland for major industries. America is one mass market for goods and services. Allen Pred (Chapter 13) suggests how this works. Major corporations are multilocational, and they distribute their goods nationally.

In this interdependent economic system, cities become creatures of the nation. Indeed, the health of the nation's economy is the single most important factor in the growth or decline of an urban area's economy. Fluctuations in the gross national product (GNP—the sum of all goods and services produced and paid for in monetary terms) are felt in the metropolis, but they have differential impacts. For some cities, national trends toward lower consumption can spell near-disaster. For others, changes in national production and consumption levels will have less impact.

International politics and economics also affect metropolitan economies. The case of Miami is instructive. "A swelling tide of Latin American visitors—and Latin American money—has turned a sleepily suburbanizing South Florida community into an international boom town, a bustling cosmopolis known from Caracas to Buenos Aires as 'el Grande Miami' " (Morganthau, 1980:36). Since over 500,000 Cuban émigrés arrived in Dade County during the 1960s, Miami has become South America's supermarket for affluent Latin tourists. The city has also become a place to invest "hot money," much of it earned smuggling drugs, according to federal officials.

How much a particular metropolitan area suffers or benefits during times of international or national economic change depends on many factors. Some of the most important are (1) the industry mix, (2) demographic and social factors, (3) geographic location, and (4) dependence on petroleum products and proximity to energy sources.

Industry Mix. The degree to which a particular urban area benefits or suffers from changes in the international and national economy depends partially on the mix of productive activities there. If the U.S. economy expands and consumers' incomes rise, they tend to spend their additional money on cars and luxury items, not cigarettes and dish towels. Hence, urban areas producing goods subject to elastic demand (cars, luxury items, durable goods) tend to benefit during times of national economic growth. But during hard times, when people make do by fixing up their old cars rather than purchasing new ones, these areas tend to suffer disproportionately. That is the meaning of the saying, "Whenever the nation catches a cold, Detroit gets pneumonia."

Urban areas that produce cigarettes, basic foodstuffs, and other products with an inelastic demand are not in favorable positions during growth periods. But they tend to suffer less during economic downturns. People don't give up eating or smoking cigarettes during hard times. Nor do they cancel insurance policies or stop going to movies.

Richmond, Virginia, is one city whose industrial mix cushions the effects of economic downturns. Tom Robbins explains why in his novel *Even Cowgirls Get the Blues* (1976:38):

> Richmond, Virginia, has been called a "depression-proof" city. That is because its economy has one leg in life insurance and the other in tobacco.
>
> During times of economic bellyache, tobacco sales climb even as other sales tumble. . . . Perhaps a cigarette gives an unemployed man something to do with his hands. . . .
>
> In times of depression, policy-holders somehow manage to keep up their life insurance premiums. . . . Perhaps they insist on dignity in death since they never had it in life.

In the next chapter, we'll compare in some detail two cities with different industrial mixes: Houston and Detroit. And we'll note how national economic trends affect boomtown Houston and bust-town Detroit.

Demographic and Social Factors. An urban area's ability to respond quickly to change (e.g., technological innovation) depends partly on its people. Cities with large proportions of unskilled, elderly, or narrowly trained people may suffer more in times of national economic slump than urban areas with a highly adaptable labor force. In addition, one-industry towns with highly specialized workers face economic disaster if new technology makes their functions obsolete. This is what happened to the railroaders in a town called Caliente; the town suffered "Death by Dieselization."

Geographic Location. "Chicago is midway between the [Wall Street] Stock Exchange and the Frontier." That is how literary critic Alfred Kazin (1970) explains Chicago's importance at the start of this century. It was, as Sandburg memorialized in his hymn to the city, "Hog Butcher for the World" and "The Nation's Freight Handler." Today, Sandburg would have to revise his lines because the stockyards have moved West. But Chicago's transport function remains important, and the world's busiest airport is located there. (For other explanations of Chicago's importance between 1900 and 1920, see Chapter 1.)

With technological change, new national needs, or the discovery of some important natural resource, cities can gain or lose strategic importance. In the 1970s, for instance, small towns like Rock Springs, Wyoming, and others in the Rocky Mountain region grew quickly as energy sources were extracted from the earth around them. Just as quickly, other towns can lose their basic reason for existence and become ghost towns. Policymakers in Alaska fear that boom towns built around the oil pipeline may suffer that fate.

Energy Needs. Availability of energy sources and easy access to transportation have played a major role in city growth for millennia. Early industrial firms, for instance, had to locate near the available sources of energy, such as water power. Technological innovations—electricity, combustion engines, telephones, and computers—brought changes in both industrial and residential location. In the process, some older urban-industrial areas in the United States found themselves victims of change.

Today, energy shortages and rising energy costs are bound to have widespread but uneven effects. Many of these effects are still unclear. Will hordes of suburbanites, fearing eternal gasoline shortages, return to the central cities? Will Rocky Mountain cities, located near important energy sources, mushroom in population? Will Western cities, especially Sunbelt centers, gain further importance while Frostbelt cities decline? The picture will become more clear in the 1980s.

To conclude: The state of the national economy is the single most important factor in determining the health of urban economies. Forces external to a city's or SMSA's control, such as the state of the nation, cannot be controlled by people in any one metropolis. But the effects of national economic change can be cushioned somewhat by local policy. To cite one instance, a declining SMSA dependent on a single industry might attempt to attract growth industries to its area. Or it might engage in massive retooling efforts for local workers. But no urban area can change forces beyond its control. Whether they like it or not, cities are economic creatures of the nation and, increasingly, the world.

Basic and Nonbasic Sectors

All productive activities which help residents of an urban area earn a living constitute that area's **economic base.** These activities include manufacturing, retail trade, sales, information and services, professional and managerial work, clerical and construction work, and transport.

Once again, the notion that cities can't exist if local residents merely take in each other's washing becomes crucial in understanding how local economies work. Interaction and exchange between the city or SMSA and the world beyond its boundaries are essential for urban existence.

Economists draw a sharp distinction between two types of economic activity: **basic** and **nonbasic.** Basic goods and services are those produced for *export* out of the city or metropolitan area. Primarily produced for export, such goods constitute the export sector. Examples include automobiles from the Detroit SMSA, steel from Gary, cigarettes from Winston-Salem, aircraft from Seattle, and refrigerators from Amana, Iowa. Nonbasic activities consist of goods and services primarily produced for local consumption. These goods and services are produced for internal markets and constitute the local sector. Examples include beauty shops, restaurants, cleaning establishments, gas stations, and dairies.

Most urban economists argue that a city's or SMSA's potential for economic growth depends on the strength of its export or basic sector. The rationale is as follows. Export goods bring money in from outside the urban area which finances the importing of goods that the urban area doesn't produce for itself. In addition, the logic goes, nonbasic activity is largely dependent on basic activity. For example, if a chemical plant closes down and the majority of a city's workers become unemployed, they will no longer patronize local retail or service establishments (e.g., restaurants and furniture stores) to the same extent, and eventually these operations will contract or fold.

Conventional wisdom about the importance of the basic sector to a local economy is

Fig. 15-5 NONBASIC SECTOR. Garage sales, gas stations, beauty shops, and cleaners are part of an urban area's nonbasic economic sector. (Brack Brown)

challenged by planner Hans Blumenfeld (1955:131). He argues that a strong nonbasic sector is the key to a strong local economy, not the reverse. He contends that the nonbasic sector's efficiency is crucial for the operation of basic sector firms.

In either case, both positions rest on an implicit assumption: that cities are like nations, self-sufficient in certain productive activities and dependent on the outside for others. For this reason, economists use international trade terms when discussing basic and nonbasic sectors. Thus, an SMSA is said to improve its "balance of payments" position if it can produce locally some product which it formerly imported. An SMSA is said to enjoy a "comparative advantage" if it can produce a commodity more efficiently and more cheaply than another urban area.

Identifying Basic Sector Industries

How can the export or basic sector activity within a city or SMSA be identified? By using either (1) the employment base method or (2) input-output analysis.

Employment Base Method. This method of identifying basic sector industries compares local and national employment patterns. To illustrate, let's look at a few economic activities in the Rochester, New York, SMSA. In the early 1970s, about 6.2 percent of Rochester's labor force was engaged in the food and kindred products industry; the national average was 1.8 percent. About 0.6 percent of Rochester's labor force produced nonelectrical machinery; the national average was 2.6 percent. Thus, we can assume that Rochester was exporting food products and importing nonelectrical machinery.

The **employment base method** can be used for either specific industries or major sectors of the economy (e.g., public administration, personal services, durable goods manufacturing, and nondurable goods manufacturing). Using U.S. census data, the percentage of the labor force employed in these sectors (and the national average for each sector) can be found. It is clear that a highly specialized area (like Gary for steel or Washington, D.C., for public administration) will show the greatest deviation from national employment patterns.

Input-Output Analysis. The employment base method gives a quick and rather simple view of a local economy's basic and nonbasic

Table 15-1 Input-Output Table Showing Interindustry Flows for a Hypothetical Region

Industry Producing \ Industry Purchasing	1. Agriculture and extraction	2. Manufacturing (light and heavy)	3. Power, communications, and transportation	4. Business, finance, and services	5. Households	6. All others	Total gross output
	(in thousands of dollars)						
1. Agriculture and extraction	$200	$300	$100	$500	$300	$200	$1,600
2. Manufacturing (light and heavy)	100	200	100	150	450	700	1,700
3. Power, communications, and transportation	200	300	200	350	200	150	1,400
4. Business, finance, and services	300	300	200	400	800	300	2,300
5. Households	200	100	400	300	100	900	2,000
6. All others	600	500	50	600	150	400	2,300
Total inputs	1,600	1,700	1,400	2,300	2,000	2,300	11,300

SOURCE: Adapted from Walter Isard, *Methods of Regional Analysis* (Cambridge, Mass., and New York: Technology Press of MIT and John Wiley, 1960), p. 312. Copyright © 1960 by the Massachusetts Institute of Technology. Reprinted by permission of the M.I.T. Press, Cambridge, Mass.

sectors. But it can't show the interconnections between local industries. Nor can the employment base method show how increases in one sector of the local economy will affect other sectors. For this kind of evaluation, an **input-output analysis** is needed.

Input-output analysis works on the following assumptions. Every good or output produced (cameras, cars, public administration, etc.) requires inputs (labor, raw materials, etc.). If expansion occurs in one industry, additional inputs will be needed; some will be obtained locally and others from outside the community. Those added inputs from within the local community will stimulate other local activity. These effects snowball; more inputs stimulate more local purchases—at restaurants, by retail outlets from wholesalers, and so forth. Using input-output analysis, these interindustry relations can be detailed.

Table 15-1 is a simplified input-output analysis of a hypothetical SMSA. All economic activity is classified into six categories. Reading across the rows, we can see how much output was produced in each category and where this output went. Reading down the columns, we can see how much each category of economic activity consumed and where the inputs came from. Thus, manufacturing consumed $1,700,000 worth of total inputs: $300,000 from agriculture and extraction, $200,000 from manufacturing, and so forth. Total inputs to any category of economic activity equal the total outputs. Consequently, manufacturing consumed $1,700,000 in inputs and provided $1,700,000 in outputs.

This is a very simple input-output table.

Fig. 15-6 GARBAGE IN, GARBAGE OUT. Some computer models were oversold to cities. San Francisco officials abandoned their expensive program and returned to tabulating census data by hand. Other computer models, simulating urban conditions, have had limited success. (© 1976 Richard Hedman)

Economists have constructed more sophisticated models to describe and predict interindustry flows within a larger region. One model, using more than 600 variables, was developed to describe the Philadelphia region. Yet such models have not been very helpful to decision makers. Problems of data collection, the complexity of real-world transactions, and theoretical problems have so far limited the practical applications of input-output analyses.

Case Study: Caliente

What happened to the town of Caliente illustrates many of the abstract notions mentioned above. As we recount this case history, recall (1) Herbert Gans's list of what determines the fate of cities (the health of their labor markets, tax bases, and the effectiveness of government support programs); (2) the factors affecting responses to economic change (industry mix, demographic and social factors, geographic location, energy needs); and (3) the basic-nonbasic sector distinction.

In 1949 sociologist Fred Cottrell studied a small desert town he called Caliente. This town, located in a county with little more than 2,500 people, had only one reason for existence: It serviced the steam engines as they moved between Salt Lake City and Los Angeles. When the diesel locomotive replaced the steam engine, Caliente's repair shops were no longer needed because diesel engines need less frequent servicing than steam engines. Geographically, Caliente was no longer strategic. This technological switch from steam resulted in "Death by Dieselization" (1951). For a city so dependent on one industry—railroading—the closing of the railroad shops and the permanent loss of railroad jobs meant the collapse of Caliente's economic base.

After the initial shock of disbelief, Caliente residents tried to find a new economic base. As Cottrell says in his update on Caliente (1972), several ventures were tried, including agriculture and tourism. Then fate took a strange turn. The federal government wanted to use land near Caliente for testing atomic devices. At the time, the potential negative externalities of this project were largely unknown, and local citizens didn't protest this land use, for atomic testing would bring jobs. In fact, only a few jobs were created in this way. Then, during the Korean War, when the primary source of tungsten was cut off, the government paid for a mill near Caliente's profitable deposit. Over time, however, the tungsten mine closed down and the nuclear test site workers moved to housing closer to their work. So, despite its effort to find a new economic base, "the economic picture is bleak" (Cottrell, 1972:76).

Given this bleak picture, one might expect Caliente to shrivel up and become a ghost town. After all, not only did it lose its economic base, it lost much of its tax base: "the railroad tore down, gave away or abandoned much of its fixed structure. In turn it demanded and got a reappraisal that reduced Caliente's tax revenue" (p. 78). And many other towns in the region did become ghost towns when they stopped exporting ore and thus could not pay for imported goods.

But Caliente did not die. It survived. It didn't exactly prosper, but it did survive. How? By providing services to residents—education, nursing, parks, and so forth. And how do residents pay for these services? In large measure through railroad retirement benefits, state pensions, Social Security payments, and other government support programs.

Cottrell (1972:84) concludes that the income of most Caliente residents does not come from exporting goods to the market. Instead, it comes from sources outside the town "who pay Caliente people for doing things mostly for each other." In this sense, Caliente represents a national trend away from producing things and toward delivering consumer services.

In the long run, can Caliente survive with no export sector? Cottrell is dubious. At some point, decisions (which will be made by outsiders—state voters, mainly) will have to be made. When the physical structures of Caliente deteriorate, will the schools and hospitals be rebuilt? Or will the stores and streets and physical structures be allowed to be reclaimed by the desert? Whatever the decision, Caliente's fate will not be determined by local residents. This, of course, is not new for Caliente. Past decisions were also made by faraway decision makers: railroad managers and stockholders.

Caliente is far from a typical town. But its story does illustrate the growing importance of state and federal support programs to help the ill health of the town's tax base and labor market. It also indicates how little control a one-industry (specialized function) town has over its own fate, particularly when technological change renders its specialized function obsolete. Outsiders have always determined Caliente's fate; now they are state voters and government decision makers instead of private railroad managers.

One irony that Cottrell stresses (see Box 15-1) concerns the deep-seated American value of individualism and belief in the market as a self-regulating mechanism. The people of Caliente are rugged individualists, believers in the "American way" of the price system and progress. Fiercely independent in an interdependent world, some Caliente people suffered more than others for their beliefs. "In short, 'good citizens' who assumed family and community responsibility are the greatest losers . . . those who were—by middle class norms—most moral were the most heavily penalized" (1951:360; 1972:68). Those who could pick up and leave the

Box 15–1

DEATH BY DIESELIZATION

What Happened when the Steam Engines Stopped

Caliente was built in a break in an eighty-mile canyon traversing the desert. . . . So long as the steam locomotive was in use, Caliente was a necessity. With the adoption of the diesel it became obsolescent.

This stark fact was not, however, part of the expectations of the residents of Caliente. Based upon the "certainty" of the railroad's need for Caliente, men built their homes there, frequently of concrete and brick, at the cost, in many cases of their life savings. The water system was laid in cast iron which will last for centuries. Business men erected substantial buildings which could be paid for only by profits gained through many years of business. Four churches evidence the faith of Caliente people in the future of their community. . . .

Average American Community

Similarly normal are the social organizations. These include Rotary, Chamber of Commerce, Masons, Odd Fellows, American Legion and the Veterans of Foreign Wars. There are the usual unions, churches, and myriad little clubs to which the women belong. In short, here is the average American community with normal social life, subscribing to normal American codes. Nothing its members had been taught would indicate that the whole pattern of this normal existence depended completely upon a few elements of technology which were themselves in flux. . . .

The Logic of Location

Division points on a railroad are established by the frequency with which the rolling stock must be serviced and the operating crews changed. At the turn of the century when this particular road was built, the engines produced wet steam at low temperatures. The steel in the boiler was of comparatively low tensile strength and could not withstand the high temperatures and pressures required for the efficient use of coal and water. At intervals of roughly a hundred miles the engine had to be disconnected from the train for service . . . . Thus the location of Caliente, as far as the railroad was concerned, was a function of boiler temperature and pressure and the resultant service requirements of the locomotive. . . .

In its demands for service the diesel engine differs almost completely from a steam locomotive. It requires infrequent, highly skilled service, carried on within very close limits, in contrast to the frequent, crude adjustments required by the steam locomotive. . . . Hence diesels require much less frequent stops for fuel and water. . . . In consequence, every third and sometimes every second division point suddenly became technologically obsolescent.

Cost-Benefit Analysis

Caliente, like all other towns in similar plight, is supposed to accept its fate in the name of "progress." The general public, as shippers and consumers of shipped goods, reaps the harvest in better, faster service and eventually perhaps in lower charges. A few of the workers in Caliente will also share the gains, as they move to other division points, through higher wages. They will share in the higher pay, though whether this will be adequate to compensate for the costs of moving no one can say. Certain it is that their pay will not be adjusted to compensate for their specific losses. They will gain only as their seniority gives them the opportunity to work. These are those who gain. What are the losses, and who bears them?

The railroad company can figure its losses at Caliente fairly accurately. It owns 39 private dwellings, a modern clubhouse with 116 rooms, and a twelve-room hotel with dining-room and lunch counter facilities. These now become useless, as does much of the fixed physical equipment used for servicing trains. Some of the machinery can be used elsewhere. Some part of the roundhouse can be used to store unused locomotives and standby equipment. The rest will be torn down to save taxes. All of these costs can be entered as capital losses on the statement which the company draws up for its stockholders and for the government. Presumably they will be recovered by the use of the more efficient engines. . . .

Probably the greatest losses are suffered by the older "non-operating" employees. Seniority among these men extends only within the local shop and craft. A man with twenty-five years' seniority at Caliente has no claim on the job of a similar craftsman at another point who has only twenty-five days' seniority. Moreover, some of the skills formerly valuable are no longer needed. The boilermaker, for example, knows that jobs of his kind are disappearing and he must enter the ranks of the unskilled. . . .

Operating employees also pay. Their seniority extends over a division, which in this case includes three division points. The older members can move from Caliente and claim another job at another point, but in many cases they move leaving a good portion of their life savings behind. The younger men must abandon their stake in railroad employment. . . . To handle the same amount of tonnage require(s) only about a fourth the man-power it formerly took. Three out of four men must start out anew at something else.

The local merchants pay. The boarded windows, half empty shelves, and abandoned store buildings bear mute evidence of these costs. The older merchants stay, and pay; the younger ones, and those with no stake in the community, will move; but the value of their property will in both cases largely be gone.

The bondholders pay. They can't foreclose on a dead town. If the town were wiped out altogether, that which would remain for salvage would be too little to satisfy their claims. Should the town continue there is little hope that taxes adequate to carry the overhead of bonds and day-to-day expenses could be secured by taxing the diminished number of property owners or employed persons.

The church will pay. The smaller congregations cannot support services as in the past. As the church men leave, the buildings will be abandoned.

Homeowners will pay. A hundred and thirty-five men owned homes in Caliente. They must accept the available means of support or rent to those who do. In either case the income available will be far less than that on which the houses were built. The least desirable homes will stand unoccupied, their value completely lost. The others must be revalued at a figure far below that at which they were formerly held.

"Most Moral" Pay Most

In a word, those who are, by traditional American standards, *most moral* . . . "good citizens" who assumed family and community responsibilities are the greatest losers. Nomads suffer least. . . .

Reactions to Technological Change

The first reaction took the form of an effort at community self preservation. Caliente became visible to its inhabitants as a real entity, as meaningful as the individual personalities which they had hitherto been taught to see as atomistic or nomadic elements. Community survival was seen as prerequisite to many of the individual values that had been given precedence in the past. The organized community made a search for new industry, citing elements of community organization themselves as reasons why industry should move to Caliente. But the conditions that led the railroad to abandon the point made the place even less attractive to new industry than it had hitherto been. There was also a change in sentiment. In the

Box 15-1 (continued)

past the glib assertion that progress spelled sacrifice could be offered when some distant group was a victim of technological change. There was no such reaction when the event struck home. . . .

The people of Caliente continually profess their belief in "The American Way," but . . . they criticize decisions made solely in pursuit of profit, even though those decisions grow out of a clearcut case of technological "progress." They feel that the company should have based its decision upon consideration for loyalty, citizenship, and community morale. They assume that the company should regard the seniority rights of workers as important considerations, and that it should consider significant the effect of permanent unemployment upon old and faithful employees. They look upon community integrity as an important community asset. Caught between the support of a "rational" system of "economic" forces and laws, and sentiments which they accept as significant values, they work a solution to their dilemma which will at once permit them to retain their expected rewards for continued adherence to past forms and to defend the social system which they have been taught to revere but which now offers them a stone instead of bread. . . .

It rapidly became apparent to the people of Caliente that they could not gain their objectives by organized community action nor individual endeavor but there was hope that by adding their voices to those of others similarly injured there might be hope of solution. They began to look to the activities of the whole labor movement for succor. Union strategy which forced the transfer of control from the market to government mediation or legislation and operation was widely approved on all sides. . . . When make-work rules contributed to the livelihood of the community, the support of the churches, and the taxes which maintain the schools; when feather-bed practices determine the standard of living, the profits of the businessman and the circulation of the press; when they contribute to the salary of the teacher and the preacher; they can no longer be treated as accidental, immoral, deviant or temporary. Rather they are elevated into the position of emergent morality and law. . . .

Justice and Market Values

Confronted by a choice between the old means and resultant "injustice" which their use entails, and the acceptance of new means which they believe will secure them the "justice" they hold to be their right, they are willing to abandon (in so far as this particular area is concerned) the liberal state and the omnicompetent market in favor of something that works to provide "justice." (Cottrell, 1951:358–85; subheads ours. Copyright 1951 by American Sociological Association. Reprinted by permission.)

community—who owned no property there and had not sunk deep roots—"the nomads," suffered least. The final irony is that for all their rugged frontier individualism, these people on the desert "must listen ever more closely to the beat of a distant drummer to whose cadence they must march" (1972:85).

The small town of Caliente was created by outsiders for technological reasons. The site happened to be located at a point on the transcontinental railroad where steam engines needed to be serviced. Technology and lack of physical barriers dictated Caliente's location. Other towns like Caliente which have a relatively undiversified economy (one that produces only a narrow range of goods and services) can also find themselves in a shaky economic position without much warning when and if technological change hits. The shutdown of a military base or a branch manufacturing plant of a multinational corporation can spell economic disaster for local residents. And such decisions are made outside the local community—by outsiders. As the people of Caliente found out, local residents have little influence over location decisions which so vitally affect their lives and livelihoods.

The case of Caliente's dependence on outsiders for its existence—both originally and now—is extreme. And the decision which originally created Caliente was not complicated. By contrast, most industrial location decisions are much more complex. Why, for instance, do business firms locate in cities rather than rural areas? Under what conditions will a group of similar economic activities cluster together or not? We now turn to such questions.

WHY ECONOMIC ACTIVITIES TEND TO CLUSTER TOGETHER

Since the emergence of the modern industrial city, both U.S. citizens and scholars have worried about the efficiency of public and private institutions. Efficiency in government was one goal of municipal reformers after the turn of the century (Chapter 11); they wanted to make politics more businesslike. By World War I, so-called efficiency experts were telling business firms how to increase production by using Frederick Taylor's principles of "scientific management." His ideas, known collectively as "Taylorism" (e.g., the division of work into small units; assembly-line techniques; time and motion studies), had international impact. Indeed, V. I. Lenin thought that Bolshevist Russia needed Taylorism.

The outcry for efficiency is still strong. However, as mentioned before, it is harder to measure in a postindustrial economy than in an economy producing stoves, cars, and other things instead of services.

Various factors influence economic efficiency. One important variable is location. For instance, if a stove factory is located far from suppliers, transport lines, and an available work force, it won't be as efficient (and thus as profitable) as one nearer to such necessary ingredients for the production and distribution of stoves. Economic logic thus dictates that the stove factory will locate in some places and not others.

Agglomeration Economies

Economists point to the cost savings which result when stove factories, clothing stores, or other firms cluster together in a physical location such as a city or metropolitan area. The term **agglomeration economies** refers to the cost savings which come from agglomeration or clustering together. Economists break down the benefits of agglomeration into three categories, each of which helps to explain why firms tend to cluster in urban areas: economies of scale, localization economies, and urbanization economies.

First, agglomeration can and often does lead to economies of scale. When the scale of an enterprise increases, the unit cost of production can drop. To build two cars, for instance, would cost more per unit than building 200,000 of the same car. One reason why firms locate in urban or metropolitan areas is that they are more likely to mount a large enough operation to take advantage of economies of scale. (There are many exceptions today, given new technologies of communication and transport. But historically—particularly during the early stages of industialization and up to World War II—advantages derived from economies of scale were an important consideration.)

Secondly, cluster effects or localization economies can benefit business firms. This means that cost savings can occur when firms of a similar nature are spatially near each other. Department stores often cluster together in the CBD or in a suburban shopping mall, taking advantage of the fact that shoppers also cluster there. With rare exceptions, investment brokers in New York City have Wall Street offices, both for the convenience of clients and for the ease of communication with other firms. Likewise, it is common for auto dealers to cluster together on Cicero Avenue in Chicago or other auto rows; they feel that locating near other auto dealers will help maximize profit, for potential customers may spill over from one lot to the next. However, some firms, like grocery stores, ordinarily don't cluster together; in such cases, the disadvantages of being too close to competitors outweigh the advantages.

Third, urbanization economies may result. That is, when a firm locates near goods and services necessary to its production or distribution processes—advertising agencies, raw materials, rail lines, or other facilities important for its particular good—it can cut costs and thus increase efficiency.

Several other factors help to explain why economic activities group together. The first is prestige. Having a high-status address (Wall Street for lawyers) or being in a popular place (New Orleans's French Quarter) may add to the firm's image and give potential customers confidence in the product. The second factor is a specialized labor force. Electronics firms have gravitated to the Silicon Valley south of San Francisco and to Boston's fringes, where a highly skilled labor force is readily available.

To conclude: Where to locate is an important decision for business firms. Economically, producers of goods and services often maximize efficiency and profit by grouping or clustering together in dense settlements. Historically, this economic fact helps to explain the existence and development of cities.

ECONOMICS OF THE FUTURE

As the United States enters the postindustrial, energy-conscious era, location decisions become more complex. Energy shortages and rising costs may force business firms and their workers to reconsider their locations. Increasing numbers of manufacturing firms may move out of U.S. metropolitan areas altogether—and into the urban areas of foreign countries. Other firms that depend on electronic communications rather than oil may scatter to the rural countryside. Large numbers of professionals and white-collar workers may be communicating rather than commuting to work, and this phenomenon will affect both business and residential location patterns.

What actually will happen is murky and much debated. Private business decisions, government policies, and international events will play a major role in whatever changes occur.

We don't pretend to be seers, but we can identify certain trends that will affect the economic life of American cities. Here are some important trends and policies. They are categorized as international, national, and regional, but it will become clear that these categories are often inseparable.

International Trends and Policies. (1) *The political economy of oil*—what oil producers and U.S. multinational firms do will impact on the nation's cities. (2) *The widening income gap between rich and poor nations*—the indirect effects of the ever-increasing gap between per capita income in the so-called First World countries and those of the Third can affect city life in the United States. Here are just a few possibilities. Even more U.S. firms could leave U.S. metropolitan areas for overseas locations, where labor is cheaper and unions are either weak or banned. The world's poor nations could boycott some U.S. products made in metropolitan areas, affecting the export sector of local economies. Poor nations could band together and sharply increase the price of their raw materials, affecting American cities in various ways, depending on the products they produce.

National and Regional Trends and Policies. (1) *Energy*—National policymakers feel that "the most important determinant of the health of the nation's economy in the future is likely to be the health of its energy policy," according to a reporter who interviewed them (Rattner, 1979: Sec. 4,1). National energy policies and energy crunches will have different impacts on the nation's cities and regions. Cities in the "energy corridor" between Houston and New Orleans are in a very different position than Frostbelt cities. And the Old West (a thirteen-state area with about 39 million people and rich energy sources) is experiencing an economic boom. Yet some officials in the Western states fear that other regions are eyeing their natural resources (oil shale, heavy crude oil, low-sulfur coal). As an official of the Council of State Governments put it, "It's the West against the rest" (in Mathews, 1979:32). Western leaders fear that national government policy will limit their growth and perhaps enrich other sections of the country. Meanwhile, one Eastern conservative chides the Old West for being the Angry West, arguing that sectionalism is outdated in the days of a national mass market (Will, 1979:116).

Several other trends are noteworthy, particularly (2) the ever-increasing *size of economic firms* and (3) the importance of *government support programs.* All these affect the fate of cities.

The precise effects of these trends and policies remain debated and debatable. But one thing seems clear: Individual cities and SMSAs have little—and decreasing—ability to control their own fate.

ANOTHER LOOK

Although theorists agree on the importance of economic factors to the fate of cities, they disagree on how the economy today really works—and how it could work better. The dean of contemporary economic conservatives, Milton Friedman, and other free market theorists look to supply, demand, price, and the market mechanism to explain how the U.S. economic system generally should work. They base their economic views on a psychological assumption: that individuals and business firms are rational, self-interested profit maximizers. Conservatives see the workings of the marketplace as a technical issue—not a moral one. Liberals like John Kenneth Galbraith point to the lack of equity in the conservative stance. If the poor cannot afford heating fuel in times of skyrocketing prices, should the market dictate that they go cold while the rich don't? Liberals think not. Furthermore, liberals point to the problems of social order and political stability that might follow from pure market doctrine. Thousands of cold, angry people might not shiver alone but rather start burning down cities in frustration or feelings of relative deprivation. Marxists—now joined by strange comrades such as Charles Lindblom—reject the notion of market sovereignty. In this view, giant corporations manipulate the market, removing uncertainties from the pursuit of profits.

It is important to note that while theorists continue to debate economic issues, American citizens in the past decade have responded to a growing sense of powerlessness over their collective economic fates by turning to a variety of answers. Some have turned inward to find their own souls via a series of "Me Decade" therapies. Others have turned to "Small Is Beautiful" and/or "Free Enterprise" politics. Many politicians who were liberals in the 1960s have since pushed for cutting government regulations, budgets, and size. This movement, fueled mainly by white, middle-class citizens, had gone full-speed ahead by the end of the 1970s with Proposition 13 in California, federal deregulation in many fields, and cutbacks in government support programs.

What's happening here? There seems to be an enormous gap between what *is* (giant private corporations and big government) and what many think *should be* (smaller government, individualism). This gap between traditional American values and modern American institutions is not easily reconcilable, at least not without dismantling major institutions. This suggests the following irony: In an era of national and international markets, of worldwide economic interdependence, comes the cry for more self-sufficiency, more local autonomy. Seeing how this contradiction is worked out in the political and economic spheres awaits us.

PROJECTS

1. **Basic sector.** Using the employment base method, try to determine what goods and services your community exports. Helpful data sources are the U.S. Bureau of the Census publications, including the decennial census material (see, for instance, the *U.S. Census of Population* summary for national averages in some categories) and the *Census of Business* (selected services, retail trade, manufactures), which is published every five years.

2. **Masters of their own fate?** Interview various members of your community (including presumed decision makers such as elected and appointed officials; the unemployed; members of different occupational groups, students, etc.). Pose the following questions:

   a. What are five or six important decisions or events that have affected the economic life of this community in the past decade?
   b. Who was responsible for these decisions? Or what forces led to them?

   Now, note the patterns of response. For instance, do interviewees tend to name local decision makers or events? Do they draw links between what happened nationally and internationally (e.g., oil policies, government support programs, new technologies) and local economic life?

SUGGESTIONS FOR FURTHER LEARNING

The first urban economics book ever published in the United States is Wilbur R. Thompson, *A Preface to Urban Economics* (Baltimore: John Hopkins Press, 1965). Although a classic in the field, it is not recommended for beginners.

Readable texts of intermediate difficulty include Robert L. Bish and Hugh O. Nourse, *Urban Economics and Policy Analysis* (New York: McGraw-Hill, 1975) which covers theory and selected issues (e.g., housing, race, environment) and urban public finance. Several books draw on urban studies literature more generally. These include Arthur F. Schreiber, Paul K. Gatons, and Richard B. Clemmer, *Economics of Urban Problems: An Introduction* (Boston: Houghton Mifflin, 1965); Douglas M. Brown, *Introduction to Urban Economics* (New York: Academic Press, 1974); and Alan R. Winger, *Urban Economics: An Introduction* (Columbus, Ohio: Merrill, 1977). James Heilbrun, *Urban Economics and Public Policy* (New York: St. Martin's, 1974), draws on concepts from other social sciences and is both readable and comprehensive.

For a very readable, somewhat iconoclastic and personal interpretation, see Jane Jacobs, *The Economy of Cities* (New York: Vintage, 1976). Among other things, Jacobs presents her scenario of how early cities developed.

Selected issues, including discussions of quantitative models for economic decision making, can be found in two anthologies edited by Harvey Perloff and Lowdon Wingo, *Issues in Urban Economics* (Baltimore: Johns Hopkins Press, 1968) and *Issues in Urban Economics # 2* (Baltimore: Johns Hopkins Press, 1978).

For a Marxist perspective, see William K. Tabb and Larry Sawers (eds.), *Marxism and the Metropolis: New Perspectives in Urban Political Economy* (New York: Oxford University Press, 1978). Of particular interest is David M. Gordon's article, "From City to Metropolis," in which Gordon theorizes that the patterns of urban development correspond to the three main stages of capital accumulation in advanced industrial countries: commercial, industrial, and corporate capitalism. Also see David M. Gordon (ed.), *Problems in Political Economy: An Urban Perspective*, 2d. ed. (Lexington, Mass.: D.C. Heath, 1977). This reader contains an excellent introduction comparing radical, liberal, and conservative frameworks of analysis. The Democratic Socialist Organizing Committee (DSOC), chaired nationally by Michael Harrington, sponsors local seminars throughout the country concerning "Marxism and the Metropolis." The Union for Radical Political Economics (URPE) compiles reading lists from courses throughout the country dealing with radical analyses of economics; the list is distributed through their New York City office.

For a discussion of the relationship of cities to their regions, see Edgar M. Hoover, *An Introduction to Regional Economics* (New York: Knopf, 1971), and Hugh O. Nourse, *Regional Economics* (New York: McGraw-Hill, 1968). For a classic case study of a city and its relationship to its metropolitan region, see Edgar M. Hoover and Raymond Vernon, *Anatomy of a Metropolis* (New York: Doubleday, 1962).

The pioneer in economic base studies, the late Charles M. Tiebout, described the nature and uses of input-output analysis in *The Community Economic Base Study* (New York: Committee for Economic Development, 1962). For an application of input-output analysis, see *Metropolitan Challenge* (Dayton, Ohio: Metropolitan Community Studies, 1959). An application of the employment base method is found in Ezra Solomon and Zrko G. Bilbija, *Metropolitan Chicago: An Economic Analysis* (New York: Free Press, 1959).

A film by Willard Van Dyke, *Valley Town* (1940), explores what happens to a town when its basic industry is made obsolete by technological change. NBC's TV film *Smalltown* (1964) looks at demographic and technological change that altered the lives of residents; it portrays towns that survived as well as some that didn't. Orson Welles's film *The Magnificent Ambersons* (1942) depicts the impact on a small town of industrialization (particularly the automobile) for economic and social life. Louis Malle's prize-winning documentary *Phantom India* (1968) contains a section on Calcutta which suggests the interrelationships between Calcutta's present plight and past history (e.g., the separation of jute fields and jute factories when partition of Bengal took place in 1947). Malle blends economic and social history in the narration with strong, often ironic, visual images.

On the specific issue of energy, see Robert Stobaugh and Daniel Yergin (eds.), *Energy Future* (New York: Random House, 1979), the best single examination of the issue in print at this writing. A report of the Harvard Business School, the book emphasizes conservation and solar energy as solutions to the energy crisis.

KEY TERMS

Agglomeration economies The clustering together of economic activities and the consequent cost savings that result. Benefits may occur from economies of scale, localization economies, and urbanization economies.

Basic-nonbasic economic activities (or **sectors**) The basic economic sector consists of goods and services produced primarily for export out of the community. Nonbasic goods and services consist of those which are produced primarily for local consumption.

Capital To a non-Marxist, machines, factories and plants, and stores and stocks of finished and unfinished goods. To a Marxist, all the above *and* the way in which they are used (the social relationships of production).

Capitalism To a non-Marxist, an economic system in which capital or wealth is primarily the private property of capitalists. Synonyms: free enterprise system, profit or price system. To a Marxist, an economic-social-political system based on private property and the domination and exploitation by capitalists of nonpropertied workers.

Demand The degree to which consumers want and will pay for a product. Demand curves illustrate that the higher the price of a good, the fewer the people who will be willing to buy.

Economic base In urban economics generally, all activities that produce income for members of a community. In Marxist social thought, the productive forces of society and the social relations of production.

Efficiency Measured (by economists) by using a ratio of units of output to units of cost. The efficiency of a business firm is related to its profitability.

Employment base method A method for identifying basic sector activities by comparing local and national employment patterns.

Equity Fairness or justice in the distribution of something, such as benefits or burdens.

Externalities Spillover effects, indirect consequences—either positive or negative—to individuals or groups not directly involved with the action.

Input-output analysis A method of measuring the interconnections between industries in a city, SMSA, or region. It attempts to show how the growth or decline in one basic sector industry will affect other industries.

Monopoly capitalism A late stage of capitalism (following the commercial and industrial stages) identified by Marxist theorists. Baran and Sweezy characterize this stage as one in which the typical economic unit is the giant corporation and the problem faced by such corporations is one of absorption of the surplus.

Price To market theorists, the financial cost of a good or service determined by the market of supply and demand. Marxist theorists stress the degree to which prices are fixed by cartels or large corporations under monopoly capitalism.

Profit To market theorists, the net income of a business firm after all expenses of production have been paid. To Marxist theorists, one form of profit derives from surplus value.

Supply The quantity of a good provided to the market at a given price. Supply curves slope upward, indicating that the higher the price, the more of a good will be supplied to the market.

Surplus value A Marxist concept, key to Marx's analysis of capitalism. He reasoned that business profits are based in the production sphere. This means that, in Marx's view, one source of profit is the exploitation of labor; that is, human labor-power becomes the source of value that goes unpaid by the capitalist employer. If, for instance, a worker spends three hours in "necessary labor" (necessary to subsist) and three hours in "surplus labor" (the time in which the worker produces exclusively for the employer), the surplus labor time is the source of surplus value.

REFERENCES

Associated Press
1980 "Most local officials say economy is top worry." New York Times (January 20):22.

Baran, Paul A. and Paul M. Sweezy
1966 Monopoly Capital: An Essay on the American Economic and Social Order. New York: Monthly Review.

Blumenfeld, Hans
1955 "The economic base of the metropolis: critical remarks on the 'basic-nonbasic' concept." Journal of the American Institute of Planners 21:114–32.

Bollens, John C. and Henry J. Schmandt
1970 The Metropolis: Its People, Politics, Economic Life, 2d ed. New York: Harper & Row.

Cottrell, William Fred
1951 "Death by dieselization: a case study in the reaction to technological change." American Sociological Review 16:358–85.
1972 Technology, Man, and Progress. Columbus, Ohio: Merrill.

Friedman, Milton
1970 "Social responsibility of business is to increase its profits." New York Times magazine section (September 13):32+.

Galbraith, John Kenneth
1968 The New Industrial State. New York: Signet.
1979 "Oil: a solution." New York Review of Books. (September 27):3–6.

Gans, Herbert
1979 Letter to the editor. New York Times magazine section (February 11):102.

Gurley, John G.
1975 Challengers to Capitalism: Marx, Lenin, and Mao. San Francisco: San Francisco Book Co.

Janson, Donald
1979 "Atlantic City's clergy say casinos hurt churches." New York Times (September 2):1, 20.

Kazin, Alfred (narrator)
1970 The Writer and the City. Distributed by Chelsea.

Leibenstein, Harvey
1976 Beyond Economic Man: A New Framework for Microeconomics. Cambridge, Mass.: Harvard University Press.

Lindblom, Charles
1978 Politics and Markets. New York: Basic Books.

Mathews, Tom
1979 "The angry west vs. the rest." Newsweek (September 17):31–40.

Morganthau, Tom
1980 "Miami: Latin crossroads." Newsweek (February 11):36+.

Rattner, Steven
1979 "Energy policy: an enigma surrounded by a riddle." New York Times (July 1):Sec. 4,1.

Robbins, Tom
1976 Even Cowgirls Get the Blues. Boston: Houghton Mifflin.

Samuelson, Paul
1964 Economics, 6th ed. New York: McGraw-Hill.

Smith, Adam
[1776]
1970 The Wealth of Nations. New York: Penguin.

Will, George F.
1979 "Wagons in a circle." Newsweek (September 17):116.

Bill Owens

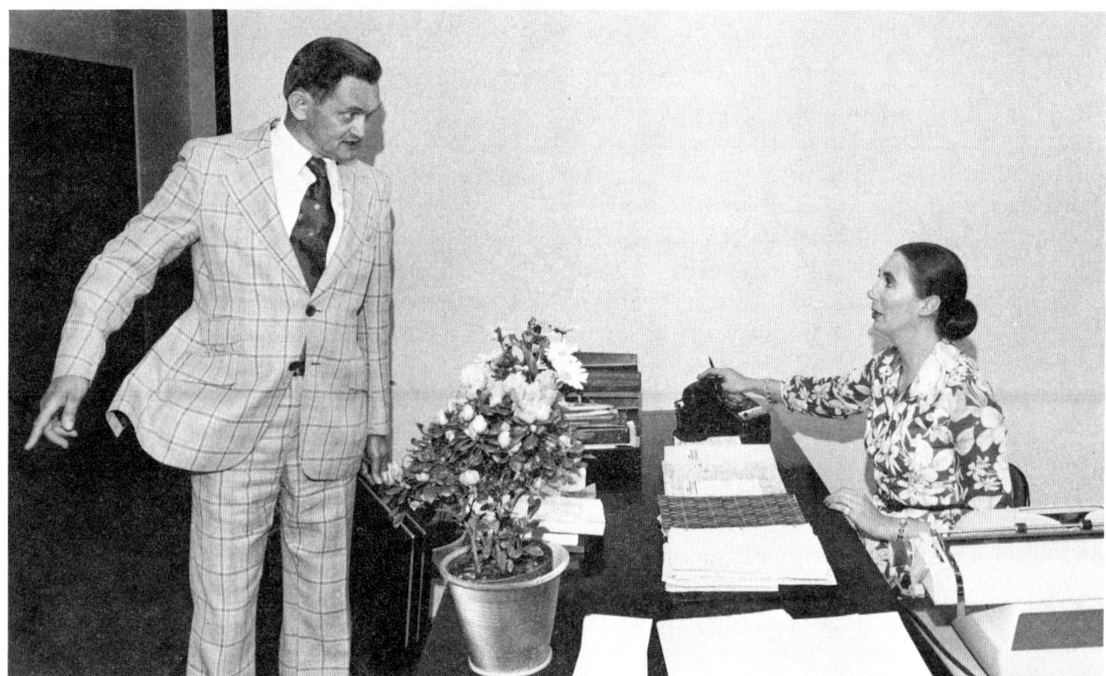

"I really enjoy being here because it's my pleasure to help people. They'd have to fire me before I'd quit. I know I'm loved and vice versa."

CHAPTER 16
Blue-Collar, White-Collar, Shirtless

"What do you want to do when you grow up?"

A first-grade teacher in Houston got the

following answers from her six-year-old students: airline pilot, soldier, rock star, police officer, President, teacher, and doctor. Interestingly, none of these American children said they wanted to collect bugs, travel to foreign lands, watch TV all day, or hike in the woods. All answered by naming *work* -related roles. Why? In the United States, people's identity has been tied traditionally to their work. Apparently these first graders had already absorbed the message: In large measure, *you are what you do*.

This situation is changing slowly for a number of reasons, both structural, social psychological, and moral. On the one hand, as the United States moves from an industrial to a postindustrial society, more people will have less work, at least traditional work, to do. By the time they grow up, these first graders may find that technology has changed the nature of much work they actually end up doing, giving them a great deal of leisure time. Indeed, we could hypothesize that in postindustrial economies, the key question for a substantial portion of the population will be "what are you into?" instead of "what do you do?" That is, many will start defining themselves in terms of their leisure interests, whether it be making videotapes for the home playback machine, surfing, or collecting old beer cans.

Moreover, in the postindustrial society, many may *have to* define themselves in terms of their leisure activities, if they wish to retain their dignity. The reason: not everyone trained in a trade or occupation will be able to practice it. This phenomenon is occurring already. Some jobs have been made obsolete by technological change and automation. Others attract too many prospective workers, causing a structural mismatch between jobs and people. In 1977, for instance, twice as many persons graduated college with teaching credentials as there were available jobs (Watkins, 1979:10). So, it's no surprise when a house painter turns out to have a Ph.D. in English literature. In a labor force that now hovers around 100 million persons (one percentage point of unemployment equals about 1 million people without jobs), countless numbers of Americans are already doing work they never dreamed of doing in order to survive.

Also, values about the meaning of work are in flux. Some Americans, mainly college-educated and professionally trained, are choosing to drop out of the "rat race" and spend more time cultivating friends and gardens instead of climbing the ladder of success. Others, affected by the "Me Decade" of the 1970s, search for self-fulfillment in narcissistic delights instead of work. And many of those who do work fulltime—the majority according to one respected study (HEW, 1973)—don't like the work they do.

At the same time, new entrants into the labor force seek meaningful work, not dead-end or boring jobs. In 1979, 50 percent of all women over age sixteen were working outside the home (*National Now Times*, 1979:10). Many of these are "reentry" women, seeking both financial and emotional rewards from their work. Yet nearly two thirds of the female labor force works in relatively low-status jobs—clerical, service, or sales—and many rush from their nonpaying work in the house to a boring, low-paying job outside the house. Some work in **pink-collar** jobs, that is, occupations in which over 90 percent of the workers are female (e.g., waiting tables, typing, secretarial work, hairdressing, sewing). If they could, some women would prefer to stay in their homes and redefine the concept of work, hoping that society will recognize the value of household labor by rewarding it in monetary terms and providing fringe benefits just like other work (see Howe, 1978: Chap. 6).

In terms of people and their work in America, the old Chinese curse seems especially applicable: "May you live in interesting times." For the 1980s promise to be most interesting and most stressful times. As the United States moves headlong into the postindustrial society, individuals will be forced to rethink their attitudes toward work.

This chapter is about the great historical changes in the nature and meaning of work. It starts with preindustrial Europe and America and then moves to postindustrial society. It examines the differing occupational structures of contemporary U.S. cities, probing what the changing location of jobs implies for cities and city dwellers. Finally, it looks at those within SMSAs who are **unemployed** and **underemployed,** or who are **employed** full-time but can't make it economically: the metropolitan poor.

THE HUMAN DIMENSION: WORK AND THE INDIVIDUAL

Traveling back a few hundred years in time and space to seventeenth-century London, we find the following situation: bakers requesting an increase in the price of bread. The bakers supported their request with the following information about their work setting and weekly costs:

> Thirteen people there were in such an establishment: the baker and his wife, four paid employees who were called journeymen, two maidservants, two apprentices, and the baker's three children. Food cost more than anything else, more than raw materials and nearly four times as much as wages. Clothing was charged up, too, not only for man, wife, and children but for the apprentices as well. Even school fees were included in the cost of baking bread. (Laslett, 1971:1)

This image—a world without complex machines or complex organizations—provides a striking contrast to that of a modern factory or office building. In preindustrial England, workers produced their bread and clothing without electricity or layers of bosses. They worked by hand, creating a finished product with co-workers who were family members or with whom personal ties were established.

This small-scale, technologically simple world of work is a world we have lost. Before mourning its passing, however, recall its less romantic aspects. Work was hard and long. Children often started productive activity at age three or four, and women played a subordinate role. There was no workmen's compensation or unemployment insurance, and few occupational standards for health or safety. People died young.

First in England, then in continental Europe, the passing of the world of preindustrial work brought sweeping changes. Urbanization and industrialization changed where people lived, how they worked, how they related to each other, and how they related to the products of their labor.

Lowell, Massachusetts: Working Conditions of America's First Female Labor Force

Let's return to one of the grand designer's cities, Lowell, Massachusetts (discussed in Chapter 14), to examine some characteristics of early industrial society. Lowell illustrates what happened in the beginning phases of America's industrialization and urbanization processes: (1) the rural-to-urban shift, (2) the increasing scale and organization of work, and (3) the changing conditions and psychological meaning of work.

Lowell was one of America's first mill towns, named after the designer of a version of a power loom, Francis Cabot Lowell. Lowell devised a mill system so that raw fiber could be manufactured into cloth under a single roof. Incorporated in the 1820s, the town of Lowell drew unmarried young women, daughters of Yankee farmers, to its mill jobs. Contrary to popular belief, it was young women—not men—who first worked in manufacturing during the period of early industrialization; they pioneered in the textile mills. Why? As Howe (1978:9) comments, "men's work" was considered more valuable and irreplaceable in the fields.

Young women came from the countryside and moved into company-owned boarding houses within walking distance of the mills. These women workers were kept under strict supervision by housemothers in their living quarters and by mill managers in their workplaces. Church attendance was compulsory, and an early curfew was enforced. Hence, the mill women—America's first female industrial labor force—exchanged countryside for city, family for housemothers and mill managers, and family concern for tight social control.

The mill women also exchanged self-paced work for labor discipline and small-scale work for large-scale industrial organization. No longer did they do chores with their family unit. Now they labored side by side with hundreds of strangers from other rural communities, each one doing a small part of the whole production process.

Writings by the mill workers themselves reveal the conditions in the mills: poor lighting, little ventilation, noise, overcrowding, long hours (eighty hours per week), and low wages. One anonymous worker describes the rhythm of her workday: "Up before day, at the clang of the bell—and out of the mill by the clang of the bell—into the mill and at work, in obedience to that ding-dong of a bell—just as though we were so many living machines" (in Eisler, 1977:161).

Modern Times

For most Americans, factory conditions have changed a great deal since those early days in Lowell, Massachusetts. (Textile manufacturing, ironically, represents an important exception; see Conway, 1979). And fewer and fewer Americans work in factories while increased numbers work in offices, many of them factorylike in the sense that they are highly mechanized (see Mills, 1951: Chap. 9). Yet some significant similarities between the work, whether office or factory, still exist. Few people, then or now, produce things with their own tools; most workers do only a small part of the entire production process; and most work in hierarchically structured organizations.

There is, of course, great variety in the working conditions of Americans today. On the one hand, there is the skilled printer in a ten-person shop who sees a job through from start to finish and the researcher who sifts data alone in the library. On the other hand, there is the auto assembly-line worker who only attaches left rear bumpers, the bureaucrat who writes memos for someone else's signature, and the waitress who takes orders from everybody.

Are people content attaching left rear bumpers or taking orders? Is it inevitable that the industrial production process breaks up jobs into tiny pieces, with each person performing a highly specialized task? If so, does this industrial process itself lead to boredom and frustration? We now turn to such questions, noting how the structure and organization of work affect the individual's feeling about his or her work.

Alienation

As societies shift from economies based on agriculture and small-scale cottage industries to relatively simple industrial economies (symbolized by Lowell, Massachusetts) or to more complex industrial organization, many changes take place in the nature of work.

Usually, the location, scale, type, and nature of work are transformed.

First, the location of work (and residence) changes. In preindustrial economies, much work must take place on or near agricultural land. Without machine-powered transport and other advanced technology, people extract a living from their natural environment and live near it. Productive activities do not cluster in cities; they are decentralized in villages and small towns. Indeed, big cities were the exception in preindustrial Europe and America. In contrast, work activities within industrial societies arise in and cluster in urban areas. Raw materials, labor to transform them into a finished product, and transport to move them become concentrated in cities. Some scholars predict that much work will again become decentralized in the postindustrial society; they argue that fast transport and new communications technologies will permit many people to work and live in small towns and rural places.

Second, the type of work changes. In preindustrial societies, the majority of people are engaged in **primary sector** activities—farming, mining, fishing, and other extractive activities. In industrial economies, **secondary sector** activities—transforming raw materials into manufactured products—dominate. In postindustrial economies, **tertiary sector** activities—services and information—dominate. That the United States is well into postindustrialism is indicated by a few statistics. In 1979, American Telephone & Telegraph (AT&T), an information-based company, became the first U.S. company in the nation's history to have assets over $100 billion. It also employed almost a million people, more than the nation's largest industrial firm, General Motors.

Third, the scale of work changes. The family farm or the thirteen-person bakery is no longer the typical production unit. Larger units of production are organized in industrial economies to take advantage of economies of scale. Even the textile mills of Lowell are small by the standards of today's auto assembly plant.

Finally, the nature of work changes. In predindustrial societies, people do not have much mastery over nature, but they do exercise some control over their work process. In handicraft and cottage industry, for instance, artisans own the tools of their trade, have traditions of craftsmanship, work at their own pace, and introduce some variation into their products. Compare that situation with modern industry, exemplified by the assembly line. The left rear bumper attacher has no discretion over how or where to place the bumper on the car; the pace of work and the product are standardized; and "the care of tools and machinery is divorced from the pride of ownership" (Bendix, 1963:204). In modern industry, the worker has little control over the work process at any level—from macro decisions about what product will be made or how much it will cost down to decisions concerning the pace of work, the arrangement of work space, or what tools are used. These conditions of industrial labor produce standardized products efficiently. And according to many observers, they also produce alienated human beings—powerless people who feel estranged from their work and themselves.

Karl Marx was the first theorist to focus on alienating work. In the *Economic and Philosophic Manuscripts of 1844* (in Tucker, 1972), Marx began to investigate the concept of **alienation**, and his ideas have exerted a powerful influence ever since on Marxists and non-Marxists alike. In fact, "alienation" has entered the social scientist's general vocabulary, regardless of discipline or ideological bent. However, not all theorists agree with Marx on its definition or causes.

Marx wonders: where does the product of the workingman's labour end up?

BY HIS LABOUR, A WORKER MAKES SOMETHING (CLOTH, MACHINERY, TYRES, BOOKS, HOUSES...). BUT THIS OBJECT, BY THE FACT OF REMAINING THE BOSS'S PROPERTY, TURNS HEY PRESTO! INTO MERCHANDISE (A COMMODITY)...

LABOUR OBVIOUSLY DOESN'T PRODUCE THINGS FOR THE IMMEDIATE BENEFIT OF THE WORKER WHO MAKES THEM. RATHER, IT IS GRIST FOR SOMEONE ELSE'S MILL...

Alienation begins with the worker being squeezed dry...

"...THE ALIENATION OF THE WORKER IS EXPRESSED THUS: THE MORE HE PRODUCES, THE LESS HE CAN CONSUME; THE MORE VALUE HE CREATES, THE LESS VALUE HE HAS... LABOUR PRODUCES FABULOUS THINGS FOR THE RICH, BUT MISERY FOR THE POOR. MACHINES REPLACE LABOUR, AND JOBS DIMINISH, WHILE OTHER WORKERS TURN INTO MACHINES..."

(Marx: "Manuscripts of 1844")

(This is how alienation makes its victims...)

ALIENATION NOT ONLY DEGRADES MAN, BUT ALSO DE-PERSONALISES HIM. WHAT CAN YOU EXPECT?

MARX STATES: THE BOSS IMPOSES THE KIND OF WORK, THE METHOD AND THE RHYTHM, BUT HE NEVER BOTHERS IF THE WORKER ENDS UP AS:

A mere appendage of flesh on a machine of iron...

(Marx)

Fig. 16-1 ALIENATION A LA MARX. (Rius, *Marx for Beginners* [New York: Pantheon, 1978], p. 79. English translation © 1976 by Richard Appignanesi. Originally published in English in Great Britain by Writers and Readers Publishing Cooperative. Reprinted by permission of Pantheon Books, a Division of Random House, Inc.)

According to Marx, alienation is not part and parcel of industrial production per se. It is inevitable only under a certain kind of social organization of industrial work—capitalist production. Here is how he came to this conclusion.

To Marx, human history proceeds in developmental stages: from primitive communities to slave states to feudalism and then to capitalist systems. Under European feudalism (the productive system preceding capitalism), serfs' labor was not seen as a commodity to be bought and sold in the marketplace; a paternalistic relationship operated between manor lord and serfs, with obligations recognized on both sides. Goods and services in the feudal system were produced mainly for personal use and local markets. Then, during the sixteenth century, a new mode of production began to undermine serfdom and the rural manor system of European feudalism: commercial capitalism. As the new class of merchant capitalists grew, so did trade, market exchanges, and towns. Over the course of several hundred years, commercial (or mercantile) capitalism developed into industrial capitalism. By the mid-nineteenth century, the transformation to industrial capitalism was complete.

In Marx's view, it was this mode of production, capitalism, that inevitably led to the worker's alienation. For the first time in human history, people became *wage labor,* selling their labor on the open market just like any other commodity. According to Marx,this transformed people into commodities, dehumanizing and depersonalizing them.

To illustrate how Marx viewed the process of alienation, let's return to the example of Lowell, Massachusetts. Marx would have viewed it something like this: Mr. Lowell buys the labor of young women, puts it to work, and treats it like any other tool of production (e.g., a machine). This labor force—or human labor-power—then becomes the source of value to Mr. Lowell, just like any other machine. How? By producing surplus value. Workers in Lowell's mill put in a thirteen-hour day. But they produce enough to pay for their own food, shelter, and other needs in only four or five hours; this is "necessary" work time. During the remaining working hours, the worker produces a "surplus product," over and above what she or he requires to meet personal needs. This surplus product is pure profit for the employer.

To Marx, private ownership of the means of production is the highest form of alienation. Marx reasoned as follows. Private ownership of the factories and other means of production results in the labor of the many being transformed into the capital of the few. It means that the very essence of human beings (*homo faber:* people as producers)—the creative act of work—is transformed into a *possession* of someone else, the capitalist employer. In this way, what formerly belonged to human beings (the products of their labor) is taken away and "alienated" from them, the rightful owners. This leaves workers dispossessed. They own nothing—neither the tools of their trade nor the finished product. In the end, people become alienated not only from their own products but from themselves. It is this process of capitalist industrial production that degrades and depersonalizes humans. Only capitalism's replacement by a new mode of production, socialism, can establish an unalienated relationship between worker and work.

Non-Marxists, Marxists, and ex-Marxists have quarreled with Marx's interpretation of the causes of alienation as well as its potential cure. Most notably, sociologist Max Weber in the early twentieth century and various contemporary theorists (e.g., Lévy, 1979) argue that the mode of production in modern society has little impact on alienation. In this view, bureaucracy, the state, and large-scale industrial organization are inherently alienating, whether capitalist or socialist. Hence, it is argued that Soviet, Cuban, or Chinese workers assembling autos or pushing pens in factorylike offices will become just as alienated from work and themselves as their counterparts in Detroit or Washington. Given this premise—that bureaucracy and hierarchy are the real culprits, no matter who owns the means of production—the cures offered to end alienation range from ending hierarchy (Thayer, 1973) to living in voluntary simplicity within smaller, more self-sufficient communities (Satin, 1978).

Much social research shows that inherently alienating tendencies do exist in the techniques of modern manufacturing and bureaucratic organization. For instance, a sociological study of textile work, auto assembly, print shops, and chemical plants by Robert Blauner (1964) contends that alienation is built into industrial work. Yet, Blauner argues, the organization of work can mitigate some of technology's effects. Technological imperatives of the auto industry may dictate a certain kind of work—fast and fragmented—but the reorganization of work (for example, job rotation) may minimize some alienating features.

At the same time, a series of recent studies claim that modern work is *not* the outcome of autonomous technical processes. Richard C. Edwards argues in *Contested Terrain* (1979) that the first large business corporations depended on hierarchical control over workers; this system of delegated authority made foremen into petty tyrants over workers, often beyond the control of their bosses. To curb the foremen's power, employers turned to another form of control: technical control, embedded in the design of production itself. Instead of obeying foremen, workers obeyed the dictates of the assembly-line process itself. In other words, the specific design of machines prestructured the work. Foremen thus became mere enforcers of prestructured work (see also Noble, 1977). Edwards thinks that most industrial workers still work under this system but that modern companies, like IBM and Polaroid, use a more subtle system of control, "bureaucratic control." Here, domination is also hidden—but it is not in the machines: "Supervisors and workers alike become subject to the dictates of 'company policy.' Work becomes highly stratified; each job is given its distinct title and description; and impersonal rules govern promotion." Other writers (e.g., Braverman, 1974) argue that work in the twentieth century has been systematically degraded not only on the assembly line but in clerical work, retail jobs, and the service trades.

Some countries, notably Yugoslavia, are experimenting with worker self-management schemes. Others have experienced the takeover of factories by their own workers, as in the Lipp watch factory in France. In the United States and Europe, "job enrichment" experiments are in process. Whether such enrichment programs actually humanize work is much debated. A former plumber, machinist, and city commissioner argues that the workplace can't be humanized until American attitudes toward authority and hierarchy *outside* of work change radically (Shrank, 1978).

The Anomic Division of Labor

Sociologist Emile Durkheim ([1893] 1966) theorized that, under normal conditions in organically solid society, the complex division of labor would bring people together in a way that made them feel interdependent (see Chapter 5). However, Durkheim warned that under abnormal conditions an **anomic divi-**

sion of labor could occur, disrupting social solidarity. If extreme specialization of function goes hand-in-hand with a decrease in communication between people doing different specialized tasks, then an anomic division of labor would result. In this situation, individuals become isolated from each other, separated by lack of understanding. In turn, this lack of communication leads to a lack of rules that define and regulate relationships among individuals, each performing a specialized job.

Durkheim's example of the anomic division of labor was the conflict between management and labor during the early stages of industrialization. At that time there were few agreed-upon rules governing their relationship. We might extend Durkheim's concept and apply it to other aspects of contemporary work. For instance, many workers now feel that their work is not only boring but meaningless. They don't see how their highly specialized task matters to the rest of society. Like characters in Charlie Chaplin's film *Modern Times* (1936), they feel like so many cogs in a machine. In addition, communities with common values and common goals are based increasingly on occupation. Such occupationally based communities—academics, doctors, race car drivers, etc.—often discourage communication with outsiders by speaking and writing in esoteric jargon and monopolizing their expertise instead of sharing it widely. In this way, gaps between expert groups and lay publics grow wider. This trend does not bode well for a democratic society. Nor does it encourage a sense of mutual interdependence.

To conclude: Industrial work, for disputed reasons, can lead to alienation from self, others, and the products of one's labor. Under certain conditions, industrial organization can also lead to an anomic division of labor in which people lack a feeling of mutual interdependence and feel their work lacks social meaning.

Worker Satisfaction

Today's bored bookkeeping assistant, surrounded by pocket calculators and other mechanical tools, is not in the same position as characters in a Charles Dickens novel who toiled from dawn to dusk for starvation wages. Nor are auto workers of the 1980s like the Lowell mill women of the 1840s, closely supervised both at work and at home. Still, worker dissatisfaction remains a serious and widespread phenomenon.

Indeed, the *majority* of American workers are not satisfied with their work. That is the finding of a study by the Special Task Force to the Secretary of Health, Education, and Welfare (HEW). Taking a long look at *Work in America* (1973), the Task Force found that, out of a cross section of American workers, only 43 percent of **white-collar** workers and only 23 percent of **blue-collar** workers would choose to do similar work again (1973:16). The study's authors report that whether a worker would again choose the same work is the best single indicator of job satisfaction.

The range of satisfaction and dissatisfaction with work in America is broad. In general, white-collar workers in the professional and technical category (as defined by the U.S. Census Bureau: see Table 16-1) report higher levels of job satisfaction than other groups. Interestingly, urban university professors are the single most satisfied occupational group surveyed by HEW; 93 percent say that they would do the same work again (1973:16). By contrast, auto assembly workers are the least satisfied. The HEW study reports that only 16 percent would redo the same work, and another study (Garson, 1973:173) reports that no auto workers—0 percent—would choose the same work again.

Table 16-1 U.S. Census Bureau Occupational Categories

White Collar
1. Professional, technical and kindred workers (e.g., engineers, doctors, teachers, radio operators)
2. Managers and administrators (except farm) (e.g., salaried managers in retail trade, self-employed managers in manufacturing)
3. Sales workers (e.g., auctioneers, insurance agents, retail sales clerks)
4. Clerical and kindred workers (e.g., bookkeepers, secretaries, typists)

Blue Collar
5. Craftsmen, foremen and kindred workers (e.g., automobile mechanics, carpenters, plumbers, pipe fitters)
6. Operatives, except transport (e.g., gas station attendants, sailors, assembly-line workers, textile dyers)
7. Transport equipment operators (e.g., bus drivers, truck drivers, parking attendants)
8. Laborers (except farm) (e.g., fishermen, garbage collectors, gardeners)

Farm Workers
9. Farm and farm managers (e.g., farmers and farm managers)
10. Farm laborers and farm foremen (e.g., farm laborers, unpaid family farm workers)

Service Workers
11. Service workers (e.g., police, flight attendants, barbers)
12. Private household workers (e.g., maids, cooks, private household housekeepers)

SOURCE: U.S. Bureau of the Census, *General Social and Economic Characteristics, United States Summary, 1970 Census of Population* (Washington, D.C.: U.S. Government Printing Office, 1972), Appendix B, pp. 19–22.

NOTE: The U.S. Census Bureau does not recognize the category "pink-collar," but it is often used popularly to refer to jobs performed mainly by women, such as typing, waiting tables, and housecleaning.

Another government-financed study (Quinn, 1978) indicates that in 1977 people under thirty years of age, black workers, blue-collar workers, semiskilled, and manufacturing industry employees liked their jobs the least. In addition, this survey shows that there was a decline in job satisfaction from the time of the HEW study in 1973, a decline that involved almost every occupational and social group.

While job satisfaction appears to be declining across the board, significant differences among professionals and blue-collar workers still remain. In general, people who do mental labor are more satisfied than those who do manual labor. Further, job satisfaction is linked to social status; the higher the status of an occupation, the more satisfied are its practitioners. Also, high pay and high job satisfaction tend to go together. However, this relationship is rather unclear because most highly paid jobs also rank high in other characteristics valued by workers (e.g., social esteem, job autonomy, challenge of the work itself, participation in decision making).

Why, then, is it that some relatively low-paid and low-prestige work does not produce job dissatisfaction? We hope to illuminate this complex issue by examining two groups of very satisfied workers, one midway on the prestige ladder (daily journalists) and one near the bottom (garbage collectors).

"I'm a rear-bumper securer. I do forty-five bumpers an hour and have had the same job for eleven years. This is a very impersonal place to work. If you had a heart attack they'd replace you in two minutes. Never fall down in front of the line, they'd run it over you. I make $300 a week but it takes a certain type of person to do this job."

"I've always been sales-oriented. If I can sell myself, I can sell the product. I take pride in my customers and have sold nine cars to one family. Everyone you meet is different."

"My father came from Japan in the 1920s because America was the land of opportunity. During World War II we were interned in Utah and had to sacrifice the farm. It has taken thirty years to build up this vegetable farm to seventy acres with eleven men helping me. My son doesn't want to farm—it's hard work with little money. He works in the Blue Chip redemption center."

'I'm a refugee from China. I sew pockets on pants. Every day I have work, and living here is easy. In China it's hard to find a job. Someone has to recommend you. I don't speak English and I'm too old to learn so I'll never get a better job."

Fig. 16-2 WORKING. (Bill Owens)

Brief Case Studies: Daily Journalists and Garbage Collectors

Daily Journalists. With the exception of TV personalities like Walter Cronkite, daily news reporters and editors have a moderate amount of social esteem. Yet unlike most American workers today, journalists working on local daily newspapers or TV and radio newscasts enjoy their work. Indeed, one survey of journalists working in nonelite news organizations (that is, organizations unlike the *New York Times* or national TV networks) reveals that less than 1 percent would not choose to do similar work again (Phillips, 1975). At the same time, most of these same journalists feel underpaid, and a considerable number dislike the bureaucratic organizations they work for. Then why are they so happy in their work?

The answers seem to be related to the nature of the work itself. One reason is that daily reporters and editors view their work as nonroutine. Another is that they feel mentally challenged by it, having a chance to be creative and constantly learning. In addition, they perceive themselves as having a great deal of autonomy on the job. To a participant-observer this may not seem the case at all, for journalists work within hierarchically structured organizations that, to an outsider, often suppress initiative. But the news workers themselves do not feel that they work under crushing constraints of bureaucratic, institutional, and stylistic pressures. They don't feel hemmed in—no time clocks to punch, no specific amount of work to do, and no absolute standards of performance. Instead, they tend to judge themselves by professional standards of inner quality controls. Finally, the craft of journalism promotes a sense of participation in events. Journalists feel that the stories they write, film, edit, or broadcast have some public impact. Thus, it seems that craft-related factors (nonroutine work, political efficacy, participation in events, etc.) account for daily journalists' high level of job satisfaction.

What's fascinating is that the journalists' relative lack of alienation from work is not dependent on their social background. Whether young or old, black or white, conservative or liberal, married or single, female or male, professionally trained or not, they like their work (despite their cynical, hard-boiled image). Their positive attitude toward work and the society in which they work seems to grow out of the journalistic craft itself (Phillips, 1975).

Garbage Collectors. Journalists practice "clean" work (that is, mental rather than manual labor), which they generally find intellectually stimulating. But what about those who do society's "dirty" work? One highly paid steel worker in Illinois says that "It's hard to take pride in a bridge you're never gonna cross, in a door you're never gonna open." For him, the problem isn't the fact that his work is dirty but rather that he feels no sense of contributing to society, no sense of achievement: "I worked for a trucker one time. And I got this tiny satisfaction when I loaded a truck. At least I could see the truck depart loaded. In a steel mill, forget it" (in Terkel, 1975:2).

The steel worker's comment suggests that the social meaning of work—not necessarily the work itself—is important for individuals. Empirical support for this assertion comes from a study of society's dirtiest work: garbage collection.

For more than ten years, sociologist Stewart E. Perry followed the history of an Italian-American cooperative of garbage collectors. By working their routes with them, talking, and visiting, Perry sought to answer some fundamental questions about the nature of work and worker satisfaction.

What Perry (1978) found was a foul-smelling, back-breaking occupation, but one which did not necessarily alienate its practitioners. The men he studied, members of the Sunset Scavenger Company in San Francisco, were not dissatisfied with their work. Perry attributes the garbage collectors' positive attitude toward their dirty work to the collective ownership and policymaking of the company. A private corporation, Sunset is owned by the workers themselves. They collect dividends and actively participate in setting company policy. Of the 315 active partners at the time of Perry's study, all but 18 were still working the trucks, and the company president received the same wage as the men on the trucks.

According to Perry, it is pride of ownership that accounts primarily for the garbage collectors' lack of alienation from work. As one scavenger told him, "a man walks through this yard here [at the Sunset Scavenger Company] and says, 'I own a piece of this; this is mine.' "

To conclude: These brief case studies raise theoretical issues important for the quality of urban life and the redesign of urban work. The case of the Sunset Scavengers suggests that no work—even society's dirtiest work—is inherently alienating; it implies that lack of control over work and lack of ownership are the roots of alienation. But the case of the journalists suggests a very different notion: that some work is intrinsically challenging and satisfying. Even if journalists work in hierarchically structured organizations, have little objective control over work, and share no monetary profits with the owners, they don't feel a sense of meaninglessness or powerlessness. These issues are controversial and unsettled. Few answers to the issue of job alienation are evident, although the number of thinkers about work (and the leisure time to think about it) has never been greater. Radical intellectuals, particularly Marxists, are going through a profound crisis of thought that turns primarily on the question of whether or not bureaucracy is inherently alienating. Ultraconservatives (e.g., de Lesquen, 1979) are returning to ideas best suited to a preindustrial, aristocratic society (see Kandell, 1979). Conservatives tend to believe that most people need close supervision and hierarchical control; this is what organization theorist Douglas McGregor (in Bennis, 1970) calls the Theory X of human behavior. In contrast, liberals tend to subscribe to what McGregor calls the Theory Y of human behavior: that work is natural, and that most people will work hard if they have a chance to fulfill their human potential.

What of the Future?

As intellectuals debate the causes and cures of alienation in learned journals, the United States is shifting rapidly from an industrial to a postindustrial economy. This means that fewer and fewer people will be engaged in manufacturing and other secondary sector activities. Thus, traditionally alienating work such as auto assembly may simply fade away for the majority, eliminated by technological change. This also means that more and more people will be **service workers** and white-collar workers, working in the tertiary or service-information sector, producing paper, ideas, and services instead of manufactured goods.

Does it follow that most work will become more satisfying in the postindustrial economy? Probably not, as Max Weber might have predicted. In Weber's perspective, Marx was right about the wage worker being separated from the products of his or her labor, but Marx did not go far enough. Weber thought that wage workers represented only one case of a universal trend toward bureaucratization. In other words, it is argued that when white-collar workers function in a bureaucratic system, they encounter a machine "as soulless as . . . machines made of iron and steel" (Simone Weil in HEW Report, 1973:39).

Already many white-collar workers in lower-echelon jobs complain of white-collar woes: boring, dull, routine jobs. Those with a college education and high expectations for self-fulfillment through work are particularly prone to high turnover and subtle forms of sabotage.

As we move into the future, there is also the problem of the anomic division of labor. A former bank clerk turned firefighter put it like this:

> . . . the firemen, you actually see them produce. You see them put out a fire. You see them come out with babies in their hands. You see them give mouth-to-mouth when a guy's dying. . . . That's real. To me that's what I want to be. I worked in a bank. You know, it's just paper. It's not real. You're lookin' at numbers. But I can look back and say, "I helped put out a fire. I helped save somebody." It shows something I did on this earth. (in Terkel, 1975:xxx)

URBAN OCCUPATIONAL STRUCTURES

Let's shift now from the impact of work on the individual to its impact on an entire community. We begin by looking at occupational patterns in different U.S. cities. Then we take a closer look at the particular kinds of manufactured goods and services produced in cities, noting what these patterns imply for both the present and the future.

City Occupational Profiles and Industrial Employment

A city's occupational profile—that is, a snapshot of its employment mix—gives clues to its social character, its economic vitality, even its recreational facilities. This kind of information is useful to scholars, policymakers, and potential investors. It can also be helpful in our everyday lives. For instance, suppose you find yourself in the enviable position of being able to choose from among five equally attractive job offers in as many cities: Syracuse, New York; Flint, Michigan; Menlo Park, California; Las Vegas, Nevada; and Gastonia, North Carolina. How will you choose? For the sake of argument, let's say that you don't care about the city's physical climate; but you do care about its cultural-aesthetic facilities. The cultural climate you prefer, of course, depends on your personal tastes and background. But whatever urban scenes you favor (hanging out on street-corners; fern bars and avant-garde movie houses; encounter groups and dream workshops; union meetings, etc.), you can get some idea if they exist by examining a city's occupational profile. (You won't be able to get a total picture without sorting through additional data on the particular kinds of goods and services produced in your potential hometown, but we'll return to that later.)

The five profiles in Fig. 16-3 show that the composition of the labor force varies from city to city. While there is no typical pattern, the occupational profile for Syracuse offers a benchmark for the mix of urban employment. This is because the proportion of Syracuse workers in the various U.S. Census categories is about the same as the national averages for each category. This chance occurrence makes Syracuse a national testing ground for market researchers trying out consumer response to new products, for it is thought to be a typical city. In Syracuse, clerical workers outnumbered all other categories in 1970. Reflecting national trends, Syracuse's rather diversified labor force is predominantly white-collar (professional, technical, managerial, sales, and clerical).

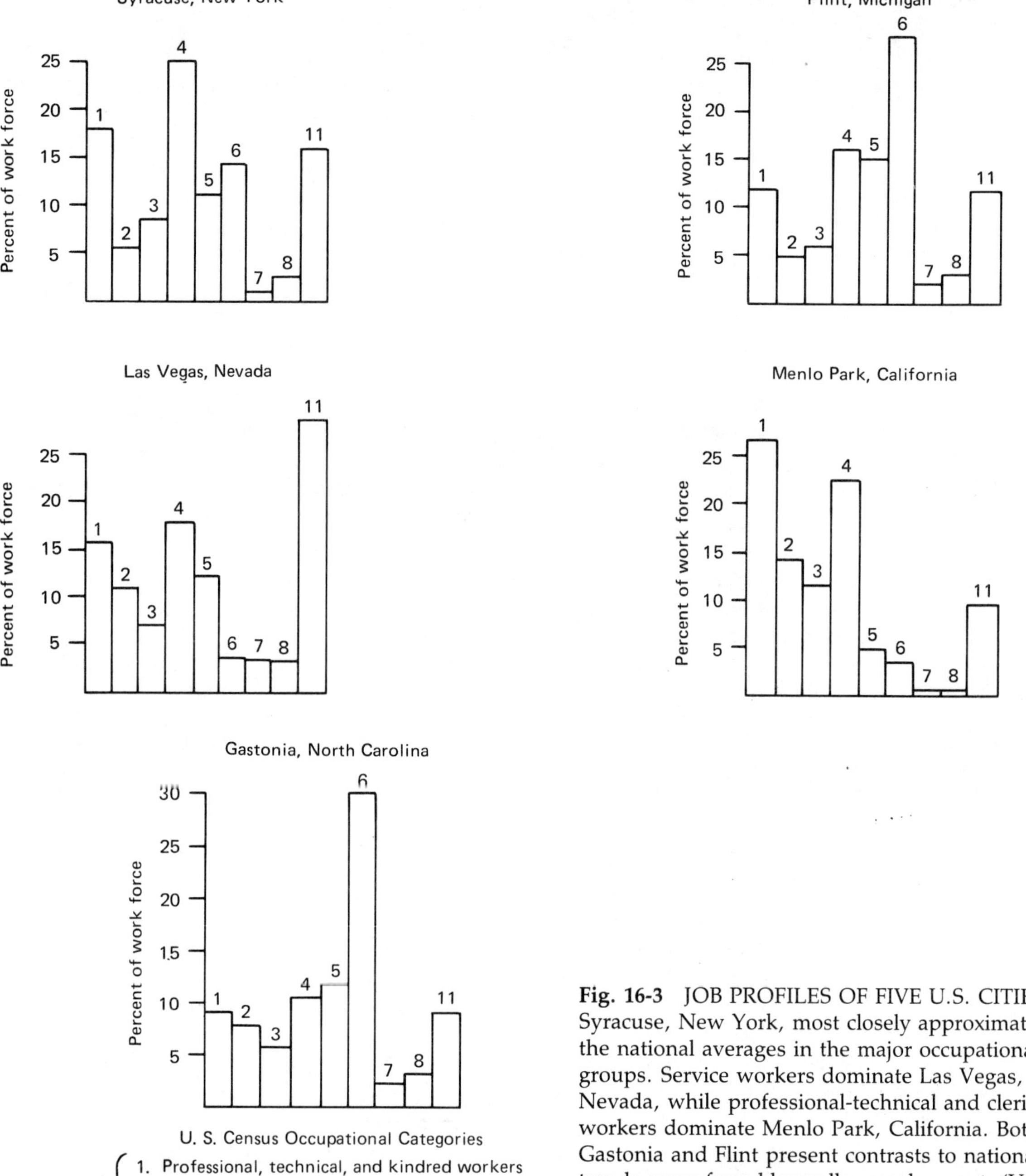

U. S. Census Occupational Categories

White Collar
1. Professional, technical, and kindred workers
2. Managers and administrators
3. Sales workers
4. Clerical and kindred workers

Blue Collar
5. Craftsmen, foremen, and kindred workers
6. Operatives, except transport
7. Transport equipment operators
8. Laborers (except farm)

Service
11. Service workers

Fig. 16-3 JOB PROFILES OF FIVE U.S. CITIES. Syracuse, New York, most closely approximates the national averages in the major occupational groups. Service workers dominate Las Vegas, Nevada, while professional-technical and clerical workers dominate Menlo Park, California. Both Gastonia and Flint present contrasts to national trends away from blue-collar employment. (U.S. Bureau of the Census, *Census of Population: 1970,* Vol. I [Washington, D.C.: U.S. Government Printing Office, 1973], Part 34, Section 1, Table 86 [Syracuse]; Part 30, Table 86 [Las Vegas]; Part 24, Table 86 [Flint]; Part 6; Table 105 [Menlo Park]; Part 35, Table 105 [Gastonia])

Less than one-third of the work force is engaged in blue-collar work, and of this, less than 15 percent work as operatives.

The four other cities show significant variations on the national theme, even some counterthemes. In Las Vegas, home of tall signs advertising tourist attractions, service workers dominate the city, serving customers in gambling casinos, drive-in wedding chapels, and other visitors' meccas. There is little manufacturing in this specialized function city. Hence, operatives account for less than 5 percent of the work force.

Menlo Park, located in California's Silicon Valley, specializes in high-technology activities such as computer systems engineering. Consequently, it is dominated by professional and clerical workers; it has relatively few operatives or service workers.

Gastonia and Flint are specialized function cities too. But they reflect earlier employment patterns: the dominance of heavy manufacturing. Historically, Flint has been a one-industry town (cars) and a one-company town (General Motors). In Gastonia, the majority of the labor force work in the textile mills.

The particular industry that dominates the local scene—for example, textiles or autos—is a key factor in that urban area's social climate. But no table of census data can reveal the relationship between what a city produces and how that city looks and feels. Only a thorough grounding in economic and cultural history can provide such insight (for instance, the textile industry's resistance to unionization and the automotive industry's widespread unionization).

To find the particular industrial mix of employment in a selected city or SMSA, researchers use the U.S. Census Bureau's *Census of Manufactures* series, published every five years. By sifting through these data, it is possible to establish the following information: The average wage of Gastonia's textile production workers in 1972 was $5,822. By contrast, the average wage of a production worker in the Flint SMSA's auto industry in 1972 was $9,090 (U.S. Bureau of the Census, 1976: Vol. III, Part 2, Table 8; Part I, Table 6).

Now, working from the occupational profiles and the data on industrial employment in the five cities, we can make several assumptions. Here are a few that might affect your choice of future hometown.

1. Flint will have a higher percentage of union members than the other cities. *Rationale:* In general, operatives are more likely to be unionized than either professionals or service workers. Gastonia, the other heavy manufacturing town, is textile-based, and cultural knowledge should suggest that this industry is not heavily unionized (see Box 16-1).
2. Menlo Park is likely to have more tennis courts per capita than Flint or Gastonia. *Rationale:* Tennis is more often played by upper-status and upper-income persons than blue-collar workers. Menlo Park has a higher proportion of its labor force in professional and white-collar jobs than the other two cities.
3. Aesthetically, Flint will appear less attractive to most Americans than Syracuse or Menlo Park. *Rationale:* One-industry, heavy-manufacturing centers tend to be built and maintained for industrial efficiency, not beauty. As one observer said about Flint, "Flint is a city of speed, a city of efficiency, but it is not a city of beauty" (Porter, [1937] 1969:34).

Now, think back to your five job offers. Which community do you think you'd prefer to live in? Before making a final choice, consider some other implications. The com-

Fig. 16-4 GASTONIA, A TWENTIETH-CENTURY MILL TOWN. (Ti-Caro Textile Mills)

Box 16-1

CITY PROFILES: ANOTHER VIEW

Hard Times in a Mill Town

The first textile mill in America was established in 1791 in Pawtucket, Rhode Island—and "ever since—with only rare and periodic exceptions—it's been hard times in the mill for the men and women (and children)—the carders, spinners, weavers, dyers, and finishers—in the textile industry. The huge sprawling textile industry has a long, unhappy history of low wages, long hours, child labor, stretch-out and speed-up, company-dominated mill towns, chronic unemployment and instability" (Fowke and Glazer, 1960:69).

In the late 1800s, New England cotton mills started moving south to take advantage of cheaper labor. People from the back woods flocked into the mill towns in North Carolina and other Southern states, attracted by the promise of a few dollars in their pocket every week. But soon the glamor wore thin, and local folk began singing the blues:

> When I die don't bury me at all
> Just hang me up on the spool room wall,
> Place a knotter in my hand,
> So I can spool my way to the Promised Land
> I got the blues,
> I got them Winnsboro cotton-mill blues . . . .

Wages stayed low, but prices of shoes and food went up. When workers followed organizers and joined unions, they were blacklisted.

In Gastonia, during a violent textile strike in 1929, Chief of Police O. F. Aderholt was killed in an attack on union headquarters. At least a dozen songs came out of this struggle, including one by a woman named Ella May Wiggins, written several days before she was shot and killed. Her song, "Chief Aderholt," contains the following refrain: "We're gonna have a union/All over the South/Where we can wear good clothes/And live in a better house./Now we must stand together/And to the boss reply,/'We'll never—no, we'll never/Let our leaders die.' "

After World War II, more mills moved South. As a former *New York Times* White House correspondent explains it, "Yankee industrialists trooped happily down from the upcountry with their little factories and mills to find a promised land flowing with the milk and honey of tax breaks, free land, cut-rate utilities, and most importantly, a cheap, docile, undemanding and unorganized labor pool" (Wooten, 1979:10).

The film *Norma Rae* (1978) tells the story of the struggle to unionize a Southern textile town. It shows why workers may still sing one of many song written to protest mill conditions, "Cotton Mill Colic":

> Every morning just at five
> You gotta get up, dead or alive,
> Every night when I go home,
> A piece of cornbread and an old jawbone.
> Ain't it enough to break your heart,
> Have to work all day and at night it's dark,
> It's hard times in the mill, my love,
> Hard times in the mill.

As *Norma Rae* shows, hard times in the mill are not gone and long forgotten. Textile manufacturing, now the South's dominant industry (accounting for about one-fifth of all jobs and $18 billion in annual sales), is the only major U.S. industry that is not significantly unionized. The story of the contemporary fight to unionize the J. P. Stevens textile plant in Roanoke Rapids, North Carolina, is told in *Rise Gonna Rise: A Portrait of Southern Textile Workers* (Conway, 1979).

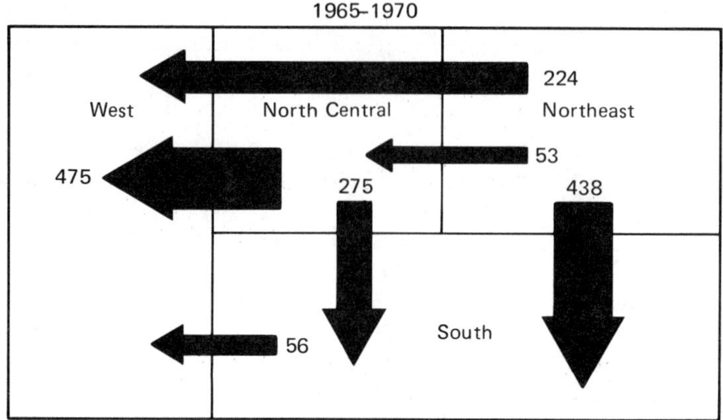

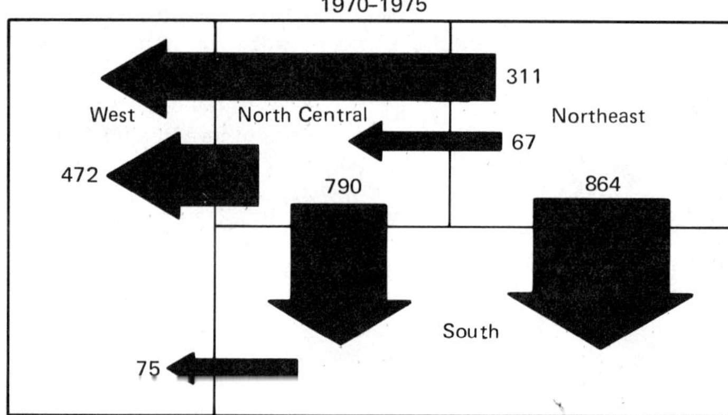

Fig. 16-5 NET INTERREGIONAL MIGRATION, 1965–1970 and 1970–1975. (President's Urban and Regional Policy Group, *A New Partnership to Conserve America's Communities: A National Urban Policy* [Washington, D.C.: U.S. Government Printing Office, 1978], p. I-5)

position of a city's labor force has some bearing on its governmental structure. As detailed in Chapter 10, city council-city manager government has not been widely adopted in blue-collar communities; it appeals more to white-collar towns. Also, the mix of industrial employment has some bearing on informal power structures. We can expect, for instance, different patterns of influence in textile-based Gastonia and high-technology, professional Menlo Park.

And what of the future? Both the occupational and industrial mix of a city have important, sometimes grave, implications for an urban area's future. A city specialized in tourist services is vulnerable to economic recession. Las Vegas, geographically isolated, is especially threatened by energy shortages and rising jet-fuel prices. Syracuse, with its more diversified economy, may suffer relatively less during periods of no growth or recession. In addition, if a city's labor force is heavily concentrated in no-growth or negative growth industries, like Gastonia and Flint, the prospects for taking advantage of national trends toward white-collar work are dim. Heavy manufacturing towns face economic disaster if and when technological change or cheaper sources of labor overseas render their workers obsolete.

Table 16-2 Civilian Employment Changes by Zone in the 15 Largest Metropolitan Areas, 1960-1970

Metropolitan Area	*Total Employment Change*		*Central-City Employment Change*		*Suburban Employment Change*	
	Number	*Percentage*	*Number*	*Percentage*	*Number*	*Percentage*
1. New York	14,000	0.3	−339,000	−9.7	353,000	24.9
2. Los Angeles–Long Beach	51,000	2.1	−137,000	−10.8	188,000	16.2
3. Chicago–Gary	277,000	11.3	−232,000	−13.9	509,000	64.4
4. Philadelphia	216,000	15.6	−98,000	−11.3	314,000	61.5
5. Detroit	170,000	13.9	−156,000	−22.5	326,000	61.5
6. San Francisco–Oakland	105,000	10.4	2,000	0.4	103,000	22.7
7. Washington, D.C.	332,000	43.9	9,000	1.9	323,000	117.9
8. Boston	68,000	7.4	−35,000	−8.6	103,000	20.2
9. Pittsburgh	24,000	3.2	12,000	4.4	12,000	2.5
10. Saint Louis	148,000	22.4	−61,000	−15.2	209,000	80.4
11. Baltimore	132,000	22.3	−22,000	−5.6	154,000	76.6
12. Cleveland	80,000	12.4	−71,000	−15.3	151,000	82.5
13. Houston	287,000	67.2	177,000	49.2	110,000	164.2
14. Minneapolis–Saint Paul	160,000	30.0	1,000	0.3	159,000	126.2
15. Dallas	186,000	46.4	114,000	37.6	72,000	73.5
Total	2,250,000	11.8	−836,000	−6.9	3,086,000	43.6

SOURCE: *New York Times* analysis of U.S. Census Bureau data, October 15, 1972, pp. 1,58. Anthony Downs, *Opening Up the Suburbs* (New Haven: Yale University Press, 1973), pp.21–22. Copyright © 1973 by Yale University. Reprinted by permission of Yale University Press and the author.

CHANGING U.S. EMPLOYMENT PATTERNS

As the United States moves into a service-consumer society of bureaucrats, gadget sellers, service providers, and information disseminators, what changes will occur in the quality of life, community morale, industrial location, and so many other aspects of urban life and culture? No one can predict with precision. But we can examine three trends in employment that merit special attention: (1) regional shifts, (2) intrametropolitan shifts, and (3) sectoral shifts.

Regional Shifts: From Frostbelt to Sunbelt

In general, employment opportunities and people are shifting away from the Northeast quadrant of the country, the Frostbelt, to that broad band of Southern states called the Sunbelt. A combination of factors, from a warmer climate to government policy and technological change, have encouraged this regional shift (see Chapter 6 for more detail).

This regional shift has led to conditions of extreme distress in some older Frostbelt cities. At the same time, it has created boomtown conditions in many Sunbelt communities.

Intrametropolitan Shifts: From Central City to Outside Central City

Within SMSAs, manufacturing and retail firms are leaving their central city locations and moving to suburbs or other areas on the urban fringe. Table 16-2 reveals the impact of this change in terms of employment. Between 1960 and 1970, the suburbs of the nation's largest SMSAs gained jobs. With certain exceptions, their central cities lost jobs. In some cases, the job shifts were extreme. For instance, Detroit lost almost one-quarter of its jobs, while Detroit's suburbs increased their employment 61.5 percent.

Sectoral Shifts: From Primary and Secondary to Tertiary

In the 1950s, for the first time in human history, more people in a single nation were thinking about things, managing things, and communicating about things than actually producing things. This momentous shift, made possible by advanced technology, signaled the beginning of postindustrial society. By 1970, about one-half of all job holders in the United States were working in the service-information sector.

In recent decades, white-collar and service work has expanded at an extraordinary rate. Professional and technical workers, for instance, increased at about twice the rate of job formation in the entire economy. Scientists and engineers increased even more rapidly, at triple the rate of overall jobs. One implication here concerns power relations. In an advanced technological society, will engineers and scientists as a group be content to remain technocrats, serving those in power as a technical elite? Or will they tire of being the tools of those on top? Will they want to dominate public decision making?

The result of these employment shifts is that only 3 percent of the labor force is now engaged in agriculture and extractive industry. Meanwhile, the secondary sector of manufacturing stagnates, and the tertiary sector of services-information continues to grow.

What are the effects of these macro-level changes? Some can be seen with the naked eye: abandoned factories dotting the inner-city landscape as blue-collar work declines; new office buildings in cities and suburbs dominating the skyline, dwarfing the factories. Other impacts are invisible to the eye but exist nonetheless. Here are just two: the growth of public sector employee unions as the tertiary sector grows, and the analytical fuzziness of the term "working-class" as low-echelon white-collar jobs increase and traditional working-class jobs in heavy manufacturing decline.

Many factors could modify present trends. Most importantly, energy shortages and rising energy costs could stimulate construction in central cities, bringing back business firms and workers from the suburbs. Alternatively, the energy crunch could increase unemployment, causing even further economic and social distress to already hard-hit Frostbelt cities.

Employment shifts in the past generation have massively and differentially affected U.S. cities. This is illustrated by the tale of two cities: Houston and Detroit.

The Tale of Two Cities: Houston and Detroit

Houston, Texas. Boomtown. Supercity. International Capital of the Fast Buck. That's what some call Houston, one of the nation's fastest-growing cities, ranked sixth in size by 1975.

A city of great contrasts, Houston is:

> twenty of the most innovative buildings in the country and 2,000 rather ordinary gas stations. It's the award-winning Grand Opera and a boisterous cowboy honky-tonk. It's the Lyndon B. Johnson Space Center and the heavily polluted ship channel. It's the Rothko Chapel and sleazy fast-food joints. But if Houston is evidence of the chaos that comes from unplanned growth, it is also a monument to the power of money, hard work and imagination. (Williams and Profitt, 1977:41)

Boomtown Houston sits in the middle of a mine of black gold: petroleum. It is located in one of nature's most abundant areas, along the Gulf Coast of Texas. Other than oil and gas, its principal raw materials include cotton, sulphur, cattle, lumber, and chemicals.

Originally, Houston's money and power were based on its primary and secondary sector activities, and it remains the international capital of oil refining, a very advanced technological process. But its tertiary sector has grown along with the general boom, so much so that in 1970 Houston was a white-collar town. Today it is corporate headquarters for many former Frostbelt firms and the home of advanced technological research. Notably, it contains NASA aerospace headquarters ("Houston control" to 1969 moonshot watchers), named after Lyndon B. Johnson, who looked after his home state by sponsoring the placement of government installations there.

As basic-nonbasic sector economic theory (described in the preceding chapter) predicts, growth in the basic sector has had a multiplier effect in the nonbasic sector. Hence, construction has boomed in Harris County, where Houston is located. About 600,000 people poured into the Houston SMSA between 1960 and 1970—an average of 5,000 per month—to take advantage of the booming economy.

One other chance feature aided the city's nearly untrammeled growth. When the economic boom began, Houston was surrounded by unincorporated areas. As the city's economy expanded, Houston annexed much of this unincorporated land to the city. In this way, Houston avoided many of the central city-outside central city disparities that typify the older Frostbelt SMSAs. In other words, Houston managed to capture much of the tax base growth stemming from its economic development rather than lose it to suburban development.

So, starting after World War II, Houston has been a big winner—a beneficiary of regional growth, federal government largesse, national energy needs, structural changes in employment, and avoidance of the central city-suburban disparity. While Houston prospered, however, Detroit floundered.

Detroit, Michigan. Detroit is no boomtown. By the mid-1970s it was so distressed that the mayor's office (1975) announced: "SURVIVAL is the issue."

As we noted before, it was once said that "When the nation catches a cold, Detroit gets pneumonia." That was in the city's past, when a national economic downturn would disproportionately hurt the sale of cars, a product with an elastic demand curve. Now so much auto manufacturing and so many skilled workers have left the city limits that Detroit's economy lags behind even in times of national growth.

Historically, the nation's fifth largest city is synonymous with cars, hence the nickname "Motown." But its dominance in auto production has been steadily eroded, and international competitors have captured an ever-increasing share of the car market as well. Nonetheless, auto jobs in the Detroit SMSA increased between 1967 and 1972. But this didn't help Detroit, for the growth took place outside the central city. In fact, Detroit's suburbs gained 50,000 jobs in the five-year period, while Detroit itself lost over 9,000 jobs. By 1972, three out of every four automotive workers were working outside the central city (U.S. Bureau of the Census, 1976: Vol. III, Michigan Tables 6, 8).

By and large, Detroit remains a blue-collar town. The service sector hasn't taken up the slack caused by declines in blue-collar employment.

As Detroit's basic sector employment declined, the nonbasic sector followed. Industry, shopping centers, movie houses, and so on left the city. So did people, particularly the wealthier, more mobile taxpayers. The result: Detroit is not only a blue-collar town but a town of low- and fixed-income people, elderly and racial minorities—what one mayor called "the dispossessed." Meanwhile, some suburbs thrive. Indeed, just forty-five minutes away from downtown Detroit, by the vehicle that once made it a vital city, lies elegant Bloomfield Hills, the home of most auto industry executives and the richest town in the nation in 1972.

Population shifts to the suburbs and negative growth in manufacturing within the city have made Detroit unable to provide high levels of public services. The city's tax base is not growing, and the downtown Renaissance Center (a hotel-convention-shops complex) has not yet lived up to its name.

The human impact of these structural and demographic shifts has been wide-ranging. Consider this catalog of Detroit's urban ills.

1. *Unemployment.* By 1975, 23 percent of the work force was jobless, the rate among young black and Hispanic males surpassed 50 percent.
2. *Crime.* A sense of paranoia about safety so gripped the city that Detroiters possessed over 500,000 handguns in the early 1970s (Holli, 1976:232). There were steep increases in murder, robbery, and rape during the 1970s.
3. *Physical deterioration.* More than 20,000 properties had been abandoned or become useless.
4. *Human services.* Only minimal levels of public services were being provided to the most needy.

To conclude: Houston and Detroit, boomtown and bust-town, illustrate some powerful job trends that are shaping U.S. cities today. Shifts from Frostbelt to Sunbelt, from central city to outside central city, and from manufacturing to services have broad implications for the economic health of individual cities.

An additional and increasingly important factor is international and national energy policy. Energy scarcities and price hikes have great but uneven impact on regions and industries. (Indeed, in 1979, Cleveland's mayor filed an antitrust suit on behalf of his city against the Organization of Petroleum Exporting Countries, charging that OPEC's price fixing had brought unemployment and inflation to his city.) For petroleum-rich, white-collar Houston an energy crunch will probably not spell economic disaster. Houston has an advantage relative to the Northeast. It depends on natural gas, not oil, to heat homes and generate electricity. Since natural gas comes from domestic wells, the city isn't as threatened by oil cutoffs or huge price increases. But Houston is spread out and almost totally dependent on the automobile. Thus, a Houston transportation expert says, "If there's a national crisis from an energy standpoint, it's going to hit hardest here" (in Stevens, 1979: Sec. 3, 5).

For the auto industry in general and blue-collar Detroit in particular, energy shortages and expense could mean even further distress. And since automobile production is the nation's single largest industry (affecting one-seventh of all private jobs), declines in that basic industry would undoubtedly have a domino effect, causing unemployment in other manufacturing cities.

POVERTY IN METROPOLITAN AREAS

Detroit's distressed condition is a stark reminder that poverty and unemployment—

not affluence and work—dominate the life situations of many city residents. We now take a closer look at the unemployed, the underemployed, and the full-time employed who still can't survive economically in the nation's SMSAs: the metropolitan poor.

Who Are the Metropolitan Poor?

Being poor in America is largely a question of definition—official government definition. That is, if the federal government's threshold for poverty changes, millions of people can be thrown out of poverty—or into poverty—on paper.

The current federal definition of poverty is based on a Social Security Administration (SSA) index. Most analysts use the SSA poverty definition, an absolute standard of dollar income. Essentially, the SSA poverty threshold is calculated by determining the subsistence food costs for a family of more than three persons and multiplying that figure by three. In 1977, the average threshold for a nonfarm family of four persons was $6,191; in 1974, it was $5,038. Families of four with an income below that threshold are classified as poor.

Another federal agency, the Bureau of Labor Statistics (BLS), uses the "standard budget" as a measure of describing minimum subsistence levels and above. Standard budgets are normative estimates of living costs. They take into account such items as food, housing, clothing, personal and medical care, and transportation. The BLS (1976a:83) makes the following assumptions in calculating the costs for lower, intermediate, and higher budgets:

> The lower budget . . . family lives in rental housing without air conditioning . . . , relies heavily on public transportation, supplemented, where necessary, by the use of an older car, performs more services for itself and utilizes free recreation facilities in the community. Compared with the intermediate budget, the life style in the high budget is marked by more home ownership, high levels of new-car ownership, more household appliances and equipment, and more paid-for services.

In 1974, the annual costs of a lower budget for a four-person family in metropolitan areas was $9,323; intermediate budget—$14,644; and higher budget—$21,381. The BLS also figures budgets for individual cities. A few 1974 examples show the inter-city variation for a lower budget: New York City—$9,852; Honolulu, Hawaii—$11,383; Houston—$8,483; and Detroit—$9,138 (BLS, 1976b: Table 28).

Now, compare the BLS lower budget for a metropolitan family of four to the SSA's poverty line for a similar family in one selected year, 1974: BLS—$9,323 and SSA—$5,038. Clearly, if the BLS standard lower budget were used as the poverty line, millions more would be considered poor.

Some radical critics of government poverty measures maintain that the standard should be based on relative rather than absolute guidelines. These critics argue that poverty is relative only to wealth; therefore, being poor in America can be measured only in comparison to being rich. Following this logic, families earning less than a BLS higher budget standard would be classified as poor.

Using the SSA income threshold, how many Americans are considered poor? The nationwide total in 1978 was 24.5 million, or 11.4 percent of the population. This was a decrease from 22.4 percent of the population in 1959.

Where do the poor live? Within SMSAs, the poverty rate inside central cities is more

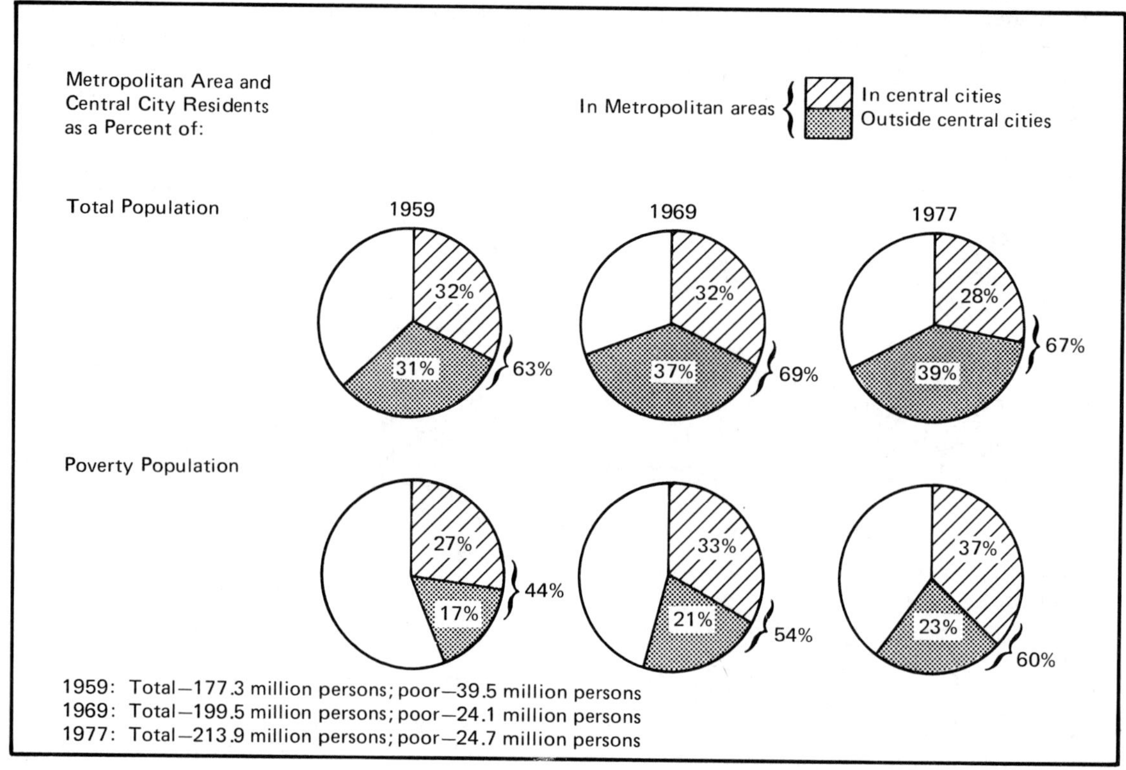

Fig. 16-6 WHERE DO THE POOR LIVE? The percentage of poor people in the nation's central cities has increased steadily in recent years. (Adapted from U.S. Bureau of the Census, *Current Population Reports,* Series P-60, No. 119, "Characteristics of the Population Below the Poverty Level: 1977" [Washington, D.C.: U.S. Government Printing Office, 1979], Fig. 3, p. 6)

than twice the rate outside central cities, and the gap has grown greater—not smaller—in the 1959–1977 period (see Fig. 16-6).

Who are the poor? Disproportionately, they are black, Hispanic, and female heads of families with no husband present. In 1977, the poverty rate was 8.9 percent for whites; 31.3 percent for blacks; 22.4 percent for people of Spanish origin; and 31.7 percent for female householders without husbands present. Among blacks, over one-half of female householders without husbands present were living below the poverty line in 1977. Almost one-fourth of white women in the same situation were poor (U.S. Bureau of the Census, 1979: Table A).

Disproportionately, the unemployed are black. In 1978, the unemployment rate for blacks was 2.3 times greater than for whites (Delaney, 1979:20). And black teenage females had the dubious distinction of having the highest unemployment rate of any group in the United States. "In the first quarter of 1975, unemployment of white teenage females stood or rather slumped at a depressive 18.1 per cent. For black teenage females the rejection, was—and this is not a typo—43 percent. A year later, while everyone was noting the great economic recovery, the rate for black teenagers had barely moved" (Howe, 1978:3).

How many poor persons work full-time or part-time and still remain in poverty? Almost one-half of all poor householders in 1977. Almost 900,000 heads of families—working full-time all year—never rise above the poverty line (Levitan in Shabecoff, 1978:19).

Before continuing, a note on statistics is needed. First, there is an active "off the books" or "underground" economy in the United States. This means that people earn cash but don't report it for income tax purposes. The federal government's General Accounting Office (GAO) estimates that 6 million people earned money in 1979 but didn't report it (*New York Times*, 1979:D6). The implication: Many classified as unemployed and/or poor may not be. Secondly, census takers tend to undercount the urban poor. This has serious results for cities, particularly the distribution of federal funds based on the number of persons below the

Fig. 16-7 THE WORKING AND NONWORKING POOR. In 1977, over 1 million male and female householders worked all year but remained below the SSA's poverty line. Over 2.7 million family householders below the poverty line did not work; the majority were taking care of young children, or were ill or disabled. (U.S. Bureau of the Census, *Current Population Reports,* Series P-60, No. 119, "Characteristics of the Population Below the Poverty Level: 1977" [Washington, D.C.: U.S. Government Printing Office, 1979], Fig. 5, p. 9)

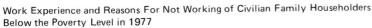

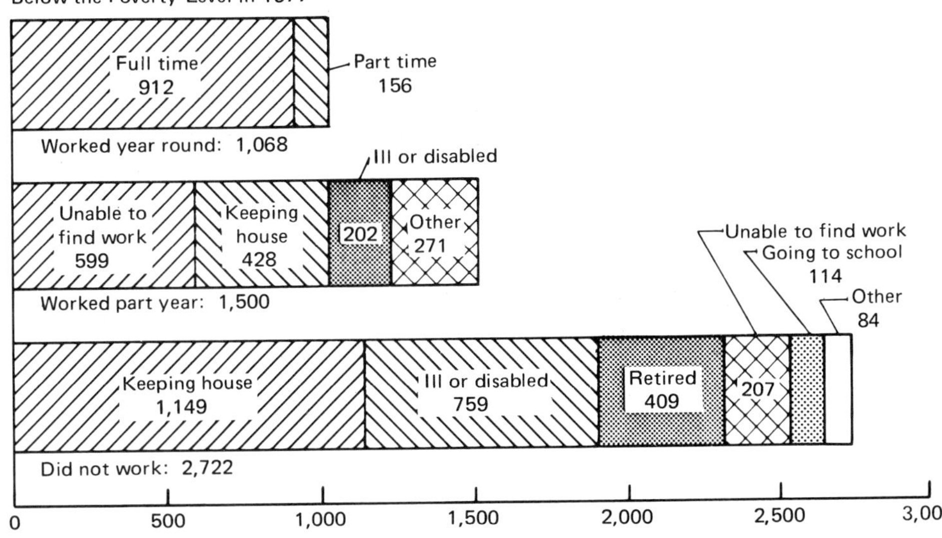

poverty line. Finally, the way of measuring employment and unemployment probably needs revision. Sar Levitan, chair of a national commission on employment statistics, says that they "come close to being straight random numbers" at the local level (in Shabecoff, 1978:19). Since this is the level at which federal public employment funds are allocated, the numbers game is crucial to cities. Further, Levitan questions whether 16- and 17-year-olds who are full-time students and look for a job a few hours per week should really be counted as part of the labor force. Meanwhile, the plaque on Levitan's office wall provides the proper cautionary note: "Statistics Are No Substitute for Good Judgment."

To conclude: In the late 1970s the metropolitan poor tended to be (1) concentrated inside central cities rather than around them and (2) disproportionately female, black, and Hispanic. The economic gap between black and white America has been widening, not narrowing, since the recession in the mid-1970s (Hill in Delaney, 1979:20).

Why Are They Poor?

It comes as no surprise that citizens and scholars alike disagree on the causes and cures of poverty. But at different times, certain notions seem to dominate social thought. And some resurface, like old wines in new bottles. For instance, about eighty years ago, the dominant belief about the causes of poverty was social Darwinist. Briefly, social Darwinism held that those who reach the top of the economic ladder are the fittest, surviving and winning the struggle for existence. By implication, the poor are unfit. This idea has resurfaced in recent years with a new twist. Some claim that poverty is linked to genetic inheritance, Exhaustive social research (e.g., Jencks et al., 1972) shows that genes and I.Q. scores have relatively little effect on economic success. Still, whether social or biological, Darwinian theories of poverty die hard.

Another notion goes even deeper in American thought: Anyone who works hard can succeed. In this view, anyone who wants a job can get one, work hard, and make it. Thus, the poor are just lazy. The Horatio Alger stories in the period of rapid industrialization popularized this aspect of the American dream and strengthened the belief in the so-called Protestant work ethic. Again, much social research (e.g., Valentine, 1979) shows that most poor Americans prefer to work and "identify their self-esteem with work as strongly as do the nonpoor" (Goodwin, 1972:112). But social science findings have done little to change firm beliefs or prejudices. No matter what social scientists find, some will undoubtedly continue to believe that poor people are lazy people.

Currently, several notions about the causes of poverty dominate academic and/or policy-making circles. Here is a brief summary of four competing notions:

1. *Poverty as personal failure.* This view—that poverty is largely the result of personal failure and lower-class attitudes—is associated with political scientist Edward Banfield (1974). According to Banfield, certain psychological traits prevent the poor from changing their status. In brief, he argues that lower-class people lack typically middle-class attitudes about planning ahead, saving for a rainy day, or pursuing an education.
2. *Poverty as a culture, passed on from generation to generation.* This view, associated with the late anthropologist Oscar Lewis, holds that the poor are present-time oriented and lack planning ability (as Banfield also says). But the reasons the poor act differently from the nonpoor have little to do with individual failure (as Banfield says) and much to do with the class-stratified, capitalistic societies they

live in. Based on fieldwork in Latin America and the United States, Lewis (1964) argues that the poor lack the means to break the cycle of poverty. So, they adapt as best they can—in a subculture set apart from other subcultures in capitalist society. This subculture—the **culture of poverty** —is transmitted from one generation to the next, making it nearly impossible to break the chains that bind.

3. *Poverty as a lack of opportunity*. This view, associated with liberals, holds that "the poor lack the skills and education to find employment in an automated society" (Campbell and Burkhead, 1968:626). Extending opportunities for the poor (without disturbing existing institutions) is the solution that follows from this stance, exemplified by the War on Poverty in the 1960s.

4. *Poverty as a structural feature of capitalism.*

Fig. 16-8 WHY DOES POVERTY EXIST? Theorists disagree. Radicals think that poverty is a structural feature of capitalism. Liberals say that poverty can be decreased within the existing institutional structure. Conservatives hold that poverty stems from personal failure and/or lower-class attitudes. (Margaret Bourke-White. Life Magazine. © 1937 Time Inc.)

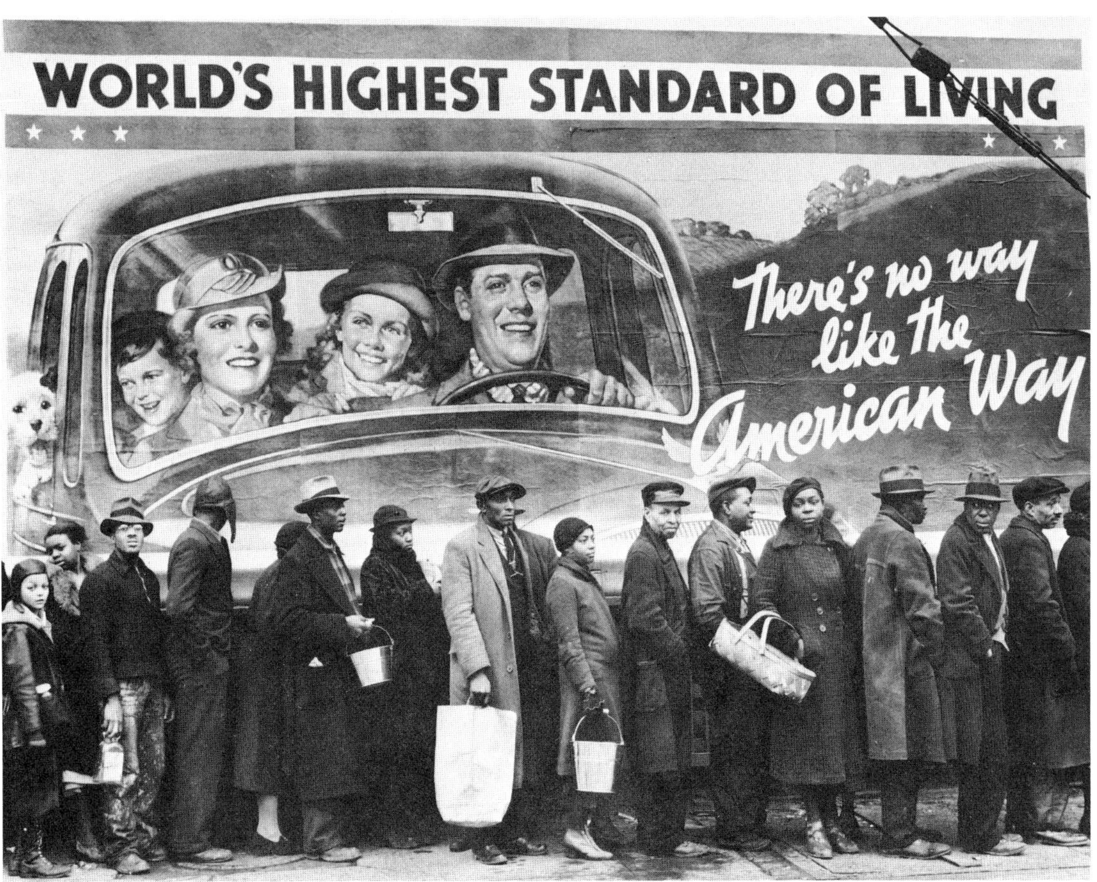

This view, held by Marxists, states that under capitalism, some are poor because others are rich. In this view, the capitalist state helps capitalists to maintain power over wage workers and thus cannot be expected to intervene meaningfully to end poverty—for that would mean speeding capitalism's downfall.

No synthesis of these four views is possible; they are too at odds with one another. But a study we've considered before, *Tally's Corner,* by Elliot Liebow, does include aspects of both the structural and social psychological perspectives.

Tally's Corner

The New Deal Carry-out shop is on a corner in downtown Washington, D.C. It would be within easy walking distance of the White House . . . if anyone cared to walk there, but no one ever does. . . . One block south of the Carry-out is a broad avenue which serves roughly to divide the Carry-out neighborhood from the downtown business and shopping district. (Liebow, 1967:17, 18)

It was here in this Zone-in-Transition, black ghetto neighborhood that urban anthropologist Liebow did his participant-observation research. One of the first questions he asked was, "Why are these men hanging out on streetcorners?" Some might think there's a simple answer: They don't want to work. That's what a truck driver said when some of the men refused his offer of work: "These men wouldn't take a job if it were handed to them on a platter" (see Box 16-2). Several streetcorner men did fit the truck driver's stereotype. Leroy prefers playing pinball to working at parking lots, and Sea Cat, "an excellent story teller," walked out on his job. Arthur, age twenty-eight, doesn't want to work. But Liebow find that most did work—at weekend or evening jobs, and thus they could hang out near the Carry-out shop during the day.

Some of the streetcorner men were doing illegal work—hustling. Liebow thinks that this makes sense, since the legal work available to the men is low-paying, low-status, and dead-end.

Interestingly, Liebow disputes the notion that the poor are present-time oriented and can't plan ahead. To the contrary, "when Richard squanders a week's pay in two days it is not because he is 'present-time oriented,' unaware or unconcerned with his future. He does so precisely because he is aware of the future and the hopelessness of it all" (Liebow, 1967:66). Thus, what may seem to others as a present-time orientation is interpreted by Liebow as a future-time orientation. The difference is that it is a future filled with trouble. He gives the following concrete example:

One day, after Tally had gotten paid, he gave me four twenty-dollar bills and asked me to keep them for him. Three days later he asked me for the money. I returned it and asked why he did not put his money in a bank. He said that the banks close at two o'clock. I argued that there were four or more banks within a two-block radius of where he was working at the time and that he could easily get to any one of them on his lunch hour. "No, man," he said, "you don't understand. They close at two o'clock and they closed Saturday and Sunday. Suppose I get into trouble and I got to make it [leave]. Me get out of town, and everything I got in the world layin' up in that bank? No good! No good!" (1967:69)

The result of their structural situation, Liebow says, is a constant awareness of a troubled future. This discourages Tally and the other streetcorner men from putting money in the bank, sinking roots, committing themselves to a family or friends, and devoting their energies to a job, for all these commitments could hold them hostage.

Box 16-2

HANGIN' OUT

Men and Jobs at Tally's Corner

A pickup truck drives slowly down the street. The truck stops as it comes abreast of a man sitting on a cast-iron porch and the white driver calls out, asking if the man wants a day's work. The man shakes his head and the truck moves on up the block, stopping again whenever idling men come within calling distance of the driver. At the Carry-out corner, five men debate the question briefly and shake their heads no to the truck. The truck turns the corner and repeats the same performance up the next street. In the distance one can see one man, then another, climb into the back of the truck and sit down. In starts and stops, the truck finally disappears.

What is it we have witnessed here? A labor scavenger rebuffed by his would-be prey? Lazy, irresponsible men turning down an honest day's pay for an honest day's work? Or a more complex phenomenon marking the intersection of economic forces, social values and individual states of mind and body?

Let us look again at the driver of the truck . . . . To him, it is clear that [most of the men] do not choose to work . . . . They confirm what he has read, heard and knows from his own experience: these men wouldn't take a job if it were handed to them on a platter.

. . . Whether or not this is true of some of the men he sees on the street, it is clearly not true of all of them . . . . It is not even true of most of them, for most of the men he sees on the street this weekday morning do, in fact, have jobs. But since, at the moment, they are neither working nor sleeping, and since they hate the depressing room or apartment they live in, or because there is nothing to do there, or because they want to get away from their wives or anyone else living there, they are out on the street . . . . Some, like Sweets, work nights cleaning up middle-class trash . . . . Some laborers, like Tally, have already come back from the job . . . because the weather was too cold for pouring concrete. Other employed men stayed off the job today for personal reasons: Clarence to go to a funeral . . . and Sea Cat to answer a subpoena as a witness in a criminal proceeding.

Also on the street . . . are the halt and the lame . . . .

Others, having had jobs and been laid off, are drawing unemployment compensation (up to $44 per week) and have nothing to gain by accepting work which pays little more than this and frequently less.

Still others, like Bumbdoodle the numbers man, are working at illegal ways of making money, hustlers who are on the street to turn a dollar any way they can . . . .

Only a handful remains unaccounted for. There is Tonk, who cannot bring himself to take a job away from the corner, because he suspects his wife will be unfaithful if given the opportunity. There is Stanton, who has not reported to work for four days now, not since Bernice disappeared.

. . . And finally, there are those like Arthur, able-bodied men who have no visible means of suport, legal or illegal, who neither have jobs nor want them. . . . Arthur will not take a job at all . . . .

The man-job relationship is a tenuous one. At any given moment, a job may occupy a relatively low position on the streetcorner scale of real values. Getting a job may be subordinated to relations with women or to other non-job considerations; the commitment to a job one already has is frequently shallow and tentative.

The reasons are many. Some are objective and reside principally in the job; some are subjective and reside principally in the man. The line between them, however, is not a clear one. Behind the man's refusal to take a job or his decision to quit one is not a simple impulse or value choice but a complex combination of assessments of objective reality on the one hand, and values, attitudes and beliefs drawn from different levels of his experience on the other. (Liebow, 1967:29–71; author's original footnotes have been deleted.)

What Should Be Done About Poverty?

Some poor townsmen were sitting around discussing the vexing question of poverty. "Poverty is hell," one man said, "but I know how to remedy this evil. People should put all they own into a common pot so that there would be enough for everyone." Another man, Hershel by name, responded, "That is indeed a fine plan, but the question is how to carry it out. I suggest we divide the task. I'll get the endorsement of the poor. You can tackle the rich."

Folk tales, like this one from nineteenth-century Russia (in Howe and Greenberg, 1954:615–6), often contain ideological visions. So do programs sponsored by government or private organizations which seek to end poverty.

Federal, state, and local government responses to poverty have long been dominated by a liberal vision. This means that the policy thrust has been toward increased funds for cities and programs aimed at widening economic opportunity. Such programmatic responses to poverty include the following: bilingual and adult education; Project Head Start, Community Action Programs, and other War on Poverty programs; the encouragement of "black capitalism" with small business loans and technical assistance; job training and CETA; fair employment practices and affirmative action laws; and incentives to encourage industries to relocate in economically depressed areas. Interestingly, programs that *potentially* threaten to do more than increase economic opportunity, notably the Community Action Program of the War on Poverty (which some mayors, as we saw, viewed as a threat to their legitimate power), are usually short-lived (see Phillips, 1971–1972). Among the liberal policies recommended over the years have been welfare reform, reduction of unemployment, and income maintenance programs.

Critics claim that liberal programs aimed at helping the "deserving poor" often end up aiding the "undeserving rich" (Boulding in Weisbrod, 1970:139). That is, as Murray Edelman (1971) notes about the War on Poverty, the "affluent recipients of public contracts" reaped the most benefits from this alleged antipoverty program. Edelman names large corporations that ran Job Corps centers, university professors who conducted poverty research, and consulting firms paid to evaluate poverty programs as some of the major beneficiaries.

For different reasons, both conservatives and radicals dispute liberal solutions to poverty. Edward Banfield, Daniel Patrick Moynihan, and other neo-conservatives think that big government can't solve the problem of poverty and shouldn't try. Their alternative: Let the market mechanism of supply and demand, not government, regulate social problems. Conservatives and neo-conservatives tend to favor removing regulations on the market so that it can work "properly." Hence, they suggest repealing minimum wage laws, reasoning that without a mimimum wage, employers would hire more low-skilled people and unemployment would decrease. They also press for laws favoring business expansion and tax reduction on the premise that money poured in at the top will filter down to the poor.

Radicals argue that pouring money in at the top doesn't help the poor. The economic pie may grow bigger, but the share for the poor remains the same (see Kolko, 1962). Radicals also point to the deceptive quality of government-sponsored antipoverty programs. They argue that the War on Poverty, for example, may convince the public that something is being done to end poverty but, in reality, it is only preserving a system of structured inequalities: capitalism. In the radical view, the idea of equal opportunity for advancement is false. It is equivalent to comparing a lottery ticket to a savings bond that always pays off. In the words of Simone de Beauvoir (1953), "any ticket may be the winning one, but only a tiny percentage of them actually do win." To end poverty, radicals argue, the institutional and class structure that perpetuates it must be changed—not just around the edges, as liberals would have it, but at its core: capitalist productive relations.

ANOTHER LOOK

While the majority of contemporary Americans are dissatisfied with their work, theorists disagree about the reason(s) and what to do about it. Behind these disagreements lie irrevocable ideological differences. Further, theorists do not share a similar view of human nature. The same could be said about causes and cures for poverty. Here again, it is not differences in disciplinary background that separate theorists. Instead, it is deep-seated ideological differences.

It is important to remember that views of human nature cannot be supported or refuted by empirical evidence. Hence, the conservative view (human beings with a "need" for hierarchy and control), the liberal view (human beings with a "need" and potential to fulfill themselves, if given a chance), and the radical view (human beings with a nature dictated by the socieconomic system into which they're born and thus changeable if that system undergoes radical change) may be called "theories" of human nature but, in effect, they are merely faith claims. What is also important is that one or another of these faith claims underlie public policy, and the results of work and antipoverty policies on individual lives are real in their consequences.

A final thought on theory and practice: more than 140 years ago, an anonymous contributor to the *Edinburgh Review* commented that "newspapers are perhaps the best representative, at any given time, of the real moral and intellectual state of the greater part of a population" (1837:197). Today, we might amend "newspapers" to "television." And what stories does TV tell us about the quality of work, the nature of poverty, and the route to success in metropolitan America? First, few people work on TV except private detectives, police officers, doctors, hustlers, and sometimes journalists. Rarely are others depicted in the actual performance of their jobs, whether in prime-time situation comedies, soap operas, or news programs. Perhaps that provides a clue to the kinds of work deemed intrinsically satisfying and exciting in our time. Secondly, liberal notions about success and poverty dominate the mass media. Typically, TV characters "get ahead" by getting an education (as in the case of Archie Bunker's son-in-law). In numerous made-for-television documentaries, people "make it" out of poverty with the assistance of government-sponsored programs. In the 1960s and 1970s, these were the stories we told ourselves collectively, perhaps reflecting the "real moral and intellectual state of the greater part of a population." As the 1980s and the era of postindustrialism progress, it will be interesting to watch TV portrayals of work, leisure, self-fulfillment, and poverty. Will the stories change? Stay tuned.

PROJECTS

1. **Occupational profiles.** Construct two occupational profiles, one for your own community (or one nearby) and another for a community of a similar size. Try to choose communities that appear to have different occupational profiles

(e.g., a manufacturing center and a white-collar town). For basic data, see the *Census of Population* series, Vol. I, "Characteristics of the Population," published by the U.S. Census Bureau.

2. **Changes in the occupational structure over time.** For the largest city in your state, construct a series of occupational profiles for the years 1940, 1950,1960, and 1970, and, if data are available, 1980. What patterns appear? How might you explain these patterns?

3. **Working—personal views.** How do people feel about the work they do? Interview people in your community who engage in different activities—professor, garbage collector, secretary, sales clerk, operative, doctor, and so forth. Try to find out if they would choose the same work again, if they had a choice; what they like most about their jobs; what they would change about their working conditions; and what they dislike about their work.

SUGGESTIONS FOR FURTHER LEARNING

How people feel about their work is the topic of numerous survey research and other empirical studies. The Report of a Special Task Force to the Secretary of Health, Education, and Welfare, *Work in America* (Cambridge: Mass.: MIT Press, 1973), reports its survey findings on worker dissatisfaction and includes suggestions for job redesign. A more scholarly treatment of these issues is Louis E. Davis, Albert B. Cherns and associates, *The Quality of Working Life* (New York: Free Press, 1975), in two volumes. Volume I contains essays on the state of the art in "quality of work" research, and Volume II contains case studies of recent experiments in redefining work. For a compilation of attitude scales used to measure job satisfaction over the years, see John P. Robinson et al., *Measures of Occupational Attitudes and Occupational Characteristics* (Ann Arbor, Mich.: Institute for Social Research, Survey Research Center, 1969).

How people feel about their work is also the subject of a number of personal statements, both in literary and interview form. Studs Terkel's *Working* (New York: Avon, 1975) presents dozens of people, speaking for themselves, about their work. Terkel interviewed a broad range of job holders, including a steel worker, newspaper copy boy, ex-Quiz Kid flower grower, and fire fighter.

Some of America's most renowned literature focuses on issues of work and its alienating effects. Most notable is Arthur Miller's haunting indictment of the economic system which results in alienation, *Death of a Salesman,* in *Collected Plays* (New York: Viking, 1957). Fiction about work by contemporary American writers, including Ken Kesey, Joyce Carol Oates, Grace Paley, and John Updike is collected by editor William O'Rourke in *On the Job* (New York: Vintage, 1977).

Work is the focus of a subfield within the discipline of sociology: the sociology of occupations and professions. For an overview of the research, see Theodore Caplow, *The Sociology of Work* (Minneapolis: University of Minnesota Press, 1954), and *The Sociology of Work in Industry* (London: Collier Macmillan, 1971) by Alan Fox.

For a sociological analysis of management ideologies in the course of industrialization, see Reinhard Bendix, *Work and Authority in Industry* (New York: Harper Torchbook, [1956] 1963). Bendix looks at the relations between employers and workers with—but not through—the eyes of those who have sought to defend and advance the development of industry. The book "deals with ideologies of management which seek to justify the subordination of large masses of men [and women] to the discipline of factory work and to the authority of employers."

How were the old mills as work places, and as places on the early American landscape? Anthropologist Anthony F. C. Wallace examines the old mills and tenements in the Rockdale region south of Philadelphia in his brilliant account of *Rockdale: The Growth of an American Village in the Early Industrial Revolution* (New York: Knopf, 1978). Tamara K. Hareven and Randolph Langenbach explore Manchester, New Hampshire's, old mills in *Amoskeag: Life and Work in an American Factory-City* (New York: Pantheon, 1978), and Steve Dunwell writes of *The Run of the Mill* (Boston: Godine, 1978).

Unemployment and underemployment are the subjects of Teresa A. Sullivan, *Marginal Workers, Marginal Jobs* (Austin: University of Texas Press, 1978). Using a "labor utilization" framework, she tests hypotheses designed to measure underemployment in the U.S..

On the nature of poverty, see David Gordon (ed.), *Theories of Poverty and Underemployment* (Lexington, Mass.: D. C. Heath, 1972), for a radical perspective and a discussion of dual labor market theory. For an account of the functions that poverty serves in society, see Pamela Roby (ed.), *The Poverty Establishment* (Englewood Cliffs, N.J.: Prentice-Hall, 1974); this includes selections from both liberals and radicals. More mainstream and conservative views are collected in Daniel Patrick Moynihan (ed.), *On Understanding Poverty* (New York: Basic Books, 1969).

The culture of poverty and a critique of this perspective are found, respectively, in Oscar Lewis's work, particularly *La Vida* (New York: Random House, 1966), and Eleanor Burke Leacock (ed.), *The Culture of Poverty: A Critique* (New York: Simon & Schuster, 1971).

Do the poor want to work? This is the topic of Leonard Goodwin's 1972 Brookings Institution study of the same name, *Do the Poor Want to Work?* Based on interviews with 4,000 people, Goodwin concludes that they do. So does Bettylou Valentine in *Hustling and Other Hard Work: Life Styles in the Ghetto* (New York: Free Press, 1979); urban anthropologist Valentine (wife of Charles Valentine, critic of the culture of poverty perspective) notes in her ethnography that the people in "Blackston" want to work.

Theories on the relationship of work and welfare from a radical perspective are presented by Frances Fox Piven and Richard Cloward, *Regulating the Poor* (New York: Vintage, 1971), in which they argue that welfare regulates both the poor and members of the labor force. A very different view of work and poverty is contained in Edward Banfield, *The Unheavenly City Revisited* (Boston: Little, Brown, 1974), now considered a classic statement of the conservative (or neo-conservative) position.

Films dealing with work, welfare, and poverty include Charlie Chaplin's classic *Modern Times* (1936) and Paul Schrader's *Blue Collar* (1978). Frederick Wiseman's documentary, *Welfare* (1975), attacks the red tape and callousness of the welfare system, showing its effects on those who work in it as well as those who depend on it. For a protrayal of the rhythm of factory life in the late ninteenth century, see the opening scenes of *The Organizer* (1964), which creates the mood of modern industrial life as workers pour into the factory to the purr of machines. Barbara Kopple's award-winning film, *Harlan County, U.S.A.* (1976), shows the rhythm of work in the coal mines as well as management-labor struggles and union problems in "bloody Harlan" County, Kentucky. *The Diary of a Harlem Family* (NET, 1968) follows the struggle for existence of a big-city black family, and *Cities and the Poor* (NET, 1966, two parts) examines urban poverty in terms of conventional theories of poverty. NBC's "white paper," *The Battle of Newburgh* (1966), describes the attempt of one New York city to crack down on "welfare cheaters" and the impact it had on their elderly citizens. A much broader attack, from a Marxist perspective, on the nature of poverty in modern society is found in *The History Book* (1975, produced for the Danish Government Film Office). The feature-length film *Salt of the Earth* (1954, producer: Paul Jerrico) intertwines three themes of exploitation from a radical perspective: management versus labor; Anglo versus Hispanic miners; and women's oppression by men. The film's director was one of the Hollywood Ten, blacklisted during the McCarthy era.

For folk songs about work and working conditions in America, listen to John Greenway, "American Industrial Folksongs" (Riverside 12-607, 1955) and "American History in Ballad and Song" (Folkways FH 5801), and a number of songs sung by Woody Guthrie and Pete Seeger.

For views on the shift from the world of preindustrial to industrial work in Europe and the U.S., see E. P. Thompson, *The Making of the English Working Class* (New York: Vintage, 1963), a painstaking work of scholarship sympathetic to the workers' struggle to nourish the tree of liberty. Herbert Gutman attempts to do for the U.S.

working class what Thompson did for the first working class (in England) in his collection of essays, *Work, Culture, and Society in Industrializing America, 1815–1919* (New York: Knopf, 1976). This book has already been influential in giving a new interpretation of American labor history. For a very different perspective, see Neil J. Smelser, *Social Change in the Industrial Revolution* (Chicago: University of Chicago Press, 1959), which takes a structural-functionalist perspective on the development of class consciousness.

For the role of professionals in industrial and postindustrial society, see David F. Noble, *America by Design* (New York: Knopf, 1977), a study of the relationship between the engineering professions, technology, and corporate capitalism. Noble's central thesis is that engineers played a significant role in protecting capitalist corporations from technological disruption. Noble debunks the idea that technology is an automatic process and presents a case study of machine tools to support his point. See Alvin W. Gouldner, *The Future of Intellectuals and the Rise of the New Class* (New York: Seabury, 1979), for the argument that the professionals (e.g., scientists, administrators, intellectuals, and technicians) are now assuming critical influence in the postindustrial society, a factor not predicted by ninteenth-century thinkers, including Marx. Indeed, Gouldner maintains that Marx was wrong when he theorized that the bourgeoisie would one day be overthrown by the workers, for culture is an important form of capital that Marx neglected.

The machine age, in which people feel like so many cogs, is reflected in the paintings of Ferdinand Leger and, some say, in the architecture of the Bauhaus school, which is rational, efficient, and unadorned. Mies Van der Rohe's glass apartment building at 880 Lake Shore Drive in Chicago is one example of Bauhaus style.

KEY TERMS

Alienation A widely used concept in social science, philosophy, and the humanities with various meanings. As used by Marx, who focused on labor, alienation is the process by which the worker is dispossessed of his or her product by the capitalist mode of production. Other theorists center on varying aspects of alienation: self-estrangement, meaninglessness, and powerlessness.

Anomic division of labor According to Durkheim, an abnormal form of the division of labor that occurs when extreme specialization of tasks is coupled with a decrease in communication between individuals performing different specialized tasks. This leads to vague rules governing relationships between groups and lack of a sense of interdependence in organically solid society.

Blue-collar A category of workers (as opposed to white-collar and service workers). As defined by the U.S. Census Bureau, blue-collar workers include the following: craftspersons (e.g., automobile mechanics), operatives (e.g., assembly-line workers), and transport operatives (e.g., truck drivers), and nonfarm laborers.

Culture of poverty Oscar Lewis's term, referring to his belief that the poor within capitalist societies possess and transmit to their children a distinct set of cultural-sociopsychological traits that sets them apart from the nonpoor. These characteristics, Lewis believed, are universal and include the inability to plan ahead, wife beating, and low levels of education and income.

Employed As defined by the U.S. Census Bureau, an employed person is a civilian sixteen years and over who (1) did any work as a paid employee or worked fifteen or more hours as an unpaid worker on a family farm or in a family business or (2) had a job but did not work during the week that the census took a count due to illness, bad weather, vacation, industrial strikes, or personal reasons.

Pink-collar Female-concentrated occupations. In the United States, the following occupations were over 70 percent female in the mid-1970s: clerical work; cashiering; bank teller jobs; nursing; elementary school teaching; private household work; and typing. In 1975, 99.1 percent of all secretaries were female.

Poverty A controversial term referring most often to lack of money and material possessions; some analysts include lack of power over decision-making processes. Most U.S. analysts use the Social Security Administration's measure of poverty which establishes a threshold by calculating the subsistence food costs for a family of more than three persons and multiplying that figure by three. Critics of this absolute standard of poverty argue that poverty is relative to wealth; hence, a relative, not absolute, standard should be used.

Primary sector Economic activities that provide the basic raw materials for existence, such as agriculture, fishing, mining and forestry.

Secondary sector Economic activities that transform primary raw materials into finished goods. In terms of employment, the secondary sector dominates industrial economies.

Service workers A category of workers (as opposed to white and blue-collar). As defined by the U.S. Census Bureau, service workers include the following: waiters and waitresses, childcare workers, fire fighters, police officers, health aides, janitors, and hairdressers.

Tertiary sector Economic activities consisting of services, wholesale and retail trade, information processing, communication, utilities, finance, insurance, public services and government, real estate, and transportation.

Unemployed As defined by the U.S. Census Bureau, a civilian sixteen years or older who was neither at work nor with a job (but temporarily not working) or looking for work during the previous four weeks and available to accept a job.

Underemployment Inadequate employment of three different types: (1) too few hours of work, (2) inadequate income level, and (3) mismatch of occupation and skills. Distinguished from "unemployment."

White-collar A category of workers (as opposed to blue-collar and service workers). As defined by the U.S. Census Bureau, white-collar workers include the following: professional and technical workers (e.g., teachers, lawyers, radio operators); nonfarm managers and administrators (e.g., business executives); sales workers (e.g., retail sales clerks), and clerical workers (e.g., typists).

REFERENCES

Anonymous
1837 Edinburgh Review 65, 132:197.

Banfield, Edward C.
1974 The Unheavenly City Revisited. Boston: Little, Brown.

Bendix, Reinhard
[1956]
1963 Work and Authority in Industry. New York: Harper Torchbooks.

Bennis, Warren
1970 American Bureaucracy. Chicago: Aldine.

Blauner, Robert
1964 Alienation and Freedom: The Factory Worker and His Industry. Chicago: University of Chicago Press.

Braverman, Harry
1974 Labor and Monopoly Capital: The Degradation of Work in the Twentieth Century. New York: Monthly Review Press.

Campbell, Alan K. and Jesse Burkhead
1968 "Public policy for urban America." Pp. 577–647 in Harvey S. Perloff and Lowdon Wingo, Jr. (eds.), Issues in Urban Economics. Baltimore: Johns Hopkins Press.

Conway, Mimi
1979 Rise Gonna Rise: A Portrait of Southern Textile Workers. Garden City, N.Y.: Anchor Doubleday.

de Beauvoir, Simone
1953 America Day by Day. New York: Grove Press.

Delaney, Paul
1979 "The struggle to rally black America." New York Times magazine (July 15):20+.

de Lesquen, Henry and le Club de l'horloge
1979 La Politique du Vivant (The Politics of the Living). Paris: Albin Michel.

Durkheim, Emile
[1893]
1966 The Division of Labor in Society. New York: Free Press.

Edelman, Murray
1971 Politics as Symbolic Action. Chicago: Markham.

Edwards, Richard C.
1979 Contested Terrain: The Transformation of the Workplace in the Twentieth Century. New York: Basic Books.

Eisler, Benita
1977 The Lowell Offering: Writings by New England Mill Women (1840–1945). Philadelphia: Lippincott.

Fowke, Edith and Joe Glazer
1960 Songs of Work and Freedom. Garden City, N. Y.: Dolphin.

Garson, G. David
1973 "Automobile workers and the radical dream." Politics and Society 3:163–77.

Goodwin, Leonard
1972 Do the Poor Want to Work? Washington, D.C.: Brookings Institution.

Holli, Melvin G.
1976 Detroit. New York: New Viewpoints.

Howe, Irving and Eliezer Greenberg (eds.)
1954 A Treasury of Yiddish Stories. New York: Viking.

Howe, Louise Kapp
1978 Pink Collar Workers: Inside the World of Women's Work. New York: Avon.

Jencks, Christopher, et al.
1972 Inequality: A Reassessment of the Effect of Family and Schooling in America. New York: Basic Books.

Kandell, Jonathan
1979 "Rightist intellectual groups rise in France." New York Times (July 8):3.

Kolko, Gabriel
1962 Wealth and Power in America: An Analysis of Social Class and Income Distribution. New York: Praeger.

Laslett, Peter
1971 The World We Have Lost. New York: Scribner's.

Lévy, Bernard-Henri
1979 Barbarism with a Human Face. George Holoch, tr. New York: Harper & Row.

Lewis, Oscar
1964 "The culture of poverty." Pp.149–74 in J. J. TePaske and S. N. Fisher (eds.), Explosive Forces in Latin America. Columbus, Ohio: Ohio State University Press.

Liebow, Elliot
1967 Tally's Corner. Boston: Little, Brown.

Marx, Karl
1972 Karl Marx: The Essential Writings. Ed. Frederic L. Bender. New York: Harper & Row.

Mills, C. Wright
1951 White Collar. New York: Oxford University Press.

National NOW Times
1979 "Women in workforce to hit record." National NOW Times 12:10.

New York Times
1979 "U.S. told six million did not file '77 tax." New York Times (July 11):D6.

Noble, David F.
1977 America by Design. New York: Knopf.

Perry, Stewart E.
1978 San Francisco Scavengers. Berkeley and Los Angeles: University of California Press.

Phillips, E. Barbara
1971–
1972 "You've repossessed my bootstraps, so brother can you spare a dime?: the liberal paradigm of political economy in theory and practice." Maxwell Review 8:59–95.
1975 "The artists of everyday life: journalists,

their craft, and their consciousness." Unpublished Ph.D. dissertation, Syracuse University.

Porter, Russell B.
[1937]
1969 "Speed, speed, and still more speed—that is Flint." Pp. 28–34 in Ray Ginger (ed.), Modern American Cities. Chicago: Quadrangle.

Quinn, Robert P.
1978 Effectiveness in Workers' Roles: Employee Responsiveness to Work Environment. Ann Arbor, Michigan: Survey Research Center, Institute for Social Research. 2 vols.

Satin, Mark
1978 New Age Politics, Healing Self and Society: The Emerging New Alternative to Marxism and Liberalism. West Vancouver, B.C.: Whitecap.

Shabecoff, Philip
1978 "Overhaul is urged in jobless figures." New York Times (July 16):19.

Shrank, Robert
1978 Ten Thousand Working Days. Cambridge, Mass.: MIT Press.

Special Task Force to the Secretary of Health, Education and Welfare
1973 Work in America. Cambridge, Mass.: MIT Press.

Stevens, William K.
1979 "Houston." New York Times (December 9):Sec. 3, 1+.

Terkel, Studs
1975 Working. New York: Avon.

Thayer, Frederick C.
1973 An End to Hierarchy! An End to Competition! Organizing the Politics and Economics of Survival. New York: New Viewpoints.

Tucker, Robert C. (ed.)
1972 The Marx-Engels Reader. New York: Norton.

U.S. Bureau of the Census
1973 Census of Population: 1970, Vol. I, "Characteristics of the population." Washington, D.C.: U.S. Government Printing Office.
1976 Census of Manufactures, 1972. Washington, D.C.: U.S. Government Printing Office.
1979 Current Population Reports, Series P-60, No. 119. "Characteristics of the population below the poverty level: 1977." Washington, D.C.: U.S. Government Printing Office.

U.S. Department of Health, Education and Welfare
1976 "The measure of poverty," Technical Paper XVIII (October 1). Washington, D.C.: U.S. Government Printing Office.

U.S. Department of Labor
1976a BLS Handbook of Methods for Surveys and Studies, Bulletin 1910. Washington, D.C.: U.S. Government Printing Office.
1976b Handbook of Labor Statistics, Bulletin 1905. Washington, D.C.: U.S. Government Printing Office.

Valentine, Bettylou
1979 Hustling and Other Hard Work: Life Styles in the Ghetto. New York: Free Press.

Watkins, Beverly T.
1979 "Number of college graduates in education drops 4 pct." Chronicle of Higher Education (July 9):10.

Weisbrod, Burton A.
1970 "Collective action and the distribution of income: a conceptual approach." Pp. 117–41 in R. H. Haveman and J. Margolis (eds.), Public Expenditures and Policy Analysis. Chicago: Markham.

Williams, Dennis A. with Nicholas Profitt
1977 "Houston." Newsweek (December 12):41.

Wooten, James
1979 "Southern conflict." New York Times Book Review (July 8):10+.

E. Barbara Phillips

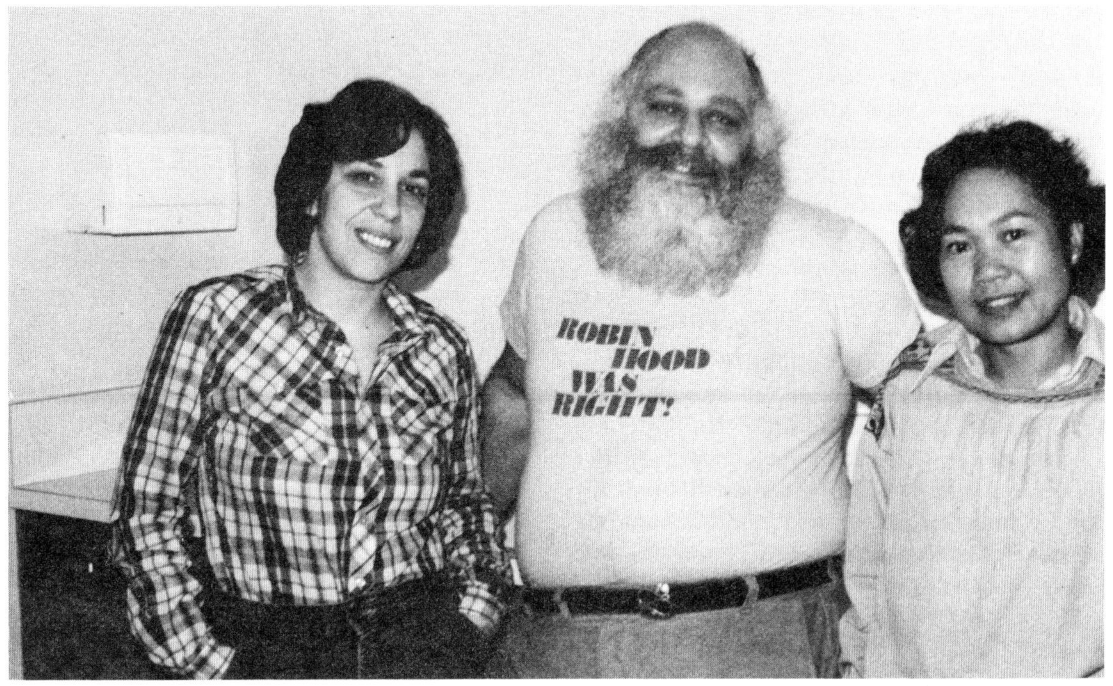

CHAPTER 17 Raising and Spending Money

"For sale: 4,058 pieces of land. Asking price: $451 million.

The seller is not a wealthy realtor but one of

the world's largest cities, Tokyo, which like many urban governments is strapped for money" (Malcolm, 1978:14).

Why are so many modern cities in financial trouble? In the U.S., should the federal government bail out nearly bankrupt cities? These are controversial issues.

This chapter provides a framework in which to consider many controversies about public funds. First, it outlines the U.S. system of local public finance—where money for local services comes from and where it goes. It discusses the varied ways local governments raise money, paying special attention to the property tax. Next, it examines a related question: What difference does it make which unit of government—federal, state, or local—provides a public service. Finally, it looks at the politics of the budgeting process and the outcomes of that process.

This chapter also reemphasizes the idea that cities exist within a complex, interdependent national system of political economy. This is important for understanding who gets what urban services, and who finally pays for them.

THE SYSTEM OF LOCAL PUBLIC FINANCE

The Multi-tiered Context

Recall that local governments in the U.S. include various political units: cities and other municipalities; counties; towns and townships; school districts; and nonschool special districts. Depending on local practice, the same service (such as the provision of water) may be performed by different types of local government. Further, a service performed locally in one state may be performed elsewhere at the state level. For these reasons, it is difficult to talk about typical revenue and spending patterns of local government.

Consider the case of three cities in New York State: Mt. Vernon, Syracuse, and New York City. If we look only at their budgets, we won't get a good idea of what public services their residents receive. True, all three cities provide police and fire protection. (None build major urban roads, for that is a New York State function.) But what about public education? Here one would be terribly misled by examining city expenditures only. For instance, in 1974–1975 Syracuse spent about 39 percent of its budget on education, while Mt. Vernon spent nothing. This does not mean that Mt. Vernon's public schools weren't operating. It does mean that education in Westchester County, where Mt. Vernon is located, is a county—not a city—function. In fact, Westchester County spent about 44 percent of its budget on education in 1974–1975 (U.S. Bureau of the Census, 1978:335).

Even these figures don't tell the whole story because funds for local education, welfare, and a host of other services also come from the state and federal governments. In other words, the total package of public services received by a city's residents comes from local, state, and federal sources. A complex, multi-tiered governmental system collects revenue, provides public services, and returns some money for local use.

Why is it important which governmental unit pays for what as long as city residents get the public services they want? The answer to that question seems obvious. It is not. The explanation requires a more indepth understanding of how a tax system works. Let us begin by looking at different parts of the local fiscal system.

WHERE LOCAL GOVERNMENT REVENUE ORIGINATES: (1) OWN SOURCE REVENUE

Generally, when statistics on urban public finance are presented by government spokes-

Table 17-1 City Government Finances

	Mt. Vernon	*New York City*	*Syracuse*
Total Revenue (mil.)	**$20.1**	**$12,828.1**	**$113.2**
Intergovernmental revenue			
Total (mil.)	$6.3	$6,763.7	$72.8
From Fed. Gov. (%)	21.5	10.0	24.1
Taxes			
Total (mil.)	$11.8	$4,852.7	$28.1
Property			
Total (%)	83.0	54.9	95.2
Per capita	$139.0	$348.0	$145.0
Sales & gross receipts (%)	13.3	24.6	—
Total Expenditure (mil.)	**$21.8**	**$11,641.3**	**$102.3**
Per capita (excl. capital outlay)	$283.0	$1,330.0	$431.0
Education (%)	—	23.4	38.8
Highways (%)	4.9	1.7	2.6
Public welfare (%)	—	24.8	—
Police & fire protection (%)	22.6	6.7	16.4
Sanitation & sewerage (%)	6.3	5.0	2.8

SOURCE: U.S. Bureau of the Census, *County and City Data Book 1977* (Washington, D.C.: U.S. Government Printing Office, May 1978), p. 725.

persons, they are based on the category "all local government expenditures." These include expenditures by cities and other municipalities, counties, towns and townships, school districts, and nonschool special districts. We use this category here to refer to "local government revenue."

Fig. 17-1 indicates the sources of local government revenue. Using 74 major SMSAs as a data base, the pie chart shows that in 1975–1976, more than one-half (54.8 percent) came from **own source revenue**—that is, money raised directly by local governments, primarily in the form of taxes and charges. The remainder (45.2 percent) came from **intergovernmental transfers**—that is, revenue raised by another level of government (state or federal) and returned to local governments.

Types of Own Source Revenue

The local **property tax** (an annual tax on land and buildings based on their assessed monetary value) accounts for the biggest share of own source local government revenue. As Fig. 17-1 shows, in the sample of 74 major SMSAs, it accounts for more than two-thirds of the revenue raised directly by local governments. Because of its vital importance, we shall return to the property tax in detail.

First, let us look at where the rest of local government own source revenue comes from. There are four other sources:

1. **User charges**—direct charges paid by the users of publicly provided services. Examples include bridge tolls, admission fees to the zoo, and metered parking.

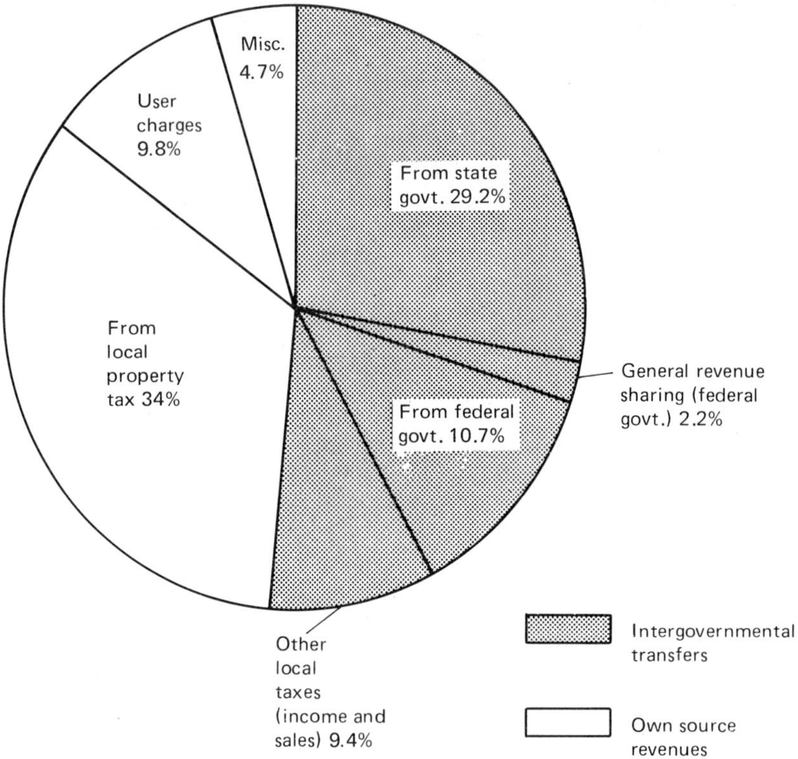

Fig. 17-1 GENERAL REVENUE SOURCES FOR LOCAL GOVERNMENTS IN 74 MAJOR SMSAs, 1975–76. (Adapted from U.S. Bureau of the Census, *Local Government Finances in Selected Metropolitan Counties: 1975–1976* [Washington, D.C: U.S. Government Printing Office, 1977], p. 7)

Virtually all local governments have some user charges, and their importance as a local government revenue source is increasing.

2. Local **sales tax**—taxes which are paid by a buyer at the time of purchase and which go to the local government. Cities in few states use sales taxes for raising revenue. However, in states where they are used (e.g., California and Illinois), sales taxes represent an important fiscal resource for local governments. (For state government, sales taxes are the main revenue source.)
3. Local **income tax**—taxes based on earned income which are paid by local individuals or corporations (not commuters) to local government. The income tax is a direct tax based on the ability-to-pay principle whereby the larger proportional tax burden is placed on individuals or firms whose capacity to pay is greater (i.e., it is progressive, not regressive). Income taxes are a small but growing source of local government revenue. In a few states, notably Ohio and Pennsylvania, they constitute an important local government revenue source. (For the federal government, income taxes are the main revenue source.)

4. Miscellaneous sources—such disparate taxes as Las Vegas's gambling tax and San Francisco's hotel tax.

Note that Fig. 17-1 gives only a general overview of local government revenue sources. It cannot give a view of typical tax-raising methods because there is no such thing. We can see this by referring back to Table 17-1. Syracuse is almost totally dependent on the property tax to raise own source revenue (95.2 percent), while New York City is not. Both Mt. Vernon and Syracuse receive over 20 percent of their total budget from intergovernmental transfers from the federal government; New York City receives less than 10 percent of its revenue from such transfers.

Competition among Jurisdictions for Own Source Revenue

Units of local government often compete for tax dollars, frequently in a highly destructive way. The reason involves the property tax and local government dependence on it for raising revenue.

Cities want a strong **tax base**—that is, valuable real property (land and structures, both residential and commercial) subject to a city's taxing power. The higher the **assessed value** (the amount at which property is valued for tax purposes) of taxable real property, the stronger the tax base is.

A strong tax base is a relative matter. There is no dollar amount over or under which a tax base can be considered weak or strong. Rather, a tax base is considered strong if it can provide revenue for public services that residents need or want (e.g., schooling, fire and police protection). For example, City A has a strong tax base, and City B has a weak tax base. Given the same demand by city residents for local services, City A will be able to provide more desired services and/or keep the **tax rate** (the ratio of the tax to the tax base) low. In contrast, City B must provide fewer services, have higher tax rates, or both.

This raises the question of what homeowners and businesses consider a reasonable tax burden. And it leads to the issue of why governments compete for property tax revenue.

Many homeowners, faced with an ever-mounting annual tax bill as their assessed valuation rises with inflation, may grumble about what they consider an unreasonable tax burden. They may join tax revolts or move to jurisdictions where the tax burden is lighter. Businesses may relocate to jurisdictions where they pay less tax for the same services.

Several points concerning homeowners' grumbles and local business property taxes should be noted. First, despite what homeowners often believe, the average residence does not usually pay its own way. That is, the average homeowner's property tax pays only a portion of what it costs to provide public services for that dwelling and those who live in it.

Second, business and commercial properties often pay *more* than their own way. "Clean" industry, particularly research and development activities, is especially attractive to localities because it generates relatively high tax revenue and requires relatively few public services. But there is an important qualification here. Business and commercial properties often pay more than their own way *if* they pay their full share. According to citizen advocate Ralph Nader's estimates (1971:16), local taxpayers subsidize commercial-industrial property owners, real estate developers, and mineral companies in the amount of at least $7 billion annually because local governments allow them to evade property taxes. For example, for tax purposes,

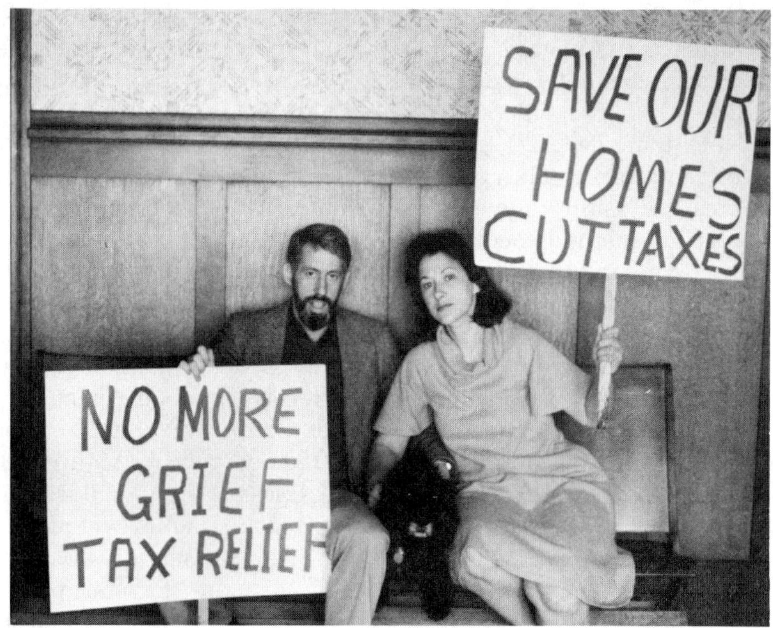

Fig. 17-2 GRUMBLING AND OTHER RESPONSES. Faced with higher annual tax bills, some taxpayers grumble or organize tax revolts. Others, including corporations, move to jurisdictions where the tax burden is lighter. (Arlene Peterson)

New York City assesses real estate at only a portion of its market value. Hence, Manhattan's third largest real estate owner in the early 1970s, Consolidated Edison, paid property tax on the appraised value of $950.5 million rather than the market value of $1,638.5 billion (*Forbes Magazine*, 1971:25).

Nader claims that large corporations withhold proper payments to governments and apply pressure on governments to "unjustifiably transfer public funds and privileges to corporate control" (1971:16). Calling this "corporate socialism," Nader says that Gary, Indiana—a U.S. Steel town—exemplifies how it works. In the 1960–1970 period, U.S. Steel's property tax assessment rose only $10 million, although capital improvements worth $1.2 billion were installed. Moreover, Nader (1971:16) says, city officials are refused permission to inspect U.S. Steel's books, and the company disobeys city law by refusing to apply for building permits, for that would make public the size of its taxable investment.

What happens if local government officials dare to enforce or even raise property taxes on corporate business and industry? Often there is the risk of immediate retaliation. Industry's most effective weapon is the threat to move elsewhere if tax breaks or subsidies are not granted or continued. This threat can serve as the rationale to keep business and industry's tax burden comparatively low.

Why are taxes lower in some local political units than others? This involves the "fit" between the strength of the tax base and the services paid for from that tax base. Within a single SMSA, for example, tax burdens are generally heavier in central cities than elsewhere. This is because there is a better fit between *demands* for public services and *fiscal resources* to meet those demands in communities outside central cities. Given two communities of the same population size, the community with highly valued industrial and residential property can provide residents with higher levels of public services with lower taxes than the community with less valuable property.

This brings us back to the issue of why local governments compete for property tax revenue. Local governments want to keep tax burdens for residents as low as possible. Thus, they compete to strengthen their tax base. A city may try to lure industry into the community by offering tax breaks or zoning variances. Frequently these efforts result in "beggar thy neighbor" outcomes. Irvine, California, provides a classic example. Located in southern California, Irvine provided numerous sites for commercial-industrial development but few for houses as it expanded in the 1960s. By attracting highly valued taxable industries and keeping its tax base strong, the city keeps the property tax rates for its relatively few homeowners low. The tax rate for commerce and industry also remains low. This development strategy, however, imposes negative externalities on Irvine's neighbors. Neighboring jurisdictions end up paying for Irvine workers' public services (such as schooling for its children) because the workers live mainly in these other jurisdictions (which enjoy none of Irvine's tax advantages). However, under the settlement order of a recent lawsuit, Irvine has promised to permit more housing construction in the future.

Central City versus Suburban Tax Bases

In general, central cities have higher tax rates than their surrounding communities. Faced with declining tax bases and escalating demand for services, central cities set higher tax rates than suburbs, which have fewer service demands and stronger tax bases. Thus, within SMSAs, taxes for similar local services or the level of local services (e.g., efficient or inefficient fire protection, regular or irregular garbage pickups) depend significantly on the community's tax base.

The case of the Milwaukee, Wisconsin, SMSA is illustrative. In the mid-1960s, the tax rate in the central city of Milwaukee was dramatically higher than the rate in Milwaukee's suburbs, whether of the industrial, mixed, or residential variety. Predictably, the tax rates for Milwaukee's industrial suburbs were lowest, for these suburbs had strong tax bases and few residents. Hence, Milwaukee residents paid a local tax rate of 13.8 mills, while residents of industrial suburbs paid a rate of 1.7 mills (Riew, 1970).

One result of the disparity between tax bases in central cities and their suburbs as well as disparities among suburban communites is this: Within SMSAs, funds spent on education differ widely from community to community. In 1976 the California Supreme Court reacted to these disparities in its landmark, nationally important decision, *Serano* v. *Priest*. This decision held that the property tax system of financing public education violated the equal protection guarantees of the state constitution. The court held that the amount of money available for a child's education should not depend on the amount of taxable real property located in his or her community. The court ordered the state legislature to devise a new system of financing public education.

Are Central Cities Bankrupt?

NEW YORK CITY NEARS BANKRUPTCY . . . CLEVELAND IN SERIOUS FINANCIAL TROUBLE . . . Banner headlines like these have become all too common in recent years. But what does it mean to say that a city is broke? What leads to such a fiscal crisis, and how many cities really face it?

A city may be unable to pay its bills for one or both of the following reasons: (1) *costs increase* (pay increases for public employees, higher prices for supplies) and/or (2) *revenues*

Fig. 17-3 CENTRAL CITY SCENE. (Ben Achtenberg)

decline (either in absolute terms or in relation to need). On the cost side, changes in demographic and physical conditions could mean increased expense. For instance, the number of people needing a local service such as a day-care center may increase. Or demands on a city for new services (e.g., the establishment of a rape prevention service) may be made. On the revenue side, the city may suffer from a declining tax base or a general economic slump. Its legal powers to raise revenue may be curtailed, perhaps under a Proposition 13–type constitutional amendment.

Before a city is pronounced broke and near bankruptcy, both the cost and revenue sides must be examined closely. Even then, of course, observers may not agree on the nature of the problem or how to solve it. This is clarified by a case study of one older Frostbelt city, New York City.

Case Study: New York City

Some observers of the American metropolis point to an urban renaissance starting in the late 1970s. They reason that the more gas prices go up, the more real estate values in central cities will climb, the more city buildings will be restored, and the more CBDs will expand. But others say that most cities are still losing substantial numbers of people, and the cycle will probably continue.

We can't predict with certainty what will happen. But we can see what did happen to the nation's largest city in the period 1950–1977. According to Sternlieb and Hughes (1977), New York City's economy stagnated, perhaps even declined in that period. The gradual worsening of the city's economic situation reflects changes in population and jobs. Most importantly in demographic terms, there was a mass exodus of middle-class whites and an influx of minority persons, often poor and in need of a host of public services. For instance, between 1966 and 1976, public assistance rolls nearly doubled, from 530,000 to 1,000,000 persons. In terms of employment, New York City lost over 73,000 jobs in manufacturing, wholesaling, and retailing alone each year in the 1950–1977 period. For example, the garment industry—famous Seventh Avenue, where thousands of European immigrants first found jobs at the turn of the century—lost about 12,000 jobs each year from 1950 to 1977. These jobs moved to other parts of the country or to foreign countries. Even classically urban kinds of work involving face-to-face communication (finance, insurance, real estate) declined, reflecting a movement of business to the suburbs or out of the SMSA entirely.

In short, New York City faced an unenviable task in the 1970s: providing increased public services, at higher cost, to increasing numbers of poor and poorly trained workers at the very time when its economy was declining. It is clear that two out of three determinants of a city's economic health—the condition of its labor market and its' tax base—were ailing in the Big Apple. Under these conditions, New York City's mayor looked to Herbert Gans's third factor for help—the effectiveness of state and federal support programs; the mayor asked for bailout money. Also, new taxes were levied to meet the service challenge. With the new taxes, including a city income tax, city revenues grew slowly in the 1970s, but expenditures rose still more rapidly. With this mismatch of high demand for services and less ability to pay for them, New York City was placed in a financial bind.

How much more per capita New York City spent in the mid-1970s than a nearby suburban community (Mt. Vernon) and a typical central city in the same state (Syracuse) is evident from Table 17-1. Note that New York City spent over four times more per capita than its suburban neighbor and three times more per capita than Syracuse.

By the mid-1970s, New York City had taken some drastic measures to deal with the financial crunch (e.g., diverting money from its capital expenditures budget to pay for day-to-day operating expenses). Eventually, the city's financial affairs were placed under the direction of a quasi-public institution, the Municipal Assistance Corporation (called "Big MAC"), which pursued a program of tough fiscal management and austerity.

Most students of New York City's fiscal situation in the 1970s agree on one essential point: The city's tax base decreased while city expenditures increased. But agreement ends there. In fact, urbanists' collected wisdom about New York City's financial situation provides a classic example of our oft-repeated maxim: What you see depends on how you look at it. Here is a sampling of ideological judgments:

Conservatives: The root of New York City's fiscal problem is the rise in expenditures. Economist Milton Friedman suggested that the city "go bankrupt. That will make it impossible for New York City in the future to borrow any money and force it to live within its budget." Friedman (in Shenker, [1975] 1977:7) added that "The only other alternative is the obvious one—tighten its belt, pay off its debt, live within its means and become an honest city again."

Liberals: The root of the problem is the decrease in revenue sources. As economist John Kenneth Galbraith (in Shenker, [1975] 1977:5) put it, "no problem associated with New York City could not be solved by providing more money."

Fig. 17-4 MOBILITY OF CAPITAL. Radicals view the flight of private capital as one source of the fiscal crisis affecting cities. (Richard Hedman)

Radicals: The root of New York City's fiscal problem is neither the rise in expenditures nor the decrease in revenue sources. Rather, the Big Apple's fiscal crisis is linked to large-scale economic trends associated with contemporary capitalism, particularly the flight of private capital to wherever it can bring the highest rate of return (including overseas). Radicals argue that New York City's government can't deal effectively with powerful local interests and the corporate political economy because "government is weaker than the corporate institutions purportedly subordinate to it. This is the politics of capitalism" (Hacker, 1965:11).

Fiscal Crisis Theory: O'Connor

As just noted, radicals don't see New York City's financial crunch as a temporary aberration. Nor do they think it can be solved either by more money (liberal solution) or belt tightening (conservative solution). Instead, radicals argue that the term "urban fiscal crisis" is misleading, for fiscal crisis at the urban level is merely a symptom of systemwide economic crisis under advanced capitalism.

Radical political economist James O'Connor has constructed a provocative theory that attempts to explain why capitalist countries like the United States are likely to be caught in a financial squeeze. In *The Fiscal Crisis of the State* (1973), O'Connor argues that the United States has moved into a new economic phase: advanced monopoly capitalism. He claims that in this phase of late capitalism, the state socializes more and more capital costs among its citizens but allows the social surplus (including profits) to be privately appropriated. This "socialization of costs and the private appropriation of profits," O'Connor (1973:9) argues, "creates a fiscal crisis, or 'structural gap,' between state expenditures and state revenues." O'Connor predicts continuing fiscal crisis in the capitalist state because the government needs to maintain and expand vital services in order to seem legitimate but will be unable to finance the services.

Do Suburbs Exploit Central Cities?

O'Connor implies that the fiscal crisis of the cities can never be solved by giving them more money or letting the market decide who gets what services. That is a very controversial idea. So is his statement that "tax finance is (and always has been) a form of economic exploitation" (1973:203), reflecting inequities in the class structure.

A further explanation of the fiscal plight of U.S. cities suggests another form of exploitation: that of cities by their surrounding metropolitan areas. Some urbanists claim that cities are in bad financial shape because their surrounding suburbs take unfair advantage of them. These observers point out that suburbanites use city streets, public buildings, and other urban amenities without paying taxes for them. John Kenneth Galbraith expresses this view in no uncertain terms:

> It's outrageous that the development of the metropolitan community has been organized with escape hatches that allow people to enjoy the proximity of the city while not paying their share of the taxes. (in Shenker, [1975] 1977)

Galbraith concludes colorfully, "Fiscal funkholes are what the suburbs are."

Other observers disagree, saying that suburbanites do contribute to the central city's economy. In particular, suburban residents provide a skilled work force and purchasing power for city business and industry.

If Galbraith is right, what should be done to stop the exploitation of central cities by their suburbs? One suggested remedy is commuter taxes. Another is the creation of metropolitanwide government. Predictably, neither of these remedies has been popular with suburbanites. Other proposed remedies focus on the transfer of tax functions from local government to regional or higher levels.

To conclude: Whether or not suburbs are "fiscal funkholes," as Galbraith claims, is a matter of debate. However, there is broad agreement that the match between fiscal resources and service demands within a metropolitan area is inequitable. This mismatch is evident in the New York City metropolitan area. Metropolitan tax sharing, adopted by Minneapolis–St. Paul, is one of many proposals to deal with fiscal equity within SMSAs.

WHERE LOCAL GOVERNMENT REVENUE ORIGINATES: (2) FISCAL FEDERALISM

Chief Justice Oliver Wendell Holmes once remarked that taxes are the price of civilization. If so, all levels of government in the U.S. federal system compete to civilize us. Local, state, and federal governments all collect taxes from their constituents. Each level places primary emphasis on different revenue sources, but each also tends to use sources employed by other competing levels of government.

The three-tiered system of revenue collection and distribution in the U.S. federal system is called **fiscal federalism.** Fig. 17-5 shows the amounts and sources of revenue collected at each level of this fiscal system for one year, 1975–1976.

Competition for Tax Dollars among Levels of Government

Local, state, and federal governments each rely primarily on one revenue source. The federal government depends most heavily on the income tax. As Fig. 17-5 illustrates, individual and corporate income taxes accounted for 85.9 percent of federal revenue in 1975–1976. State governments rely most heavily on sales and excise taxes. (Essentially, an **excise tax** is a sales tax imposed on selected goods such as liquor and cigarettes.)

FEDERAL GOVERNMENT ($323.5 billion)

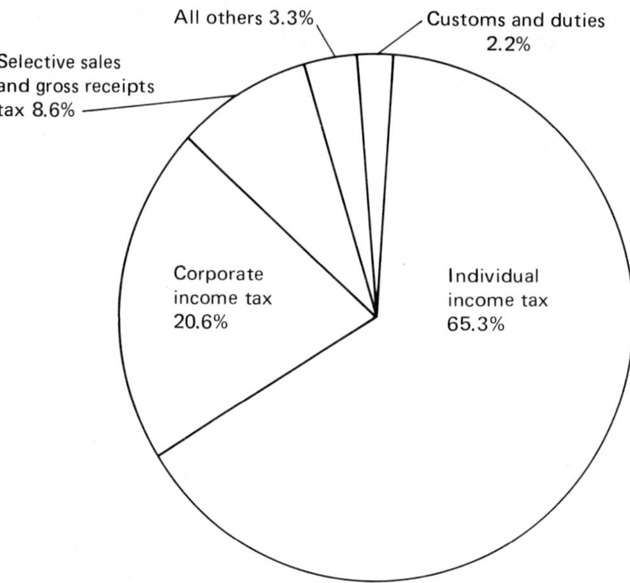

STATE GOVERNMENT ($140.5 billion)

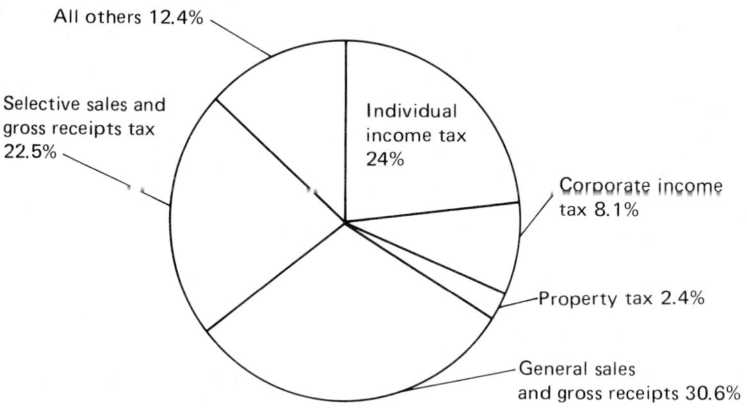

LOCAL GOVERNMENT ($108.6 billion)

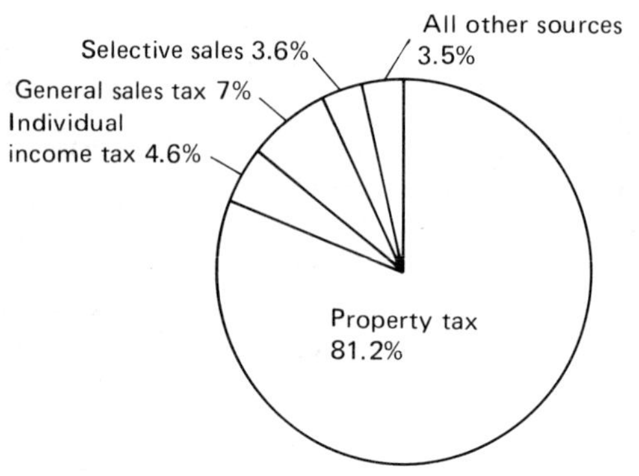

Local governments rely very heavily on the property tax for own source revenue. In 1975–1976, 81.2 percent of their own source revenue came from this source.

It is clear from Fig. 17-5 that the federal government's tax pie—and tax bite—is the largest. In 1975–1976, the federal government raised more than twice as much tax revenue as all the states combined and almost four times as much as all local governments.

Does it matter which level of government takes the biggest tax share? Does it matter which level of government raises and spends money, as long as taxpayers get the public services they want? Yes, very much. Both the sources used to raise money and the level at which taxes are levied have profound consequences. Some consequences are easier to understand than others. We'll start with the easy-to-understand effects and then return to those requiring some background in economic concepts.

First, taxes are limited by the ability to pay. Thus, when one level of government takes money from a taxpayer, other levels must take a smaller share—unless (1) the total amount of tax is increased and/or (2) tax funds are redistributed to other levels of government. Needless to say, increasing the total tax amount is not a popular idea.

Secondly, and a bit more complicated, is the issue of intergovernmental transfers. The federal government gives back to states and local governments some revenue that it collects. Similarly, states return some revenue to local governments. When all these transfers are netted out, the extreme differences between the size of the federal, state, and local tax pies are diminished. In this redistribution process, local government is the biggest winner.

Fig. 17-5 AMOUNTS AND SOURCES OF OWN SOURCE REVENUE: FEDERAL, STATE, AND LOCAL GOVERNMENTS, 1975–1976. (U.S. Bureau of the Census, *Governmental Finances in 1976* [Washington, D.C.: U.S. Government Printing Office, 1977], p. 4)

State-Local Intergovernmental Transfers

Local governments receive more than one-third of their total budget from their state governments. As Fig. 17-6 shows, the largest share of state transfers goes to education and welfare. Since school districts are legally separate entities in most communities, the bulk of the funding in one selected year, 1972, went directly to them, not to cities.

Generally, funds are transferred from state to local governments on the basis of objective formulas. In the case of education, funding for local school districts is usually based on complicated formulas that take into account such factors as the average number of children in daily attendance and the number of children with special educational needs.

Federal-State and Federal-Local Transfers

The federal government, through its various agencies, transfers revenue to both state and local governments. What enables the federal government to redistribute funds to lower levels? Primarily, revenue from the federal personal income tax. Since it was authorized in 1913, the income tax has become the single largest revenue producer for the nation.

In recent years, there has been a dramatic increase in federal aid to state and local governments. This increase, as well as the general pattern of federal aid, is charted in Fig. 17-7.

Federal funds flow to state and local governments in three different forms: (1) categorical grants, (2) block grants, and (3) general revenue sharing. Categorical grants are the most strictly limited. They are given for a narrow, specified category of activity such as urban park acquisition. Block grants

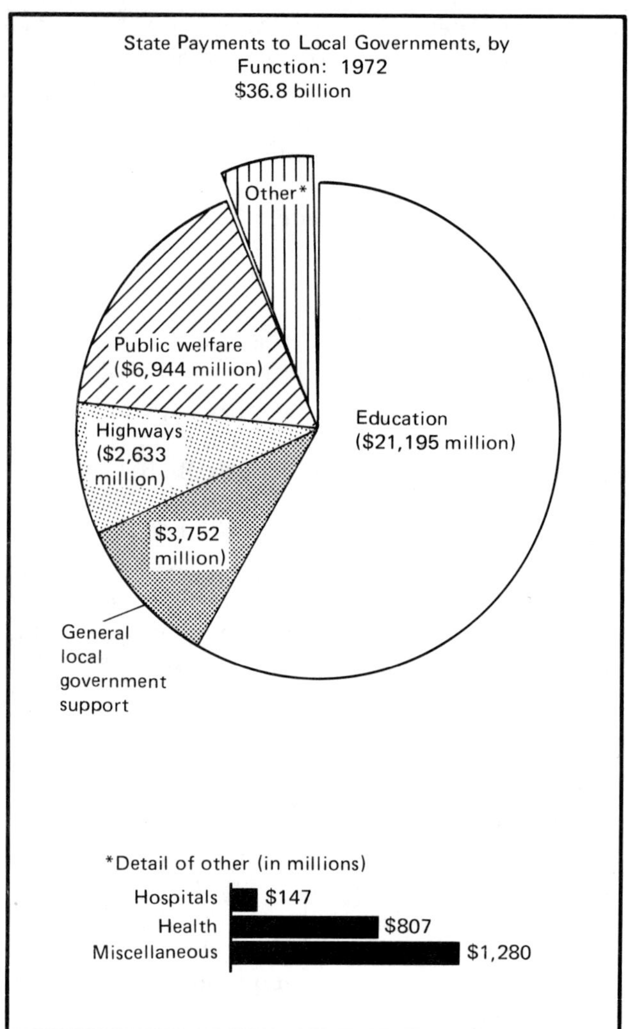

Fig. 17-6 STATE PAYMENTS TO LOCAL GOVERNMENT BY FUNCTION, 1972. (U.S. Bureau of the Census, *Census of Governments, 1972,* Vol. 6, No. 3 [Washington, D.C.: U.S. Government Printing Office, 1977], p. 7)

are given for a general category of activity such as community development or law enforcement. General revenue sharing funds have the fewest limitations. State and local governments can use them to supplement their own source revenue as they see fit.

WHY THE METHOD OF RAISING REVENUE IS IMPORTANT

Why is the method of raising revenue important? This is a complicated issue. Before addressing it, some economic background is useful. Thus, we begin with three relevant concepts: tax incidence, progressivity, and elasticity.

Tax Incidence

The **incidence** of a tax refers to who finally pays it. At first, this seems simple. The taxpayer sending a check to the Internal Revenue Service by April 15 pays the federal income tax; the purchaser laying out an extra four, five, or more cents on the dollar pays the sales tax; and the property owner remitting money to local government bears the burden of the property tax. Simple, but not necessarily so. Those who ultimately pay the tax may not be the same persons who pay it directly. For instance, if a jurisdiction raises the property tax rate, apartment building owners there must pay higher taxes. The incidence of the tax *appears* to fall on these building owners. However, the owners may simply pass on the increases to their tenants by raising the rent.

Measuring shifts in tax incidence raises difficult empirical and conceptual problems. While economists agree that it should be done, they disagree on how it can best be accomplished.

Progressivity

Once it has been established who really pays a tax (that is, tax incidence), another question arises: Is the tax progressive or regressive? A **progressive tax** is one that takes a larger and larger percentage of income as one moves up the income ladder. In other words, it affects the affluent more than the poor. Thus, a progressive income tax might take 2 percent from the person earning $5,000 annually, 10 percent from the person earning $12,000 and 25 percent from the person earning $30,000.

Fig. 17-7 THE GROWTH OF FEDERAL AID TO STATE AND LOCAL GOVERNMENTS, 1969–1979. (U.S. Office of Management and Budget [OMB], *Special Analyses of the Budget of the United States, Fiscal Year 1979* [Washington, D.C.: U.S. Government Printing Office, 1978], p. 175)

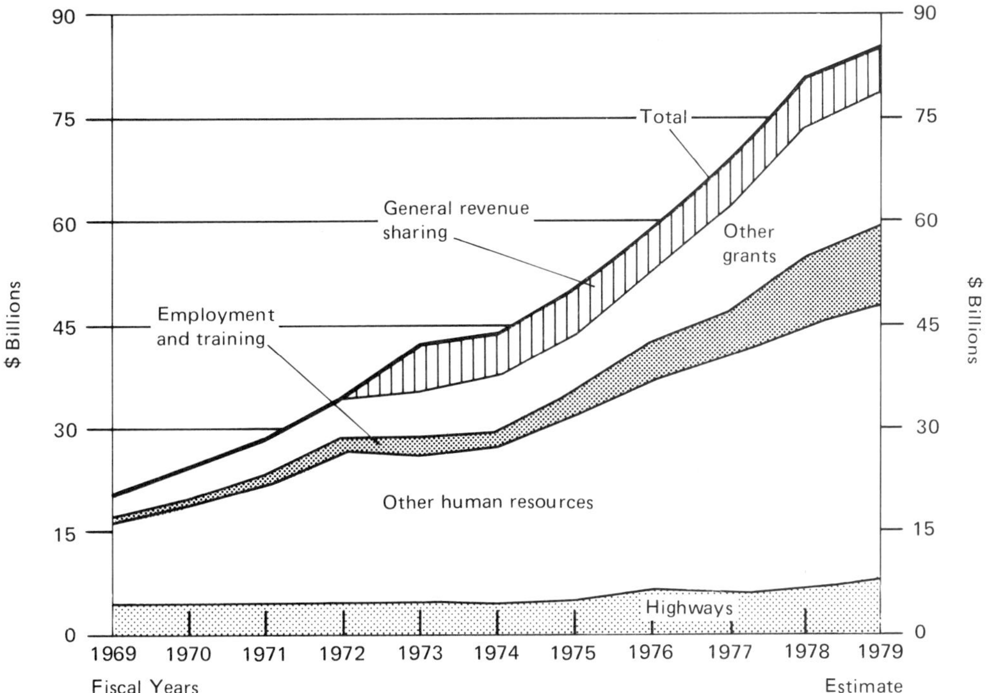

A **regressive tax** works the opposite way; its incidence falls more heavily on lower-income than higher-income persons. For instance, whether a person earns $3,000 or $30,000 a year, the tax on a pack of cigarettes or a pair of shoes is the same.

There is a great deal of ideologically based debate on tax progressivity. Radicals tend to dispute the alleged progressivity of many taxes, particularly the corporate income tax. They claim that a considerable part of the tax is passed on to lower-income people via higher prices. Further, radicals argue that the present tax system is largely an indirect subsidy to corporations and other privileged groups. Liberals, on the other hand, see some taxes as progressive, and progressive taxes have long been a mainstay of their general reform program. Usually liberals point to the federal personal income tax as "the big gun of the equalizer"—that is, the major tool for the redistribution of resources from the more to the less affluent. Conservatives take another tack. Generally they fear that taxes which are too steeply progressive (particularly corporate and personal income taxes) will dampen people's incentive to take risks, slow economic growth, and curb the profit motive.

Elasticity

Elasticity refers to the ability of tax revenue to grow as an economy expands or shrinks. If revenue from a tax grows more rapidly than income, the tax is considered elastic. If revenue from a tax grows more slowly than income, the tax is considered inelastic.

Economists have a formula for calculating elasticity. Tax elasticity is expressed as a coefficient by dividing a percentage change in tax revenue by a percentage change in income. For example, if, in a given year, personal income in the United States increased 20 percent and revenue from the tax on that personal income increased 40 percent, a tax elasticity coefficient would be calculated as follows:

$$\frac{40\% \text{ (change in revenue from personal income tax)}}{20\% \text{ (change in personal income during the same period)}} = 2$$

In this example, the tax "stretched" more rapidly than the income. Thus, it has a high coefficient of elasticity. However, when tax revenues grow more slowly than income (i.e., the coefficient is less than 1), the tax is considered inelastic. In other words, the more elastic a tax source, the more revenue it will generate as the economy expands; the more inelastic a tax source, the less revenue it will generate in an expanding economy.

It is common sense that governments favor elastic taxes over inelastic ones in times of economic growth. Likewise, in periods of no growth or recession, an inelastic tax is often preferred because it continues to yield almost as much revenue despite general economic decline.

Rethinking the Property Tax

With the concepts of tax incidence, progressivity and elasticity in mind, let us return to the question at hand: Why is the revenue source important? We begin by analyzing the bulwark of local public finance—the property tax—and then we consider other taxes in the intergovernmental system.

To investigate the true incidence of the property tax, one must examine the extent to which the original taxpayers (persons and firms) later shift its burden to others. Some economists (e.g., Netzer, 1966) insist that the burden of the property tax falls on consumers of property—owners and renters. For instance, a homeowner and her two children live alone in a house; there is no one to whom she can pass on the burden of the property tax. But owners of rental property are in a somewhat different position. They can shift some of the tax incidence to renters. Thus, in this view, the property tax can be seen as a tax on the consumption of shelter with an incidence falling on landowners, homeowners, and renters. Since the rich pay a smaller percentage of their income for shelter than do the poor, the property tax appears quite regressive. Other economists do not agree. Indeed, some (e.g., Aaron, 1974) believe that the property tax is progressive. This debate continues, awaiting methodological refinements for tracing the shifts in tax incidence. Meanwhile, two highly respected economists say that the property tax is somewhat regressive but less so than previously believed (Musgrave and Musgrave, 1976:430–39).

The next question about the property tax is this: How elastic is it? The answer depends on two factors, one economic and the other essentially political: (1) the increase in property value compared to increases in the Gross National Product (GNP) and (2) the amount of that increase that community residents want to spend on taxes.

In economic terms, the value of taxable property for the first half of this century has grown more slowly than the GNP, making the property tax inelastic. However, since World War II it has grown slightly more rapidly than the GNP, making the property tax modestly elastic in recent years. Yet, there is great variation. Land in economic growth areas, such as many Sunbelt cities, has provided an elastic tax base, while real property in distressed central cities has generally provided an inelastic tax base.

In political terms, the elasticity of property tax revenue reflects local voters' preferences and pressures. At least in theory, local government expenditure patterns are tied to constituents' demands for services. Local governments decide how much own source revenue they *need* to collect after they determine how much they will receive from other revenue sources, including general revenue sharing.

Property tax rates vary widely from one jurisdiction to another. This variation reflects value differences as well as differences in the strength of the tax base among communities. Some communities want—and are willing to tax themselves for—higher levels of service.

The last question about the property tax is this: How does it compare to the prime money raisers for state and federal goverments in terms of tax incidence, progressivity, and elasticity? The answers here have broad implications for public policy.

To answer this question, it is necessary to compare the property tax to state and federal taxes. Throughout the nation, state taxes are regressive. Sales and excise taxes, which yield about two-thirds of state revenue, are largely responsible for this regressivity. Available data point to the conclusion that lower-income people pay the heaviest state taxes (see Herriott and Miller, 1971).

As for federal tax policies, the single largest revenue producer, the federal personal income tax, is elastic. Many liberals (e.g., Pechman and Okner, 1974) claim that the overall distribution of federal taxes is substantially progressive. Others are not so sure. A pioneering study in the concentration of wealth in America concludes that the degree of progressivity in personal income tax rates has not been steep enough to change substantially the shares of income received by different income groups (Lampman, 1962). Historian Gabriel Kolko ([1962]) 1971) goes further. He claims that between 1910 and 1959, the income share of the lowest income-fifth (the bottom 20 percent of the population in terms of income) actually *declined.* That is, the liberals' hope—the federal income tax—has not been the "big gun of the equalizer." It has not worked to redistribute income to the poorest citizens.

Apart from the federal income tax, the only other substantial tax thought to have a progressive effect is the corporate income tax. Yet, especially in periods of inflation, corporations pass on much of this tax to consumers (Lampman, 1962).

To conclude: Most scholars find that government tax policies at local, state, and federal levels have not served to change the relative distribution of income and wealth in the United States over the past decades. In part, this is due to regressive state-local taxes (although there is debate over the regressivity of the property tax). Further, state-local taxes are relatively inelastic compared to federal income taxes. One implication here concerns the relative growth of different levels of government. Particularly in periods of economic growth, the federal level can be expected to expand its revenue bases faster than state-local levels. This fact is of prime concern to those who fear that more and more functions will be transferred from lower to higher levels of government.

Another implication concerns government's role in the redistribution of income from the affluent to the poor. This ideologically loaded issue has very practical consequences. Liberal economists stress government's legitimate function in correcting the market distribution of income. Critics argue that this redistribution has not really happened. Conservatives argue that it should not happen; that is, government does not have the legitimate role of correcting the market distribution of income. Radicals claim that the tax system, particularly the state-local system, ensures that the poor stay poor and the rich remain rich; conservatives argue that the government should not intervene to make the rich poorer; and liberals think government should intervene but don't agree on how effective tax policy has been in achieving income redistribution.

Finally, we return to our original questions: What difference does it make which revenue source is used? What difference does it make which level of government—national, state, or local—raises it? By now, the answers should seem complex, entangled with a host of political, socioeconomic, and moral concerns. And the answers *are* complex.

Cities exist within an interdependent system, buffeted by macro-level forces beyond their control. These include the movement of people and industry to more profitable areas and structural changes in the economy. Yet cities must deal with many of these large-scale forces armed only with meager weapons, particularly meager in comparison with federal resources. Many older central cities, including New York City, have tackled what are essentially national problems, such as poverty, by attempting to redistribute income from richer to poorer individuals via an extensive welfare system and low-cost university education. However, over time, these city policies have helped to drive away middle-income people and businesses that feel overburdened by taxes. This exodus reduces the city's inelastic own source tax base even more. Attempts to raise city taxes to even higher levels only hasten the retreat of more people and industry. And so the cycle goes. What we are suggesting here is that the fiscal crisis of the cities is best understood in a national framework.

ALLOCATING THE PUBLIC BUDGET

Once tax revenue wends its tortuous way to the public coffers, a drama unfolds: the annual ritual of allocating the budget. This process can be as complex as the mating ceremony of the giant elephant seal. To make the behind-the-scenes budgetary process more comprehensible, we turn to studies by scholars of urban public finance, public budgeting, political science, and policy analysis.

Public Budgeting: A Basic Vocabulary

Public budgeting may elicit groans or yawns. It does sound rather dry. Generally, it is not reported in the news media because it is a complex story to tell, because it happens behind closed doors (and thus is difficult to show on TV), and because it is what *New York Times* columnist William Safire calls a MEGO (My Eyes Glaze Over)—a bore to audiences. As a result, local news media give broad coverage to what mayors, county legislators, and other elected public officials do or say publicly, but they offer little reportage on the bureaucratic politics of public budgeting. This is unfortunate for citizens because budget making is a political process that can reveal a great deal about local priorities and power relations.

In fact, the core of local politics—who gets what from the public purse—is hammered out in the budgetary process. Will city revenue be used for day-care centers or a rape prevention center? Will money be spent to spruce up sidewalks in affluent residential neighborhoods, plant trees in the CBD, or add a police officer to the force? These are the kinds of issues addressed in the budgetary process. Clearly, the answers have great impact on local residents.

Before considering the budgetary process, the following terms are helpful: program budget, line-item budget, operating expenses, and capital expenditures. A **program budget** organizes information relating to expenditures by specific program areas. Thus, all expenses involved in running a fire department would be grouped and totaled under a program budget. Included would be such disparate items as capital expenditures (e.g., a new fire truck), personnel costs (firefighters' salaries), operating expenses (supplies, phones), and so on. A **line-item budget,** on the other hand, views each component of cost as a separate category, regardless of program. A city's line-item budget might group together capital expenditure costs for all agencies and so on. Another important distinction is between operating expenses and capital expenditures. **Operating expenses** include costs associated with the ongoing work of the city, primarily salaries and other personnel costs. **Capital expenditures** include such items as the purchase of new equipment and building construction.

What is the single most costly item in most local government line-item budgets? Operating expenses, overwhelmingly. Personnel costs account for nearly 80 percent of most local government budget outlays because local government is extremely labor-intensive.

The Politics of the Budgetary Process

We have already hinted that understanding the politics of budgeting is a key to understanding government. Aaron Wildavsky, a political scientist and public policy analyst, points out the reason in his influential book *The Politics of the Budgetary Process* (1974). According to Wildavsky (1974:2–5), a government budget "may be characterized as a series of goals with price tags attached. Since funds are limited . . . the budget becomes a mechanism for making choices among alternative expenditures. . . . If politics is regarded in part as a conflict over whose preferences shall prevail in the determination of . . . policy, then the budget records the

SPEAKING FOR TRANSPORTATION I WANT TO SAY WE WHOLEHEARTEDLY AGREE THAT RATIONAL PLANNING METHODS SHOULD BE APPLIED. YOU ALL KNOW OUR TRANSIT SYSTEM IS IN A STATE OF **ACUTE CRISIS!** WITHOUT NEW EQUIPMENT **NOW** WE WON'T BE ABLE TO OPERATE, IN FACT I HAVE HERE A RECENT REPORT

AHEM!

Fig. 17-8 LET US REASON TOGETHER. (© 1976 Richard Hedman)

outcomes of this struggle." He concludes that "in the most integral sense, the budget lies at the heart of the political process."

While Wildavsky analyzes the federal budgetary process, some of his insights are helpful in understanding local government budgeting as well. First, Wildavsky notes that budgeting is **incremental.** In other words, this year's budget is likely to be very much like last year's with small increments in various categories. This means that "the largest determining factor in this year's budget is last year's budget" (1974:13). Second, Wildavsky points out that much game playing is involved in budgeting. For instance, in deciding how much money to request, government agency bureaucrats pick up cues from legislative and/or executive officials and then devise plans to get as much money as they can reasonably expect. They may play it straight, presenting a budget request already cut to the bone. They may pad their request, anticipating budget cuts. Or they may include items favored by those who review the budget as their lowest priority so that the reviewers won't eliminate funds for the bureaucrats' real concerns. In addition, a public agency may try to build and use constituencies that independently put pressure on legislators and executive officials to fund their pet projects.

As Wildavsky describes it, the federal budgeting process is fragmented, incremental, and highly specialized. Reacting to the apparent irrationality of such a decisionmaking system, reformers in the 1960s called for changes in the budget preparation process. Subsequently, various reform measures (e.g., **zero-based budgeting**) were enacted at the federal level. All of them aimed to make the consequences of alternate spending policies clear and comparable on a cost basis. But Wildavsky thinks that any such efforts to bring rationality to budget making fly in the face of political exigencies and thus are doomed to failure.

Case Study: Oakland, California

Meanwhile, some of the ferment for budgetary reform reached local government. Various systems for greater rationality were instituted in many cities. But as one of Wildavsky's colleagues lamented while doing budget research, "I found myself working in the city of Oakland, California, where the total budget was small enough to have been a rounding error in the Department of Defense" (Meltsner, 1971:ix). In fact, Oakland's city manager discouraged a study of the city's budget, saying that "there was no budget problem because there was no money!" All the elaborate systems analysis techniques could not create something from nothing, especially money.

Oakland's case confirms the incremental nature of local government budgeting. Each year, only marginal adjustments are made in the budget. There is little flexibility in the budget because resources are scarce and commitments to personnel are almost binding.

As in most city budgets, the largest single amount of money in Oakland (70 percent) goes to personnel salaries. Modest annual salary increases, an infinitesimal growth in the number of city employees, and a few more pencils take up virtually all the city's slowly expanding revenue—with no new programs (Meltsner, 1971:18–19).

In Oakland, the tug of war over the budget involves three main participants: the city council, the chief executive, and individual city departments. The negotiating process among these budget makers is dominated by a lack of policy initiative on anyone's part. That is, instead of deciding what needs to be done and then trying to fund it, local decision makers look at last year's budget to see what

Box 17-1

HOW TO CUT A BUDGET

Rules of Thumb in Oakland

1. Cut all increases in personnel.
2. Cut all equipment items which appear to be luxurious.
3. Use precedent; cut items which have been cut before.
4. Recommend repairing and renovation rather than replacing facilities.
5. Recommend study as a means of deferring major costs.
6. Cut all nonitem operating costs by a fixed percentage (such as 10 percent).
7. Do not cut when safety or health of staff or public is obviously involved.
8. Cut departments with "bad" reputations.
9. When in doubt, ask another analyst what to do.
10. Identify dubious items for the [city] manager's action.

(Meltsner and Wildavsky, 1970:336. Copyright © 1970. Reprinted by permission of the publisher, Sage Publications, Inc. [Beverly Hills/London])

has already been done and then struggle over any money left over.

Implicit rules of thumb are commonly applied to budget cutting in Oakland. (See Box 17-1). The first—"cut all increases in personnel"—lends support to Wildavsky's skepticism about rational budget making.

Oakland's case is not unique. A study of the budget process in Cleveland, Detroit, and Pittsburgh found that rules for decision making are well established and seldom vary (Crecine, 1969).

To conclude: The picture of municipal budgeting that emerges from various studies is not one of rationality, imagination, or intellectual debate over alternatives. Instead, budget matters are guided by historical precedent—the previous year's appropriations. There is little concern for substantive policy issues or much attention paid to citizens' views. Unlike the federal budget process (which is typified by real struggles over alternative spending policies), the municipal budget process is dominated by gloom over lack of revenue.

Where Local Government Revenue Goes

What mix of local government activities gets funded via the incremental budgeting process? The largest slice of local funds goes to education. The remainder is divided among numerous services ranging from sewage to administration. Fig. 17-9 shows how local government spent its money in 1975–1976.

Because Fig. 17-9 groups together all local government spending, it can't reveal the spending patterns of individual cities. A look at other U.S. census data reveals wide variations in budgeting among cities and other municipalities. Predictably, the single most important determinant of spending level is the availability of money. But a number of other factors—political environment, income and age distribution of residents, and so forth—also help explain differences in spending levels and service mixes among urban communities.

To conclude: We all know people who claim to be committed to some cause, perhaps saving the environment or promoting social

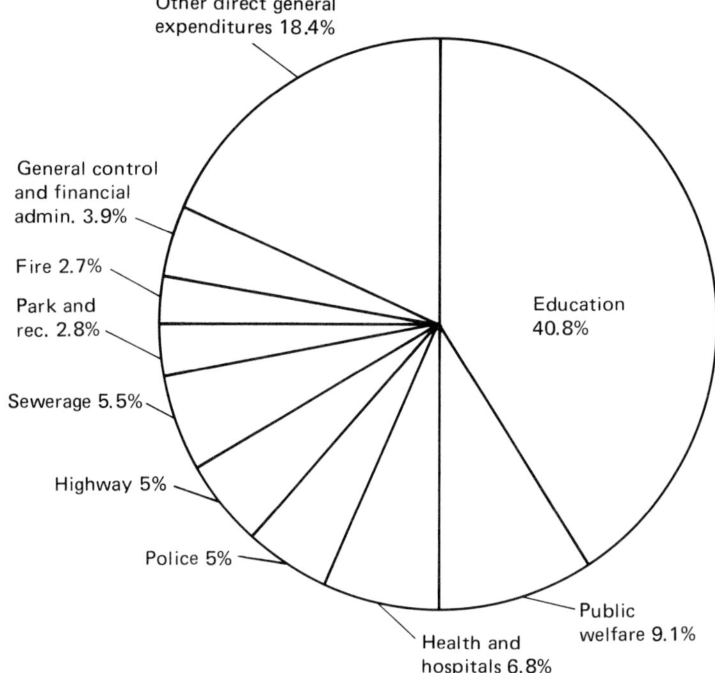

Fig. 17-9 LOCAL GOVERNMENT REVENUE PIE. This chart shows all direct general expenditures of local governments. (Adapted from U.S. Bureau of the Census, *Local Government Finances in Selected Metropolitan Areas and Large Counties: 1975–1976* [Washington, D.C.: U.S. Government Printing Office, 1977], p. 7)

justice. The way they actually spend their time and money reflects their level of commitment and priorities. So it is with governments. A budget is a value statement reflecting the priorities and real commitments of a collectivity—or, theoretically at least, the majority's preferences. Thus, whatever values taxpayers claim to hold can be measured against how much money they're willing to commit to these goals relative to others.

In the United States, local public finance reflects traditional commitments to locally controlled education and basic services like sewers and water. But the local budget alone cannot reveal the total package of value preferences. For a more realistic assessment of what taxpayers both want and get in terms of public services, we have to examine federal, state, and local expenditure patterns.

ANOTHER LOOK

Ultimately, local public finance is tied to metropolitan, state, and national production and consumption, as well as local value preferences. How much is produced in a city, state, and the nation as a whole affects the public services citizens receive. The public goods and services citizens want to consume—and pay for collectively—reflects their values. How much surplus is available for public allocation determines the limits of public spending.

Theorists disagree on many normative questions of political economy: What, if anything, should be done to encourage fiscal equity between central cities and their suburbs? Should the federal government take over all fiscal responsibility for welfare assistance via a national tax? Or should the federal government decrease its involvement in traditionally local functions? Should government at all levels lower its voice and tighten its belt, letting the market decide who gets what services? The answers depend on the theorist's political ideology.

Policy analysts not only disagree on what should be; sometimes they can't agree on what is. The debate over who finally pays the property tax is illustrative. Methodological problems, particularly in the area of data collection, lead some researchers to conclude that the property tax is regressive, while others claim that it is somewhat progressive.

Of course, even if policy analysts agree on the effects of a particular tax policy, it doesn't follow that their findings will have public policy impact. One example is sales taxes. Researchers have collected mounds of empirical evidence showing that sales taxes are regressive, affecting the poor more than the affluent. However, unless those empowered to change tax policy want to do so, the evidence has little significance. In other words, theorists propose, others dispose.

PROJECTS

1. **Local revenue sources.** Using census data, construct a pie chart of local government revenue sources for two different cities.
2. **Local expenditures.** Using census data, construct a pie chart of general expenditures for the same two cities.
3. **Comparison of revenue patterns.** Compare the data collected in Projects 1 and 2. Are there differences between the two cities in terms of own source revenue and intergovernmental transfers? Are there differences between the cities in terms of spending patterns? What hypotheses might you construct to explain any differences?
4. **The budgeting process.** Attempt to find out as much as you can about the budget-making process in your community. Using interviews with city officials, any relevant newspaper clippings, and informal talks with knowledgeable academics, try to determine who the major actors are and what interest groups seem to have some input into the budgeting process.

SUGGESTIONS FOR FURTHER LEARNING

The leading text on urban public finance is Richard A. Musgrave and Peggy B. Musgrave, *Public Finance in Theory and Practice,* 2nd ed. (New York: McGraw-Hill, 1976). While difficult reading, it does not presuppose a background in economics.

Other public finance books include J. Richard Aronson and Eli Schwartz, *Management Policies in Urban Public Finance* (Washington, D.C.: International City Managers Association, 1975), an anthology of short, readable articles on public finance intended for practitioners; Robert L. Bish, *Financing Government* (New York: Holt, Rinehart & Winston, 1973), a more compact treatment of urban finance issues; and Robert Pettingill and Jogindar S. Uppal, *Can Cities Survive?* (New York: St. Martin's Press, 1974), a more popular treatment focusing on the fiscal crisis of American cities.

The debate over the nature of the property tax is explored in Dick Netzer, *Economics of the Property Tax* (Washington, D.C.: Brookings Institution, 1966), which argues that the property tax is essentially regressive as a tax on consumers of shelter. See also Henry Aaron, *Who Pays the Property Tax?* (Washington, D.C.: Brookings Institution, 1974). It summarizes the view that the property tax is less regressive than was formerly thought.

A readable, journalistic account of the New York City fiscal crisis is Jack Newfield and Paul DuBrul, *The Abuse of Power* (New York: Penguin, 1978). The authors focus on manipulation of the New York City bond market by bankers and the subsequent back-room deals struck by members of various city power blocs. A more scholarly anthology, which focuses on the New York City crisis from a radical perspective, is Roger E. Alcaly and David Mermelstein (eds.), *The Fiscal Crisis of*

American Cities (New York: Random House, 1977). This work contains analyses by several radical academics, including David Gordon, John Mollenkopf, and William Tabb.

A book that has greatly influenced public policy analysis is Aaron Wildavsky, *The Politics of the Budgetary Process,* 2nd ed. (Boston: Little, Brown, 1974), a witty, urbane, and readable book. Wildavsky deals with public sector budgeting behavior at the national level, but many games local budgeters play can be understood by the rules Wildavsky has decoded.

Local budgeting is described in Arnold Meltsner, *The Politics of City Revenue* (Berkeley and Los Angeles: University of California Press, 1971), an informed tour of the drab and frugal offices of city budgeters in Oakland, California, and John P. Crecine, *Governmental Problem Solving: A Computer Simulation of Municipal Budgeting* (Chicago: Rand McNally, 1969).

A filmstrip that explores urban public finance issues is *Cities in Financial Trouble* (Englewood Cliffs, N.J.: Prentice-Hall Media, 1976), which contrasts the financial problems of older cities to the situation in newer, thriving ones. *One Way to Better Cities* (Association-Sterling Films, 1970) attacks the current operation of the property tax as promoting urban decay and suburban sprawl. The film argues for site value taxation in place of the property tax. A film which explores intergovernmental fiscal relations and defends the concept of revenue sharing is *Cities Are People: How Dare We Not Save Them?* (Ralph Hall Productions, 1971). Three mayors describe the problems of their cities and the need for revenue sharing. The film was made one year before the passage of general revenue-sharing legislation.

Why and how economists disagree is the theme of an episode of the PBS television series *Economically Speaking.* Produced by the PBS station in Erie, Pennsylvania, the episode (telecast in spring 1979) features liberal economist Walter Heller and conservative economist Milton Friedman in conversation with Marina Whitman (moderator).

In *Problems in Political Economy: An Urban Perspective,* rev. ed. (Lexington, Mass.: D.C. Heath, 1977), editor David M. Gordon brings together writings from the liberal, radical, and conservative points of view on such topics as public expenditures theory and governmental impact on the distribution of income.

KEY TERMS

Assessed value The amount at which real property (land and structures) is valued for property tax purposes. Frequently the assessed value of property is set at some fraction of the full market value, such as 25 percent.

Capital expenditures Money spent for capital goods, such as new equipment and building construction.

Elasticity A measure of the degree to which a revenue source will stretch as an economy expands or shrinks. It is expressed as a coefficient by dividing a percentage change in tax revenue by a percentage change in income.

Excise tax A tax on the sale of a specified type of good, such as cigarettes, liquor, and gasoline. An excise tax, unlike a sales tax, is limited to specified items rather than applied across the board.

Fiscal federalism The system of intergovernmental fiscal relations within the U.S. federal system in which different layers of government (federal, state, or local) collect and spend revenue.

Incidence The final resting place of a tax after all shifting has occurred. A statement of tax incidence shows who finally pays the tax.

Income tax A tax levied on individual and corporate income. Theoretically it is a progressive tax based on the ability-to-pay principle, whereby a larger tax burden is put on individuals or firms that have a greater capacity to pay.

Incremental Refers to small units. Public budgets are not constructed anew every year. Rather, they are incremental in nature; policy makers make small increases or decreases in some budget categories.

Intergovernmental transfer A transfer of revenue from one level of government to another.

Line-item budget A budget that breaks down expenditures by nonprogram categories, such as personnel or capital expenditures.

Operating expenses Money spent for the city's on-going work, primarily salaries and other personnel costs.

Own source revenue Revenue raised by a jurisdiction directly from income sources that it controls, such as a local property tax.

Program budget A budget that breaks down expenditures by program categories, such as police department costs.

Progressive tax One in which the rate of the tax increases as the taxable base grows—for example, 5 percent tax on an income of $1,000; 8 percent tax on $5,000; and 25 percent tax on $30,000.

Property tax A tax on real property: land and such improvements on land as housing and commercial-industrial buildings. The amount of tax paid is based on the assessed value of the property and the tax rate is set by the jurisdiction.

Regressive tax One in which the rate of the tax remains the same while the taxable base grows; the opposite of a progressive tax. Thus, the proportion of tax paid by a person earning $5,000 is greater than that paid by a person earning $25,000. Sales and excise taxes are regressive.

Sales tax A tax based on a flat percentage of the selling price. It is paid at the time of sale by the purchaser, collected by the seller, and subsequently turned over to some level of government.

Tax base For a community, refers to the total assessed value of all real property within its borders. It also refers to the value at which a tax rate is applied to determine the tax owed. In property taxes, for instance, the tax base is the assessed valuation of real property.

Tax rate The rate applied to the assessed value (in the case of the property tax) or to earnings (in the case of the income tax) for tax purposes.

User charge A tax paid by the person who actually uses a publicly provided good. Examples include bridge tolls and admission fees to city museums.

Zero-based budgeting A technique whereby an organization (e.g., a federal agency, a city) examines the total amount of expenditure for each type of activity on an annual basis. This technique attempts to force decision makers to justify expenses and think through alternatives in terms of costs and benefits.

REFERENCES

Aaron, Henry
1974 Who Pays the Property Tax? Washington, D.C.: Brookings Institution.

Crecine, John P.
1969 Governmental Problem Solving: A Computer Simulation of Municipal Budgeting. Chicago: Rand McNally.

Forbes Magazine
1971 "Who owns New York?" (June 1):24-32.

Hacker, Andrew (ed.)
1965 The Corporation Take-Over. Garden City, N.Y.:Anchor.

Herriott, Roger A. and Herman P. Miller
1971 "Who paid the taxes in 1968?" Washington, D.C.: U.S. Bureau of the Census, Population Division.

Kolko, Gabriel
[1962]
1971 Wealth and Power in America: An Analysis of Social Class and Income Distribution. New York: Praeger.

Lampman, Robert J.
1962 The Share of Top Wealth-Holders in National Wealth. New York: National Bureau of Economic Research.

Malcolm, Andrew H.
1978 "Tokyo on the brink of bankruptcy, facing central government rule." New York Times (February 4):1.

Meltsner, Arnold
1971 The Politics of City Revenue. Berkeley and Los Angeles: University of California Press.

Meltsner, Arnold and Aaron Wildavsky
1970 "Leave city budgeting alone!: a survey, case study, and recommendations for reform." Pp. 311–358 in John P. Crecine (ed.), Financing the Metropolis: Public Policy in Urban Economics. Beverly Hills, Calif.: Sage.

Musgrave, Richard A. and Peggy B. Musgrave
1976 Public Finance in Theory and Practice, 2nd ed. New York: McGraw-Hill.

Nader, Ralph
1971 "A citizen's guide to the American economy." New York Review of Books, 27, 3 (Sept. 2):14–18.

Netzer, Dick
1966 Economics of the Property Tax. Washington, D.C.: Brookings Institution.

O'Connor, James
1973 The Fiscal Crisis of the State. New York: St. Martin's.

Pechman, Joseph A. and Benjamin A. Okner
1974 Who Bears the Tax Burden? Washington, D.C.: Brookings Institution.

Riew, John
1970 "Metropolitan disparities in fiscal federalism." Pp. 137–161 in John P. Crecine (ed.), Financing the Metropolis: Public Policy in Urban Economics. Vol. 4, Urban Affairs Annual Reports. Beverly Hills, Calif.: Sage.

Shenker, Israel
[1975]
1977 "Urban experts advise, castigate, and console the city on its problems." Pp. 5–10 in Roger E. Alcaly and David Mermelstein (eds.), The Fiscal Crisis of American Cities. New York: Random House.

Sternlieb, George and James W. Hughes
1977 "New regional and metropolitan realities of America." Journal of the American Institute of Planners, 3: 227–41.

U.S. Bureau of the Census
1978 City and County Data Book 1977. Washington, D.C.: U.S. Government Printing Office.

Wildavsky, Aaron
1974 The Politics of the Budgetary Process, 2nd ed. Boston: Little, Brown.

Richard Hedman

FINALE
To Be Continued

Imagine a huge blank wall.

"How boring is a blank wall," sigh the City Council members. Moving quickly against boredom, they vote funds for 500 paint brushes and truckloads of paint. Then they invite men, women, and children from each city block to transform a blank wall in the CBD into a giant mural about city life.

The idea spreads. Soon muralmania grips the nation's cities. People everywhere are painting city scenes on blank walls.

"Cities grow curiouser and curiouser," sniff the urbanists. "This muralmania deserves our undivided attention," they decide. So, grant proposals are written—and funded.

The social scientists swing into action. An economist collects data on the time spent painting instead of working at paid employment and the consequent rise or fall in the GNP. Teams of participant-observers join paint crews in twenty-two selected cities. A political scientist studies the relationships that develop between City Hall flaks and neighborhood block groups. A geographer charts the location of blank walls in small, medium, and large cities. A sociologist gathers data on the social backgrounds of those who paint skyscrapers and those who paint playgrounds. A mass communications researcher examines the impact of muralmania on prime-time TV programming. An organization theorist explores how paint crews divide their tasks. And on and on . . .

One year passes. Everywhere people are painting blank walls. Or they're talking about what's painted on walls that used to be blank. Throughout the nation, conferences on muralmania are held. Scholars present learned papers, including "Ethnic Styles of

Depicting City Hall," "The Spatial Relation of City Murals to Transport Nodes," "How Paint Crews Handle Conflict on Scaffolds," and "A Cost-Benefit Analysis of Muralmania with Emphasis on Changes in Consumer Buying Patterns."

Meanwhile, political commentators reflect on the deeper meanings of muralmania. According to one radical pundit, "Muralmania presents a strong case against capitalism. Here we have nonalienated labor, working collectively in their own interest, to creatively humanize the cities. The lesson is clear: We can end alienation if we end capitalism." A liberal draws a different lesson: "Muralmania presents a strong case for equal opportunity. Given an equal chance to express themselves and a little on-the-scaffold training, all Americans—regardless of social background, color, or creed—can rise to the top rungs of the ladder." A conservative columnist doesn't agree, writing that "Muralmania presents a strong case for letting the free market work without government interference. Responding quickly to consumer preferences, the market was responsible for providing gallons of paint at cheaper prices and for employing the jobless in paint factories. The message is self-evident: Keep the government out of running and regulating our lives, and the nation will prosper."

Other voices are raised. A decentralist comments, "How beautiful is smallness. Muralmania presents a strong case for local community action. Just imagine what energy would be released through neighborhood government." A centralist, on the other hand, argues that "Muralmania presents a strong case for central coordination and economies of scale. Without regional paint buying and the vast administrative effort that went into organizing paint crews, muralmania would have fizzled out."

Clearly, muralmania has captured the nation's imagination. Amid the TV talk shows, editorials, parades, and block parties, social scientists continue their analysis. One team of content analysts carefully examines photos of all city scenes painted by all the people on all the cities' walls. Grounded—rather, flooded—in data, they construct a typology to make sense out of the infinite variety of urban images painted on once-blank walls. Seventy-five categories of images are devised. Here are just a few:

1. *Types of people depicted by occupation* (several thousand subcategories, taken from the U.S. Department of Labor's job title dictionary).
2. *Types of people depicted by race and ethnicity* (fifteen subcategories, taken from the 1980 U.S. census).
3. *Types of technology depicted by energy source* (seventeen subcategories, including feet and hands, electronic, and appropriate).
4. *Types of ideas expressed by symbols* (ten subcategories, including religious, political, and economic).

After constructing this typology of urban images painted during muralmania, the social scientists look over data about the muralists themselves. Then, as is their bent, they construct numerous hypotheses. Here's one about differential perceptions of urban life: Big-city radicals tend to paint public buildings, while small-town conservatives tend to paint private homes and small businesses.

During a coffee, tea, or frozen yoghurt break, the urbanists sit around and wax poetic. "Isn't it amazing," says one, "that each city speaks with a distinctive voice. Take Los Angeles and San Francisco, for example. Their murals have very different images. Frankly, I have never felt comfortable in L.A."

A colleague chides, "Really, you are so

Bostonian! I bet you feel right at home in San Francisco. After all, it's an Eastern look-alike. Its personality was created by enterprising Easterners, bitten by the gold bug and out to strike it rich. It just doesn't feel like L.A., that space-age Autopia, that Western Surfurbia to its south."

"Good grief," moans an aged urban theorist. "Your discussion of San Francisco and Los Angeles is disturbing. All my scholarly life, I've been searching for the fundamental forces that govern modern urban life. I have tried to discover the structures and institutions that underlie modern cities everywhere. Now you remind me of vast differences between two cities, both located in the same outpost of postindustrial society, that state of the (imagi-) nation called California. Is there no hope of constructing a theory that can explain urban life and behavior in Los Angeles, San Francisco, Boston, Moscow, Beijing, and Keokuk, Iowa?"

Others chime in. One says, "Physicists have recently discovered the gluon—apparently, the vital component of matter in the universe. But for us to search for the fundamental component of urban life—the City Gluon—seems less fruitful. In my view, no one element and no one theory can possibly explain how all cities work at any historical point in time."

Another adds, "I agree. First off, what we label a 'city' is not a single beast. The name 'city' covers administrative capitals, commercial-trade centers, military garrisons, religious shrine settlements, and rather small trading posts. How can any single theory explain urban existence in these various kinds of cities? Clearly, being an urbanite in New York City and Crescent City, California, is a qualitatively different experience. Furthermore, cities aren't single units. Take a big city like Chicago. It's got diverse neighborhoods. It's got urban villages and cosmopolitan corners. It's got breadmakers in small shops and computer programmers in the Prudential Building. It's got folks like my grandparents, who came to the city from a Mississippi farm, and it's got my kids, who think that milk comes straight from a carton."

A political sociologist enters the discussion. "Yes, yes. Even so, some key concepts can help us to understand how cities work. These concepts concern underlying structures and institutions, whether they're experienced in people's heads or not. My candidates for key concepts include economic and social interdependence, specialization, and differentiation."

An anthropologist suggests that "Population size and growth and population density could be added to the list. Of course, theorists since the ancient Greeks have pointed to the importance of population size and density for human relations. Now, there are some anthropologists who claim there are such things as 'magic numbers' which influence, even determine, human behavior. Some even claim they have the exact number in the game. For instance, the magic number for hunting-gathering bands is twenty-five; over that, people risk conflict and fighting. In early villages, the magic number is one hundred; over that, villagers tend to split into two villages. And so on."

"Hmm," a skeptic wonders aloud. "This magic number business is a bit too deterministic for my taste."

"Well," says the anthropologist, "I can show you evidence from one hundred two societies—including baboons and Bushmen—where the numbers work."

The skeptic responds, "You can show me all the evidence you want. My intuition tells me it's plain nonsense."

The discussion heats up. At this point, one of the urbanists tries to lower the temperature level. "Colleagues, let us give our imagination free play. How might you explain how cities work to a person who had never seen or lived in one—say, a Tasaday tribesperson in the Philippines today?"

The first scholar answers, "I would use the analogy of the human body. Each organ of the body performs a particular function. The heart, for instance, pumps the blood through the human system, and the brain coordinates motor activity. Each organ is useless on its own. Organs function together in harmony, and together they form a living, organic system. This living system can't be described merely by talking about each separate organ because the body is more than the sum of its parts. It is the same with cities. The lifeblood of cities—goods, services, ideas—is circulated throughout the metropolitan system by networks of transport and communication. Managers and administrators, like the human brain, coordinate human activity. And just like the human body, the city is more than the sum of its parts. In addition, just as the body grows and becomes differentiated into specific organs and systems, so do cities grow more complex and become differentiated internally."

The second scholar answers, "Your analogy is elegant and simple to understand. That is why it is so seductive. Yet it lacks a certain dimension. It doesn't convey the possibilities for change and conflict. Someone once said that cities are places where unexpected things happen. Your metropolitan system-as-human-body metaphor neglects this sense of spontaneity. Also, human bodies have boundaries that everyone can see. Cities don't. Where, for instance, do the boundaries of New York City begin and end? On a map, the political boundaries are clear. But the eyes and ears of the Big Apple stretch across the globe. No, your metaphor is misleading. The metaphor of the city as a machine—with meshing gears and parts all working in harmony—suffers from similar shortcomings, in my opinion."

The third scholar answers, "Let me offer another metaphor from the world of biology. This is only fair, since Charles Darwin took his idea of the survival of the fittest from Herbert Spencer, a sociologist (who, incidentally, gave us the metaphor of society as a human body). I think the city is most like a single cell. Just as it is in the nature of cells in the body to pool their resources and to fuse when possible, I think it is in the nature of urban life for people to come together and to join with each other in common activity whenever possible."

"Colleagues," a fourth injects, "I prefer to return to our empirical evidence for our metaphor. Murals all over this country show the city to be a swirl of nonagricultural activities. So I offer this image: the city as collage."

Another urbanist speaks up. "This discussion reminds me of old elephant stories. One person looks at the city and sees bodies and systems. Another sees single cells trying to fuse together. Still another sees a collage or a mosaic. Similarly, one searches for underlying structures and institutions. Another focuses on subjective meanings of city life. Still another seeks fundamental elements of city life everywhere. And some stick to the available evidence, while others depend on intuition. Each approach has its merits—and limits. The trouble is, they don't seem to lend themselves to synthesis. So, what is to be done?"

"No doubt some of us will continue to dissect small pieces of the urban scene," answers a former plumber-turned-theoretician. She continues, "Some will focus on substantive issues—urban transport, terrorism, pollution, etc. Some will explore particular parts of urban culture. Others will try to make the connections between the small pieces and the theoretical issues. Still others will try to merge theory and practice, applying their knowledge to improve the quality of urban life. Whatever we do, I hope we remember John Gardner's admonition: 'We must have respect for both our plumbers and our philosophers or neither our pipes nor our theories will hold water.' "

Hopefully, all of us will continue the long search for knowledge by sharing our evidence and insights and by asking better questions. That is why we cannot say "The End." That is why we say instead, "To Be Continued . . . "

Brief Biographies

Any list of notables is bound to dissatisfy some, offend or outrage others. This relatively short list reflects our judgment of persons whose ideas, research, and/or actions have significantly contributed to urban theory or practice, either directly or indirectly. Thus, we include Max Weber, Emile Durkheim, Karl Marx, and other macro-level social theorists because their conceptual frameworks have had an important impact on urban studies. Others, including Robert Moses and Frederick Law Olmsted, are known primarily as doers rather than thinkers, and their doings influenced the shape of modern urban America. Still others, such as Milton Friedman and John Kenneth Galbraith, are included because they represent points of view to be reckoned with.

Who is systematically underrepresented or excluded from this list? There are few behind-the-scenes urban policymakers. We would have liked to include Abraham Levitt and sons of Levittown, David Rockefeller of the Chase Manhattan Bank, and others whose decisions (e.g., suburban development, redlining of urban areas) have had enormous impact on twentieth-century urban America or on particular cities, but that is a list in itself. Also, there are few poets, artists, or writers of the city; a more complete listing would include Georgia O'Keefe, Woody Allen, Tom Wolfe, John Ashbery, Walt Whitman, Saul Bellow, Thomas Wolfe, Finley Peter Dunne, Frank Norris, and many, many more.

Thus, this list is necessarily incomplete. It is merely a list of *some* notable contributors to the study or practice of things urban.

Jane Addams (1860–1935) College-educated, well-traveled social reformer. Founder of Chicago's Hull House in 1889, first president of the Women's International League for Peace and Freedom, and co-winner of the Nobel Peace Prize for 1931, Jane Addams started at Hull House and moved into a wider political arena of social reform. She helped to promote labor legislation, set up juvenile courts, sponsor municipal government reform, and agitate for women's suffrage.

Christopher Alexander (1936–) Innovative architect-designer whose book *A Pattern Language* (1977) summarizes an alternative vision of design: highly participatory and decentralized, with attention to symbolism and overlapping (nontreelike) structures.

Edward R. Banfield (1916–) Neo-conservative urbanist best known for his controversial book *The Unheavenly City* (1968), which drew a storm of criticism from liberals and radicals for its gloomy view of human nature and government's ability to do much about urban problems. Earlier works include co-authorship of a classic study of city decision making—*Politics, Planning, and the Public Interest* (1955)—and *City Politics* (1963). Banfield is currently Shattuck Professor of Urban Government at Harvard University.

Brian J.L. Berry (1934–) A preeminent urban geographer of the twentieth century, Berry has conducted empirical studies on numerous topics, including central place issues, commercial city structure, suburbanization, racial segregation, and spatial aspects of the Indian economy. A champion of quantitative geographical techniques, he is presently the Williams Professor of Urban and Regional Planning at Harvard University and director of the Harvard Laboratory for Computer Graphics and Spatial Analysis.

Ernest W. Burgess (1886–1966) Formulator of the Burgess hypothesis. Burgess hypothesized that U.S. industrial cities are structured in concentric zones. Burgess was a principal figure in the University of Chicago's school of sociology and urban theory. *The City*, co-authored with Robert E. Park and Roderick D. McKenzie, exerted a powerful influence on urban sociologists, geographers, economists, and other students of the city.

Daniel Burnham (1846–1912) Architect, city planner, and highly skilled propagandist for his own ideas, Burnham is best remembered for building according to a preestablished plan. He was the inspiration behind the Columbian Exposition Fairgrounds, called the "White City," at the

Chicago World's Fair of 1893. Later, he devised the Chicago Plan of 1909, gaining business support for his notion of the "City Beautiful." He has been called the predecessor of New York City's Robert Moses because of his obsession with highways and his policies which led to the eviction of poor people in order to widen Chicago thoroughfares. Burnham's vision is revealed in his quip: "Make no little plans. They have no magic to stir men's blood."

V. Gordon Childe (1892–1957) Australian-British archeologist whose thesis stressed the importance of environment (capable of producing an agricultural surplus), technology, and social structure (emergence of a governing elite) to the origin of cities in ancient Mesopotamia. He was Abercromby Professor of Prehistoric Archeology at the University of Edinburgh in Scotland.

Walter Christaller (1893–1969) The developer of central place theory, Christaller published a seminal book, *Central Places in Southern Germany* (1933), describing the size, spacing, and number of so-called central places in a region.

Robert Dahl (1915–) Author of the influential study of urban decision making, *Who Governs?* (1961), which presents a pluralist view of community power structure. Professor of political science at Yale University, Dahl joined the Democratic Socialist Organizing Committee (DSOC) in the late 1970s.

Richard J. Daley (1902–1976) Chicago's late mayor (1955–1976) and boss of the Cook County Democratic Party machine, often considered to be the last surviving old-style city machine in American politics. Daley was a second-generation Irish-American and self-made man who never moved from his small neighborhood house or lost his working-class accent and malapropisms. Daley was undisputed master of ethnic politics in Chicago during his tenure as mayor. However his various policies are interpreted, observers agree that Daley had political clout.

Emile Durkheim (1858–1917) Eminent French sociologist who asked a key question: How do individuals make up a stable, cohesive society? In his first book, *The Division of Labor in Society* (1893), Durkheim addressed this question by examining two forms of social solidarity, mechanical and organic. He theorized that in modern (organically solid) societies, social cohesion results from, or is expressed by, social differentiation (division of labor).

Walter Firey (1916–) Best known for his 1947 book, *Land Use in Central Boston,* in which he developed a theory of cultural ecology. Firey argued against the economic determinism of the classic models of urban spatial structure, contending that cultural values and symbolism play a significant role in the way cities are structured. He is professor of sociology at the University of Texas and a specialist in human ecology and regional planning.

Milton Friedman (1912–) The leading spokesperson for U.S. economic conservatives today. A pure market theorist, Friedman proposes market solutions to national and urban problems. He taught at the University of Chicago and is presently at the Hoover Institution at Stanford. *Newsweek* carries his column on current issues, alternating with his partner in columny, liberal Paul Samuelson.

John Kenneth Galbraith (1908–) A self-proclaimed "abiding liberal," Canadian-born Galbraith has long served as a member of Harvard University's economics department. He has produced numerous books, including *The New Industrial State* (2nd rev. ed., 1971), and played policy roles, including Ambassador to India during the 1960s. (Ironically, his ideological opponent, Daniel Patrick Moynihan, followed him at the New Delhi Embassy several years later.)

Herbert Gans (1927–) Author of *The Urban Villagers* (1962) and *The Levittowners* (1967), sociologist and city planner Gans disputes Wirth's notion that urbanism is a way of life. Currently, he is professor of sociology at Columbia University.

Erving Goffman (1922–) Called "the Kafka of our time" for his vision of routine encounters, Canadian-born sociologist Goffman is known for his dramaturgical model of social interaction: People present themselves or perform in various masks, depending on the audience and the impression they wish to manage. To Goffman, social interaction in public and semipublic places is guided by unspoken rules (norms) which help maintain public order. At present, Goffman teaches at the University of Pennsylvania.

Homer Hoyt (1896–) Real estate economist Hoyt is best known for his development of the sectoral model of internal city structure, published by the Federal Housing Administration in 1939: *The Structure and Growth of Residential Neighborhoods in American Cities.*

Floyd Hunter (1912–) Author of *Community Power Structure: A Study of Decision Makers* ([1953], 1963), a classic statement of the elitist model of community power, and an update, *Atlanta's Policymakers Revisited* (Chapel Hill, N.C.: University of North Carolina Press, 1979). Formerly professor of community organization and social science research, he is currently living on the land in Sonoma County, California.

Jane Jacobs (1916–) Popularizer of unconventional ideas about cities and city planning. As a journalist and later editor of *Architectural Forum,* Jacobs grew increasingly critical of planning which destroyed communities, separated land uses, and rebuilt sterile areas. Her best-selling book, *The Death and Life of Great American Cities* (1961), presents an alternative view in which planners should protect neighborhoods, mix land uses, and pay attention to design details that matter to people. In *The Economy of Cities* (1970), she argues that the first cities led to agriculture, not vice versa. Presently she is an independent writer in Toronto.

Oscar Lewis (1914–1970) American anthropologist who did much of his work in urbanizing societies. A critic of Louis Wirth, he found that people adjust to urban life in various ways, and that the city is not the proper unit for analyzing social life.

Elliot Liebow (1925–) Author of *Tally's Corner* (1967), a study of black streetcorner men in Washington, D.C. Anthropologist Liebow hung out with the unskilled urban men and, based on his firsthand observation, drew a portrait of their social and work situation linking their way of life to macro-level social forces.

Kevin Lynch (1918–) A key figure in urban design, Lynch invented a vocabulary which dominates urban design today. He is concerned with making cities more imageable so that their residents find them understandable and reassuring. After an apprenticeship with Frank Lloyd Wright, Lynch turned to teaching. His best-known work is *The Image of the City* (1960). Currently, he teaches in the Department of Urban Studies and Planning at the Massachusetts Institute of Technology.

Malcolm X (1925-1965) Second in command of the Black Muslim movement in the U.S. during the early 1960s, he left the party after a policy disagreement with party leader Elijah Muhammad. He was believed to have been forming a new movement when he was assassinated in 1965.

Karl Marx (1818–1883) Revered by many, feared by some, and loathed by others, Marx's ideas are inescapable. Although his ideas have not been widely popular in the United States, he was known to Americans in the nineteenth century through his articles for the *New York Daily Tribune* between 1852 and 1862. Further, Marxian concepts, particularly alienation, have become part of the working vocabulary of social scientists, whatever their attitude toward Marx's work. Marx's major writings include the early work, *The German Ideology* (1846) and the three-volume, magisterial *Capital* (1867, 1885, 1894).

Robert Moses (1888–) Master builder of U.S. cities, Moses used his base as head of public authorities in New York City to establish a new kind of political machine, lubricated by money but rooted in bureaucratic power instead of ward-level politicians. He mobilized banks, contractors, labor unions, the mass media, insurance companies, and churches to shape the physical structure of New York City and social policies. He has been called the single most powerful man in New York and the chief influence on American cities in the twentieth century.

Daniel Patrick Moynihan (1927–) Democratic Senator from New York and leading spokesperson for the neo-conservatives, Moynihan formerly served as U.S. Ambassador to India, urbanist at the Joint Center for Urban Studies at MIT and Harvard University, Nixon's policy advisor, and U.S. Ambassador to the United Nations. A prolific writer, Moynihan is the author or co-author of numerous urban studies, including *Beyond the Melting Pot* (1963), a study of five ethnic groups in New York City. Moynihan is known for his forthrightness, wit, and phrase-making ability ("benign neglect" was his term—his policy advice to the Nixon administration for certain social issues).

Lewis Mumford (1895–) A charter member of the Regional Planning Association of America in 1923 (whose studies influenced the eventual building of Radburn, New Jersey, and other greenbelt towns). With the publication of *The Culture of Cities* in 1938, Mumford gained a worldwide reputation. In the course of writing more than twenty books, he has come to represent a particular view of urban life and urban "solutions." In his own words, "the city should be an organ of love; and the best economy of cities is the care and culture of men . . . . Otherwise the sterile gods of power, unrestrained by organic limits or human goals, will remake man in their own faceless image and bring human history to an end."

Richard Musgrave (1910–) Co-author, with his wife, of *Public Finance in Theory and Practice* (1976), the best-known urban public finance textbook. He is presently the H. H. Burbank Professor of Political Economy at Harvard University.

Dick Netzer (1928–) An urban public finance scholar who takes the position that the property tax is quite regressive. He is presently Dean of the Graduate School of Public Administration at New York University.

Michael Novak (1933–) Slovak-American author of *The Rise of the Unmeltable Ethnics* (1971). He has taught at Stanford and Syracuse Universities and is a leading advocate of white ethnic politics as a challenge to WASP power and lifestyles. In 1980 he was resident scholar in Religion and Public Policy at the American Enterprise Institute.

James O'Connor (1930–) A radical economist-sociologist who developed the theory of the *Fiscal Crisis of the State* (1973). O'Connor is presently professor of sociology at the University of California, Santa Cruz.

Frederick Law Olmsted (1822–1903) Pioneer American landscape architect. Olmsted was the moving force behind many projects to make the natural environment accessible to urbanites, including Central Park in New York City before the era of Boss Tweed. Olmsted left his mark on countless American parks, waterfronts, and civic areas.

Robert E. Park (1864–1944) Member of the Chicago school of sociology and collaborator with Ernest W. Burgess in developing the ecological perspective on urban phenomena, Park was a news reporter and social reformer-turned-sociologist. He taught sociology at the University of Chicago from 1914 to 1933.

Pericles (c. 490–429 B.C.) Led citizens of the Athenian polis to overthrow a ruling oligarchy in about 463 B.C. Under his democratic leadership, Greek culture flourished, producing what is often called the "Golden Age of Pericles." His most famous speech, the "Funeral Oration," was given on the occasion of a funeral for soldiers who had died in the war between Athens and Sparta.

Henri Pirenne (1862–1935) Belgian economic historian who advanced a thesis tracing medieval European cities to the revival of commerce in the twelfth century.

George Washington Plunkitt (1842–1924) A cracker-barrel philosopher of machine politics. A lifelong Tammany Hall politician in New York City from the days of Boss Tweed until his death, Plunkitt gave a classic description and defense of the city machine, including "honest graft."

Carl Sandburg (1878–1967) Born in Galesburg, Illinois, to Swedish immigrants, Sandburg was a poet, Lincoln scholar, humanitarian, and newspaper writer. *The People, Yes* (1936) is often considered to be his epic. Sandburg's bold images of industrial cities are double-edged, noting both the promise and the problems they portend. But in general, he celebrated urban industrial society and the countless Americans who created it.

Gideon Sjoberg (1922–) Best known for his attempt to classify cities in a two-term typology: preindustrial and industrial types. Sjoberg is presently professor of sociology at the University of Texas.

Adam Smith (1723–1790) Known primarily for *An Inquiry into the Nature and Causes of the Wealth of Nations* (1776), considered the first comprehensive system of political economy. A professor at the University of Glasgow, he used the concept of the invisible hand, whereby the individual seeks his or her own personal gain and thus promotes the public interest. Smith viewed the world as a well-ordered, harmonious mechanism. His ideas lie at the base of laissez-faire economics.

Robert Sommer (1929–) Psychologist who observes how people actually use airports, classrooms, convalescent homes, and other spaces in order to provide guidance to architects and other design professionals. His study of *Personal Space* (1969) is a seminal work on the way in which people relate to their immediate space. Currently, Sommer is professor of psychology at the University of California, Davis.

Lincoln Steffens (1866–1936) A muckraking journalist and antimachine crusader, Steffens authored a series of magazine articles exposing "The Shame of the Cities." He concluded that "the source and sustenance of bad government [are] not the bribe taker, but the bribe giver, the man we are so proud of, our successful businessman." Later in life, Steffens studied, wrote, and lectured in defense of the Russian Revolution. His autobiography is a notable literary contribution.

George Sternlieb (1928–) An influential scholar on a range of urban policy topics, including the Frostbelt-Sunbelt issue, housing ownership and finance, rent control (of which he takes a dim view), and regional planning policy. He is presently professor of urban and regional planning and Director of the Center for Urban Policy Research at Rutgers University.

W. I. Thomas (1863–1947) Contributed the concept of "the definition of the situation" to social psychology. His best-known book (with Florian Znaniecki), *The Polish Peasant in Europe and America* (1918) details the connections between the individual's definition of the situation and his or her family and community background. For Thomas, the interrelationship of individual personality and social order was a key concern.

Ferdinand Tönnies (1855–1936) German sociologist who identified two contrasting types of society and mentality: *Gemeinschaft* (community) and *Gesellschaft* (society). Tönnies, like Marx, traced social development as an evolutionary transition from primitive communism and village-town individualism to capitalistic urban individualism and, in the future, to state socialism. Tönnies's concepts, although not original, have influenced generations of scholars.

William Marcy Tweed (1823–1878) Boss of the New York City Tweed Ring from 1866 to 1871 and the symbol of a corrupt machine politician. Originally a chairmaker and voluntary fireman, Tweed became an alderman (1852–1853), sat in Congress (1853–1855), and was repeatedly elected to the New York State Senate. In 1870 he was made commissioner of public works for the city. But his real power came informally as the grand sachem (head) of Tammany Hall, New York City's Democratic Party machine. He was criminally and civilly indicted for various frauds and eventually jailed. After a brief escape to Cuba and Spain (1875–1876), he was recaptured and died in a New York jail while suits were pending against him for recovery of $6,000,000.

Edward L. Ullman (1912–) Together with Chauncy Harris, Ullman developed the multiple nuclei model of internal city structure which holds that city space is organized around a number of independent centers of commercial, manufacturing, and residential activity. He taught geography at various universities, including the University of Washington and Harvard University.

W. Lloyd Warner (1898–1970) With his research associates, social anthropologist Warner set the pattern of research for future generations with the "Yankee City" series, studies of urban social stratification. Warner developed two techniques for studying what he called social class, but he actually measured social status, not class. In general, Warner found that American cities have a "system of open classes" (that is, status groups).

Samuel Bass Warner, Jr. (1928–) Urban historian whose particular fascination is the interplay between social history and physical space. Among his books are *The Private City* (1968) which examines Philadelphia's society and physical form in the late eighteenth, mid-nineteenth, and early twentieth centuries and *Streetcar Suburbs* (1962) which describes the social and physical dynamics of Boston's pre-automobile suburbs at the end of the nineteenth century. He is presently professor of history and social science at Boston University.

Max Weber (1864–1920) A classic figure in the European liberal tradition whose sociological work ranged from the theory of bureaucracy and authority to the methodology of social science. His essays on *The Protestant Ethic and the Spirit of Capitalism* (1904-05), *The City* (1921), and "Status, Class, Party (1922)" continue to stimulate debate even today. Rationalization of modern life was a theme in Weber's political sociology. He envisioned the dawn of an age in which bureaucracy would be like an "iron cage," reducing the individual's role within an ever-expanding network of management and control.

William H. Whyte (1917–) A social scientist by avocation instead of vocation. He is the author of *The Organization Man* (1956), an influential study of the ethics, ideology, and lifestyle of the "new middle class" that runs big business and public organizations. In the section on the organization man at home in the suburbs, Whyte details his fear that the norms of the suburb, like those of the corporation, violate the spirit of individualism.

Aaron Wildavsky (1930–) Author of *The Politics of the Budgetary Process* ([1964] 1974), a classic study of the games budgeters play at the federal level. Wildavsky is also a leading figure in the field of policy analysis. Formerly, he was Dean of the Graduate School of Public Policy at the University of California, Berkeley.

Louis Wirth (1897–1952) Member of the Chicago school of sociology and disciple of Robert E. Park. He is best remembered for his classic essay, "Urbanism as a Way of Life" (1938), in which he argues that large size, heterogeneity, and high density in the city lead to a particularly urban way of life.

Index

EP62